Foundations
of Political
Sociology

Foundations of Political Sociology

Irving Louis Horowitz

With a new introduction by the author

Transaction Publishers

New Brunswick (U.S.A.) and London (U.K.)

New material this edition copyright © 1997 by Transaction Publishers, New Brunswick, New Jersey 08903. Originally published in 1972 by Harper & Row, Publishers.

This book is printed on acid-free paper that meets the American National Standard for Permanence of Paper for Printed Library Materials.

Library of Congress Catalog Number: 96-48069
ISBN: 1-56000-912-8
Printed in the United States of America

Library of Congress Cataloging-in-Publication Data

Horowitz, Irving Louis.
    Foundations of political sociology / Irving Louis Horowitz ; with a new introduction by the author.
        p. cm.
    Originally published: New York : Harper & Row, 1972.
    Includes bibliographical references and index.
    ISBN 1-56000-912-8 (pbk. : alk. paper)
    1. Political sociology. I. Title.
JA76.H67   1997
306.2—dc21   96-48069
                                                                  CIP

In memory of Sam Melville (Grossman)

CONTENTS

LIST OF TABLES

INTRODUCTION TO THE
TRANSACTION EDITION

Reissuing a work a quarter of a century after its initial publication requires some sort of justification. Usually, this takes an explanatory form of two sorts: claims as to the unique worth of the book in question; or charges that the works produced in the interim do not measure up to the standards set by and in the earlier volume.

Either approach is risky, involving appeals to egotism more than to intellect. Of course, one can always appeal to the demands of the marketplace. In the case of *Foundations of Political Sociology*, such claims are not entirely without merit, but they tend to beg rather than answer the questions: why this book, and why now? So let me take the bull by its horns, so to speak, and deal with the two kinds of claims described in the opening paragraph.

When *Foundations of Political Sociology* was first published it met a curious reception. Established sociology journals dealt with it in a less than friendly way. Political science journals were enthusiastic. I found this curious because I had worked so hard to convince the reader that because sociologists have a strong interest in issues of social class and stratification, and how these impact mass participation and voting behavior, they are more likely to deal with political sociology. Political scientists, I indicated, are more likely to be concerned with political socialization, that is, how a citizenry becomes identified with a nation and/or a party through the processes of legitimacy and participation. Further, I made it quite plain that my own preferences were slanted toward the sociological end of the political process—that is, issues related to class, race, ethnicity, and nationality—rather than types of rule and forms of legitimacy.

What then explains this topsy-turvy response? Let me venture a response to an outcome that has long vexed me. The sociological tradition, by the start of the 1970s at least, had become enamored of ideal types and formalization procedures of all sorts. Systems and processes—whether in Weberian or Marxian terms—had been extracted from Weber and Marx as such. What remained was less a study of actual systems than a scheme for identifying forms of domination and legitimation. We began to see books on modernity and the state written at such a high level of abstraction that the sense of the empirical was all but lost. As a result, political sociology fell victim to this thirst for formalization. In the process, it was also victimized by general theories so removed from actual processes of domination and legitimation as to lose any commonsensical meaning or relevance to grounded theory.

In the professional world of the early 1970s, sociology was viewed as some sort of a pie, to be divided into slices called economic sociology, political psychology, military sociology, and, of course, the subject of this book, political sociology. While this neat division of labor permitted developing new frameworks of analysis, it did not offer much in the way of synthesis. This process of balkanization, called specialization, within social research has continued well into the 1990s. One major goal of *Foundations of Political Sociology* was to identify the critical integrative issues that gave flesh and blood to the field. In retrospect it is easy to see why the book was viewed as less than successful by some of my sociological colleagues.

Political scientists, for their part, resonated to the book, despite its being clearly biased toward classical themes in sociology, for a variety of reasons. A large portion of the book was given over the study of actual political systems—fascism, socialism, liberalism, conservatism—and this emphasis on "isms" was very much a part of the work study habits of political scientists. From my point of view, I was simply aiming to return to a more sober, common sense of "systems"—one that took as a starting point the way organization and ideology were integrated into the structure of political domination.

An additional irritant to some sociologists of the time was my avoidance of the emphasis—then quite fashionable—of voting behavior as a measure of Left-Center-Right behavior, moving from that point into the study of a thing called "political man." What was dubiously gained in this attempt to correlate public opinion with political rule was profoundly lost in avoiding the simple fact that, for most nations and systems on earth, voting was not a central agenda item in the organization of political life. Fashioning general theory on such shaky premises was self-defeating at the outset.

Again, the political scientists came to the rescue. They inhabited a far richer world in which voting was problematic rather than given, and in which key issues of elites and masses, legitimacy and illegitimacy (political that is), and national interests and global organizations were themselves essential frameworks for studying the political dialectic. For political scientists, a book like *Foundations of Political Sociology* made good sense, or at least reasonable sense. In this, my book is surely a firm bridgehead between disciplines—one that emphasizes major stratification variables, but does so in a context of varieties of political systems.

The work also served as a bridgehead between cultures. It had the distinction of being published in fine editions by major firms in the German, Spanish, and Portuguese languages. It was even issued in Hong Kong in a so-called "pirated" edition. The continuing use of the book in these foreign language editions serves to buoy my belief that its issuance in English—even without urgently needed corrections and changes—is not simply a function of vanity. Indeed, I would say that whatever reputation I have in Germany, which, after all, was a founding home for the discipline of political sociology, is largely based on the five-volume paperback edition of the book—an effort made possible by my personal friend and political adversary, the late Petra Kelley.

Much has happened in the past quarter century. Indeed, much takes place every day to either confirm or disconfirm a wide variety of assumptions and beliefs about the nature of the world. In this, *Foundations of Political Sociology* is clearly not exempt from this process. In parts, it has a creaky feeling and in others yet, a cranky quality. I will spare the reader, and my ego, from identifying which is which. However, several key changes have taken place that define the century and not just a quarter century. These must be acknowledged if the book is to be read in context and with fairness.

Foremost among these changes is the reconfiguration of the geo-political map with the collapse of European Communism. As I wrote soon after the events themselves, 1989 is equal in importance, in world historic importance, to 1789. The demise of the Soviet Union closed out what had been opened up two hundred years earlier: a belief that dictatorship can cure the aches and pains of ordinary people by the simple act of removing a class irritant, be it the aristocracy in France or the bourgeoisie in Russia.

The direct rule of the body politic, without mediation by the normal process of the economic marketplace, not only failed to resolve disparities, but made them sharper and greater. Political despotisms displaced class iniquities with human frailties. Issues of life and death displaced those of wages and hours—to the greater glory of the political system but to the calamitous consequences of the ordinary people who had dedicated their lives to revolutions and their leaders.

As a result, the ground of political sociology has shifted from discussions on communism, fascism, anarchism, and assorted time specific systems to a more fundamental, albeit older tradition of equality and inequality as polarized expressions of ideals and realities. Thus, there has been a rediscovery of how a tradition in politics that extends from John Locke to Harold Laski argues for equity as a right no less than as a remote ideal. But there has been a corresponding rediscovery of another element of that older tradition, extending from Plato to Alexis de Tocqueville, that argues the naturalness of some forms of social inequality, and the obligations of citizens to commonwealth. *Foundations of Political Sociology* might have benefitted from showing how conservatism and liberalism in particular provide a series of domain assumptions for the other "isms" of the century. In this way, the excessive relativism of the book might have been dealt with, if not entirely overcome.

Despotism has hardly vanished from the face of the earth in the past quarter century. Indeed, it might be argued that the killing fields have become institutionalized—from Cambodia to Rwanda to the parts of an entity formerly called Yugoslavia. But at the same time, democratic institutions have been immeasurably strengthened the world over—ranging from Russia to South Africa, and in places like Algeria and Egypt where expectations for normalization scarcely existed a quarter century ago.

Economic freedom is not imposed from the top, not simply a product of "positive" (read statist) reforms, but a matter of choices and decisions made by ordinary people unfettered by the political systems in which they may find themselves. This understanding is an equally enormous development of the past quarter century. The tremendous efforts of nonpolitical sociologists—people as far removed as Peter Berger and Michael Novak—must be mentioned as having brought to a high level of consciousness acceptance of the significance of the free market in the creation of the free society. While these people were following in the footsteps of Milton Friedman, Friedrich von Hayek, Michael Polanyi, and others, they were far better prophets of the present than professional sociologists and political scientists alike.

A final area that needs far more amplification than provided in the earlier edition of *Foundations of Political Sociology* is the interaction of technology, information, and social action—or what, as a shorthand, I would call the Orwellian Dimension. The political process is now carefully calibrated to a world in which information and propaganda are constantly intermingled. While other works of mine deal with these issues, I confess that this book gave far too little weight to such epiphenomena. The production of ideas, perhaps even more than the production of goods, now determines the character of political regimes. Exploration of that enormous and irreducible fact deserves a work unto itself.

To the catalogue of paired issues that I did deal with—elites and masses, legitimacy and illegitimacy, specific interests and general values—would have to be added publicity and privacy. Especially in democratic and quasi-democratic regimes, the relationship between what an individual can claim as a private domain and what a society can claim as the public's right to know requires far greater attention than is now found in the literature of political sociology. Clearly, such an issue is central to defining societies. The authors of *The Federalist Papers,* Hamilton, Madison, and Jay, understood this cluster of concerns well—certainly far better than sociologists, who in their almighty arrogance simply assume a special knowledge of what is good for ordinary people to know and not know. Worse, they rarely take seriously a realm of life in which that which is not required for the exercise of the commonweal remains the personal preserve of the private person.

That the issue of publicity and privacy was hardly examined was less an oversight on my part than a huge shift in the fault line of politics as such. The new technology, which has fueled an explosion of information and data, has also been central in determining social relationships: who shall read and/or write, what shall be read and written, and where and when. Tensions between individuals and authorities have resulted in a recasting of who should have power over certain types of information; such guidelines continue to be outstripped by real world events. Clearly, to reflect upon a treatise on political sociology a quarter century after the fact is to appreciate the fact that it is not only personal limits and proclivities that must be examined, but some impersonal limits that reshape ideas and cultures no less than systems and structures.

Democracy versus totalitarianism. Free markets versus command systems. The public right to know versus the personal right to privacy. These three vast areas have undergone great changes in the past quarter of a century. *Foundations of Political Sociology* does little to shed light on these areas, in part because of changes in the world at large. In all truth, they are also a function of weakness in the evolution of my own political formation at the time. Had I looked more closely and precisely at the Anglo-American traditions, or if one prefers, the empirical frameworks, and less critically at the Continental European tradition, or if one prefers, rationalist frameworks, *Foundations of Political Sociology* would have been a better book.

Having said all this, I do emphatically believe that this long unavailable title continues to merit present-day consideration. That it failed to predict cataclysmic events is not much of a criticism. It was never its purpose to do so. That my volume failed to take into proper balance the extant literature of the time— especially the anti-totalitarian literature that abounded—is more justifiably a criticism. In this, I must plead ignorance more than guilt—unless, of course, the two words are convertible currencies.

Were I to undertake the huge task of preparing a new edition of *Foundations of Political Sociology*, recent political configurations and ideological shifts would take front and center. At the same time, the vast literature of political philosophy, with its emphasis on policy-making and decision theory, would play a far larger role. I would also need to distinguish that which is permanent and that which is transient in all things political. This would require a far deeper analysis of such phenomenon as nationalism and how even matters related to class, race, gender, and party may be subsumed under much larger moorings, such as the presumed clash of civilizations and cultures. Perhaps at some point in the future, such a task will be feasible. But for the present, I hope that this introduction makes clear my own sense of the limitations no less than worth of *Foundations of Political Sociology*. But clearly, I also hope these brief remarks will provide a framework to guide others in future integrative efforts, and in the process, secure a respectable place for itself in the field in which I have so much enjoyed working and living.

IRVING LOUIS HOROWITZ

Princeton, New Jersey
November 1996

ACKNOWLEDGMENTS

There is nothing more ritualistic in preparing a book for publication than the acknowledgments page. It is more like paying dues than offering homage. Yet the fact remains, as the great F. O. Matthiessen once remarked, that all of us who write a great deal, owe a great deal. And our acknowledgments are something of a side bet covering at least part of that indebtedness.

Until the hideous episode at Attica which took the life of my old friend Sam Melville Grossman, I had intended to dedicate this book to my father, a long overdue debt. Let me begin, then, by acknowledging his role:

> To Louis Horowitz, immigrant, laborer, organizer, whose slap across my face for distributing Republican Party campaign literature in the 1936 Presidential campaign gave me my first lesson in the social passion behind political power.

Since *Foundations of Political Sociology* emerges out of my two decades of teaching what I feel to be the core subject matter of political sociology, the key to the success of the book is, of course, the ceaseless questioning of the premises and content of my work by students and colleagues. This has been a shield and a buckler against error, and the fertilization that has occurred across time and place hopefully has made this a better book. I can only thank those countless people—at Hobart and William Smith, at the Universities of California, Wisconsin, Rochester and Stanford, at Washington University and, for the past three years, at Rutgers University—who raised the right questions and demanded more than feeble answers. I doubt seriously that this book will satisfy all of those who had to endure my lectures, or that the personal learning process will now translate itself into collective conscience. After all, the nature of knowledge, not to mention the nature of academic interests, would make such an outcome impossible and probably unhealthy were it possible. Yet I do believe, with all my heart, that what is presented here is a synthesis no less than a symposium—a way of looking at the world, no less than a way of carving up classroom assignments.

In this task I have had the help of many scholars, many friends and many institutions. I hope, with this book, that I can now repay the contributions of scholars, friends and institutions, however imperfectly.

Two people, who each co-authored a chapter with me, deserve special recognition. First there is my former wife and good friend, Ruth Leonora Horowitz, now of the University of Washington in Seattle, who I belatedly realize was at least as much an "influence" on my work, as I on her work —indeed probably more so. Second is my former student at Washington University in St. Louis, Martin Liebowitz, who more nearly than any other student in the mid-sixties I was privileged to teach, understood the points of intersection between intellectual commitment and political activity.

The following people have read, criticized or helped rewrite one or more chapters:

> Donald G. MacRae (London School of Economics)
> Daniel Bell (Harvard University)
> William H. Friedland (University of California at Santa Cruz)
> Richard R. Fagen (Stanford University)
> David Mechanic (University of Wisconsin)
> Robert Hamblin (The University of Arizona)
> Henry Riecken (Social Science Research Council)
> Pio D. Uliassi (United States Department of State)
> Aaron Wildavsky (University of California at Berkeley)
> Howard S. Becker (Northwestern University)
> Lee Rainwater (Harvard University)
> Tom B. Bottomore (University of Sussex)

I take their kindness and solicitude as vital inputs to my efforts. I only hope that they are not held responsible for the book as a whole, or any of the errors in part. I am painfully aware that this list is partial; perhaps all that it really succeeds in doing is providing the reader with a range of influences.

I must acknowledge the tremendous technical help I received in preparing this manuscript for publication. As anyone who does this sort of work comes to realize, writing the manuscript is roughly 50 percent of the work. The other 50 percent rarely receives its just due because of its definition as proletarian labor. And in the case of the world of books, such "dirty workers" more often than not turn out to be women workers. The manuscript was typed and retyped in a nearly endless stream of versions by Lois McGarry, Rayne Ayers and Mary Wilk. Each of these people, with their sensitivities and sensibilities, spared me more than a few errors. The manuscript was copyedited twice: first by an anonymous male at Harper & Row, and second by Mary E. Curtis, who, when she has nothing better to do, serves as executive editor of the book division at *trans*action. The production editor for the book at Harper & Row was Kathleen Mac-Dougall and rarely has an author been more fortunate in his choice of accidents. Finally, there is my good friend and loyal supporter at Harper & Row, Jim Clark, who has put up with my nonsense through thick and thin and three different publishing firms.

I gratefully acknowledge permissions granted by the following publications to use materials from articles originally published by them. The citations are to the original articles, with the chapters of the book containing material from these articles given in parentheses following citations. These articles have been revised, either slightly or substantially, depending on their age and their applicability to the overall design of the book. For the most part, each original article represents only a fraction of each final chapter.

"The Hegelian Concept of Positive Freedom," *The Journal of Politics.* Volume 28, Number 1, February 1966 (Chapter 4).

"The New Conservatism," *Science and Society.* Volume 20, Number 1, Winter 1955-56 (Chapter 6).

"Natural Man and Political Man," from *The Anarchists,* ed. Irving Louis Horowitz. New York: Dell Publishing Company, 1964 (Chapter 8).

"The Military as a Subculture," from *Protagonists of Change,* ed. Abdul A. Said. Englewood Cliffs, N.J.: Prentice-Hall, Inc., 1971 (Chapter 14).

"Social Deviance and Political Marginality" (co-authored with Martin Liebowitz), *Social Problems.* Volume 15, Number 3, Winter 1967 (Chapter 15).

"Social Science and Public Policy: The Political Foundations of Modern Research," *International Studies Quarterly.* Volume 11, Number 1, March 1967 (Chapter 16).

"The Academy and the Polity," *The Journal of Applied Behavioral Science.* Volume 5, Number 3, July-September 1969 (Chapter 17).

"Social Science Mandarins: Policymaking as a Political Formula," *Policy Sciences: An International Journal.* Volume 1, Number 3, Fall 1970 (Chapter 18).

"Tax-Exempt Foundations: Their Effects on National Policy" (co-authored with Ruth Leonora Horowitz), *Science.* Volume 168, Whole Number 3928, April 1970; Copyright 1970 by the American Association for the Advancement of Science (Chapter 19).

"Deterrence Games," from *The Structure of Conflict,* ed. Paul Swingle. New York and London: Academic Press, 1970; Copyright 1970 by Academic Press (Chapter 20).

"La Condition de la classe ouvrière aux États-Unis," *Sociologie du Travail.* Volume 13, Number 3, July-September 1971 (Chapter 23).

"On Alienation and the Social Order," *Philosophy and Phenomenological Research.* Volume 27, Number 2, December 1966 (Chapter 26).

If the acknowledgments page is ritualistic, so too is the inevitable disclaimer that comes at the end, gracefully accepting all responsibility for the contents of the book—the errors are mine, the truths are thine. Which for all its sanctimonious hypocrisy is probably the way things should be, since we all inhabit a world of human frailty rather than a world of divine guidance.

PREFACE

The famous South African novelist, Nadine Gordimer, has recently reminded us that "a writer writes one book all his life; whether consciously so or not, his work is of a piece." The more I thought about what makes *Foundations of Political Sociology* different, the clearer it became that the book was a piece with all of my other basic writings over the past fifteen years beginning with *The Idea of War and Peace, Radicalism and the Revolt Against Reason,* and, above all, *Three Worlds of Development* and *Professing Sociology.* Because she postulates a unitary character to the intellectual career of a person, Miss Gordimer also provides whatever rationalization might be needed for a book. "For this reason the writer is entitled to present as the provisional entity between two covers, which is what any single book is, any combination of writing that he sees as that entity." Indeed, even though I confine myself to writing about political sociology in this book, it is plain that this is not a first codification of the subject, or even a last ultimate statement, but rather my most systematic exposition of problems that I have and undoubtedly will continue to address my attentions and energies to.

Foundations of Political Sociology is at its core a statement about the transformation of a past-oriented series of reflections into a goal-oriented series of prescriptions. The book further shows how this becomes possible by a shift of emphasis from a political economy of the nineteenth century based on history, to a political society of the twentieth century based on policy. This is a fundamental alteration. Today our realities are dictated by problems of allocation as much as by problems of production. They are guided by the articulation of interests as much as by the stampeding of masses or the sullen alienation of individuals. In whatever direction one looks, the increase in the role of political life with respect to economic life becomes clear.

It is more apparent to me now, than at the beginning of this long intellectual journey, that the distance between things political, social, military and economic has narrowed dramatically through the century. This diminishing gap does not, however, signify that the relationships have simplified. Quite the contrary; relationships between large-scale factors have become more complex over time, despite, or perhaps because of, the concentration of activities in fewer and fewer major institutions. What I am discussing throughout this book is the function of power in its various and sundry guises. And if many aspects of power seem linked to the activities of economic conglomerates and the goals of military institutions, this itself is a reflection of what is increasingly a basic political and sociological reality: namely, the rise of the military factor as intertwined with the economic factor in the codetermination of the social and political life of men and nations.

To talk of a military-industrial complex is to take for granted an engineered political arrangement; to talk about the overthrow of state power is to assume the essentially political goals of insurgency and counterinsurgency; to talk about what policy does to people is to believe that they can be molded into something other than what they are by the political apparatus. In short, economics does not disappear, but rather becomes the limiting factor of political sociology. There are still things that cannot be answered by political sociology, but there are a great many more things that cannot be answered by assuming the primacy of economics over other areas of social intercourse.

This means that idle chatter about "base" and "superstructure" has become an anachronism. Politics and economics move in and out of each other throughout society, like the ebb and flow of an ocean. They are no more subject to the determinations of classical mercantile capitalism than is socialism simply a new mode of monetary exchange. Everywhere the state becomes more powerful. Everywhere the forces that move the state increase in strength. Everywhere the essential rhetoric of the state, nationalism, is on the incline. The effects of political structures on the affairs of ordinary men in their everyday activities has become the essence of any sound social science.

If we are confined by reality to clustering large-scale factors in contrast to analysis of small-scale factors, this is not indicative of a cloudiness of vision. Quite the contrary; it shows that we have finally gotten beyond the monistic point of view that any single variable satisfactorily explains all other variables in the functioning of social life. To deal with the realities of politics, economics and militarism, is to unfold a subtle mosaic of social life that has become more complex and even more opaque as the century moves along. Under the circumstances, artificial precision at the expense of truthful representation, serves the ends of dogmatism and obscurantism—forms of special pleading that social scientists are dedicated in principle and in practice to remove. The conventional pluralistic formula of political sociology has been reduced to class, status and power. For my part, if reduction is necessary, I prefer the formula of econor.y, polity, and military. How the "big three" as a whole and then in parts inteisect and interact with problems of social stratification and social structure is the essence of *Foundations of Political Sociology*.

Nor am I harkening a return to "sociological imperialism," in which all economic, political and psychological realities are subsumed under a tautological category called "interactions." Rather, it is an appreciation that new absolutisms, along with new relativisms, have sprung up. And the world is not simply a wide open universe in the pragmatic Jamesian sense, but rather a rigorously deterministic one in the Hegelian idealistic sense. We have, over time, moved from economic self-regulators to political regulators, from economic classes to categories of political elites. It is not a simple-minded reversal of base and superstructure. The political life is no longer the base and the economic life is no longer the superstructure. It is rather that such rhetoric, such language, so soothing in the nineteenth century, no longer explains the fusions of social welfare and policy making, no longer explains the interconnection of men of power across class lines, united against men without power, again often grouped across class lines.

Conventional models of the social system rely on levels of generalization that are either too abstract to have political meaning, or too ambiguous to provide policy guidelines. Thus, we have functional frameworks based on the social system as the whole, with economic, political and psychological variables as the parts. Or we are given the received wisdom of social systems as being identical with a dominant social class, as if the ruling class is omnipotent or omniscient, and as if expressions of its interests and values are perfectly isomorphic with the character of the social system at any given moment in time. The newest claimant to our attentions and affections is the phenomenological denial that a social system exists at all; rather, what is real are only atomic particles called individuals who interact and make demands upon one another through an exchange network. My own position compels a different starting point: Just as we have moved over time from political economy to political sociology, so too have we moved to an understanding of social systems as essentially political in definition and demarcation. Commonsense triumphs over nonsense. Fascism, communism, liberalism, anarchism, etc., constitute the appropriate level to deal with the social system. These "isms" permit an appreciation of the interpenetration of the social organization of economic life with the ideological mobilization of political life. This treatment of social systems is carried through in my analysis of military systems and also stratification systems.

While taking full cognizance of model construction and historical stages, one must begin with a concrete realization that the political sociology of growth is the central organizing pivot for any modern discussion of social systems. This book is a foundation of political sociology, not in the simple-minded sense that no one has before put together such a package, although strange to say, this too is seemingly the case; but a foundation in that the book takes seriously the dissolution of political economy as a unique explanatory model, and its replacement with political sociology as a central tendency in the study of how the state functions in relation to the society.

I have been teaching a course based on at least some aspects of these pages since 1957. Indeed, during the last fifteen years not a year has gone by that I have not been privileged to teach such a course. And each environment was a challenge. In the United States I taught this course for a decade, at Washington University and now at Rutgers University. And even before then, I had the opportunity to teach political sociology at the State University of New York at Buffalo, Syracuse University, Hobart and William Smith Colleges and the University of Rochester. More recently, I've offered the course on visiting appointments at the Universities of California and Wisconsin and Stanford University. And then there were the remarkable opportunities to test out this material in such different environments at the National University of Mexico, the Hebrew University in Jerusalem, the University of Buenos Aires and, most recently, at the University of Sussex in England.

Everywhere I went, I learned something new. Everywhere I taught, I was made to appreciate the need for greater clarity and specificity. Everywhere I confronted the same intellectual problems, albeit in different specific guises. To all of the people in the past of my life, and in the present of my life, goes my deepest sense of obligation and gratitude. For if the words are my own, and the errors even more emphatically my own, the ideas expressed, insofar as they accurately reflect and portray social realities, belong to the collectivities with whom I have had the opportunity to interact.

Political sociology has arisen, like a phoenix, from the dry bones of political economy. There is no adequate text on the political economy of contemporary socialism, or for that matter the political economy of contemporary capitalism, for no such book can be seriously written—since sociological and political aspects have conspired to determine, at least as often as they are determined by, economic factors and thus, to shape the substance of our social world. This then is the message of my book. The rest is elaboration.

IRVING LOUIS HOROWITZ

New Brunswick
Christmas Day, 1971

HISTORIES

CHAPTER 1

AN HISTORICAL INTRODUCTION TO POLITICAL SOCIOLOGY

The purpose of this work is to explain the relationship between the basic social variables of class, caste, ethnicity and race and how they intersect and interpenetrate the key political variables of power, authority, sovereignty and representation. Political sociology, the general rubric under which such studies are categorized, should not be confused with political socialization, which is the examination of how people become socialized into political behavior. The desperate search for the different rather than the distinctive has led to a profound overestimation of the "civic culture" at the expense of the "political culture." Whatever the merits of this adult reworking of basic civics for Everyman, it cannot and should not be confused with political sociology.

The questions that political sociology can attempt to answer are quite distinct. For example: How does social class affect voting patterns? What is the relationship between religious fundamentalism and political conservatism? Why should the generational factor have any bearing on political ideologies? Who determines political destinies—elites or masses, influentials or ordinary citizens? When does political behavior become most significant —under electoral conditions or under dictatorship?

As political sociology differs from political socialization, it also can be distinguished from voting analysis—for political life often becomes most decisive and intriguing precisely at points when and where electoral processes break down (if indeed they ever existed). In this sense, the psychological aspects of socialization on the one hand and the aspects of voting behavior on the other represent the outer limits rather than the core of the study of political sociology.

Political sociology as a quasi-formal enterprise begins in the eighteenth century. At that historical point, the dialogue between society and state was begun in earnest. In fact, the eighteenth century can be divided, at least the French portion, into two parts: (1) the period of the *philosophes* and (2) the period of Rousseau. Such a division may seem to set up an uneven contest between one man and a whole school of thought, but I think not. The contest was quite evenly matched, and the dialogue meaningful. From it emerged the basic terms of political sociology, with a clarity and precision that haunts the twentieth century.

For the Enlightenment in general, the most important single premise was the idea of man as a social animal, or the reassertion of the Aristotelian premise that the way to understand man was through the study of society. In itself, this was an empty platitude; but the notion of man as a social being was not so vague and vacuous. Underlying the idea that man is a social animal was the notion of civilization, or, in modern terms, social responsibility for the individual. The essence of man as a social animal, unlike the Aristotelian polity in opposition to it, was that man was social not by virtue of his biological composition, but rather by virtue of the responsibilities that a society assumed for its citizenry.

This was an immense change from classical capitalist doctrines of the seventeenth century, and certainly from the medieval world's parochial concept of society as a set of obligations that lords and serfs had to one another. In the eighteenth century, Enlightenment doctrine, or "illumination," was that the individual fulfilled himself through society. Because of that, society assumed a role with respect to the individual's welfare. The Rousseauian rejoinder in some measure was that the notion of man as a social animal did not come to terms with the problem of the general will. And the general will was not so much a matter of the individual with respect to the society, but rather of the commonweal with respect to the person. The exchange agreement, in *The Social Contract* (Rousseau, 1913), ironically, was not a social contract, but a political contract, a firm contract with the state. The appropriate name for the book would have been *Contrat d'etat* rather than *Contrat social,* because in effect the arrangements made and worked out for mutual protection and exchange were not with the society; therefore the commonweal was not concerned with the problem of man in society, but that of man in the state.

What makes this such a potent and important notion is that the state, in the eighteenth century at least, did not have a myth of glorification about it—that is, the notion of society was a much more generous one than the notion of the state. "Society" did not involve any concept of coercion; nor did it entail negative obligation. The notion of the society's responsibility for its citizens was a positive concept: society doing things for people in a beneficient way revolutionized all notions of personal behavior. The notion of the state and its concordat with the person has an almost Faustian ring—that is to say, the bargain is a devil's bargain. It is extremely important to note that Rousseau well understood the diabolical nature of the relationship of the person and the state, whereas the men of the Enlightenment saw only the optimistic aspects, namely, the social response and fulfillment of responsibility to its citizenry. The relationship between the individual and society, which was developed by the *philosophes*, is fundamentally different from that between the person and the state, which was developed by Rousseau.

Another enormous area of difference between the eighteenth century and earlier epochs was that the kingdom of reason displaced the preeminence of custom in the affairs of men. This difference was primarily what made the eighteenth century the age that brought about a political sociology and raised the questions that later became paramount in the discipline. Both the *philosophes* and Rousseau were fully cognizant of the irrationality of the person. Men like Diderot, Holbach and Helvétius were not fools. The assumptions by the *philosophes* were several: that society curbed man's natural propensities, and man through society became reasonable; that society, in effect, was a rationalizing agency; that society acted on the natural man or on the individual presocialized agent in such a way as to mold the person into a rational form. The highest expression of that rationality was utility, or the notion of what we call utilitarianism. In effect, utility theory argued the rationality of the bargain. It was bourgeois. Man and society made an agreement to perform certain obligations in order to get certain things in return. It was a thoroughly commercial notion of rationality. Why should man be good in society?—this was the kind of question Helvétius asked. The answer was that an exchange network would be to his advantage. Every man having the faculty of reason (reason being, in effect, utility, or hedonistic self-interest) knew that, in order to fulfill his self-interest, he became a member of society, and that society was the collectivized expression of the rational ego. Man could now be reasonable because he could now be utilitarian, and vice versa; his rationality was defined to the very degree that he participated in the exchange network.

The early nineteenth century brought forth hedonistic Bentham and his calculus, where utility principles were the ultimate measurement. The point of view of the utilitarians was very appealing and commonsensical. It was not an abstract idealistic notion of reason. It was not a Hegelian notion; it was an exchange notion—the reason of the stomach, the reason of the marketplace, the reason of wealth, the reason of status, the reason of utility, the reason of selfishness. Selfishness would prove out the rationality of men. The ego was not a bad thing for the *philosophe*. He saw in the exchange network the very touchstone of reason. What could be more reasonable than self-interest and the natural fulfillment of it through the agency of the society, which would help resolve the problems that blocked the realization of self-interest?

The Rousseauian response to this interesting development was as follows: Even if one could warrant the rationality of the ego, even if one could demonstrate that in all cases the person acts in terms of his own interests, how would one unify those interests into a collective whole? How would one express through the general will the rationality of so many conflicting interests? And at what point would the interests that men have move contrary to one another and break down any notion of rationality in society? So ultimately, the question for Rousseau was not the rationality of the ego; rather, he called into question the rationality of the state. Even if man was reasonable, the state, the economy, the general overall polity was unreasonable because the general will stood over and above its particular manifestations. It was a summation of all its parts and was therefore something else—and that something else rose in opposition to the reason of the person and the reason of the state. It became in itself such an irrational driving force that the very historical development, the very evolution of a society, the very attempt to resolve certain problems, did not lead to reason, but rather to exploitation, to unreason. To paraphrase Rousseau's *Discourse on Inequality* (1964, p. 218): For every solution to the problem of finance or money, the way we live commands as its asking price surrendering part of ourselves. The ego itself is often the asking price for the solution of these fundamental problems of civilization.

Another notion that divided the rationalists from the romantics was the notion of progress—that civilization could be measured step by step, brick by brick, building by building, dollar for dollar, pound for pound. These were obvious measurements of progress; progress was real and not only material but spiritual. Indeed, for Condorcet progress was measured by the spiritual development of the mind, not just by vulgar economics or materialism, but by the generosity of the person, by his increasing civilization, his increasing emergence from savagery. The future looked promising —music, art, literature, all of the cultivated fields. They seemed to betoken an age of universal progress, where the wisdom of necessity would be transformed and the wisdom of freedom would be realized, where the utopian solutions would become a matter of everyday life.

There was good measure and good reason to feel that way. It was not only the coming of the French Revolution but also the life of letters, the rise of a leisure class that was nonparasitical, intellective, independent of the sources of production, but at the same time not indolent. Nothing disturbed the enlightened nobility more than the notion of being wastrels. They understood the theory of automation, or how to be productive with one's life. Progress was measured by the growth of this leisure class and at the same time by the growth of their productivity. These men dedicated themselves to the life of the arts. It was a world, as Diderot put it in his most fervent moment, in which intellect itself was the basic form of action. The life of ideas was itself a means of activity in transforming the world. This was the ultimate in the evolution of bourgeois consciousness—and the ultimate that was ever expressed about the life of ideas. It was not that ideas led to action. It was not a crude assertion of praxis. Nor was it the relationship of theory and action. It was that ideas themselves were a species of the act. The ennobling impact of the *Encyclopedia* (Diderot, 1965) was itself an activity; it did not simply lead to activity.

This faith in a positive development of civilization was later picked up by Saint-Simon and became the rhetoric of European romantic sociology. It was also a main point upon which Rousseau based his criticism of the doctrine of equality, in the name of the general will. Rousseau's ultimate critique of egalitarianism was that inequality was the price of progress, Rousseau was a marvelous calculator of the costs of all social change. In effect, he held that civilization was attained by suppressing personality. It was the first expression of the Freudian theory of civilization and its discontents. Discontent was absorbed by the progress of civilization, and, in effect, progress was achieved by transforming the individual. In order to sustain himself, the individual became part of a collective whole. The only answer to the collectivization of civilization was the personality, and the personality was what Rousseau wanted to preserve. He was far from being a collectivist. The outcome of his thought was collectivism, but the input was individualism. The real juxtaposition was of man to all notions of civilization. For the romantic, progress was a highly personal and even private concept. Progress in any purely economic or material form necessitates a surrender on the part of the person to the role of growing civilization and the suppression of personality—that very personality that defines humanity; but for Rousseau the answer to civilization was the concept of man.

Several additional points need to be mentioned. In order to gain a society that was reasonable and at the same time became part of a general progress of civilization, the men of the Enlightenment held to the notion of class stratification. The irony, and it is an irony, is that all of the upholders of egalitarianism were at the same time believers in class stratification—Diderot, Voltaire, Holbach, Condorcet and every other writer of the Enlightenment. They all believed that the notion of class stratification as an axiom, as a way of life, had to be preserved. On the subject Voltaire was most forthright. He said a cook would always be necessary—how else would he, Voltaire, be served? How could he write his discourses on the egalitarian society unless there were people to serve him? He used Gallic wit but stated clearly that there were masters and there were slaves. In a world of equality how could there be secret transactions? How could there be private lives? How could there be room for the most personal acts, for the most intimate problems? For Voltaire and Diderot it was very clear that differences would be preserved. The human world depended on the necessity of a doctrine of social stratification. Is it any wonder that the *philosophes* (who started out proclaiming a doctrine of emancipation, a doctrine of the social necessity to solve individual problems) ended up by participating in a middle-class celebration after the French Revolution? As Harold Laski indicated, after the French Revolution of 1789, the state became a means of disciplining and mobilizing the working class. The notion of egalitarianism was not incommensurate with the notion of stratification, nor would it be for the next two hundred years.

In contrast to this was Rousseau's concept of liberty. The answer to equality was always the personal ability to say no. And liberty, unlike equality, was the freedom to be negative. It was the freedom to respond in a way that was not part of the march of civilization. Ironically, that notion of personal liberty, which Rousseau upheld, ended in a denial of stratification. In the world of Geneve, distinctions would be based only upon knowledge, and even that would be liquidated in time because, in the world of Geneve, the better students would teach the poorer students and there would be a whole rotation of people learning from one another so that eventually all would develop in their own ways. But Rousseau's idea of liberty was in some sense a rebuke even to this notion of class distinction. This brings us to two final points.

The eighteenth-century *philosophes* were at their source ideologists of liberalism. It is impossible to read any of them and walk away with any feeling but one of their liberalism—a liberalism that involved an extensive degree of compromise and depended in great measure on the arts of compromise: the coexistence of different social and economic classes, bringing about collective change of progress and civilization in a consensual way. The Rousseauian option was at one and the same time one of reaction and radicalism. That is why no one has solved the Rousseauian problem—because Rousseau was an expression within himself of reaction and radicalism. If there is any lesson to be derived from him, it is that the gulf between radicalism and reaction is much narrower than the gulf between either of those two and liberalism. It is liberalism that is a monstrosity from the point of view of either a Right or Left Rousseauian. Rousseau is the highest expression of the notion of totalitarian democracy and the neurotic man. With Rousseau, reason became the doctrine of assault on social custom. Reason was based on necessity and yet was the cement of the state.

From a methodological point of view, it was a struggle between the materialism of the *philosophes* and the dialectics of Rousseau. As far as the secularists and naturalists were concerned, the world was reasonable precisely because of the banality and ordinariness of human wants and desires. For Rousseau, the irrationality, the unreasoning properties of men, the endless questioning made him necessarily a dialectician, a cost accountant. Rousseau was a bookkeeper of society. He evaluated the debits and credits and never made any assumption that the good and the true were always found to coexist. He always had a sharp eye for measuring the costs of every step forward. So here, too, we have the methodological struggle between scientism and dialecticism—a struggle that was not to be resolved easily. But this is the framework of a world of totalitarian democracy or liberalism.

A final point to consider here is the manner in which we tend to re-evaluate and reestimate the world of the past. In the 1930s and perhaps even in the 1920s, when one spoke of the eighteenth century, when one thought of the characteristic figure, Voltaire came to mind. Voltaire was the man of the century, the expression of its wisdom, characterized as the age of liberalism. But by the 1960s, the characteristic figure was Rousseau, as our problem became the interpenetration of radicalism and totalitarianism. What this does is shift our vision of allocation of responsibility for the failures of the century; because if there is one thing that must be said, it is that the eighteenth century was a failure. The Revolution failed; it was betrayed. The question became: Who betrayed it? Why did it fail? What went wrong? And beyond the obvious issues: What is the difference between betrayal and accommodation, between failure and success, between right and wrong in politics?

These questions were raised in precisely the same manner when later spokesmen, ideologists and social investigators spoke about the Soviet Revolution. The answers usually were framed in terms of the failures of the Revolution to fully implement its own rhetoric. In theory, brotherhood, equality, liberty were universalistic; in practice, they were restricted to members of certain classes, races and castes. Political sociology became viable precisely to the degree that the eighteenth century made explicit *political* promissory notes to redeem *social* injustices and yet failed to do so, or better, did so partially. Therefore, the earliest problems of political sociology were both quantitative and qualitative: the measurement of the extent to which the French Revolution created the basis for universal enfranchisement, and the restraints imposed by the very successes of the Revolution. This was a problem not only in simple measurement but also in complex human choices. The makers of the Revolution were often the betrayers of the Revolution. Whether such treason was a function of altered circumstances, altered consciousness or some combination of the two has become a focal point for contemporary political sociology, the difference between real history and imaginary history, the difference between pre-revolutionary societies and postrevolutionary societies, the difference between a revolution made in the name of all mankind and one that benefits selective portions of the elite. And if the victory of the French Revolution spawned the rise of political socialization, the abortive and limited characteristics of constitutionalism did more: They spawned the rise of political sociology.

REFERENCES

Diderot, D. (1965) *Encyclopedia: Selections by Diderot, d'Alembert and a Society of Men of Letters,* trans. N. S. Hoyt and T. Cassirer. Indianapolis: Bobbs-Merrill.

Rousseau, J. J. (1913) *The Social Contract,* trans. G. D. H. Cole. New York: Dutton.

Rousseau, J. J. (1964) *Discourse on the Origin and Foundations of Inequality: The First and Second Discourses,* ed. R. D. Masters and trans. R. D. and J. R. Masters. New York: St. Martin's Press.

CHAPTER 2

A THEORETICAL
INTRODUCTION TO
POLITICAL SOCIOLOGY

Political science has a strange lineage. Its intellectual antecedents are bifurcated between the utopian (Platonic) inheritance involving the image of the perfect polity, and the pragmatic (Machiavellian) inheritance involving the image of the perfect scoundrel. The ancestry of political science has a double element of futurism: the utopian longing after political perfection, and, in contrast, an exact evocative picture of how one rules satisfactorily on an everyday basis. What fused these two utterly disparate frameworks, what prevented their dissolution over time, is that both utopists and pragmatists served the same elitist masters. Political science is united, therefore, not so much by abstract theory, but by its specifically elitist response to the needs of those who rule or who seek to rule.

This split between the Platonic and the Machiavellian within the historical development of political science is a dialogue that takes place just as much within Plato and within Machiavelli as between them. Machiavellianism really contains the seeds of utopianism just as, conversely, Platonism contains the seeds of the so-called policy of Machiavellian orientation. Machiavellianism took the form of a search for a united Italy, Caesarism—the vindication of the national destiny of the Latin peoples, especially the Italian peoples. It was more than a program for a crude nationalism or on how one should behave in power; such lessons had been provided long before Machiavelli. Furthermore, even in the Platonic heights there are Machiavellian depths, for Plato was a conspirator, a man who was connected to the land oligarchy yet dedicated in his political behavior to the democratic polis. This dialectic is important to recognize because while the schisms that a science develops have certain points of overlap with other sciences, they also have certain autonomous elements. The autonomous problem for political science has been policy orientation for the present versus the long-range programing of the good society.

Another related large-scale schism unique to political science is the notion of political *philosophy* in contrast to a notion of political *science*— or as Leo Strauss (1959, pp. 9–55) put it, political science can be viewed as a higher form of political philosophy. This position is in marked contrast to the empirical descriptive view that in the main prevails in political science, as indeed it does in most social sciences. The empirical view is that political science, insofar as it is a science, has to behave like the other social science disciplines. It is obligated to study man in the same way with the most up-to-date tools available and as far as possible with the same kind of value neutrality toward the object under consideration.

The political philosophers within political science who are critical of empiricism, esteemed and prominent figures like Daniel Boorstin, Russell Kirk and Leo Strauss, tend, interestingly enough, to be highly conservative in their ideological moorings. They want a political science of meaning or value content. There is a curious similarity between the political philosopher in search of meaning and the more recent tendencies toward a sociology of large-scale meaning. However, in the field of political science, unlike sociology, the revolt against empiricism is an antiscientific revolt led by men of conservative orientation. Within sociology the revolt against empiricism is a radical or liberal revolt. It may be a matter of historical timing, or due to the internal characteristics of organizations, but the revolts against empiricism seem to be coming from opposite sides. As a result of the conservative nature of the political science revolt, the empiricist orthodoxies have been largely successful in claiming that such assaults on orthodoxy are a disguised revolt against science itself. However, if this has delayed the emergence of a radical critique within political science, it has not alleviated the sources of discontent common to all the social sciences (Surkin and Wolfe, 1970).

To summarize, the central characteristics of political sciences are (1) a tension between the utopian orientation and the political orientation, and (2) large-scale, or macro-, antiempiricism versus micro-scientific tendencies. Bearing in mind all the nuances and contradictory aspects involved, one may then ask, What is the relationship between political science and sociology?

One would have to start by saying that the political scientist believes in

EMPIRICAL: EXP GAINED ON EXPERIMENT RATHER THAN THEORY.

the state in the same proportion and to the same extent that the sociologist believes in society. The question is, in effect, What is of larger importance? Which is the most significant feature of human life? The Greek philosophical inheritance never satisfactorily resolved this question. Within the Platonic-Aristotelian framework one moves directly from society to polity to ethics, but at the level of social life one is never told whether the state is the capstone of the society, or the society embraces or is larger in its significance than the state.

The decision one reaches on this question in great measure determines whether an individual's fundamental orientation, not just department affiliation, is that of a political scientist or a sociologist. For if the state is the supremely important variable in contrast to the society, several consequences follow. The most important is that the formal organization of society that the state embraces becomes central to any study. The state, after all, is a formal arrangement, a legally sanctioned sovereign entity with a well-defined set of legal structures, not just normative structures. If, however, the choice is made in terms of sociology or in terms of society, then the informal, normative, culturally bound phenomena, the nonlegal or sublegal aspects, become important—those things in the life of man that are not covered by any legal contingency.

The choice between state and society is not simply a choice between words; it is a choice between two monumental concepts. It is this problem that divided the nineteenth-century classical social scientists. The schism was always between those who accentuated state power, people like Hegel and Gumplowicz, and those who emphasized social power, like Durkheim and Simmel. Interestingly, on this question Marx was very ambiguous and extremely vague. In his early writings (his 1846 *The German Ideology,* for instance), Marx opposed Hegel, saying that society is greater than any state, that the state form is only the distorted reflection of those in power. However, in the *Critique of the Gotha Program,* written thirty years later, in 1871, Marx talked about the state as the definition of the revolutionary situation and emphasized that state power, not social power, determines when or if the revolution is successful (Marx, 1938, chap. 1). The problem can be posed in terms of whether civic obligation or social action is the touchstone for defining the outer limits of human behavior.

Whether one studies civics or sociology is really a matter of what one considers important to study. Does one study the constitution and the laws or the norms of everyday behavior? Sociologists tend to take for granted that normative behavior is somehow central, simply on the basis of the time they devote to normative behavior. The sociologist assumes that because he spends a great deal of time with norms, norms are therefore more important than that with which he spends a small amount of time—the laws. It is doubtless true that most people can go through an entire lifetime without encountering law as a form of pressure, but most political scientists answer that what we call normative is merely that which is tolerated after the laws are set forth. Establishment of behavior as normative is a lower form of establishment of authority. It is tolerated precisely because of its unimportance. Manners and mores do not rock the structure of polity. Adolescent behavior, for example, is extremely important to the sociologist. It figures in the pages of most publications and communications. But from political scientists the sexual revolution of the adolescent evokes a loud yawn, and properly so from their point of view. Why should they care about something that has no effect on the essential nature of the political system? Only when normative behavior is related to the political system does it become important for the political scientist. This is an important difference in the vision of the two disciplines. Sociologists see annual revolutions—in sex, dress and so on—but political scientists still hold a rigorous notion of revolution as a change in legal order and power constraints.

The sociologist tends to talk in terms of values and value systems. Because he is concerned with the study of normative behavior, the derivation of normative behavior assumes cardinal importance. The political scientist does not indulge in that language because he does not usually study those norms. His big concept is interests. What concerns him, in the words of Lasswell, is who has power and how much, or, as Robert Dahl asks, who governs? In other words, interest becomes central because the question of political power is always a question of interests, not values. In Weber's *The Protestant Ethic and the Spirit of Capitalism* (1958), this is most explicitly demonstrated. The value decision on behalf of the Protestant ethic changes the interests that men have in the kinds of social systems they live in. In contrast to this is Tawney's position (1926), which starts from the premise that the values of the Protestant Reformation derive from the social system. The notion of causal derivation is very critical. If we assume that values are primary, it is natural to expect that a revolution of values will create a revolution of interests. If we assume that interests create values, a revolution in the social order is primary. The gulf between Tawney and Weber on the Protestant ethic is not simply a difference in their intellectual equipment, not simply a difference in their stature, but rather, a difference in their premises—what they consider to be the sources and what they consider to be the residuals. Whether one considers interests or values, the roots determine one's picture of the universe. It affects one's attitude toward moral suasion, toward the efficacy of trying to convince people of a position. Sociologists are notorious utopians in that sense; they act under the assumption that they will be able to convince all people once they present the facts. Political scientists do not make assumptions of moral suasion. On the contrary, they tend to assume that no matter what the facts, interests will tend to win out over the evidence. Sociology tends to be more reformist because it makes assumptions that political science does not. However, the very concern with political primacy tends to polarize political scientists most sharply on questions of everyday life.

This general focus emerges in the political scientists' definition of their field as almost intrinsic and organic to the study of elites. The word *elite* is for the political scientists what the word *class* is for the sociologist. For the political scientist, the makers of history are generally few in number— 9 Supreme Court justices, 435 members of the House of Representatives and 1 President. They are distinguishable person-objects. When one speaks of an elite within the Lasswellian framework, one means those who can be observed, those who have a high percentage of visible power. Power is defined by the political scientist almost in physical terms, by movement. How many men can be moved by how many men? As in physics, this does not mean energy expended; it implies objects moved or displaced. Likewise in political science—power is defined not by the efforts expended by masses, but by the objects moved. Therefore, for the political scientist, 200,000 demonstrators mean much less than one individual well situated who has the good ear of the man of power. For the political scientist, decisions, not causations, are key, because volition rather than determinism is the episte- mological framework within which he tends to operate.

Sociology tends to assume that spontaneous or collective dynamics is very important, that the behavior of 200,000 may not be vital, but only because they are not 400,000 or more. The sociologist assumes a quanti- tative response to the question of the nature of power, which is why, even when he concerns himself with politics, he prefers electoral data. Sociolo- gists who work with political science material gravitate almost instinctively to the study of the electoral process because that yields material they are amenable to, namely, the stated beliefs of masses. Political science tends to be more concerned with the nature of appointive than with that of elec- tive office, and more interested in the characteristics of expertise or the qualifications of office than in the procurement of that office in a public arena.

In part this represents more than a difference between elite concepts and class concepts, but further, a notion of elites in contrast to publics. The sociologist deals with publics, with select groups of people performing a variety of activities. He assumes that publics, whether they be Wall Street lawyers or street corner louts, have their own structures and their own elite groupings. The political scientist tends to be concerned with the elite rather than smaller publics of power holders and with the power broker instead of the more localized publics. The traditional literature of political science is linked to the study of the elite of elites, of those groups that have power on a national or even international level. This is not simply a gap between the language of antidemocratic strains in political science or the presumption of the inherently democratic tendencies in sociology. The antidemocratic strain of political science emanates from the characteristic features it sees as important in the society: the appointed official, the elite, the interested group, the *civitas*. The state itself is an antidemocratic institution because it represents only a small fraction of the people, and since the burden of political science is to study the state, its essential ideology has been molded by the materials it deems essential.

Within political science the notion of being popular or of appealing to a wider public counts for much less than it does in sociology. The sociologist's penchant and belief is in publics, in numbers, in masses, which is a characteristic stamp of its base in a broad-ranging constituency. The work of sociologists in the study of mass leisure, mass work, bureaucracy and organizations concerns wide sectors of the population. Even those who study small towns in mass society have a large public compared to the publics of the political scientist. The miniscule nature of the political scientist's constituency leads to discounting the role of the popular will or the mass public. Political science, for the most part, lacks that kind of mass concern and mass interest. Its concerns are policy decisions, and such decisions do not require numbers, but the right person, and the right appeal to that person.

The modern-day problem for the political scientist is the registration of power by the political scientist himself. On the one hand, the political scientist wants a science that is divested of values and removed from the problems of applied social science, but on the other hand, he needs to be aware of policy needs because his elite constituency forces him in that direction. Ultimately, if he believes that the right person, not numbers, is decisive, that right person will have to be himself. In other words, underneath the political scientist is a politician, no matter how denunciatory his general attitudes—toward lower echelons, not politics itself—are. He finds local politics distasteful, but he rarely fails to respond to the call of Washington because that is not just a form of ward-heeling politics but an elite activity, which is natural if one believes in elites as a solution to the problems of political life. In contrast to this, the sociologist tends to be far more value-conditioned, more concerned about the implications of the form of this behavior and more vitally interested in how society functions. He is more interested in distinguishing between the therapeutic needs of the systems; the same caution does not seem to be present in political science. The ever-widening separation between politics as a mass activity and policy making as an elite activity has created a larger market for political scientists as an occupational group, but at the same time, made them considerably more vulnerable to elitist pressures and elitist interpretations of events. The very fact that many political scientists have come to assume a touching faith in political socialization, in clear contradistinction to political sociology, is itself a reflection of a consensualist set of assumptions that posits the infinite viability of the present-day policy-making machinery. The sociologist, for his part, has had some difficulty in recognizing the importance of political sociology because he still tends to assume that nonconformist behavior is primarily deviant in nature, rather than political in ambition.

The orthodoxies of sociology still encourage a framework that seeks to isolate rather than tie together the study of social deviance and of political marginality. But it is precisely this new linkage that makes political sociology of such paramount contemporary importance. For the very extension of the vocabulary of both social and political motives makes the entire range of human actions subject to radical reinterpretation.

Perhaps another way of stating the problem of developing a true political sociology is that too often sociologists have insisted upon the primacy of social stratification variables, while political scientists have, in turn, insisted upon the primacy of party participation or voting preferences. In a sense, the need is to arrive at an interactionist framework in which the question of causal primacy is precisely what is left open, and not prematurely settled by professional fiat. As Sartori (1969, p. 89) put the matter recently: "As long as we take for granted that cleavages are reflected in, not produced by, the political system itself, we necessarily neglect to ask to what extent conflicts and cleavages may either be channeled, deflected and repressed or vice versa, activated and reinforced, precisely by the operations and operators of the political system."

The marriage of sociology and political science is to be understood as a marriage of convenience rather than of affection—a relationship thrust on each by the stubborn inability of either discipline to cope with the interpenetration of elites with masses, constitutionalists with confrontationists, democrats with totalitarians, and, above all, with how social classes confront political realities and attempt to translate their special "deviant" interests into the general values of the state and society.

The fact that political sociology has come to the fore is an indication that political economy has strangely receded in importance. It is the tacit recognition that the realm of the society has come to displace the realm of the economy as the essential turf and terrain of political struggles. It is in the wide area of habits, customs and mores, and not just the impersonal behavior of the marketplace and the regulation of trusts, that the political system becomes central. This represents a broadening of the powers and aims of the state to shape the future—and, some might add, the deepening threat of the state to disrupt that future. Nonetheless, few still doubt that the state does operate in this wider area of social controls, and that, in turn, deviant social movements translate themselves with increasing frequency into political movements of opposition to the state and its policy-making potentials.

The implications of this for the rise of political sociology may be disquieting, particularly because they represent a response to the widening instruments of coercion, the fact is that political sociology has come to define the twentieth century with the same fundamental importance as political economy defined the nineteenth century. For that reason alone, the field must be ranked a foremost innovation of social science in our age.

REFERENCES

Marx, K. (1938) *Critique of the Gotha Program.* New York: International Publishers [written in 1871].

Marx, K., and F. Engels (1964) *The German Ideology,* trans. R. Pascal. Moscow: Progress Publishers [written in 1845–1846].

Sartori, G. (1969) "From the Sociology of Politics to Political Sociology," in S. M. Lipset, ed., *Politics and the Social Sciences.* New York: Oxford University Press.

Strauss, L. (1959) *What Is Political Philosophy and Other Studies.* New York: Free Press.

Surkin, M., and A. Wolfe, eds. (1970) *An End to Political Science: The Caucus Papers.* New York: Basic Books.

Tawney, R. H. (1926) *Religion and the Rise of Capitalism: A Historical Study.* New York: Harcourt Brace Jovanovich.

Weber, M. (1958) *The Protestant Ethic and the Spirit of Capitalism,* trans. T. Parsons. New York: Scribner.

CHAPTER 3

POLITICAL PROGRESS: THE ENLIGHTENMENT PIVOT

THE ENLIGHTENMENT
DOCTRINE OF PROGRESS

The French Enlightenment gripped all strata of the third estate by the close of the eighteenth century. The fundamental explanation for this is embedded in the relation of Enlightenment to the social and economic situation in France. In the latter part of the century, middle-class democracy found its development hampered by the restrictions of the *ancien régime*; France was confronted with political, religious, moral and philosophical problems, all growing out of clashing economic interests. These problems of a society in flux stimulated people to think of creating a mode of life in which everyone would be enlightened as to the possibilities inherent in social life.

The revolutionary nature of French eighteenth-century thought was an accurate reflection of the social revolution then in progress. Enlightenment became the ideological justification of revolution. But it was also an instrument to further the cause of revolution. Unlike their contemplative forebears, the *philosophes* understood that theory becomes a genuine factor only when it propels masses into action. The dependent political position of the middle classes made them antagonistic to the feudal regime and its religious-philosophical foil. The feudal system found its security in looking to a bygone era when noblemen were truly noble. The merchant and industrial classes knew that the determinant of future progress rested upon the social universe and its variegated elements. The altered status of the urban bourgeoisie, and their increased wealth and power, suggested endless social advances. This fostered the notion of progress as the central theme in the philosophical literature. Indeed, unswerving faith in progress was the one point that all conflicting schools of Enlightenment thought held in common.

> The conviction that humanity, at least at the present moment, moves on the whole in a progressive direction has absolutely nothing to do with the antithesis between materialism and idealism. The French materialists equally with the deists Voltaire and Rousseau held this conviction to an almost fanatical degree, and often made the greatest personal sacrifices for it. (Engels, 1941, p. 31)

Ideas that in their content were obviously products of the emergent bourgeoisie began to appear. In particular, the commercial classes applauded individual achievement and success. The fetish of egotism did not emerge with Freud. It was materialism, not idealism, that initiated the anthropocentric movement in modern philosophy. The French Enlightenment appealed to the social world, the sensuous world, turning its back on the political conservatism fostered by idealism and supernaturalism. The ethics of the Middle Ages were determined to be contrary to emotional and rational elements in human experience. Feudal mores seemed bloodless and lifeless, the color and imagery invested in the angels and saints having faded considerably by the eighteenth century. The social standards of the new classes were held to correspond with the productive nature of man. For scholasticism, contemplation made great men. The encyclopedists were dedicated to the idea that great passions make great men. There was a powerful Enlightenment tendency to interpret "morality in the empirical terms of pleasure and pain with the characteristic bourgeois tang of calculating" (Grossman, 1926, pp. 12–13). All evidence indicates that the source of utilitarianism's popularity during the eighteenth century was its adaptability to newly introduced categories of economic exchange.

Criticism of the monarchy urgently required philosophical justification. The utilitarian doctrines provided just that conception of life that could render in measurable terms the irrationality of a decadent feudal regime and also work for the formation of a more rational society based on personal needs and interests. French utilitarianism did more than argue for a society in which the happiness of the greatest number would decide everything. It described the possibility of actualizing the potential of an environment through education and legislation. These were to be the levers of future progress. In France the Enlightenment received its most advanced sociological expression. As the hub of eighteenth-century intellectual life, France provided such tenets of Enlightenment as the belief in the supremacy of science, human reason and social progress. The Enlightenment was a movement with both national and cosmopolitan features. It generated and was in turn sustained by a rising middle-class European culture. Yet its roots were such that the Enlightenment not only assumed different national forms but also developed fundamental cleavages in the content of the philosophic message. A brief survey of the path of the Enlightenment throughout the remainder of Europe will serve to show both continuous and discontinuous factors.

The Enlightenment in France owed a particular debt to English thought, especially its doctrine and theory of knowledge. The fact that English theory gloried in a Revolution already concluded, while French theory glorified in a revolution which, though it seemed inevitable, had yet to come about, did not prevent the *philosophes* from drawing heavily on progressive English philosophy. George Sabine (1937, pp. 546–547) has warmly described the principal features of this debt:

In the seventeenth century, French philosophy and science had been relatively self-contained; in the eighteenth, as Cartesianism hardened into a kind of scholasticism, it was deliberately supplanted by the philosophy of Locke and the science of Newton. In political thought such a result was a foregone conclusion after the revocation of the Edict of Nantes made religious toleration a major part of any reforming philosophy. With the residence of Voltaire in England between 1726 and 1729, and of Montesquieu ten years later, the philosophy of Locke became the foundation of French enlightenment, and the admiration of English government became the keynote of French liberalism. Henceforth, the "new way of ideas" was the rule of philosophical and psychological speculation, and the principles of the *Treatise of Government* became axioms of political and social criticism. These principles were very simple and very general. The law of nature, or of reason, was supposed to provide an adequate rule of life without the addition of any revealed supernatural truth and was believed to be imprinted in essentially the same form upon the minds of all men. As a result of Hobbes and Locke, the content of the law of nature had become enlightened self-interest, but because of the harmony inherent in nature a truly enlightened self-interest was thought to be conducive to the good of all. In accord with these general ethical principles, governments were held to exist only to further liberty, security, the enjoyment of property, and other individual goods. Hence political reform must aim to secure responsible government, to make it representative, to limit abuses and tyranny, to abolish monopoly and privilege—in short, to create a society in which individual energy and capacity are the keys to power and wealth.

The commercial and industrial classes in England, after being in the forefront of a protracted and victorious revolution, were forced to conclude a union with the older aristocracy, primarily in order to head off popular resistance movements. From the Diggers to the Chartist movement, peasants and workers demanded democratic reforms that the middle classes were unwilling to grant. Under pressure, the bourgeoisie was inclined to effect compromises with idealism and orthodox theology, even in philosophy. The English Enlightenment made its representatives glorifiers of an achievement rather than prophets of revolution. The radically different uses the utilitarian self-interest doctrine was put to in France provide ideological corroboration of this. While English intellectuals were presenting utility doctrines as a natural ally of theology, the French were attempting to prove the natural hostility of utilitarianism to theology. The "cool" self-love of Joseph Butler was a far cry in theory and in practice from the "passionate" self-love of Helvétius. Superficial formal similarities cannot disguise the intense hostility of their doctrines. Reconciliation was the leitmotif of English thought in the latter half of the eighteenth century. Like Bentham, most English theorists contented themselves with advising the French on how to "remodel" their government along parliamentary lines.

The radical strains of English thought were largely confined to framing a theology compatible with democratic and naturalistic thought. Even John Toland did not venture to link his critique of supernaturalism and his exposition of naturalism with criticism of the social origin and role of religious concepts. In France such a procedure was considered incredibly timid, if not downright naïve. Critics of established religion and theology such as Voltaire and Helvétius saw the "religious evil" as more profoundly an outgrowth of "social evil." Except for Holbach and Condillac, the Enlightenment in France paid scant attention to the metaphysical problems inherent in any system of theology. The challenge to church authority had to be popular not aristocratic, social not metaphysical

The conclusion of the "Glorious" English Revolution in 1688 and the publication of Locke's studies on the nature and function of government brought to a climax (and some insist a halt) the form of democratic political theorizing typical of the period of civil war. But the Enlightenment carried on long after the class that gave it its initial impetus became dominant. The entire century after the Revolution was also one of immense intellectual fermentation. Interestingly enough, the Enlightenment in the postrevolutionary period was the property of the aristocracy on one side and democratic elements whose ambitions remained unfulfilled by the Revolution on the other. The bourgeoisie temporarily forfeited the realm of new ideas in order to initiate an industrial revolution which shifted power to itself.

The blueprints the middle class drew for the rest of society did not, however, work out as expected. By the time the English bourgeoisie gained political power (1832), it was clear that the much heralded benefits of industrialism had not found their way down to the masses. Taking advantage of the difficulties faced by the bourgeoisie, the aristocracy renewed a vigorous intellectual battle. Engels described how the dynamism of the aristocratic ideology "shocked the pious feelings of the middle class." He noted that "with Bolingbroke, Shaftesbury, etc., the new deistic form of materialism remained an aristocratic, esoteric doctrine, and, therefore, hateful to the middle class both for its religious heresy and for its anti-bourgeois political connections. Accordingly, in opposition to the material-ism and deism of the aristocracy, those Protestant sects which had furnished the flag and the fighting contingent against the Stuarts, continued to furnish the main strength of the progressive middle class" (Engels, 1940, p. 19). The intellectual power of the aristocracy came through with particular force in literature. The work of Dryden, Addison, Scott, Wordsworth, Pope and Southey gave clear warning that although the English Revolution was ended, the struggle for supremacy was not. But the basic limitation of the aristo-cratic reaction was that it hearkened to days past and never to be retrieved. It appealed to the material and spiritual havoc caused by the industrial revolution, unable to comprehend the other and more crucial side of capi-talist rule, namely, that capitalism had brought products into being that could lay the foundations for a really human order. It was the concreteness and immediacy of these products that ultimately outweighed the torrent of aristocratic reaction.[1]

A popular strain also forced its way to the surface of English Enlighten-ment. The writings of Gerard Winstanley, leader of the extreme left wing of the Revolution, were published as early as 1696 through the medium of John Beller's *College of Industry*. The philosophical essays of Toland, the artistic work of William Hogarth, the poetry of Thomas Gray, William Blake and Robert Burns—these were among later independent outbursts against the bourgeoisie that helped instill middle-class rulers with a lively fear of real democracy. The Enlightenment in England was saved from middle-class practicality and triviality by spokesmen for the old aristocracy and by the scattered expressions for justice and true liberty from the amor-phous laboring classes.

The "Enlightenment" in Scotland ended up not by enlightening, but by severely restricting the abilities of men either to understand or alter their material existence. Though their criticisms of classical idealism were pene-trating, Scottish intellectuals offered no resolution for the dilemmas they pointed to. The very doubts raised concerning the powers of science and a philosophy based on its achievements led the Enlightenment back to the religion it supposedly started out to overthrow.

The Enlightenment in Germany was a protracted affair, extending from the seventeenth century well into the nineteenth century. And while it underwent many developments, it still retained certain very definite features that distinguished it from the French Enlightenment. Germany's *Aufklärung* was persistently formal and academic. Too weak to form a united phalanx

---

[1] An article by Hicks (1937) develops in workman-like fashion the aristocratic ideological reaction to the English bourgeoisie.

against foreign invasion and domestic squabbles, Germany attempted to philosophize a cohesive nation into being. The conception of an omnipotent state existed long before material conditions brought absolutism to power. It is not farfetched to imagine that Leibniz' "absolutely isolated and independent monads" served to characterize a Germany of absolutely isolated and independent principalities. The "monad of monads," which was to bring all pluralities in nature into unity and harmony, could easily be transferred to a "state of states," which was to bring all pluralities in society into unity and harmony. In fact, this is exactly what Hegel (1956) was later to do in his *Philosophy of History*. Rationalism, coated over by a heavy layer of romanticism, dominated the German Enlightenment, keeping it eternally locked in the "airy realm" of speculation disconnected from fact.

A scant decade separates Helvétius' (1810) revolutionary *Treatise on Man* and Immanuel Kant's (1882) *Critique of Pure Reason,* a work sufficiently compromising in social intent that it won the unrestrained plaudits of the German professorial bourgeoisie. Kantianism was as much a reaction to the implications of French naturalism as it was to the skepticism inherent in British empiricism. The French middle class was forging the tools for a monumental revolution, and the English middle class was assuming the leading position in world trade and industrial production.

> While all this was going on, the powerless German burghers were only able to carry things as far as the "good will." Kant assumed the realization of "good will," the harmony between it and the needs and desires of individuals would be achieved in the *hereafter*. This "good will" of Kant's outlook corresponded completely to the degradation and misery of the German bourgeoisie who were never capable of developing their petty interests into common national interests and who as a result were continually exploited by the bourgeoisie of other countries. These petty local interests corresponded, on the one hand, to the genuinely local and provincial limitations of the German bourgeoisie, and on the other, to its cosmopolitan pretensions. (Marx and Engels, 1964, pp. 175–176)

French philosophies of Enlightenment were based on genuine class considerations and were directed to the material functioning of society. Kant, as a typical product of the German Enlightenment, represented similar class interests, but abstractly, without understanding that his categorical imperatives were not universal and transcendent, but localized and narrow expressions of a timorous middle class.

> Kant consequently separates the theoretical expressions of these (class) interests from the interests themselves. He transforms the materially motivated will of the French bourgeoisie in a *pure* self-determination of the *free will,* of the will in and of itself, of the human will. In this way he converts it into a purely ideological determination and moral postulate. The German petty-bourgeoisie in consequence, shudders at the practice of this energetic bourgeois liberalism just as soon as it asserts itself either

in the reign of terror or in shameless bourgeois competition. (Marx and Engels, 1964, p. 177)

In contrast to the main currents of Enlightenment in England, Scotland and Germany, the French Enlightenment was both a prophecy of things to come and a practical political instrument. The bourgeoisie provided the *lumières* with the material means of existence while they, in turn, provided the bourgeoisie with an appropriate philosophy of civilization. The basic intellectual sources of the French Enlightenment came from all over Europe. But its political momentum developed strictly out of contradictions native to France. Interest in social theory increased in proportion to consciousness of its new role in the affairs of men. By the first half of the eighteenth century, this interest blossomed forth with a large and varied output of books touching upon a thousand and one problems and venturing as many solutions.[2]

In the latter half of the century, both the tempo and depth of the varied forms of intellectual activity quickened. George Sabine (1937, p. 544) pointed out that "every branch of literature—poetry, the drama, and the novel—became a vehicle of social discussion. All scholarship was bent in this direction. A poet like Voltaire or a novelist like Rousseau, a scientist like Diderot or d'Alembert, a civil servant like Turgot, and a metaphysician like Holbach produced political theory as naturally as a sociologist like Montesquieu wrote satire." Nevertheless, the *philosophes* differed profoundly both in temperament and aims from the court literati, the courtiers of the genteel tradition. They differed just as sharply from the pedants who were so immersed in the past for its own sake that they could neither understand the present nor mold a bright future. Above all, philosophers like Helvétius must be distinguished from university metaphysicians, from men who held official posts by acceding to scholasticism. The philosophical leaders of the Enlightenment were forerunners of the modern revolutionary intellectuals. It was from these men that the *Tiers* learned to divorce theoretical principles from idealist premises and to employ theory as an instrument of social practice. Democratic movements of the nineteenth and twentieth centuries gave proof of the validity of this approach.

In periods of their decline, exploiting classes often become "skeptical" of the possibilities for further social advancement. The pundits of the *ancien régime* bitterly attacked every tenet of Enlightenment. They preached

---

[2] Historical works appeared on the ancient customs and institutions of France, such as Volney's (1811) *The Ruins,* Fontenelle's (1932) *De l'origine des fables* and Dupuis' (1872) *The Origin of All Religious Worship;* descriptive works on the nature and duties of government, the most famous of which is Montesquieu's (1949) *The Spirit of the Laws;* books that described the moral and political institutions of foreign nations, such as Raynal's (1782) *The Revolution of America* and Maillet's (1797) *Teliamed: or, The World Explain'd;* and philosophical discourses dealing with the foundations of human society, such as Rousseau's (1913) *The Social Contract* and Condorcet's (1955) *The Progress of the Human Mind.*

the natural stratification of men, and argued that divine appointment rather than the general will was the ultimate source of political power. They insisted that democracy would bring on anarchism—that is, the rule of the filthy mob and the uncultured money-grubbing middle class. In the same Parisian *salons* that fostered the spirit of free discussion, the circulating library, the popular newspaper, the Society of Free Masons, which provided channels for the flow of *philosophie démocratique* to a wide audience, there was also to be found a sophistry amiable to the thought processes of decadent social forces. Helvétius' theory of the equal capacities of man, an outlook that was to become the touchstone of democratic movements the world over and was to receive juridical recognition in the *Declaration of the Rights of Man,* was rejected by some "scholars" because it exalted man at the expense of animals. Enlightenment ideological currents revealed the bifurcation of classes in French life.

The *philosophes* were the first to conceive of the social utility of sound ideas and their human carriers. No longer were intellectuals to be viewed as alienated from the mainstream of social battles. The *philosophes* represented the role of the intellectual as providing leadership to the demands of the people. The defense made of the freedom of the press, the right of women and youth to a full measure of social power and responsibility and the need for a democratic reorganization of the educational system attested to the newfound maturation of the intellectuals. Knowledge was no longer viewed as a special province of the chosen few, but the property of all to some degree and the right of all to every degree. That is why the *philosophes* were in a position to become an organizing force for the revolutionary classes.

Enlightenment thinkers aimed at providing a philosophy of man rather than a philosophy for privileged men. A passage from the *Encyclopedie* (1777–79, vol. 12, pp. 382–383) examines the new relationship of man to nature and society:

> One consideration especially which we ought not to lose sight of, is that if we banish man, the thinking and contemplation being, from the surface of the earth, this pathetic and sublime spectacle of nature becomes a scene melancholy and dumb. Silence and night take possession of the universe. Everything is transformed into a vast solitude in which unobserved phenomena move in an obscure and secret manner. It is the presence of man that makes the existence of beings interesting. Can we propose anything better in the history of these beings than to submit ourselves to this consideration? Why should we not introduce man into our work as he is placed in the universe? Why should we not make him a common center? . . . This is what has determined us to find in the principal faculties of man the general division to which we have subordinated our work.

The leaders of Enlightenment considered that the belief in human omnipotence distinguished them from their counterparts in antiquity and feudalism. But in their efforts to provide a philosophy for all humanity, they had to go beyond the bounds of social reality, of bourgeois reality. They were not aware that the philosophy of Enlightenment was tailored to bourgeois specifications. Unlike the Marxian thinkers of the nineteenth and twentieth centuries, the *philosophes* remained unaware of the class basis of their views. In his work on Diderot, Henri Lefebvre (1949, p. 163) made an acute judgment of the avant-garde philosophers that stands up equally well as a characterization of the philosophy of the age: "The incomplete materialism of the eighteenth century, still mechanistic and vulgar, was unable to make itself clear as to its aims, because it did not comprehend the consciousness of the class struggle as a motive force in history nor its own class character. Thus the *philosophes* could not arrive at an understanding of their own struggles and abnegations."

Philosophes like Helvétius, Diderot and Condorcet viewed themselves quite apart from the actual class positions they occupied. Their moral dedication to "humanity" rather than any particular class reflected the temporarily compatible relationship between all sectors allied against the aristocracy. They regarded the rise of technology, the natural and social sciences and the crafts as powerful social weapons. The shift in economic forces that made possible this expansion was not comprehended by them. This is revealed by their curious idea that they, the *philosophes,* and not the bourgeoisie, were the trustees of science and the guardians of progress. The fact that they remained unaware of the class foundations of their world view was indicated in their conception of themselves as a distinct and unified class, with a program of social reconstruction different from that of any other group in French life. This was the grand illusion harbored by the *lumières,* and strangely typical of professionals in later periods.

This lack of class consciousness was a historical limitation, and not a personal failing. Certainly it in no way prevented the new philosophical leaders from playing a revolutionary role in helping to bring about the downfall of the *ancien régime.* Those who worked mainly with their heads overcame the supposed "alienation of the intellectual from his fellowmen" and joined in the struggles of the rest of humankind. Diderot emphasized that in the *Encyclopedie* (1777–79, vol. 25, pp. 668–669):

> Our philosophy is full of humanity. Civil society is, so to speak, a divinity for him on earth; he burns incense to it, he honors it by probity, by an exact attention to his duties, and by a sincere desire not to be a useless or embarrassing member of it. The sentiments of probity enter as much into the mechanical constitution of the philosopher as the illumination of the mind. The more you find reason in a man, the more you find in him probity.

While Diderot was pointing out the necessary social duties of the intellectual, Helvétius was busy defining what these duties specifically were. Throughout *Treatise on Man,* he showed that a philosopher plays a useful role only by criticizing despotic, corrupt and dying regimes while generating a love for truth, honesty and usefulness.

> A writer who is desirous of the favor of the great, and the transitory applause of the present hour, must adopt implicitly the current principles of the time, without ever attempting to examine or question their authority. It is from this source that arises that lack of originality so common among literary productions. . . . There are periods in every country when the word *prudent* bears the same meaning with *vile;* and when these productions are esteemed only for their sentiments, which are written in a style of servility. In all nations there are certain periods when the citizens, undetermined what measures they ought to take, and remaining in a state of suspense between a good and bad government, are extremely desirous of instructions, and are disposed to receive it. At such a time, if a work of great merit makes its appearance, the happiest effects may be produced. But the moment it passes, the people, insensible to glory, are by the form of their government irresistibly inclined towards ignorance and baseness. Such is the present condition of France. (Helvétius, 1810, pp. vii–viii)

With few exceptions, philosophies of classical antiquity and the Middle Ages were not concerned with the intricate relationship between theory and social practice. The "contemplative" attitude dominated from Plato and Aristotle to Bruno, Descartes and Spinoza. It had always been an accepted axiom that the highest philosophic activity is the "exercise of the mind," which served to justify the split between head and hand, mental and physical labor. The pervasive animosity of many people for "philosophy and speculation" stems from their understanding that ruling-class philosophy—the only philosophy they are permitted to learn much of—has only scorn and condescension for physical labor. Intellectuals earned the scorn of wide masses. Even today, when they attempt to be popular instead of contemplative, they fail miserably. For the pseudoprofessionalism, lack of meaningful ideas and esotericism make even "practical" business theory a dull puzzle to the mass of people who live by a combination of head and hand.

An initial step in overcoming this historically evolved dichotomy between theory and practice was made by the encyclopedists. Their viewpoint neither implies the antiintellectualism of modern pragmatism, nor implores the scholar to stop thinking and become "one with the people." On the contrary, as Charles Frankel (1948, p. 9) so ably wrote:

> It lies in a new recognition that science and criticism have a social function even if the individual thinker is unaware of it. The *philosophes* were conscious that they were living through an intellectual revolution—a revolution among intellectuals—and they did not feel that the result of this revolution was simply that the man of books had come to be reminded that he had other obligations and that he also ought to be a man

of action. Rather, the revolution lay in the discovery that when a man is properly intellectual he is in that way performing a social function and engaging in a species of social action.

The encyclopedists understood that by turning theory to the concrete needs of the age, it became at once both revolutionary and truthful. Intellectuals addressed themselves to practical tasks precisely by their dedication to work toward aims common to all, not just a tiny segment, of humankind.

> Our philosopher does not believe in exiling himself from this world, he does not believe that he is in enemy country; he wishes to enjoy with wise economy the goods which nature offers him; he wishes to find pleasure with others, and in order to find it, he must make it: thus he tries to be agreeable to those with whom chance and his choice have thrown him, and at the same time he finds what is agreeable to him. He is an honest man who wishes to please and to make himself useful. . . . This love of society, so essential to the philosopher, makes us see how very true was the remark of Marcus Aurelius: "How happy will the people be when kings are philosophers or philosophers are kings!" (*Encyclopedie*, 1777–79, vol. 25, p. 669)

Theorists of the French Enlightenment carried the burden of being mocked and despised as outcasts courageously, because they wished to serve a social, not an ornamental, purpose. They hoped to awaken popular animosity toward the major social and political enemies.

The *philosophes* showed the middle class the value of science and the virtue of liberty; they actually represented the philosophic spirit of the bourgeoisie, although they thought they represented the common spirit. The two "spirits" were harmonious only because at this stage of French history the bourgeoisie was able to speak for "humanity" in general. The Enlightenment in France in this way became a movement among intellectuals to assert themselves as a political force by introducing the significance of ideology as a decisive factor in human evolution. The worldly philosophy of the French Enlightenment found its fulfillment in ideas of equality and progress. The words of Condorcet (1955, p. 251) provide a forthright statement on this matter: "our hopes, as to the future condition of the human species, may be reduced to three points: the destruction of inequality between different nations; the progress of equality in one and the same nation; and lastly, the real improvement of man." Translating theory into social activity, the *philosophes* became the high priests of the coming bourgeois democratic revolution. It was not for nothing that the *philosophes* often compared themselves to the Old Testament prophets. They had the same revolutionary zeal, the same faith in the omnipotence of their message, the same hatred for oppressors. They made little use of the Bible, but they had teachings that were calculated to rout out the money-makers and fear-makers from their feudal temples—the scientific theory of Newton and the social theory of Locke. And like the social prophets, they met with overwhelming success.

It would be impossible to discuss the Enlightenment without bringing forth the distinctive part played by the encyclopedists—the vanguard spokesmen for radical thought, and of the Revolution itself. The encyclopedists inherited from the past a desire to synthesize all useful knowledge in a series of volumes. Pierre Bayle's *Dictionnaire historique et critique* (1697) prefigured to a certain degree the *Encyclopedie,* which reached final completion in 1820. Another indication of the "encyclopedic" approach was presaged in the works of Voltaire. The main difference between the works of Bayle and Voltaire on one side and the *Encyclopedie* on the other was not only in scope but, also in the organized method of work.

The *Encyclopedie* was a collective undertaking in two basic aspects: (1) it was an intellectual current in which many thought streams were welded together; and (2) these views were advocated in common. Not only did the encyclopedists have a joint source of ideas, but also this very source was the product of the interaction among these thinkers. French revolutionary philosophy was not the world outlook of Fontenelle, Montesquieu, Condillac, Voltaire, Rousseau, Diderot and Holbach, to name but a few of the contributors, but a philosophy these men shared, out of the discussions and criticisms resulting from the intellectual cooperation of these *philosophes.* They held in common the goal of freedom from sword and cloth. And to the actualization of this goal they united in common endeavor (See Soboul, 1951). Condorcet (1955, p. 256) described the nature of this eighteenth-century popular front: "The philosophers of different nations, embracing in their meditations the entire interests of man, without distinction of country, of color, or of sect, formed a firm and united phalanx against every description of error and every species of tyranny."

What welded the *philosophes* together more than abstract theoretical agreements were the tasks of writing and publishing a universal compendium of human knowledge that would lead to an unleashing of libertarian sentiments. In the *Preliminary Discourse* of the *Encyclopedie,* d'Alembert (1821–22, vol. 1, p. 185) indicated the dual purpose of this great venture in literature; it was to be a dictionary of the arts, sciences and crafts,[3] expounding the basic premises of each in such a way as to "really reach the mind of a people rather than merely the surface." Furthermore, it was to be a work aimed at exhibiting the order and connection of all human knowledge, "encompassing in a single system the infinitely varied branches of human science." The construction of the *Encyclopedie,* d'Alembert noted (1821–22, vol. 1, p. 186), was actually begun when the contributors agreed to bypass inherited scholastic categories and "return to the origin and gen-

---

[3] The position occupied by the "crafts" is indicative of the transformation that the French economic base underwent in the eighteenth century. For only in a society on the road to industrialization would the crafts or technology merit such thoroughgoing concern.

eration of our ideas," to nature (See also the *Encyclopedie*, 1777–79, vol. 1, pp. liv-lviii).

No one was more sensitive to the ideological needs of the day than Denis Diderot, the guiding genius who conceived and edited the major portion of the *Encyclopedie*. He believed the practice of free and disciplined criticism to be crystalized in this work, and hoped that, as the institutionalization of the Enlightenment, it would be an antidote to the infections caused by church and state (*Encyclopedie*, 1777–79, vol. 25, pp. 660–670). Diderot hoped that his advanced views on human knowledge would become common currency among the readers of the *Encyclopedie*.

> Truth is not for the philosopher a mistress who corrupts his imagination and whom he believes is to be found everywhere; he contents himself with being able to unravel it where he can perceive it. He does not confound it with probability; he takes for true what is true, for false what is false; for doubtful what is doubtful, and for the probable what is only probable. He does more, and here you have a great perfection of the philosopher: when he has no reason by which to judge, he knows how to live in suspension of judgment. The philosophic spirit is, then, a spirit of observation and exactness. (*Encyclopedie*, 1777–79, vol. 25, p. 667)

The *Encyclopedie* aimed at overthrowing the "edifice of mud" and putting in its place the "edifice of truth."

The *Prospectus* prepared by Diderot (1875–77, vol. 13, p. 130) reveals that he viewed this organ of liberal thought as more than a polished compendium of information that would disabuse men of their prejudices: "It is also an attempt to establish and exhibit the unity of science as a whole; the mutual help given by the individual sciences to one another; and the historic continuity of the scientific enterprise." I. K. Luppol (1936, p. 49) makes a most interesting observation on the *Encyclopedie*:

> Although the French bourgeoisie of the eighteenth century neither created nor caused any political tribune, it did, through the hand of Diderot consider the *Encyclopedie* "the holy confederation against fanaticism and tyranny," agreeing with an expression of Cabanis. It was a living synthesis, superior to anything heaped together in the archives. In so far as it is a collective work, composed of seventeen volumes, to which must be added e'even volumes of engravings without counting the supplements and the index written without Diderot, the *Encyclopedie* is not only an example of a period in knowledge but a veritable plan of action.

The eighteenth century witnessed the sharp delineation of various disciplines, and philosophy was not an exception. Just as it was the century of immensely important scientific discoveries, so, too, it was the century of new social theories. The *Encyclopedie* was conceived as the tool that would weave these intellectual advances into an integral whole. In a sense, the *Encyclopedie* was the first unified science movement.

> Our Century has called itself the *philosophic century* par excellence. From the principles of the profane sciences to the foundations of revelation, from metaphysics to questions of taste, from music to morals, from the scholastic dispute of theologians to commercial affairs, from the rights of princes to those of peoples, from the natural law to the arbitrary law of nations, in a word, from the questions that affect us most to those that interest us least, everything has been discussed, analyzed and disputed. (d'Alembert, 1821–22, vol. 2, pp. 10–11)

This statement by d'Alembert illustrates the temper of the age. The *Encyclopedie* systematized the enthusiastic optimism of revolution and Enlightenment. Above all, agreement on dislikes made the encyclopedists the cohesive force they were. In positive theory there was a wide divergence between Voltaire's panpsychic deism and Diderot's physiological materialism, or d'Alembert's agnostic positivism and Helvétius' sociological materialism. Yet these scholars maintained the closest possible association throughout their lives. This philosophic front was made possible by the alignments of class forces. The forces of reaction, having not yet "discovered" the merits of British subjectivism, grouped about the philosophy of clerical idealism. The forces of progress were, in the main, grouped about sociological materialism and mechanical deism.

The leading scholars of Enlightenment, the encyclopedists, were not "professional" philosophers. They were down-to-earth persons whose ideas grew out of the soil of new social alignments in the making. These men echoed the sentiments of the bourgeoisie: "free commerce, free industry and free men." The theoretical precepts of the *philosophes* issued out of the problems of the day and therefore were amenable to the classes in France that had the most to gain from the advocacy of new ideas. For this reason, everyone not a member of the privileged groups regarded one or another of the encyclopedists as his personal advocate.

Despite the practical harmony among the encyclopedists, there were persistent and significant differences reflected in their thinking. The same Rousseau who contributed brilliant studies to Diderot's *Encyclopedie* was not above slandering him, along with Grimm and Holbach, in the *Confessions* (Rousseau, 1953). Divergences between the *philosophes* were one aspect of the contrasting social fabric that blended to overthrow the *ancien régime* and establish capitalism. These classes exhibited marked ideological differences resulting from different levels of social maturity and relations to existing productive forces. There was a profound difference between the social role of, say, a financier and that of a farmer producing for the urban market, a proletarian at work in a new established machine industry or a collector of feudal tithes turned banker. Such a heterogeneous combination of classes, although united for the single purpose of destroying the politico-economic power of the dominant feudal classes, would naturally at the same time have certain independent aspirations. The *Cahiers de doleances* of 1789, which presented a list of grievances against the *ancien régime,* give an accurate picture not merely of the general antagonism between the *Tiers* and the old classes but also of specific class demands and levels of class consciousness of each segment of the *Tiers.*

In a literal sense, the conscious defenders of the bourgeoisie's interest —property interest—were with their limitations more correct in their appraisal of social conditions than were the more theoretically advanced *philosophes.* Voltaire, Rousseau and d'Alembert had an advantage over the materialists in that they knew, to a greater extent at any rate, the class nature of the conflagrations they were entangled in, whereas Helvétius, Holbach and, to a lesser degree, Diderot tended to arrive at utopian conclusions to absolve the harsh realities of class conflict. A deep contradiction between the two basic segments of the encyclopedic school showed that those dedicated to the liberation of humanity, though offering a more democratic and consistent doctrine, suffered under the illusion that the outcome of their struggles would end conflicts between men once and for all. Those who were clearly dedicated to the liberation of capital, though presenting an outlook limited in its democratic implications, were not encumbered by the vain hopes of utopianism. Therefore, those who were theoretically less consistent were more consistent in relation to the class practices and understanding of the period.

The sociological tendency in the encyclopedic group had a twofold derivation. On the one side, there was the English naturalism of Francis Bacon, Thomas Hobbes and John Locke ready at hand. The other source was embedded in French traditions from the rationalist-naturalist school of Peter Ramus, Pierre Gassendi and Blaise Pascal to the more developed insight provided by Pierre Bayle and René Descartes. The duality of sources of encyclopedic materialism is an empirical and meaningful fact. Both French and English philosophic tendencies intersect and come into organic union with French materialism. This knowledge is important, for there have been attempts to minimize and distort the materialism of the encyclopedists and the materialist tendencies of their predecessors.

Encyclopedic materialism instantaneously took up the legacy of past materialist philosophies and vigorously rejected past metaphysics. "True philosophy" was set diametrically against "false metaphysics." This approach, a recurrent motif in Helvétius' philosophy, found initial expression in the Voltairian conflict between reason and superstition. For this reason, the French Enlightenment,

> particularly French materialism, was not only a struggle against the existing . . . religion and theology but was quite as much an outspoken struggle against the metaphysics of the seventeenth century and against all metaphysics, especially that of Descartes, Malebranche, Spinoza and Leibniz. Philosophy was set up in opposition to metaphysics; just as Feuerbach, when he first came out decidedly against Hegel, placed sober philosophy in opposition to intoxicated speculation. (Marx, 1845, p. 85)

THE FRENCH REVOLUTION AND THE
POLITICALIZATION OF SOCIETY

The French Revolution instituted the rule of the middle classes. But the contradictions inherent in the new society initiated a fresh series of class antagonisms. With the rise of a powerful bourgeoisie and the appearance of a bourgeoisified monarchy, the coalition of class forces came to an end. Just as the popular masses were no longer needed by the bourgeoisie, so, too, democratic theory was no longer required. Instead of revolution, the French bourgeoisie in the nineteenth century took the path of restoration. The ruling bourgeoisie half-heartedly and half-consciously reinstated the world outlook of feudalism as a bulwark against the Enlightenment.

Political practice under the *ancien régime* can best be described as Machiavellianism gone mad. Had the court nobility been more aware of Machiavelli's "directives" for ruling-class conduct, they would have seen that only their extinction would cleanse French society. The rusty feudal political mechanism ran on a combination of venality, court intrigue, sexual debasement and duplicity of all sorts. It had, by the eighteenth century, sullied even medieval mores. Honor, courage and faith were notions dragged out for window-dressing purposes only. The nobility had formalized such debasements; even the dressing and undressing of the king were performed with amazing pomp and ceremony, involving literally hundreds of people. Fundamentally though, these were superficial means of disguising the real basis of feudal domination, the exploitation of the peasantry. The reaction to the narrow and barbarous state of political affairs grew with each new indication that neither the first nor second estate was in a position to solve the pressing problems the French masses faced daily.

The complete collapse of serfdom by 1715 and the gradual decay of the feudal state in France gave rise to various efforts to solve the conflicts of political power. They all revealed a particular class orientation, and all were locked in fierce battle with each other. The first important political reform doctrine, one that captured the imagination of most *philosophes,* the *thèse royale,* saw the salvation of France in a powerful monarchy, which would eliminate the strength of the feudal nobility by basing itself thoroughly upon the middle classes. In 1734, this view was presented by Abbé Dubos in his *Histoire critique de l'etablissement de la monarchie Francaise.* For Dubos, feudalism was nothing but a corruption of the roots of the monarchical institution, which, in its origin and by its nature, practiced Roman law. This view left clear the path for a marriage of the monarchy with the rising bourgeois class. It was this type of political viewpoint that the *philosophes* generally came to accept as their own.

The *thèse nobiliaire* also based its appeal on history. The upholders of this doctrine believed that the reconstruction of French society rested upon the recognition of feudal automony, and that once the power of the nobility was recognized as absolute and omnipotent, the corrupt monarch could be curbed if not deprived entirely of power. This would enable the nobility to fulfill its social responsibilities by acting as guardian of the laws of France and the rights of its citizens. This doctrine, then, placed responsibility for the weakened condition of the nation on the court nobility. The *thèse nobiliaire* was first presented in 1827 by Count Boulainvilliers in his *Histoire de l'ancien gouvernement de la France*. Twenty years later, these views were refined and broadened by Montesquieu (1949) in *Esprit des lois*, his effort to formulate a science of government. Boulainvilliers and Montesquieu attempted to supply evidence for the original and autonomous powers of the aristocracy. Feudalism was for them as old as the Frankish monarchy. When the Franks conquered Gaul, they supposedly brought with them from their Teutonic background not the absolute monarchy, but a feudal lordship with diffuse powers. Therefore, in its origins the monarchy was only as powerful as the lords permitted it to be. The history of the French monarchy was considered by this second group of political philosophers to be the history of their usurpation of legitimate feudal powers. The obvious solution was a retention and strengthening of feudality (Neumann, 1949, pp. xxiv–xxviii).[4]

A third group of thinkers, who became influential in the latter half of the century, opposed the solution of the royal and nobiliary theses in two basic respects: They were against any exclusive concern with forms of political domination, and, even more significantly, they approached the problem of social reorganization not from the viewpoint of the bourgeoisie or the aristocracy, but from the vantage point of broad popular elements gathered in the third estate. It was a conception held in common by Meslier, Mably, Morelly, Helvétius and Argenson. In his *Considerations sur le gouvernement ancien et present de la France* (1765), Marquis d'Argenson capably put forth the ideology of this group. He saw as the major need the transformation of the monarchy into a force that could act on behalf of the masses of people. Franz Neumann (1949, p. xxvi) briefly describes the essence of Argenson's position:

> The monarchy must be strong, its power must be undivided; autonomous and feudal rights must be crushed, and the monarchy be reoriented toward the third estate. A rational administration of France, her division into districts, boroughs and municipalities, appeared to him indispensable. Local and regional administrators were to be appointed from lists elected by the communes; provincial estates, deliberating in one chamber, were to integrate the absolute monarch and the self-governing municipalities. All internal tolls and duties were to compete with all feudal privileges. . . . The philosophic basis was found in the Physiocrats' theory of a completely free and competitive society held together by an absolute monarch.

[4] An exceptionally valuable guide to the ideology of the political Enlightenment is Franz Neumann's (1949) introductory essay to Montesquieu's *The Spirit of the Laws*. My comments on the royal and nobility theses are based on Neumann's essay.

The outstanding feature of this approach, and that taken by Mably in *Parallele des Romains et des Francais par rapport au gouvernement,* is its socialist orientation. It keynotes the needs of the third estate as a whole rather than those of the middle classes alone.

To Voltaire, Diderot and even Holbach, social progress was the political progress of all humanity. The encyclopedists, while admiring the benefits yielded by English bourgeois constitutionalism, believed that a strong and intelligent monarch would be better able to achieve a smoother functioning middle-class state by eliminating the procrastination inherent in the parliamentary system of government. The *philosophes* did not assume that parliamentary government was the same as democratic government. They were, if anything, far bolder in advocating civil liberties than their English counterparts. Nor should we forget their absolute respect for and defense of the "rights" of private property against both the "greed and envy" of the masses and "arbitrary confiscation" by a hereditary aristocracy. Voltaire, Diderot and Holbach were democrats to be sure, but democrats who at their very best fought a two-sided battle. As long as the *ancien régime* remained in political power, the land-owning nobility and their compatriot, the Roman Catholic Church, bore the brunt of their slicing attacks. But even before the Revolution of 1789, these *philosophes* held that their democratic and egalitarian goals were inaccessible to the ordinary people, who they imagined were more cattle-like than human. Only a minority in French intellectual circles had any understanding of the natural endowments of all men. Their attention was devoted to the possibilities for peace and prosperity under a government operated by these troublesome beasts who were men.

Voltaire's intellectual development would indicate that his outlook was much more than a mirror-like idealization of English constitutional traditions. In stressing the necessity and advantages of an alliance between bourgeois and monarchical elements, his views were well adjusted to the realities of sociopolitical life in France (Luporini, 1950). For a revealing insight into Voltaire's middle-class bias, we should recall his comment on equality in the *Philosophical Dictionary* (1945, p. 117):

> The human race, such as it is, cannot subsist unless there is an infinity of useful men who possess nothing at all; for it is certain that if a man who is well off will not leave his own land to come to till yours; and if you have need of a pair of shoes, it is not the Secretary of the Privy Council who will make them for you. Equality is at once the most natural thing and the most fantastic.

Natural, that is, to the exploited masses, quite fantastic to the bourgeoisie and Voltaire. He continues with the statement that "all men have the right in the bottom of their hearts to think themselves entirely equal to other men: it does not follow from that the cardinal's cook should order his master to prepare him dinner" (Voltaire, 1945, p. 117). In other words,

Voltaire would allow all men to *think* themselves equal as long as they do not try to put such thoughts into *practice*. Like Hegel after him, Voltaire made use of the master–slave parable. A man may be enslaved to another materially, but he, in turn, holds the master captive in spirit. Because the master is dependent upon the slave for his wealth, he must always be a slave to the human slave's whims, fancies, desires and dreams. What this play on words always ignores is that the free spirit *is* free, precisely in his effort to be so—materially, socially and politically.

Similarly bound to the ideology of the *thèse royale* was Diderot. He may have started out by fulminating against the exploitation that personal wealth breeds, but he remained in the end a firm adherent of the view that property rights are eternal: "It is property that makes the citizen; every man who has possessions in the State is interested in the State, and whatever be the rank that particular conventions may assign to him, it is always as a proprietor; it is by reason of his possessions that he ought to speak, and that he acquires the right of having himself represented" (*Encyclopedie,* 1777–79, vol. 17, pp. 15–16).

The logic, though not the sentiment, of the position developed by Voltaire and Diderot, is to make the fight for liberty equivalent to the bourgeoisie's struggle to establish the liberty of property ownership in fact and in law. In Holbach's (1822, p. 3) definition of "true liberty," the sentiment is brushed aside, and the logic is followed to its better end: "True liberty consists in conforming to the laws which remedy the natural inequality of men, that is, which protect equally the rich and the poor, the great and the small, sovereigns and subjects. In a word, to be free is to obey only laws." Here, Holbach confused laws made by men, who have vested interests, with the laws of nature. Once again, we have the appearance of what we must term, for want of a better phrase, "spiritual equalitarianism." The propertyless peasant is little comforted to know that his nonexistent property will be given the same attention in "law" as that of the propertied squire. Holbach assumes that private-property relations are sacred.

How is it that these revolutionary theorists could begin by indicting class iniquities and end by appealing to a monarch for elevation of private property owners to a dignified and ranking social status? One answer seems to be that although they despised the exploitation caused by the *ancien régime,* which men like Diderot and Rousseau knew full well would be continued by the middle class, they accepted middle-class leadership because no other group in French society was in any position to take power away from the old privileged feudal classes. A strong proletariat was still a thing of the French future. Thus, the revolutionary theorists made no demands other than that the needs of the peasantry be considered—and the peasantry was first and foremost concerned with land ownership, with property rights. Then why did they turn to the bourgeoisie for a solution and away from the peasantry? The answer is not simple. Indeed, a strong strain of peasant communism persisted in their writings. These *philosophes* did not accept enlightened despotism as a goal of social relations, but rather as an instrument, a means for reaching More's *Utopia* (1955). In truth, the very real limitations of the bourgeoisie were outdistanced by the visions of the *philosophes*.

The relation of Helvétius to his encyclopedic associates on the question of political power is twofold. While paralleling their concept of the enlightened monarch as the dispenser of law and order, he disagreed with their faith in the healing powers of the bourgeoisie. He developed his theory of political rule along the lines of the *thèse démocratique*. But he gave it a "proof" and a "popularity" it lacked in the hands of Morelly, Mably and Argenson—namely, the utilitarian motivation of all humanity. If everyone is driven to seek his own best interests, and those interests could only be served in social intercourse, the monarch could really be enlightened only if he served the interests of every man in every class. It is this broad humanism of Helvétius that so sharply differentiates him from his colleagues. Legislation was to be in the name of all people, without class prerogative. The criterion of the success of a legislative program is the amount of happiness it brings each and every person. This is the final test of political progress. The monarch will be a good instrument for political advancement only as long as he abides by the dictums of utilitarianism. The test of his success is the mass of people—not a privileged class or sect, but the measurable wealth in the hands of the producers. All rulers, all laws and all customs must demonstrate their services to present needs. What fails in this test should be discarded, without fanfare and certainly without regrets. Find out what people desire or need, and frame laws aimed at securing just that—these were the elemental principles of Helvétius' juridical and political reform program. It was his deep-felt concern with the needs of the great mass of society that prompted Helvétius to scorn the maze of juridical precepts and political edifices inherited from the old order. These inherited evils, which both the adherents of a bourgeois monarchy and a feudal monarchy would subtly preserve, in effect only "preserve the errors accumulated since the origin of the human race" (Helvétius, 1818, pp. 259–267). If the world had to be made over, let it allow for the happiness of all, not just for the enjoyment of a new privileged class.

It is important to examine Helvétius' Enlightenment theory because it is at one and the same time a perfect representation of sociological materialism and also a clear example of the collective aspirations of the most politicized group of men ever to join forces in common goals.

In his analysis of past theories of politics, Helvétius sharply called to task the apriority inherent in the views of Plato's (1968) *Republic* and Augustine's (1963) *City of God*. They discussed what "heaven ordained" or what "should and would" be, but they hardly took the trouble to examine what *is*. Such political abstractions deal not with real problems and real solutions, but with distant problems and impossible solutions (Helvétius, 1810, vol. 2, p. 278). "If there is a method to fix public attention on the problem of an excellent legislation, it is by rendering it simple and reducing it to two propositions" (Helvétius, 1810, vol. 2, p. 279). Helvétius thought those propositions were of such a useful nature that no person could fail to recognize their critical significance.

> The importance of the first should be the discovery of laws proper to render man as happy as possible, and consequently to procure for them all the amusements and pleasures compatible with the public welfare. The object of the second should be the discovery of means by which a people may be made to pass insensibly from the state of misery they render men as happy as possible, and consequently to procure for them. (Helvétius, 1810, vol. 2, p. 279)

Helvétius goes on to suggest that we should follow the example of mathematicians to resolve the first proposition: "When a complicated problem in mechanics is proposed to them, what do they do? Simplify it; calculate the velocity of moving bodies without regarding their destiny, the resistance of fluids that surround them, their friction with other bodies, etc." In similar manner, to resolve the problem of excellent legislation, one should pay no regard to the prejudices or friction caused by the contradictory interests, or to ossified mores, laws and customs. "The inquirer should act like the founder of a religious order, who in dictating his monastic laws has no regard to the habits and prejudices of his future subjects" (Helvétius, 1810, vol. 2, p. 279). Helvétius did not realize that he was setting a standard no less abstract and a priori than Plato. He, too, was telling the "inquirer" to disregard the existing levels of human development and frame a perfect utilitarian theory of legislation having no relation to historical reality.

But to discover how people can pass from conditions of misery to those of happiness, Helvétius offered entirely different criteria: "It is not after our own conceptions, but from a knowledge of the present laws and customs that we can determine the means of gradually changing those customs and laws, and of making a people pass through by insensible degrees, from their present legislation to the best possible laws" (Helvétius, 1810, vol. 2, pp. 279–280). Thus, thesis two, unlike thesis one, was based completely on laws of history. Helvétius recognized that there was an essential difference between these two propositions. When the first, unhistorical proposition is resolved, its solution becomes general, the same for all peoples and nations, while the resolution of the second differs widely according to the form and level of social development of each people and nation. Satisfactorily overcoming the problems generated by these contradictory but equally real propositions will inevitably lead to political progress. They provide for the universal happiness of people, while at the same time taking into account basic differences between people. Progress therefore has two elements: the transient forms any search for happiness takes, and the universal desire of all men for happiness as an end in itself.

In a series of 31 "Questions on Legislation," Helvétius (1810, vol. 2, pp. 281–290) put forth the essential features of his theory of legislation and politics. The propositions are so worded that there is little question he intended them not to raise doubt, but to demonstrate the correctness of his conception of political progress.

In order to achieve political progress, it behooves us first to understand the motives that unite men in society. To this problem Helvétius devoted much time. Society is formed when men realize that the scourges of nature cannot be overcome singly, but only by individuals banded together in common struggle. Therefore, the necessities of material conditions force men to be essentially social in spite of their essentially egoistic natures. Mankind once *united against nature* becomes *divided against one another.* The result is a division of labor, an economically torn society. With the crystalization of these economic and social divisions, people are then "obligated to form conventions and give themselves laws" (Helvétius, 1810, vol. 2, p. 281). These laws have as their foundation "the common desire of securing their property, their lives, and their liberty, which, in an unsocial state, is exposed to the violence of the strongest" (Helvétius, 1810, vol. 2, p. 281).

The stage of savagery was likened by Helvétius to modern despotism. Both had in common the destruction of all bonds of social union. Despotism, like its primitive ancestor, substituted might for right, the lash of the ruler for the law of people. He then suggested that a certain equilibrium of power among the different classes of citizens be introduced, as it was during the English revolutions of the preceding century (Helvétius, 1810, vol. 2, p. 282). Once this relative harmony of social interests comes into existence during a revolution, the class and individual strife of those on the same side is minimized. After the revolution has achieved its aims, however, Helvétius noticed that there is a resurgence of the very social antagonisms that the revolution had sought to abolish. Just as prior to the revolution, so, too, after the revolution, a polarization of class interests reemerges.

The despairing insight of Helvétius concerning the harmony and polarization of social and class interests led him to posit a political order that could finally end this cyclical path of development. His conception of the future society may best be characterized as an early form of utopian socialism, in the traditions established by Mably, Morelly and Linguet. "Have the poor really a country?" he asked.

> Does the man without property owe anything to the country where he possesses nothing? Must not the extremely indigent, being always in the pay of the rich and powerful, frequently favor their ambition? And lastly, have not the indigent too many wants to be virtuous? Could not the laws unite the interest of the majority of the inhabitants with that of their country by the subdivision of property? After the example of the Lacedemonians, whose territory being divided into thirty-nine thousand lots,

was distributed among thirty-nine thousand families, who formed the nation, might not, in case of too great an increase of inhabitants, a greater or less extent of land be assigned to each family, but still in proportion to the number who compose it? (Helvétius, 1810, vol. 2, p. 283)

Little imagination is necessary to perceive that Helvétius was not posing questions, but rather was providing fundamental answers as to necessary preconditions for achieving a harmonious, equalitarian society.

Helvétius passed on to a different phase of political progress, the development of the legal codes of a state. Pointing out that a great number of involved legal statutes are not infrequently a maze of contradictions made useless by their abstraction from real-life situations, Helvétius indicated that such multiplicity of laws leads to ignorance and a failure on the part of governing classes to execute the public will. The only purpose they serve is to institutionalize the oppression of the people and to confuse them concerning what their true interests actually are. "The multiplicity of laws, often contrary to each other, oblige nations to employ certain men and bodies of men to interpret them. May not these men or bodies of men, charged with their interpretation, insensibly change the laws and make them the instruments of their ambition? And lastly, does not experience teach us, that wherever there are many laws, there is little justice" (Helvétius, 1810, vol. 2, pp. 284–285). Therefore, in repressive governments, the laws serve directly as an instrument of oppression.

In a good society, in a rational political arrangement, one that is concerned with the welfare of people, a small number of clear and self-evident laws are sufficient. Complicated laws that are interpreted and reinterpreted by elitist aspirations serve only to further political reaction. Where there are no private interests there will be no need for a complex legal scaffold to keep down the public will. Simple laws are sufficient to establish the simple goal of all humankind, happiness (Helvétius, 1810, vol. 2, p. 284). Just as land should be divided up among all people for the purpose of doing away with conflicts between rulers and ruled, Helvétius advocated dividing up nations into small federations equal in size and political power. In this way, wars, national oppression and territorial aggrandizement could finally be abolished.

May not a certain number of small republics by a federative compact, more perfect than that of the Greeks, shelter themselves from the invasion of an enemy, and the tyranny of an ambitious citizen? If a country as large as France were to be divided into thirty provinces or republics, and to each of them a territory nearly equal (in size) were to be assigned, and if each of these territories were circumscribed by immutable bounds, or its possession guaranteed by the other twenty-nine republics, is it to be imagined that any one of those republics could enslave all the others, that is, that any one man could combat with advantage against twenty-nine men? (Helvétius, 1810, vol. 2, pp. 285–286)

To prevent an aggressor nation from commencing warfare against a nation constituted in a democratic federation, Helvétius would impose certain safeguards.

[On the supposition that these democratic republics] were governed by the same laws, where each of them took care of its interior police and the election of its magistrates, and reported its conduct to a superior council; or where the superior council composed of four deputies from each republic, and principally occupied with the affairs of war and politics, should be yet charged with observing that none of those republics changed its legislation without the consent of all the others: and where, moreover, the object of the laws should be to improve minds, exalt courage, and preserve an exact discipline in their armies. On such a supposition the whole body of the republics would be sufficiently powerful to oppose efficaciously any ambitious projects of their neighbors, or of their fellow-citizens. (Helvétius, 1810, vol. 2, p. 286)

As long as the legislation of such a federated republic renders the greatest happiness to the greatest number of people, procuring for them all the pleasures compatible with public welfare, these republics could be sure of continued political progress. Helvétius' interest in peace and prosperity overshadowed the utopianism of the plan.

Laws are good if they equalize the material basis of human welfare and extirpate all possibilities of special class interests and wars of aggression. It was through peace and social equality that Helvétius saw the vast possibilities open for political progress. Legislation is moral if it secures peace and equality. It is immoral if it does not do so. "Whenever the public welfare is not the supreme law, and the first obligation of a citizen, does there still subsist a science of good and evil; in short, is there any morality where the public good is not the measure of reward and punishment, of the esteem or contempt due to the actions of citizens?" (Helvétius, 1810, vol. 2, p. 288) Helvétius recognized that political progress is measured by more than the democratization and equalization of the material sources of pleasure. It is measured also in terms of the ideals and attitudes it instills in people. Therefore, the good society and the good laws provide for emotional and psychological pleasures as well as for material goods. In fact, in a quite real sense the ideas and opinions of men help mold and shape the future course of civilization. This strain in Helvétius' thought is made explicit.

Is it enough for a government to be good, that it secures to the inhabitants their properties, lives, and liberties, makes a more equal partition of a nation's riches, and enables the people more easily to obtain by moderate labor a sufficiency for themselves and their families, if the legislation does not at the same time exalt in the minds of men the sentiment of emulation, and for this effect the state does not propose large rewards for great talents and great virtues? And might not these rewards, always consisting of certain superfluities, and which were formerly the source of so many great and noble actions, again produces the same effects? And can the rewards decreed by government be regarded as a luxury of pleasure adopted to corrupt the manners of the people? (Helvétius, 1810, vol. 2, p. 289)

Helvétius argues →

The answer is obviously that they cannot. Government has to provide for the all-around security of the people. Only by so doing can political progress be ensured.

Helvétius' progressive conception of development in the political–legal structure of society, presented as it was in an epoch of decomposition, cynicism and corruption of the *ancien régime,* stood forefront in the cause of the rights and dignity of man. The weaknesses in his presentation stemmed from an inability to conceive of the causal relationship between a country's political institutions and its precise economic stage of development. Plekhanov's description of the utopian socialist search for *the* enlightened lawgiver as the "joyless chase of some happy historical accident" serves equally well in delineating an essential weak spot in Helvétius' thinking. Plekhanov considered this "search" as basic to Enlightenment philosophy:

The chase of the happy accident was the constant occupation of the writers of the Enlightenment in the eighteenth century. It was just in hope of such an accident that they sought by every means, fair and foul, to enter into friendly relations with more or less enlightened "legislators" and aristocrats of their age. Usually it is thought that once a man has said to himself that opinion governs the world, he no longer has any reason to despair of the future: *la raison finira par avoir raison.* But this is not so. When and in what way will reason triumph? The writers of the Enlightenment said that in the life of society everything depends, in the long run, on the "legislator." Therefore they went on their search for legislators. But the same writers knew very well that the character and views of man depend on his upbringing, and that generally speaking their upbringing did not predispose the "legislators" to the absorption of enlightened doctrines. Therefore they could not but realize that there was little to be hoped from the legislators. There remained only to trust to some happy accident. Imagine that you have an enormous box in which there are very many black balls and two or three white ones. You take out ball after ball. In each individual case you have incomparably fewer chances of taking out a white ball than a black. But, if you repeat the operation a sufficient number of times, you will finally take out a white ball. The same applies to the legislators. In each individual case it is incomparably more probable that the legislators will be against the philosophers: but in the end there must appear, after all, a legislator who is in agreement with the philosophers. This one will do everything that reason dictates. Thus, literally, thus, did Helvétius argue. *The subjective idealist view of history* ("opinions govern the world"), *which seems to provide such a wide field for man's freedom of action, in reality represents him as the plaything of accident.* That is why this view in its essence is very *joyless.* (Plekhanov, 1947, pp. 75–76)

The impatience of Helvétius in the face of questions concerning social evolution and revolution, the nature of historical change, revealed his political philosophy to be one-sided and ultimately idealist. In his view of history, he opposed God as a *deus ex machina* only to substitute a monarch as the *deus ex machina.* However useful this notion may have been in combating antiquated political dogmas, it had serious scientific value only insofar as it attempted to explain the ideological content of politics. Like other *philosophies,* Helvétius made a remarkable effort in this direction only to end in failure. The materialist Helvétius, in his view of political growth, adopted an idealist position—that opinions rather than economic and social conditions ultimately determine the course of civilization. When materialist considerations forced their way to the surface of Helvétius' thought, they did so mechanistically and at the risk of destroying the spirit of his efforts. Social science and humanism found themselves divided in his political outlook. When he concentrated on making politics a science, he lost touch with the human participants in the struggle for progress. When he concentrated on humanizing politics, he lost touch with the material roots of progress. At one point, social consciousness becomes an accidental response to atomic particles whirling about in the mind, and at another, it becomes the prime mover. This is the tragicomedy of mechanical materialism. In the first act, humanism battles cannibalism. In the second act, science battle supernaturalism. But this doctrine never finishes the play because it never finds the proper resolution and solution to the conflicts posed (Gay, 1969, pp. 529–552).

Irrespective of what Helvétius did to make sociological naturalism a vital political philosophy, the attempt failed because of his attachment to metaphysical slogans that made history a stage prop to the "individual" and forgot that the individual can read only those lines written by social history, the accumulated and collective endeavors of mankind. The reproach of idealism from Plato to Hegel—that materialism was inherently ossified and static—was a proper reproach to the extent that materialism operates within a physicalist vacuum. Spinoza attempted to make political science as rigid as geometry, La Mettrie compared human society to a monster machine, and Holbach thought that men, like atoms, responded to the requirements of Newtonian physics. Each new effort to explain scientifically the political life of man made it that much clearer that one would first have to find that set of laws that specifically controls human behavior. This was a task the Enlightenment threw at the coming nineteenth century. Hegel grappled with the task and failed. Marx grappled with it and succeeded. Why? Because he alone started with sensuous man, but man rooted in relations he is part of, not voluntarily but necessarily, not haphazardly but organically. He alone was capable of linking man to his economy, science to its technology and materialism to methodology. With him that elusive third act the Enlightenment never finished is complete.

It is certainly true that the political thought of Helvétius was of immeasurable aid in justifying bourgeois social and state power. This is, however, hardly a unique distinction. The significant point is that in the eighteenth century he was able to write from the standpoint of all exploited publics. He avoided the trite and typical political theorizing of the Enlightenment. The narrow "career open to talents" egalitarianism found no favor in Helvétius' outlook. Politics cannot remain the exclusive preserve of an aristocratic elite or of professional civil servants and still claim democracy as its method or goal. His considering politics as the domain of the people as a whole is an achievement that has to be deemed a peak in the development of French democratic political thought. His approach contained an element of negating the very class that assumed the reins of government in this type of equalitarian doctrine. As soon as the French bourgeoisie became the ruling political body, it no longer required, and eventually came to resent bitterly, the possible consequences of an application of utilitarian theories of social and political equality.

Helvétius neither understood nor had patience with political theorists who were preoccupied with forms of government. In his view, governments were either good or evil, the standard of judgment being their social utility. This view presupposed yet another idea, which was to gain increasing prominence in the nineteenth century, namely, that the *content* of society is its material resources—natural and human—and that the *form* of society are in such a relation to the content as either to propel or retard the growth of the material base of society. Since, in Helvétius' view, all previous forms or stages of society rested on securing an abundance for private selfish interests, a good (useful) economic and political system was a thing of the future lacking any historical precedence. Helvétius' failure to concern himself with the political forms of government may be deplored as a negation of political science, but none can deplore the reason behind this. It stems from his revolutionary attitude toward problems of social progress. The prime goal of man being happiness, all political institutions must be adapted to satisfy this aim. Political progress is not the slow, gradual and haphazard adaptation of old institutions to meet new situations, but their revolutionary transformation under the guidance of a providential monarch. As against Montesquieu, Helvétius (1807, Discourse 3, chap. 30) taught their veneration of ancient laws and credos is not only a naïve rejection of the requirements of the present but also dangerous to a scientific comprehension of politics. For him, the individual alone is capable of determining his interest at any particular moment. The integration of these various individual interests into a common political organization makes possible a democratic society. It is this very meshing of individual interests that revealed to Helvétius the necessity of an equal distribution of wealth, labor, education and, above all, political control (Helvétius, 1810, vol. 2, p. 119).

The desire to frame a democratic theory of politics rests on a comprehension that men must first change their environment if they are to bring about any profound change in their psychology. Materialism and causal determinism are the heart of the utilitarian science of morality. But this faith in the self-corrective powers of "man" went only so far. Unfortunately, the utilitarians attributed to an enlightened monarch powers of social change that are the sole property of society as a whole. This exaggeration in utilitarian political doctrine of the role played by a princely ruler stemmed from the almost sacred belief that once enlightened, the ruler would be a dispassionate dispenser of law and justice, thereby becoming the prime agent of social progress. This view implies that a king in relation to social institutions acts as a mechanic does in relation to a run-down machine, the separate parts of which can be reordered through purely external intervention. This is what Plekhanov (1934, p. 168), in an essay on Marx, called "the transformation of a phenomenon into a fossilized thing by abstracting it from all the inner processes of life, the nature and connection of which it is impossible to understand." The utilitarians were caught in a web of their own design. They developed a theory of politics that expressed the democratic yearnings of the masses of Frenchmen. But the theory remained tied to a helpless metaphysical view of political progress, which rested on changing society through the enlightenment of a king. In the last analysis, Platonism won out; the search for the philosopher-king was on. It mattered not to the encyclopedists that they were trying to prove that the impossible was the necessary, that it was in the best interests of a monarch to act judiciously toward the very subjects he exploits and must continue to exploit if he is to remain a monarch. Such a view is the antithesis and negation of a theory of politics that rests on first altering the social conditions of life if progress is to be realized.

POLITICAL SOCIETY:
THE ROUSSEAUIAN PIVOT

The contribution of Rousseau to a theory of political society is as great as those made by the other *philosophes* as a group. *A Discourse on the Origin of Inequality* (Rousseau, 1950) occupies a place of honor in the historical genesis of political sociology. At the most general level, Rousseau succeeded in showing that the difference between the political society and the moral man, a distinction made by Plato and Aristotle, and one that has continued to grip thinkers in the vise of dualism, is largely fictitious. The political and the moral are equivalent; both are aspects of human socialization. Legal relationships are as binding or as limiting as moral persuasions permit; similarly, moral relationships are as binding or limiting as legal persuasions permit. The key to both is legitimacy; and for authority to be made legitimate, a cluster of norms and values must be mutually agreed upon by all parties involved in a social contract. The point here is to move beyond the theory of the social contract and into Rousseau's general theory of the history and evolution of political society.

The critical significance of Rousseau inheres, not in his idea of original goodness, which was, in the long run, but a ploy with which to beat back the theological critics, but rather in his ideas that the human origins in an empirical context do not entail a settlement of the idea of original evil or goodness. Indeed, his critique of Hobbes in *A Discourse on the Origin of Inequality* comes exceptionally close to the post-Enlightenment sensibility on this question.

> Above all, let us not conclude, with Hobbes, that because man has no idea of goodness, he must be naturally wicked; that he is vicious because he does not know virtue; that he always refuses to do his fellow-creatures services which he does not think they have a right to demand; or that by virtue of the right he truly claims everything he needs, he foolishly imagines himself the sole proprietor of the whole universe. Hobbes had seen clearly the defects of all the modern definitions of natural right: but the consequences which he deduces from his own show that he understands it in an equally false sense. In reasoning on the principles he lays down, he ought to have said that the state of nature, being that in which the care for our own preservation is the least prejudicial to that of others, was consequently the best calculated to promote peace, and the most suitable for mankind. (Rousseau, 1950, p. 222)

Rousseau understood that the primary human drives have little to do with the moral questions and a great deal to do with the social question —the question of survival.

> Man's first feeling was that of his own existence, and his first care that of self-preservation. The produce of the earth furnished him with all he needed, and instinct told him how to use it. Hunger and other appetites made him at various times experience various modes of existence; and among these was one which urged him to propagate his species—a blind propensity that, having nothing to do with the heart, produced a merely animal act. (Rousseau, 1950, p. 235)

But as the long gestation period of human survival was resolved, then —and only then—did the period of social survival emerge. The act of people valuing each other created the conditions for human obligation to each other, and with that man moved on from the idea of society to that of polity or, as Rousseau called it, civility.

> As soon as men began to value one another, and the idea of consideration had got a footing in the mind, every one put in his claim to it, and it became impossible to refuse it to any with impunity. Hence arose the first obligations of civility even among savages; and every intended injury became an affront because, besides the hurt which might result from it,

the party injured was certain to find in it a contempt for his person, which was often more insupportable than the hurt itself. (Rousseau, 1950, p. 292)

Rousseau moved on from that to a brilliant appreciation of how political men tend to perceive of the idea of liberty in precisely the same terms as philosophical men conceive of the idea of nature. Just as there is no meaning to any notion of the "natural" propensity of men toward evil, so, too, there is correspondingly no basis to speak of the natural propensity of social man to a condition of slavery.

> Politicians indulge in the same sophistry about the love of liberty as philosophers about the state of nature. They judge, by what they see, of very different things, which they have not seen; they attribute to man a natural propensity to servitude, because the slaves within their observation are seen to bear the yoke with patience; they fail to reflect that it is with liberty as with innocence and virtue; the value is known only to those who possess them, and the taste for them is forfeited when they are forfeited themselves. (Rousseau, 1950, p. 255)

The idea of legitimacy serves to make men political as well as sociable. In the absence of such legitimate authority, one has slavery. But that condition is not natural: It is a consequence of despotism and unfulfilled promises.

It follows, then, that for Rousseau the emergence of inequality had nothing to do with the original state of human degradation or ignorance; rather, it was a direct consequence of imperfectly conceived political rule. In point of fact, the state encourages inequality precisely to the degree that it enshrines the social and economic inequalities found in a society.

> If we follow the progress of inequality in these various revolutions, we shall find that the establishment of laws and of the right of property was its first term, the institution of magistracy the second, and the conversion of legitimate into arbitrary power the third and last; so that the condition of rich and poor was authorized by the first period; that of powerful and weak by the second; and only by the third that of master and slave, which is the last degree of inequality, and the term at which all the rest remain, when they have got so far, till the government is either entirely dissolved by new revolutions or brought back again to legitimacy. (Rousseau, 1950, p. 263)

Rousseau was unable to perceive the possibility that it was in the very essence of the state to enshrine inequality through law. But he did get beyond the easy identification of progress with equity, of abundance with happiness and the other simple identifications that the men of Enlightenment were, in fact, prone to make. If the Enlightenment, in these very drives toward a theory of measuring progress, gave rise to the sociological imagination, then Rousseau, in his answer to this touching faith in measurable change, gave rise to the political imagination—to an appreciation of how man surrenders his rights to society, only to find out that society then cedes its own rights to the state.

The *Discourse on Inequality* is only superficially an essay on looking backward. Rousseau was no Edward Bellamy. He recognized that the impulse to examine antecedents is more profoundly an effort to know the future. Both historical and utopian longings stimulate discontent, but they can never be more than feelings. And sentiments can never really bring us back into the past. They can only be a stimulant to living in the present. Rousseau concluded the opening section on an optative note: the worth of looking backward and the necessity of going forward. Historicity plays a critical role in Rousseau's work; indeed, his sense of historicity is rare for the Enlightenment period.

Rousseau described the backward condition in terms of the savage man. The savage man, or the noble savage, is an obvious fiction, and no one knew this better than Rousseau. However, out of that fictionalized and highly personalized account of what the savage man is supposed to be came some very interesting theories. It should be added that the eighteenth century, the French Enlightenment in particular, stimulated all the *philosophes* to concern themselves with anthropology, and to worry about the origins of man. This came about, in part, through the concern with the origins of nature as a source for overcoming theology. Many *philosophes* were concerned with the relationship of geological time to divine providential statements about the beginning of the world. This led to further inquiries into the origins of man, all of which were dedicated to one principle, the overthrow of divine truth. That is to say, Rousseau, along with the rest of the eighteenth-century Enlightenment, was interested in those subjects that would help overthrow organized religion. Toward this task geology and anthropology became important. That was the source of concern with the origins of man in his original form. And in this, Rousseau was very much a man of "his times."

Rousseau's concern was not with the savage man, but with alienation in modern man. The wholeness of original man was being contrasted with the fragmented quality of modern man. This was the first inkling of the marvelous dialectician (or bookkeeper, if you will) that Rousseau was. At every advance in technological proficiency there is a loss of basic skills. The more one rides in an automobile, the less capable he is of walking. The more one uses electrical equipment, the less adept he becomes with mechanical skills. When there is a massive power failure, the social world grinds to a halt. Men stop. They have nothing at their disposal. Everything called "civilized" has in some sense become external to them, and their sheer physical prowess has become separated from themselves. Men become alienated from their physical condition the less savage they are. The first premise of Rousseau's outlook was the notion of alienation in modern man, not in the form of the factory machine, not in the spiritual form of reasoning, but in the basic raw Spartan form of man's physical prowess separated from himself. In this schism between mind and body one can see how the origins of inequality emerge. The struggle becomes the control not of the man, but of those forces external to man upon which he depends for his existence. The struggle for control is not for one's own body, but for the communications network, the electrical network, the mechanical apparatus. The forces of production and consumption, which are alien to men, become the essential focus of revolutionary struggle— although whatever interest group wins, man as a self-controlling element loses.

Original man is all man in that he controls his possessions, and that which defines him is not isolated from what he uses. To that degree, he is able to say yes or no with relative free will, but the more civilized he becomes, the more the definition of civilization becomes the external relationship he has to the object, the more he becomes brutalized—brutalized not simply in the sense of being incapable at the lower end of exercising free will, but incapable in the upper end of exercising free will, so that like a brute he no longer has a share in his own operations. He loses his character as a free agent; so the highly civilized man is not simply effete, though he may be very worried about being effete, he is brutish in that he is without command over his free will.

> The body of a savage man being the only instrument he understands, he uses it for various purposes, of which ours, for want of practice, are incapable: for our industry deprives us of that force and agility which necessity obliges him to acquire. If he had had an axe, would he have been able with his naked arm to break so large a branch from a tree? If he had had a sling, would he have been able to throw a stone with so great velocity? If he had had a ladder, would he have been so nimble in climbing a tree? If he had had a horse, would he have been himself so swift of foot? Give civilized man time to gather all his machines about him, and he will no doubt easily beat the savage; but if you would see a still more unequal contest, set them together naked and unarmed, and you will soon see the advantage of having all our forces constantly at our disposal, of being always prepared for every event, and of carrying one's self, as it were, perpetually whole and entire about one. (Rousseau, 1950, p. 201)

Rousseau, in the face of a celebration of progress, interjected a cautioning note, quite horrible in its prospects. He turned to the subject that the whole of the eighteenth century was taken with, namely, the reasons and the passions. In eighteenth-century literature—especially in Diderot and Helvétius—the passions and the reasons were in fine balance. Man is made up of some kind of mix between them, and they had no doubt that to the extent reason overwhelms the passions, to that extent man is rational and reasonable. Only one voice argued this point. Rousseau, almost in a Dostoevskian way, issued forth a reminder of their irreducible character.

Rousseau argued that reason is not the enemy of the passions, but indebted to the passions. There are several important ideas here: One is that the notion of reason as the enemy of passions is overthrown. In order to have a reasoning being, one must have a passionate animal. Passion is the handmaiden of reason because the purpose of knowledge is never knowledge itself. It is instrumental in the person because it aids one to attain a personal sense of glory, satisfaction or happiness. Rousseau was not presenting a critique or ethic on the idea of reason, but was merely asserting that reason is related to the passions in such a way that both become essential for the survival of man. Indeed, his position is very much like the twentieth-century notion of Schumpeter and Weber—that science is not the enemy of ideology, but the handmaiden of ideology. But to speak thusly is to speak of the end of science itself.

One of the problems in this period of writing was the notion of a natural state or an original state. While many of the *philosophes* were anti-religious in their ideology, they imbibed from the theology of their times the notion of an original state. They might argue whether the original state was good or bad, but that there was such a thing as a natural state was never doubted by Augustine, Hobbes or Rousseau. In part, one has to understand by the concept of the original state the parallel to natural law, the idea of some kind of sociological a priori, some kind of anchor point that is known to all men logically, something that is not merely empirically found out, but is revealed to man. The function of the concept of the natural state was that it revealed to man his original condition.

In the end of the first section on Hobbes' ethics, Rousseau examined the idea of the natural state being a state of war. In effect he said, in response to the Hobbesian view, that the natural state, far from being a state of war, is actually a state of peace. The arts of war are cultivated only when objects are alienated or externalized from man. Insofar as man is in self-possession and in self-command, his concerns are not so much fixed upon the liquidation of an enemy as upon his own survival. Hobbes was wrong, inductively, because a man does not attack another man simply to beat another man; he attacks him to gain something so that the death of the other man is an advantage for the killer. But if there are no objects externalized from the man, what advantage can there be? Only in a condition in which objects are possessed does killing become a premium and war a value, so that the deeper the alienation of the man from the objects of his life, the more likely the possibility of war.

In effect, Rousseau believed that depravity comes into being when there is something for which to be depraved, when there is an object of desire and when men falsely assume that force creates right, rather than assuming that free men exercise free choice. The nobility of the savage stems in part from his self-possession, his completeness as a person and, at the other end of the spectrum, from the absence of a need to agree because of his self-completeness. The notion of depravity comes into being only when there are objects that have to be agreed upon. Depravity existed for Rousseau, but only to the extent that man is not in control of his own personality.

Plentitude and abundance and the struggle over these, according to Rousseau, make for regional, national and international strife. For Rousseau, the revolution of pain could never be the liquidation of another person, but only self-improvement. There will never be sufficient material objects because "enough" is a thing that man, as a creature of passions, always pushes further and further away. Within the framework of any situation, the character of the person determines the kind of behavioral pattern he will set forth.

The pure Rousseauian state is a state of pure and perfect self-possession. To the extent that one needs objects and things, one is a slave of the passions. This is almost a neo-Christian view, as is true of the whole transcendentalist movement. Part of the inspiration for that movement was Rousseau. They embellished his ideas with the idea of reason derived from the Hegelian world view, so that one lived not only in the state of nature but also in the state of mind—a state of mind purged of selfishness and greed.

The issue here is also the question of egoism. Egoism is linked to society as the self-aggrandizement of men. This emphasis on self-respect is a Spartan notion, and it was linked by Rousseau to "nature." Nature provides self-respect; society provides self-aggrandizement. The context of the origins of inequality is in this dialectic of the displacement of the feeling of wholeness and totality one finds in nature over and against the egoistic feeling one finds prevalent in most societies. The tasks of the good state then become clear: to restore the natural wholeness to the social tasks. This became the leitmotif of all political writings of the nineteenth century— a task raised to the level of practice by the French Revolution, but realized in theory only by those who meditated and contemplated the ruins of that Revolution.

REFERENCES

Alembert, J. L. R. d' (1821–22) *Oeuvres,* vols. 1, 2. Paris: A. Belin.

Argenson, R. d' (1765) *Considérations sur le gouvernement ancien et présent de la France.* Paris: M. Rey.

Augustine (1963) *City of God,* trans. J. W. Wand. New York: Oxford University Press.

Bayle, P. (1702) *Dictionnaire historique et critique,* 2nd ed., revised and augmented. Rotterdam: Reinier Leers [written in 1697].

Condorcet, M. J. (1955) *Sketch for an Historical Picture of The Progress of the Human Mind.* New York: Noonday Press [1796].

Diderot, D. (1875–77) *Oeuvres complètes,* ed. J. Assezat, vols. 2, 13. Paris: Garnier.

Diderot, D., and d'Alembert, J. L. R., eds. (1777–79) *Encyclopedie, ou*

Dictionnaire raisonné des sciences, des arts et des metiers, par une société de gens de lettres, vols. 1, 12, 17, 25. Geneva: J. Pellet.

Diderot, D. (1955) *Supplement au voyage de Bougainville.* Geneva: Droz.

Dupuis, C. F. (1872) *The Origin of all Religious Worship.* New Orleans: privately printed [written in 1795].

Engels, F. (1940) *On Historical Materialism.* New York: International Publishers.

Engels, F. (1941) *Ludwig Feuerbach and the Outcome of Classical German philosophy.* New York: International Publishers.

Fontenelle, Bernard Le Bovier de (1932) *De l'origine des fables.* Paris: Felix Alcan [written in 1724].

Frankel, C. (1948) *The Faith of Reason.* New York: King's Crown Press.

Gay, P. (1969) *The Enlightenment: An Interpretation,* vol. 2: *The Science of Freedom.* New York: Knopf.

Grossman, M. (1926) *The Philosophy of Helvétius.* New York: Teachers College Press.

Hegel, G. W. F. (1956) *Philosophy of History.* New York: Dover.

Helvétius, C. A. (1807) *Essays on the Mind,* trans. W. Mudford. London.

Helvétius, C. A. (1810) *A Treatise on Man, His Intellectual Faculties and His Education,* trans. W. Hooper, 2 vols. London: Vernor, Hood and Sharpe.

Helvétius, C. A. (1818) Letter to Montesquieu, in *Oeuvres complètes,* 5 vols. London: privately printed.

Hicks, G. (1937) "The Literary Opposition to Utilitarianism," *Science and Society,* vol. 1, no. 4.

Holbach, P. H. T., baron d' (1822) *Systeme Social,* vol. 2. Paris: Niogret.

Hook, S. (1950) *From Hegel to Marx.* New York: Humanities Press.

Kant, I. (1882) *Critique of Pure Reason.* trans. J. M. D. Meiklejohn. London: Bell.

Lefebvre, H. (1949) *Diderot.* Paris: Hier et Aujourd'huit.

Luporini, C. (1950) "On the Lettres Philosophiques of Voltaire," *Societa.*

Luppol, I. K. (1936) *Diderot: See idées philosophiques,* trans. V. Feldman and Y. Feldman. Paris.

Maillet, B. de (1797) *Teliamed: or, The World Explain'd.* Baltimore, Md.: W. Pechin.

Marx, K. (1845) "On the History of French Materialism," from *The Holy Family;* Appendix in F. Engels (1941).

Marx, K., and F. Engels (1964) *The German Ideology,* trans. R. Pascal. Moscow: Progress Publishers [written in 1845–1846].

Montesquieu, C. L. de Secondat (1949) *The Spirit of the Laws,* trans. T. Nugent. New York: Hafner.

More, T. (1955) *Utopia and A Dialogue of Comfort.* New York: Dutton.

Neumann, F. Introduction to C. L. Montesquieu (1949).

Plato (1968) *Republic,* trans. A. Bloom. New York: Basic Books.

Plekhanov, G. V. (1934) *Essays in the History of Materialism.* trans. R. Fox. London: Bodley Head.

Plekhanov, G. V. (1947) *In Defence of Materialism: The Development of the Monist View of History,* trans. A. Rothstein. London: Lawrence and Wishart.

Raynal, G. T. F. (1782) *The Revolution of America.* Philadelphia: Robert Bell.

Rousseau, J. J. (1913) *The Social Contract,* trans. G. D. H. Cole. New York: Dutton.

Rousseau, J. J. (1950) *A Discourse on the Origin of Inequality,* trans. and ed. G. D. H. Cole. New York: Dutton.

Rousseau, J. J. (1953) *The Confessions of Jean Jacques Rousseau,* trans. J. M. Cohen, bks. 9, 10. Baltimore, Md.: Penguin.

Sabine, G. (1937) *A History of Political Theory.* New York: Holt, Rinehart & Winston.

Soboul, A. (1951) "L'Encyclopedie et le mouvement Encyclopediste," *La pensee,* no. 39 (November–December), pp. 41–51.

Volney, C. F. C. (1811) *The Ruins; or, A Survey of the Revolutions of Empires,* 5th ed. London: T. Tegg.

Voltaire, F. M. A. de (1945) *Philosophical Dictionary,* trans. H. I. Woolf, abridged ed. London: Allen and Unwin.

CHAPTER 4

POLITICAL ORDER:
THE ROMANTIC PIVOT

STATE POWER AND SOCIAL ORDER

Traditional sociology tends to assume that the state is part of the social system, and that a system of power operates only at some levels within the system. This is not the only possible or plausible vision of human interaction. If the dialectical tradition culminating with Hegel did nothing else, it established the unique place of political theory in the study of culture. Hegel's analysis of freedom is distinguished by a firm separation of civil society from polity. His approach is theoretical in that throughout he is concerned with basic properties of social and political structures. Social phenomena are not viewed empirically as going entities, but selectively, through logical, that is, dialectical, distinctions. The Hegelian approach assumes completeness in that all relevant concepts and relations that would be required in empirical undertakings are worked out. This special sense of methodology as ideal typification should be kept in mind when examining Hegel. What we are provided with is a systems approach rather than empirical analysis.

Few commentators have viewed the directly political and social writings of Hegel as an extension of his more abstract works. A British analytic philosopher has even suggested that Hegel's *Philosophy of Right and Law* (1953), in which the social and legal basis of political freedom is central, represents an aberration, "a deep loss of integrity both in his character and in his thinking" (Findlay, 1958, p. 320).[1] My purpose in this chapter is to show that such a view represents a misreading of Hegel. If taken literally, it would result in a view of him as a thinker who lacks the skills of even a keen social ethnographer. I shall try to demonstrate the reverse: that for Hegel the social and political issue of freedom represents *die Weisheit*, the sociological expression of philosophic wisdom.

Hegel shared with the *Sturm und Drang* movement and its romantic aftermath a dissatisfaction with the utilitarian impulse to define freedom in terms of a calculus of individual interests. Yet he was not willing to consider the notion of a *Volksgruppe* to be a replacement for a practical theory of individual freedom and responsibility. Hegel's contempt for abstract notions of freedom, and for freedom as a defense of property rights, places him in contrast to Novalis, Muller, Schleiermacher and other representatives of German romanticism during the Napoleonic era. In attempting to locate the specific ethical coordinates of freedom, Hegel laid the basis for a new view of political man.

Prussianism as a ninetenth-century ideology was quite different from what it was to become during the age of national socialism. In the years in which Hegel wrote, Prussia appeared as the least compromised part of Germany. Although defeated by the Napoleonic armies at Jena, Prussia retained a distinct moral advantage in the eyes of nationalists for having defended German interests. Other German states became French satellites in the Rhine Confederation. Austria capitulated to Napoleon through court maneuvers. Prussia alone remained an unwilling partner to the Continental System. The Prussianization of Germany was viewed by many of the intellectuals as the exclusive means for achieving the feeling, if not the fact, of sovereignty. The ultimate defeat of the Napoleonic forces served to enhance Prussian separatism. What should be appreciated is that the options for men like Fichte and Hegel were narrowed to Prussianism or Bonapartism. And whether Hegel was "pro-Bonaparte" or "pro-Prussian" represents an ideological irrelevance. The breakthrough of a democratic option did not take place in Germany until the second half of the nineteenth century, fifty years after Hegel died (Krieger, 1951, pp. 125–138).

Even if we are to consider Prussianism in its incipient forms as reactionary, it does not follow that the social thought of Hegel was proscribed by ultimate values about the *Volksgeist*. If it is proper to consider Hegel's ontology in terms of system and method, a position Engels maintained

---

[1] The view of Findlay is an extension of the position taken by Karl Popper (1945, chap. 12) and seems a characteristic of English philosophical opinion generally.

(Engels, 1934), it is no less the case that his social theory can be interpreted along similar lines. Hegel's concept of freedom was not simply an afterthought to his disaffection with Bonapartism. In its theoretical side it was an effort to overcome the antinomies created first by Hobbes' mechanical rendering of the question of political power in an egocentric world, and second by Kant's abstract, rationalist approach to politics in a cosmopolitan, universalist world. History became Hegel's way out of the dilemmas created by both mechanism and transcendentalism.

The problem of the scope and nature of political freedom occupies a technical status in Hegel's thought analogous to that of the issue of causality in natural philosophy. Hegel was faced with the task of reestablishing the grounds of causality in order to make history scientific and overcome the indeterminism of Locke's *Essay Concerning Human Understanding*. He confronted a similar problem of demonstrating that (contrary to theories based on custom and volition) freedom is inextricably tied to social necessity.

To demonstrate this, Hegel drew heavily upon the work of Aristotle, Spinoza and, to a lesser extent, Bacon. From Aristotle, Hegel learned that freedom is essentially social and political, rather than individual—freedom in the absence of organized social systems being a logical as well as an empirical contradiction for Aristotle. From Spinoza, he derived the determinist view of freedom as the comprehension of necessity—freedom being impossible in isolation from knowledge of the real and rational relations of human societies. From Bacon, Hegel derived the idea that there is a clear identification of positive freedom with the power to transform knowledge into social goods through the beneficent agent of science and experiment. These men clearly do not exhaust the philosophic influences that generated Hegel's desire to bring about an explicit context for discussing freedom. One would also have to reckon with the line of the German *Aufklärung* moving from Lessing to Kant. Nevertheless, the writings of Aristotle and Spinoza serve to indicate the intellectual network within which Hegel operated. More so than with most philosophers, the intellectual lineage of Hegel is of decisive importance; as his lectures in philosophic history make plain, he set himself the task of reconciling as well as comprehending the totality of the history of ideas (Hegel, 1955).

The romantic view of Hegel's doctrine of freedom was a caricature. In Germany, there were the well-known efforts by the monarchy to appropriate Hegel's theory of freedom by making it part of a system paying homage to the state. The writings of semiofficial ideologists such as F. J. Stahl are characteristic. They denounce Hegel only at those points when his writings serve no statist ends. There were the equally abstract efforts to make the Hegelian theory of freedom serve as a touchstone for a wholesale critique of German society. The work of the left-Hegelians, Bruno Bauer and Arnold Ruge, purged Hegel of his particular philosophical message by reducing "*human* emancipation" to "*political* emancipation" (Marx, 1956).[2]

Outside Germany, Hegel's work underwent similar transformations. There were the feeble attempts of Anglo-American high culture to establish a simplistic formula: The free man is one who comprehends the necessary limits of history, nature and mind. Left as a formula, it is little wonder that Royce saw human freedom as circumscribed and defined in terms of the need for loyalty to the established social order (Royce, 1908, p. 213). This same formula led Bosanquet to implore man to suffer and be strong in the face of the higher necessity of preserving security and order (Bosanquet, 1917, p. 300). The alternative to this somber, symbiotic isomorphism between freedom and the state was Kierkegaard's freedom from society, truth as subjectivity, the notion that man's abiding happiness is to be found in human freedom in conscious opposition to the physical world as such. The individual became the only reality, the only free entity (Kierkegaard, 1944, pp. 291–299, 505–512).

While the fragmentation of Hegelian social theory makes it plain that even the firmest edifice will crack with time, and become obsolete under changing conditions, there remains the need to explore the rubble to see if there are any usable parts, and to understand what went wrong in the construction of the Hegelian social-philosophic system.

THE METAPHYSICAL NECESSITY
OF FREEDOM

The category of freedom pervades all areas of Hegel's philosophy. Every phase of life and logic is said to reveal the impulse toward freedom. In logic, which for Hegel encompasses the structure of the universe of mind and matter, the doctrine of notion, the core of his nonsyllogistic logic, is equated with the necessity of development and self-development in the process of life. Freedom is knowledge, a symbol of "pure self-consciousness"—the absolute and unfettered awareness of the logical relations underlying the generation and regeneration of life (Hegel, 1929, sec. 3). Logic is considered as an ontology, a description of a rational universe in motion. Further, this objective rationality is determinate because it is real.

The essence of freedom is thus a derivative of logic—a comprehension of the forms of actual development. The assumption that the expansion of freedom can happen outside or in opposition to reality is, in Hegel's imagination, a violation of the purpose of philosophy, the cognitive search for concrete truth. Hegel was compelled to satisfy the requirements of his idealism by ultimately conceiving of freedom metaphysically, as "absolute self-security and self-repose" (Hegel, 1929, sec. 3). However, this does not alter the fact that he considered logic as a product of the free con-

---

[2] There exists a vast and worthy literature on the growth of "right" and "left" Hegelianism in Germany. The following works in English are good representative samples: Hook (1936); Löwith (1949); Cornu (1957); and Speier (1952).

science, since only such a conscience is in a position to establish scientific truths. In *The Science of Logic* (1929), we receive our first indication that Hegel's view of freedom is not reducible to political totalitarianism or to personal idiosyncrasy. An uncontrolled system of power, like pure individualism, is irrational; and, by definition, what is irrational cannot be transformed into a mode for realizing freedom.[3]

In the *Phenomenology of Mind* (1931), the knot of freedom is untangled in carefully evolved stages that demonstrate the logical bases of consciousness. For Hegel, the evolution of human thought is no less an evolution in the positive freedom of civilization. Freedom comes through precision and exactitude. The social role of science, no less than its essential content, is the expansion of freedom through knowledge. This identification of philosophy with science provides mankind not only with a love of wisdom but also with wisdom as such. In the act of transforming potentiality into actuality, abstraction into specificity, man changes from a plaything of causality into its master. Real freedom then, for Hegel, is emancipation through the "scientific" control of events—science not yet seen as differing from the ontological.

The *Phenomenology* offers an intensive description of the development of consciousness. The unfolding of ideas, true as well as false, has its autonomous history. In Hegel, rational thought moves from the logical to the phenomenological—that is, from form to content. He is concerned with carrying the conclusions of the *Logic* to a higher stage, from a description of the forms of nature's laws to analysis of the content of thought. Consciousness is more than a quality of intellect, it is a category of society and its institutions. Freedom of spirit comes not by simple recognition of external objects as a mysterious event alien to thought; nor does freedom of spirit offer proclamations about personality development. Absolute knowledge is that which binds objectivity to subjectivity; it unfolds as law, ethics and religion—that is, knowledge as a social function.

Hegel had an unyielding respect for this object–subject formula, considering such a relation more capable of yielding truth than either the individual or the group taken separately. He made the subordination of the knower to universal reason a guiding principle of his work. As in his *Logic,* so, too, in his theory of science, what is important in the evolution of mankind is the concrete conditions of social life (especially its institutionalized forms), which give substance to the quest for freedom.

No sooner had the *Phenomenology* been completed than a paradox revealed itself which relentlessly pursued Hegel. If the essence of freedom

---

[3] The best explanation offered of the tripartite relation of science, idealism and freedom in Hegel is that of Edmund Husserl (1954, pp. 56–57). He noticed that Hegel, in his effort to consecrate philosophy in the name of science and in the name of rigor, precision, and truth, only succeeded in falsifying the character of science. Husserl noted that Hegel thus falsified existence through his idealist persuasion, by exalting rather than explaining the nature of science.

is the identification of individual reason with universal reason, the true realm of freedom is pure thought. Far from yielding freedom as concrete activity, freedom once more assumed the classic contemplative pose. Marx had to examine the core of this dilemma to arrive at an independent standpoint:

> It is precisely abstract thinking from which these objects (Wealth, State, Power) are alienated and to which they stand opposed with their pretension of reality. The philosopher, who is himself an abstract form of alienated man, establishes himself as the yardstick of the alienated world. The whole history of estrangement, the whole reappropriation of this *Entausserung,* is therefore nothing more than the history of the production of abstract thinking, that is, absolute, logical, speculative thinking. (Marx, 1959)

Hegel grasped the *idea* of freedom. But since only the idea had reality, he effectively sealed himself off from a naturalist appraisal. As a result, as Feuerbach expressed it, Hegel was led to convert freedom into a religious artifact by incorporating things into thoughts about existence (Feuerbach, 1903–11).[4]

Since we have introduced the assessments of Feuerbach and Marx, it is worthwhile to show how historical sociology evolved in distinctive stages around the idea of alienation. First, Hegel saw man as separated from reality as the personal conscience is isolated from objective consciousness, or better, as ideas are separated from truths. Next, Feuerbach considered the alienation problem in so-called anthropological terms, that is, as man separated from his own biosocial nature, and in consequence, having no direct experience of nature *qua* nature. To overcome this alienated condition, man invents a religion in order to conquer nature artificially, and evolves a theology to justify this anthropomorphism. Finally, Marx examined alienation as an economic condition rather than a philosophical condition. Alienation became a consequence of iniquitous, exploitive productive relations; man, the inventor of machines and/or labor-saving instruments, becomes captive to the machine. The problem becomes radically altered in modern psychoanalytic doctrine. To save labor-time becomes a special case of the large-scale task of emancipating man. The intellectual movement from Hegel to Feuerbach to Marx can be described as a movement from a sociology of knowledge into a sociology of religion and finally into general sociology, or the criticism of social institutions as such.[5]

Our main concern is with how Hegel worked out his sociology of knowledge, or, for those who stoutly insist that sociology begins with

[4] This Marxian point has been made in greater detail by Alexandre Kojève (1947, pp. 412–441) in examining phenomenology as a movement from the logician to the sage in Hegel's thought.

[5] For a further elaboration of the place of German nineteenth-century philosophic ideas in the evolution of political sociology, see Aron (1957, chap. 2) and Horowitz (1961, chap. 2).

Comte, with Hegel's phenomenology of freedom in society. Hegel was not unaware of the impasse into which his *Logic* and *Phenomenology* placed him. It was not just that he pictured freedom as the unity of thought and reality; Kant before him and Kierkegaard afterwards shared this belief. Hegel's real problem was his assumption that concrete reality is revealed through philosophic contemplation. This view left little room for social activity as a legitimate enterprise on the road to freedom. Hegel himself understood that metaphysical emancipation was not the same as emancipation from metaphysics. He attempted to overcome this paradox by retaining the belief that although the foundations of freedom are delineated by logical and phenomenological *forms,* the manifestations of freedom are social, economic and legal, and hence practical. The actual expression of Hegel's dilemma is that his attempt to develop a meaningful political philosophy came twenty years after his direct attention to political practice.[6]

FROM MORAL FREEDOM
TO LEGAL NECESSITY

Hegel's *Philosophy of Right and Law* considers the problem of freedom in terms of social structure and historical process. In it, the individual is conceived of not only as consciousness, but also as economic, political and legal activity. The repository of human knowledge is the social institution, from kinship units to international relations. The resolution of the dilemma between thought and action was bridged by making the thinking part of freedom philosophical, and the practical part of freedom social. The trouble with this bridge lies in its faulty construction. Social phenomena were seen to supersede one another, rather than to coexist. Personal morality is "resolved" into the family, which in turn is "resolved" into civil society, which in turn is "resolved" into the state. The structure of society ultimately became its process. Once again, freedom became linked to the notion of metaphysical perfection.

Most evidence adduced to prove Hegel's attraction for statism is derived from the *Philosophy of Right.* In its uncritically high estimate of the German Reformation, its desperate efforts to give a philosophic basis to militarism with which to counter the effects of Kant's pacifism, and its attempt to derive historically the necessity of nationalism with which to counter Rousseau's conventionalist idea of society, this work represents a classic defense of conservative political theory, overshadowing the less systematic efforts of Burke in England. Nevertheless, such a judgment, even granting its correctness, mistakes the political posture of Hegel with the quality and goals of his analysis.

[6] It is significant that Hegel's (1953, 1931, 1929, 1956) *Philosophy of Right and Law* [1821] comes much later than either the *Phenomenology of Mind* [1807] or *The Science of Logic* [1812]. For that matter, it precedes in time only the publication of the posthumous work on the *Philosophy of History* [1822].

In this work are to be found such cardinal concepts as the functional role of economy in the development of social systems, the conflict between economic and political interests in periods of crisis, and a precise description of the psychology of alienation. Furthermore, in the Preface to the work, which is said to stand as a monument to Hegel's unyielding reaction, he candidly declares that while the state is something rational in itself, such rationality is gained most readily by giving the person a chance to become a personality. Hegel rejects the Platonic critique of Greek democracy (and by extension all democracy) by declaring that his view led him to "violate most deeply . . . the free and limitless personality" (Hegel, 1953, Preface). Such a free personality is considered to be the basic direction and aim of social action. That this idea of the free personality is at variance with the ideal of the historical state should not prevent an acknowledgment that Hegel was concerned with how to gain concrete emancipation and to stipulate the conditions in society that would make this possible.

The *Philosophy of Right and Law* is divided into three parts. The first two deal with the nature of abstract right and morality, property and welfare "considered intrinsically." The third part, which has as its chief divisions the family, civil society and the state, is the core of the book. It traces the meaning of freedom in its "social forms."

Freedom is initially considered in its most cellular form as personal, undifferentiated caprice. Next, the individual is examined in terms of the forms governing his relationships to other individuals, possession, property, contracts and moral obligation. From this, Hegel develops the idea of freedom in terms of law and ethics. The ethical life makes possible socialization of the person in that it evaluates the notion of freedom to the forefront of self-consciousness.

> Ethical life is the idea of freedom in that on the one hand it is the good becomes alive, the good endowed in self-consciousness with knowing the willing and actualized by self-conscious action—while on the other hand self-consciousness has in the ethical realm its absolute foundation and the end which actuates its effort. Thus ethical life is the concept of freedom developed into the existing world and the nature of self-consciousness. (Hegel, 1953, par. 142)

Hegel desires to move beyond personal freedom to universal freedom. He proceeds, via the dissolution of the family and community associations, to a consideration of freedom in terms of civil society and the political state which represents the social realization to rise above private interests and mediate conflicting private claims in terms of a larger national purpose. The idea of the rule of law, rather than men, did not, of course, originate with Hegel; it is a fundamental juridical principle of Western societies. What Hegel did do was convert this juridical principle into an ethical absolute. Law was provided with a mystique. Ethics was thereby to be codified like law. The sameness of law and ethics is not just a peculiarity of Hegel, but of the language as well. The word *Recht,* the German equivalent to *jus* in Latin, *droit* in French, or *derecho* in Spanish, can be translated as either "right" or "law." Hegel himself declares that by *Recht* he means not only civil law, but also morality, ethics and, at times, world history—that is, in the sense of the dialectical pattern of human growth (Hegel, 1953, par. 33).

Throughout Hegel's *Philosophy of Right,* a deceptively commercial imagery is used to describe freedom. Individual freedom becomes the right to private ownership, use and exchange of property. Civil society has as its essential core "the protection of property by law" (Hegel, 1953, par. 188). Even the heralded state, which genetically displaces society, is said to have a middle-class basis. Indeed, "that this middle class be formed is a main interest of the State" (Hegel, 1953, par. 297). The structure of society is economy considered historically. This fact is central in understanding Hegel's social thought. He makes plain that whatever his reservations about the moneyed classes, he was never willing to adopt a nostalgic view of the German landed aristocracy. While Hegel mistrusted the *burgerliche Gesellschaft,* he preferred it to restorationist politics, or for that matter, feudal economic policies.[7]

The intention of Hegel is clear: to unite a fragmented Germany in awareness of need for action. By logical extension, other aspects of Hegel's world view become equally evident: that the touchstone for measuring human emancipation is history, and that social function, therefore, cannot be considered apart from historical design. Because of this double aspect, Lefebvre (1956, p. 59) wrote: *"Pour poser correctement notre problème, des rapports entre necéssité et liberté, remontons à Hegel."* Hegel presents a "positive" concept of freedom in relation to law and social order that stands apart from and yet embraces a pronounced conservation. The *Philosophy of Right* is an attempt to evaluate critically all past estimates of the nature of the free society and the free conscience; but it is also an effort to settle the issue for all future ages.

The most challenging social question taken up in the *Philosophy of Right* is the relation of egoism to sociality. Hegel rejects the utilitarian theory that decisions are best resolved by the pleasure–pain principle. The challenge is made in terms of the French Revolution. Before he had formulated the polarity of egoism and altruism, Hegel was convinced that the Revolution was a vision of an age of true justice. However, it was no less a desire for freedom that moved men everywhere to become critics of existing establishments. For Hegel, the French Revolution, like the Protestant Reformation, was a world revolution, and not simply a national up-

---

[7] With obvious approval, Hegel (1934, p. 18) took note of the fact that the system of representative government was common to all of the newer European states, irrespective of outward forms of monarchism or republicanism. The Hegelian distinction between family society or community, and civil society or society as a whole, had a particularly profound effect on the development of historical sociology in Germany (Tönnies, 1940).

heaval. Its specific content ended in death and despair, while its radical aims nurtured a generation of rebellion. But the ultimate betrayal of the purposes of the Revolution, by one class after another, one political faction after another, caused him to evaluate the liabilities in those Enlightenment tenets that were converted into slogans of the Revolution (Hegel, 1953, par. 273f.; 1956, chap. 3).

Starting from the premise that the individual makes his future only in ways calculated to expand personal happiness, utilitarianism is a negation of freedom because it can envision no purpose to life beyond individual pleasure. As a doctrine about society, the principle of utility reduces itself to the assertion that rulers should act with Olympian detachment to offset the follies of selfish ambition. To Hegel, this confusion between the "ought to be" and the "is" of politics was made because the Revolution, following Rousseau, saw in the state a General Will, popular consensus, and not what it actually is, the historical unfolding of Rational Will (Hegel, 1930).[8] This resulted in an irrational insistence that the state reflects a system of stratification—for example, Montesquieu's system of checks and balances. The utilitarian notion that laissez faire should be the leading political principle because it is economically viable represented the first step in the demise of the Revolution. For Hegel, it demonstrated that French social theory could not distinguish politics from economy (Hegel, 1930, par. 272).

In its utilitarian usage, freedom is only the egoistic right of the person over and against the collective will of humanity. Real freedom, freedom as rational, negates egoism because its point of departure is the spirit of the avant garde (the state) and not the general spirit of the people (the society). The vogue of hedonism represents, to Hegel's way of thinking, not the achievement of freedom, but the alienation of man from freedom. This is a necessary outcome of a perspective that regards the products of history as both subjective and capricious, responsible more to an irrational general will than to law. Here we have the first indication that Hegel is dissatisfied with a pure theory of society; and that instead he will seek to create a "synthetic" political sociology.

FROM THE GENERAL WILL TO THE WILL OF THE STATE

The French Revolution, and particularly its intellectual forerunner, Rousseau, are primary targets of Hegel's efforts to frame a political sociology, precisely because the Revolution and Rousseau announced the birth of reason in society. The opposition to Rousseau is expressed first in his condemnation of rule by men rather than rule of law, second in his

---

[8] Some of Hegel's most succinct comments on French social theory were not included in the main body of the *Philosophy of Right*, but were rather appended later. They appear in the literature as *Hegel's eigenhandige Randemerkungen zu seiner Rechtsphilosophie* (1930).

criticisms of the principle of social equality, and third, in his opposition to establishing the popular will as a basis for political life. Beneath Hegel's disenchantment with the course of the French revolution was his larger theoretical concern over the relationship of social contract to natural right. In Rousseau, Hegel saw the essential forerunner of his own view of freedom and its relation to political authority. In the betrayal of the revolutionary impulse, he saw a need to reassert reason in the state in order to replace reason in society. Hegel's extended polemic is worth quoting to appreciate the character and extent of his revolt against political nominalism.

> If the state is confused with civil society, and if its specific end is laid down as the security and protection of property and personal freedom, then the interest of the individuals as such becomes the ultimate end of their association, and it follows that membership of the state is something optional. But the state's relation to the individual is quite different from this. Since the state is mind objectified, it is only as one of its members that the individual himself has objectivity, genuine individuality, and an ethical life. Unfortunately, however, as Fichte did later, Rousseau takes the will only in a determinate form as the individual will, and he regards the universal will not as the absolutely rational element in the will, but only as a "general" will which proceeds out of this individual will as out of a conscious will. The result is that he reduces the union of individuals in the state to a contract and therefore to something based on their arbitrary wills, their opinion, and their capriciously given consent. . . ." (Hegel, 1930, par. 258a)

What Hegel meant by sociality is not easy to discern. First, it involves integration with other individuals in family, clan and group relations, and second, the processes of civil society. Third, at a more developed state of universal history, sociality entails the rationalization of ideals through the state. In terms of problems of the state, Hegel becomes most demanding. We cannot will our connection to the state any more than we can will our alienation from it in periods of decay. Rousseau's advice to simulate the moral qualities of primitive man, if not the social conditions of antiquity (prehistory), is to Hegel tantamount to the illusion that man can escape his historical commitments. Hegel's organicism rejected the possibility of a complete dissolution of ties and relations between men and nations. When this takes place, you are no longer dealing with social forces as such, but with random persons. The freedom of the social contract is, therefore, an illusion of those who cannot rise above civil society. To Hegel, the social contract is vicarious freedom ending "in the maximum of frightfulness and terror" (Hegel, 1930, par. 258a).

The alienation of the *honnête homme* from rotting feudal society made of Rousseau a critic. But his voluntarism gave to his thinking a nostalgic glow and an irrational substance, which cast doubt on the possibilities of ever reaching the good society. Hegel, starting from a strictly formalistic desire to place man in a total system of historical infallibilism, frowning upon the waste and horror of revolution, nonetheless (if inadvertently) became a crucial link in modern theories of social revolution. He paid strict attention to the real sources of historical generation: the economically sanctioned civil society and the politically sanctioned state. Once the Hegelian social system was complete, with its hierarchical chain moving and grinding its way from the individual to the state, it was but a step away to frame a historical hypothesis that moved from nationalism to international-ism and from the middle-class state to the classless society, or antistate. And this bold step Marx took.

The connection of law to freedom is twofold for Hegel. In one capac-ity, law has as its actual content the processes that form the evolution of society independent of human will. In this way, freedom is related to neces-sity in that it presupposes an elemental conformity with objective, historical ideals. But the relation of laws to freedom in civil society seemingly has for its chief content the customs, rules and traditions through which freedom becomes linked to coercion rather than to nature's way. If the spirit of law embodies the spirit of freedom, and if freedom cannot exist without duties and obligations in the juridical sense, we are once more left with the polari-zation of individual autonomy and political responsibility.

In one sense, the existing law of the state becomes the archetype for the conduct of individual wills. The theory of freedom thus becomes an elaborate scheme for maintaining the status quo, of keeping political power in the possession of those in a position to maintain and interpret the mean-ing of law. Reason becomes nothing but the reality embodied in the state structure; freedom, the knowledge that the state is the foundation of con-sciousness and self-consciousness (*bewusstsein und Selbst-bewusstsein*). These were indeed the conclusions of the *Philosophy of Right* emphasized by the neo-Hegelians Kilthey, Glockner and Trietschke in their quest to prove the ideal origins of the political state (Lukács, 1953; Marcuse, 1941).

A different meaning emerges from a more balanced appraisal of Hegel's analysis of freedom and the legal superstructure. If there is, *in fact,* a correspondence between a social system and a moral–legal order, then to move contrary to the spirit or content of law is to move against freedom itself; for it would destroy that unity of the people under the state upon which law is based (Hegel, 1953, par. 153). There is strong evidence that Hegel himself preferred to place a liberal construction on legal matters, as in the case of his analysis of civil rights for religious groups (Hegel, 1953, par. 270a). Hegel assumes a condition of society under law that would overcome the alienation that stems from a world without justice, a universe of collective authority. Under the impulse of creating an ethical social order, men can achieve a form of freedom having greater durability than the spurious demand for the direct abolition of social order. It is this aspect of Hegel's theory of law that accounts for post-Hegelian efforts to locate more precisely the connection of law and social emancipation.

Hegelianism was sundered at just this point: If the emphasis was put on law and social institutions, a conservative result was guaranteed; if the emphasis was placed on the changing contents of law and society and the steady need for human emancipation, then a radical result was assured.

Ethics, in the same way as law, is for Hegel the essential content of freedom. In this he is perhaps closer to the Judaic than to the Greek tradition, since there is no functional difference in his thought between law and morality. Implicit in Hegel's position is the proposition that the good is defined by the free conscience, whether such a conscience resides in the self, the state or the universe. Since the ethical world of concrete social life is the idea of freedom, morality no less than logic has for its objective content the doctrine of necessity (Hegel, 1953, par. 142). If we accept the premise that moral obligation is the human response to objective necessity, the absence of responsibility (even in the juridical sense) implies the absence of moral choice. The presence of necessity in human events limits our options to what is possible, but it does not destroy options as such. If every act is a free act, there can be no question of sorting right from wrong. The right becomes amoral, something settled by arbitrary coercive power. Hegel was thus led to reject Hobbes' power thesis because it rested on the same sort of psychological hedonism that disregards the norms and values of society and the state. The right to make decisions is the characteristic of an ethical man—that is, a free man. This right, operating within a vortex of historical necessity, is considered by Hegel as a hallmark of the free man vis à vis the slave. Nietzsche, to challenge this system of ethics, was compelled to challenge the entire history of rationalist philosophy (Nietzsche, 1957).

As in the theory of law, much depends on whether we define the Hegelian ethical system to mean that freedom exists because an objective telos directs man to his goals (almost in the Calvinist sense of predestiny), or whether freedom is an expanding category the contents of which change in direct proportion to human evolution. To satisfy the demands of his system, Hegel concludes with an absolutist prescription: freedom as consciousness of moral–legal obligations. To satisfy his sense of social process, he employs a historical ethos: freedom as consciousness of rational and real possibilities.

Hegel endowed freedom with a metaphysical content because he desired to carry his historicism to its ultimate conclusion: the identification of historical evolution and moral purpose. Because of this, freedom, however ingeniously interpreted as a stage of socially based self-consciousness, was unable to get beyond a metaphysical parallelism. Within this system are to be found the root premises of political realism and political idealism. The ethical can have a content only in relation to human action. But action is itself dissolved into spirit, the idea, universal history. Whether man defines his ethical system, or is defined by it, is something Hegel does not resolve, since he would then also have had to declare that history is not the only framework within which to consider the problem of freedom.

In terms of personal morality, freedom remains an insecure abstraction. Freedom requires a "concrete ground" that is, the union of the individual and the universal. Hegel's concrete ground was the state. While law and morality offer freedom within an objective frame of reference, and in this fashion overcome the capricious freedom which is "the will free only in itself," such objectivity remains formalistic and indeterminate (Hegel, 1953, pars. 29, 30). The social locus of human activity is represented by the growth of the state, the true representative of the collective will. Hegel grants the reality of personal, inner freedom, Luther's freedom of the soul. But freedom to be organic must be objectified, the impersonal responsibility of a nonsectarian institution. Without such an impersonal force, freedom would be reduced to a psychologically naïve peace of soul, or an equally unheroic pecuniary freedom of the economic marketplace. What is needed is a cancellation of such egoism, its transformation into a set of higher truths. Hegel's emphasis on these higher truths of the reasoning mind clearly demarcates him from a shallow romanticism, from efforts to subsume reality with a feeling of *Geist*.

The identification Hegel makes between personal will and the will of the state was considered a necessary curative to the flaws in civil society. Civil society represents the superficial world of money relations, the area in which the individual strives for the private accumulation of wealth. Civil society represents the core of degradation, the "spectacle of excess, misery, and physical and social corruption" (Hegel, 1953, par. 185). In civil society, the full horrors of the exchange market are unfolded, the basis of which is the accumulation of private wealth proceeding through the impoverishment of the laboring classes (Hegel, 1953, par. 243, 244).

Civil society embodies values contrary to those of the state; its own inadequacies generate the Leviathan. Civil society, which is clearly identified with the German bourgeoisie, has as its main human denominator the entrepreneurial personality. The state has for its proper concern those universal laws and principles guiding all citizens. The latter is therefore freedom as such (Hegel, 1953, par. 258). The state therefore replaces either the atomized individual or bourgeois civil society as the chief organizing force of men; polity replaces society as the form for realizing freedom (Hegel, 1953, par. 260).

To support this position, Hegel presents a damaging empirical characterization of the bourgeoisie as an economic and social force. At the same time, he also offers an idealization of the landed nobility and court aristocracy in charge of the state machinery. In this way, Hegel mirrors the cleavage in German life at the start of the nineteenth century between commercial and inherited aristocratic interests. In his work, one gets a keen sense of how threatened the Prussian emperor must have felt by the machinations of the bourgeoisie, its pressuring for a greater share of political power as compensation for its "economic burden." Hegel participated in the Prussian celebration by convincing himself that the political state could somehow stand apart from and above the socioeconomic cleavages in its historic role as the carrier of freedom. Like equilibrium and consensus doctrines of the present era, Hegel was more interested in the immediate conditions for maintaining political stability than in the long-range linkages between the state and the dominant economic sectors.

Hegel represented the idea of freedom as organically related to the political state, and to the inevitable unfolding of a *Weltgeschlichte* which makes certain the attainment of absolute truth. In his analysis of civil society, Hegel adopts the arguments of English classical political economy to ensure the state a metaphysical position at the expense of the divisive influences of commercial bourgeois interests. This was a return to freedom in its abstract form; a retreat from a scientific concept of social structure to ideological deliberations on how best to preserve conservative political values. History became historicism, a tool for proving this or that emperor to be the bearer of the historical essence. History ceased to serve as a majestic framework for locating outstanding problems of man, and served instead to enshrine the state as the vehicle for realizing equilibrium.

However emphatically Hegel turned the concept of freedom to the sacred interests of the state, there remains the kernel of "self-consciousness" and "self-creation" which enabled him to consider freedom as residing in the social process. Man in his continuing self-creation, the steady growth of civilization through consciousness, provides a firm basis for total emancipation. Only formal freedom reduces everything to the General Will. The General Will reveals itself as an assortment of conflicting individual wills, each insisting on holding itself up as the model for all men. If this process continues indefinitely, tyranny prevails. Inevitably, a shallow liberalism allows for the Will of the One to displace the General Will. Such a tyranny would offer the shadow of freedom in place of a substantive freedom—for example, the right of judgment and criticism (Hegel, 1956).

POLITICS AS A COSMIC VOCATION

A great deal of attention has been given to the way Hegel subsumed society into universal history, and in so doing, drowned the individual in a cosmic vocation. Hegel realized, nonetheless, that there remains an impulse toward individuality. In his directly political essays, written two decades before the *Philosophy of Right,* Hegel attempted to retrieve for the area of social personality the "smaller" liberties of dissent, difference and even disaffection from the general commonweal. Hegel was critical of efforts to curb individual liberties needlessly because this entailed the risk of destroying freedom in general. Reason and knowledge mediate freedom. The rational constitution does not seek to impose the abstract will on every member of society at every level of social intercourse for the obvious reason that such unanimity of opinion is impossible, and for the less obvious reason that personal liberty is the precondition for the formation of general emancipation. It is not that Hegel conceived of personal freedom in contradistinction to necessity, but that true freedom must always allow a measure of freedom *from* authority—that is, liberty.

In Hegel's early view, liberty is denied in two ways: The hedonist negates it, making it a matter of caprice and private will, thereby depriving it of a meaningful historical setting; while the abstract rationalist negates liberty by ruling out the variables in human-formed ideals and standards, and placing a premium on abstract duties and obligations. Hegel offered his theory of negative freedom (liberty) to overcome especially the one-sided conclusions of Kant, Rousseau and Fichte. Positive freedom corresponded to Hegel's theory of history and philosophy as scientific disciplines, while negative freedom corresponded to the practical judgments men must daily make about economics and politics.

The transition from *Selbstbewusstsein* to the *Staat* as the perfect embodiment of consciousness in Hegelian terms is the transformation from freedom as contemplative to freedom as active. In the realm of praxis, if a people desire negative freedom alone, freedom from institutional responsibility, they can never achieve moral or political heights. The built-in egoism of the *burgerliche Gesellschaft* would cut the ground out from under freedom, reducing society to freedom *of* rather than *from* market competition. This was the condition of German society at the start of the nineteenth century. As Hegel says: "The obstinacy of the German character has not yielded to the point where the separate parts would sacrifice their particular interests for the whole society, where all would be united in one general body and where freedom might be achieved in common with free subjection to the supreme political authority" (Hegel, 1934, pp. 11–12). Germany, trapped by the small middle-class faith in political particularism (*Kleinstaaterei*) achieved freedom only in the realm of abstraction rather than in history. This charge became a battlecry for the remainder of the century, socialism declaring that this victory in the realm of ideas prevented the growth of democracy, and restorationism declaring that this same condition made Germany effete and lacking in national purpose. Hegel himself saw the problem in stricter terms of universal freedom: Germany should have been the freest of nations. Hegel did not believe that "self-centered activity" makes rational political authority impossible, that society must be at the mercy of brute physical power.

Once positive freedom is anchored to the state, negative freedom, "the self-centered activity," should be allowed to develop unimpeded. The function of liberty is to heighten the prospects of knowledge. This being so, the suppression of liberty carries with it the threat of positive freedom, itself being corroded and its historic mission derailed. Hegel insisted upon the free activity of the citizens "in the field of administration and adjudication." Autonomy within a larger national policy is a guarantor of social organization. Hegel was a constitutional monarchist and not just a crude advocate of the discredited divine rights doctrine. And this bias in favor of legality was a constant in his writings. Although he could present no solution other than a conservative solution, he never retreated to the specious comforts of feudality. We owe to Hegel the complete separation of the conservative conscience from the feudal mind. "Society should leave to the people their maintenance according to law, and each class, city, village, community, etc., the freedom of doing and executing what lies within its sphere" (Hegel, 1934, pp. 24–25).

The young Hegel emerged as an unequivocal inheritor of the *Aufklärung.* "Nothing should be more sacred (to government) than to leave to the free action of the citizens all these matters and to protect it without regard to utility. For this freedom is sacred in itself." Hegel goes on to explain the virtues of individual liberty. "We consider that people happy to which the State leaves much freedom in the subordinated, general activities, and that political authority infinitely strong which will be supported by the free and untrammeled spirit of its people" (Hegel, 1934, p. 25). Hegel's theory of freedom and liberty amounts to a safety-valve principle of government, since unlimited expression of criticism, far from weakening the state, gives it its unlimited strength. Hegel did not show the way in which the negative and positive poles of freedom can be joined without lapsing into the authoritarianism of the God-State. What prevents the leader of state from placing a cap on the valve of criticism when he so pleases? The sectioning off of residual political power into the hands of various elites made it difficult for any "subordinate" activities to be registered. But the problem of the dysfunction of reason was not considered by Hegel, any more than it was by Rousseau.

With the passage of years, Hegel was unable to resist the blandishments of linking his theory of freedom to the authoritarian state. He indicates that negative freedom is "periled" by its inherent tendency to excess. In this way, Hegel blames the existence of economic inequality and political repression, not on the messianic state, but on the "excesses" of the popular elements. The *vox populi,* expressing itself through dirty monetary advantage and revolutionary unrest, makes necessary a powerful state (Hegel, 1934, pp. 39–40). His position reflected a political situation in which Germany was divided in fact between a political power ruled by Junkers and landed nobility, and an economic power rooted in urban commerce and industry. In this context, the state did indeed "mediate" the claims of each. But with the subsequent expansion of the business classes, and their amalgam with the major "old families," the facade of state neutrality was quickly dispelled. History became synonymous with the manifest destiny of the mythic German Empire, and the state became the vehicle through which history would be realized and through which criticism would be distilled.

The leitmotif in Hegel's social thought is the distinction between anarchy and freedom. The movement from society to polity is an obvious effort to get from one to the other. But no such distinction is made between liberty and the state beyond a rather tepid reminder (in the twilight of his career) that "people must participate in legislation and in the most important affairs of state." In the fluid conditions of German life, an effective statement would have at least implied, not simply participation, but opposition to the nation-state. This transition from the freedom to participate in the Prussian celebration to opposition to any of its pronouncements was one Hegel could not make once he had staked out the territory of society as the struggle between anarchy and authority. By the close of his career, when he was more concerned with wrapping up his system than in opening up new issues, Hegel fell victim to his own admonition: "When philosophy paints its grey in grey, then has the shape of life grown old." Thus it is that the close of his *Philosophy of Right and Law* is neither summation nor conclusion, but an introduction to the Introduction of the *Philosophy of History* (Hegel, 1953, pars. 341–360).

Neither political science nor political economy can contain the Hegelian "world mind." History alone is the anchor point and proving grounds of freedom. Social life is a "mundane interest," and the "absolute mind," discontent with the mundane, "prepares and works out its transition to its next higher stage" (Hegel, 1953, par. 344). While one is left with the disquieting knowledge that the "absolute mind" is nothing more than Hegel's own mind, there is nonetheless a nobility of spirit motivating his decision to locate the springs of freedom in historical process rather than in philosophical speculation.

Freedom is essentially a changing phenomenon. The more mankind develops spiritually, that is, in the sense of the world mind, the more it becomes aware of its generic self and genetic unfolding. The historical growth of consciousness is thus itself the source of freedom. "World history is the progress of the consciousness of freedom." The role of the *philosophy of history* is to explore the progress of the idea of freedom, while the function of the *history of philosophy* is the "actualization of freedom." World history in Hegel's sense is the progress of freedom because it is the process of the self-realization of the spiritual content of social existence. And conversely, "freedom is itself its own object of attainment and the sole purpose of spirit. It is the ultimate end toward which all world history has continually aimed" (Hegel, 1956, Introduction). At this point, Hegel's kinship with Platonism is most clearly revealed, since just as spirit and freedom are linked, so, too, slavery and dead matter are fused.

Every slackening of spirit involves a retreat to material inertia. Only through history are gaps in the fortress of freedom overcome, nowhere else. Once freedom becomes manifest in spirit, it becomes practical, something taken up by the *Volksgeist*. Freedom can thus be viewed as the propelling force of hitherto existing societies. When freedom is fully realized through the identification of consciousness and history, society in its profane ceases to exist. What we are left with is a sacral collectivity of human spirit. Before the tide of freedom everything gives way. In his early years, Hegel interpreted this in a radical fashion. Those institutions and constitutions that did not correspond to the *Volksgeist* were doomed because they provided an unreal, irrational bond. "The owl of Minerva spreads its wings only with the falling of the dusk" (Hegel, 1953, Introduction). Here Hegel cautions against a predeterminist view of social existence. The task of displacing the old involves the ability "to rise above one's little interest." Egoism conflicts with social change. "Too often a reservation is hidden behind the eager concern for the general welfare as long as it coincides with our own interest. Such eagerness to consent to proposed reforms gets discarded as soon as a demand is made upon it" (Hegel, 1934, pp. 9–10).

Contrary to the common view, Hegel did not consider either social or political freedom as abstractly inevitable. Freedom is real, but conditional in its forms. It is thus an active process rather than a passive series of events. In this way, Hegel provided his sociological followers from Marx to Mannheim with a methodological basis for posing the conditions of man's material freedom, just as Hegel himself had traced the evolution of the idea of freedom as spirit.

To the degree he was concerned with human emancipation, Hegel tried to hold with one rein chariots moving in opposite directions. He hedged on an expansive view of freedom by first identifying freedom with the established political order, and then assuming that such an order is spiritually sanctioned by the gods of reason. In this system, spontaneous social change becomes "the spirit of negation, *i.e.*, the negation of freedom" (Hegel, 1953, par. 151).[9] But Hegel, the devoted servant of the concrete, introduced a more sociological concept of freedom than had previously been known in the history of ideas. He filled the issue of freedom with historical detail, while at the same time showing that the context of freedom is social and human and hence realizable. In so doing, he revolutionized the study of freedom by going beyond the psychological frame of reference which had bottled up political theory from Hobbes to Rousseau.

What Hegel sought had nothing in common with political quietism. He felt that the proper end of men, freedom, can be achieved because it is rooted in both the human personality and in the historical *Geist*. If the further growth of mankind is our self-declared purpose, freedom is not simply what is desirable but what is necessary. Indeed, Hegel's theory of freedom in its panpsychic immensity easily allows for a chiliastic interpreta-

---

[9] It should be recorded that Hegel's opposition to civil conflict and political revolution held only when there exists an organic connection between a conquered people and its prince, or more simply between a ruler and the ruled. Where no such connection obtains, rebellion and revolution may be warranted. Hegel (1953, par. 281, addendum 172) also noted the distinction between external aggression and internal order: "A rebellion in a conquered province in war is a different thing from a rising in a well-organized state. In such a case, there is only a contract, no political tie, *'Je ne suis pas votre prince, je suis votre maître'* Napoleon retorted to the envoys at Erfurt."

tion. He himself forestalled such a view by limiting its practical application to the growth of Germany from absolutism to constitutionalism. But the uses of Hegel's social theories outweigh these pragmatic abuses. It was Hegel who finally separated the issue of political freedom from personal liberty: the moral absolutists on one side and the amoral atomists on the other. In so doing, Hegel, no less than John Stuart Mill, set the terms of discourse for the nineteenth-century struggle between liberal and conservative ideologies.

REFERENCES

Aron, R. (1957) *German Sociology.* New York: Free Press.

Bosanquet, B. (1917) *Social and International Ideals: Being Studies in Patriotism.* London: Macmillan.

Cornu, A. (1957) *The Origins of Marxian Thought.* Springfield, Ill.: C. C Thomas.

Engels, F. (1934) *Ludwig Feuerbach and the Outcome of Classical German Philosophy.* New York: International Publishers [written in 1845].

Feuerbach, L. (1903–11) "Gedanken uber Tod und Ensterblichkeit," in *Sammtliche Werke,* ed. by W. Bolin and F. Jodl, vol. 3. Stuttgart: Bad Cannstatt Fromann Verlag.

Findlay, J. N. (1958) *Hegel: A Re-examination.* London: Allen and Unwin.

Hegel, G. W. F. (1929) *The Science of Logic,* vol. 2, trans. W. H. Johnston and L. G. Struthers. London: Allen and Unwin.

Hegel, G. W. F. (1930) *Hegel's eigenhandige Randemerkingen zu seiner Rechtsphilosophie,* ed. G. Lasson. Leipzig: F. Meiner.

Hegel, G. W. F. (1931) *Phenomenology of Mind,* trans. J. B. Baillie. London: Allen and Unwin; New York: Macmillan.

Hegel, G. W. F. (1934) "Die Verfassung Deutschlands," in *Hegel heute; Eine Auswahl aus Hegel's politischer Gedankenwelt.* Leipzig: F. Meiner.

Hegel, G. W. F. (1953) *Philosophy of Right and Law,* trans. T. M. Knox. Oxford: Oxford at the Clarendon Press.

Hegel, G. W. F. (1955) *Lectures on the History of Philosophy,* trans. E. S. Haldane, vol. 1. London: Routledge & Kegan Paul.

Hegel, G. W. F. (1956) *Philosophy of History,* trans. J. Sibree. New York: Dover.

Hook, S. (1936) *From Hegel to Marx: Studies in the Intellectual Development of Karl Marx.* New York: Reynal & Hitchcock.

Horowitz, I. L. (1961) *Philosophy, Science and the Sociology of Knowledge.* Springfield, Ill.: C. C Thomas.

Husserl, E. (1954) *La philosophie comme science rigoureuse,* trans. Quentin Lauer. Paris: Presses Universitaires de France.

Kierkegaard, S. (1944) *Concluding Unscientific Postscript,* trans. D. F. Swenson and W. Lorie. Princeton N. J.: Princeton University Press.

Kojève, A. (1947) *Lecons sur la Phénoménologie de l'esprit, professées de 1933 à 1939 à l'école des hautes-études réunies.* Paris: Gallimard.

Krieger, L. (1951) *The German Idea of Freedom: History of a Political Tradition.* Boston: Beacon Press.

Lefebvre, H. (1956) "Lois objectives et forces sociales," *La Nouvelle Critique* (May), pp. 59–73.

Löwith, K. (1941) *Von Hegel zu Nietzsche.* New York and Stuttgart: W. Kohlhammer.

Löwith, K. (1949) *Meaning in History.* Chicago: University of Chicago Press.

Lukács, G. (1953) *Die Zerstörung der Vernunft.* Berlin: Aufban-Verlag.

Marcuse, H. (1941) *Reason and Revolution: Hegel and the Rise of Social Theory.* New York: Oxford University Press.

Marx, K. (1956) *The Holy Family; or Critique of Critical Critique* [written in 1845], in K. Marx and F. Engels, *Gesamtausgabe,* abt. 1, band 3, Berlin: Bietz Verlag.

Marx, K. (1959) *Economic and Philosophic Manuscripts of 1844,* trans. M. Milligan. Moscow: Foreign Languages Publishing House.

Nietzsche, F. (1957) *The Use and Abuse of History,* trans. A. Collins. New York: Liberal Arts Press.

Popper, K. (1945) *The Open Society and Its Enemies.* London: Routledge & Kegan Paul.

Royce, J. (1908) *The Philosophy of Loyalty.* New York: Macmillan.

Speier, H. (1952) "From Hegel to Marx: The Left Hegelians, Feuerbach and 'True Socialism'," in H. Speier, ed., *Social Order and the Risk of War.* New York: Stewart.

Tönnies, F. (1940) *Fundamental Concepts of Sociology,* trans. C. P. Loomis. New York: American Book.

CHAPTER 5

IDEOLOGICAL
AND HISTORICAL
SOURCES OF
CONTEMPORARY
TOTAL POLITICS

The rise of political sociology has been announced from two sources, each an unlikely candidate for such pronunciamentos: first, the survey researchers who have come to employ electoral and opinion data as the basis for determining the beliefs of men, but more, the validity of such mass measures for the decisions political leaders must make about society as a whole; and second, the grand European theorists who have announced a century of total politics—that is to say, the growing belief that classical capitalism may have been an aberration, that in fact the political structure is the base of society, while the economic system is part of the superstructure. The theorists have given at least as much impetus to the study of political sociology as have the survey researchers. We shall focus on three such monumental figures and frameworks in this chapter.

DEMOCRACY, TOTALITARIANISM
AND MESSIANISM

The brilliant critique of Enlightenment notions of political democracy offered by Jacob Talmon (1960) in *The Origins of Totalitarian Democracy* is a healthy antidote to the optative mood set in the thirties by Harold Laski. But Talmon represents the dangers as well as the realities of the present revulsion for utopian dreams corrupted by antiquarian leaders. However, before the critique comes the explication of Talmon's framework. His basic formula is that political messianism is a continuation of totalitarian democracy. A more generic purpose is to establish a continuity over centuries on the framework of the concept of democracy. Toward that end, he singles out five points that link nineteenth-century political messianism and eighteenth-century totalitarian democracy.

The first point is that for both the eighteenth and nineteenth centuries, reason was the necessary replacement for tradition. The world of democracy was a world of reason per se, and the world of tradition was held to be the world of unreason. Insofar as the nineteenth century presented a notion of democracy at all, it pushed forward an idea of universal reason embodied in the revolutionaries of the eighteenth century.

The second point Talmon makes, an important one, is that the consciousness of revolution dominated intellectual thought in both eighteenth- and nineteenth-century versions of democracy. A similar feeling pervaded the French Enlightenment and the later German romanticism of Kant and Hegel: The notion of consciousness of revolution fed the revolution of consciousness. The idea of romanticism itself was in this sense an extension of the idea of conscious behavior or revolutionary behavior. A religion of revolution was contained within the French Revolution, the industrial revolution and the Protestant Reformation; it was this religion that provided continuities between them.

The third point that Talmon adduces is rather subtle in shading. It rests on a recognition that the individualism of eighteenth-century rationalists and the collectivism of nineteenth-century romantics really were not far apart. They both shared what he calls a perfectionist attitude toward man: Man is capable of growing; he is capable of getting better. Ultimately, this was an insistence on getting better as mandated by an intellectual elite.

This idea feeds into yet a fourth point, namely, that the democrats of both centuries had in common a notion of man's essential greatness. The perfectability of man was itself ultimately translated into a concept of goodness. This idea already meant something radically different from the religion of early Christianity, which in some sense predetermined a negative outcome from the Fall—the inevitable failure of humans to achieve all that they hoped for on earth. The secularization of morals meant the rise of an optative mood in all decisions about the political ambitions of men.

Finally, what both centuries had in common—the fifth point—was a metahistoricism rather than a faith in history. The worlds of Condorcet and Hegel were very much the same worlds in their attitudes toward the rational potential of man. Both eighteenth- and nineteenth-century democrats really believed in preordained outcomes to history, much more than in the vagaries of empirical history. Given these five points, Talmon deals with political messianism as a continuation of the eighteenth-century French concept of totalitarian democracy.

Talmon's points are profoundly and properly made. But there are discontinuities that, in my opinion, separate the nineteenth century from the eighteenth century in terms of the problem of political democracy; and on balance these discontinuities conceptually outweigh the continuities. Talmon alludes to these discontinuities throughout his work. Theoretically, he does not come to terms with them, but practically, as a historian, he cannot avoid them. Even when he attempts to express himself in terms of continuities, he actually makes allusion to numerous discontinuities.

A most important point of difference, ideologically at least, is that the eighteenth century was French and the nineteenth century, German. It is impossible to avoid the fact that the locus of intellectual activity shifted. The eighteenth century had Voltaire, Rousseau, Condorcet, Diderot and Montesquieu. The early nineteenth century could boast no such French intellectuals of equal stature. It belonged to the Germans—Kant, Schilling, Marx, Feuerbach. Social thought shifted to Germany for many reasons, not the least of which was that Germany itself became a major political power during the nineteenth century—the outcome of the Prussian wars, the settlement of water disputes with Russia, the collapse of Napoleon and industrial development. Whatever the causal reasons for the nineteenth century's belonging to Germany, it was a fact. Therefore, the national characteristics of the writing have to be taken into account. The national characteristics of people have serious political consequences. Acting and thinking are very different; the expressions and modalities of ideas are different in each nation. The essential differences, as it was announced by Lessing even before the end of the eighteenth century, was not over the question of Enlightenment, but over the question of history: Historicity dominated German thinking, from Lessing to Marx; empiricism characterized French thought in a way that blunted revolutionary feelings from emerging. The preordainment of historical outcomes is supposedly much more important and verifiable than the outcomes of the capriciousness of leaders such as Louis XIV. Only in Condorcet was there historicity, and in reality that was phenomenology. The closest the French came to history was in the geological debates over theology and in the chronicles of Voltaire, which were more in the nature of exposé than exposition.

The eighteenth century witnessed an argument between the individual and the personality. At its highest and most sophisticated levels, this involved the relationship between the person and the state, either from the point of view of the person or the point of view of the general will of society. But the focus of all theory and discussion, the nature of democracy, was on the man, on the person, on the individual. What the nineteenth-century notion emphasized was class struggle, race, warfare and group conflict. In other words, political democracy was no longer an interactionistic scheme of man's place in the secular realm, but the reverse—a demonstration of impersonal cosmic forces that prevail over man, of which man is an organic part. The basic analogy was organicism rather than atomism. The organ was the person, but the organism was the state or the society. The language of German romanticism reflected a profound change in the structure of politics, and it was no longer the same kind of discussion. Therefore, it is extremely hard to accept Talmon's notion that political messianism, given its legitimacies, is really the same as totalitarian democracy.

The eighteenth century was one in which the intellectual was integrated, where his activities were involved with the production of either spiritual or material things leading to the change of society. The Enlightenment witnessed the prototype of the expert. Diderot (1965) genuinely felt that the production of the *Encyclopedie* would have a compelling effect on the legislative composition of France. It was the beginning of the notion of political jurisprudence. Enlightenment figures worked not only pragmatically but ideologically; they had the idea of changing their society. This was quite different from the nineteenth-century German idea of alienation which was the prevailing form of discourse among intellectuals. The man of ideas had to realize himself first as a man of ideas, and to realize himself, he became alienated—in other words, positive alienation. There was a complete revolt against the political science approach. They had no interest in what educators and legislators were going to do; they looked upon them as baboons. The notion of positive alienation as a source of inspiration, as a basis of intellect, was entirely different from the eighteenth-century notion of the integrated intellectual. When Montesquieu (1949) wrote *The Spirit of the Laws,* he believed very much that the system of laws he was working out would be carried through by the end of the century. It was written in a kind of pedestrian, involuted way to make it acceptable to lawyers. That was not the way Hegel wrote. In *Philosophy of Right* (1953), it is evident that Hegel had not the slightest idea of the implementation of the system. These are two books that can be readily compared because they are both concerned with the structure of society: the French with changing, the German with understanding, that structure.

The emphasis in the eighteenth century was on legislation and education, on the rulers and the ruled. The eighteenth century focused profoundly on the polity. It had a politicalized orientation. Therefore, the Robespierrian world seemed quite natural, very much an outgrowth of the Enlightenment. This is not quite true of the first half of the nineteenth century. There the emphasis was on property, on business, on commerce—it was not on changing the legislative characteristics of a society, but an attack on the economic base of that society. It was very different from that of the eighteenth-century *philosophes,* whose notion of economics was primitive and did not even rise up to that of the physiocrats. The notion of the economy became important for German romanticism only because the romantic movement saw class interests as somehow destructive of and discordant with national interests.

The difference between Enlightenment and romantic movements was well summarized on the cultural sphere, specifically in art and music. Classicism was a concern with the form and the elements of form—a lively interest with logic. Romanticism in its inherent nature was a concern with content. That is why Hegel and Marx wrote tendentiously about art—because they were romantics, not because they were monarchists or socialists. Romanticism directed its energies to the feeling and the content of an object. To Mozart, feeling was expressed best through the musical line. Bruckner's focus was on the musical tone. There was a different way of interpreting music—the single line, or the composition in its entirety. One cannot omit from a discussion on political messianism or its related subjects an appreciation of the cultural distinction between classicism and romanticism. What is meant by democracy itself is at stake. Hannah Arendt (1963) stated this in comparing democracy to the difference between compassion and passion. The classicists were compassionate. The romanticists, however, were passionate. There is a vast difference between a compassionate and a passionate view of other people and other destinies. To have compassion for a *person* is different from being passionate about a *cause*. What is at stake is more than the different attitudes and different feelings involved. At the root is a concept of the political life moving from partial explanation to total explanation, from partial resolutions to total solutions.

The distinction between psychologistic and interactionist frameworks is fundamental to how societies are examined. It is a choice between a stochastic and deterministic framework. Positivism is the study of society as a contrivance. The nineteenth century did not have that viewpoint; organicism did not permit it. For romanticists—for Hegel as well as Marx —man was a product of society. This was the alpha and omega of the change from self-help to social help. What could society do for the individual? To talk about society as such was not to talk about man, but to talk about systems; whereas in the eighteenth century, to talk about democracy was to talk about individuals. How to go about making a ruler become democratic was a real problem for a man like Voltaire. How could one go to the court and convince him that he should behave differently? The nineteenth century did not take a personalistic attitude toward emperors or dynasties. It already considered them obsolete and doomed by the dictates of history. In that sense, the French Revolution, which started with eighteenth-century premises, quickly passed over to nineteenth-century premises, once the Revolution actually became an accomplishment.

Consequently, the eighteenth century was an age of leaders, and a concept of individuals as elites was paramount. The nineteenth century was not a century of men; it was a century of forces, not of leaders, but of history. That is why political messianism is different from totalitarian democracy. The messianic element itself became a historical aspect of political life, and not merely a notion of elites or men. Politics became impersonal, a question of forces moving about. Marx labeled it "History operating behind the backs of men." The unmasking tradition thus replaced the empirical tradition in this transition from classicism to romanticism.

The eighteenth century was a century of exhortation which depended in large measure on the ethical variable, on the assumption of the purification of men, on the notion that class interests were not as important as personal values. The nineteenth century was a century not of values, but of interests. It was a century of fragmentation where personal values could not be promulgated. The basis of a rich man's wealth stemmed from his *not* breaking bread with a poor man. Not everyone could be convinced to change the structure of society. They were entirely different frameworks, the one of interests and the one of values. That conflict was one of the great divides of the two centuries. For it made the rehabilitation of societies and man subject to political necessity rather than good will. Redemption became historical; and the person to be redeemed had, in turn, to assume the requisites of history over and against any personal morality or utility.

What the two centuries reveal in terms of manifest political ideologies is a basic competition between libertarianism and egalitarianism. The eighteenth century was libertarian, and the notion of democracy was introduced as a form of being liberated *from* obligations. Conversely, the nineteenth century focused on the notion of the necessity *of* doing one's duty. There is a vast difference between these two perspectives. This emphasis on a theory of obligation extends from Hegel through Durkheim (1933). One cannot fail to see the austere, necessitarian qualities in *The Division of Labor in Society*. Democracy comes through order—this was asserted as a moral prerequisite for democracy. The eighteenth-century notion, however, was much more anarchical and represented a freedom from tyranny. For the Enlightenment, man was a social being; whereas for Romanticism, man was a statist being.

Talmon has considerable difficulty dealing with the eighteenth-century notion of universal brotherhood based on a libertarian principle. He lacks any significant theory of class, and, above all, has scant appreciation of how the rise of nationalism in the nineteenth century served to fragment the Enlightenment faith in universal brotherhood. Class consciousness was converted into nationalism—the brotherhood of men under the same flag. The politicalization of brotherhood even served to cement antagonistic classes. Patriotism is an extremely different concept from the notion of equality. The full force of this shift came one hundred years later with the complete disintegration of the socialist movement when confronted by all-out European warfare. When the showdown came, men behaved as Frenchmen and Germans, not as universal brothers or as members of the same social class suffering a common imperialist exploitation.

The nineteenth century perceived the universal revolution of the century to be a national bourgeois revolution. The rise of the bourgeoisie, of industrialism and urbanism, and hence of new iniquities, led more to a breakdown of faith in democracy than to any new forms of political messianism. Indeed, it was not until the twentieth century that the ideology of Enlightenment was spent, and romanticism turned irrational in its quests for political reconstruction.

The French Revolution of 1789 was a complete event. There was something *sui generis* about its form. It was perfect in what it destroyed and perfect in what it brought into being. It destroyed the "old order" in a permanent way. Future revolutions of the nineteenth century—1830, 1848, 1871—were all incomplete; they were widespread, but they did not conclude anything decisively. They did not make the role of the bourgeoisie paramount—they ended in compromise. The bourgeoisie recognized a new threat in the proletariat. Once their own revolution against the aristocratic classes had been completed, they turned to compromise, not consolidation. The great charge made by the nineteenth-century idealists was that the universal revolution of the eighteenth century was a chimera. It, too, was based on class interests. They reinterpreted past universalistic claims and saw them all as a facade. The bourgeoise state reinterpreted the universal claims in highly particularistic, interest-bound terms, thus putting an end to middle-class radicalism as a dominant force in political history. But the unquenchable nature of man's desire for perfection, even political perfection, is such that the search for total solutions persisted—long after the embers of the French Revolution and the German consolidation died away. If political perfection could not be achieved in reality, it could at least serve as a rallying cry in social practice; hence the move toward political totalism was preceded by a resurrection of political myth as a guide to such practice.

POLITICAL MYTHS AND
MYTHOLOGICAL POLITICS

According to Raymond Aron (1957), the people of the late nineteenth century transformed political realities into myths: the myth of the Left, the myth of the revolution and the myth of the proletariat. I would add two others: the myth of history and the cult of personality. But more important than these myths are the reasons why and the methods by which what once was seen as a reality came to be viewed as a myth. Perhaps as a prelude to that we ought to know what a political myth is. The one thing it is not is a series of shattering statements about Greek gods and their behavior. Quite the contrary. It is the profanation of polytheism; it is the secularization of faith. Beyond this, the political myth comes after the breakdown of faith as such. The emergence of the political myth represented a subtle recognition that the rationalist phase of the eighteenth century and the romantic phase of the early nineteenth century no longer obtained.

For the intelligentsia, the late nineteenth century represented a time of betrayal and a time of failure. The fact is that for other sectors, the late nineteenth century was a time of industrial success and the institutionalization of major political reforms; the paradox is that loss of faith on the part of the intelligentsia coincided with the attainment of the industrial takeoff point in Europe. Up to the middle of the nineteenth century, Europe wore its industrialism almost like a costume; there was something superficial about it. Even today one can feel the feudal pulse underneath the industrial base, for in Europe the feudal traditions are profound. However, by the late nineteenth century, Europe experienced not just industrialism, not just an increase in the rate of production, but the rise of mass consumption. The economy of Middle Europe was transformed from an agricultural to an urban base. In the labor movements of Italy, Germany and France, the concept of a working class working for itself became a power factor. The numbers in the labor movement increased dramatically during this period—all of the quantitative indicators of development were exhibited. One might have predicted a period of tremendous celebration. From the material indicators, one should assume that the intelligentsia would be enthralled by the achievement of the age. But they were not. And it is important for us to understand why they were not. In some measure, the very success of the industrial pattern was its ultimate failure. Affluence bred contempt among the intellectuals and contentment among the masses. The achievements of industrialism were poorly distributed; and the cultural biases of the intellectuals were repelled by the price in sensibility that was extracted by the industrial juggernaut of Europe.

What failed? One system that failed, obviously, was socialism, most dramatically in the Paris Commune. That provided the most significant demonstration to date of the international solidarity of the bourgeoisie, and the parochial divisions of the revolutionary factions. The Paris Commune was the crowning achievement of socialism in the late nineteenth century, and also its greatest failure. Elsewhere revolution, socialism and radicalism enjoyed even less success than in France. The prognostications for socialism and revolution collapsed under the weight of the success of the industrial system—the very success that had been predicted even by Marx and Engels, but could not be accepted precisely because bourgeois rationality tended to blunt any social revolutionary movement.

In the eighteenth century, the notion of revolution as a prelude to industrialism was the slogan and general expectation. But by the end of the nineteenth century, the call for revolution against the industrial system had begun. This nineteenth-century notion was quite sophisticated: the Revolution now was not to be done in the manner of the Luddites or Canutes. It was not to be an assault on production, on the bourgeoisie, on the managerial estate or on the holders of power. In effect, it was to be an assault on the successful, and that was the critical factor. The assault failed: The bourgeoisie did not crumble; the industrial system was not transformed;

the working class did not seize power. The question of the moment then became, How could one possibly make a revolution? How was socialism to be attained?

I should stress again that in the eighteenth century the synonym of radicalism was reason. If one idea dominated the century, if one notion inspired the men of the Enlightenment, it was the concept of reason: that men were reasonable, that political men were reasonable, that social institutions were reasonable in their functioning. The existence of mass social institutions was itself a claim for the primacy of reason. The Hegelian synthesis was based on the notion of reason. Reason equaled itself in its phenomenology, while in the final *Gotterdammerung,* Germany equaled reason and reason equaled Germany. Marxism was also a system of reason. The working class overthrew the shackles of the past, whether they be religious or ideological. The machine became reasonable. Workers presumably figured out their exploitation in relation to the machine. They then organized reasonably. Marxism assumed a people who were political, not spontaneous.

By the end of the nineteenth century, not only did the concept of irrationality enter the picture, it dominated. And it dominated political discourse in two forms: first, as a statement of the way people behaved, and second, as a statement of the way revolutions were gotten and begotten. Men like Sorel, Pareto and Michels represented ultimately and lastingly the final assault on the Age of Enlightenment. Indeed, Sorel knew better than perhaps anyone else, save Gaetano Mosca, that the notion of reason had to be overthrown if one was to continue to have a revolutionary standpoint in an age of affluence. One must appreciate the degree of shock created by this position. Even now, if most revolutionists, communists or socialists pride themselves on one thing, it is their reasonableness. It is the inevitability of a socialist system based on the rationality of production. But at the end of the nineteenth century, the new revolutionists confronted that tradition diametrically. They claimed that to uphold the future meant to become mad in the present. To be a revolutionist was to be a madman. One could not go into the marketplace and assert the reasonableness of political radicalism. The crippling blow aimed at the socialist formulation was the argument that the working class could no more be convinced of its destiny by Marx than the bourgeoisie has been convinced of its destiny by Voltaire. One could not go to the workers any more than one could go to the emperors, nor could one make assumptions of rationality on the basis of interests.

This clear gap between interests and values was later developed by Weber and Michels. They observed that a value commitment may be irrational. A pronouncement of an individual interest does not necessarily mean that the person will pursue those interests. A statement of a man's class position is not the same as the performance of a man's class behavior. To tell a man he is exploited is not to convince him that he must become a member of a warring class. He can react in several ways: He may like exploitation; or better, he may believe it to be a natural state. "I am a worker because I am foolish. I know I am foolish because I am a worker." There is no answer to this reasoning. It is very potent among peasants and ethnic minorities, no less than proletarians. The attempt to put the worker to the test, and tell him how equal he is, itself represents an act of inequality of a gargantuan proportion. But of course the history of rational revolutions moved exactly in that direction. At the end of the nineteenth century, revolutionists perceived a great, shocking, horrifying truth—that rational instruction in the nature of exploitation was a hoax, that such activities were not the way to bring about a revolution.

The schism between social democracy and political revolution was not just a tactical struggle between Eduard Bernstein and Rosa Luxemburg; it was a fundamental schism based on different philosophies of life and different political assessment. It finally became apparent that industrialism would not lead to revolution, but away from it. For example, French revolutionaries went to Clemenceau and made demands. And he granted such demands. The revolutionists responded in confusion to Clemenceau's suggestion that they organize unions, join the government and participate in political organizations. The working class was asked to participate; they were not thrown out of the French Republic. On the contrary, they were invited into the government. This was the ultimate in the diabolical corruption that the bourgeoisie heaped on the revolutionists. It coopted them. It castrated the revolutionary movement until there was nothing left of its revolutionary zeal. The same process of mobilization and cooptation took place in Germany. And essentially because of this, when the showdown came in 1914 between class and national identifications, the choice was clear—nationalism.

The early stages of the civil rights movement in the United States had that quality. The government invites black people to join them in the government to make a collective war on poverty. The activist becomes a special adviser to the President, whom he never sees, yet he is supposedly a leader of the government reform policies. The civil rights leaders have not "sold out," but they do live well; they have been co-opted through a process of accommodation. All of this takes place by a process of informal arrangement. Meanwhile, the working class, far from becoming revolutionary, becomes content. New alliances are forged with the middle classes, revealing once more the terrible power of nationalist identification in the advanced countries of the world.

The advanced countries have not had a revolution since the abortive ones of 1848. Call the system capitalism or whatever, it works well enough not to be overthrown. It gives more and more people basic kinds of advantages: high income, high mobility and high access to the sources of power. It might be said it does not work well enough, that Germany had a counterrevolution of fascism. But over time, class arrangements and political structures remained as they were before World War II, even in

Germany. Men of ideas in the nineteenth century were confronted by a diabolical bourgeois devil that did not disappear and above all did not pursue
expected terrorist tactics in relation to the working class. The system did
not become brutish; it became clever. That was one of the irritants which
drove the revolutionists first to madness, and then to myths.

The first quest was to look for the revolutionists. Who would they be—
which men, what sector of society? One must have an agent for a revolution,
a physical person, an entity. What was the profile of the revolutionist? The
working out of that profile became the key to the entire discussion that
ensued through the late nineteenth century and that continued between
Sartre, Camus and others. It was the search not for the social system, but
for the personal agent; the instrument of the revolution. To discover his
contours and his characteristics became the abiding passion of men like
Sorel, Pareto and Michels. The emphasis changed from the revolution to
the revolutionary man. The factory workers presumably "sold out" revolution, through traditionalism or through trade unionism. The question became, Where and how is revolutionary man developed? And here the question of myth came into play; and here the intriguing observations of
Aron become meaningful.

The transformation from actual history to mythological history is
described by Aron with great skill. It needs to be emphasized, however,
that his vision is itself extrapolated from a long line of Franco-Italian social
theory that took command between the death of Marxism and the birth of
Leninism—at least in their pure forms. Indeed, the rise of mythological
socialism can be said to be a response to a special period in European
political history, a period between the collapse of the Paris Commune and
the success of the Bolshevik Revolution. Yet, in a larger theoretical context,
the issues generated have come to plague political sociology throughout the
present century.

The Myth of Being Left. What kind of man was the Left man? First of all,
he was a man who believed that the past was good. He had a Rousseauian
quality to his thought. He believed that there was a time when things were
right and that this was a time when things were wrong. He believed in a
beatific past, in the noble savage; he assumed that in order to have something better it was necessary to understand that the past itself gave firm
guidelines, that the past "primitive communism" was perfect and the present
advanced socialism was imperfect. This was the basic Left sentiment that
was believed necessary to revolutionary man.

The Myth of Revolution. Revolution was not good for what it brought, for
the benefits that ensued or the vulgar material advantages; revolution had
value as a form of life, as a form of struggle and as a kind of antiseptic to
the infections that the wealth and affluence of a society continued to cause.

Revolution provided purification of the soul far more than purification of the society.

The Myth of Work. Aron calls this the myth of the proletariat, but I think that had dissolved by the end of the nineteenth century. In Sorel, the idea of labor was transcended, and it took on a grotesque form in which any kind of work was good. Peasants were good because they worked hard. The therapy of effort was believed to be a tremendous factor in forging revolutionary action. The radical man was someone who believed in the therapy of work, who was not idle, but who acted out certain Spartan virtues.

The Myth of History. Not only was history seen as perfection of the past but also it was believed that the future society would be as good as, if not better than, the past. Above all, the revolutionary man had to believe that the future held in store a political system so unlike the present as to be worth the trouble of its achievement. History was not simply what came into being, but what was constructed, created; it was an act, rather than a fact. History was not a set of events, but a set of things one did. The sense of making history, creating history, was an essential property of the myth-making man. It was not just what occurred, but what he made occur. It was the expression of the ego in history. Why do revolutionists have to have activity? Why do they not accept the historical inevitability of socialism and wait for it to come? It is inevitable because men act, not because men declare in favor of a metaphysical system of inevitability. This answer rallied the Russian populace to socialism. It made them antideterminists. It made them actors, not just shadows in history books.

The Myth of the Person. By the close of the century, the irrational man was celebrated as the new revolutionary. Such a man was alienated not only from the work source but also from all sources in the industrial society. The Nietzschian image was dominant, not the Marxian image. And revolution took something other than such mild forms as Hegel's notions of alienation; it became things that nasty-tempered and brutish men did precisely because they should not do them. Because there was no possibility of a revolution, they had to make a revolution. The revolutionary did not look at the rationalistic prescription; he drew upon ego inspiration. What was good for him was good for the world. This was ultimately the myth of the person over and against the society.

These requirements, which were determined by the end of the nineteenth century, came to define the radical or revolutionist. The properties of the radical were the myths just outlined. What made them mythical was not that they were implausible, but that they were all rallying cries. The myth is a symbolic organizing center. It is a sphere of unification having nothing to do with science. Although these men were the forerunners of so much modern sociology, they really posed as antiscientists, at least in terms of social sciences. They took the positivist view that a social system is never a scientific system, that talk of scientific planning is therefore absurd. Social systems, whatever they may or may not be, are not of themselves rational or scientific. What transpired was not the end of the revolutionary syndrome; it was not the end of the notion of change. What did occur, however, was a dramatic alteration of ideas about (1) the human advantages of change, (2) the character of the change they were going to bring about, (3) the political systems involved in bringing about this change, and (4) the notion of the intellectual, fundamental quality of change. These alterations led intellectuals of the last half of the nineteenth century to renounce the tradition of reason, for to uphold the notion of revolution they had to mythify.

Reason became the ultimate betrayal because they had begun with a concept of reason as the real touchstone of what the present lacked, the idea that one was a revolutionist because the present was not reasonable enough. The very men who asserted the necessity of irrational judgment or the existence of this, the need for the myth, themselves betrayed the original reason for making a revolution, namely, a higher society or a more perfect union. And that is why the last half of the nineteenth century was somewhat disappointing. Compared to twentieth-century radicals, these men were giants, but compared to their forerunners, they were secondraters. Because of the monumental contradiction that to assert the reality of the future they had to mythify the kind of men who make social change, a great paradox arose. The bifurcated poles of this thinking have provided modern political theory with its fundamental problems. Briefly stated, the major propositions of the new revolutionists rested on action, rather than cognition.

1. The essential field of human activity was political activity, yet the contents of their political sociology represented a denial that the existing frame of politics contained either the solutions or the problems of men.
2. The evidence for socialism was said to rest upon the historical requirements of humanity, that is, upon the belief in history as an objective and verifiable process. Yet the basis of mass action was asserted to be antihistorical, based on subjectively held myths and not history, upon a view of history as simply an extension of individual imagination and fantasy.
3. A psychology of action was developed in order to realize the goal of human liberation. But since human liberation itself was merely a continuation of an action psychology, the aim of scientific psychology, rationality, was submerged in an instinctual pool. Human practice, Sorel's basic prophylactic of civilization, in this way lost a sense of meaning, direction and value.
4. The polarities of reason and unreason, mythology and science, and sociality and individuality were contained in their inability to supply

a set of basic values by which men might live harmoniously. The further they sought the basis of integrated society, the more deeply committed they became to an irreducible alienation and atomization of the human situation.

5. Emancipation itself was a major stumbling block. At one and the same time, emancipation was conceived of strictly as emancipation from the nation-state and also more broadly as human emancipation from the uniformity and mediocrity of class relationships and class existence. Yet at no point did they show the interrelation between political emancipation and human emancipation, between freedom at the objective and subjective levels alike. These men were unable to reconcile emancipation at the political level with what they held to be human emancipation, and they were tormented that every gain in the political arena was seemingly at the expense of human emancipation. The very reification of what is political and what is human held a formula for rejecting both industrial and political organization and led to no resolution. This is one reason, of course, for their being irrationalists.

The words *irrational* and *revolution* have always been strange bed-fellows. They generate a very intense pulling together and apart, a strain, representing the ultimate outcomes—fascism and communism. Neither of these groups were simply leftists, or even primarily leftists. They were the very expression of the pure polarization that came about at the end of the nineteenth century. It is no accident that nonrational rhetoric is used with equal facility by the Right and by the Left. The only political sectors who are unable to use it are the liberals. The second half of the nineteenth century was the age of liberalism. But liberalism could not be accepted by the intelligentsia in search of transformation. As both right and left pulled at the liberal element that existed and coexisted in these men, by the early twentieth century the bourgeois synthesis collapsed and the political world was once more in a state of perpetual flux.

PASSION AND COMPASSION IN TWENTIETH-CENTURY POLITICS

Most social scientists pay little attention to historical details; their analysis is thus generally cross-sectional rather than longitudinal. One gains certain advantages from looking at a society in that way, but loses others. My purpose here is to indicate what I consider to be the essential problems of the present historical period.

The fundamental question is: What is new about the twentieth century? Hannah Arendt (1963) has said that basically the age is characterized by nationalism, by imperialism and ultimately by totalitarianism. While she has written a brilliant book defending her thesis with enormous insights and very good points of selection and points of focus—if rather poor organization—these are not features of just the modern age. Nationalism is certainly not a twentieth-century phenomenon, nor is imperialism; and even totalitarianism has enough ancestry to raise certain doubts about its novelty. Arendt leaves unanswered the question of the twentieth-century period, namely, whether it is novel. *On Revolution* (Arendt, 1963) is a continuation of discussions first broached in *The Human Condition* (Arendt, 1958) and *The Origins of Totalitarianism* (Arendt, 1951). Because the concept of revolution is something less than social science and something more than mere speculation, perhaps a prosaic ordering of Arendt's materials is not only forgivable but also necessary. I shall state her position in propositional form and offer some lines of disagreement and further inquiry.

War and revolution have violence as their common denominator. Conflict derives from fratricidal instincts, while political organization has its roots in crime. Crucial to revolution in the modern age is the concurrence of the idea of freedom and the experience of new social beginnings, of apocalypse.

Revolution gains a new significance as war, its partner in violence, becomes an implausible way to effect social change. Total annihilation has transformed the character of the military from protector of civitas into a futile avenger. Even prior to the nuclear age, wars had become politically, though not yet physically, a matter of national survival because of the widespread fear that the vanquished power would suffer the subjugation of its political organization. Nontechnological factors in warfare have been eliminated so that the results of war may be calculated in advance with perfect precision. Foreknowledge of victory and defeat may well end a war that need never explode into reality. If we are to survive, this cannot become a century of warfare, but it most certainly will become a century of total revolution. The universal goal of war is revolution. But even without the possibility of limited agreements, revolution will come to define the character of the modern uses of violence and the present impulse toward freedom and liberty.

Revolution in the modern age has been concerned with two distinct drives: liberation (absence of restraint and increase in social mobility) and freedom (political level of life). While liberation is consonant with various forms of government, freedom is only possible through a republican form of government, which explains why the American, French and Russian revolutions all adopted this form of rule.

The two fundamental models of revolution are the American and French revolutions—though only the French Revolution became *the* basic model for Marxism. The American Revolution adhered to the original purpose of revolution making—freedom—while the French Revolution abdicated freedom in the name of historical necessity. The American Revolution was thus profoundly political and antihistorical, while the French Revolution was historical and profoundly antipolitical.

The French revolutionary model, the model adopted by Marxism and which penetrated the ideological and organizational aspects of the Russian Revolution, was concerned with the social question—with problems of exploitation, mass alienation and poverty. It was inspired by the idea of compassion. The American revolutionary model was concerned with the political question—with problems of policies and the predicaments that flowed from an elitist theory of mass human nature. Its revolutionary passion did not give way to compassion.

The weaknesses of the "classic" French model are revealed in the abortive aspects of the major revolutions of the modern era—the Paris Commune, the Russian Revolution, the Hungarian uprising. In each case, there was the rise of two distinctive forces: the party, acting in the name of the people, and the voluntary associations (workers' councils, soviets, communes), or the people as a collective. In the betrayal of the revolution, the force of power over the people came through the consecration of political parties, while the council system, because it failed to realize itself as a new form of government as such (as in the American Revolution), tended to be short-lived. It is this fact that accounts for the perfidy of modern revolutionary movements—the breakdown of voluntary association and its replacement by a swollen bureaucracy. And it is this fact which is central to the Maoist Chinese efforts to maintain the impulse toward revolution in a post-liberation climate of accommodation and consolidation of State power.

These propositions indicate Arendt's morphology of revolution. While it is not possible to argue her book's thesis in terms of "right" and "wrong," a number of questions arise. The key problem of On Revolution is the relative absence of evidence.

Arendt displays little knowledge of modern warfare (and slender awareness of the ambiguities of modern conflict—counterinsurgency, paramilitary struggle, police action, guerrilla action) that would show that war is becoming obsolete, that it is like a gun with two barrels pointing in opposite directions with the triggering mechanism designed to kill the gunman as well as the victim. But the absence of any distinction between war and annihilation throws all of the weight of her discussion of revolution onto the questionable assumption that war is obsolete by reason of self-interest. The absence of knowledge of problems of contemporary warfare is excusable—war and peace studies are dismal—but conceit is no reply. And when the author states that "the only discussion of the war question I know which dares to face the horrors of nuclear weapons and the threat of totalitarianism, and is therefore entirely free of mental reservation, is Karl Jaspers' The Future of Mankind" (Arendt, 1963, p. 287), she is only revealing her lack of awareness of a widespread and valuable literature that has just this relationship as its central concern. Nor is her definition of revolution sufficiently operational. To see revolution as having everywhere a violent quality is to fail to distinguish between change in social structure and impulsive strategies sometimes used in such changes. Even if we assume that Arendt is speaking exclusively in terms of political revolution, it is *not* the case that violence is a necessary or sufficient component.

Contradictory statements blemish her profound insights in the revolutionary process. "The part of the professional revolutionists usually consists not in making a revolution but in rising to power after it has broken out, and their great advantage in this power struggle lies less in their theories and mental or organizational preparation than in the simple fact that their names are the only ones which are publicly known" (Arendt, 1963, p. 263). Elsewhere she states that "without Lenin's slogan 'All power to the Soviets' there would never have been an October Revolution in Russia" (Arendt, 1963, p. 269). Therefore, the relationship between cadre and charisma remains unresolved. Arendt's assertion that the consequence of revolution is always less freedom and liberty than previously existed is belied by an appreciation of the *positive* outcome of the American Revolution. Indeed, it is precisely her dislike for revolutionary process that causes her to search out special features in the American Revolution not found in Europe.

Hannah Arendt belongs in the unusual category of a revolutionary conservative. For although she is bent on demonstrating the negative aspects of Thermidor and Robespierre and the positive aspects of the *Federalist Papers* and the founders of the American Republic, she nevertheless is seeking at the deepest level for a way to make revolutionary movements responsible to revolutionary men. Thus it is that councils of workers, soviets and the like are held to be useful models of voluntary control. The revolutionists constitute a "new aristocracy" that would properly spell the end of general suffrage. As she puts it, only those who as voluntary members of an "elementary republic" have demonstrated that they care for more than their private happiness and are concerned about the state of the world would have the right to be heard in the conduct of the business of the republic (Arendt, 1963, pp. 234–251). The revolutionary elite would be the guardians of the nation. How this differs from the "betrayal" of revolutions by political parties, how this guardianship could avoid becoming a political party, is not amplified. Arendt respects the "spirit of revolution" but scorns its failures to find an "appropriate institution." She has located such an institution in the voluntary councils that accompany revolutions, but what is amazing is her unwillingness to support her theory with evidence; for example, there is no discussion of the functioning of the Yugoslav worker councils or of the Israeli kibbutzim. This is the result of a failure to confront real contemporary revolutions, to take up the political revolution of freedom in relation to the economic revolution of abundance. Her comments in this direction reveal an awareness of the potential antagonism between economic development and political freedom, but not a consistent understanding of how and where they intersect. The big question of revolution is precisely the "mix" between economic rationalization and political reason. Polarization of these may make a stimulating treatise, but it cannot define the experimental character of most contemporary revolutions. For Arendt, the French and American revolutions are diametric opposites. For peoples of revolutionary lands, they both stand as beacons in the search for the new. Perhaps politics and people have been polarized in European models, and bureaucratic and voluntary associations have become sundered. But if massive revolution has defined the century, might it not be wiser to reach for new combinations of policy and publics rather than to look with nostalgia upon the Greek city-states and their prudent elitism which rested, after all, on a slave base?

Many constraints within Arendt's perspective result from an exclusive focus on Europe as a model. What is really new from a historical point of view is that the play no longer is in the hands of those nations and those figures she emphasized in her earlier works. Characteristic aspects of the twentieth century, even of twentieth-century totalitarianism, cannot be found by studying Central Europe or southern Europe or England. The twentieth century must be perceived with the recognition that the power locus has shifted from Europe to the United States, the Soviet Union, and the Third World. What is novel about the twentieth century is that Western tradition, which was developed in a particular geographic area, is now being acted out in different ecological locales. Intellectual and political problems are not new, but their important locus is. And when the locale changes, nuances develop in the problem itself.

Hans Kohn (1957) has indicated that one of the interesting things about America's arrival in world history is its lack of consciousness about that arrival. America failed to recognize that it was a world power; from the evidence Kohn adduces, Americans were so unaware of the American presence that after World War I the major impulse was to return to prewar times. The critique of Wilson and Wilsonianism that was successful throughout the age of Harding and Coolidge, during the decade of the twenties, represented a profound attempt by American politics to return to its parochial and provincial origins. The United States did become a world power economically as a result of its international involvements between 1848 and 1919, but the recognition of this internationalism and its own role in the new colonialism never came in a direct form. It was rarely manifested ideologically. To this day, Americans are uncomfortable with self-definitions of colonialism and imperialism; they are ill at ease with an explanation system that is based on raw power. The United States has always been a country of moralists, and that tradition has continued to the present. The recognition that what is new about the twentieth century is the United States' presence is not quite as commonplace as one might expect. The bulk of the American people do not envision their country in that way, or at least they did not until the termination of World War I.

The coming into power of the Soviet Union was an entirely different issue, because the Soviet Union consciously worked for world power. It became a power in an overt way through its revolutionary ideology of internationalism; the growth of the Soviet Union was never unconscious, but it was even less often self-conscious. The true irony of the situation is that a relatively weak power, the Soviet Union, became a world historic force in a very conscious way and that a relatively powerful nation, the United States, became an international power in a relatively unconscious way. In retrospect, elements of consciousness, self-consciousness and unconsciousness have loomed much larger in the cold war period than they did in the forties or fifties. Indeed, the twentieth century witnessed the last attempt of western Europe to be an internationally powerful arena, to retain its hegemony; that last gasp was an ugly one—the Nazi German attempt at hegemony.

The only way that Europe could retain its world status ultimately became through a Nazi totalitarian system. Those smaller nation-states that did not possess the capacity to search for power passed into historical oblivion. They are with us still in rhetoric only. Like final acts of romantic plays, the Nazi drama carried a desperation with it, a distorted recognition that the collapse of the Third Reich was the collapse of Europe—the collapse of world history itself according to the Nazis. The English were urbane and could explain this collapse with equanimity because they had seen many civilizations come and go and were quite prepared to wait another thousand years to become a power again. In the meantime, the English were able to sustain the myth of their own empire, and paper over its demise.

The force of the rhetoric of European civilization is exemplified in the form of its last great man, Charles de Gaulle. There can be no doubt that he was an echo out of the past, however functional for France was his postwar position vis à vis the United States. De Gaulle's ideology, was from an age only a short time past, but his rhetoric was long outmoded. De Gaulle was dominated by the vision of an age when everyone in the Russian court spoke only French, and when Americans were like Benjamin Franklin, appealing to France for support in its democratic ambitions. De Gaulle gave voice to France's final aspiration to her past history. From a historical point of view, this is what is new and what is old. It is obvious that the de Gaulles are old, and that the control of power is no longer in the hands of Europe, or certainly France. As a consequence, Europe's institutions, whatever their merits or demerits, either wane or die on the alien soil of both Russia and America. Europe can be viewed as the *un*continent of the twentieth century. It is a playground for tourists, for people who like historical monuments and for masochists who like to visit graveyards. It interests people who want to see what the medieval world was like, or what Athens was when it was directing ancient slavery. What Europe ultimately has to sell is its history. Tourism is an appeal to the historical sense. That is why Russia is bad for tourists, and the United States expensive for and unconcerned with tourists. Their importance and interest lie in the future. One would not go to Smolensk or Cleveland, for example, to see the sights. Tourism is but a single instance of attitudes toward power and history. Nations on the move tend to disparage, if not discourage, a view of itself as historical—such self-definitions are left to glorious achievements that were, rather than dreary statistics that are.

Arendt and others report that the twentieth century represents a period of tremendous polarization. It is not only that the United States and the Soviet Union came into being as world powers, but also that they came into being as negations of each other. The period is the very antithesis of the pluralistic internal development of many of these societies. Every area exhibited a breakdown of pluralistic styles, of ideals—fanaticism. Totalitarianism seemed to emerge in some great measure from this impetus toward polarization. There was struggle in philosophy, and it was always the struggle of positivism versus metaphysics; in social science, empiricists versus rationalists; in economics, capitalists versus communists. Everywhere the middle ground gave way at critical moment. The liberal standpoint no longer seemed possible. It was not so much that the ideals of liberal democracy had given way as that these ideas became operationally implausible.

The old had durability and the new had fragile qualities—for example, the fragility of political institutions. Again and again, that nineteenth-century invention, the party system, gave way. Not only in Africa did the party system fail; not only in Asia was there a uniparty structure. In Europe, there was a premonition of this. The growth of bolshevism took place outside the framework of political parties; so did fascism in Italy. Germany had its ultimate political party crisis in 1932, and a uniparty system appeared a year later. The ideals of freedom of conscience and free speech correspondingly gave way to the decline of the party system. The notion of free speech was replaced by ideological definitions. The definition of a man increasingly became fanatic; one had to know a man's ideology before he could be trusted. His currency was first demonstrated by his ideological correctness; everything else was secondary. The natural sciences came to be determined by ideological conditioning rather than by intellectual conditioning. This, too, was a return to traditionalism; it was not something new so much as a reemergence of the very old.

The model of African states increasingly emerged as a uniparty in which the party process is linked to the ideological system, and the party functions as the operational clearinghouse for decision making, as an arena not for a contest of wills, but of different strategies or philosophies of life. This is true in Asia and Africa and increasingly true in Latin America, where the model of an operational social system is something similar to that of Mexico, which is a system with several parties but only one operational government party. In the old societies, the party system broke down throughout Central Europe; in Germany, Italy, Russia and France, the party system collapsed. The party system was reinstalled in Germany and Italy, not by any effort of will on the part of their peoples, but as a consequence of defeat. The Americans wanted them to have a party system; the Americans won. The institutionalization of party life is not an internally derived necessity. It is an externally imposed obligation. The collapse of party life has been a very profound phenomenon. Arendt (1963, pp. 280–285), has said there "is only one party that survived the twentieth century intact and that is the Communist Party in Europe. The rest of the parties have come and gone, but ultimately the only party which exists is really an antiparty apparatus. It is not a party but a system of rule."

In Africa, the uniparty system has frequently degenerated into military dictatorships. One of the characteristics of such regimes is their instability. They are strong enough to seize power, yet not strong enough to retain it. The active institutionalization of the military exposes the need for some party apparatus. The tendency to smash the uniparty results from the lack of a notion of succession. As a consequence, there is no way of dealing with the problem of political change. The systems can be overthrown only by violent means. The Bolshevik model has had the elasticity of managing succession. Rulers do change, and policies do become outmoded, so in certain countries succession is managed by forbidding one to succeed himself after a certain number of years in office. When the office is vacated, the pent-up criticism is released. In Mexico, when a man is president he is also beyond criticism. But he leaves office to torrents of criticism of his regime. This is one way of managing the problem of succession. The Africans have yet to do this. There are several reasons: The National Liberation leaders are still alive, and they are generally headmen; the ideological leader may not be a good bureaucratic leader. In the case of Ghana, Nkrumah is a good example. If he had died in 1965, he would have been successful, but he lived a year too long. He was an ideological leader, who took out full-page ads in the international press urging investment on the basis of low labor costs. This contradiction caught up with him eventually. The National Liberation image broke down, but there was no breakdown of the uniparty system.

The model of factionalism within a party requires something other than internal dynamics. It has been said that the kinds of factional change develop within a party or within the uniparty that in previous ages were represented by political parties. But what is really involved is the development of elitism, not democracy, and not value alternatives. Interest groups are very different from the value centers that a party in its pure form ostensibly represents. In the American party system, values are embodied in the parties. Within the party, interests are at stake with an assumption of common valuational norms. This, of course, is the Bolshevik model. The Bolsheviks mean by democracy that within the central authority of the party, assuming a commonality of values, these pockets of interest will express themselves and develop an internal cohesion and consensus. This definition of democracy is the very negation of nineteenth-century political democracy. Political elitism is different from political democracy. Reason became practical, and nonreason became theoretical. Technology was reason, and the social sciences were nonreason. Diabolical schemes were developed for doing away with masses of men in elaborate and costly ways; these were based on reason, but any overall purpose in society could only be called nonreasonable.

Bettelheim pointed out that only in the twentieth century did economics become unimportant in how to deal with people. For example, the gas chambers were expensive, elaborate mechanisms that involved whole hosts of cost factors that were serious liabilities for the *Wehrmacht*. Truckloads of Jews for the ovens were more vital cargo than cargo or troops for the front, and took priority over troop movements. The gas chambers were rationally planned irrationalities. It was not just a matter of killing, but the symbolic significance of the murders. It had to be done rationally, or else the beasts would be deprived of their real goal. A suicide represented the failure of reason in the system. The system was reasonable only if one was put to death, not if one put himself to death.

It was not just total politics, but total annihilation that increasingly became the defining hallmark of the age. This contributed to the fragility of institutional life. All men came to realize that total annihilation is possible, because men have achieved this goal on a limited scale. The meaning of Hiroshima was not that it was a city that was decimated—it was the cataclysm of total destruction. Total annihilation was possible because institutional life was fragile. One could destroy total populations scientifically and with impunity.

Less frightening, but equally impressive, is the wide appreciation that the relationship of the parts of a social system to the whole have changed. The eighteenth and nineteenth centuries were centuries of political economy. The twentieth century is a century of political sociology, not because the word *sociology* has become important, but because the word *political* is important. The relationship involved between "base" and "superstructure" is an inverse one from the past, in which there was no regulation of the market, other than the unconscious self-movement of parts of the economic system. The age of classical capitalism was legitimized precisely by the absence of governmental regulation. In the case of Ricardo, the supremacy of people with property and people with real factory wealth was emphasized. In the case of Marx, it was revolution stimulated by oppression. But the classical political economists never challenged the market as the determining factor in social change. Economic determinism was not the exclusive property of the Marxist; more importantly, it was the property of the classical political economist.

Inexorably, in many different forms, whether it be the bureaucratic forms of Germany or Russia or the United States, the political role became important—not directly, not as an assertion of the primacy of voting or democracy, but as management, as the assertion of the primacy of regulation. This is not the resurrection of politics in its constitutional form; it is politics not of the party, but of the expert. It is almost nonpolitical politics. It is a system of control and expertise, a political system. Economics is determined, and it is a political determinant. There is no such thing as economic determinism. This insight was already observed by Michels but became a reality when economics was fragmented. Economics became partial; it separated out into class antagonisms, and these roles had to be managed. It was not the division of labor that was important, it was the management, as unionism or whatever other form. Total politics emerged, without the party system; politics was finally separated from parties.

Americans continue to treat politics as if it has to do exclusively with parties. Political scientists often do not deal with politics, but with voter data. The twentieth century is a topsy-turvy world where economics collapses, politics takes over, the party system vanishes and the control systems take over via political mechanisms. Political sociology is a great deal more than the politics of party voting. The kind of political sociology that is often done, that rests so heavily on formalist criteria, reveals a view of politics as specialized, and a view of sociology as generalized. This peculiarly American solution only serves to disguise the essential unity of politics and sociology at every institutional level from law to marriage. There is a double problem in allowing science to substitute formal elegance for real knowledge. One cannot just present materials that would move beyond voting analysis without recognizing the collapse of the party system as such. Not to recognize this phenomenon is simply not to deal with politics as an everyday event. The twentieth century, and its polarities and totalities, is one in which the fine distinctions between causally primary economic factors and secondary political factors have dissolved under the pressure to program, plan, and predict the future.

REFERENCES

Arendt, H. (1951) *The Origins of Totalitarianism.* New York: Harcourt Brace Jovanovich.

Arendt, H. (1958) *The Human Condition.* Chicago: University of Chicago Press.

Arendt, H. (1963) *On Revolution.* New York: Viking Press.

Aron, R. (1957) *The Opium of the Intellectuals,* trans. T. Kilmartin. Garden City, N.Y.: Doubleday.

Aron, R. (1968a) *Democracy and Totalitarianism,* trans. V. Ionescu, New York: Praeger.

Aron, R. (1968b) *Progress and Disillusion: The Dialectics of Modern Society.* New York: Praeger.

Diderot, D. (1965) *Encyclopedia: Selections by Diderot, D'Alembert and a Society of Men of Letters,* trans. N. S. Hoyt and T. Cassirer. Indianapolis: Bobbs-Merrill.

Durkheim, E. (1933) *The Division of Labor in Society,* trans. G. Simpson. New York: Macmillan.

Hegel, G. W. F. (1953) *Hegel's Philosophy of Right and Law,* trans. T. M. Knox. Oxford: Oxford at the Clarendon Press.

Kohn, H. (1957) *American Nationalism: An Interpretative Essay.* New York: Macmillan.

Montesquieu, C. L. de Secondat (1949) *The Spirit of the Laws,* trans. T. Nugent. New York: Hafner.

Talmon, J. (1960) *The Origins of Totalitarian Democracy.* New York: Praeger.

SYSTEMS

CHAPTER 6

POLITICAL CONSERVATISM AND CONSERVATIVE POLITICS

THE OLD CONSERVATISM AND THE DEFENSE OF POLITICS

In this chapter, we shall examine conservatism as a model ideological movement rather than as an inherited Platonic philosophy. Conservatism was perhaps the first political movement that was directly involved with politics as such; Bernard Crick's (1962) *In Defense of Politics* makes this quite clear. That is to say, one of the important aspects of conservatism in its modern classical form (that of the eighteenth and nineteenth centuries) is that it grew out of the very soil of politics. It was the product of political policy-making and of men who were directly involved in the making and breaking of nations. Examination of the leadership of the conservative movement indicates how radically different it was from that of the liberal forces: Edmund Burke was one of the shining lights of the English Parliament; Prince Metternich was the kingpin figure in the Congress of Vienna of 1815 and one of the most significant personages of this period; and in this country were John Adams and Alexander Hamilton—the Federalists. In other words, the conservative movement, unlike that of its critics, grew out of very practical politics. It did not spring to life as an ideological movement with a plan to change the world. It did not begin with a design for the future: it came into being as a result of the effort to maintain the status quo, to maintain the order intact. In effect conservatism was concerned primarily with order because the men who were identified as conservatives were concerned with order, a consequence of their functional position in the eighteenth-and-nineteenth-century period.

But one would have to say that the twentieth-century conservatives, or neoconservatives, are in a sense the very opposite of their classical predecessors. Perhaps this is the most serious problem in any analysis of conservatism. In its classical form, conservatism is linked to the consequences of political involvement, but twentieth-century conservatism is a response to alienation from that kind of involvement. Russell Kirk or Peter Viereck (as is evident in the literature they produce) are very much the outsider looking in. Twentieth-century conservatives, as an organized body, are outside the power system. The conservative rhetoric has not penetrated the halls of power, and furthermore the conservative point of view is no longer a consequence of holding power. In its classical form, conservatism represents a position of dominance; in its modern form, it is in a subordinate, external, alienated position. An analysis of conservatism shows that while, in terms of doctrine, there may be lines of continuity between its classical and modern forms, functionally and politically there is incredible discontinuity. This is the result of many events that have taken place in Western Europe and the United States—principally, the rise of liberalism, socialism and communism. From 1848 until the present, the political mood has been within that framework rather than within a conservative framework. The breakup of the old aristocratic order upon which the conservative view is based, coupled with the collapse of visions of empire and the end of monarchy as a viable system, all helped to destroy conservatism as a political force; but it has lingered on as a political ideology.

In the United States, from 1775 (the period of the Revolution) until the Clay-Calhoun era (about 1840) conservatism, whether it be English imported Toryism or Whiggism, was in a remarkably powerful position. Conservative strength is reflected in the character of the United States Constitution, in the division of government into three separate and equal branches and in the nature of who voted and monetary requirements for voting. It is reflected in the division of the legislative branch into two Houses, one based on unequal representation, in the strict constructionism of the Supreme Court and in the strong Hamiltonian money and banking policies. In other words, one could say that up to and perhaps including the age of Jackson, conservatism was not alienated from mainstream politics and so was very much an authoritative force. It is not that it lacked opposition, but that the opposition was in the main not quite so strong as the conservative forces.

Not until the Jacksonian period did the kind of populism emerge that

led to the breakup of conservatism as a movement. The Jackson administration was especially important in this break-up—even more important
than the Civil War—because it spearheaded a strong populist tradition.
Later, with avowedly conservative Presidents, even with conservative Democrats or Republicans, there was an unshakable commitment to liberalism,
which meant a commitment to rapid progress and to national growth.
During this long period of time, the early status quo proclivities declined,
even with the most conservative writers. They were revived much later in
the literary work of people like Irving Babbitt and in the political work of
senators like William Borah. At the end of the nineteenth century and in
the twentieth century they reemerged as a claim against the liberal society,
but this time it was criticism rather than establishment sentiment. The
power of conservatism in its new form, in contrast to classical conservatism,
took root first in the period of Reconstruction, when conservatives criticized
the way that the revolutionary aspect of the Civil War was handled—the
fact that the Negro, once freed, was really more enslaved by capital than
he had ever been by the aristocracy—and, furthermore, criticized the industrial system. Conservatism became a savage counterpart to modernization
as such. Over the long span of time the old conservatism became separated
from the new conservatism by its functional posture with respect to the new
order of things: it started as a majority doctrine and ended up as a minority
one.

Several factors were involved in this reversal. First, conservatism is an
ambiguous doctrine. Comparison of Peter Viereck's (1949) *Conservatism
Revisited* with Russell Kirk's (1953) *The Conservative Mind* shows them
to be very different. Both books are representative of the conservative
movement, but they are different to such an extreme degree as to raise the
question of whether a definition of conservatism is possible. Furthermore,
even if we can arrive at a satisfactory settlement of the conservative ethos—
such as mistrust of rapid change, faith in faith, a concern for reason over
the passions, a belief in natural law rather than social contract—we could
not quite be sure whether a conservative thrust is possible without a conservative class. Conservatism is a movement, an ideology, but has no class
to give it support. The middle classes—this is especially true in the United
States—are liberal. The labor classes are liberal. There is no need for a
class to hold to a conservative rhetoric because the conservative ideology
serves no class function (although it may, of course, render intellectual
services). What happens to the conservative mood is that it tends to become
very badly divided, with one wing moving very close to a kind of neofascism
and the other wing moving toward a vague kind of liberalism. To a degree,
there may even be an accommodation with left-wing ideology. In either
case, there is a movement away from the conservative position, and the
conservative movement rends itself by moving Right or Left. This does not
happen within the speculative realm, within the realm of marginal men,
but with men who have tradition, who have English ancestry, who have

Episcopalian connections. But their relationships to each other are vague rather than powerful, and vague linkages do not make for satisfactory politics. The difficulty with conservatism is that as a political force it is not supported by class forces either within American or European life. At the same time, as an ideology of intellectuals, it must suffer the same criticisms that it launches against its opponents—namely, that it is abstract, egghead, vague, irrelevant and not tied to the real issues. In other words, the very premises that move people toward the conservative view also tend at the same time to break their connection with the conservative style; the very justification for entering a conservative framework is somehow made self-defeating by the fact that conservatism cannot escape its own criticism of other ideologies. All ideologies face dilemmas in America, but none more than conservatism because it peculiarly makes a claim to political relevance yet has no real claim or relevance. It must accept the framework set by a cosmopolitan liberalism, while steering clear of the ultranationalism of nativistic reaction.

Every ideology seems to carry within itself a mass concept and an elite concept. Marxism, which is supposedly a doctrine for the masses, harbors the deepest kind of elitist assumptions. This is also true of socialism, anarchism and every other kind of doctrine. There is no doubt that the rise of a class of bureaucratic experts is a kind of conservative triumph. But one should not confuse elitism in general with conservatism as an ideology. Conservatism is eschewed by almost every man of power. The Democratic party, for instance, has rested its case on the popular classes and on the popular will. Concern about the popular will and the democratic majority has been so overwhelming in recent times that the government has determined from the results of the most recent survey whether a war should be escalated. So in a functional sense the conservative philosophy of Edmund Burke hardly governs present-day men of power. There is no open recognition of conservative ideology of any faction representing conservatism, only people who say "Slower" or "Faster" instead of "No." Ultimately, conservatism is reduced in political terms to a cry against minority groups, social welfare and government involvement; yet, in the extreme, it verges toward neoanarchy—the attack on the state as such. The frenetic attacks by certain conservatives upon the so-called communists in government in large part stem from their feeling that all state power or state authority is intrinsically communistic. Insofar as there is pervasive government control, they argue, the state has been moved much closer toward a "communist" solution.

Too often, when one speaks of conservatism, he develops a rhetorical definition instead of a useful one. The fundamental definition of conservatism is the minimization of state authority and the maximization of individual opportunity and autonomy. Every bona fide conservative takes the standpoint "that government that governs least governs best." But very few labor leaders or businessmen—whom one would expect also to be committed to free enterprise—will rest their case on that position. Quite the contrary. The liberal position dominates in most business circles; those who are making the dollar know better than to act against their own interests. Every stratum of business above that of petty shopkeeping is concerned with positive, affirmative government intervention in the struggle for government contracts, for grants from state institutions, and so forth. What has happened is that conservatism has collapsed as a movement; at best it is a posture. If one examines political funding in recent presidential elections (1948–1968), he will find that the major business organizations supported the Democratic Party at least as often, and to the same extent, as the Republican Party. Even organizations such as the National Association of Manufacturers, which is relatively to the Right of the various chambers of commerce, were unable to support the idea that government intervention should be entirely eliminated. The idea of government intervention and state and federal supports has become so thoroughly institutionalized that the ideological cornerstones of conservatism have become an academic matter. Criticism of rising state authority is no longer justified, because in a historic sense the conflict of interests from a practical point of view is now a struggle between liberalism and socialism. Our own vision of the situation is distorted. Every chamber of commerce is committed to progress, not to the status quo. The argument for planning or not planning is the argument between liberals and socialists; it is not an argument between conservatives and liberals. Fragmented planning is exactly what liberalism is about.

The irony is that some aspects of conservative criticism have a great deal of merit. Although it is rarely taken seriously, there is much to be said for the argument that federal governments have an incredible amount of power, that instead of states withering away, as Marx suggested, they became more powerful. That absolute power tends to corrupt absolutely is a more realistic formula than that the states will wither away when the classes wither away; it is certainly better supported by evidence. It seems unlikely that conservatism will die away. It will live on as other kinds of doctrines, such as anarchism, continue to live: it will persist as a critique of the social order. The social origins of the conservative critique are different, perhaps, but it functions to call to mind the fact that the present order of things is not idyllic. State power is indeed a form of creeping socialism; but only in the special sense that socialism readily acknowledges the planning and programming of economic systems.

More important, conservatism has staying power because it is the only nonradical or nonsocialist way of handling certain problems. In the social sciences it provides an ideologically meaningful framework and avoids the demons of socialism; it is an important device for galvanizing concern with macro problems in the social sciences. Large numbers of political scientists, economists and sociologists, if not enamored of the conservative frame of reference, at least give it serious thought, because it does provide a perspective on serious problems without a commitment to revolutionary thought. Thus conservatism's main modern function has been as a preliminary to important social science research; movements such as that led by Leo Strauss in political science have at their core a desire to attack the most significant problems of the age without embracing radical points of view. For certain types of men the problem becomes how to criticize society and how to evaluate social systems without seeming to become radical, and without making commitments to utopia. One might say of present-day conservatism, at least as it applies to social science, that it is a counterutopian response to the need for large-scale research. This is a far cry from its beginnings in the halls of power, from Metternich's settlement of European affairs, but, in all truth, this may be the necessary end of any doctrine that no longer has a social base.

There are, after all, only two ways to avoid being typed as a liberal or a member of liberal society. One can identify with the socialist or communist vision of social utopia, which defines an optimal end point. The other way is conservatism. Conservatives are in the awkward position of being without a viable social utopia, since the corporative state and system crumbled long ago, after the Burke era. As a result conservatism has substituted a kind of therapeutic politics, in which the state is rejected. It is this war on politics, if you will, that gives strength to the conservatives. Negativism carries them very far; it is true that conservatives have no ideal design of a social system and that the world of Christian faith has collapsed, but they remain convincing in terms of their approach to the policial society. There remains a rather marked interest in conservatism among college students and among intellectuals in general. The ideology fulfills urgent psychological requirements, and, from that point of view, is extremely important.

The conservative anticommunist posture, for instance, has as its deeper source the mistrust of any external power imposed on the individual. Its thrust and bite is not anticommunism, but the fear of being taken in. It is based on the fear that manliness will be destroyed by the state, that the value of work will be replaced by the desire to be taken care of. This indicates not simply an "anti" sentiment, but a profound feeling of disgust and revulsion with the control of men by impersonal bureaucratic institutions. That is why present-day conservatism always emerges as critique. Of course it is negative; it should be negative, because the positive affirmations all come in the form of destruction of the personality, in dehumanization. The sentiment that conservatism appeals and gives deep significance to is an idealization of the person. The grounds are relatively irrational—tradition, faith, religion, symbol systems—and they ostensibly enable the individual to come to terms with himself as a person and to become a defined personality. Conservatism in the present period is a form of therapy; as such, it is extremely important and not to be taken lightly.

Economically and socially, American society is moving in the direction of statism rather than toward an atomistic pure liberal society. This movement can be partially seen in the growth of bureaucracy. In the field of business, many areas are dominated by three or four huge corporations that seek to preserve themselves rather than compete in the free marketplace. Individuals find their position within the market, not simply by economic choice but by all sorts of status criteria. As the business world increasingly comes to depend upon government, it decreasingly loses its power of autonomous decision-making. And this makes conservatism increasingly anachronistic, despite the weaknesses of liberalism.

There are those who argue the thesis of the end of ideology within the West. If this is true, it is the first time in history that a social system has presented no more conflicts. Certainly it is the case that traditional kinds of divisions no longer obtain. For example, the socialist party is now very much like the liberal in rhetoric, just as classical conservatives have the same problem of distinguishing themselves from liberalism. The character of the competition and conflict is very different. For example, the struggle for power may well involve relatively few men who control relatively few machines; it may take on an international character between have and have-not nations. In truth, liberalism as an ideology has triumphed. It is difficult to accept that fact, however, so we say that all ideologies have been abolished, as Lipset claims, or we decry the bureaucratization of life. Liberalism's triumph is that its age is the twentieth century, not the eighteenth century. Everybody is a liberal. Everybody believes in the free exchange of ideas. Everybody believes in restricted planning, but not national planning. Everybody believes that democracy is a good thing, but not at the expense of social order. Everybody believes that the rich should be taxed, but not to the point of eliminating profit incentives. The eccentric solution is the conservative or socialist option. Ideology has not dissolved, nor is there any firm evidence for the dissolution of western society. Rather, we are profoundly committed to the liberal point of view and we are genuinely outraged by the nonfulfillment of complete material satisfaction for all citizens. The liberal belief is so profoundly rooted that the interesting question is how the triumph of liberalism took place so thoroughly, and what its long-range prospects are.

Why is the liberal formulation vague, and the conservative formulation not; why is liberalism the basic political style in the Western world? There are several possible reasons:

1. The middle classes form their own historical vantage point; in some deep measure, incorporate the liberal policy of the French Revolution, German Enlightenment, English Revolution and American Revolution. The middle sectors have always been involved with liberalism as the justification of their behavior and point of view. Therefore, it is natural that once they did come into power their rhetoric would survive and triumph.

2. Activities in the world of science throughout the eighteenth and nineteenth centuries also gave support to liberalism instead of conservatism. For example, Darwinism, the idea of evolution, the entire notion of change in types and structures and their effects, became a rallying cry for all believers in the ultimate equality of men through equal opportunity. Inevitably, in the nineteenth century, Darwinism came to mean progress. Darwinism had the added advantage of describing a struggle for survival rather like a stock market exchange system. Scientific activities also had the effect of supporting the liberal framework.

3. The challenge of the nineteenth century was no longer an aristocratic challenge. The working classes were interested in unionization and independence from the middle class so that the center of interest became how extensively liberalism could permeate the working class and prevent revolution. The biggest threat (to the middle classes) was socialism, not conservatism, and therefore they offered up as much as possible without giving up their sovereignty and so tried to minimize class friction without encouraging revolutionary violence.

There is no mystery about why liberalism emerged victorious. The only mystery is how liberalism in the twentieth century was able to reconcile the uses of any degree of state power with its faith in individual freedom of action. Here one comes upon some very interesting possibilities—namely, the breakup of the hegemony and strength of the bourgeoisie to determine, without intervention, the goals of all social classes. Isolationism, which deepened in the United States in the twentieth century as manifest destiny and Pax Americana, supplied ideological continuation for the conservative framework. By 1964, a very powerful challenge took form, in the guise of Goldwaterism and a general deepening conservatism within the Republican party. The domination of this conservatism doomed the Republican party to minority status, but more important is the fact that present-day conservatism again has a practical concern with politics. It also has the problems that go along with these concerns.

The most difficult thing for opponents of conservatism to understand is that underlying the antipathy to communism is the strong feeling that it is equivalent to total regulation. Conservatism is nostalgic rather than utopian; the past rather than the future holds the key to conservative solutions. There are, however, values to conservatism's nostalgic ruralism, and, whether ideal or otherwise, genuine in application. It is easy to dismiss nostalgia and ruralism only if one ignores considering how deeply we all are involved with nostalgia—both as a frame of reference and as a belief that the dim past was really better than the present. Conservatism may not answer certain kinds of needs, but one must take seriously its claims upon men, and consider why, without an undergirding social class, conservatism prevails among a large portion of minority groups. The answers given to these questions are all too often oversimplified. Furthermore, they tend to be based on liberal rather than scientific assumptions, and take for granted that conservatism is absurd. I argue that conservatism is a serious position that will continue to be represented as American society matures. Twentieth-century conservatism demands a mature industrialized society. An under-developed or developing society cannot afford the time, the leisure or the effort required to work within conservative frameworks. Conservatism is both a consequence and critique of industrialism.

THE NEW CONSERVATISM AND
THE CRITIQUE OF POLITICS

One of the leaders of the conservative revival in America has admitted that "conservatism is among the most unpopular words in the American vocabulary" (Viereck, 1949, p. x). It is also one of the most persistent currents of thought. Conservatism's unpopularity and persistence are not unrelated: the history of modern conservatism in large measure is the history of conscientious defiance of every major advance shaped by popular democracy. The renewed popularity of the conservative philosophy of civilization is therefore of more than casual interest.

In recent intellectual history, conservatism's most effective prophets have been Russell Kirk and Peter Viereck. In educational theory, the conservative school is represented in its many facets by Arthur Bestor, Bernard Bell and Gordon Chalmers. There is also the ascendency of antinaturalist philosophies such as those of Eliseo Vivas, John Wild and Jacques Maritain. And there is the school of history propagated by Allan Nevins, which is attempting to rewrite American history in terms of the business class. Perhaps the high-water mark was the publication of a multivolumed study of the Standard Oil Company. This task, undertaken by the Harvard School of Business Administration, made the a priori decision that the Rockefeller portrayed by past historians never really existed, that he was a blameless hero who transformed the oil industry from anarchy to scientific organization.

The number of intellectual areas traversed by the new conservatism is as widespread and ramified as American society itself. It is my aim to explore the historic roots and essential premises of an outlook that is making a strong bid to replace pragmatism as the philosophy of American business civilization (Rossiter, 1955).[1]

Ultimately, modern conservatism faces the same theoretical opposition that older conservatism did. Burke attempted to defeat the menacing principles of the French Enlightenment and Revolution, and the hopes it aroused in the masses of men: complete social and political equality, a recognition of the right of man to economic well-being and happiness, the

[1] To my knowledge Rossiter's is the best attempt by a theorist to summarize conservatism's current status.

supreme authority of men to judge their mode of life independent of theological edict, and belief in the possibilities of the endless and inevitable advancement of society. Since these remain goals to be fought for rather than achievements registered, the conflict between conservatism retains its vitality. What has drastically changed are the forms Enlightenment precepts have been taking through the world, the urgency of the conflict and the classes that embody these contrary intellectual traditions.

EDMUND BURKE

The spiritual fountainhead of conservatism, as most writers agree, is that English statesman Edmund Burke. He serves the new conservatism well, for his age, like our own, was one of enlightenment and revolution. In large measure, modern conservatism attempts to apply to the Russian Revolution the stigma attached to the French Revolution. There was the pietism that held that since society was but a fragment in the cosmological hierarchy, the basis of human relations must be theological. The foundation of material prosperity should be the recognition and veneration of private property. It was Burke's intention to prove that the social division would be tantamount to flouting Providence itself. He also taught a moral absolutism, an eternal order of values that could never be experimentally verified, but only revealed. This moral hierarchy was graded from the highest religious ideals to the lowest leveling sentiments. And last in theory but first in actuality was Burke's social elitism, a stress on the inherent worth of socioeconomic stratification and the attendant duties and rights of class to class and man to man. All three aspects, pietism, absolutism and elitism, were claimed to be valuable in their promotion of social harmony and stability. And for the contemporary conservative, as for Burke, "Harmony, not struggle, is the ruling political objective" (Hogg, 1947, p. 32). Because Burke defined the various principles of conservatism so diligently, his "ideas did more than establish islands in the sea of radical thought: they provided the defense of conservatism" (Kirk, 1953, p. 61).

The approach of Burke set the classic pattern of conservatism as a reaction to the main direction of social life. In his own time, he reacted as any man of economic substance did, but with greater eloquence and vituperation, to the French Revolution. The tendency has been to overlook the fact that it was not the "excesses" of the Revolution that Burke countered; the Revolution was itself an excess because it settled matters with the *ancien régime* outside the framework of tradition and convention. Burke was adamant on this point. For in the partnership of social forces, "all men have equal rights, but not to equal things. He that has but five shillings in the partnership, has as good a right to it, as he that has five hundred pounds has to his larger proportion" (Burke, 1854–57b, pp. 331–332). Once this precept of the right of the rich to be rich and of the poor to remain poor is accepted, revolution becomes a political equivalent of theft. The Enlightenment announced the doctrine of popular sovereignty as the inherent right of man in civil society. This was the excess that Burke (1954–57b, p. 335) could never forgive: "Men have no right to what is not reasonable, and to what is not for their benefit." Ordinary men being unable for want of the "leisure to read, to reflect, to conserve," only those who do, "what I should call a *natural* aristocracy," can properly judge what is reasonable and beneficent for the whole of society (Burke, 1854–57a, p. 85). For Burke, economic paternalism was the answer to popular revolution.

The quality about the French Revolution that was perhaps even more disturbing to the natural aristocracy than the event itself was that its ideas spread. British Jacobinism as represented by such sturdy democrats as Priestley, Paine and Godwin offered a serious challenge to the "great compromise" of 1688. The ideas of liberty and universal fraternity opened up the possibility that the exploited could act as a social force for themselves and not just remain an amorphous mass. Burke grasped the meaning of these international ramifications of the Revolution. The cry of anarchism was sent up as a flare in the night. Only obedience, sacred and profane, could save official society from the excesses of the masses. Burke's admonitions to the empowered classes were heeded.

The nineteenth century dawned with reaction triumphant throughout Europe. But the enthroned sat restlessly. The idea of the French Revolution remained potent, its canons strengthened rather than refuted by Schiller and Hegel. Hegel (1929, Preface), though a faithful servant of the Prussian state, perceived that "the spirit of the age has broken with the world as it has hitherto existed." He had a "foretelling that there is something else approaching." The emperor of Austria, the king of Prussia and the czar moved swiftly to counteract this "something else"; and Metternich supervised the formation of the "Holy Alliance."

The transmission of Burke's ideas to Metternich was direct. Some of Metternich's most trusted advisers introduced English conservatism to central Europe. Metternich's Concert of Europe was an attempt to effect a "great European compromise" by the application of conservative doctrine designed to cement relations between a functionless aristocracy and peripheral portions of the professional and middle classes. But he was very much aware that the grand conservative concern was doomed (Viereck, 1949, p. 108).

The Revolution of 1848 brought down the aristocratic house of cards. The top elements of the middle class took command of the political machinery. At the same time, workers were undergoing a period of rapid maturation. From the time Metternich's conservative synthesis collapsed, it became clear that the future social events would no longer rest on aristocratic claims of legitimacy and law. The old conservatism became painfully aware that it was fighting for a losing cause. Its main economic props were collapsing. Theology, too, found itself unable to compete with the social and scientific revolutions of the period. In the latter half of the century, there was little left for conservatism to do but follow Cardinal Newman's lead in abandoning the world of material relations entirely, and in contenting itself with a pseudosacred realm of values and feelings.

The conservative philosophy came to consider itself the guardian of traditional values against the encroachments of science and industrialism and the bourgeoisie that promoted them both. "Let Benthamism reign, if men have no aspirations," Newman (1878, p. 280) said acidly. Newman presented the bourgeoisie with an impossible choice: "We must make our choice between risking Science, and risking Religion" (p. 280). Profits dictated that the middle class risk religion. For this, conservative philosophers have never forgiven industrial society. For as they warned, science and secularism, the rejection of belief and faith, would one day become an instrument of the propertyless mass. W. E. H. Lecky pointed an accusing finger at the bourgeoisie who acquired "vast wealth by shameful means." It was they, the businessmen living by the utilitarian credo, who were laying the seeds for the destruction of society. "When triumphant robbery is found among the rich, subversive doctrines will grow among the poor. When democracy turns, as it often does, into a corrupt plutocracy, both national decadence and social revolution are being prepared" (Lecky, 1896, pp. 501–502).

Having only memories, aristocratic conservatism became very historically minded, but it was a sterile historicism. It was not an effort to understand the processes of human societies, but an apologia for the continued existence of a whipped aristocracy. Conservatism, old style, revealed, as did Newman and Lord Acton, a desire to return to an "organic Christian society." But by the beginning of our century, this was all that was left to traditional conservatism. The conservative became a critic without portfolio. It remained for modern American conservatism to demonstrate the unexplored possibilities of this philosophy in making a forthright appeal to the new aristocracy of industrial wealth.

CONSERVATISM IN AMERICA

Historically, with the exception of its use by the southern slaveholding class, the conservative philosophy has always played a secondary role in American thought. This is not surprising when one recalls the absence of a feudal economic structure. Convention and status were concepts hardly calculated to fire the imagination of a civilization that had to be carved from the wilderness. When Alexis de Tocqueville (1900) in his *Democracy in America* noted that Americans were the most fully realized expression of Cartesian practicalism, and yet managed to remain the least philosophic people, this is essentially what he meant. Nonetheless, conservatism has persisted in the form of an "aristocracy of mind." From the time of Jonathan Edwards (with his idea that the rulers of society and theology should be those who have been granted divine grace with a "supernatural sense") to George Santayana (who would promote a society ruled by men who can transcend "animal faith" and lead the "life of reason"), American conservatism has been oriented toward an aristocracy of knowledge. Eighteenth- and nineteenth-century conservatism in America imagined it had overcome the problems faced by its European counterparts by augmenting Burke with Harrington. The natural inequalities of man could not be touched by political reformers and philosophic radicals because, as John Adams (1850–56, p. 382) observed, no human legislator can ever eradicate inequalities implanted by Divine Providence. Natural inequality, for Adams and his successors, implied the existence of a natural aristocracy that could withstand social upheaval because it was presumed to be providential rather than social in character. This shrewd bifurcation of the ideal and the material enabled conservatism to thrive on American soil despite adverse conditions. But by the same token, its stress on an aristocracy of knowledge deprived it of the support of the great mass of Americans of all classes. In past centuries, the United States had little regard for contemplative pietism and elitism, approaches that in no way could be instrumental in the feverish effort to catch up to and surpass European industrialization. Conservative philosophy, therefore, spent much time criticizing the expansive business civilization. Whatever was of value in this critique was unfortunately dissipated in conservatism's incapacity to measure the actual historical movements in American life. In substituting the formal values of the past for what such values represented in a new world, conservative philosophy reached a pinnacle of intellectual isolation.

Instead of succeeding in its aim of providing a stream of intellectual continuity to match the continuities in nature, conservatism championed a bifurcation of the past and present. The battleground of ideas assumed the character of the glorious past resisting the encroachments of a decadent present. This dualism was brought to full focus in Henry Adams' (1957) *Mont-Saint-Michel and Chartres*. In establishing the idol of the past as a sure way to protect the "harmony" of future generations, conservatism severed the real and the ideal, the material and the spiritual, the continuous and the novel elements in society. Such an alienation ultimately served to destroy an understanding of and respect for the achievements of the past. It fostered a utopianism lacking an essential democratic content.

It should not be strange to find the new conservative literature uncritically praising the admittedly minor tradition of John Adams, John Randolph and Irving Babbitt. These figures have served as a bulwark of the status quo. They shared a condemnation of the "materialism" of a modern industrial society that turned its back on heavenly values. Conservatism attempts a miraculous inversion of the historical process. The movement of life creates new problems demanding new solutions. The utility of previously defined theories is severely circumscribed by current needs. It is not a question of "deserting the past," as the conservative has it, but of keeping pace with the present. In its mistrust of the incessant movement of American life, conservatism has rejected the great fact that the world of man is not exempt from the process and progress of the universe.

Adams opposed the inevitable broadening of the democratic base by pointing to the heavenly basis of social stratification. Randolph and Calhoun opposed any termination of Negro slavery by appealing in a platitudinous fashion to state sovereignty. Southern conservatism in the nineteenth century was barbed criticism of northern capitalism in a frenzied effort to prove that chattel slavery was not as brutal as wage slavery. Southern conservatism preferred to ignore the requirements of an American business economy. It paid for its ignorance in humiliating defeat. Early in this century, Babbitt opposed technological growth because he felt it destroyed the beauty of the labor process. In his case, as with prior conservative doctrinaires, what is being rejected is the forward movement of life itself.

The spark of the new conservatism is what Harold Laski aptly termed the business civilization in decline. Present conservative philosophy has meaning only if it is viewed in the context of a business class in search of some outlook less shapeless than pragmatism. Oscar Handlin (1954), in his preface to *Elihu Root and the Conservative Tradition,* notes that the twentieth century is a "critical juncture in American history," a period in which "the evolving industrial economy of the nation produced men of wealth who needed the support of a conservative tradition." It could not be otherwise. The lack of a rooted aristocracy made conservative doctrine distasteful to the earlier American middle class. It is only in the modern era that conservative thought becomes politically significant because only in this period is there a middle class that finds comfort in looking backward. The significance of the current dearth of literature on the "new capitalist revolution"[2] and the attempt to write the history of business practice in adulatory terms lies in the linking of the middle class to an explicit conservative philosophy. It is hoped that from this class a new aristocracy can emerge, playing the same role in confounding revolutionary attitudes that the older conservatism attempted in a less favorable atmosphere. The remaining problem is to show the business class how to avoid the same dismal fate as the nobility.

It should not be thought that the new conservatism is less critical of middle-class morality than its historical counterparts. Its rapier-like criticism finds comparable expression only in the literature of American radicalism. From Brooks Adams to Robert Hutchins, two of the finest representatives of the conservative "Left," the "Coca-Cola civilization" has been severely criticized. However, the critique made of capitalism is with an eye toward its preservation. As a biographer of Brooks Adams puts it, it is an attempt "to preserve as much as possible of the old way of life and at the same time to reconcile the velocity and extent of mechanized change with responsible administration for the general welfare" (Anderson, 1951, p. 200). It is this aspect of conservatism that drives many of its advocates

---

[2] For the most important recent contribution to economic conservatism, see Berle (1954).

to the precipice of fascism. In its frenzied efforts to preserve the old, conservatism may surrender to corporatism, ruralism and ultimately fascism itself.

The new conservatism has no desire to see the downfall of a business economy, but simply to make its board of directors more conscious of ultimate goals. In this way, it is hoped that the wealthy classes will be able to provide a world leadership that can insure American hegemony. The difficulties in the conservative position arise when in the name of tradition it attempts to dam up that very tide in human affairs that gives worth to the past.

The conservative revival in the United States could appear to have a dual derivation. One is the present aberration in the relationship between the capitalist and socialist worlds. The international struggle for the minds of men has produced on the national level conditions of mass fear of alterations in the socioeconomic structure. There is an almost pathological identification of change with socialism. This has provided a proper soil for nourishing a conservative "renaissance." The new conservatism has merely transformed the nineteenth-century critique of socialism by Lecky and Spencer to the effect that "socialism is slavery" into a tendentious first principle. The current labeling of all manner of reform tendencies, from abolitionism to the New Deal, with the "egalitarian" and "leveling" curse is adequate testimony of the extent to which the new conservatism attempts to satisfy the appetites and prejudices of a business civilization.

The other major source of contemporary conservatism's power issues from the widespread disillusionment engendered by bourgeois existence. While making it perfectly clear that they stand on the side of property rights, conservatives are nonetheless critical of those tendencies that produce excess corruption of the moral fiber of the people. The stress on the rural life as the good life, when considered in this way, is a sort of bourgeois asceticism calculated to engender a love rather than a revulsion for societies built on private property. The following comment by Eliseo Vivas (1950, p. 314) is typical of the character of the forms of criticism launched by the new conservatism:

> I see no reason to assume that there is more love in this scientifically enlightened and humanitarian age of ours than there was in those ages which partisanship and historical ignorance dismiss as the days of the Inquisition. All the evidence points with some clarity the other way. Let us remember that it was left to our generation to invent the fact, no less than the term "genocide."

The new conservatism is a search for meaning, an attempt to anchor the middle class to something more fundamental than the shifting sands of James's pragmatism, something more worthy than a philosophy of will that reduces moral righteousness to success. In this way, the new conservatism hopes to replace the pluralistic world of pragmatism, with its many truths, with a monistic world that charts an absolute and theologically sanctioned truth.

Because contemporary conservatism realizes that to go forward means to embrace the socialist ideal, it chooses to look backward to a more ethically stable climate—to the high point of thirteenth-century feudalism if possible, or if not that far back, then to the England of the Great Reaction (1790–1832). These are specific historical directions that the new conservatism pursues. The enormous theoretical issue this raises, that is, the maintenance of the past *qua* past in the face of steadily advancing material culture, is usually resolved by coming down on the side of the hoary past against the main currents charted by the natural and social sciences. If a portion of pragmatic doctrine rests upon resolving dilemmas through expediency, the new conservatism demonstrates the lengths to which it can carry the pragmatic method while revealing a profound disenchantment with its system.

ELITISM

Elitism is not a modern innovation. It gained currency with the first definite political and economic divisions between men. In Greek antiquity it had already hardened. Plato presented elitism as being in the nature of biological reality, while Aristotle shifted the basis of his elitism to sociological grounds. With some justification, Aristotle noted that the growth of knowledge is stimulated by a leisure class that has time to think and rule. Elitism was, and remains, a theoretical justification for the existence of a society with ruling and ruled classes. In its philosophic pretensions, earlier American conservatism stands very close to Aristotle's social elitism, while the new conservatism has rediscovered the use of a biological fixing of status first developed by Plato. The new conservatism is in theory a series of footnotes to Platonist teachings. And it should not be overlooked that the present output of "defenses" of Platonism parallels efforts in other areas of thought to reduce the history of culture to the history of conservatism (See, for example, Wild, 1953; Levinson, 1953).

Contemporary conservatism is, like its ancestors, far more a negative reaction to continued social development than a positive enunciation of principles. In Burke, we find a violent reaction to the French Revolution; Henry Adams reacted with equal vigor to the expansion of American industry; Jacques Maritain and George Santayana react, each in his own way, to the heresies of socialism and secularism. This negativism is especially pronounced in conservative efforts to resurrect elitism as a fundamental social law. The "desperate naturalism" of Santayana is an attempt to resolve the conflagrations of modern life by absolving a rational elite from any worldly dilemmas. The rational–intellectual life "is no fair reproduction of the universe, but the expression of man alone" (Santayana, 1953, p. 174). Reason exists in man alone because only man is conscious and ideal-forming. The life of reason is a life of contemplation, of harmony. This view bears a strong spiritual kinship to the dominant philosophy of the medieval age. Yet it is presented to contemporaries as a plausible solution to current affairs. This solution is achieved by making reason the exclusive preserve of the elite. In order to maintain the delicate balance of society, the aristocratic elite must be preserved—being that group that alone can rise above the contradictions of reality to rational contemplation. In his last work, Santayana (1951, chap. 42) made clear his hope that the American industrialists will form the backbone of a contemplative elite. Any effort to destroy an elitist society would mean a reversion to biological levels of existence that would involve men in a series of struggles for the progress of the "rabble." Santayana's elitism is a calculated reply to the Enlightenment faith in progress as the extension of equality. "Progress, far from consisting in change," insists Santayana (1953, p. 82), "depends on retentiveness." The conservative spirit beat hard in Santayana's breast. Rather immodestly, the new conservatism assumes that the destruction of elitism would automatically result in the destruction of society itself—because it identifies society with capitalism, and itself with both.

However, it is both possible and desirable to develop social forms without either an elite or a leisured aristocracy. Nor does the absence of elitism logically imply the "leveling curse." The faith in radical democracy is not a desire for deadening uniformity. On the contrary, the extension of economic equality would make possible a genuine intellectual diversity, because it would allow for the development of the potentialities of the massive proletariat, what one conservative calls "an ugly modern word for an ugly thing" (Kirk, 1953, p. 392). In the analysis dealing with the machinery for preserving culture, the new conservative avoids discussing ways of extending this precious culture, for a society of 30 million Shakespeares and Newtons, such as Saint-Simon envisioned, would only destroy elitism. Any admission that knowledge and action belong to the community of man in common undercuts the basis of conservative philosophy. In the choice between preserving either elitism or culture, the modern conservative faces a problem that cannot be resolved by platitudes. To those who identify conservatism with political stability, like Peter Viereck, elitism becomes central, while for those who identify conservatism with the preservation of cultural values, like Robert Hutchins, elitism is secondary. The attitude adopted toward the issues of elitism and past traditions is one of the cornerstones dividing the new from the old conservative.

The undifferentiated frontal attack on democracy and socialism generally takes the form of flaying the heresy of revolution. Cromwell, Robespierre and Lenin, and the movements they led, are provided with a set of immutable qualities. "Impatience and ignorance are characteristic of democratic ages" (Kirk, 1953, p. 189). It is therefore no surprise to find a treatment of the differences between democracy in seventeenth-century England, eighteenth-century France and modern Russia reducing itself to an examination of the extent to which "violence replaced law" and "barbarism replaced custom." If American democracy is opulent and ignorant, Russian democracy can only be described as more opulent and ignorant. Abstract ethical dogma replaces factual analysis of the nature of social classes and the expansion of political democracy. Conservative social philosophy consists in evaluating the relations of men in terms of its own unique moral commitments. The "life of reason" cannot be led by the majority because most people are regarded as animal-men. Democracy is held to be inferior to either theocracy or timocracy. The extent to which the new conservative is willing to gauge the worth of a political system by its treatment of the elite reveals a profound distaste for the democratic form of rule.

Since the American middle class has been saturated with the antispeculative nourishment provided by pragmatism, the new conservatism has had to manufacture its elitist aristocracy out of that portion of the middle class that can temper its acquisitive bent with contemplation. Its recruiting grounds are often found in the educated and professional elements. Because the new aristocracy is in large measure an *ersatz* group, modern conservatism has devoted great energy to developing a philosophy of education. It is through its educational philosophy that the new conservatism attempts to define a set of postulates that can appeal to those who may gain from being part of an American elite. Even here, however, they must look backward. In Plato's categories of bronze, silver and gold men, the new conservatism finds its "positive" philosophy. H. M. Magid offers Plato's elitism as the only realistic approach the rulers of society can take toward political and educational philosophy. First, for the mass of men "loyalty" is essential. In a dynamic society, loyalty cannot be taken for granted; it must be promoted. The young are taken in hand before they can have achieved intellectual maturity and critical skill, and they are taught how to be loyal and what to be loyal to. This is achieved through indoctrination of carefully written history, stories of heroes and by example and enforced ritual. In educating an elite, we are urged to "get beyond the myths and stereotypes of education for loyalty to a presentation of the actual facts of political life, how our political institutions function" (Magid, 1955, p. 37). Hand in hand with the ruling elite march those granted an "education for understanding," individuals who have the task of searching for the "truth about the foundations, normative as well as factual, of political life itself" (Magid, 1955, p. 42). The philosopher in this way forms a superelite, the only group seriously allowed to conduct an inquiry into the basis of society. The stratification in this system of educational philosophy is, we are assured, a guarantee of harmony because it makes clear the bifurcation of the theoretical and the practical. Such political realism sounds peculiarly like the ideals advocated by extreme reaction. It canonizes the separation of head and hand fostered by every dominant class in history.

The elitism advocated by the new conservatism differs but quantitatively from the biological stratification preached by European fascism. It is of small consolation that the elitism of an intellectual aristocracy is said to be more benevolent than that of a "race" or "nation." The principal premise of man's natural inequality is challenged by neither. In any such arrangement, the schisms of humanity would be made a permanent feature of social existence, rooted in either "natural law" or "divine law." Thinking and doing, like rights and duties, would be severed. In theory, the conservative position flows evenly from the pursuit of knowledge to the achievement of dynamic thinking, to the right of rule. In actuality, the procedure is somewhat different. Because the proletarian monolith is held incapable of anything greater than believing myths propagated by men of silver and gold, their efforts must remain confined to doing what they are told. The great bulk of civilization conveniently eliminated politically, the right of rule falls naturally to those classes already ruling. Because the giants of thought are deemed by conservatism to be also the giants of industry, the elitist scheme becomes an elaborate justification of the status quo. We are presented with an eternal separation of men into fixed economic and intellectual molds, a large price indeed to pay for "harmony."

The recognition that inequality is an existing fact is no special knowledge of the new conservatism. It is equally clear to contemporary democratic philosophies that this is so. The essential difference is that the liberal and socialist traditions consider the inequality inherent in class stratification as something to be opposed. In this sense, they, too, struggle for harmony by pointing out that antagonistic industrial relationships prevent harmony. The new conservatism considers economic stratification necessary and beneficial to the public welfare. It would mitigate whatever evils result from social disparagement gradually, so as not to disrupt the basic composition of classes. "Conservatism derives its inspiration and seeks to base its policy on what conservatives believe to be the underlying unity of all class . . . their ultimate identity of interest, their profound similarity of outlook" (Hogg, 1947, p. 31). Having already rejected any view maintaining that class divisions at the productive base cannot yield a community of interests, it is a simple jump to the proposition that "the nation, not the so-called class struggle, is at the base of Conservative political thinking" (Hogg, 1947, p. 32). Because "harmony, not struggle," is the principal political end of the new conservatives, the values of elitism become self-evident to the ruled as well as the rulers. Patriotism, love of God and mythical heroes become important facets because they promote the stability of the state.

The new conservatism does not restrict its theory of harmony to the political realm alone. In economics, we find it applying a similar thesis. "Since the industrial revolution," writes Viereck (1949, p. 12), "conservatism is neither justifiable nor effective unless it has roots in the factories and trade union." Frank Tannenbaum (1951) attempts to provide these roots by presenting the trade union as a far-reaching repudiation of reform and revolution. It is for him "the great conservative force of our time." He resurrects the economics of the corporate state as the inevitable outcome of the natural conservatism of both labor and capital. "The corporation and the union will ultimately merge in common ownership and cease to be a house divided. It is only thus that a common identity may once again come to rule the lives of men and endow each one with rights and duties recognized by all" (Tannenbaum, 1951, pp. 198–199). In consideration of conservatism's commitment to elitist precepts and its utter contempt for labor, it is doubtful whether such a "partnership" can lead to anything different from the Nazi experiment, namely, the absolute and relative deterioration of the workers' conditions. What the new conservative doctrine is actually offering is a joint stock company of an aristocracy of management and labor. It simply extends the joys of elitism to a select portion of labor.

The metaphysic of present-day conservatism is the idea of harmony. However, nowhere is this metaphysic better refuted than in the pages of its own growing literature. To maintain, on the one hand, that society is a bundle of conflicts between classes, nations and social systems, and to hold, on the other, that a transcendental spirit is at work blending these conflicts, so that the whole pattern emerges as a teleological symphony, requires a privileged degree of credulity. The evidence of the historical sciences points in the opposite direction. In his constant looking back toward the imposing edifice of thirteenth-century feudalism, for example, the new conservative somehow fails to notice that in the very century the City of God had been declared to exist, the seeds of feudal decay had already assumed large-scale proportions. In truth, the new conservatism desires harmony in a social matrix where men are bitterly divided in their interests. The recognition that different socioeconomic interests prevail is perhaps the reason why the new conservatism presents a *deus ex machina* to work out what men are unable to resolve in present circumstances. In its belief that individual harmony is a prerequisite for the achievement of social harmony, it is akin to those forms of utopianism that sought to transform society by educating its rulers in the principles of utilitarianism. The idealism inherent in both dooms each to utter failure.

William Ralph Inge utilizes the *deus ex machina* to demonstrate that the state based on private interests is an eternal verity, "whose type is laid up in heaven." The state becomes the secular expression of Divine Will, "The unifying force which keeps the citizens of a country together" (Inge, 1946, pp. 154–155). The state is an absolute good because it draws its "vitality from the deepest instincts and most firmly rooted habits. Private property, the family, religion, patriotism. . . ." And for modern conservative doctrine, any repudiation of such a state must result in a "fiasco" (Inge, 1946, p. 155). In this form, philosophical conservatism reveals its awareness of social contradictions. For were society a naturally harmonic balance between classes and nations, there would be no need for a state to keep "the citizens of a country together." When conservatism calls upon the divine inspiration of a God-state to maintain an elite in power, it is asking Providence for a restoration of harmony to capitalism, not showing that harmony already is rooted in private-property relations. The appeal to prejudice, myth and supernatural edict cannot alter basic facts of economic history. To ask Providence to do what men cannot is not to reveal a love of God, but a failure of nerve in human powers.

THE CONSERVATIVE ETHIC

The moral absolutism of the new conservatism is as much a reaction to the "open society" and "open morality" of pragmatism as it is an attempt to forge a heuristic principle against Marxian ethics. The inherent pluralism of pragmatism makes it impossible to utilize ethics for a predetermined social goal. The steady stream of criticism the new conservatism has directed at Dewey's instrumentalism is pointedly oriented at his "means–ends continuum." The question John H. Hallowell (1954, p. 131) poses for pragmatic ethics cannot be evaded: "How is happiness possible without some rational principle in terms of which we can differentiate good pleasures from bad?" A universe without fixed ends, always locating goals in the immediate activities of men, is a universe lacking purpose. It fails to develop criteria for judging both means and ends in terms of a wider setting than individual biological needs. The new conservatism seeks desperately for purpose, for a teleology of morals. What its advocates continually refuse to admit is that purpose can exist without being predetermined.

Modern conservatism is aware that direction is of either one of two varieties: the direction of history, what Maritain derisively calls the historical god, or the preordained direction of cosmic will. Since even current conservative doctrine admits that the historical flow forecasts the extinction of absolutist, theologically conditioned morality, there remains but one alternative. To restore purpose into the life of society, it is necessary to give moral law a paramount role, exempting it from the laws of history. Democracy itself is conceived by Hallowell as a series of duties based "upon the reality of a universal obligation to obey moral law." To be disobedient to moral law becomes synonymous with disrespect for democracy: "If the validity of the moral law is an illusion, so is the validity of democracy" (Hallowell, 1954, p. 124). The moral sanction becomes God's sanction, the moral will becomes God's will, and the moral choice becomes the choice of God. Morality becomes a matter of finding out the divine pattern and obeying its dictates. Purpose is to be restored to the lives of people by lifting them from the ignoble choice of adopting either a pluralist, directionless ethic sanctioned by a bourgeoisie saturated with utilitarianism or an ethic with a range of applications circumscribed by history and sanctioned by a materialist proletariat. It is a conflict between the idea of history as the interaction and conquest of natural and social obstacles by men and the idea of history as redemption from original sin. History, we are told, "is not as Marx declared it to be, 'the activity of man pursuing his own aims' but rather a dialogue between God and man, with God taking the initiative and man either fleeing or responding to His call. The essential meaning of history is the restoration of personality through redemption from evil" (Hallowell, 1954, p. 100). It is the obvious task of the new conservative to make sure that men respond to rather than flee from this providential call. Here the professor has turned preacher.

The recurrent dilemma of the new conservatism is that in its rejection of a "shallow liberalistic" ethic it moves away from any realistic criteria for judging the worth of acts and attitudes. An objective ethic becomes equivalent to a normative and transhistorical ethic. In this form, morality is seen as a matter of discovery rather than a process of development. The determination of who has discovered the True Ethic becomes the focal point of value analysis. The absolutism of this approach does not admit to the existence of alternative ethical programs which are basic for certain periods and for specific social purposes. Instead, it is compelled to adopt a rigid theological dogma. Those accepting such a dogma are said to have discovered the True Ethic; those who have not are said to be lacking an ethic altogether.

The moral authoritarianism of modern conservatism represents a deep mistrust of a scientifically grounded ethic. It is the substitution of an ethic of allegiance for one of empirical procedure. It denies that the framework of human values is human society. The conflict in ideas that exists between social forces is revolved by reference to supernatural dogma. In the footsteps of Saint Augustine, contemporary conservatism bifurcates society into "two cities." The city of man is held to be based upon an egoist morality, while the heavenly city is based on love of God and contempt for self. The possibility of escaping the egocentric dilemma, of acquiring a humane moral code through secular methods, is ruled out. Man, according to the new conservatism and the old theology it mimics, is, in his origins, evil. Redemption comes through renunciation of the worldly and acceptance of the heavenly. The ethical norm in this way comes to be identified with a nonhuman authority: "The effect of this teaching is not only to distinguish the secular from the spiritual spheres but to place the secular authority under the sanction of a higher authority" (Hallowell, 1954, p. 117). We are presented with gradations of being. The "highest authority" being spiritual in nature is only indirectly transmitted to the individual. The "secular authority" is the state. The state becomes God in nature. It is the level of being that interprets the normative ethic for the individual. Morality in this fashion becomes a matter of respect for authority, and authority becomes a matter of allegiance. Because the secular state is the disseminator of the providential moral code, any challenge to it becomes heretical.

By lifting the problem of choice from human society, the conservative ethic is able to demand unswerving allegiance to that state on the basis of religious sentiments. For insofar as the secular authority is the reflection of theological authority, the state must be judged as absolutely good. Criticism of such a Christian state can properly be viewed as an attack on the religious basis of civil society itself. The new conservatism promises a militant defiance of those Jeffersonians who dare preach the separation of religious and political institutions. It "will seek to expose the reckless vanity of political principles that ignore or deride the quest of God" (Rossiter, 1955, p. 372). This theocratic goal is the natural result of moral absolutism. If the initial premise of human decadence is accepted, if ordinary men are creatures of sin, and if absolution is possible only through a rigorous calculus of duties and allegiances, then indeed to reckon the possibilities of achieving a steadily expanding democratic society is, as the conservative says, a supreme sin.

The entire strength of conservatism's closed ethical system is the ability to sever values from actions. The impact of modern science has convinced the new conservative that in the realm of physical and social events all is flux. The *raison d'être* of conservatism, however, is to emphasize that which it insists is permanent in life. Faced with a changing world, it must lift the spiritual side of things from its base in material relations. If the conservative philosopher can show that ethics is not subject to change, he can go on to establish a realm of immutable values. If, in the spirit of Neoplatonism, he can further demonstrate that that which is subject to causality (materiality) is unfree, whereas the spiritual is alone connected to free will, he can show that spirit alone gives man freedom. Man as "flesh" is a "creature of habit, of impulse, of passion, driven here and there by the forces of nature which are beyond his control" (Vivas, 1950, p. 341). Any efforts at material improvement are therefore wasted, according to Vivas. "But, insofar as he [man] is spirit, he is free. And the law of causality cannot be said to apply to him" (Vivas, 1950, p. 342). The moral law, not subject to causal determination, is thus "above" the laws of nature altogether. In this form, the path is clearer for the supreme edict of the new conservatism, the bedrock of its moral absolutism, the view that "the ethical is otherworldly." It turns us away from our social loyalties and conflicts and "toward the source of our freedom and the goal of our salvation" (Vivas, 1950, p. 346).

While Eliseo Vivas is elusive about the exact "source of our freedom," other naturalists doing penitence are not as squeamish. The source of freedom is held to be God. The goal of our salvation is regarded as the establishment of the heavenly city on earth. Although this city will establish "moral equality," it cannot change the lordly "conviction that civilized society requires order and classes" (Kirk, 1953, p. 8). But having learned that only the moral realm provides for freedom from enslaving causal relations, we can only bear the iniquities latent in civilized society. The elaborate moral canons of the new conservatism have a quite secular goal of securing a harmonious society based on private property—a hardly novel outcome of a hardly novel philosophy.

Despite the bifurcation of men committed in the name of moral law, the new conservatism does face mankind with a choice that is inescapable.

Either the realm of values is subject to causality and scientific analysis or science and values are mutually exclusive. If the former is true, then the possibilities of developing an organic, naturalistic conception of human nature exist. If the latter viewpoint is true, then any efforts undertaken to change man or his external circumstances are doomed to failure in advance. Morally, the conflict between conservatism and democracy is between the view of human nature as fixed and human nature as plastic. To deny the malleability of human ethical conduct is to deny the reality of the endless struggle of mankind to utilize an advanced ethic to further alter his social conditions. To assert that man is governed by rigid, predetermined moral dogma is to make social action suspect. It is this sort of resigned belief in the futility of human efforts at improvement that the new conservatism seeks to inculcate. And it seals this resignation with an anti-scientific trust in cosmic design.

PIETISM

The pietism of contemporary conservatism finds its inspiration, like so many of its basic tenets, in the doctrines of Burke. Providential guidance is considered the cornerstone of the sociopolitical structure. Prescriptive rights flow from the nature of God in the same way that natural rights are held to flow from the nature of man. The individual is held to be simply an instrument of Divine Will. The historical evolution of society is regarded as the Divine Will asserting itself in nature: "History is the gradual revelation of supreme design—often shadowy to our blinking eyes, but subtle, resistless and beneficent. God makes history through the agency of man" (Kirk, 1953, p. 36). Not a small amount of attention is focused on humanist and materialist philosophies that have made man his own proper study. The cosmic pietism of the new conservatism is a direct assault on the principle that men, since they are, in fact, independent of supernatural control, have the task of adjusting values so as to enable men to alter as well as comprehend the nature of their lives. To the conservative, this position involves the heresy of self-sufficiency. And the self-reliant individual is not likely to be pious or desirous of supernatural instruction. A naturalistic view of man is a democratic view of man. And as Kirk (1953, p. 119) informs us: "The pure democrat is the practical atheist: ignoring the divine nature of law and the divine establishment of spiritual hierarchy, he is the unconscious instrument of diabolic powers for the undoing of mankind."

Modern conservatism emphasizes religion as duty rather than religion as social justice. This is indicated by such remarks as: "the first rule of society is obedience—obedience to God and the dispensations of Providence, which work through natural processes" (Kirk, 1953, p. 59). However, the pietism of the new conservatism must contend with more than the relations of men to Providence. It attempts to show the epistemological basis for such a relation. In the conflict between reason and superstition, conservative doctrine finds its answers. The naïve Enlightenment faith in reason as the path to a higher democracy is castigated as a false idol that promotes only the cause of radical incendiaries. Conservatism perceives a great truth, namely, that the nature of man as thoroughly rational expels the transcendental from social decisions. Action based on reason is judged by Kirk as akin to belief in atheism and materialism. And for the conservative, "the experience of the species is treasured up chiefly in tradition, prejudice, and prescription—generally for all men, and sometimes for all men, surer guides to conduct and conscience than books and speculations." There is a strong current of antiintellectualism in conservative preachings. It relates reason "to a wasteland of withered hopes and crying loneliness." Irreligious ideas become a sign of "intellectual vanity" (Kirk, 1953, p. 36). At this point, conservatism and pragmatism meet. The antiintellectualism of both is based on a depreciation of human faculties of reason.

The thoroughness of the conservative attack on reason would shock Thomas Aquinas little less than Denis Diderot. Reason is not even allowed to exist as a theological handmaiden. The new conservative knows "man to be governed more by emotion than by reason" (Kirk, 1953, p. 8). We are warned by the leader of the natural rights school, Leo Strauss (1953, p. 6), that "the more we cultivate reason, the more we cultivate nihilism." To appreciate the extremeness of this view, we should recall the classic defense of Catholicism offered by Aquinas. He bolstered the case for revelation on the power, not the negation, of reason. The great scholastic opposed the idea that myth is a surer guide to Providence than reason. The orientation of present-day conservatism, however, is more compatible with the mystery cults of antiquity and the irrationalism of Sorel and Pareto than with the sophisticated rationalism of Aquinas.

Our main concern, however, is not the medieval defense of reason, but the present conservative assault on it. Reason is linked with "degradation, the rebellious will of man" (Hallowell, 1954, p. 128). In place of the heady powers of human reason, we are urged to remember that man is bathed in original sin. And if the plunge to a socialist hell is not to be final, we must return to the singular source of goodness, religion. Between Enlightenment and scholasticism the choice must be made. Modern conservatism chooses the latter. The Enlightenment forgot what John Hallowell (1954, p. 128) remembers: that "man is not an autonomous being but the creature of God, his moral weakness is his own, but his moral strength is born of the love of God. What the modern world has almost forgotten is the reality of spirit that ultimately triumphs over material power." Such sentiments rest on the assumption of a human incapacity to solve the problems of social existence. The full-scale attack launched on Enlightenment principles is on the surface a logical extension of Burkeism. They are that certainly. But more profoundly, the new conservatism sees in Enlightenment thought the taproots of American democracy. The resurrection of pietism requires a negation of the democratic tradition. It is, therefore, important for conservatism to train its sights on the concepts of self-interest, natural goodness, reason and happiness—concepts that received dynamic expression in documents such as the Declaration of Independence and the Bill of Rights.

The candor of the new conservatism, its recognizable identification with antiintellectual and fascist currents, is somewhat jarring to the American saturated in traditions of Enlightenment and utility. American democracy has taken the tenets of eternal progress and happiness, not as abstractions, but as a guide to daily living. A reaction to this tradition on American soil, while clearly not novel, has also quite definitely been a subdued tendency. Even the older forms of conservatism made their opposition to reaction and irrationalism clear. John Adams could still play a vital part in the progress of the American Revolution. What modern conservatism confronts us with is a definite choice between a materialist tradition of freedom through the rational uses of technology, science and social institutions and a philosophy of myth and prejudice artifically grafted onto the American scene from the backwaters of European idealist currents.

"Absolute democracy" is said to have failed because it leads toward "social disintegration," which in turn raises the specter of "oppressive collectivism." The new conservatism wants to be saved from the consequences of the proposition that society is itself the root source of human happiness and misery. V. A. Demant offers as his salvation from political realities "an organic relation between man's secular and spiritual life." The idea of religion propagated by the new conservatism sheds its monastic garb long enough to tell us that "the 'primacy of the spiritual' must be upheld, not as a retreat from the secular tasks of life, but as a condition of handling them aright" (Demant, 1947, pp. 65–66). In plainer language, religion is to be the foundation of society itself.

Conservative pietism is a ladder moving toward the theocratic state. Only a "Christian society" can save mankind from the twin horrors of reason and revolution, from the "old spurious God of the lawless Empire bending everything to his adoration" (Maritain, 1951, p. 187). The perplexing qualities of this position are clear even to some conservatives. If broad social conflict and change result from the iniquities of the material conditions of life, how is it possible for spiritual forces to do more than help us bear iniquities? If genuine change is providential, man is necessarily passive in the face of his everyday socioeconomic relations. It is precisely the fact that men are not simply passive, refusing to await the call of Providence before acting, that makes the conservative dish unappetizing to all but those comfortably situated. At great cost, the overwhelming majority of men have become aware that, although faith may soothe their burdens, it cannot remove them. It is this overwhelming fact of an age of social and scientific revolution that the new conservatism has refused to acknowledge.

Cosmic pietism, with its emphasis on myth and superstition, is translated into practical affairs as a reawakening of the Crusading Spirit. We are presented with a thorough identification of God with nation, race and class—particularly the American nation, the Anglo-Saxon race and the business class. The new conservatism is basically different from its ancestors in that it no longer makes paramount the critique of the bourgeoisie. Instead it places a theological *imprimatur* on the activities of American financial interests, while damning forever rational and egalitarian societies based on "collectivism." Allan Nevins musters all the tendentious zeal of the new conservatism in practically conceding the inevitability of war with "communist tyranny." Instead, he would have us believe that such an unthinkable holocaust would entitle the American civilization to take its place beside Athenian civilization (Nevins, 1954).[3]

Contemporary conservative pietism is, in fact, employing the idealist philosophy as a screen to promote a New Holy Alliance. The Atlantic Community is to become a twentieth-century version of Metternich's European Union (Viereck, 1949, pp. 132–136). Far from being a humane or judicious conception of the spiritual, the new conservatism uses religion cynically, for adventurist ends. Theoretically, it holds that religion is the basis of society. Practically, it holds that religion is a pragmatic device for maintaining intact a society based on private property, order and duty. It attempts to provide a cosmic scope to imperialist pretensions. A more ironic use of theology is hardly imaginable.

REFERENCES

Adams, H. (1957) *Mont-Saint-Michel and Chartres.* New York: Heritage Press.

Adams, J. (1850–56) "Discourses on Davila," in *Works,* vol. 6. Boston: Little, Brown.

Anderson, T. (1951) *Brooks Adams, Constructive Conservative.* Ithaca, N.Y.: Cornell University Press.

Berle, A. (1954) *The Twentieth-Century Capitalist Revolution.* New York: Harcourt Brace Jovanovich.

Burke, E. (1854–57a) "Appeal from the New Whigs," in his *Works,* vol. 3. London: Bohn.

Burke, E. (1854–57b) "Reflections on the Revolution in France," in his *Works,* vol. 2. London: Bohn.

Crick, B. (1962) *In Defense of Politics.* Chicago: University of Chicago Press.

Demant, V. A. (1947) *Our Culture: Its Christian Roots and Present Crisis.* London: Society for Promoting Christian Knowledge.

---

[3] This is an expansion of the position Nevins (1953) expounds in the introduction to his book *Study in Power: John D. Rockefeller, Industrialist and Philanthropist.*

Hallowell, J. H. (1954) *The Moral Foundation of Democracy.* Chicago: University of Chicago Press.

Handlin, O. Preface to R. W. Leopold (1954) *Elihu Root and the Conservative Tradition.* Boston: Little, Brown.

Hegel, G. W. F. (1929) "Phenomenology of Mind," in *Selections,* ed. J. Loewenberg. New York: Scribner.

Hogg, Q. (1947) *The Case of Conservatism.* Baltimore, Md.: Penguin Books.

Inge, W. R. (1946) "The State, Visible and Invisible," in W. R. Browne, ed., *Leviathan in Crisis.* New York: Viking Press.

Kirk, R. (1953) *The Conservative Mind: From Burke to Santayana.* Chicago: Regnery.

Lecky, W. E. H. (1896) *Democracy and Liberty,* vol. 2. London: Longmans.

Levinson, R. B. (1953) *In Defense of Plato.* Cambridge, Mass.: Harvard University Press.

Magid, H. M. (1955) "An Approach to the Nature of Political Philosophy," *Journal of Philosophy,* vol. 52, no. 2 (January 20), pp. 37–42.

Maritain, J. (1951) *Man and the State.* Chicago: University of Chicago Press.

Nevins, A. (1953) *Study in Power: John D. Rockefeller, Industrialist and Philanthropist.* New York: Scribner.

Nevins, A. (1954) "Should American History Be Rewritten?" *Saturday Review,* vol. 37, no. 6 (February 6).

Newman, J. H. (1878) *Discussions and Arguments on Various Subjects,* 3rd ed. London: Pickering Co. [originally published in 1827].

Rossiter, C. (1955) "Toward an American Conservatism," *Yale Review,* vol. 44 (March), pp. 354–372.

Santayana, G. (1951) *Dominations and Powers.* New York: Scribner.

Santayana, G. (1953) *The Life of Reason; or The Phases of Human Progress,* rev. ed. New York: Scribner.

Strauss, L. (1953) *Natural Right and History.* Chicago: University of Chicago Press.

Tannenbaum, F. (1951) *A Philosophy of Labor.* New York: Knopf.

Tocqueville, A. de (1900) *Democracy in America,* trans. H. Reeve, rev. ed. New York: Colonial Press.

Viereck, P. (1949) *Conservatism Revisited: The Revolt Against Revolt.* New York: Scribner.

Vivas, E. (1950) *The Moral Life and the Ethical Life.* Chicago: University of Chicago Press.

Wild, J. (1953) *Plato's Modern Enemies and the Theory of Natural Law.* Chicago: University of Chicago Press.

CHAPTER 7

THE
LIBERAL TRADITION
AND
EVOLUTIONARY
POLITICS

Classical liberalism is connected in history to the general emancipation of western Europe from the fetters of class structures. The liberal position stemmed from a concern for economic equity no less than from an interest in liberty. In this sense, nineteenth century liberalism is closer in appearance and in substance to the socialist claims of fraternal brotherhood than to the emphasis of conservative thought upon the right to rule of those with custom and wisdom. Liberalism defined its claims in universalistic terms; it spoke of freeing mankind as a whole. The bourgeoisie, which came to embrace liberalism, was not, however, in complete accord with the doctrine. The bourgeoisie's relationship to liberalism was closer to a kiss of death than an embrace of eternal love—since at precisely the point that the bourgeoisie discovered liberalism, the doctrine ceased having total critical value and meaning to wide numbers of people. This was the case, at least in the context of western Europe during the nineteenth century.

Liberalism does not preceed socialism as an ideology. Historically, it is parallel in time to the maturation of socialist doctrine in Europe. The rivalry between liberalism and socialism is especially bitter and acrimonious precisely because socialists could not place liberalism in the same historical ash can as they did the capitalist system. Their attempts to engage in the subterfuge of equating liberalism and capitalism failed to convince anyone.

Liberalism does not precede socialism in political life as capitalism is assumed to have preceded communism in economic life. If one examines the history of early capitalism—in sixteenth-century Italy, or seventeenth-century Holland, or even eighteenth-century England, it is evident that the early ideologies of the bourgeoisie had precious little to do with liberalism as a national policy or a public ideology. In fact, the bourgeoisie often bitterly fought those early reform legislations that in history became connected with their class mission. Even the ideology of latter-day capitalists can only by a considerable stretch of the imagination be connected to liberalism.

Liberals are often persuaded by their adversaries that they simply reflect and represent the capitalist ethos of *laisser-faire et laisser-passer*. But on close examination, one may discover that liberalism and capitalism represent parallel growth patterns. It may be that the liberal tradition has come to stand for capitalist styles and capitalist economies; but if so, this is a very late development in the history of capitalism. There is little historic correspondence between the liberal ideology and its presumed capitalist economic base. At the same time, it is important to recognize that the roots of many forms of socialist ideology, as Marx himself pointed out, lie deep in the feudalistic tradition and in the guild tradition. Thus, socialist ideology also does not necessarily stand as the ideological surrogate for the modern socialist economy. There is an autonomous realm to political ideology that is too often made short shrift of. Not to recognize the autonomous development and the special properties of ideologies is to falsify political sociology, to make of it a dialectical monstrosity where every doctrine has its place and every person knows his place.

Let us therefore proceed on the assumption that the time of pure capitalism was in a state of relative decline corresponding to an incline of liberal ideology. As a matter of fact, if we take England as our prime illustration of this hypothesis, the rise of liberalism corresponds with the rise of the political enfranchisement of the masses. And the major victories of the liberal parties in England from the midnineteenth-century Factory Legislation Acts to the midtwentieth-century Nationalization Acts came at the expense of the bourgeoisie. It may be said that liberalism functioned throughout the century as the advanced ideology of the most enlightened sections of the class that despised it. This is as true of twentieth-century United States as of nineteenth-century England. The liberal forces—the New Deal, for example—were despised by the bourgeoisie, and by the establishment sectors, even though these groups benefited most in the long run from the liberal reforms. If we understand liberalism in this way, we can better appreciate the tensions, ambiguities and uncertainties that have pervaded the liberal tradition in politics and society.

After making a somewhat ambiguous rejection of the extreme individualist view of libertarianism and opting for a more societal view of liberty within the framework of human obligation, the liberals turned their energies toward a theory of measurement. Societal development through liberalism became the measurement of progress. It was a way of defining where men were, where men are, and where men ought to go. Thus, the degree of liberalism become the measure of growth. Liberalism was the developmental ideology of the nineteenth century, and because of this, it became more than a bourgeois system; it also tried to account for the fact that there were other social classes in ascendancy such as the factory working class. The appeal of tne liberal ideology to broad sectors of society, especially in the urban sectors, was an appeal made on behalf of the progress, not simply the spiritual achievements, of the human race. It relied upon measurable commodities: the number of literate people, the number of educated people, the rate of gross national production, the growth and spread of urbanism, the growth and spread of secularism. These quantifications were characteristic hallmarks of the liberal measurement of progress; and they were the bedrock benchmarks of industrial Europe and America.

If we turn to the question of the essence of liberalism itself, we come upon what Isaiah Berlin (1954) properly calls two types of liberty: positive liberty and negative liberty. He means by a negative theory of liberty, the desire not to be impinged upon, to be left to oneself. Negative liberty is a recognition of the private self as being sacred and inviolable and the right of a man to a private self, that a man is more than a corporate entity. It acknowledges a private soul with private longings and with certain inalienable rights that do not stem from any contractual arrangement with state authority. The negative theory of liberty is the measurement of how much autonomy a man has in a society. The measure of that autonomy can be very practical: What are the conditions under which a person is penalized and what are the conditions under which a person is praised? Liberalism is an advanced form of calculus, not of hedonism, but of an exchange system based on the assumption that everyone has the capacity to assist and to be assisted. Given the fact that society makes certain demands upon a man, how many demands and on what bases? What is a man penalized for? Ethnicity? Nationality? Lack of patriotism? Race? Not voting? Within the framework of ideology, there can be violations of liberty in the name of libertarianism. If one is penalized for not voting, in what way is this an abbreviation of personal liberty? Those nations that boast that 99 percent of the citizenry participate in the vote are perhaps the most suspicious examples of antilibertarian attitudes. Perhaps a nation with 48 percent of its people voting is a better example of the right of the private citizen not to participate. In other words, a negative theory of liberty is concerned with the degree to which personal autonomy is preserved in society. Generally speaking, this cult of the individual has characterized both western European and American varieties of liberalism.

The central European tradition has been different. Its concerns are linked with a positive theory of liberty—that is, the liberty to perform tasks with efficiency and effectiveness. This view can be traced in a direct line from Spinoza through Hegel; and it can be found in Marx and many of the European socialist figures of the nineteenth century. This positive theory of liberty has to do with the notion of mastery, of control, rather than autonomy. The liberty to play an instrument, for example, can only be derived by mastery of that instrument. This notion of liberty carries over into a concept of the state. One cannot be at liberty in a state unless one knows the effective rules of that state, so that liberty depends in part on an appreciation of that system that enables men to survive. Political liberty thus becomes identified with political participation. These are very sharply divergent notions of what liberty means. Liberty from (liberty in the sense of autonomy) and liberty to (liberty in the sense of control) provide the poles of the libertarian framework.

These traditions are not easily resolved. To be sure, Isaiah Berlin does his best, but he fails; in the end he is content to stand with a negative theory of liberty derived from the utilitarianism of John Stuart Mill. However, the ambiguities within the liberal tradition are imposed not simply by other forms of political ideologies, but by the metaphysics of the concept of liberty itself. The liberal literature, insofar as there is a conscious liberal literature of the nineteenth or twentieth century, shows that the contradiction between negative and positive theories of liberty becomes increasingly pronounced as liberals become engaged in the political arena. For once the issues are joined at the level of instrumentalities, and the gloss of common agreement on goals is pierced, liberalism is subject to the same stresses and strains as any other political doctrine.

Liberalism as a nineteenth-century doctrine is essentially linked to the belief that each person should count as one irrespective of his property holdings or irrespective of his monetary worth, that in the political arena one citizen is as important as any other citizen. In this way, elitism was challenged, in effect, by maintaining the equality of men in the political arena, irrespective of differences in the economic arena.

But there was a curious anomaly that arose: The fathers of liberalism wanted more than a minimum amount of liberty. Their real goal was maximum noninterference. But they also understood that it is unlikely that such a demand for liberty has ever been made by other than a small minority of highly civilized human beings. If only a small, articulate group of human beings can recognize their right to liberty, in what way can it be said that liberalism is any less an elite doctrine than the conservative doctrine it sought to replace. In short, if the liberal intent is to convince people capable of the exercise of free conscience, and if it is true that the exercise of free conscience in all situations is perhaps the most difficult and impossible task for all but the smallest minority, then liberalism is only another variant of elitism. To be sure, the elite is dedicated to values which command mass support, and even mass sympathy. Nonetheless, while the purposes of liberalism insofar as they are not undermined by the elite formulations themselves remain dedicated to the democratic ethos, there is a recognition that only a small minority of highly civilized men can be liberals in any profound sense.

By the end of the century, the classical liberal position was as much a minority point of view as any other ideology. It was not only that liberalism resolved itself into a bourgeois position; but rather that even the bourgeoisie was incapable of maintaining itself in a liberal framework. The class anomaly concerning liberalism continued well into the twentieth century; even at present this dilemma continues to exercise decisive intellectual constraint within the political framework and the state.

What liberalism represents now is, in a theoretical sense, not that much different from what it represented in the last century. But the challenges and the threats are different. The nineteenth-century threat to liberalism was aristocratic. The twentieth-century threat is from the masses. It is not so much that liberalism has changed as that the opposition to liberalism has changed and broadened.

In comparing an enlightened twentieth-century liberal like David Riesman with the best of the nineteenth-century liberals, one finds less difference and more intellectual continuity than in most other political traditions. The shifts in conservative thought between the nineteenth and twentieth centuries were numerous primarily because early conservatism was marginal. There is less discontinuity within the liberal tradition.

Take the question of optimism, or the optative mood, as C. Wright Mills liked to call it. The liberal point of view conveys a long-standing infectious optimism, for liberalism has always been connected with the doctrines of progress and evolution. When liberals speak of change, they usually assume that the organism is susceptible to alteration, and they rarely think of the organism as requiring an exorcism or elimination. Therefore, when liberals speak of men of power, the tendency is to speak of how this power can be acted on.

This strong optimistic mood historically has pervaded liberalism as an assumption, among even the most sophisticated of its adherents—things can be changed by direct action, and the sources of power are divided enough and open enough so that it is possible to act on these sources of power and make the appropriate changes in the system. This is precisely the point in the twentieth century that has so sharply divided the socialists from the liberals. Socialism represents a form of historical pessimism. It represents a statement about the impossibility of change or of effective political action from within. Liberalism makes precisely the reverse assumptions about the openness of the system. Indeed, one might say that optimism enables liberalism to function as a dominant force within current American life, because liberalism provides reinforcement for the theory that the American system is an open system and viable and subject to change.

This optimism within the liberal framework has to do with effective

interaction between selective groups. It is more elite than mass oriented—
dominated by the belief in the impact of a letter upon a congressman, or
the effectiveness of a private session between a man of knowledge with a
man of power. It is faith in legal procedures, in the rule of the law. Liberalism in its own way celebrates the ideals of the system. Liberals always act
as if the definitions of the social system are circumscribed by constitutional
limitations and constraints; as if the formal rule of law is always and everywhere upheld. As a result, no one is more thwarted by the realities of the
situation than those who accept the ideals of the system as the norm. Thus,
the liberal, acting as if the Bill of Rights exists fully, and as if all constitutional safeguards are upheld, often mistakes normative behavior with
juridical ideals.

Liberalism makes the assumption that the rule of mind or of reason
will uniformly win out over raw power. Perhaps this is its great virtue;
unless men act as if the ideal were at least possible to implement, the ideal
can never be realized. It is, therefore, no accident that the victories of
liberalism have been legalistic. Organizations such as the American Civil
Liberties Union are its ultimate achievements in the practical realm of
politics because they take law as sacred and demand that powerful people
and the agencies they direct live up to law. It is liberalism's strength that
it makes this demand, because this provides an idealistic fervor within it
that is sometimes thought to have vanished in the dust of English constitutional history.

Lippmann (1922, pp. 414–415) summed up with particular clarity
the relationship between social stability and faith in reason.

> It is only on the premise of a certain stability over a long run of time that
> men can hope to follow the method of reason. This is not because mankind
> is inept, or because the appeal to reason is visionary, but because the evo-
> lution of reason on political subjects is only in its beginnings. Our rational
> ideas in politics are still large, thin generalities, much too abstract and
> unrefined for practical guidance, except where the aggregates are large
> enough to cancel our individual peculiarities and exhibit large uniformities.
> Reason in politics is especially immature in predicting the behavior of
> individual men, because in human conduct the smallest initial variation
> often works out into the most elaborate differences. That, perhaps, is why
> when we try to insist solely upon an appeal to reason in dealing with
> sudden situations, we are broken and drowned in laughter.

Lippmann never tells his readers whether this derision of reason and stability is to be endured in silence, or somehow met full force. It is clear that
Lippmann sensed that liberalism functions best in consensus situations, when
conflict is low and outbursts at a minimum. But, of course, the evolution
of the twentieth century has denied ideal conditions for the perseverance
of liberalism.

Within the legal framework of a democratic society, the liberals have no problems; they simply assume that the law must be obeyed at all times. But suppose the demand of the moment is for an illegal act of conscience, not necessarily political but yet clearly illegal—such as the activities surrounding absolute laws of sex, marriage and divorce. Here the liberals have a genuine dilemma. Namely, do they support free conscience or established precedence? The right of the free conscience stems from roots that are often extralegal in character. Then how does the liberal behave? Does he behave in terms of extralegality or within the framework of law?

If one conceives of liberalism as both a morality and a polity, when the morality is identified with the polity, there is little dilemma in action; but when the demands of the morality contradict the demands of legality, the liberal position either vanishes into a form of acquiescence in law or a rejection of law, and therefore a form of radicalism which presumably the liberal seeks to move beyond. The rule of law or the rule of men is the liberal's dilemma. He celebrates the former, but is often compelled to act in terms of the latter.

The student movement deserves to be examined from the point of view of liberalism. In many cases, the administration wants civics and the students want politics. The peculiarity of civics is that the norms of legality are always upheld. The administration in such a situation does not always want a rejection of activity as such. They are, rather, interested in civic action. But they fail to appreciate that the student movement is often a demand for politics and that politics in contrast to legislation is often extralegal. Every demand for a change in law is a demand for something other than what presently governs men. The extralegal wing has become the radical wing. Such specialized interest-group movements presume a kind of moral conservatism, even though they exhibit an ideological radicalism. Interest groups reveal a demand for reduced organizational constraints. It is a demand to be irrational, if for no other reason than to deny the rationality that the society wishes to impose. In this way, social protest often is compelled to move beyond liberalism, not so much on ideological grounds, but simply as a means of organizational survival. Often the leading figures in political protest are not always the most judicious figures. For many, liberalism becomes a fetter to action, and hence a poor ideology for generating social protest.

For its critics, liberalism offers partiality, fragmentation and indecisiveness. It offers a middle range between whatever is at one extreme end and whatever is said to be necessary at the other. It accepts the partiality of the world in a way that no other doctrine of the twentieth century does. Here again, what appears to critics as weakness is perhaps the ultimate strength of liberalism, for underneath the shibboleths and rhetoric of liberalism is something important. It is the assumption that one can live a life without knowing all the answers. The strength of liberalism is that it does not offer fanaticism, that it makes the assumption that the world is not always going to be fully known, and that men can yet act within a

SYSTEMS

partial frame of reference. The more one emphasizes the fragmentation of
the world, the more one must insist on the pragmatic values of men, the
less can an argument be made for action as good in itself.

Every action depends in some measure on the belief that the act will
bring about the desired change. If there are no warrants that an act will
result in the anticipated goals, then how can one assume the necessity for
the act as such? The liberal position is dangerous above all for the liberal
himself, because at the same time that he must acknowledge the fragmentary
quality of the world, he must act at least as vigorously as those who have
a dogma, who have firm solutions. This is where the liberal tradition has
had its gravest trials and tribulations. To the degree that it emphasizes the
act, to that degree it moves toward fanaticism. To the degree that it emphasizes fragmentation it leads to resignation. So that, at the end as at the
beginning, whether from the point of view of action or quietism, positive
versus negative theories of liberty, liberalism is a gigantic ambiguity, and
perhaps for that reason both a success and a failure—depending on what
criteria are used for measuring success and failure.

Charles Frankel (1956), who himself must be ranked a firm advocate
of the liberal system of organization and action, appreciated the degree to
which the belief that science represented the consolidation of empirical
methods became the great spur to the liberal outlook. He also appreciated
the extent to which this identification of liberalism to science was in fact
the Achilles heel of that ideology.

> The disasters already accomplished by technology, and the greater disasters
> that are threatened, have undermined the genial assumption that there is
> a simple connection between engineering and happiness. The belief that
> there is a necessary connection between progress in knowledge and
> progress in morality has been shattered by the spectacle which the Fascists
> and Communists have placed before us of bestiality joined with technical
> efficiency. We see that disinterested science means the gradual elimination
> of mythological codes of thought has been challenged by the emergence,
> in this most "scientific" of ages, of mythologies whose intellectual quotients
> are in inverse proportions to the primitive character of the passions they
> evoke. (Frankel, 1956, pp. 39–40)

And while Frankel, like Lippmann before him, appreciates that the special
divination that provides a scientific rationalization for liberalism is simply
beyond redemption, lacking any alternatives, he still insists on the need for
a nonsanctioned liberalism, something that at least deserves a "fighting
chance." In a sense, Frankel, like many articulate liberals, is himself engaged in the task of unmasking the limits of the liberal doctrine—only, upon
examining alternatives, the liberal group remains intact precisely because
the options appear to be so gruesome to the cultivated mind lurking behind
the commodity fetish.

The traditional liberal theory of government rests not so much on a theory of checks and balances but, more purposely, on the weighting given to each of the factors that comprise governance. For the essence of liberalism is not simply a division of powers between executive, legislative and judicial branches; nor is it simply the mechanisms for adjudicating the relationships between all three. More profoundly, the nature of liberalism implies the representative will of the people, as expressed in the legislative branch and in the judicial check. This is so over and against potential presidential abuses of power. It is no accident that the traditional liberal formulations always involve the assumption that government governs best when it governs least. Nor is it an accident that from an empirical point of view the liberal credo has found itself, more often than not, opposed to executive power and supportive of judiciary power.

Indeed, the central difference between traditional and contemporary variants of liberalism is the shift from legislative to executive emphasis. As liberalism has become increasingly linked to the amelioration of social problems, and not just the defense of individual rights, this shift from a suspicion of government to a celebration of government has become pronounced. In a sense, the traditional liberalist formulation was far closer to the modern conservative formulation than either is to a modern liberalism from the New Deal period onwards. The stimulus to such a reformulation of liberalism was the manifest weaknesses of a business civilization that could no longer sustain a laissez faire posture and survive. Under the circumstances, it is quite understandable why liberalism, the cardinal ideology of such a business civilization, also changed its orientation toward federal government.

Louis Hartz (1955), writing at a time when it was still fashionable to declare "that the Bolshevik Revolution represents the most serious threat in modern history to the future of free institutions" (1955, p. 302), nonetheless best appreciated the reasons for the thriving of liberalism in American soil. "America represents the liberal mechanism of Europe functioning without the European social anatagonisms." In elaborating this point, Hartz indicates that the main danger to the liberal society is not the principle of majority rule, "but the danger of unanimity, which has slumbered unconsciously behind it." That is to say, Hartz has ably understood that liberalism is not simply a credo of the wide-open Jamesian universe, but a fixed dogmatic position that comes close to identifying itself with Americanism and the course of Empire.

> Surely, then, it is a remarkable force: this fixed, dogmatic liberalism of a liberal way of life. It is the secret root from which have sprung many of the most puzzling of American cultural phenomena. Take the unusual power of the Supreme Court and the cult of constitution worship on which it rests. Federal factors apart, judicial review as it has worked in America would be inconceivable without the national acceptance of the Lockian

creed, ultimately enshrined in the Constitution, since the removal of high policy to the realm of adjudication implies a prior recognition of the principles to be legally interpreted. (Hartz, 1955, p. 9)

This special brand of liberalism takes root in the United States because the democratic system is not one to be fought for, but simply part of the birthright of the American. It is for this reason that liberalism is both so ingrained and yet so dogmatic within the American context.

Conservatism has largely based its claims on elites, and therefore on the will of the executive. Radicalism, too, has based its claims on vanguards who are uniquely qualified and endowed to feel the pulse of the masses. These pulse takers are, in effect, a totalitarian equivalent of executive power. But within this framework, liberalism has uniquely seen the legislative and executive branches as those agencies of power that insure legitimate authority and also the rights of the people. This emphasis on the will of the people as individuals, with every man counting as one, better explains the staying power of liberalism as a practice than the simple division of powers incorporated in the theory of checks and balances. Liberalism has come upon hard times, in part as a consequence of the emergence of executive power as supreme.

Liberalism stands, too, for a sharp demarcation between state power and government power. That is to say, in marked contrast to either extreme conservative or extreme radical regimes, the expression of powers implies a separation of those who have decision-making power—namely the political branch—from those who carry out the everyday affairs of ordinary men, or what can be called governmental power. That is why the liberal society has come to be clearly demarcated by its separation of the political and the bureaucratic. For separation of the political man and the policy-making man, was in its own subtle way, the extension of the doctrine of separation and the balance of powers. What has taken place over time to erode this situation, is the emergence of bigness itself, and the veritable collapse of representativism. For one man to represent a constituency of 1,000 is quite different from one man representing a constituency of 500,000. As a result, society's political apparatus has grown distant from the people, and more and more socio-political functions are lodged in the hands of policy personnel or bureaucratic officials. Thus a gap emerges between the elected official and the appointed official, a gap that once again adds to the strain on the liberal ethic of every man counting as one. The origins of ilberalism are linked to a petty bourgeoisie era of small handicrafts industries, small factories, small-size management firms, and the like. Its ethic rests heavily on a town hall doctrine of visible elites performing visible tasks. The emergence of antiliberalism—at least as a systematic arrangement—coincides with the enormous growth of technology, large-scale factories, assembly-line production, and the like. When the individual, in fact, counts for less than the running of a society. The very emphasis on bureaucratic efficiency sets in motion all sorts of potential for anomie and alienation, thus also opening the way for the demise of classical liberalism.

In this same vein, liberalism as a classic doctrine rested not only on individualism but also on proprietary rights in a world of small-scale homeowners with small-scale plots of land. The individual's value to the social system was determined, in part, by the value of his property. The erosion of property as a source of wealth—at least as the main source of wealth—and of the rights of the commodity as the key to the creation of wealth, removed a major underpinning of the liberal ethic. Thus the shift from small-scale property based capitalism was itself a main factor in the change in the nature of liberalism (cf. McClosky, 1969).

But if liberalism suffered as a result of the displacement of property relations by industrial relations, it also gained at another end—at the sociological end. It opened up vast new channels of mobilization and participation in the social system for the nonpropertied person. The extension of the educational apparatus became the key to upward mobility. It raised a question not of birth, but of performance—and beyond that, introduced the notion that competence rather than excellence was the essential criterion in an achievement society.

Robert Paul Wolff (1968, p. 149) shrewdly points out that contemporary liberalism is more than merely a ritual preference for the middle of the road: "It is a coherent social philosophy which combines the ideals of classical liberalism with the psychological and political realities of modern pluralistic society." Wolff goes on to state the social purposes served by a pluralistic liberalism in America.

> It eases the conflict among antagonistic groups of immigrants, achieves a working harmony among the several great religions, diminishes the intensity of regional oppositions, and integrates the whole into the hierarchical federal political structures inherited from the founding fathers, while at the same time encouraging and preserving the psychologically desirable forces of social integration which traditional liberalism tended to weaken. (Wolff, 1968, pp. 149–150)

A number of commentators have seen the partial character of liberalism, or better, its failure to acknowledge the possibility of the wholesale reorganization of society. Wolff makes this point with telling effectiveness.

> Pluralism is humane, benevolent, accomodating, and far more responsive to the evils of social injustice than either the egoistic liberalism or the traditional conservatism from which it grew. But pluralism is fatally blind to the evils which afflict the entire body politic, and as a theory of society it obstructs consideration of precisely the sorts of thoroughgoing social revisions which may be needed to remedy those evils. Like all great social theories, pluralism answered a genuine social need during a significant period of history. Now, however, new problems confront America, prob-

lems not of distributive injustice but of the common good. We must give up the image of society as a battleground of competing groups and formulate an ideal of society more exalted than the mere acceptance of opposed interests and diverse customs. (Wolff, 1968, p. 161)

It is interesting to note the degree to which discussion of twentieth-century liberalism seems inevitably centered on the United States. The locus of political experimentation has shifted from England, the model of classical liberalism, to the United States, the locus of pluralistic liberalism. And in the shift is also the transformation of liberalism from a political doctrine of ruling through consensus, to a sociological doctrine of accomodating through interest-group determinations. And while it is proper to note that the core problem of liberalism has shifted from law (distributive justice) to economy (the common good), none of the critics has thus far indicated what a better society would look like. For nearly all the critics of liberalism are themselves liberals, or at least antitotalitarians, and this very fact indicates that if liberalism is in deep trouble, its critics are no less in a bind of coming up with a social system that "works" better.

In an American social order in which everyone counted as one, competence was sufficient; excellence was viewed as an elite importation. Liberalism underwrote the idea of upward mobility with a corollary idea: that all men can do just about all jobs, given half an opportunity; they may not be able to do the job brilliantly or perfectly, but they can do it competently. And in this way, education became a touchstone of the new liberalism—the nonproprietary type.

What has shaken the roots of this new liberalism is that the very fact of mass education in the achieving society has created once again a search for distinctness and difference, or an attempt to get beyond competence and once again into something unique. What this has meant is a return to concepts of property—this time, in the form of suburbia and the antiurban patterns of living. Beyond that, it has also meant the return of ethnicity, race and all of the demarcations of a special sort that set people apart from each other and that are not subject to egalitarian definitions or educational mobility. Thus, the challenge to the new liberalism is not so much the massification of society as its mythification. The desperate search for individuation in a mass society has taken a distinctively nonliberal turn, and the new ways of racialism and ethnicity certainly demonstrate this fact.

The emergence of a system of checks and balances and educational mobility, introduced a further refinement in the liberal credo, namely the notion of institutional autonomies—or what has since come to be known as pluralism, in which religion, education, legislation, and the like, all coexist alongside each other in harmonious balance, and in which every person can participate—whether he is a member of the Parent Teachers Association or a member of a professional society. The very plethora of voluntary associations in America seems to underwrite an era of good will—

an era in which pluralism and liberalism became fused into a single uniform doctrine.

And, in point of fact, examples of this do abound for a society of a plurality of organizational forms and differential memberships. But what has taken place simultaneously, to deprive liberalism of its glorious victory, is a fusion of economic, political and military institutions. Whether or not one adheres to a doctrine of power elites, the concentration of power and the disproportionate role played by economic and military institutions has prejudiced the liberal faith in educational, religious and social institutions. That is to say, the pluralism exists, but it exists within a larger context of concentrations of power, which is ferocious in size and has nothing to do with liberalist notions of mobility and success.

The liberal position, in terms of law and order, is basically a faith in the concept of authority; that is, in the internalized, individualized expression of wants and needs, in the behalf of the legitimacy of those who hold power—not just a faith of those who hold power. Liberalism exists within a delicate mosaic where power exists—but only because it is fair in its execution. And in a world where every man does count as one, and where every man does hold property, and every man does vote—such a system of authority can indeed be said to have prevailed.

What took place, however, is the rise of the delegitimation process along with the mass society itself; the reliance on force and violence rather than rational decision making, both by those who are the holders of power and those who contest such power, immediately changed the name of this social game from authority to power. The question of law was subsumed under a question of force, and the question of legislation became subsumed under the question of voting blocs and special interest groups. In such a world, liberalism lost much of its clout, for the whole concept of liberalism as a juridical event rests upon a concept of benign participation and benevolence rooted in education and legislation, and moderated by the consensus that prevails between those who rule and are ruled. In fact, liberalism never really admitted the gap between those who rule and are ruled, but rather presumed that all men ruled and all men are somehow ruled by others. The very breakdown of a system of balance, the very disequilibrium between the powerful and the powerless, rendered liberalism very weak—if not simply a rationale for the powerful. The hatred exhibited for liberals, from both the conservative and radical sectors, in no small part stems from the unwillingness of liberalism itself to confront a system which is not based on harmonies and equalities, but one rather based on elites and masses, and ruled and rulers, and so forth.

Liberalism survives basically in a situation where long-range goals are feasible and where these goals can be actualized by a consensus apparatus. But to have long-range goals presupposes the social system that has time, and presupposes a network of fundamental agreements and a series of disagreements only on tactical questions. To the contrary, radical and conservative doctrines tend to deny the existence of this long range, and function rather in terms of a series of crises or the assumption of crises. They tend, therefore, to set up the ideal of immediate gratification and immediate reform, and in this sense, it is simply an empirical issue—whether, in fact, the society has a long time to survive and grow. For if it does, the capacity of liberalism is increased, but if it does not, its capacity is seriously reduced. To a considerable extent, the rise and fall of liberalism in America has to do with assumptions about the long-range viability of the American society itself. The heyday of liberalism coincides with assumptions of that long-range viability, and that means the whole of the nineteenth century, until up to World War I. But in a century of total war and in a shrinking imperial system, this same liberalism yielded and buckles before conservative and radical thrusts.

The very items that made liberalism great in the past cause it great anguish in the present. For liberalism was identified with open-ended theorizing, with evolution, and above all, with the goals of science and its products. All of the shibboleths of science were linked into one network of fact and theory; evolution, industry, growth, progress, technology and science itself. And all of these had a ring of goodness that provided easy-to-demarcate signposts of growth, and each growth testified to the worth of liberalism itself.

But here, too, liberalism was cursed at the moment of its highest successes because the very artifacts produced by technology, and the very theories produced by science, were seen to be at least as destructive of human impulse and human goodness, as creative. That is to say, the ability to create mass annihilation, based upon the systematic use of science and technology, was a shocking illustration of the gulf between science and society, between the goods that men produced and the uses to which they are put.

Mills (1963, pp. 187–195) outlined five assumptions of liberalism which made this ideology a force in the past, but which are no longer viable as a result of changed social structure. First, it assumed a coalescence of freedom and security that tears apart when security no longer is assumed to rest on small holdings, but rather on big absentee ownership—the very sort of ownership that has as its asking price personal freedom. Second, it assumed the preeminence of rural areas and rural values, and this has simply been outstripped by the growth of centralized cities. Third, it assumed the autonomous development of political, social and economic factors, factors that in the present have been melted and blended. Fourth, it assumed that individualism is the seat of rationality, but the growth of a bureaucratic organization of knowledge had led to buying and selling of knowledge as a collective community. Fifth, liberalism assumed a ready identification of the holders of power and authority; and it is precisely this that has become difficult to locate and explicate.

But Mills's most telling point is that liberalism, long opposed to Marxism for its severance of means and ends, has simply reversed matters, and divested ends from means.

> Liberalism, as a set of ideals, is still viable, and even compelling to Western men. That is one reason why it has become a common denominator of American political rhetoric; but there is another reason. The ideals of liberalism have been divorced from any realities of modern social structure that might serve as the means of their realization. Everybody can easily agree on general ends; it is more difficult to agree on means and the relevance of various means to the ends articulated. The detachment of liberalism from the facts of a going society make it an excellent mask for those who do not, cannot, or will not do what would have to be done to realize its ideals. (Mills, 1963, p. 189)

The most telling weakness in liberalism comes about through the gap between science and society. Many of its theorists, from James to Dewey to the present, assume automatically that the spirit of science is good and that the spirit of liberalism is scientific. But the clear and obvious demonstration that all social systems, fascist or communist, can make use of basic science and can maintain a network of scientific programming and planning, sent shock waves into the liberal world. It made it evident that the canons of science do not automatically translate themselves into canons of liberalism. And the recognition of this fact, whether it be through the camp at Auschwitz, or the bombs of Hiroshima and Nagasaki, ended once and for all the liberal monopoly on science and instead created the possibility of a scientific monopoly of liberalism.

Lowi's (1969, pp. 288–314) four counts against the liberal ideology, followed by three counts against its pluralistic rationalization, constitute perhaps the most succinct and damaging indictment delivered thus far. As such, they deserve extensive statement.

> [1] Interest-group liberalism as public philosophy corrupts democratic government because it deranges and confuses expectations about democratic institutions. Liberalism promotes popular decision-making but derogates from the decisions so made by misapplying the notion to the implementation as well as the formulation of policy.
> [2] Interest-group liberalism renders government impotent. Liberal governments cannot plan. Liberals are copious in plans, but irresolute in planning. Nineteenth-century liberalism was standards without plans. This was an anachronism in the modern state. But twentieth-century liberalism turned out to be plans without standards.
> [3] Interest-group liberalism demoralizes government because liberal governments cannot achieve justice. . . . They cannot achieve justice because their policies lack the *sine qua non* of justice—that quality without which a consideration of justice cannot even be initiated.
> [4] Finally, interest-group liberalism corrupts democratic government in the degree to which it weakens the capacity of government to live by

democratic formalisms. Liberalism weakens democratic institutions by opposing formal procedure with informal bargaining. Liberalism derogated from democracy by derogating from all formality in favor of informality.

By far, the most interesting criticism of liberalism is contained in the third and fourth points. Liberalism has long held that the trouble with most theories of power is that they denigrate or simply ignore the forms of judicial review upon which power is checked by the will of the majority. Here, however, we find Lowi saying that liberalism, by reducing laws to a series of informal norms and interest-group balancing acts, is little else than a veiled form of power concentration theory. The difficulty with this argument is that Lowi is forced into the position that conservatism alone is the defender of the legal framework and the formal polity. But precisely this position serves to partially blunt, if not entirely compromise, Lowi's radicalism; since at the very least, radicalism is no more concerned with the preservation of the legal edifice than is liberalism.

The criticisms Lowi offers of the pluralist component in liberalism seem more telling. They reduce to three interrelated propositions (Lowi, 1969, pp. 294–296):

[1] The pluralist component has badly served interest-group liberalism by propagating and perpetuating the faith that a system built primarily upon groups and bargaining is perfectly self-corrective.

[2] Pluralism has failed to grapple with the problem of oligopoly or imperfect competition as it expresses itself in the political system.

[3] Finally, the pluralist paradigm depends upon an idealized and almost totally miscast conception of *the group*. Laissez faire economics may have idealized the firm and the economic man but never to the degree to which the pluralist thinkers today sentimentalize the group, the group member, and the interests.

It is intriguing to note the extent to which all discussions of modern liberalism are linked to pluralism. And it is clear that it is precisely the difference between the old-fashioned analysis of whole systems from the new-fashioned analysis of actions within the system that demarcates the old from the new liberalism.

REFERENCES

Berlin, I. (1954) *Two Essays on Liberty.* New York and London: Oxford University Press.

Frankel, C. (1956) "Liberalism and the Imagination of Disaster," in his *The Case for Modern Man.* New York: Harper & Row.

Hartz, L. (1955) *The Liberal Tradition in America: An Interpretation of American Political Thought Since the Revolution.* New York: Harcourt Brace Jovanovich.

Lippmann, W. (1922) *Public Opinion*. New York: Macmillan.

Lowi, T. J. (1969) *The End of Liberalism: Ideology, Policy and The Crisis of Public Authority*. New York: Norton.

McClosky, R. G. (1969) *American Conservatism in the Age of Enterprise*. Cambridge, Mass.: Harvard University Press.

Mills, C. W. (1963) "Liberal Values in the Modern World," in *Power Politics and People: The Collected Essays of C. Wright Mills,* ed. I. L. Horowitz. New York: Oxford University Press.

Wolff, R. P. (1968) *The Poverty of Liberalism*. Boston: Beacon Press.

CHAPTER 8

ANARCHISM: FROM NATURAL MAN TO POLITICAL MAN

From its historical beginnings, a linguistic ambiguity resides in the term *anarchism*. The ambiguity is not exclusively a failing of language. It is a consequence of the claims and counterclaims, currents and crosscurrents that necessarily plague a social movement simultaneously dedicated to "propaganda of the deed" and "scientific liberation from political myth." For the anarchists are theorists and terrorists, moralists and deviants and, above all, political and antipolitical.

The concept of anarchy conjures up two contrasting visions. On one hand, it describes a negative condition—that which is unruly or disorganized, that which is not controlled or controllable. Sociologists might say that a condition of anarchy prevails when any event is unstructured, or lacking in norms, such as spontaneous crowd behavior. These negative connotations of anarchism have penetrated the scientific no less than the popular literature. Nonetheless, there is also a popular positive notion of anarchy as conscious rebellion, which entails a view of anarchy as "unrule" because formal rule systems are unnecessary and superfluous in the governing of normal men. The phenomenon of altruism, or self-sacrifice of personal ambition, indicates that spontaneous behavior is not synonymous with irrational behavior. We are thus confronted with a negative concept of anarchy as a condition of unruliness in contrast to a positive view of anarchy as a response to the superfluity of rules.

Anarchist negation is embodied by an event, or an agency of events, such as the group that rejects external pressures in the form of adjustment to a context of prevailing norms of superimposed rules. Conversely, positive anarchism, anarchy as affirmation, means the "internalization" of rules to such a high degree as to do away with the need for external constraint altogether. This ambiguity in anarchism has as its theoretical underpinning an idealization of natural man in contrast and in opposition to civilized man.

At least one of the confusions is not so much the work of anarchism as of the commentators on anarchism who consider it to be exclusively a historical movement or a political organism. Some historians see the demise of anarchism in 1914, or with the absorption of anarchist ideals by social reformers and the awakening of "social conscience" in the middle classes (Tuchman, 1963). Others consider anarchist ideas to have been absorbed by mass union and political movements (Cole, 1954, pp. 315–360). And still others place the final death throes of anarchism in 1939, with the collapse of the Spanish Republic (Woodcock, 1962, esp. pp. 393–398). What seems to unite the historical school is a consensus that, however fuzzy the origins of anarchism might be, there is no question about its definite terminal point. The plain truth is that as a historical force anarchism never had much of a reality. When Bakunin remarked upon 3,000 anarchists in Lyons, he considered their number an extraordinary achievement. And even in republican Spain, the anarchist "organization," Federación Anarquista Ibérica, could claim only a fractional (and factional) membership.

What characteristically distinguishes anarchism from other radical movements is precisely the low premium placed on immediate political success, and the high premium placed on the fashioning of a "new man" in the womb of the old society. The great Italian anarchist Errico Malatesta, who bridges nineteenth- and twentieth-century European thought as few of his peers did, put the matter directly in *Le réveil:*

> Our belief is that the only way of emancipation and of progress is that all shall have the liberty and the means of advocating and putting into practice their ideas—that is to say, anarchy. Thus, the more advanced minorities will persuade and draw after them the more backward by the force of reason and example. (Quoted in Cole, 1954, pp. 356–357)

The classical anarchists, Bakunin, Malatesta, Sorel and Kropotkin, share a concept of anarchism as a "way of life" rather than as a "view of the future." What is offered is a belief in "natural man" as more fundamental than and historically prior to "political man."

Civilization is viewed as a series of impediments and obstructions preventing the natural man from realizing himself. This represents an inversion of Hobbes' doctrine of the "war of every man against every man." In Hobbes, the Leviathan exists for the exclusive purpose of curbing "the solitary, poor, nasty, brutish, and short" character of natural man. From the anarchist standpoint, Rousseau's doctrine of the natural goodness of man is only a partial solution to the problems presented in Hobbes' view of human nature. For whether man is "good" or "brutish" is less important to the anarchist than what men do to preserve their inner core. Rousseau shares with the power theorists the idea that self-preservation requires men to contract out their private rights. The Rousseau paradox is that to gain survival entails a loss of humanity. Rights are swallowed up by obligations. The state absorbs civil society. Natural man is outflanked and outmaneuvered by society.

The anarchist rebuttal to this line of reasoning is that to make a contract, which is an involuntary act to begin with, is really to compromise the natural man. If man is really good, then the purpose of life, in contrast to the purpose of politics, ought to be the restoration of the natural condition of human *relations* at whatever level of human *development* thus far achieved. This is not exclusively a matter of internalizing felt needs, but, no less, a form of shedding that which is superfluous and unnecessary. Intrinsic to anarchism is an asceticism and an ascetic mood. One finds the anarchist as a historical figure to be a person very close to "natural" values and "fundamental" living conditions. Their attitudes toward matters of food, shelter, sexuality and the generalized expression of human needs in the social economy are simply that all needs can be satisfied once the "natural laws of society" shed the impediments of civilization. This sublime faith in the natural in contrast to the social accounts to a considerable degree for the central peculiarity of anarchism—the absence of a well-worked-out commitment to economic development.

Precisely because economics in its advanced form must necessarily cope with problems of affluence, consumer and producer demands, distribution of goods, allocation of natural resources and the like, the anarchist tends to consider economic prognostication as catering to both the impossible (because prediction is unfeasible for future social systems) and the unnecessary (because any "rational" economy would center on "production for use"). Even in its specifically economic form, such as in the work of Pierre Joseph Proudhon, anarchism makes little attempt to chart the contours of a rational economy. Proudhon's critique of property relations is everything Marx said it was: abstract, grandiose in statement and rhetorical in content. Piecework is described as the "deprivation of the soul," machinery becomes the "protest against homicidal labor," and economic history as such becomes a "sequence of ideas" (Proudhon, 1846 and 1891).[1] Even those later figures, like Bakunin and Kropotkin, who accepted the main contours of socialist economics, did so more as an instrument by which

[1] In contrast, see the critique by Marx (1935).

the restoration of the feudal workshop could be achieved than as a guide to the study of economic realities.

There is a perennial tension between the naturalistic character of anarchism and its emergent participation in socialist currents. On frankly moral grounds, the anarchists opposed the stratification of men into classes. Social classes violate the natural equality of men in their psychological–biological characteristics. Anarchism tends to distinguish wage laborers from factory owners in terms of the moral properties of work rather than the alienative features of class relations. A strong pietistic religious element is present: work is good, idleness is evil; the poor are noble, the rich are sinful. Men are naturally equal, but they are socially stratified. Real and legitimate differences are obscured by social position and by family property. Anarchist man sees differences in terms of the quality of mind of each person, the degree of self-realization and self-fulfillment and the extent of socialization. Capitalist man is the accommodating man: solicitous when profits are at stake, brutal when workers are at stake, cruel when the social system is at stake.

The anarchist image of life is in terms of a moral drama—a drama in which individuals are pitted against social systems. It is little wonder, then, that the anarchist has an apocalyptic attitude toward social classes. Abolish class relations, and the natural man will come to fructification. This attitude toward classes is comparable to the approach that nudists take to clothing. Eliminate clothing, and all people will immediately perceive the absurdity of clothing, as well as its harmful psychological by-products such as repression and guilt. So, too, runs the anarchist argument. Abolish social classes, and the absurdity of class distinctions will immediately become manifest. The absurd by-products of the class system—oppression of the poor by the rich, impoverishment of the many on behalf of the few and so forth— will give way to the new dawning. Just how this process will install an economy of abundance and distributive justice becomes a matter for future generations to discuss. Just as it would be metaphysical to discuss the problems that would occur in a world of naked people, so, too, the anarchist holds that socialists are metaphysicians for attempting to anticipate the problems as well as the contours of society without exploitation and an economy without classes.

This tension between "naturalism" and "socialism" is also present in the anarchist stance toward politics. The whole world of politics is itself an embodiment of authority, or arbitary power. At some level, the definition of politics is necessarily linked to the exercise or restraint of power. The whole concept of politics has as its perfect social expression superordination and subordination, just as in the previous illustration the whole notion of economics has as its basis mastery and slavery. Once again, then, the reason the anarchists take an antipolitical position, not simply against certain forms of politics but against the content of politics as such, is that the notion of superordination and subordination, resting as it does on a social concept to justify power, is a superfluity, a civilized manner for expressing the social fact of inequality. The point of view of most anarchists is that the doctrine of self-interest arises only at that point when the interests of society are schismatic or bifurcated. When it is seen or felt that the self is something other than the society, only at that point does hedonism become a force.

The political doctrines of anarchism are totalistic. They are anti-egoistic, because egoism is an expression of civilization. They are antifatal-istic, because fatalism violates individual liberty. The propensity of natural man is voluntary association based on the practice of mutual aid. The concept of mutual aid, while sharing many properties of altruism, differs from the latter because altruism implies conscious surrender of self in an egotistical milieu. Mutual aid is socially systematized. There is no longer any psychology of egotism in anarchist society, and therefore there can be no altruism, for it would have no psychological basis. One would not perform an altruistic act; one would perform social acts at all levels—whether in defense of self or on behalf of other persons. Egoism as a division among men would be broken down in the anarchist world, creating the possibility of a truly human association that at the same time overcomes the distinction between the public and the private.

This utilitarian "mutual aid" aspect of anarchism is dominant and fully expressed from Godwin to Tolstoy. It was particularly suitable as the ultimate expression of the plight of the modern peasantry. Collectivist anarchism departs from this social stress to the idea of the individual's war against the state as a form of self-preservation. The ever-enlarged scope of bureaucratic domination had led anarchism to emphasize the need to survive under the pressures and censures of society.

What characterizes contemporary anarchism, as contrasted with earlier forms, is the highly personal nature of the revolt against authority. There might very well be a sense in which the anarchism of intellectuals is a very special variant of anarchism. It possesses three distinguishing qualities: (1) emphasis on individual responses, on the "politics of truth"; (2) rejection of professionalism and departmental academicism; and (3) belief in the sanctity of the "private life." In the intellectual's powerful sense of the distinction between public and private, which D. H. Lawrence in particular has pointed out, and the image of the fighting private intellectual, there is an anomic kind of anarchism, if one may speak of *anomie* in this connection.

In its classical model, the notion of the fighting romantic against the world is antithetical to anarchism as a theory, but quite in keeping with the psychological characteristics of anarchists as people. The anarchist as a person tends to be highly deviant, closely allied to the criminal sectors in European society and to the lumpenproletariat in the United States, the tramps, hoboes and rummies. While the anarchist does not define himself as a criminal (criminality is seen as a form of lower-class egotism—excus-able rather than practicable), he does not consider the criminal, as does the bourgeoisie, to be "an enemy of society." Indeed, they have close dealings; anarchists have at times hired out as professional criminals to commit assassinations and bank robberies in Italy and Spain. But the anarchist who steals does not do so for his own self-interest. He carefully allocates funds, making sure that nothing is used for creature comforts. He will kill, but he is very careful not to harm anyone who is innocent from the viewpoint of the class struggle. He will cajole, but not for the purpose of keeping the reins of power. The goal, however ill defined, is all-important. And the means used in its attainment (the overthrow of the state and of the class system) are moral by virtue of these aims. Therefore, the means used are conditioned only by the question of their efficiency; no ethic is attached to them. Clearly, the anarchist is not a pragmatist. He does not accept the idea that there is a means–ends continuum. The purposes of violence determine its good or its evil character—and not the fact of violence as such. This dichotomization gives to the anarchist the appearance of criminality, while distinguishing his essence. It also provides for a life style that is often awkward and difficult to manage—since he must work with egotists while maintaining his altruism, and cooperate with derelicts while urging a "new man" theory of social change; and he must oppose totalitarianism in theory while maintaining authoritarian personality traits in personal habits and behavior.

The fundamental development of anarchism as a social agency for change and as an intellectual mood reached full expression in the nineteenth century. It is not inconsequential to take note of the philosophical climate and technological level surrounding this development. The philosophical point of view underlying classical anarchism is not so much Hegel's dialectics as it was Kant's ethics. The only true morality that the anarchist would recognize is one in which there would no longer be a distinction between what is done for oneself and what is done for others.

A derivative of this is the antitechnological claims of anarchism. These turn out to be fundamentally petit bourgeois or peasant. The notion of community was very strong in utopian varieties of community life. Small-scale farming and small-scale industry, where there was indeed intimacy and rapport between the people at work, where work itself was an organizing principle and a viable one, were a vital principle of life writ large. This combination of the technology of the small factory and the small farm, linked as it was with a highly rationalistic Kantian image of what a moral man defines the communal obligation to be, reveals the anarchist as antitechnological in his stance just as previously he is described as antipolitical and antieconomic. He is total in his commitment to a social ethic in which the personality is part and parcel of that social view. And the alienation of men from the sources of their labor, and from the machine directly, violates this social ethic. Because anarchism in its most distilled form is the idea of the brotherhood of man and the *naturalness* of this equality, any separatist movement, such as nationalism or racialism, that has imaginary pressures from the exploiting strata of every state has to be sharply opposed. The main evil of nationalism is not solely that it breeds wars, but that it does so because nationalism is *unnatural.* Civilization sets up arbitrary differentiations so that national distinctions intensify and exaggerate factors making for conflict: patriotic gore, class animus, racial purity. They are unreal and susceptible to dissolution and alteration. Their only reality derives from the power relations that are caused by class domination and legal rationalization.

The philosophic stance of anarchism is juxtaposed against the power relations of society. Anarchism is a commitment to the idea of nature, to the belief that nature is an "essence," while society is an "accident." It stands in contrast to the idea of existence because the concept of existence, as it has unfolded in both Marxist and existentialist thought, involves problems of revolution, of change in terms of other men, in terms of a fundamental theory of the redistribution of power, in terms of the redistribution of wealth rather than the notion of wealth as such. So that the difference between socialism and anarchism is primarily a difference between those who would abolish the forms of social relations as they now exist and those who would abolish the content of all hitherto existing class society. The socialist has ultimate visions of future society through the redistribution of power, property and so on. The anarchist sees any such compromise as stillborn and doomed to perpetuate in new form the same divisions that have riven society historically. For the anarchist, the root of the problem is society; for the socialist, the root of the problem is class. This helps explain, in addition to the fierce personality clashes, the bitterness between socialists and anarchists. Their philosophical and ideological premises differ despite the superficial acceptance by both of a communal economy. It is shallow to say that the difference between anarchists and socialists is tactical, that is, that socialists would postpone the abolition of the state while the anarchists want to abolish the state now. What underlies this tactical difference are contrasting theories of human nature.

Anarchists regard socialists as corrupted by the political structure because they accept the premises of the bourgeois state—order, constitutional limits, parliamentary procedure and the like—in order to wrest power. By failing to destroy power, they are corrupted by it and perpetuate the state they are pledged to overthrow. The anarchist assumption is that to better civilization is a subtle form of corruption, of self-delusion. What is required is abolition, not improvement. Not even the word "revolution" really encompasses the anarchist ideal. Revolution is the idea of the radical change in the forms of life. The anarchist notion of abolition is more profoundly radical in its implications because of the distinctions between contamination through the acceptance of the forms of civilization and regeneration through the breaking of such civilized forms. The socialist changes society, leaving inherited civilization intact. He reforms its worst abuses. His arguments are for a higher development of civilization. The anarchist rejects the inherently constricting and corrupting nature of civilization and demands total reconstruction of the human condition. He means to annihilate the sociological, economic and political features of human life that we have come to consider fixed. The practical socialist claims no more than the right to humanize and equalize the power structure. The impractical anarchist claims to do no less than liquidate state power as such.

THE ANARCHIST AMBIGUITY

We inherit many stereotyped notions about political movements. Perhaps one of the most common is that of the bearded, bomb-throwing and blasphemous anarchist. And though the more priggish devotees of anarchism would wish to deny that any truth inheres in the stereotype, even historical truth, it must be admitted frankly that, like most stereotypes, this one has much to recommend itself. From the *Narodniki* in czarist Russia, to the anarchist mine workers of Catalonia and Asturias in Spain, to the Wobblies of the Industrial Workers of the World (IWW) in the western part of the United States, anarchist social movements have been violent in practice if not always in "theory." To be sure, anarchism traditionally counterposes the "force" of the nation–state against the principled "violence of the great unwashed" (Sorel, 1929, p. 67; and 1950, pp. 247–248). But the brute fact remains that a cornerstone of anarchism has been its militant and spontaneous activism.[2]

On the other side, the anarchist literature (and we must face the fact at the outset that anarchism exists in this day and age more as a literature than as a movement) frequently operates out of a sweeping stereotype of its own: a view of the social system as inhabited by alienated proletarians, anomic professionals and anxiety-ridden policy-makers. This, too, is a stereotype with considerable punch behind it. Indeed, the two-pronged anarchist attack—upon a bourgeois society become insipid and infirm with age, and upon a socialist state become more corrupt and bureaucratized than even the most ossified form of capitalism—is not restricted to anarchists by any means. A spate of literature, from analytic to poetic, bristles with the same charges. The social sciences have taken over the anarchist claims against bureaucracy with their trenchant critique of the dysfunctional nature of the organizational life.[3]

We do not settle what anarchism stands for by a simple cataloging of the social systems it opposes. For on such matters, anarchism stands close to the entire frontal assault made on capitalism—from nostalgic conservatism to utopian socialism. The classic definition of anarchism is as an ideology and as a philosophy standing for the immediate liquidation of all

---

[2] Even so humane an anarchist as Emma Goldman (1931, p. 88) wrote: "Does not the end justify the means? What if a few should have to perish? The many could be made free and could live in beauty and comfort."

[3] For recent examples, see Presthus (1962, pp. 287–323) and Whyte (1956, especially pp. 155–185).

state authority. But the close observer will immediately perceive that this is a negative recommendation rather than a positive option. It is a central purpose of this chapter to elicit, through both text and commentary, the chief principles and aims by which anarchism as a body of social theory either stands or falls.

The American now lives in what sociologists have termed the "overdeveloped society." Social scientists have sternly warned us that the bureaucratic machinery that makes this overdeveloped society tick is fast approaching a condition of diminishing returns. The organizational complex has substituted a chain of command for individual initiative, automatic salary escalations for promotions based on personal merit, problems of communication for differences of class and an overall bureaucratic pathos in place of treating issues as they arise in each instance. The psychiatrists have put us on notice that this bureaucratic machinery has taken a huge toll in disrupting normal human impulses and relations. The economists have been no less clear in pointing out that the costs of supporting this Leviathan are paid for by keeping the largest portion of humanity in a socially underdeveloped condition.

In the face of this matrix of public issues and private agonies, the dominant human response to giganticism has been a retreat to the private world of friends and nuclear family, where the home becomes not so much the castle as the fortress against any further penetration by the monster state. But at the same time, this dichotomization of life rests on the total separation of public policy and personal ethics, on an acceptance of the permanent existence of the manipulative state and the manipulated man. Recent studies of the American electorate indicate how complete is this passive acceptance of the situation. Political parties are described as having "no differences," while outrages to public sensibilities are met with the resigned statement: "You can't fight City Hall." In this situation, the good American becomes the clever American: the man who can "stay out of trouble," the man who can "work within the system" rather than one who fights the system.

Given such a set of public factors—of the complex organizational apparatus, of the deterioration in citizen participation through voluntary association—it scarcely requires any feats of mind to show that modern industrial life is incompatible with the anarchist demand for the liquidation of state authority. Anarchism can be no more than a posture. It cannot be a viable political position. The anarchist reader concerned exclusively with problems of political decision making should return this book and demand a refund—indeed, if a refund can be made without wild snarls of credit memorandums. One can afford to be forthright about discouraging the political minded anarchist because this audience, potential or otherwise, is miniscule. It is precisely this fact—the ineluctable separation of the American overdeveloped society from the underdeveloped science of politics —that still makes anarchism an interesting, if ambiguous, point of view.

For the bulk of our public have little beyond postures by which to live in any event. And perhaps it is useful to explore a literature that unpretentiously declares itself nothing but a posture, an attitude of mind and a style of life. Indeed, anarchism has become, in this generation, an effort to stay the hand of the "iron law of bureaucracy," an attempt to fashion a personal code of ethics that consciously refuses either to abide by the rules or to work such rules to personal "businesslike" advantage.

In terms of the social forces utilizing the anarchist credo and posture, a remarkable transvaluation of values has occurred. In the eighteenth century, the chief advocates of anarchism were recruited from the European peasantry, with its plethora of utopian communities, religious societies and aristocratic idealists, all poised against the onslaught and inevitable victory of the industrial capitalist system and its political affiliate, the Leviathan. In the nineteenth century, anarchist doctrine found a new home among the working classes of industrial Europe. In the specialized trades, in the trade unions and in working-class voluntary social associations, anarchist pirnciples took on new vigor. But once again the wave of organization swept "spontaneous" working-class anarchism into the dustbin of history. The complete victory of trade unionism and social democracy in Western Europe, and of bureaucratic state socialism in Eastern Europe, further separated anarchist doctrine from proletarian practice.

Nonetheless, anarchism has proven to be a stubborn if self-conscious minority posture. Modern life has created its own standards of success and failure. And there are enough "failures" to fill any ten mass movements. The rebirth of anarchism in the twentieth century has been due to a general disaffiliation of "intellectuals" and "professionals" from the general celebration of the affluent society. This portion of society, while enlarged as a consequence of the growing need for expertise and exact knowledge, has also been the most defeated victim of overdevelopment. The man of knowledge has been "on tap," but rarely "on top." Knowledge has been effectively separated from power, just as clarification has been isolated from manipulation.[4]

In consequence of this very bifurcation, modern society has created the first collectivity of natural anarchists, people who are resistant to absorption within the establishment and whose antipolitical rejection of affiliation is part of the self-definition of an intellectual. The bases of intellectual activity require spontaneity in a world of precision and order, individuality in a universe of collective responses, risk taking in an organizational arrangement geared to "line" and "staff." Because of this polarization of social life, anarchism has remained a factor in modern societies. The intellectual is antipolitical by social training and personal habit. The anarchist is antipolitical by intellectual conviction. The wedding of these two elements defines the scope of present-day anarchism.

---

[4] Cf. C. Wright Mills in Horowitz (1963, pp. 599–613).

The great anarchist Peter Kropotkin (1912, pp. 92–93) anticipated this fusion of intellect and anarchy when he outlined the basis of scientific activity:

> There is one point on which Anarchism is absolutely right. It is in considering the study of social institutions as a chapter of natural science; when it parts forever with metaphysics; and when it takes for its method of reasoning the method that has served to build up all modern science and natural philosophy. If this method be followed, errors into which Anarchists may have fallen will be easily recognized. But to verify our conclusions is only possible by the scientific inductive-deductive method, on which every science is built, and by means of which every scientific conception of the universe has been developed.

Whatever its defects, anarchism has attempted to adhere to the canons of scientific method. And whether by conscious decision or by indirection, intellectual activity has become increasingly anarchist in posture. Thus, however "ambiguous" the anarchist legacy may be, it remains a useful one and a needed one.

A TYPOLOGY OF ANARCHIST STRATEGIES AND BELIEFS

However contemptuous contemporary anarchists may be of the ordinary standards of political success and failure, within its own frame of reference, anarchism reduplicates this general concern for political realities no less than political truths. This is expressed with admirable clarity by Kropotkin (1909, pp. 579–580) in his work on the French Revolution. He points out that anarchism is not only a series of brilliant ideas but a historical entity as well:

> All through the Great Revolution the communist idea kept coming to the front. Fourierism descends in a direct line from L'Ange on one side and from Chalier on the other. Babeuf is the direct descendant of ideas which stirred the masses to enthusiasm in 1793; he, Buonarotti, and Sylvain Maréchal have only systematized them a little or even merely put them into literary form. Blanqui and Barbés conspired to create secret *communistes matérialistes* organizations under the *bourgeois* monarchy of Louis-Philippe. Later on, in 1866, the International Workingmen's Association appeared in the direct line of descent from these societies. . . . There is therefore a direct filiation from the *Enragés* of 1793 and the Babeuf conspiracy of 1795 to the International Workingmen's Association of 1866–1878.

In examining the basic forms of anarchism, we do not mean to imply the existence of distinct doctrines. What is at stake is not so much alternative models of the good society as distinctive strategies for getting there. Therefore, the differences in forms of anarchism involve details of priority rather than programmatic rhetoric. Should the first step include or exclude violence? Should the state be liquidated as a consequence of the workers' organization from below, or must the first stage in organizing a system of mutual aid in terms of liquidating the state? Should anarchism strive for victory through numbers or through conspiratorial techniques? It might appear strange that an *ism* that has generally never been in a position to muster any significant political support should be so preoccupied with principles and programs. Yet, historically, it is a characteristic feature of minority movements, unburdened as they are with problems of the exercise of political power, to be schismatic and factional in relation to their principles and precepts. The struggle for purity is as essential to political messianism as the sacrifice of principles is characteristic of actual rule.

Furthermore, it is evident that while anarchism has undergone integral transformations in terms of changing demands placed upon it by the inner dialogue, the converse is no less the case: Anarchism is subject to changes in terms of differing historical circumstances. The Godwinists' concern for universal justice was a direct outgrowth of the English bourgeois revolution with its exceptional concern for the juridical forms of change. The Bakunists' sanction of organizational terror was likewise framed in the spirit of Russian *Narodniki,* who saw no other possible means of toppling the autocracy. The impulse behind the doctrines of violence propounded by Malatesta and Sorel was clearly a disillusionment with organizations as such, with their "oligarchical" tendencies that Robert Michels (1949) so brilliantly summed up in *Political Parties.* Present pacifist varieties of anarchism likewise reveal a response to the concentration of armed power in the hands of the emissaries of government, and hence a need to fashion tactics that can circumvent this monumental fact without destroying anarchists as such. The "rage to live" that is witnessed in the writings of literary anarchists is just as true to the canon of rebellion to state tyranny as earlier forms; however, it sees individual acts of terror as hopelessly meaningless in an age that takes systematic extermination of populations for granted.

The types of anarchism that have evolved represent a double response: to the internal tensions and strains of doctrine, and no less to the changing social circumstances in which anarchism found itself at given historical periods. What is revealed in the varieties of anarchism are different seats of social and class support, contrasting attitudes toward the utility of political combat, different psychological and philosophical support and contrasting organizational methods. This may not produce theoretical coherence or, for that matter, success in the public arena, but it does prevent the kind of doctrinal stultification and stagnation that has overcome a good many *isms* that at one time or another could claim a far larger number of adherents. And this very fact must appear as a central feature of the anarchist tradition.

UTILITARIAN ANARCHISM

The first conscious form of anarchism represented a compound of nostalgia and utopianism—a natural enough consequence of a doctrine developed by an enlightened sector of the aristocracy and later employed by the sansculottes. Utilitarian anarchy ever remained an expression by the déclassé wealthy on behalf of the underprivileged of society. The poor had not yet learned to speak for themselves, so an element of surprise is ever present in the writings of Helvétius, Diderot and Godwin, that there should be an ever-widening distinction between rich and poor, between social gain and social responsibility. The utilitarian anarchism even of a Saint-Simon was not so much a form of rational consciousness as it was a form of embarrassment in search of guilt alleviation. The solution was to be reason—the manufacture of reasonable creatures from below, and the appeal to rational authorities from above. Self and society, private and public, ruler and ruled were all to be united under the banner of reason, in the path of which stood the accursed state.

As befitted men of sensibility and good sense, not the direct action of masses, but the edict of rational rulers was to be the central agency for eliminating, first the iniquities of the State, and later the state itself. The equation was relatively simple: Education plus legislation equals the good society. The present tendency is to offer a perfunctory dismissal of these earliest expressions of anarchist sentiment; and clearly, modern experience offers sound reasons for this. Nonetheless, it should be recalled that utilitarian anarchism did a great deal to shape the modern vision of human nature as plastic and progressive. It understood, indeed, that men can be rendered happier by a more reasonable social order and that they would be more orderly rather than less so, given a more equitable distribution of power and wealth.

This eighteenth-century form of anarchism suffered from the deformations and exaggerations of the aristocratic sector that gave it original shape and that remained present even when it was taken over by the conspiratorial elements within utilitarian anarchism. So volitional a creature was man, according to this view, that historical forces simply dissolved. Just as the slate could be wiped clean, so, too, was society to be cleansed of its repressive mechanisms. Cultural antecedents, malignant classes, vested interests, competition for power—each and all were to be eliminated in the wave of reasonableness that was to overtake rational and responsible men. From Helvétius to Godwin, the assumption was clearly that knowledge and truth could overcome ignorance and interests. What Kingsley Martin (1929, p. 191) wrote of the utilitarians in general has a particular relevance in understanding the apocalyptic antihistorical basis of the early anarchists: "They never dreamed that if men were offered the truth they would not leap for it, that if they were told ugly facts they would prefer pleasant lies, that if reasonable ideals were offered them they would continue to act as their fathers had done; they did not see that the follies of the past were not only imposed but ingrained, that men carried their history not only on their backs but in their heads." It might be added that when the recognition of these historical truths became manifest, the aristocracy that fashioned the early versions of antistate chose to sacrifice its revolutionary awareness and to preserve its inherited privileges. The decline of utilitarian anarchism was a consequence of a double force: the rise of the consciousness of poverty by the propertyless and the growth of compromise rather than criticism as the path chosen by the dwindling aristocracy to maintain its privileged place in the empire of capital.

PEASANT ANARCHISM

The other major current in early anarchism had as its basis the gigantic European peasantry, which, despite the process of industrialization, remained the largest single class in Western society down through the nineteenth century. Indeed, the process of industrialization led to a celebration of the verities and the virtues of the land. From Thomas Munzer to Charles Fourier, there was a pervasive and widespread sentiment that capitalism meant the growth of external authority and not the age of progress the bourgeois spokesmen were so fond of heralding. Unlike the utilitarian anarchists, the peasant anarchists put little faith in reform from above. Instead, they urged a withdrawal from the state as such and the setting up of informal communities based on principles of mutual assistance and social service.

The anarchist communities represented an effort to escape the profanation of all values under capitalism, and to avoid the liberalist solutions put forth by capitalist apologists. The industrial process and the wealth it produced, far from being a liberating agent, was for the peasant anarchists the ultimate form of human degradation.

In describing the individual and organization in utopian ideology, J. L. Talmon (1960, pp. 127–136) shows what the peasant spirit held to be most sinful in the capitalist spirit. In it one can see the moral bases of later socialisms:

The capitalist system, which claims to be wholly purposeful, encourages wasteful parasitism, and is in turn to a large extent fed on it. There are the throngs of innumerable middlemen, agents, lawyers, useless clerks, who eat at the expense of others, without producing anything useful. Their whole raison d'être is to incite their begetters and bread givers to greater and more refined acts of rapacity and fraud, and to stultify the victims thereof. The State machinery, gendarmes and army, tax collectors and magistrates, customs officers and civil servants, allegedly existing to "protect" society from commercial piracy and abuse, are in fact the accomplices and instruments of the fraudulent conspiracy.

In such a situation, any appeal to the reasonableness of the holders of power and wealth must appear absurd. The peasant anarchists had little regard for the philosophers and their liberal sophistication. They tended to emphasize the curative power of work, especially of productive cultural work.

But in this emphasis on peasant verities, they came upon the inherited concerns of the Church and its interests in preserving and salvaging the souls of the poor. Thus, peasant anarchism was compelled to pay special attention not only to the bourgeois liberal enemy but also to the religious and conservative "enemy." In Fourier, it took the form of a critique of ascetic and repressive morality. Such an outlook only perverted the truly human gains of mutual aid in the communities of land by making man into "a creature of insatiable cupidity." The goodly peasant must therefore avoid not only the lures of the City of Man but also the perversions of the City of God—or rather the construction of Providential Will given by corrupt, property-holding clerical forces.

The high regard in which later anarchist spokesmen, such as Proudhon and Bakunin, held the peasantry, marks one of the great watersheds between anarchism and bolshevism. For what is involved is nothing short of the difference between a theory of peasant revolution and a theory of proletarian revolution. The polemics of Lenin against Sismondi, and of Stalin against the Russian *Narodniki,* can only be appreciated in a context in which the peasantry remained the largest portion of backward imperial Russia—a portion that not a few socialists felt was being dangerously downgraded in the formation of a revolutionary movement.

The anarchist vision of the European peasant as an independent, hard-working, creative and potentially radical creature contrasted most sharply with the official socialist vision of this same creature as a "troglodyte," a self-seeking petit bourgeois, whose vision of the world was restricted to the sight of his fields. Leaving aside the special features of the western European peasantry (which tended to confirm the Marxist image rather than that held by Bakunin), it remains a fact that most present-day revolutions in the Third World have a very definite peasant character. The theory of proletarian revolution has had to be bent to a considerable extent to take account of this mass peasant force—that far from being a selfish and willing pawn of industrial capitalism, it has proven to be far more revolutionary than the Marxian tradition has ever officially acknowledged. Nevertheless, it must be acknowledged that the anarchist view of the western European peasant was far more rosy than the facts warranted. And even though anarchism may not have worshiped at the shrine of petit bourgeois life as such, through the medium of a "bourgeoisified" peasantry, it certainly did respond to petit bourgeois values—individualism, enterprise, dissociation and antipolitics. The failure of the peasantry of Europe to respond to anarchist impulses was, after all, the definitive answer to those who saw the solution in a withdrawal from, rather than combat with, the state.

ANARCHOSYNDICALISM

If the anarchism of aristocratic utilitarians was often aggressive and intellectual about the less vital questions of the day—such as vegetarianism, free love and a universal language—and the anarchism of the peasants moved in a narrow and parochial circle entailing negative attitudes toward the processes of industralization and urbanization, the anarchism practiced and preached by radical trade unionism proved of a sounder variety. It was first and foremost based on the realities of nineteenth-century European life; and it drew its support from the struggle between classes that was at the center of the historic drama. As one writer put it: "Anarcho-syndicalism is *par excellence* the fighting doctrine of the organized working class, in which the spirit of enterprise and initiative, physical courage and the taste for responsibility have always been highly esteemed" (Moulin, 1948, p. 137).

The marriage of unionism and anarchism in Europe was a natural consequence of the fear and hostility the more articulate factory workers felt concerning the bourgeois state. The organizational apparatus of skilled workers, in particular, often developed in conscious opposition to the state. The *Bourses du Travail* in France became a state within a state, as did the Swiss watchmaking guilds. The expansion of union activities within working-class life contributed to a mass political awakening by virtue of its very emancipation from politics as such. Fernant Pelloutier (1902), in particular, gave theoretical substance to anarchosyndicalism by connecting the economic struggle of classes with the direct political struggle to emancipate mankind from the state. The new men of labor were to assume all positive state functions, from the protection of proletarian rights to education in the possible forms of mutual cooperation. Anarchy was to be made over into a social force first and an ideological force second. The proletariat was to replace the peasant and the ideologue alike as the central element in the struggle against the bourgeois state.

The growth of anarchosyndicalism was greatly assisted by a new turn toward the problems of tactics in social revolution—something notable for its absence in older anarchist postures. The fusion of socialism and unionism was seen as functionally complete in the general strike. This was not viewed either as a strike for summer wages or as a widespread attempt to garner political concessions from the state. While the possibilities of immediate gains were not denied, the essence of the general strike was to evoke the deepest class allegiances and obligations of the workers. As economic strife between classes would become more intense, the meaning of the general strike would become manifest. The anarchosyndicalist strike would entail direct worker participation in a board social and economic upheaval. It would become an instrument for compelling the state to abandon its place on the historical stage to the direct association of the wage-earning class. For the most part, revolutionary unionism, such as that practiced by the IWW in the United States and the General Confederation of Labor in France, did not view the general strike as a replacement of the traditional economic strike. Rather, it was to supersede all pragmatic short-run strikes. Keynoting this approach was an intense disdain and a flat rejection of anything that the government or opposing politicians were willing to concede the workers. The general strike was antipolitical, conceived of as part of the permanent social revolution (Horowitz, 1961, esp. pp. 23–38).

The new wave of optimism that gripped anarchist circles in the late nineteenth century soon gave out. The workers cared less for political strikes than for economic strikes, less about the general strike and more about the wages of sin and the hours of leisure. The state proved quite as adept at absorbing proletarian interests as it earlier did bourgeois interests. The state as a mediative power obviated and blunted the sharp edge of anarchist criticism of the state as oppressor. The immense growth of an impersonal bureaucracy, the extension of the administrative aspects of state authority to cover worker interests, cut deeply into anarchist pretensions at forging a spontaneous mass movement of insurgency (See Pelloutier, 1902, esp. pp. 70–71, 184–189).

It was not simply the continued vigor of the state that caused anarcho-syndicalism to be short-lived. Nor, for that matter, can the dismal failure of this form of proletarian anarchism be attributed to the moral corruption of the working class as such. The deeper answers are to be found in the faulty formulations of the anarchosyndicalists themselves. Their problems ran along three pivotal paths. First, they tended to approach socialism as a reality around the corner, rather than as a long-range process of social reorganization. Beyond the general strike no precepts or principles were enunciated. Second, anarchosyndicalism abandoned the tasks of organization, preferring ready-made agencies of working-class life that were essentially unprepared (and unwilling) to engage in direct revolutionary action. Revolutions are not spontaneous events; they are made by men. And men, in their turn, either lead them to the promised land or turn them away from the implications of large-scale revolution. Finally, anarchosyndicalism failed to offer sound sociological or psychological reasons for getting men to act. It failed to distinguish between the ends of action and the stimuli to action. The simple announcement that a world without a state will be the outcome of a general strike neither proves that this will indeed be the result nor is likely to stimulate men to maintain and sustain a political act beyond the initial failures.

Anarchosyndicalism, which was itself a response to the disillusionment with appeals to monarchical rulers, and with parliamentary socialists, created its own forms of disillusionment as the workers increasingly turned toward the state as a mediative force in their conflict with the bourgeoisie. Anarchosyndicalism sought to engage in mass politics, while at the same time it wanted to escape the evils of political contamination. The paradox proved too great for the doctrine to resolve, and it was increasingly compelled to flee from the state, rather than defeat the state in a general contest of class wills.

With the collapse of anarchosyndicalism, anarchism as a class ideology increasingly gave way to anarchism as personal–moral redemption. Anarchism became a form of conduct rather than an instrument of class politics.

COLLECTIVIST ANARCHISM

Anarchism had within itself one remaining burst of *political* energy, that with which the names of Bakunin, Kropotkin and the First International are connected. This "collectivist anarchism" is to be distinguished from communist anarchism as preached by Malatesta. What it really hinges very much upon is "freeing" anarchism from a class base and placing it upon a mass base. The rhetoric of class is retained, but it is clear from the contents of the Bakuninist message that the concept of proletarian is more a matter of self-definition than of economic position in the factory system. In collectivist anarchism, the words "proletariat," "peasantry," "rabble," "people" and even "lumpenproletariat" are interchangeable. The battle line was drawn between the people and the state. Nationalism replaced the bourgeoisie as the great *bête noire* of the century. What was begun by the French Revolution of 1789 was to be completed by modern revolutions such as the Paris Commune—the destruction of the nation–state. Collectivist anarchism took firm hold of the humanist aspect of socialism—and accused the class theorists of violating the double purpose of socialism: the "smashing" of state power and the creation of voluntary associations along internationalist lines.

The position of Bakunin is particularly emphatic in summing up collectivist anarchist sentiments. The central elements are that the poor already carry the germs of true collective life and that the social revolution is prefigured by the life style of the very poor. The passage is worth quoting in full, since the differences between Bakunin and Marx were stated with full clarity.

By the *flower of the proletariat,* I mean above all, that great mass, those millions of non-civilized, disinherited, wretched and illiterates whom Messrs. Engels and Marx mean to subject to the paternal regime of *a very strong government,* to employ an expression used by Engels in a letter to our friend Cafiero. Without doubt, this will be for their own salvation, as of course all governments, as is well known, have been established solely in the interests of the masses themselves. By the flower of the proletariat I mean precisely that eternal "meat" for governments, that great *rabble of the people* ordinarily designated by Messrs. Marx and Engels by the phrase at once picturesque and contemptuous of "*lumpenproletariat,*" the "riff-raff," that rabble which, being very nearly unpolluted by all bourgeois civilization carries in its heart, in its aspirations, in all the necessities and the miseries of its collectivist position, all the germs of the Socialism of the future, and which alone is powerful enough today to inaugurate the Social Revolution and bring it to triumph. (Bakunin, 1950, p. 48)

At the core of collectivist anarchism lies the consideration that the state claims as its victim society as a whole, and not just any particular class. To be sure, under certain conditions the factory workers may receive the harshest treatment, but it is no less the case that historic conditions exist in which the factory worker may suffer far less as a result of the manipulative capacity of the state than other social factors. Therefore, the task of socialism is a collective one, since communism is a collective need. The purpose of the state is to break up the solidarity of all the oppressed— from the lumpenproletariat to the peasantry—and hence the role of the anarchists is essentially to prevent this catastrophic process from gaining success. It can do this best by exposing the hoax of patriotism, the chauvinism inherent in the system of nations, the duplicity involved in doling out favors to one exploited group over another.

Collectivist anarchism is thus seen as a continuation of the human as against the inhuman, a break with class theory and class solutions. The state principle is particularistic—favoring one group over another, exploiting the many on behalf of the few. The anarchist principle is its dialectical opposite. It is universalistic—favoring society as against the state, the great mass as against the very few. Collectivist anarchism is basically a midpoint between the class consciousness of the early pioneers and the humanistic consciousness of the present century. In Bakunin, one sees the constant swing of a pendulum: an attempt to broaden it so as to be universal in its inclusiveness. Here one also finds the effort to develop a broad-based politics, but no less an appeal to individual integrity and initiative as against politics in its profane practice.

The moralization of politics takes place through the general application of the principle of freedom (people) as the chief force opposed to the principle of authority (the state). Unfortunately for collectivist anarchism, the appeal to everyman had even less success than the appeal to class man. Its very universalism and moralism deprived it of any fighting core, of any "advanced sector." A wish-fulfillment element was clearly present: Collectivism was viewed not so much as a future condition of man as a present status assigned to the masses by the state. The powerless, designated as noble, good, true and healthy, really had no need of further organization in such a theory. In their very wretchedness, they were internally purified. Those furthest "outside of civilization," those most deviant with respect to conventional norms of behavior *were* good. In such a situation, the need for specific measures became unnecessary. The dissolution of Bakuninist organizations in Spain and Italy was perhaps brought about as much by the celebration of the poor as by the damnation of the rich. In short, it lacked a theory of alienation, and hence the need for practical steps to overcome this condition.

The insight of collectivist anarchism concerning the character of state power was its moralistic and petit bourgeois outcry against state authority. The fact was that political solutions did not resolve the paradox of authority by simply transferring coercive power from one class to another. The people's state or the proletarian dictatorship did not exactly mark a vast improvement over the aristocratic state or the bourgeois state, in terms of the reduction of public intervention over private lives. On this point, Bakunin scored heavily. The widening of the state apparatus, whether through evolution or revolution, to include the proletariat and the displacement of one class by another class does, indeed, have significance of a libertarian character.

The French Revolution may have been "aborted" by the bourgeoisie, but it is hard to doubt that significant changes would have taken place to better man's lot. Universal enfranchisement, a system of juridical checks on power, vast improvements in the services rendered by the state to its citizenry may not constitute real improvement. In this sense, collectivist anarchism missed the point of social revolution—which is that revolution is an adventure into new possibilities, and not an ultimate resolution. It continues historic processes, but does not resolve them in a final messianic burst of popular virtue. In opposing the "cult of the state" with the "cult of freedom," collectivist anarchism sharpened the differences between Behemoth and anarch—but it contributed little to maximize the area of human options and social reorganization.

CONSPIRATORIAL ANARCHISM

The general failure of anarchism to make an impression upon the population as a whole, and the corresponding growth in the centralization and bureaucratization of the nation–state, placed anarchism in a crisis condition. By the close of the nineteenth century, certain clear patterns had emerged: (1) Class membership no longer corresponded to class *interests* —the factory workers were not so much concerned with the acquisition of political power as they were with gaining a "fair share" of economic wealth; and (2) industrial technology undermined and outflanked anarchism by transferring the seat of power from the small artisan workshop to the big impersonal factory. What was increasingly required was counterorganization and not withdrawal from political society. Under such conditions as these, the anarchism of involvement received a new emphasis.

Conspiratorial anarchism acts on the premise that the state exists by force, by the actual or legal terrorization of the masses. The state is able to do this with small numbers because it has the force of arms behind it. Conspiratorial anarchism thus sought to emulate and simulate the techniques of the ruling class. The role of the state would be met with the violence of the anarch. The conspirators hoped to speed up the collapse of state power by a process of systematic assassination of the rulers and by stimulating widespread insurrection. The last part of the century saw the techniques of violence raised to a principle throughout Europe and America.

The United States has the distinction of having the most violent and turbulent labor history in the Western world and, at the same time, one of the least theory-involved publics (Hofstadter, 1963). In this situation, the United States offered fertile soil for conspiratorial anarchism. The arrival in the United States of Johann Most provided just the sort of theoretical support necessary to inflame working-class violence. Most's booklet of 1885 has as its instructive and definitive title: *Science of Revolutionary Warfare—A Manual of Instruction in the Use and Preparation of Nitroglycerine, Dynamite, Gun-Cotton, Fulminating Mercury, Bombs, Fuses, Poisons, Etc. Etc.* One can only wonder what the et ceteras refer to. He was most clearly infatuated with the direct response of force to the bourgeoisie, as can be seen in the following eulogy offered by Most:

> In giving dynamite to the downtrodden millions of the globe, science has done its best work. The dear stuff can be carried in the pocket without danger, while it is a formidable weapon against any force of militia, police, or detectives that may want to stifle the cry for justice that goes forth from the plundered slaves. It is something not very ornamental, but exceedingly useful. It can be used against persons and things. It is better to use it against the former than against bricks and masonry. It is a genuine boon for the disinherited, while it brings terror and fear to the robbers. A pound of this good stuff beats a bushel of ballots all hallow— and don't you forget it. Our lawmakers might as well sit down on the crater of a volcano or on the point of a bayonet as to endeavor to stop the manufacture or use of dynamite. It takes more than justice and right than is contained in laws to quiet the spirit of unrest. (Quoted in Adamic, 1934, p. 47)

The use of violence to counter the force of the state, wherever it occurred—in the Haymarket affair, in Coxey's Army, by the American Federation of Labor Dynamiters, in the Centralia Steel unionization, by the Wobblies of the West—all came to a frustrating and dismal end. The organizational power of the state could not be overwhelmed by the disorganized power of direct action. In America, as in Europe, the conspiratorial anarchists were hunted as criminals and punished with a vengeance reserved for murderers and kidnappers. The state unleased a steady stream of counterviolence that finally dissipated anarchist strength (and not incidentally, a good deal of socialist power). The state, in the form of the legislative groupings, for its part began to respond to industrial violence by increasing the pressure on all sides for nonviolent methods of resolution. Laws protecting the rights of workingmen considerably mitigated the class war of the previous period. In addition, new forces of unification arose. Nationalism, engendered by World War I, superseded labor strife. Class unity was restored. The Union was saved.

A serious drawback to conspiratorial anarchism lies in the difficulty of establishing the difference between ordinary murder and political assassination. The bomb outrage of Emile Henry in 1894 was condemned by fellow conspirators as the act of an ordinary bandit. Confusion was always occasioned by a division of opinion on this or that assassination. The assassination of Princess Elizabeth was condemned by some as foolish and considered by others as necessary. Similarly, the assassination of President McKinley had the same effect in the United States. Violence simply has no definition of limits. As Masaryk (1955), reminds us: "We must not forget that anarchism is a menace to the very anarchists themselves, that Kropotkin and Reclus were [themselves] threatened with death by anarchists." The line between egoistic criminality and altruistic assassination was crossed so often that this type of conspiratorial approach degenerated into sheer chaos. "The Metaphysics of anarchism becomes indeterminist; miracle plays its ancient role in the anarchist chaos; anarchist philosophers become poets; anarchist politicians develop into utopians" (Masaryk, 1955, pp. 393–399).

One might readily consider conspiratorial anarchism a short-lived failure. And measured in terms of the achievements it registered, this is so. The conspirators, however, raised to a new level of consciousness the plight of the lower depths of society. It produced extensive protective labor legislation. It implanted the juridical problem of the special quality of politically inspired coercion in contrast to the egoistic terror of the professional criminal. Above all, it accelerated a consideration of social and economic legislation relating to women, children and minority and immigrant groups. If this took place in an atmosphere of hostility to anarchism, it must also be said that anarchism, for its part, made a more radical posture feasible throughout Europe and America.

But for the anarchists themselves, conspiratorial techniques created yet an additional schismatic and factional element. The needs of the twentieth century moved revolutionaries into a more concerted effort to connect strategies to general ideologies. This, in turn, led to an extended period of working-class political organization that had little to do with the anarchists. Drawn from déclassé elements in society, from students, intellectuals, semiprofessionals and artisans, conspiratorial anarchists never had the kind of connection to proletarian life that could produce any kind of direct impact that might allow for a socialist renaissance. Violence gave way to organization. In the United States, Eugene Victor Debs's socialism took a commanding post. In France, Jean Jaures became the acknowledged leader of proletarian action (over and above the animosities of his anarchist critics). In Russia, the *Narodniki* gave way to the Marxism of Plekhanov, Martov and Lenin—to organizational socialism. What further insured the abandonment of conspiratorial anarchism is that the organizational socialists absorbed, rather than canceled, nonparliamentary methods. The tactic of illegality, while rarely resorted to in European socialism, was never abandoned as a possible ploy. The rhetoric, if not the content, of violence was thus made part of the general program of contemporary socialism—of Marxism.

COMMUNIST ANARCHISM

The cross-fertilization of radical ideas produced a form of anarchism that was at once a theoretical response to the extreme antiintellectualism of the conspiratorial factions and no less a practical response to the extreme intellectualism of the First International. The leading exponent of communist anarchism is unquestionably Errico Malatesta. Malatesta attempted to apply the principles of direct action early in his career. In a movement characteristic of Francisco Juliano's Peasant Leagues in Brazil, he headed a small group of armed men in 1874 that had the explicit purpose of liberating the peasantry of southern Italy from the domination of state and church. He encouraged the peasantry to seize the land and set up workers' collectives. This experiment in political independence through direct action was a constant theme in Malatesta's life. The fact that the insurrectionary movement was suppressed and overwhelmed each time it was attempted did not discourage Malatesta or, for that matter, lead him to revise his positive estimate of the possibilities of revolution.

The main point in the principles of communist anarchism is that violence should be intrinsic and organic to the goals sought. First, if force was to be used, it should not be a hit-and-run affair, but a concerted effort by the entire social class or sector of that class that had achieved revolutionary consciousness. Second, Malatesta sought to eschew the heavy premium on parliamentarianism that was ever characteristic of the First International. Third, there was a rejection of the anti-Marxism of Bakunin and Kropotkin. While no criticisms were made directly, a large gulf existed between the collectivism of Bakunin and the communism of Malatesta. The fact is that Bakunin hardly could be said to have escaped the leadership cult that gripped most anarchist factions in the First International. Malatesta and his allies Sergei Stepniak and Carlo Cafiero saw themselves as activists first and as leaders last. It was to be an activism conditioned by scientific socialism, by the laws of historical evolution and by the exacting labors necessary to forge a revolutionary apparatus—in short by Marxism rather than Bakuninism.

Communist anarchism was not opposed to violence on principle, but it was opposed to a form of violence that was not at the same time educative and instrumental in gaining lasting advantages for the oppressed.

> Certainly, in the present state of mankind, oppressed by misery, stupefied by superstition and sunk in degradation, the human lot depends upon a relatively small number of individuals. Of course, not all men will be able to rise in a moment to the height of perceiving their duty, or even the enjoyment of so regulating their own action that others will also derive the greatest possible benefit from it. But because the thoughtful and guiding forces at work in society are few, that is no reason for paralyzing them still more, and for the subjection of many individuals to the direction of a few. (Malatesta, 1949, p. 38)

If Bakunin sought to be the Marx of anarchism, so, in like manner, Malatesta can be considered the Saint-Simon of anarchism. The focus of communist anarchism was on organizing the mass of exploited for a general assault on the capitalist-feudal bastions. And to do this, "armchair" techniques were no better than "violent" techniques. Both had to be subsumed in a sociological appreciation of the general struggle between classes.

Communist anarchism comes close to urging some form of political organization if anarchism is not to be dissolved by parliamentary maneuvers. When Malatesta (1949, p. 29) asks rhetorically how to solve the problem of self-government and self-regulation, he inquires bitingly: "To elect a government of geniuses by the votes of a mass of fools?" While this is a sword intended to cut through the arguments of parliamentary socialists, it also reflects his belief in political action, which is at the same time organized action.

Theoretically, the main energy of communist anarchism is in proving that human nature is plastic enough for self-regulation without the need of state authority. As such, he anticipated Lenin's distinction between techniques of command and techniques of administration. Unlike many of his fellow anarchists, Malatesta distinguished between legitimate authority and illicit power. And as such, communist anarchism gave special priorities to separating those who have a "functional" role in society and those who have an "explosive" role.

> A governor is a privileged person, because he has the right to command others, and to avail himself of the force of others to fulfill his own ideas and desires. An administrator or technical director is a worker like others, in a society where all have equal opportunities of development, and all can be at the same time intellectual and manual workers; when there are no other differences between men than those derived from diversity of talents, and all work and all social functions give an equal right to the enjoyment of social advantages. The functions of government are, in short, not to be confounded with administrative functions, as they are essentially different. That they are today so often confused is entirely on account of the existence of economic and political privilege. (Malatesta, 1949, p. 30)

Communist anarchism distinguishes itself from collectivist anarchism by urging the abolition of government by the proletarians in the name of all mankind. Malatesta (1949, p. 32) felt that "it would be better to use the expression 'abolition of the State' as little as possible," since the state is only the federal expression of governmental rule. And what anarchism ought to strive for is the elimination of external coercion at any level—local, regional or national—and hence, for the elimination of government of men and its displacement by the regulation of things. The arguments adduced against those who maintain that men are selfish by nature, that regulation inadvertently spills over into rule and that the state may be manipulated to workers' demands are treated in the customary anarchist way. Psychological plasticity, social altruism and self-consciousness are all bastions against the corruption of anarchy.

There is an interesting anticipation of Durkheim's (1933) ideas on the *Division of Labor* in Malatesta's work. Anarchism is to be guaranteed in the first place, by each person's performing a useful function; in the second place, by elimination of all distinctions between town and country; and in the third place, by what Durkheim called the "collective conscience"—that form of social solidarity guaranteed by a consensus of interests and sentiments. Underlying communist anarchism is the same sort of philosophical telos operative in mercantile capitalism. Since each man knows that his own interests are directly plugged into social interests, he will himself assure accord with the principle of the greatest happiness for the greatest numbers. But it is precisely the factual dubiousness of utilitarianism that casts a long shadow over anarchism on the Left no less than mercantilism on the Right. It was difficult enough to cast a net and catch *one good man,* as the encyclopedists sought to do. But for a net to be large enough to catch *all good men* was more than doctrine could support. The equation of all society with the common search for happiness leaves out of the reckoning the alternative definitions of happiness that men harbor. As a result, the theoretical collapse of communist anarchism was inevitable. What held it in its course for any length of time proved to be the saintly charismatic qualities of its leaders; the rational behavior of its followers had little importance. The irony of communist anarchism is that in practice it rested so heavily for its support on the strength of its leaders, and so little on the revolutionary mass of the poor. The advantages of Leninism, of communism without anarchism, is that it made no such felicitous assumptions about the goodness of men, the spontaneity of social revolution or the capacity of a quick conversion from one social system to another without strife. That such advantages dissolved with the emergence of Stalinist absolutism may show just why Malatesta mistrusted any form of state communism. But in the course of events, this has to be reckoned a small comfort to one who made such great sacrifices for his convictions.

INDIVIDUALIST ANARCHISM

At the same time that European anarchism was undergoing a steady ramification, with an emphasis on mass strikes and general revolutionary violence, and developing some of the organizational features of political life, there arose a highly personalistic anarchism in America. Inspired more by Max Stirner than by Bakunin, Kropotkin or the "Latin" wing of anarchism, this variety of anarchism is distinguished by viewing the "ego" or the "person" as the repository of all that is human and self-determining, and the state as the repository of all that is inhuman and oppressive. Individualist anarchism shares with utilitarian anarchism a reliance on utilitarian philosophy, but it is distinguished by the extremely personalistic turn it gave to utility theory. Similarly utilitarianism in general is marked by two distinct stages: the French "sociological" variety and the English "psychological" variety. And like the English school of utilitarianism, the point of crossover between individualist anarchism and extreme conservatism was not always easy to define. Indeed, if Stirner provided individualist anarchism with its original rationale, it was the conservative critique of the state made by Jeremy Bentham, and later by Herbert Spencer, that provided this strain of anarchism with its sense of righteousness.

Individualist anarchism shared a vocabulary of sentiments and a theory of natural law with the classical conservatives. A cataloging of what this form of anarchism involved is not unlike a reckoning of the features one encounters in reading Lord Acton, Alexis de Tocqueville or Brooks Adams. Rather than recount the separate achievements of the leading figures of individualist anarchism, let us see what such disparate figures as Max Stirner and his American exponents, Josiah Warren, Lysander Spooner and Benjamin R. Tucker, have in common.[5]

1. The individualist anarchists believed that a collective society in any form was impossible without leading to an authoritarian system. They thus adhered to the concept of private property or individual proprietorship, insofar as this embraced no more than the total product of individual labor.

2. The purpose of society is to preserve the sovereignty of every individual without exception. Thus, all human associations based on limiting sovereignty, particularly the state, must be curbed and eventually eliminated.

3. The principle of mutualism was to be arrived at on a voluntary basis and in this way: through a withdrawal from all agencies and institutions of an involuntary kind, undermine all juridical and legislative authority.

4. The principle of individuality requires the absolute equality of the sexes, the absolute equality of the races and the absolute equality of labor for its success. Thus, anarchism must seek the extinction of interest, rent, dividends and profits, except as represented by work done.

5. The system of democracy, of majority decision, is held null and void. Any impingement upon the natural rights of the person is unjust and a symbol of majority tyranny. No rightful authority can be external to individual consent, and all such authority legitimizes civil disobedience, resistance and even destruction.

6. Any definition of liberty begins and concludes with the liberty of the weaker party in a nation. Since the majority always appropriates the right to legislate and enforce legislation, the true and basic test of liberty is always the right to disobey and violate such legislation.

[5] For a most useful compendium, see Martin (1953). See also Schuster (1932).

In many ways, individualist anarchism found its natural home in the frontier spirit of America. It was the perfect embodiment of "worldly asceticism" and represented a secularization of the Protestant ethos and the capitalist spirit of thrift and trust. In Europe, the anarchists found themselves involved increasingly in socialist politics and adopting a class position. It was the socialists, especially the Marxists, who attempted to purge the anarchists from the radical ranks. In America, the situation was reversed. The anarchist found himself increasingly espousing petit bourgeois causes, the rights of individual proprietorship. As such, the anarchists became the first consistent critics of socialism in America.

William Bradford Greene (1849, pp. 70–71) expressed the anti-socialist bias most directly. "In socialism, there is but one master, which is the State; but the State is not a living person, capable of suffering and happiness. Socialism benefits none but the demagogues, and is emphatically, the organization of universal misery. Socialism gives us but one class, a class of slaves." This passage might as easily have been written by William Lecky. And indeed, the *History of European Morals* (Lecky, 1870) contains not a few phrases of such an order. Benjamin Tucker, perhaps the best known and certainly the most prolific of individualist anarchists, said of Marx at the time of his death that he was the most "bitter of all enemies of anarchism." And, in turn, Tucker pledged anything that would combat Marxism, which "represented the principle of authority which we live to combat" (quoted in Martin, 1953, p. 219). Nor were the differences between individualist anarchism and all forms of collectivism matters of principle alone. The tactic of violence—propaganda by the deed—was vehemently opposed by men like Tucker. Speaking of the violent wing of American anarchism, of Spies, Parsons, Fischer and Berkman, he wrote that "if the revolution comes by violence, and in advance of light, the old struggle will have to be begun anew" (Quoted in Martin, 1953, p. 255).

Individualist anarchism sought to preserve the principle of rights over law and hence supported, at least passively, the anarchists indicted by the law courts for their acts of violence. But it also sought to make anarchism a respectable doctrine. And so it opposed the principles of violence and the acts defined as criminal that the European wave of collectivist and conspiratorial anarchists brought with them to the new world. Anarchism thus carried within itself a microscopic reflection of the general struggle going on throughout the nineteenth century in America between nativism and cosmopolitanism. Tucker went to rather desperate lengths to show anarchism in the most respectable light. He presented an analysis of the subscription list of his publication, *Liberty,* according to occupational and professional ranking (perhaps the first such example of mass communications research done in the United States!) to show that anarchists are not criminal either in fact or in theory.

The anarchism of Tucker, Spooner and Josiah Warren disintegrated for many reasons. Among the most immediate was the loss of nativism as a progressive value. Increasingly, it became subject to chauvinistic and conservative leanings, and correspondingly, it came to fear and loathe the introduction of unionism and political organization of the foreign-born as the direct consequence of mass democracy. Individualist anarchism thus joined intellectual bonds with know-nothingism—with that variety of anti-intellectualism that soon lost the need for intellectualist postures as such. Second, the very individualism of the American nativist anarchists made the establishment of "a central clearinghouse" out of the question. Pockets of anarchism soon became transformed into small literary clubs. The championing of private enterprise as the bulwark of state monopoly, made by near anarchists like Karl Heinzen, rendered anarchism useless for the advancement of working-class interests and superfluous, even absurd, as a rationalization of the ideology of laissez faire capitalism.[6]

If individualist anarchism made sense in 1870, with the rise of political boss rule, the collapse of Reconstruction and the centralization of authority through the liquidation of local self-government, it lost all meaning in an era of uncontrolled big business. In the early 1930s, with the country in a catharsis over the Depression and with mass unemployment on an unparalleled scale, the last voice of individual anarchism, that of Charles Erskine Scott Wood, was being raised in an outcry: "too much government" —this at a point when even corporate barons were ready to support federal legislation for the amelioration of the crisis in the American economy. The conclusion of Wood's (1931, p. 266) work makes plain the pathetic outcome of individualist anarchism:

We are interfered with and accustomed to control and dictation from the cradle to the grave in thought, speech and act, in work and play, in morals and manners, in habits and costumes. If in anything we seem free, it is only because our despot is indifferent and has not yet chosen to dicate. Always there was a measure of freedom left to the most servile peoples. The soul of freedom, the understanding of what is the true sphere of government, the aroused defiance against all tyranny, the resentful, angry resistance of free men to every invasion of their god-given rights, is dead. . . . We do not fight that others may have freedom in the opinions we hate. We reverence the policeman's club because it is "law"—when in fact it is generally only the policeman's will, conscious of the brutal power of the State back of him; and every instinct should teach us that most law is oligarchic despotism, and no law is entitled to blind obedience.

But pathetic or not, this kind of minority report cuts two ways. If it resists the encroachments of government in such matters of welfare as social security legislation and federal health insurance, it no less stands as a constant reminder that the state has no right to tyrannize minority opinion under any conditions—since, in fact, the state has no "rights" per se that

[6] See Wittke (1945, pp. 247–249). See also Schuster (1932, pp. 124–125).

are not surrendered by or expropriated from individuals. Libertarianism and conservatism are the paradoxical consequences of individualist anarchism: Roger Baldwin and Barry Goldwater are both products of its ideology to one degree or another. And if no doctrine could possibly survive such dichotomous results, it remains true that individualist anarchism put the case against Behemoth most starkly. The aberration and absurdity it yielded is hence nothing but the logical outcome of the arguments it put forth.

PACIFIST ANARCHISM

While most anarchists did not avail themselves of terrorist tactics, few spokesmen of classical anarchism cared to deny its efficiency. But with the historical collapse of anarchism and its complete separation from political involvement, it became possible for their remaining number to return to a more pristine, if pietistic, view—all the more so since the absence of any fruitful intercourse with the socialists limited the range of their dialogue and still further the range of their influence. Those among the anarchists whose position rested on persuasion attempted to create models of community action to prove that the "vision" is attainable. Indeed, in the work of Gandhi the idea of pacifism as the essential way to a truthful life is casually related to the view that a truthful life must itself exclude proprietary and monetary claims of any type.

The view of the state found in anarchist pacifism corresponds to that of most traditional varieties of anarchism. In Gandhi's view, the state has three functions in the exploitative process: It serves, first, as a mechanism for the distribution of goods and services; second, as a mechanism for the resolution of conflict among its members; and third, as an instrument for safeguarding the "national interest" in a world of competitive and conflicting petty interests. But it was also his view that these functions that the state performs are corrupted by the very nature of the state as sovereign. Nation-states rest on coercion, not reason or humanity. Constantly, even the positive ambitions of the state are being thwarted by the means it must employ, by force and violence. The problems of a society are no different from the problems of the individuals a society contains. Since the very nature of state authority is the enrichment of private wealth and not the public good, the only legitimate task of the state is its self-liquidation. In place of state power, there is to be a "world federation established by agreement" (Cf. Jack, 1951, pp. 120–121).

A similar viewpoint emerged in the work of Tolstoy. Tolstoy was confronted by a "holy Russia" in which the collective conscience of the wealthy classes was reserved for Sunday sermons, while during the rest of the week they were concocting ways to exploit further the nominally emancipated peasantry. But in the bosom of this growing Leviathan, a popular anarchistic ethos emerges. For Tolstoy (1905, p. 199), it takes the form of pure Christianity, a religion that substitutes for the irrational and the violent "a new comprehension of life" in which no person will "employ violence against anyone, and under no consideration." But anarchist pacifism is aware that this new comprehension of life is none too readily appreciated by state power, by those benefiting from coercion. This is the basis of political terror.

> The governments and the ruling classes do not now lean on the right, not even on the semblance of injustice, but on an artificial organization, which with the aid of the perfections of science, encloses all men in the circle of violence, from which there is no possibility of tearing themselves away. (Tolstoy, 1905, p. 199)

This circle of violence is made possible by the use of several means. The first is the massive intimidation of the people by falsely representing the state as inalienable and so "inflicting the severest penalties for any attempt at changing it." Second is the bribery by the state of civil bureaucracy and military officialdom. These bribes are ultimately paid for in the heavy taxation of the populace. Third is the hypnotic effect of the state— its concerted effort to distort and deprive common men of cultural and scientific knowledge. The circle of violence is completed by the brutalization of a certain segment of the people into unthinking beasts, willing to do the bidding of any master. Given these new idols of the cave, any attempt to change social systems through violence ends in the abyss of a bloodbath. The world of the state is one in which virtue is made synonymous with force and irrationality (Cf. Horowitz, 1957, pp. 89–106).

For both Tolstoy and Gandhi, the history of class society bears witness to the fact that violence has never established its opposite, a consensual society. It only intensifies and institutionalizes the uses of violence. The impasse of violence can only be broken in the triumph of conscience, in the release of the natural propensities of people to cooperate with one another and to love each other. The anarchist element emerges in pacifism as a direct confrontation of man and the state. Obedience to a government is considered a negation of religious principles. As Tolstoy (1955, p. 13–14) put it: "A man who unconditionally promises in advance to submit to laws which are made and will be made by men, by this very promise renounces Christianity." The individualism inherent in the pacifist reply to violence becomes a pronounced renunciation of the social contract and of state authority as such. In this way, anarchism and pacifism were wedded in history and in theory.

At the basis of anarchist pacifism is the idea that as long as sovereign nation–states exist, the possibility of resolving the dilemma of egoism and altruism, force and harmony, war and peace, remains nil. The very existence of separate states implies the use of force to resolve every major issue. Just as individuals must strive to go beyond the passions of the ego, Tolstoy and Gandhi implore men, as political beings, to move beyond the confines of the state and its by-products—force and aggression. Universal Man can be fulfilled only in the Universal Society.

The difficulty with pacific anarchism is that it can no more escape the commitments to a specific milieu in which the state exists than can other forms of the doctrine. Whatever its subjective intentions, it is clear that pacific anarchism is a politically involved position. Historically, it was the basic instrument for achieving national liberation in India. But in that very act emerged the Indian *state*. Pacifism, while a call to nonviolent action, was no less an instrument of large-scale social conflict. And to insure the success of the revolutionary movement meant the consecration and sanctioning of the coercive state after the revolution. The use of armies, policemen and "agents of the state" had to be given a large priority. Hence, pacifism in the state of political victory involved itself in the betrayal of its anarchist premises.

The problem of anarchist pacifism is not simply that the anarchist aspect tended to be submerged in the hue and cry of nationalistic passions, but no less in its assumptions about the *fixed* goodness of man. The pacifist techniques, elevated as they were to innate principles of human nature, came into conflict with the fact that pacifism is a *learned* technique. It no more demonstrates the superiority of pacifism's gaining its victory than conspiratorial anarchism demonstrated the superiority of violence. The argument from human nature always comes upon the possibility of being contravened by the facts of human behavior. Thus it is that the anarchist position as a "pure" doctrine gave way to a series of tactical preferences— violence, pacifism, conspiracy, collectivism, communism and so forth— that only further emphasized the contradictions between anarchy as a way of life and as a goal of men. The very victories of pacifist techniques only further exposed the anarchist dilemmas. It is perhaps in the nature of anarchism that it can never have any real "victory" without sacrificing its principles. By the same token, it can never suffer any ultimate defeats either.

THE REVOLUTIONARY DEED AND
THE REDEMPTIVE SPIRIT

If, as Santayana says, anarchy is a momentary sporadic enjoyment of change underlying a paradise of order it is equally true that for the anarchist the Leviathan is but a celebration of order underlying a world of change. Basic to anarchism is a general theory of action. And the test of significant action is the rejuvenation of personal existence. Significant change occurs only through the direct confrontation of class actors. The dialogue is determined by social interests, the stage setting provided by the state, and the resolution guaranteed by the absurdities of the present.

The necessity for participation, for direct action, is a modus operandi of anarchism. Action may not guarantee the successful conclusion of a conflict, and long-range prediction is out of the question for most anarchists; what is guaranteed is personal redemption. Social equilibrium tends to be viewed with a certain suspicion and alarm, not because of political factors so much as personal factors. Equilibrium resolves itself in terms of rationalized authority. The "rules" of a society tend to become deified into the "rights" of society. The very perpetuation of formalistic rules thus comes to depend upon the willingness of men to become alienated with respect to work processes and anomic with respect to social interaction. The anarchist demand for action is at its source an insistence on the psychological values of spontaneity. The revolutionary deed is useful *in its nature,* over and above political success of failure, precisely because action with a moral purpose is redemptive.

What should not be confused are the terms "action" and "conflict." The existence of conflict is a consequence of incompatibilities of class and power. The existence of action is a volitional response to conflict. As such, humanized man, active man, dedicates himself to the removal of sources of conflict. What underlies the anarchist faith is indeed a restoration of order. It is a holistic view in which the desirability of voluntary association provides the ground of social action. The host of anarchist "little societies" —from agricultural associations in Catalonia to proletarian *Bourses* in France—was an attempt to put into practice the idea of moral redemption through the release of natural impulses. The socialization process is held essential to personal liberty. The concept of personal redemption through a counterprocess of withdrawal is alien to the anarchist tradition.

The belief that the closer one is to natural behavior, the more proximate man is to the good society is a common theme of nineteenth-century romanticism. The anarchists, along with the utopians, simply sought to put this strain of romanticism to the test. The secretary of the Social Freedom Community of Chesterfield, Virginia, filed the following report in 1873:

> We hold to the unity of interests, and political, religious, and social freedom; and believe that every individual should have absolute control of herself or himself, and that, so long as they respect the same freedom in others, no one has the right to infringe on that individuality. We have no constitution or by-laws; ignore the idea of man's total depravity; and believe that all who are actuated by a love of truth and a desire to progress (and we will knowingly accept no others), can be better governed by love and moral suasion than by any arbitrary laws. Our government consists in free criticism. We have a unitary home. (Nordhoff, 1960, p. 357)

Nor should it be thought that such principles can have no application to industrial society. The argument from the inherent egoism of human nature is clearly the weakest link in the critique of anarchism. The Council of Aragon was an illustration in pre-Franco Spain of anarchist organization along "natural" lines.

> Libertarian principles were attempted in the field of money and wages. Wages were paid by a system of coupons exchangeable for goods in the cooperatives. Wages were based on the family unit: a single producer was

paid the equivalent of 25 pesetas; a married couple with only one working, 35 pasetas, and four pesetas weekly additional for each child. This system had a serious weakness, particularly while the rest of Spain operated on a system of great disparity in wages between manual and professional workers, since that prompted trained technicians to migrate from Aragon. For the time being, however, ideological conviction, inspiring the many technicians and professionals in the libertarian organizations, more than made up for this weakness. (Morrow, 1938, pp. 142–143)

It is undoubtedly the case that such social and economic equalization runs counter to the general tendency toward differential reward for differential work. But it must likewise be noted that it is precisely this general tendency toward status factors (urban rather than rural, engineer rather than technician and so on) that anarchism sought to challenge.

The idea of a natural man continues to inform the heirs of anarchism. There is a considerable body of European social scientists, especially the Franco-Italian group gathered about the Center of the Sociology of Cooperation, who have made the concept of voluntary association a cornerstone of their researches. The problem of getting people to make sound use of their time, the task of overcoming the anomic characteristic of industrial society, the forms of stimulating the spontaneous action of small groups in a world of bureaucratic manipulation, planning to overcome the gaps between peasants and city dwellers—all of these, while now stripped of apocalyptic trappings and ideological baggage, remain central tasks of social theory and social practice alike (Cf. Meister, 1958, pp. 123–126).

Most anarchists would question the possibility of successfully reconciling the impulse to voluntary association with a society increasingly determined by impersonal mechanisms of persuasion and coercion. The continuing preeminence of associations guaranteed by coercive measures—by either the force of arms or the symbolic power of law and contract—only intensifies the alienation of industrial man from his natural inclinations. Supporting this anarchist line of reasoning is the steady decline of the influence and nuclear membership in voluntary associations. The town council has given way to the urban planner; the political party has given way to the policymaker; and the voluntary association as such has given way to centralized bureaucracy. Impersonalism and professionalism, essential features of a developed industrial society, have perhaps done more to deprive anarchism of any contemporary vigor than all of the repressive measures of all of the modern garrison states.

In this situation, the anarchist appeal might appear helpless were it not for a singular fact of our times: The very weight of modern industrial organization reveals a series of dysfunctional elements. Work becomes routinized. Bureaucracy tends to dull initiative. Automation intensifies the difference between effort expended and results achieved. And leisure tends to be anomic, tending toward excitation without meaning, to a breakdown in long-range goals as such.

The large problem that comes into focus at the sociological end of the spectrum is therefore the possibility of rejuvenation. What is the effective scope of change? Is change possible at the purely individual level? Can a voluntary basis of agreement be reached at the national or international level? Traditionally, anarchism has been a failure, in part because it was never able to see the practice of men as extending beyond face-to-face relations. Organizationally, it never got beyond immediate primary group associations. And when it did foster and formulate an organizational network, it then became subject to the structural features of a social system that it ostensibly set about to overturn. When anarchism became large scale, as it did in Italy in the nineteenth century and in Spain during the twentieth century, it employed the techniques of mass persuasion, which made it subject to Michels' "iron law of oligarchy."

Part of the dilemma is built into the anarchist ethos of voluntarism. The scope of rejuvenation is always highly restrictive and restricted. It was restricted to that level of primary associations that would allow for the interplay of forces without the creation of a bureaucracy or a rationalized hierarchy. However, it was also restrictive in the sense that whatever its aims of becoming a national movement managed to gain in terms of support, it laid itself open to the charges of exercising the known pressures of the existing social order for its own ends. Interestingly enough, a movement of such vast scope and anarchist potential as Gandhism, in a period when it became a consolidated political force, when it had the responsibility of running the society, at that point the ideal of a "cottage society" gave way to the clamor of industrial society, and pacifism itself gave way to a new form of benevolent statism. The whole purpose of anarchistic pacifism became subverted in the practical everyday needs of manning borders, training an army, developing a bureaucratic force, becoming a world power. Anarchism seems to have intrinsic to itself a contradiction between a sociological view of personal redemption and a belief in the ultimate subversion of individuality by a society.

The anarchist concept of internationalism was never made clear. Rather, it developed the notion of the breakup of nationalisms. The shape of international order or the idea of international cooperation is held to be a consequence of the absence of competition between dictatorial involuntary associations. In contradistinction to bourgeois notions of internationalism, such as protective associations on a multinational level (for example, the European Economic Community) or the Marxist socialist view of national self-determination of proletarian states, the anarchists juxtapose the idea of internationalism as a necessary consequence of voluntary life. The liquidation of involuntary activity means the liquidation of nationalism and the maturation of the true community of man. But there is no anarchist scheme in most varieties of universalism or federalism. Available instruments of peace such as a world court are themselves held to be agencies of supercoercion. And supercoercion is not a realized internationalism because competition between nations would remain. Class exploitation is a form of superordination, but not the exclusive form. The anarchist idea of revolution has two phases: The first phase is the abolition of social classes, and the second is the rising force of voluntary association among men, bringing about a rejuvenation. The anarchists were among the first to be critical of industrialism in its capitalist forms. They were the first to explore the weaknesses in Bolshevik revolution. There is a *theoretical* soundness to most anarchist criticism of existing social orders. If one reads Berkman or Goldman on the repressive character of bolshevism, one cannot help but admire their predictive acumen. However, one is always left a bit discontented by the type of criticism that can never be wrong because it is always dealing in the realm of what *ought* to be. Anarchism is an argument of perfection against an imperfect world. It scoffs at attempts to make an imperfect world a little less so. Its very totality gives it a rightness in the abstract. But this totality deprives it of concreteness. Anarchists are right in their critique of existing social orders. But the issues are not quite joined. How does one get from an oppressive social system to one a little less so?

The victories of industrialism and urbanism led to considerable changes in anarchist doctrine. The Proudhonian critique of property had an appeal to propertyless peasants, whereas the later Kropotkin emphasis on an anarchism of social need both universalized it and served to reorient it toward proletarian aims. Withdrawal from harsh bourgeois realities into Stirner's *Gemeinschaft* paradise of total egoism—the community of fate, which sustained the early anarchist belief in the natural goodness of man —gave way to increased involvement in *Gesellschaft* imperfections, to the society of interests based on mistrust of this natural goodness, to a contractual relationship. And it must be said that the only time anarchism became a "world historic force" coincided precisely with this new emphasis on class exploitation and class redemption.[7] But this historic period proved as ineffectual in general as the wranglings of Bakunin in the International. The anarchist doctrine of *smashing* state power never admitted to a strategy and theory for the *maintenance* of power. The purpose of involvement was continually beclouded by a strong moralizing belief in the dangers of contamination that stem from such involvement.

Liberation in the anarchist lexicon always retained a negative quality. It remained liberation *from* rather than liberation *through*. Tolstoy wanted to be liberated from all national governments. Sorel wanted to be liberated from all political parties. Stirner wanted to be liberated from all social requirements. In this way, anarchism insured its marginality, which was not unlike the marginality of coffeehouse European intellectuals. Both pre-

---

[7] That anarchism reaches its maximum practicality in relation to a concept of class rather than personal exploitation is made clear by comparing such different forms of anarchism as those preached in China and Latin America. See and compare Scalapino and Yu (1961) and Simon (1946).

ferred the underground to the firing line of politics. Redemption was to be personal. Like the intellectuals, immortality was insured by moral rightness rather than by political victory.

The ideology of negation is not an adequate tool for class rebellion. It is a fact of the age that no class *qua* class can exist without the action generated by ideological thinking. For that reason, intellectuals as a class can never be galvanized into a form of independent activity. However, it is the only class that can survive strictly on the unmasking tradition—on the tradition of uncovering the weaknesses in political myth and social ideology as such. Given the anarchist propensity to this kind of exposé, an "alliance" of anarchism and intellectualism might have been expected to materialize.

What prevented an association of intellectuals and anarchists is therefore a complex question. Two processes in particular seem to attract attention. In the first place, the historic tendencies of intellectuals were to cancel themselves in the direction of academicism and professionalism; that is, the intellectuals were the historic forerunners of the present-day teachers, welfare workers, researchers and so forth. And while a tension remains between the intellectual and the academic, the process of cross-fertilization between them served to enhance the status of both. And more, it tended to make the intellectual increasingly cautious and responsible in the types of criticism he offered. His view of life became separated from his work performance, with the latter increasingly defining his "role set." The slogan of the modern intellectual became the separation of fact and value. More and more, the search for facts gave the intellectual the kind of special information and special consciousness that made professionalism possible. And from professionalism to respectability is a short hop indeed—especially since the striving for professionalism is itself partially motivated by precisely the impulse to respectability—to a high status ranking.

The second master trend that prevented too close an association with anarchism is the historic apathy, indeed antipathy, for deeds, and certainly for the "propaganda of the deed." Anarchist and socialist shibboleths about the unity of theory and practice remain largely mythical. The intellectual sees political action as corrupting thought. Indeed, the whole of the sociology of knowledge from Dilthey to Mannheim can be seen against a background that believed that action is the fundamental basis for the "distortion of truth." Intellectualism developed its own ideology—the guardianship of the truth over and against political ideologies. Social myths, political slogans and propaganda of destruction were viewed by anarchists as techniques for manipulating the rebellion of the oppressed. Anarchist martydom always seemed to carry with it infliction of suffering upon others —particularly men of learning. As such, the anarchist was viewed as a slave of his own activism—violence always threatened to spill over into regicide, and self-sacrifice into the sacrifice of others. Anarchism was viewed as a labyrinth of tactics and terror, which it was the job of intellectuals to transcend if not actually to eliminate. Thus, the process of redemption for intellectuals came to be defined as the politics of exposé rather than liberation from politics as such.

On the other side, the anarchists were undergoing certain sociological processes that similarly moved them away from any informal concordat with intellectuals. We have already spoken of the marginality and negative definitions of freedom that anarchists are bound by. These definitions, when translated into action, made the anarchists arch "norm breakers." They became the foes of organized society and the friends of social deviance. As such, they were hardly distinguishable from criminals. Certain "nonutilitarian" theories of crime—crime committed not to secure the direct objects of theft and vandalism, but as a reaction against bourgeois society— share with anarchism a principled attitude toward crime. Even if we accept Emile Durhkeim's brilliant commentaries on the necessity of crime for social change, and the definition by a given society of what a crime is, it is clear that anarchists can hardly accept the indecisiveness of intellectuals —of a portion of society that remains relatively low on any risk-taking scale. Anarchists thus rationalized the gap between themselves and intellectuals by indicating that the indecisive nature of intellectual behavior stemmed from their hazy interests as a social subclass. Therefore, even their sanctimonious doctrine of separating facts from values was held to be a reflection of weakness rather than of principle.

This directly feeds the plaint of anarchists that intellectuals are betrayed by their own quest for knowledge. When Dostoevski noted that the "direct, legitimate fruit of consciousness is inertia, that is, conscious sitting with-the-hands-folded," he gave expression to this antagonism of the anarchist for men who could never be direct. The consequence of reflection is ultimately self-reflection, and this soon leads to an academic narcissism. The whole force of anarchist antiintellectualism is not so much a critique of ideas as it is a condemnation of the man of ideas. The "deed" was, after all, what stimulated new ideas, and so the deed was held paramount.

While the social sources of intellectualism are profoundly antimoralistic in contrast to anarchism, they turn a full circle, moving in opposite directions, and meet. The meeting place is their shared critical view of the present, a common need to see the present as *a moment* in history rather than as *the moment* of history, and a common need to make the better serve as the critic of the good.

REFERENCES

Adamic, J. (1934) *Dynamite: The Story of Class Violence in America.* New York: Viking Press.

Bakunin, M. (1950) *Marxism, Freedom and the State,* trans. and ed. K. J. Kenafick. London: Freedom Press.

Cole, G. D. H. (1954) *Socialist Thought: Marxism and Anarchism, 1850–1890*. London: Macmillan.

Durkheim, E. (1933) *The Division of Labor in Society*, trans. G. Simpson. New York: Macmillan.

Goldman, E. (1931) *Living My Life*. New York: Knopf.

Greene, W. B. (1849) *Equality*. West Brookfield, Mass.: privately printed.

Hofstadter, R. (1963) *Anti-Intellectualism in American Life*. New York: Knopf.

Horowitz, I. L. (1957) *The Idea of War and Peace in Contemporary Philosophy*. New York: Paine-Whitman.

Horowitz, I. L. (1961) *Radicalism and the Revolt Against Reason*. London: Routledge & Kegan Paul.

Horowitz, I. L., ed. (1963) *Power, Politics and People*. New York: Oxford University Press.

Jack, H. A., ed. (1951) *The Wit and Wisdom of Gandhi*. Boston: Beacon Press.

Kropotkin, P. (1909) *The Great French Revolution: 1789–1793*. London: Heinemann.

Kropotkin, P. (1912) *Modern Science and Anarchism*. London: Freedom Press.

Lecky, W. (1870) *The History of European Morals*. New York: Appleton-Century-Crofts; reissued by George Braziller, 1955.

Malatesta, E. (1949) *Anarchy*, 8th ed. London: Freedom Press.

Martin, J. J. (1953) *Men Against the State*. Dekalb, Ill.: Adrian Allen.

Martin, K. (1929) *French Liberal Thought in the Eighteenth Century*. London: Ernest Benn.

Marx, K. (1935) *The Poverty of Philosophy*. New York: International Publishers.

Masaryk, T. G. (1955) *The Spirit of Russia: Studies in History, Literature and Philosophy*, 2d ed., vol. 2. New York: Macmillan.

Meister, A. (1958) "Community Development and Community Centers," *International Review of Community Development*, no. 1, pp. 38–57.

Michels, R. (1949) *Political Parties*. New York: Free Press.

Morrow, F. (1938) *Revolution and Counter-Revolution in Spain*. New York: Pioneer Publishers.

Moulin, L. (1948) *Socialism of the West*, trans. A. Heron. London: Gollancz.

Nordhoff, C. (1960) *The Communistic Societies of the United States*. New York: Hillary House Publishers.

Pelloutier, F. (1902) *Histoire des Bourses du Travail*. Paris: A. Costes.

Presthus, R. (1962) *The Organizational Society*. New York: Knopf.

Proudhon, P. J. (1846) *Systeme des contradictions economiques ou philosophie de la misere*. Paris: Guillaumin.

Proudhon, P. J. (1891) *What Is Property: An Inquiry into the Principles of Right and of Government*. New York: Humboldt Publishing Co.

Scalapino, R. A., and G. T. Yu (1961) *The Chinese Anarchist Movement.* Berkeley: Berkeley Institute of International Studies, University of California.

Schuster, E. M. (1932) *Native American Anarchism: A Study of Left-Wing American Individualism.* Northampton, Mass.: Smith College Studies in History.

Simon, S. F. (1946) "Anarchism and Anarcho-Syndicalism in South America," *Hispanic American Historical Review,* vol. 26 (February), pp. 38–59.

Sorel, G. (1929) *Materiaux d'une theorie du proletariat,* 3rd ed. Paris: Marcel Riviere.

Sorel, G. (1950) *Reflections on Violence.* New York: Free Press.

Talmon, J. L. (1960) *Political Messianism: The Romantic Phase.* London: Secker and Warburg.

Tolstoy, L. (1905) *The Kingdom of God Is Within You.* New York: T. Y. Crowell.

Tolstoy, L. (1955) "Gandhi–Tolstoy Correspondence," *Iscus,* vol. 2, no. 1, pp. 12–41.

Tuchman, B. W. (1963) "The Anarchists," *Atlantic,* vol. 211, no. 5 (May), pp. 91–110.

Whyte, W. H., Jr. (1956) *The Organization Man.* New York: Simon & Schuster.

Wittke, C. (1945) *Against the Current: The Life of Karl Heinzen.* Chicago: University of Chicago Press.

Wood, C. E. S. (1931) *Too Much Government.* New York: Vanguard Press.

Woodcock, G. (1962) *Anarchism: A History of Libertarian Ideas and Movements.* New York: World.

CHAPTER 9

THE POLITICALIZATION OF SOCIALISM

FROM SOCIALISM TO MARXISM

Socialism and Marxism are both nineteenth-century phenomena, and fittingly enough, they share a political base quite different from the conservative base. If conservatism began in the heat of political involvement and was central to decision making in the eighteenth and nineteenth centuries, socialism and, even more profoundly, Marxism, were alienated, marginal features of early nineteenth-century life. The doctrines reflect that fact: Socialist writing tends to be strident and polemical, whereas the work of conservatives tends to be almost euphoric in its quietude and self-possession.

It is almost as if conservatism, reflecting the psychology of the political insider, is calm, relaxed, knowing, worldly, capable of exercising compromise, capable of judicious behavior; certainly to read Metternich (and there are 19 volumes to read) or to read Burke is to read almost an elegiac attitude toward the political life. On the other hand, socialism, and especially Marxism, is militant, insecure about worldly behavior, or as Engels would say, subject to proletariat asceticism or anger. These are not simply the psychological consequences of dialectics or polarized styles of thinking, but of being entirely outside the framework of political life; for socialism attacks the present, and refuses to compromise with what is.

Nineteenth-century ideologies, like the classes of that period, confront each other with stylistic differences as well as differences in content. Indeed, stylistic differences are sometimes more instrumental in distinguishing between conservative and radical thought than are substantive issues.

The hallmark of socialist action is the stance toward the world rather than the substance of the critique; for if one thing unites conservatives and socialists it is the attack on the present moment as truth. On the conservative side, the attack is on behalf of the past, while socialists attack the present as proponents of a utopian future. The style of attack is thus as important as its substance; socialists such as Eduard Bernstein are frequently less severe in their condemnation of bourgeois society and liberalist theories of democracy than are conservatives such as Brooks Adams. That the socialist legacy consists of style as well as substance is too often overlooked, primarily because one rarely engages in direct conversation with either socialists or conservatives, and their books, no matter how passionately written, inadequately convey their respective stylistic poses.

Perhaps the best way to understand nineteenth-century socialism is to present it in terms of its Comtian and its Saint-Simonian phases, or what one could call the conspiratorial phase and the legalistic politicalized phase; for in this distinction between Saint-Simonian socialism and Marxian socialism lies the seeds of the failure of nineteenth-century socialism. Apologists for socialism too often blame that failure upon the bourgeoisie, the power of the middle classes, the strength of the capitalists or how clever the opponents were, as if the world conspired to defeat the nobility of the socialist aims. While there may be some truth in that view of the demise of classical socialism, it is more nearly correct to say that socialism was doomed from the very outset.

In its Saint-Simonian, or pre-Marxian, phase, socialism held, in common with every other political doctrine, a belief in elites. The works of Comte and Saint-Simon are as elitist as any conservative, reactionary or liberal writing in the nineteenth century. Saint-Simonian or Comtian socialism is based on the principle that elites or ruling groups of advanced men will virtually bring up the rest of humanity by the bootstraps. In this sense, socialism is the product of the romantic period as well as of the classical period. The role of the individual is extremely pronounced, until he almost seems to be an Archimedean lever picking up and carrying society into the brave new world.

Saint-Simon betrays this in his approach to art and science. Shakespeare and Newton are his models of the new socialist man; yet they can hardly be considered representative of socialism. The former is a medieval writer, perhaps the best writer in the English language, but certainly not a socialist. And Newton could not be considered, by the wildest imagination, a liberal, much less a socialist. He was a great physicist, but he was a mystic; he worried about the Book of Daniel; he worried about excluding materialists who did not even exist from the Royal Academy of Science. The fact that Saint-Simon came closest to a mass version of socialism before Marx indicates the extent of socialism's delinquency.

Marxist theory argued, for the first time in the history of literature and social science, that the principle of the mass was the natural enemy of the principle of elites. The essential motor of life was the mass as a force. History thus became the history of masses, not the history of kings; the history of forces, not the history of individuals. Above all, history was inexorable for Marx, and not subject to the whims or the fallacies of individuals no matter how brilliant; so the Marxian assault was, in fact, an assault on the socialism of the Enlightenment, of the utopians, of Hegel, Feuerbach and the materialists. Marx cleared away the debris of elites and of theories whose movement depends on elites.

The theory of elites still has a number of adherents in the modern world—for instance, David McClelland and his high achievers, or the entrepreneurial version of Bert Hoselitz and Wilbert Moore, in which society is mobilized because an entrepreneur has a vision and acts upon it. Another is the functionalist theory of deviance—that the deviant is the one who mobilizes the society (Lipset, 1967, pp. 3–49). Even the socialist is presented as a marginal man who moves the society. In other words, within social science the theory of elites remains preeminent. No one in political science, for example, can contest that elitism is the *sine qua non* of every theory in the field.

Marx deserves recognition for presenting the first genuine alternative to elite theory. The socialist movement prior to Marx represented an extreme form of psychologism, while Marxism can be said to represent an equally extreme form of sociologism. That is to say, the role of the individual in creating the new society was as important for the pre-Marxian socialist as it is for every other elite theorist, and the notion that the masses' accomplishments depend upon forces—forces that are made up of more than one, that are always social—is the essence of Marxism.

One reason why Marxism has been such a poor resource psychologically, excluding for the moment the theory of alienation, is that it has never really contended with the individual as a maker of forces. The individual for Marx is part of the historical force but could never *be* the force; the force was always larger than the person. Indeed, when Marx spoke of social science he always meant the science of the many; he never meant the science of the individual, for man is a microcosm of the whole. Social psychology is the outermost limit to which Marxian thought will extend, but even it annoyed Marx or left him basically unconcerned. For unlike previous socialists, he was interested in the other end of the spectrum. The first socialists were interested in alienated man, in alienated labor, in the role of the individual in history. They were interested in creating a society with 30,000 Shakespeares and 30,000 Newtons. But Marx was not particularly interested in these goals as an end unto themselves; he was interested in politics. The Marxist system works because of its politics of involvement, not its psychology of alienation.

Marxism and socialism differ in their attitudes toward economics and politics. Socialists have been notorious economic determinists, but Marxism and Marx are characterized by emphasis upon politics and political determinism. Revolution for Marx was never simply the stage of economic transformation, but rather the direction of political control. Thus, he dated the French Revolution from 1789 and not later. Serfdom ended in Russia in 1905, but the Revolution did not come until 1917. Another example is American society from 1775 to 1781; American political independence took place in the late eighteenth century, whereas its economic independence took place later. Thus, by 1840, the gross national product in the United States was estimated as being equal to that of England. Indeed, the United States became a new sort of model for socialists—since in the western European experience feudalism fettered capitalist growth, and the bourgeois state came about after the solidification of the capitalist class, whereas in the United States, the bourgeois state assisted in the formation and development of capitalism (See North, 1966, pp. 86–87; and Baughman, 1971, pp. 282–285).

Marxist periodization has to do with the political conquest of power; again this is a fundamental ingredient of Marxism socialism in contrast to earlier forms of so-called scientific socialism. It was not, as has been widely and erroneously thought, that Marx stressed economic bases; it was that Marxism recognized the role of politics as the early socialists did not. Consequently, Marxism made its heaviest impression and deepest impact at the political end of the spectrum rather than at the psychological end. Economic determinism had already been enunciated by Ricardo and Smith, who believed all decisions to be furtively guided by the economic balance and equilibrium in the society, with the equilibrium asserting itself against man under all circumstances. For Smith, no political machinery could possibly change the impact of the economic equilibrium. Economic determinism obviously cannot be considered the hallmark of Marxian socialists.

The socialist tradition is, however, concerned about the position of labor in society. Socialists have always been involved with the improvement, amelioration and liberation of the working class. This was the basis of socialism before, during and after Marx. Sometimes it took the form of a direct attack on capital, an attack on the state or the growth of trade unionism. Because socialism has been so largely involved with the condition of the working class, as that condition changes, so the doctrine changes. This is evident in the English Labor Party and in some of the Scandinavian Labor parties. But Marxian socialists have not been solely concerned with labor, but more primarily with drawing off a portion of that labor power for the purpose of party organization. Marxism becomes a doctrine unto itself, with its concern about the party of labor rather than the act of laboring, about the conquest of state power, not the maintenance of better conditions for workers in industry.

There are great differences between a political labor movement and an economic labor movement. One of the characteristic differences can be observed in the present-day remnants of the political labor movements in Europe and Latin America, in contradistinction to the economic labor movement in the United States. In the latter, politics is a highly professional concern, and the essence of the movement is organization of workers for more money, rather than the conquest of state power. The gap between the economics of socialism and the politics of Marxism is extremely profound and has, since the time of Marx, separated socialism into revolutionary and reform wings.

The fundamental source of disagreement is whether the purpose of working class organization is economic or political. The Marxist system is a system of political determination, because the definition of Marxist purpose is the conquest of state authority. With Marxism we are clearly dealing with the role of the party, the organization of the party and the conquest of the state.

It is clear that Marx and Engels' vision of the *International Working Men's Association* was that it represented a formal response to the economic realities of an International Business Men's Association (Marx and Engels, 1971, pp. 35–49). The difficulty was not in their assessment of bourgeois interlocking interests, but rather in the assumption that this would create the basis for a durable counteralliance among the workers of Europe. In the solidarity forged by the Paris Commune such an optimism was warranted. The international character of the struggle was vouchsafed on both sides. But by the time of World War I, the contradictions between the ambitions of the European bourgeoisie produced a wave of nationalist responses that overshadowed and former semblance of bourgeois unity. Similarly, this same rise of nationalism produced serious rifts within the socialist ranks. Thus, the process of nationalism took precedence and priority over the need for working-class solidarity. And in this ineluctable fact, the transformation of socialism from an economic movement to a political movement was carried out within the span of thirty-five years. This search for political control represented socialism without tears, for it is not based upon humanistic statements about alienated labor, how workers are exploited and the bleedings of the weak and the poor and the downtrodden. Marx was not a humanist as a man or as a writer. Those qualities were attached to him by his later interpreters, who wanted to make Marx the new Erasmus. The problem is that once Marxism is humanized, it becomes a matter of sentiment rather than theory. It is true that the poor suffer, that there is oppression, and that it is terrible to be exploited. But these concerns are not the essence of Marxism, nor do they characterize the Marxian socialist approach.

The basic rules of the nonutopian socialist approach would be don't

sentimentalize and don't brutalize. One should not brutalize the condition
of people, but above all one should not sentimentalize. Marx invented a
new class of people in order to stress that maxim; he called them the
lumpenproletariat. No one was more severe, more vicious, in his condemnation of these poor than Karl Marx. His word "lumpenproletariat" refers
to scum who do not work, who do nothing, and he is more severe toward
them than one would expect of a Puritan parson. No one, not even Cotton
Mather, was more disgraceful in his attack on the very poor and the deviant
than was Marx. Marxism is not to be confused with love of the deviant or
the outsider; it is a stringent, almost Lutheran doctrine. Anyone who has
read Luther and his attack on the papal emissaries will appreciate the comparison: Marx was a superior convert from Judaism, to whom very few
aspects of Judaism can be attributed.

FROM MARXISM TO LENINISM

Engels serviced the needs of Marxism by providing the ideological
contours of the future socialist society. Being less prudential than Marx, he
was able to provide the linkages between general theory and personal
therapy. In Engels' work three things are important: history, economics and
communism. Engels states that what distinguishes Marxian history from
all previous perspectives is that history begins when men move to satisfy
their needs. The progress of history and the progress of men is the movement from the satisfaction of needs to the satisfaction of wants. When there
are large bodies of men whose needs are satisfied, they go on to satisfy
their wants. When this occurs, there is a condition of affluence. When there
is affluence, one has communism. Marx gave no other indication of its
essential germane characteristic.

Engels describes communism as neither a state of affairs, nor a system,
nor an ideal to which reality has to adjust itself. "We call communism the
real movement which abolishes the present state of things" (Engels, 1934,
pp. 20–21)—the large number of deprived and those who have wealth.
Communism is the struggle itself, not the goal to be achieved. This, too,
distinguishes Marx's work from the work of the early socialists, which is
why he almost had to call it by a new name; for their socialism was a state
of affairs, a system. Marx's socialism is a process; people struggling for the
future embody communism. Marx, in effect, acknowledges that he is not
fighting to bring into being a new state of affairs or a new social system;
rather, the struggle is itself the state of affairs that is essential to the defini-
nition of the system or of the situation. Marx once told movingly why he
could not accept the elite theory of history or of society; those who write
history in terms of the princes of a society, or in terms of the ruling elites
of a state, he stated, can only write in terms of what he called the "shared
illusions of that era." Thus, if an era imagines itself to be actuated by purely
political or religious motives, the historian of elites accepts this idea al-

though in fact religion may be only a medium by which the true motives are actualized.

The political illusions or the religious or economic illusions of the dominant class and the class that writes the history of the period can never be true history or true social science. To deal with problems from the point of view of social science rather than from the point of view of illusion is to escape the illusion. To be outside the illusion means to be outside the system itself, that is, outside of nationalism, outside of patriotism, outside of the ruling class, outside of the ideology of the state. The premises here are posited very nearly in terms of the actual role of the nineteenth-century revolutionary, who was, in fact, outside the power system and justified that outside position as a means to acquire self-consciousness.

The dilemma of the Marxian system in its most generalized expression has to do with the fact that Marx himself was an elitist. However strongly he advocated the cause of the mass, he could not escape the premises that he opposed. The party system was the vanguard of the working class. It was to be the flower of that class. The leaders who were to make the new ideology, the new intellectual history, the new science, were drawn from a small narrow segment of the total society. The revolutionary leadership itself was to be drawn from a small sector, so that the ultimate problem remained, despite the formula, the safeguard, that Marx offered—namely, that the elites of the new revolutionary class would constantly be prey to the failings and to the needs of the poor. This formula was closer to a sop to the intellectual system Marx worked out than representative of his genuine political feeling. Throughout the First International, the arguments against the peasantry, like the arguments against the bourgeoisie, were elitist in essence—an elitism of a different variety but elitism nonetheless. The elite would be the factory class, which Marx endowed with certain necessary virtues and with destiny. They were indeed to be the chosen people—chosen for the task of liberation, but unwittingly, unlike other elites. From within this factory elite would be drawn the political elite. This formulation provides the intellectual basis of the neo-Marxist breakaway called fascism. The Franco-Italian school of socialism derives its energy from a recognition of this dilemma between historical inevitability and personal volition. Within the framework of this participatory dilemma, the problem of Marxian socialism becomes fused with the problem of twentieth-century Freudian psychologism.

The transition from "socialism" to "communism" took place formally almost as an accident. Lenin was in search of a name that would distinguish his movement from that of the Social Democrats. The discussion took place as early as 1911 and the decision was made in 1912; there was no great urgency to this matter. The irony is that such a minor decision should become so profoundly significant in the later history of the evolution of socialism, when the Revolution in Russia became the essential divide, the great watershed between the history of socialism and the beginning of a socialist society. The consecration of the name "communism" was in many ways symbolic of the historic victory of revolutionary doctrine in at least one country. One would have to say that the Russian "communist" Revolution was viewed as having such enormous significance because the socialists had not yet achieved any victories. Europe did not become socialist, and the vague leanings toward victory were always fraught with compromise and treachery and doubt.

World War I was, in fact, the great defeat of western types of socialism, from which it has yet to recover. Based as it is on class doctrine and the international solidarity of the working class, socialism came upon the impossible anomaly of nationalism within the working-class movements of western Europe and was unable to stem the tides of war, or convince its own membership that workers have more in common with one another than Frenchmen have with Frenchmen or Germans with Germans.

The Communist party for its part was able to muster a settlement on the basis of the new doctrine of the homogeneity of working classes. It was able to absorb a tremendous military defeat and to sustain enormous battle losses. The resolution of the war in the Treaty of Brest Litovsk was by all odds one of the most humiliating defeats that a big power has sustained in the twentieth century. With every day of procrastination, which the Bolsheviks chafed at, the German terms cost Russia even more territory. Ironically enough, this defeat for Russia meant success for the Bolsheviks. The dialectic of World War I is the nearly concurrent victory of socialism in one country and the postponement of communism throughout the rest of the world, the success of Russian nationalism and the defeat of European internationalism. Not to appreciate this is to fail to appreciate the hopes and reservations that the Bolshevik Revolution inspired throughout the world. Socialism as an economic system became rapidly pragmatized, while communism as a moral ideal became rapidly obsolete.

The success of the Soviet Union illustrates what may be described as an iron law that ideology is transformed into organization. Every revolution has this as an essential law. The function of ideology in the prerevolutionary era is the smashing of organizational power, and the function of the successful revolutionist is the restoration and maintenance of organization, whatever the basis of that organization, and the smashing of ideology. To examine the fifty-year history of the Soviet Communist Party is to see this operating clearly. All discussions prior to the Bolshevik Revolution from 1905 to 1917 had to do basically with the ideology of socialism and the ideology for the revolutionary forces: How does one prevent the dictatorship of the proletariat from becoming the dictatorship over the proletariat? How is the state to wither? Do its functions wither, or does the state apparatus? What is the role of democratic opposition? What will be the nature, the characteristics, of the opposition?

These kinds of questions, which of course were in many ways the kinds of questions asked by socialists in western Europe, formed the basis of relating party apparatus to the party system. But even before this occurred, western European parties began to form their own ideological lines, taking as prototypes the Mensheviks and Bolsheviks. These lines were made possible by certain ambiguities in the writings of Marx. So committed were the Menshevik and Bolshevik parties to ideological correctness, that doctrinal sanction became extremely important. For example, the Mensheviks claimed that nowhere in Marx's writings is there any real sanction for a notion of dictatorship or for an elite. They argued that Marxism is an expression of the masses, and that because it is a mass doctrine it must be based on the labor movement to succeed, or even to fail. Lenin argued that there was a warrant for an elite and that Marx did understand the need for a party apparatus that is recruited independently of trade-union recruitment. The early stages of the struggle in Russia were a struggle between spontaneity and organization, both of which were fought out ideologically.

One could say that the early history of the Russian Social Democratic Party and then the Bolshevik party was concerned with ideological argument—argument for the purity of doctrine. The purpose of purity was action. Until 1917, these arguments were very interesting; an examination of *The Origins of Early Russian Bolshevism* (Haimson, 1951) shows that these are still problems understandable within the context of Marxist ideology. With the assumption of power by the Bolsheviks, all of this came to an end, and a new set of problems emerged, having to do with organization.

The nature of the Bolshevik Revolution was special in two respects. The ideological struggle itself convinced the men who engaged in it of the rightness of their cause. After all those years of struggle, all those years of combatting the oppositionists and all those years of bulletins, pamphlets, essays and newspapers, they were successful. The success that crowned those years of ideological struggle also convinced the leaders of the Bolshevik movement that their enemies had been wrong. That was even more important.

During the Civil War period, there was an amorphous kind of transition from the old regime to the new. The ten days that shook the world that John Reed wrote about (1935) were hardly earth-shattering. The revolution was a long-brewing affair that lasted from February to November, and then four more years into a civil war in which no one could make any claim of having central authority. This, too, helped forge the special qualities of dogmatics within Soviet life. If ideologically the Bolsheviks had dominated from 1905 to 1917, then between 1917 and 1921, they persevered militarily in the first phase of the conquest of power. And again it appeared that all opposition was wrong. The cadets, the Social Democrats, the various local leaders and regional leaders—all fumbled and crumbled one after another. Private armies like that of Denikin collapsed; the White Guard collapsed, so that in the second phase—the phase of actual revolutionary combat—the Bolsheviks again persevered.

In both these stages—1905–17 and 1917–21—the Bolsheviks were remarkably successful. The memoirs of the old Bolsheviks reveal their amazement at the success of the Revolution. Lenin himself, for example, made the claim that were it not for a nurse on the bench who said this was the moment to strike he would have gone back on the train and slept that night. One can imagine how confused and divided were the lower echelons.

The German Imperial Army must be given some credit in the success of the Revolution. They had no intention of fighting on two fronts, and they wanted to get the Russians out of the war. The Russians were being massacred; hardly a man from that period did not sustain injuries in battle. In the eyes of the German Imperial Army, the Bolsheviks were not so much the party of peace, but rather the instrument for getting Russia out of the war. (Katkov, 1968, pp. 63–88). It was they who placed Lenin in that famous sealed car and shipped him through Germany to the Finland station in April 1917. Thus in some measure the Bolshevik Revolution was a child not only of internal developments in Russia but, also of the decisions of the German Imperial Army. From this point of view, the accidental properties of the revolution loom large. Very little appears to be inevitable about the revolution when one bears in mind that it could not have been carried out without the clear passage given Lenin by Germany. All of this the old Bolsheviks knew well; so their reaction to this accident of history was a certain amount of insecurity.

The Bolshevik Revolution unfolded as an accident that set off a great deal of activity. The ordinary people really did not know they had attained power. The Imperial Guards ran away. The czar stood fast like an idiot, and they shot him. All those years of planning were resolved by the convergence of a series of unbelievable accidents: the stupidity of the czar, the cowardice of the White Guards, the Palace Guard's confusion, the German Imperial Army's sending Lenin through in a car. Revolution was obviously not made by Soviets rising all over Mother Russia; everything went on so much as if a revolution had not occurred that it could not be denied that the seizure of power had been accomplished by an elite group.

This awareness had enormous bearing on the shape of the Revolution, because the Bolshevik's insecurities led them to doubt (1) that they really had won, which could only be resolved by saying to someone else, "Put X to the wall"—if this is done, one has really won; and (2) suspicion of fellow conspirators, as if several men had found the "bag of money" and each might make primary claims on it.

FROM LENINISM TO STALINISM

In the first days of the Revolution, the tasks of rule were relatively simple. Lenin had the kind of authority invested in his person to enable him to control the situation. But with his demise in 1924 came the beginning of organizational problems, both within the Party apparatus and the burgeoning bureaucratic apparatus. The early movement and the mood of this time are ably described in E. H. Carr's (1950) first volume, *The Bolshevik Revolution*. The first stage showed all the earmarks of socialism triumphant. In Lenin's attitude on November 7, when he announced the triumph of the workers and the peasants, one can see the emergence of the Trotsky problem; namely, when Lenin said, "we in Russia at once must occupy ourselves with two tasks," what was involved was an unwillingness or an incapacity on Lenin's part to come to terms with the possibility that the victory of world socialism might well imply the collapse of the Soviet Republic and, correspondingly, that the victory of the Soviet Republic could come at the expense of the world socialist movement. This became the very center of the dilemma in the first post-Lenin phase. The problem became, in effect, where does one make his investment—in international revolution or in a national revolution? In either choice are risks.

The Stalinist faction claimed that the essential task was the building of socialism in the Soviet Union. Once this was finished, one would have a base from which to give support to the other revolutionary factions around the world. With the collapse of this base, one would return to a bourgeois state and to conditions that prevailed before 1917, as well as halt the democratization of the working class, which had been deeply weakened by the World War.

The Trotsky faction argued that the consolidation of power in one state would lead to the corruption of that state and that instead of a workers' society one would have a bureaucratic society. Instead of providing support for the international working-class movement, the international working-class movement would be drained in order to sustain the bureaucratic apparatus that would grow up in that one nation.

The arguments on both sides have certain prima facie intellectual strengths. It is clear why Lenin avoided the problem: When it became clear that one could not perform a double task, he made the decision on behalf of nationalism. As the socialists decided on behalf of the nation during World War I, so, too, the Bolsheviks decided to support the nation. Whatever the ideological paraphernalia, the decision was made to sacrifice the international working-class movement rather than the Soviet Union.

While this split was novel, in a Russian context, it corresponded more or less to the split between the Social Democrats and communists during the World War I period. However, the Russian case concerned the control of state power, not the seizure of state power. The Russian schism of nationalism and internationalism took place not as an ideological discussion of outsiders, but as an organizational discussion of insiders. That is why it was so wicked in its implications and in its outcomes.

This struggle within the Bolshevik party made necessary the kind of purge that took place. If I may draw an analogy, we live in a world where we know there are criminal elements, and we know that they annihilate one another, but they do not disturb those of us who are not within that society.

If one does not gamble, if one does not frequent racetracks, if one does not deal in hard drugs, one rarely hears about these people, and they are not of practical concern. Only within the confines of the criminal subculture are there purges.

Similarly, in the Soviet Union, the purge was not directed against the society, because all parties recognized that a purge against society would cripple the economy and morale. So there was never a purge in the Hitlerian sense, in which whole ethnic groups were wiped out. The purges took place within the Party apparatus itself over questions of whether one was a Trotskyite, a Zinovievite, a Stalinist or belonged to one of the other factions within the party. All efforts were made to purify the party, not to purge it; that the purification process involved a purge was a consequence of the need for purity. It was a slightly different view from that in Nazi Germany —for example, the SS destroyed in one night a whole city because the shopkeepers were Jews. The gap between party and society was much greater in the Soviet Union than in Germany. Thus the character of repression was more confined. In this sense, the early stages of Bolshevik consolidation profoundly differed from the earlier struggle between the professionals and politicals within the German *Wehrmacht*. The purge and the purification both occurred as a struggle within the party, not within the society at large. They may have frightened ordinary people but did not demobilize them in any economic sense.

This is important to bear in mind because of the notion of terrorism that even fairly prominent writers have developed about this period in Russia has tended to confuse the object of terror. The object of terror was not the working class or the peasantry. On the contrary, the purpose of this terror was always to purify the party so that it would do more for the people. It was recognized that this was terribly hypocritical, but it did allow Soviet society to function normally despite turmoil and chaos. If one was a good Stakhanovite worker, one was genuinely rewarded. A photograph might appear in the newspaper, with a worker's arm around Stalin. The worker would go home thousands of miles away, with a renewed faith in the personal concern of the system with individual needs, and not simply political tasks.

The economic structure within which Soviet life operates, has remained untouched by the continual political scramble. Soviet politicians operate much like the criminal in relation to general society. One rarely feels the impact of criminal society unless he engages in those acts that directly impede the operation of state power. That was the situation throughout the late twenties and early thirties. Even the various purge trials did not touch the general society. There was a quietude, a certain amount of concern, which no doubt ramified throughout the society, but no extreme worry. The existence of the purges was known, but this knowledge did not affect the functioning of most lives. Terrorism itself did not seriously effect the rate and character of production. The argument that terror threatens economic development forgets the important fact that in Soviet life terrorism was largely confined to the political arena. Thus, there was a negligible influence of political structure upon variations in economic performance— a strange truism common to the Third World countries along with the socialist bloc. (Adelman and Morris, 1967, pp. 237–251).

What happened to the military, to the party, to the state, to the nation? To take over a society is not to liquidate the established organizational patterns of life. The first thing that indicated the shape of the Bolshevik system and its essential conservationism had to do with the army. Bolshevism, or socialism in general, is antimilitary. The problem then became, how is the problem of a standing army to be handled? What is the role of the armed forces to be in the new state? It was taken for granted that a decision had been reached concerning the larger society, but there were consequences for each sector in society. The development of a permanent standing army was repugnant to the Bolsheviks. In effect, in the early stages the Red Army was comprised of advance units of the Soviets. The control of the army was indeed in the hands of the masses in whose name the revolution was made. But over the long run, and certainly by the end of the Lenin period, a professional armed force had been consolidated. As long as the masses had the weapons, they were in a position to rebel. The 1917 Revolution became consolidated only when the weapons systems changed, only when the Soviets were considerably weakened and the armed forces became independent and dominant.

Leonard Schapiro (1960) points out in *The Communist Party of the Soviet Union* that a permanent standing army was against Social Democratic tradition and that there were demands for a state militia. The professional army came into being for two reasons: the confining of the militia to the Soviets would enable a defensive localistic armed force to emerge; it would not enable the Soviet Union to defend itself nationally. That is to say, the coordination would be taken out of the hands of the local Soviets in order to guarantee the sovereignty of the nation as a whole. Once the decision was made that socialism in one country is going to be inexorable, the next decision, to divide the professional army from the economic proletariat, was inevitable. That was the first move in organizational Bolshevism, long before many others that confirmed the transition from ideology to organization. All the ideological arguments vanished before the need to keep the state intact. Had Trotsky perceived the true nature of the problem at that time, things might have been different in the historical evolution, though that is highly speculative.

It is clear that the development of a professional standing army was the first vital thrust into the socialist ideology made by the Soviets. The second vital thrust was in relation to the problem of nationalism. Here, too, ideology violated the needs of the day, and finally yielded to organizational necessity. The formula of nationalism was the right of each nation to self-determination; the notion of self-determination of nations was not originated in the United Nations, but was a Bolshevik slogan. The formula was to be: each nation—and that meant 200 or more national or ethnic groups within the boundaries of Russia—would have the right to affiliate. In exchange for this affiliation, the group was granted language and legal rights within the boundaries of the national unit. In effect, a kind of barter and exchange system developed whereby, for the right of national consciousness, groups granted the Soviet Union the command of the society. It was almost like a social contract, in which certain rights were guaranteed—for example, the right of military forces—and in exchange for which one received the right to a grammar. It seems trite to express it so simply, but it was a formula that enabled the Soviet Union to maintain its homogeneity in a nationalistic and separatistic world.

This formula was very much like the resolution achieved in the United States during the post-Civil War period. States' rights were upheld, but they became largely mythical when they clashed with national needs. The person had an obligation to the state that he would pay dues, buy insurance and licenses and pay all kinds of taxes to the local authority, but he always had a sense of belonging to a larger whole.

The notion of Russian self-determination reduced itself to an acceptance of states' rights as long as those rights never impinged on the national sovereignty. Indeed, this resolution was so advanced that it enabled the Soviet Union to grow with rapidity almost with the announcement of national policy, because it afforded a resolution early and without bloodshed of that which historically had divided the Russians, namely, sectionalism—the kinds of struggles that made for Civil War in the United States. If we bear in mind that the industrial takeoff period in the United States was accelerated after the Civil War, it becomes apparent how profound the settlement of these issues was for the growth of Russia.

The solution was similar to what the United States did after the Civil War. There were threats to the system from the Leningrad group and the Georgian and Ukrainian groups, and even during World War II, Ukrainian nationalism was successfully appealed to by the Nazis. But by and large, the system of decentralization had succeeded in making the regions feel they have autonomy while they hold national allegiance.

The settlement was, of course, a federalistic settlement, based on the claims of the sovereign state upon its subjects and upon its states. The solution was a federated republic, not a socialist republic. Once again, the ideology of the national self-determination was produced as a federalist solution. Here, too, the ideological was transformed into the organizational.

The Soviet Revolution was not doing away with the state, but with socialism as such. The revolution that was to announce a triumph of society over polity was altered almost immediately after the Revolution. Instead of the liquidation of state power and authority, the slogan was "the workers' state." For example, Lenin pointed out immediately after the Revolution that the worker himself now administered the state. This statement still had a populist flavor; but in an address called "To the Population" (Lenin, 1955), the argument was no longer presented negatively as the liquidation of state authority, but positively—for the authority of the Soviets. Needless to say, the notion that the party was the administrator of the state was soon introduced, and then the idea that the party council would administer the state. The state, far from moving toward dissolution, became more important as the lines between party and state were blurred.

The key was that the legal forms had to be protected because the society rested on ideology. However, the polity always upstaged society. One of the most bitter outcomes for the revolutionists was that their expectation of the victory of society over polity was not fulfilled, but quite the reverse. There took place the development within Bolshevik life of the complete mastery of the political system over the economic system.

What was involved here was an end of ideology in the East. The Party discussions after the Revolution, which were so marked and heated, finally came full cycle to a point where organization dominated and ideology either vanished or became subterranean, as in the current artistic rebellions in the Soviet Union. The fact that the Soviet Union has made very slender theoretical innovations within the framework of a socialist or Marxist ideology is itself indicative of the degree to which the ideological has given way. The reforms of the economy are all in the direction of competition, and all move in terms of a social psychology which supposedly characterizes capitalist man rather than socialist man. After fifty years of Bolshevism, perhaps in no country on earth is the United States so much admired as in the Soviet Union.

The difficulties with socialism have proven to be far less serious at the economic level than at the political level. Under capitalism, through the system of gaduated taxation, wages have been equalized and profits curbed; through the system of social welfare, monetary distribution similarly has been made more widespread; and through technological rationalization, productive tasks have become less onerous and distinctions between head and hand have been sharply curtailed. This is not to say that the gaps between socialism and capitalism have been obliterated. They clearly remain. It is to say that a more significant gap has developed between forms of political rule, under socialism, or more precisely, between the political methods for attaining socialism.

The process of gaining state power has driven a breach between democratic and authoritarian socialism that is at least as deep as the breach between capitalism and socialism. The relative autonomy of political power, its clear and distinct realm apart from economic performance, has compelled decision-makers to be cognizant of a double interchange system of decisions: capitalism and democracy, capitalism and totality, socialism and democracy, socialism and totality. This model of economic base and political superstructure has collapsed, and given way to a model based on political sociology. Decision-making takes place in a universe in which economic activities are part of a larger network of sociopolitical decisions. The nature of the socialist commitment has changed. As cadres began making a choice either in favor of socialism with democratic politics, or socialism with totalitarian politics, the decision at the level of political form rather than economic content became the critical point determining alliances and allegiances among these cadres.

In a strange sense, the fact that politics rather than economics increasingly has come to underwrite the Soviet system, no less than the American system, worked to the advantage of the Bolshevik leadership. Socialism may have stagnated, but statism has not. Fundamental problems of production went unsolved and often unheeded; whereas in the political realm, bureaucratic techniques of rule were elevated to a level of sophistication unimagined by the early pioneers of Russian socialism. A brief comparison of the ineptitude in handling the agrarian sector, in contrast to the cleverness in handling the administrative apparatus, offers clear evidence of this transformation of socialism from a doctrine of economic equities to a dogma of political priorities.

The early Soviet leadership appreciated the need, not just for industrialization, but for a method to reduce the Russian dependence on agricultural produce as a primary source of wealth. As a result, a great assault was mounted on the social structure of peasant relations and of farm technology as well. The American approach has been to outflank the farm class by reducing its numbers in proportion to the total society. In American society, the agricultural base has diminished, until today it is 7 percent of the population in the United States. In the Soviet Union, it is still 50 percent. One of the bizarre consequences of the ideology of smashing the feudal remnants was that it took precedence over common sense. The sacrifice of the agricultural sector was enlarged rather than diminished by making the agricultural sector the experimental playground for the Bolshevik Revolution. Terrorism took place in the agricultural sector to a very large degree. The wealthy peasant class was wiped out and the bourgeois class was eliminated. Where terrorism directly affected these classes, the level of production remained stagnant. The amount of livestock produced in 1964 was the same as in 1917. But the purge and the terror were mainly intraparty phenomena. The conventional justifications for de-Stalinization may have been formulated among the leaders to get rid of an institution that threatened them.

The question of terror and the Soviet Union, however, cannot be easily resolved. What seems to have happened in the Soviet Union is that those workers who were highly politicalized did take risks, but Stalin was an intelligent organizer. He had a second and a third echelon training every man to do every other man's job. The party base expanded very rapidly, with new jobs for new personnel. A half million new bureaucratic jobs were created during the purges. The death of every man multiplied the available jobs. The party thus was made more attractive. The terroristic formulas operated primarily within the politicalized sector. Their depth of penetration has been so badly overestimated that some kind of redress of balance is in order. Academic people have been prone to the worst generalizations about terrorism, speaking as if it were the primary factor in Soviet society, without taking into consideration the countervailing effects. At the very time of the purge, 1934–39, Soviet literature was filled with the need for inner party democracy. There was a national intellectual effort to get people to become more candid. It is very complicated. No society succeeds if it relies solely on terror, for it is very dysfunctional; there must be more terrorists than workers. A society succeeds because of rewards to those who produce more than anyone else.

The emergence of bureaucratic socialism produced a profound de-politicalization of Soviet society. And it also had the same economic effects as bureaucratic capitalism in the West: reformism and revisionism in the working classes. With the deepening (instead of lessening) of the division of labor within the socialist system, special interests manifested themselves throughout the social subsystem. As a result, instead of the administrative apparatus withering away or dissolving, it hardened into a bureaucratic apparatus linked by its higher functionaries to the Party apparatus. But if the goals of self-management became less important to the socialist ethic, the goals of economic planning became more important. And in the ful-fillment of these plans, the administrative apparatus played a central role. The bureaucracy became the functional equivalent in the economic realm to the Party in the political realm. The real brilliance of socialism in the Soviet Union is how airtight the two compartments of government and politics have been kept—a compartmentalization broken only at the top echelon leadership levels, where the art of governing and the power of ruling were thoroughly isomorphic (See Hegedüs, 1969, pp. 237–252).

Milovan Djilas (1957, pp. 124–146) believes that Soviet leadership had no new ideas to offer. There is an inverse correlation between political terror and ideological innovation. The Soviet leaders became more or less a stable conservative force. They were the regulators of the society, the bureaucratic members of the society. They certainly cannot be considered men of ideas, for they were the managerial estate of the society. In the Soviet Union, when a basic decision had to be made between ideology and the functional requirements of the nation, there was a 100 percent resolu-tion in terms of the functional requirements of the nation. Invariably, the argument that the nation must survive won out over any and all other kinds of considerations. It is not that ideas or ideology as such vanished; it is that meaningful competition in ideas vanished and ideological innovative-ness tended to disappear. There is no longer any argument about socialism in one country.

It might be said that from an ethical viewpoint Trotsky was right, but that is not an arguable premise in Russian life. Ideology is no longer a factor. The rhetoric of Marxism will be referred to once in a while, but without any new approaches to economic development or new concepts of the economy. There is no improvement on or criticism of *Das Kapital*

(Marx, 1967). The Soviet Union may have ideological discussions, but never is there a resolution of ideology into organization. The purpose of ideology is to smash organization; therefore all organizations are against ideology. The Soviet Union is the most perfect case on record of the collapse of ideology in the face of the bureaucratic pathos.

REFERENCES

Adelman, I., and C. T. Morris (1967) *Society, Politics, and Economic Development.* Baltimore: Johns Hopkins Press.

Baughman, J. P. (1971) "New Directions in American Economic and Business History," in G. A. Billias and G. N. Grob, eds., *American History: Retrospect and Prospect.* New York: Free Press.

Carr, E. H. (1950) *The Bolshevik Revolution, 1917–1923.* New York: Macmillan.

Djilas, Milovan (1957) *The New Class; An Analysis of the Communist System.* New York: Praeger.

Engels, F. (1934) *Ludwig Feuerbach and the Outcome of Classical German Philosophy.* New York: International Publishers.

Haimson, L. (1951) *The Origins of Early Russian Bolshevism.* Cambridge, Mass.: Harvard University Press.

Hegedüs, A. (1969) "Marx's Analysis of Bureaucracy and the Socialist Reality," in *Marx and Contemporary Scientific Thought,* Proceedings of UNESCO Conference, jointly sponsored by the International Social Science Council and the International Council for Philosophy and Humanistic Studies. Belgium: Mouton and UNESCO.

Katkov, G. (1968) "German Political Intervention in Russia during World War I," in R. Pipes, ed., *Revolutionary Russia.* Cambridge, Mass.: Harvard University Press.

Lenin, V. (1955) *To the Population. On "Democracy" and Dictatorship. What is Soviet Power?* Moscow: Foreign Languages Publishing House.

Lipset, S. M. (1967) "Values, Education, and Entrepreneurship," in S. M. Lipset and A. Solari, eds., *Elites in Latin America.* New York: Oxford University Press.

Marx, K. (1967) *Capital,* ed. F. Engels. New York: International Publishers.

Marx, K., and F. Engels (1971) *Writings on the Paris Commune,* ed. H. Draper. New York: Monthly Review Press.

North, D. C. (1966) *Growth and Welfare in the American Past: A New Economic History.* Englewood Cliffs, N.J.: Prentice-Hall.

Reed, J. (1935) *Ten Days That Shook the World.* New York: Modern Library.

Schapiro, L. (1960) *The Communist Party of the Soviet Union.* New York: Vintage Books.

CHAPTER 10

THE
MILITARIZATION
OF COMMUNISM

An explanatory model emphasizing similarities between communist revolutions considers phenomena like Leninism, Maoism and Castroism to be variations on a theme composed by Karl Marx, and caused by a set of circumstances generally described as underdevelopment. A failing capacity to control the social environment, aspirations to modern industrialization, a politically unassimilated, discontented intelligentsia ready for revolutionary action, a recent history of real and imagined grievances against foreign imperialism—these are taken as the constitutive elements of communist revolution. Indeed, communist revolutions are taken to be much like national revolutions everywhere in the underdeveloped world, except for their more extreme methods, goals and doctrinaire commitments.

A contrasting explanatory model points out the unique character of each communist conquest, and justifies this observation on the grounds that the anticipated socialist fraternity of nations and interests has clearly been wracked by enmity. Different socialist systems have shown differing patterns of behavior toward capitalist systems and neutralist antisystems. Different national communist leaderships met the exigencies of practical administration and the universal struggle over scare goods in such a way as to lead them inevitably to regard self over others and thus to subsequent ideological battle among themselves.

To adopt a rigid morphological standpoint and claim that one communist revolution is like any other is to say that basic precepts and methodologies do not change, that each cataclysm, however far-reaching, is sufficiently like its predecessor to require little more than an explanation for a few adjustments (such as creating a Leninist party to assure the "inevitable" outcomes of historical law or allowing peasants to fulfill the historic destiny of the sometimes scarce proletariat). Although each adaptation to circumstances may be viewed as a unique event, it is best comprehended as one of a number of common responses to a set of common conditions. The explanatory model favoring similarity thus assumes a number of commonalities of social cause.

The explanatory model based on comparative differences focuses on postrevolutionary behavior. It is guided by the belief that the revolutionary event may have been based in a general social cause, such as underdevelopment, but that a dynamic "paradigm" for international politics demands that imbalance and conflict arise from a universal and self-interested competition for goods, and that irrespective of initial similarities, over time, national interest must disturb the socialist community.

While these broad explanatory approaches have been generally accepted, they tend to ignore many fundamental problems essential to comprehending communist revolution and policy. It is necessary to "step outside" them both to pose fresh problems. Therefore, we require a third and more inclusive way to understand the communist revolutionary phenomenon: to see it as a strategy, not for industrialization and political control of the social environment alone (vital as this is), but for the seizure of government power in order to institute a modernizing social order. The communist believer has a picture of the future. It is one legitimized by history. How does his vision of emerging history influence his strategies for acquiring the power of government?

An important aspect of the communist world picture is a belief in the inevitability of the laws of history. These "laws" promise the communist ultimate ascendancy and victory and assure him of the progressiveness of the values he holds. The communist's commitment is based upon his understanding of an objective tendency toward world socialism, which is to relieve the universe of a capitalism dying of its own contradictions. His decision to cast his lot with history is thus "good," in scientific accord with "material reality." At the same time, he seems himself as a political actor, making decisions and plans, charged with the task of bringing historical law to actual fruition. Given that this "law" guarantees his future victory, what must he, as a political actor, do in the meantime? The communist is committed to a deterministic model of history while he is pressed to rationalize his role as a conscious, willful political man. How does he link "law" and "will" so that the operation of both will be realized through the actions of men, and then only if they organize to act properly? Organizing for appropriate action is the way to prove that there is indeed a socialist tendency "inherent" in modern capitalist systems. Nothing proves this so certainly as victory, of course, and so it is necessary to organize for political victory. But organization for victory over what? Over abstract "capitalism"? No. Rather, over the political agents that represent it in a ruling government. The communist world picture thus comes to include the idea of seizing the power of government as the appropriate political action sanctioned by the laws of history.

"Organization" in communist theorizing thus means revolution making. But this concept, so central to communist political approaches to power, has fragmented into a number of strategies for power seizure. This fragmentation has created many dilemmas for communists. What follows from conceptualizing "organization" as a centralized political "party"? What follows from conceiving it as a "guerrilla band"? How did communists come to produce different interpretations of the same solution to the problem of "law" and "will"? What conditions have favored a party concept? Which have favored guerrilla warfare? Can a communist movement, committed to international solidarity, tolerate a party and a guerrilla organization? What do these distinct organizational models imply for communist cooperation internationally?

In considering these problems it is vital to employ a methodology that views the communist idea of organization as a strategy for the seizure of power, and to observe its changes over time and its implications for relations between national communist movements. For in the long run, a communist organization devoted to party idealizes its model. One devoted to guerrilla warfare idealizes its resistance to model construction. Because each is legitimated by instances of success, these idealizations enhance the polycentric tendencies in the communist world. Problems of conflict within and between segments of the communist movement may be illuminated by examining the problem of communist conceptualization. We do not always need to rely upon the much worn "national interest" device for making observations. In addition, the idea of various styles of communist organization explains similarities in the communist political vocabulary without having to reduce all matters to those deriving from "underdevelopment."

THE SOVIET MODEL

The first spectacularly successful step in the direction of "organizing" Marxism was taken by Vladimir Lenin. Lenin accomplished his organizing mission despite a doctrinaire Marxist commitment to historical law because he squarely faced up to three problems. First, he confronted the fact that "capitalist productive relations" could not be relied upon to lead the proletariat to a revolutionary consciousness; rather, it led them no farther than to group interest politics and the art of compromise. Second, he tried to understand how or why it was the "bourgeois intellectual" instead who appeared to be revolutionized by the capitalist system. Third, he tried to solve the problem of how to bring this intellectual to the factory worker, and how to unite them in organized action that would lend history a hand by seizing the political power of government.

Many of Lenin's critics asked, If socialism is inevitable, why work for it? Why not leave workers' organizations, such as trade unions, to achieve what they can and rely on "historical evolution" to carry their awareness further at a later time? Lenin answered that the growth of capitalist production creates in the proletariat only that mentality that makes trade union tactics possible. The Marxist principle, that all ideology is a superstructure built upon the foundation of productive relations, implied to him that trade unionist politics is the proletariat's final answer to capitalism. To rely, therefore, on the working class to "evolve" into a self-consciously revolutionary force is quite out of the question. Moreover, according to Lenin, the socialist theory of Marx and Engels was created by educated representatives of the bourgeois intelligentsia. It was even introduced into Russia by this group. Clearly, then, only socialist intellectuals had formalized a revolutionary theory properly sifted from working-class experience and properly able to extend working-class consciousness to revolutionary socialist consciousness.

Implying that class position did not wholly determine class mentality, Lenin traveled far from Marx and Engels who accepted the deterministic connections between class identity and class ideology. He did not pursue the matter of how he arrived at this voluntaristic position. Lenin read Marxism as a call for socialist revolution, one that proscribed the *aims* of popular politics and not its means. He could, by concentrating upon Marxism as a theory of political *goals*, (not action) legitimized by historical law, take considerable theoretical liberties in formulating the means of achieving them. Faced with the problem of bringing together socialist intellectuals and the small, powerless, but still essential, proletarian agent of historical destiny, he sought a rationale for uniting them. Lenin had not, of course, gotten to the point that others did later, that of substituting one popular mass (a large-scale peasantry) for another (the scarce proletariat). He was trying to mobilize the only socialist revolutionary elements that he, as a Marxist, understood to be possible. He thus combined his version of an observed political reality with Marxist goals, worrying little about doctrinal consistency. By focusing upon the revolutionary intent, the goals of Marxist theory, he quite ignored the violence he did to one of its basic propositions.

Lenin could thus come to conceive a professional revolutionary staff of working-class intellectuals, a Communist party dedicated to power seizure, as the object of Marxist theory. Marxism ceased to be, for "Leninists," either a futuristic image or a technique of social criticism. It could not even survive as the mere ideological position of an interested group. It had become a theory about the goals of modern politics and how to attain them without complacent subjection to the historical law that legitimized them. Marxism as formulated by Marx and Engels, and reemphasized by Lenin, came to be thought of as a scientific theory providing men, interested in honest understanding, with a means of consulting history and the present in order to draw valid conclusions about how people do and ought to behave politically. But like all scientific theory, it remained for men to prove it by application. Thus, Lenin proposed a theory of communist organization as an essential part of Marx's theory about goals. He insisted that it was required in order to prove the validity of those goals. After all, a scientific theory needs validation in practice—in a laboratory situation when that is what is called for, in human action and organizational experiment when that is called for. Communists acquired the idea that a scientific theory must be tested. If it is correct, it will survive. Scientific socialism, if correct, will show itself in victories stemming from properly organized implementation of goals.

The fullest expression of the Leninist idea exists as *What Is To Be Done?* (Lenin, 1929). In this work, Lenin attacks a propensity of the Marxist intellectuals to consider and employ Marxism as a technique for sociological analysis and criticism. "Freedom of Criticism" advocates among socialists apparently found mutual criticism so absorbing they thought it a primary activity. Not only that, they were led by such predilections to imagine that the height of political action was the issuance of flaming public statements demanding that Marxism be recognized as a legitimate position, entitled to "rights" to be heard. The outcome of this, Lenin warned, would merely be that the environment could absorb such a demand and lead Marxism down the path of adaptation to the continuing existence of a bourgeois order. Since Marxism is not primarily an analytic tool, it is worse than dangerous to "plead" a cause on this basis. Marxism is a revolutionary plan to be implemented. To treat it otherwise is to corrupt it. Moreover, "free critics" engaged in hair-splitting battles with one another over points of principle were creating mere diversions from revolutionary goals. These ought, if they were really scientific socialists, to suppress their differences, turn from endless critical activity and organize to implement the plan, to make revolution. For "those who are really convinced that they have advanced science, would demand, not freedom for the new views to continue side by side with the old, but the substitution of the old views by the new views" (Lenin, 1929, p. 96). No excuses for intellectualizing or prayerfully awaiting a new dawning could be tolerated. No excuses limiting the revolutionary intelligence to support of worker trade union claims, economic benefits, spontaneous demonstrations (Lenin is chiding the "economist") can be considered anything less than a betrayal of revolutionary victory (p. 107). Only a Communist party, organized for revolution making, cultivating the skills to effect it, guarding the ideas to illuminate the path, can validate Marxist "science" (p. 110). Failure to employ Marxism on behalf of winning power for the proletariat strengthened the hand of the bourgeoisie. To suggest that socialist ideology is critical activity or commands revolutionaries to await a day when the proletarian consciousness will have grown up, is to strengthen a bourgeois power: "to belittle Socialist ideology in any way, to deviate from it in the slightest degree means strengthening bourgeois ideology" (p. 123).

The characteristics of a centralized Communist party, which Lenin considered the realization of Marxism, are clearly defined. It must be "all-national," not parochial, in the range of issues it engages (Lenin, 1929, pp. 167–168). It must possess mastery in Marxist theory (p. 180). It must establish a class of revolutionary scientists, professional revolutionists, who are less concerned for socialist rhetoric than for victory (pp. 181, 185). To make these a cohesive group, all class distinctions between intellectuals and workers within the party must be abolished (pp. 187–188, 204). This party must survive a hostile environment and restrict its numbers to the most loyal cadre, who will formulate policy for a dispersion of local party workers (pp. 187–188). This will give continuity to the struggle, for a large, democratic party is unwieldly and vulnerable to police destruction (pp. 196, 199). It must provide a channel of mobility for talented workers otherwise denied means to exercise their political talents (p. 205). Such men the party will educate and broaden, universalizing their thinking beyond the limits of personal or merely group interest (p. 206). There may be in all of this a risk of authoritarianism. But the compensations for taking this risk are too great to be foregone. Besides, such a party will provide good substitutes for formed democracy, such as the fact that trusted people will be better supported than if they had been formally elected and subject to the constant will of a large membership (pp. 213–217).

Lenin never systematically examined the matter of arming or militarizing the party organization. There was no need to. The Bolshevik power base was located in urban areas, and from positions in the Soviet, the communists could advance their revolutionary plan. Moreover, Kerenski's regime lost support so quickly that in seizing upon the "moment," Lenin did not also elaborate a theory of armed seizure. Time did not allow for it.

This does not mean that Lenin did not exhibit a considerable tolerance for violent action. One of his ablest biographers indicates that

> Lenin hoped that the revolutionary squads would seek out members of the Black Hundreds (reactionary monarchists and pogromists), "beat them up, kill them, and blow up their staff headquarters." Sometimes one person would have to do this "at his own risk." This was the way to fight for freedom, he insisted. All other democrats were merely "quasi-democrats" and "liberal chatterboxes." (Fischer, 1964, p. 120)

Violence was in the Russian air. Tkachev and Nechayev were principal advocates of violence with whose writings Bolsheviks were familiar. Lenin was not repelled by them. Peasant outbursts, riots and looting had become a "tradition." Still, to Lenin and his followers, these showed lack of method. They represented mere randomness, easily spent, romantic, but ineffective, individualism. Lenin did show a desire for "methodizing" violence. But neither the Bolsheviks' access to urban political machinery nor the speed with which the Kerenski regime disintegrated encouraged the extension of Marxism in the direction of theorizing about armed battle. Thus, Leninist organization was left as primarily "party" organization, an outward emulation of a traditional European organizational form, but directed toward a revolutionary coup.

Some military base for the Bolshevik party was in evidence, and it could operate with the force of precedent for the future.[1] Organized on an ad hoc basis, it was nevertheless significant for Bolshevik victory in 1917. The medium through which the Bolsheviks organized their forces for a final coup was the Military Revolutionary Committee of the Petrograd Soviet. It channelized revolutionary possibilities as the chaos of the liberal bourgeois factions increased. Bolsheviks were not prepared with a military theory for the November Revolution, but they were aware of the need for a military adjunct to the party. With the Bolsheviks in control of the Petrograd Soviet, a resolution to create the Military Revolutionary Committee was carried on October 29, 1917, and the committee itself was staffed some four days before the insurrection (including a few sympathetic Left Socialist Revolutionaries). The president of the soviet, Leon Trotsky, was also chairman of the committee, and he established liaison with the Bolshevik Central Committee through a secret "military revolutionary center," consisting of five members (Sverdlov, Stalin, Bubnov, Uritsky and Dzerzhinsky).

Although the Central Committee had met on October 23 to set up a Political Bureau, (including Stalin, Trotsky, Sokolnikov and Bubnov, overlapping membership with the Military Committee), intended as a temporary measure until the uprising, there is no evidence that it ever operated. Real organization of the insurrection was in the hands of the Military Revolutionary Committee of the Petrograd Soviet. This "general staff" of the revolution maintained control over the military units in the capital and controlled revolutionary squads called the Red Guard (probably an inspiration for Mao Tse-tung at a later time). The Red Guard had been organized as early as June through factory and shop committees controlled by the party's Central Committee and had come to number some 200,000. The Military Revolutionary Committee directed the revolutionary "plan" in its last days. It acted through lesser "commissars" (several hundred by November 5). The commissars were appointed to military units in the capital to exhort, mobilize and lead them to shops and factories to arouse the Mensheviks and Left Socialist Revolutionaries influential there to action or sympathy. The party's Central Committee had, for a time, become a Military Committee, supervising sectors of revolutionary activity

---

[1] The events described are digested from the work of Fainsod (1953) and Shapiro (1960).

such as railways, posts and telegraphs and coordinating activity with other areas such as Moscow.

In its preparations for insurrection, the Military Revolutionary Committee relied on developing a sufficient Bolshevik political organization. It already had approximately 1,000 members in the Petrograd area alone, among them young officers and others with military experience. Through this organization, commissars were assigned to the Petrograd garrison's combat units, as well as to arsenals, warehouses and other such structures. Arrangements were made through the commissars, who were in charge of issuing arms, to prevent the arming of Junkers, or cadets in the military schools, and at the same time to divert military equipment to themselves. Some resistance followed. The Bolshevik commissar could not establish his authority in the important Fortress of Peter and Paul which commanded the Winter Palace. But on the afternoon of November 5, Trotsky appealed to the soldiers of the fortress. Resistance was overcome. With their peaceful surrender also came a prize of some 100,000 rifles.

The Provisional Government tried to quell the tide. The Bolshevik newspapers *Rabochii Put'* and *Soldat* were closed down. Criminal proceedings against the Military Committee were initiated. Kerenski tried to summon his own military strength. He went before the "preparliament" to proclaim a national crisis and ask for unqualified support. Menshevik Martov, approving the suppression of the Bolsheviks, nevertheless framed a resolution, upon which the debating body could agree, but which publicly held Kerenski's ambivalent land reform policies and his persistence in the world war responsible for the crisis. The Provisional Government rapidly lost face. Lenin was hiding, impatient, issuing a stream of directives. Events rushed to a climax. Trotsky addressed a meeting of the Petrograd Soviet. During the night of the sixth and the morning of the seventh, the Bolsheviks moved rapidly to seize the strong points of the city, which the Military Revolutionary Committee had staked out. Kerenski's military support melted away. Seizure was accomplished with no bloodshed. So vital had the role of the Military Revolutionary Committee been that it remained the center of government until its dissolution on December 18, 1917.

Through all of this, there was never any concept that this military core comprised anything but armed party action, undertaken by party members (significantly not true in the later Cuban case). There was no separate military and party leadership to coordinate. Thus the Military Committee was subject to retraction when the party officially took power. The revolutionary plan was lodged in the party mind. No mere military individual could have carried it out or comprehended it. It could not be wrested from its secure place. Certainly, then, no special theory of military power seizure needed to accompany the organized party which found no contradiction in coordinating its military with its political personnel.

Over the decades of rule, Soviet communists, idealizing their own revolutionary experience and accommodating *realpolitik* as a mode of maintaining their governing status, have never fully acquired a military concept of revolutionary organization and have been unable to provide parties looking to their leadership with a legitimized model of military seizure. Communists in a new experiential setting do not find in the Soviet lead anything but a "party" model of organization, a "political" model for seizure by penetration of government machinery, waiting for urban insurrection, accompanied then, perhaps, by military improvisations. Communist parties were either "Sovietized," accepting the Soviet model, or found it necessary to challenge USSR leadership. This Soviet tendency has been even further strengthened by the USSR's big power status and its stake in world stability as a possessor of nuclear power.

THE CHINESE MODEL

Following the directives of Stalin, the twenties proved a disaster for the Chinese Communist party. As a result, its greatest leader, Mao Tse-tung, was forced to formulate a new organizational plan for the communist seizure of power. In the process, Mao carried Communist "reorganization" to points of considerable departure from the Russian model.

On Stalin's instructions, at this time, Chinese Communists were to maintain a distinct party organization and, as individuals, enter the revolutionary nationalist Kuomintang (KMT). They were to support the establishment of the KMT's Canton power base and its northern military expedition for the unification of China. Beyond this "united front" tactic, they were instructed to try to build a mass organization of workers and peasants under their own direction, to fill key positions in government and the army and to work for the cementing of Chinese–USSR relations. Thus the Chinese Communists were led to seek compromise and cooperation with the commander-in-chief of the Kuomintang army, Chiang Kai-shek. But Chiang broke with the Communists in 1926 and thereafter began to destroy Communist organizations and exterminate their cadres. Confused, the Chinese Communist party reacted with desperate insurrectionary attempts in several South China cities. But they were isolated, lacking in high prestige among the workers, and were easily defeated.

Mao Tse-tung, then only an official of the Communist party in Hunan Province, led a remnant force, made up of rebel units from Chiang's army, a number of Communists and uprooted peasants, to temporary safety in the mountain stronghold of Chingkanshan. At first, this was little more than an act of self-preservation. But in defeat, Mao began to consider the possibilities of rural partisan warfare for which so few other Communists saw any future; they still believed in the centrality of the factory proletariat.

The Leninist-oriented Comintern policy was devoted to the idea that only an urban working class could carry out a proper Communist revolution. The Russian example was supposed to have demonstrated that even where the proletariat formed a small minority of the population, its concentration in the big cities would enable it to determine the outcome of a national crisis. After that, peasant "allies" would follow. Li Li-san, head of the Chinese party, was pressed to pursue this line. Stalin, in the name of Leninism, demanded that the Chinese party aim to take provincial capitals, from Mao's countryside base, and provide the communist movement with vital "proletarian centers." But Mao's attempt to comply with the demand, for the sake of party discipline and despite his doubts, by the occupation of Changsha in July 1930, ended in one of the most serious defeats for the Communist partisans. When Wang Ming continued Stalin's policy, despite the failure of the "Li Li-san line," one disaster continued to follow the other. At last, Mao sought to explicate his doubt into theory (which became official party policy when he became chairman of the party in 1935, a development the Russians finally accepted, but grudgingly).

Given the support and sympathy for the insurgents exhibited by the peasantry, a Chinese Communist revolution, Mao reasoned, could be realistically anticipated if it was based upon that peasantry. Given also the size and disunity of the Chinese nation, a slow process of conquering and establishing one soviet after another among the peasantry, until national power was encircled and vulnerable, was unavoidably a military process. Mao knew that China's traditional peasant uprisings had never been victorious unless educated leaders from the outside helped the peasant to overcome his limitations and establish political bases of opposition to the regime. Now, he concluded, this would be the role of *armed* Communists under Chinese conditions. Just as Lenin had built up the Bolshevik party as an organization of professional revolutionaries in order to introduce conscious revolutionary struggle into the young Russian labor movement, just so, the Chinese Communists would build up an organization of armed revolutionaries to do the same for the peasant.

This conclusion had been long in the making in Mao's mind. It grew out of largely personal observation, betrayal by the KMT, Soviet masterminded catastrophes and ultimate isolation in the southern mountain region. Even as early as 1926, Mao showed his penchant for seeking out the peasantry as China's revolutionary class. In his *Analysis of the Classes in Chinese Society* (Mao Tse-tung, 1962), he had begun to redefine the peasantry as a "semiproletariat" and ripe for revolution. And in his somewhat later "Report of an Investigation into the Peasant Movement in Hunan" (Mao Tse-tung, 1954–56, vol. 1, p. 31), the result of his tour of inspection in Hunan from January 4 to February 5, 1927, he describes the peasant mass as having "risen to fulfill their historic mission . . . to overthrow the rural feudal power . . . the main force in the countryside which has always put up the bitterest fight is the poor peasants. Throughout both the period of underground organization and that of open organization, the poor peasants have fought militantly all along"—this because they had no stake in protecting the established society. Sections of the report indicate clearly that Mao regarded the poor peasant as the main force, "the vanguard of the revolution" (Mao Tse-tung, 1954–56, vol. 1, p. 29). Even Leninist rhetoric about organizing progressive elements under the "hegemony of the proletariat" or the "leadership of the Communist party" does not appear (although some version of this does become a latter-day source of Mao's "New Democracy").[2] Clearly, then, the poor peasant had nothing to lose by socialist revolution. Organizing him for revolution implies that all other prerequisites for socialism will eventually take shape. This shift from proletarian to peasant-based revolution was no end in itself, nor was it without great organizational implications. For it was significantly and necessarily accompanied by a concept of revolutionary warfare that created important distinctions between Soviet and Chinese concepts of organization and strategy.

After he was routed by the KMT forces in the midtwenties, Mao showed his growing awareness of a need for the Chinese party to form military detachments. His writings on the "Second Revolutionary War" show his desire to develop a party, *armed* for military revolution and power seizure.[3] This he understood to be a long, arduous locale-by-locale affair. As military advances were made in the provinces, small-scale local revolutions would have to be carried out and "liberated areas" established. There, representative government would be set up (only the idea of a "soviet" conveyed the representative concept to Chinese Communists) and serve as the unofficial but real popular government of the area. And the "soviet-ized" area would be strengthened even more if surrounding provincial elites became frightened and divided. Once in existence, it should aim at establishing economic self-sufficiency, a sound and popular Communist party organization and a strong Red Army unit capable of self-defense (Mao Tse-tung, 1962, p. 60). Thus, a *military* struggle for the peasantry would have to be conducted in order to establish a Communist government within the existing system until the national government fell from want of support.

In this strategy, the Communist party supplies, recruits, trains, educates, but still controls a military personnel. For military struggle is still seen on the level of tactics. Only a scientific Marxist reading of power configurations, manifesting stages of historical law, can show to what uses the tactic may be applied. Only the party, the committed, educated Marxists, can perform this reading. Then, too, it is particularly congenial to party control that party and military leadership is largely the same (as in the Russian case). The Communist party may thus continue to act as "head"

---

[2] See Schwartz (1951, pp. 73, 76) for a view of Mao's Hunan report as an indication of a unique Maoism. Karl Wittfogel, however, has insisted that Maoism is just warmed-over, Sinicized Leninism. Most commentators accept Maoism as an innovative extension of Marxism. See also Brandt (1958, p. 109) and Fairbanks (1958).

[3] Mao's military theory is expanded upon elsewhere here but is available as "Strategic Problems of China's Revolutionary War," an "Interview with James Bertram," "Strategic Problems in the Anti-Japanese Guerrilla War," "On Protracted War" and "Problems of War and Strategy," all in Mao Tse-tung (1954–56).

of the armed "body," for the leadership echelons of party and army can find no contradiction in the unification of functions. Thus, a budding guerrilla organization can remain subject to party supervision and political intelligence (Mao Tse-tung, 1962, p. 68).

Even late in 1938, Mao reiterated a basic rule when he stated that "our principle is that the Party commands the gun, and the gun will never be allowed to command the Party" (Mao Tse-tung, 1962, p. 71). They ought, instead, to be "reeducated" to party doctrine, and thus party educators must always accompany military personnel. Of course, inhuman or irrational violence ought to be out of the question also because it diverts the party from real strategy and makes it sink to the level of blindness and immorality of the enemy. Violence is to be avoided in order to display the high moral fiber of the Communist party, but it should be avoided as well in the interests of party dissemination of political enlightenment.

In the course of struggle, however, the party "head" could not read events with the tool of scientific and classical Marxism alone. Rationality dictated that Marxists come to know the "laws" of war as they had come to know the "laws" of political society. And these they may know only by fearlessly encountering war, by exploring all of its sides, all of the experiences it yields, all of its points of uniqueness from and likeness to other kinds of events. Without pressing into war as far as possible, the party shall never understand it and never triumph. For the first time, valuable knowledge for Party Marxists is that gained from experiencing the "laws" of war, for such experience validates and gives final proof of actual strengths and weaknesses of the power protagonists. Thus, while pleading the cause of rational party control of random violence, Mao is able to say that

> war is the highest form of struggle, existing ever since the emergence of private property and social classes, for settling contradictions between classes, between nations, between states, or between political groups at given stages of their development. Without understanding the circumstances or war, its characteristics, and its relation to other things, we cannot know the laws of war, cannot know how to direct it, and cannot win victory. . . . a revolutionary class war or a revolutionary national war has its own special circumstances and characteristics of war in general. Thus besides the general laws of war, it has some special laws of its own. . . . without understanding its special laws, we cannot direct a revolutionary war and win victory in it. . . . Therefore we must study the laws in general, we must also study the laws of revolutionary war, and finally, we must study the laws of China's revolutionary war. (Mao Tse-tung, 1962, p. 75)

It is hard to believe that any part of this statement could have been consciously formulated by Lenin, even in the heat of the last days of the revolution and while directing the operations of the Military Revolutionary Committee. For Lenin, there were just wars on behalf of popular rights or national sovereignty and unjust wars for economic and power redivisions to suit the interests of ruling classes. Theorizing about war, for Lenin, never proceeded beyond establishing what a Communist's attitude ought to be toward one of these given kinds of war. Mao, in the midst of prolonged war, had to stretch his Marxism much further in the direction of military theorizing, and so he explored its organizational value and finally turned up a "military Marxism."

We must note the vital fact that the Japanese invaded the Chinese mainland in 1931. That event significantly advanced Mao's military thinking (and further linked it to survival, for Chiang was still more interested in destroying communists than he was in defeating the Japanese). But the degree toward which this sytematized Mao's thought is clear in Mao's strategy for Japanese defeat. Here he evolves his famous theory of "protracted" and "mobile" warfare. Mao assumes that the size of Chinese territory is so vast that the enemy will spend himself in conquering it. Thus, the decisive battles will be fought in China, and China's fighting men need not aim at the Japanese mainland. Japan, Mao observed, was a powerful imperialist power, politically, economically and militarily well organized. But it was the aggressor in the war. This gave the Chinese their first advantage—namely, both Chinese and world opinion will not favor Japan. Second, weak and divided as China was, its land mass was vast and its manpower infinite. So, China could count on world opinion and the size of its lands and armies to favor it over time. The war was a contest between a modern, rationalized, aggressive force without infinite resources for prolonged battle and a weak, traditional nation, able to absorb infinite attack until the attacker was exhausted (Mao Tse-tung, 1954–56, vol. 2, pp. 167–168). Thus, war on China's mainland would be protracted, but if China made no disastrous strategic errors, it would, despite its weakness, win decisively. The army's retreat would stop and its full advance begin. The war would thus pass through three stages: "the enemy's strategic offensive and our strategic defensive, the enemy's strategic defensive and our preparation for the counteroffensive, and the enemy's strategic defeat" (Mao Tse-tung, 1954–56, vol. 1, p. 197).[4]

The enemy would be allowed to advance with little resistance, then encircled, cut off from mainland supplies, be forced to fight inexhaustible human reserves. But, along the way, China must *never* fall to pure defense. It must always be preparing for the offense. It must build exterior lines for minor offensives while fighting a defensive war on interior lines. Exterior lines must constantly force the enemy's rear to become his battlefront. The enemy, even after a tactical victory, would need to rest. He would tire. He would stop heavy fighting for a short while. At this point, guerrillas must harass the enemy's rear, from the Chinese "exterior lines," then run off quickly, returning unexpectedly to harass again. Guerrilla harassment from

---

[4] See also Mao Tse-tung (1954–56, vol. 2, pp. 182–184).

unexpected points on the enemy's rear lines must be constant, but must be particularly unceasing during the enemy's moments of rest. Always the aim must be to turn the Chinese rear lines into front lines, and the enemy's front lines into his rear lines. The Chinese guerrilla band could thus prevent any clear idea of a Chinese front or rear from forming in the enemy's mind while he was doing battle with Chinese army regulars (Mao Tse-tung, 1954–56, vol. 2, pp. 194–195). Chinese tactics must follow a jigsaw pattern throughout the war. The enemy encircles; the Chinese counterencircle, but making sure to do so in such a way as to cut off segments of the enemy's army in the process. Mao elaborated at length on encirclements and counter-encirclements, which fall into too complex a range of types for repetition here (Mao Tse-tung, 1954–56, vol. 2, p. 195). But so it goes: the "enemy advances, we retreat, we retreat, enemy halts, we harass; enemy tires, we attack, enemy retreats, we pursue" (Mao Tse-tung, 1954–56, vol. 1, p. 212). In the earlier stages of the war, mobile warfare (the jigsaw pattern) is primary, guerrilla warfare secondary. In the latter stages, guerrilla war-fare (harassment, conversion of rear and front lines) is primary, mobile warfare secondary. Although mobile warfare in the third stage will not be undertaken entirely by the original guerrilla forces, they will by then have been raised from fighting guerrilla war to fighting mobile war (Mao Tse-tung, 1954–56, vol. 2, pp. 224–225).

Mao insisted that guerrilla warfare must be carefully planned, but not so rigidly as to endanger maintenance of the initiative and flexible adapta-tion to circumstances. Apart from routine planning, the strategic operations should be commanded centrally by the general staff and the war zone commanders, while the specific dispositions in a campaign should be made by lower ranks to maximize elasticity (Mao Tse-tung, 1954–56, vol. 2, pp. 154–155). Also, the guerrilla must plan for bases, for his preservation and in order to turn the enemy's rear into his front so that he has to fight ceaselessly throughout the areas he occupies. In order to create a base, a guerrilla unit should have extensive knowledge of the locality in which it operates, strong support among the people, the ability to repulse the enemy in that area and the skill to organize and arm the people for the consolida-tion and defense of the base. "Roving insurgents" winning victory were a groundless illusion. But above all, popular support insured success. And as the war dragged on, the quality of the guerrilla units would improve politi-cally and organizationally as well as militarily. When the war of attrition is won, these units could be absorbed into the regular army and take part in the final counteroffensive (to be launched with KMT cooperation, finally possible on the eve of World War II when Chiang decided in favor of driving out the Japanese with an all-out effort).

Several points in Mao's military thinking must be emphasized. First, armed military action was inseparable from party action and was conceived as an issue from the party leadership's Marxist understanding. Party appli-cation of Marxist theory coupled with military experience could master the "laws of war." Proper measures for victory would be further formulated in conformity with these dialectical laws. For example, for interior lines of battle, there must always be maintained exterior lines. Offensives were carried out along with defensive action. Procrastination was warranted as well as swiftness. Initiative was valuable; then, too, so was passivity. Mobile warfare contrasted with the building of guerrilla base areas. Troops must be concentrated and dispersed. Planning was as necessary as flexibility. For every encirclement there was a counterencirclement. And all objectives, all of these opposite modes of action, must be brought into play at once. Heavy battle produced a new synthesis of all these opposites. The "laws of war," like the laws of history, would thus be brought to fruition by armed party action in order to bring forward the only actors selected to win by history. Second, Mao's elevation of guerrilla warfare to the level of strategy must be counted an original contribution to military thinking, and like the idea of Communist peasant revolution, is involved in the concept "Maoism." Third, Mao's pattern of planning showed his relegation of KMT troops to a secondary function in the war, revealing his contempt for them as patriots and fighters (though he clearly avoided open clashes with them at this time). The level of guerrilla warfare was one in which only the Communist could participate. It became identified with higher communist political morality and identity. Fourth, Mao was deeply conscious of the international significance of the Chinese–Japanese conflict, and the extent to which the world scrutinized and evaluated his strategy. He was thus vehement about identifying higher Communist morality and practical prowess as an example for other oppressed nations and as a warning to other oppressors.

> Thus the protracted and extensive Anti-Japanese War is a war of jigsaw pattern in the military, political, economic and cultural aspects—a spectacle in the history of war, a splendid feat of the Chinese nation, a world-shaking achievement. This war will not only affect China and Japan, strongly impelling both to advance, but also affect the world, impelling all nations, first of all oppressed nations like India, to march forward. (Mao Tse-tung, 1954–56, vol. 2, p. 272)

The upshot of all this is that the Chinese party learned the value of initiating and controlling armed combat and ceased to frown upon the conduct of war as a legitimate political instrument.

> Every Communist must grasp the truth: "Political power grows out of the barrel of a gun." Our principle is that the Party commands the gun, and the gun will never be allowed to command the Party. But it is also true with guns at our disposal we can really build up the Party organization, and the Eighth Route Army has built up a powerful Party organization in North China. We can also rear cadres and create schools, culture and mass movements. Everything in Yenan has been built up by means of the gun. Anything can grow out of the barrel of a gun. (Mao Tse-tung, 1954–56, vol. 2, p. 272)

Vital as the peasantry was seen to be to insure the success of the communist revolution, it is hard to say whether a party-controlled guerrilla force, armed with guns, exceeded their value. Mao refers not only to a Marxist political line but a Marxist military line as an indication of the importance of military action and organization for the Chinese party (Mao Tse-tung, 1954–56, vol. 2, p. 274).

The Chinese revolutionary model has militarized the party organization while it had left the concept of party-controlled revolution unchallenged. Victorious in 1949, the Chinese scheme seemed vindicated as a better adaptation of Communist organization to the context of underdeveloped countries than could be gained from following the Russian example. By incorporating a theory of party-led military initiatives into the Marxist literature, the Chinese experience promised party organizations elsewhere the victories that reliance upon the Soviet model had failed to produce. It thus competed with the Soviet Union for prestige among communist revolutionaries all over the world. The Chinese model influenced most strongly those who saw little stake in stability, who sought a revitalized mode of Communist organization which included military initiatives and guerrilla warfare as a matter of principle, as an instrument emphasizing willful decision making over too strict an adherence to deterministic social laws.

THE CUBAN MODEL

The strengthening of military organization as a basis for communist revolution was greatly enhanced by the Cuban revolutionary experience. Indeed, a theorist of the Cuban Revolution (Debray, 1967) has gone so far as to elevate the guerrilla band into a prominence that subordinates, even denigrates, Communist party political organization. What was it about the Cuban Revolution that made a nonparty, guerrilla revolutionary model possible in the name of communism?

First, the Cuban Revolution was carried out by a pragmatic and theoretically unself-conscious leadership. It did *not* "apply" Lenin or Mao to its Cuban context. Consequently, directly military means of overthrowing the old regime could be advocated or employed without conceiving of any need to subject guerrilla actions to the discipline of a party. Because Castro and Guevara operated without benefit of a Leninist or Maoist model, they did not need to curb the military by party discipline.

Second, the Cuban Revolution eventually brought about an alliance between two distinct leaderships, that of the revolutionary guerrillas' military band and the Communist Party. Unlike *any* previous communist revolution, military and party leaderships were not the same and did not overlap. Thus, the guerrilla leader could continue to see himself as a military, not a political, actor, even under conditions of coordinated action with the Communist party.

Third, the primary revolutionary role of initiation and sustained insurrection was played by one and not both of these distinct entities—by the guerrilla band, not the Communist party. Ex post facto theorizing has elevated this new set of circumstances to the level of a new revolutionary principle favoring the enlarged role of a popular military force in Communist revolution making.

Castroism can be located historically from July 26, 1953, the date of the unsuccessful attack on the Moncada army post in Santiago de Buba, a year and a half after Batista's seizure of power. Fidel Castro emerged from this event as an independent figure with a personal following. The "July 26 movement" gained some definition thereafter, although it remained broad and vague at best. During Castro's improvement on the Isle of Pines from October 1953 to May 1955, he wrote his "History Will Absolve Me" speech (Castro, 1968). It came to stand as the articulation of the reforms sought by the 26th of July movement. There is little clear-cut ideology in it, aside from a general pleading for reform and justification of militant action toward that end. Then, in a pamphlet published clandestinely in June 1954, Castro took hold of reform a little more firmly. He promised to restore Cuba's 1940 constitution, hold popular elections and carry out land reform, including the restriction of large land holdings and an increase in the number of smaller ones and made some promise for vaguely defined "agricultural cooperatives." Moreover, in 1954, Castro wrote something less well known, which affords considerable insight into his motivation and conception. In that year, he sent a number of letters to Luis Aguero, an *ortodoxo* leader and radio commentator, to whom he confided some of his thoughts about his developing movement.[5] On August 14, 1954, Castro thought that he ought to "organize the men of the 26th of July movement"; he wanted to unite them "into an unbreakable body" of fighters. They must constitute "a perfectly disciplined human nucleus" for the "force necessary to conquer power, whether it be by peaceful or forcible means." He pointed out that

> the indispensable preconditions of a genuine civic movement are: ideology, discipline and leadership. The three are essential but leadership is most fundamental. I do not know if it was Napoleon who said that one bad general in battle counts more than twenty good ones. It is not possible to organize a movement in which everyone believes he has the right to issue public statements without consulting the others; nor can anything be expected of an organization made up of anarchic men, who at the first dispute find the easiest way out, breaking and destroying the machine. The apparatus of propaganda, or organization, should be so powerful that it would implacably destroy anyone who tries to create tendencies, cliques, schisms or rebels against the movement. (Aguero, 1959).

[5] Under President Ramon Gran San Martin's ruling Partido Revolucionario Cubano there had been a split in which an opposition group was formed, the Partido del Pueblo Cubano. The original party was known as the *auténticos* and the latter, Partido del Pueblo Cubano, as the *ortodoxos*.

Of the three conditions, Castro was least concerned with ideology. Discipline, and especially leadership, occupied him most. "La jefatura es basica" had the force of a first principle with him. Thus, Castro showed himself not to be ideology-bound at the very time he was organizing revolt. He could freely pursue the path of nonparty military or "guerrilla" rebellion, when the time came, with little concern for party rules, traditions and doctrine.

Even guerrilla warfare techniques and rationales came to him slowly. Neither he nor Guevara sought out the likely example Mao Tse-tung might have provided for them. The consistent failure of Cuban Communists to produce a revolution, the failures of spontaneous uprisings and romantic conspiracies, finally convinced Castro to consider guerrilla warfare and preparation for a protracted struggle. Still, despite his general drift, in the early months of 1957, not even Castro believed wholly in this plan. Castro had gone into the mountains still believing that he would probably merely harass the regime until the day when a great urban strike would paralyze Batista and cause his downfall. It was in course of battle, when his "strike" failed to materialize, that Castro, in late 1957, became convinced that guerrilla military operations were the path to power. Late as this development was in Castro's revolutionary career, it is of the greatest significance that he began with little ideology, independently of the Cuban Communist party, which was still thinking in 1917 terms, and learned from his experiences to follow a nonparty guerrilla warfare solution to the problem of power seizure. Not even an alliance with the Communists could overcome the significance of this lesson.

The Castro–communist alliance was first realized sometime in 1958. This does not mean that some Castroites and some Communists did not labor for such an alliance before this. But they were inhibited from working together as long as an important section of the 26th of July movement was anti-Communist in principle and the Communist leadership was antiinsurrectionist in practice. By the summer of 1958, however, the 26th of July movement suffered a major blow by virtue of procrastinating for an urban strike which did not materialize. And the Communist Party in the meantime had come around partially to an insurrectionary policy. The dividing line between Castro and the Communists narrowed down to that the overall value of armed struggle. The *fidelistas* could not surrender this issue. But the Communists could assimilate it as "tactics." This meant that they would have to cross the line and go over to Castro's side in order to make an alliance possible (Debray, 1970, pp. 31–46).

Castro's ideological "void" began to be filled by this alliance. At first, Castro seemed to identify himself with a vague "humanism," something distinct from capitalism or communism, some third way (it would be interesting to trace his possible studies of European history for the sources of this influence), some style of citizen participation. Communists tried to avoid clashing with him over his humanist "vogue." Yet it gained some stature and especially frightened the older Communist Party when the 26th of July trade union section swamped the Communists in union elections on a "humanist program." Still, Anibal Escalante criticized it as "ideological confusion" (a deed for which Castro was never altogether to forgive him). And Escalante prevailed. Castro dropped the term to preserve the alliance (Escalante was "purged," however, in 1962). The gradual increase of communist ideological influence upon Fidel, which grew out of the exigencies of alliance, convinced him that he was carrying out a socialist revolution. In 1959, with victory, he could declare it so. Despite such influences however, the July 26 movement and the Communist party remained distinct. By whatever degrees Castro came to accept communism, he never gave an inch on the matter of guerrilla insurrection (See Horowitz, 1970).

Escalante, then secretary of the Cuban Communist Party, could say on June 30, 1959 in *Hoy* that

> Fidel proclaimed that our revolution was socialist, that it had entered its socialist phase. He was not making a promise such as "we are going to make a Socialist Revolution." No. He explained an event which has already taken place. The Cuban Revolution has passed through its first stage, the first phase of national liberation and anti-feudalism it has completed. It fulfilled its tasks with honor and entered into a new, higher stage of social development; the socialist stage. And Fidel quietly and simply so declared it to the four winds. And we must advance in the direction of complete socialist transformation of our country. (Quoted in Tang and Maloney, 1962, pp. 2–3)

Castro's ideological pliability enabled communists to make common cause with him. Castro himself professed to Marxism in a speech on December 20, 1961, when he said, "we have acted in a Marxist-Leninist manner." He went so far, in this same speech, as to indicate he had always been a Marxist-Leninist. "Of course, if we stopped at the Pico Turquino [a height in the Sierra Maestra] when we were very weak and said 'We are Marxist-Leninists' we might not have been able to descend from the Pico Turquino to the plain. Thus we called it something else, we did not broach this subject, we raised other questions that the people understood perfectly" (Quoted in Tang and Maloney, 1962, p. 6). In fact, in his speech of December 1–2, 1961, Castro claims that he had been something of Marxist-Leninist since his student days:

> We began in the university to make the first contacts with the *Communist Manifesto*, with the works of Marx and Engels and Lenin. That marked a process. I can say an honest confession that many of the things that we have done in the revolution are not things that we invented, not in the least. When we left the university, in my particular case, I was really

greatly influenced—not that I will say I was in the least a Marxist-Leninist. (Quoted in Tang and Maloney, 1962, p. 10)

Castro climaxed this speech with the cry "I am a Marxist-Leninist, and I will be one until the last days of my life" (p. 11). Many other available statements would only be redundant. But the evidence shows that Fidel lacked a strong ideological "character." He could absorb Marxism-Leninism while at the same time viewing his earlier thinking as a process of evolution toward it, justifying his earlier belief in *jefatura* and his "humanism" as youthful expressions of the mature communist. Yet Castro did not appear to display an early understanding of Marxism-Leninism. He certainly never accepted nor advocated the idea of a party-led revolution (definitely a "first law" with proper Leninists). Not even the writings of Ernesto Guevara, his revolutionary companion, whose communist sympathies were never open to doubt, show an ideologically defined personality, much less the strictures of Marxist-Leninism. For Guevara was more the companion to Fidel than he could ever have been to the Communist party. His entire attention appears to have been occupied by an unorthodox concept of guerrilla action into which a Communist party organization never insinuates itself as vanguard over the popular will.

Far from unraveling the intricacies of Marxism-Leninism for the Cuban environment, Guevara (1961) was content to combine a practical, little guidebook on guerrilla warfare with a simple revolutionary theory: (1) popular forces can win against a regular army; (2) it is not always required to wait for "objective conditions" to be appropriate for revolution; the insurrectional focal point can create them; and (3) in Latin America, the countryside is the main locale of the armed struggle. In addition to offering some technical guidance for the "popular war," Guevara's work does little more than elaborate these three points. Gone are the "phases" of "class" revolution we are accustomed to hearing from a Mao or Lenin. Only phases of military combat exist. "Stages" are merely conditions of closeness or distance from victory. But importantly, though not with Guevara, the conscious issue of unorthodox rebellion against traditional Marxism—an armed guerrilla band—is loosely and indiscriminately conceived as a popular vanguard. "The guerrilla band is an armed nucleus, the fighting vanguard of the people" (Guevara, 1961, p. 10). The guerrilla figure himself is conceived in such a way that he might have been mistrusted by a Lenin or Mao as a romantic individualist with a muddled intellect, perfectly incapable of analyzing his society, his goals, his historic role.

> We must come to the inevitable conclusion that the guerrilla fighter is a social reformer, that he takes up arms responding to the angry protest of the people against their oppressors, and that he fights to change the social system that keeps all his unarmed brothers in ignominy and misery. He launches himself against the conditions of the reigning institutions at

a particular moment with all the vigor that circumstances permit to breaking the mold of these institutions. (Guevara, 1961, p. 17)

And far from being knowledgeable about the "stages of history" so as to master a "science of society," he need know little more than what is required of a good man and good soldier. What the guerrilla needs to have is a "good knowledge of the surrounding countryside, the paths of entry and escape, the possibilities of speedy maneuver, good hiding places," and "naturally" in all of this he must "count on the support of the people" (Guevara, 1961, p. 17). He should be willing to die for nothing more defined than "an ideal" (p. 18) and "social justice" (p. 20). Moreover, "Whoever does not feel this undoubted truth cannot be a guerrilla fighter" (p. 22). It is not even a truth that men can know. The good revolutionary "feels" it as an overpowering force. There is much talk devoted to guiding the fighter through the countryside, the intricacies of his weapons, supplies and so forth (pp. 28, 30–31). But the mystic "feeling" is accompanied only by a practicality that verges on inhumanity. Quite unlike Mao's stress on persuading, reeducating or returning captured enemy, Che suggests that "he should be eliminated without hesitation when he is dangerous. In this respect the guerrilla band must be drastic" (p. 37).

Mao Tse-tung was attempting to exploit the contrast between a ruthless Kuomintang army and a humane Red Army. Guevara came down to a focus upon the credibility of guerrilla power and the practical steps that enhance it. The guerrilla need not trouble himself with "contrasts" or party directives about his behavior toward enemy or peasantry. He is stoic, saintly, a "teacher-fighter," ready for supreme sacrifices out of the sheer intensity of his conviction (Guevara, 1961, p. 49). His reward for all his pains are violence and battle themselves: "Within the framework of the combatant life, the most interesting event, the one that carries all to a convulsion of joy and puts new vigor in everybody's steps, is the battle." Indeed, the "battle" is "the climax of the guerrilla life" (p. 50).

We may justifiably accuse Guevara of romanticism, of a lack of analytic skill and vigor, of a lack of commanding style, of excessive preoccupation with the details of combat, of sketchiness and a dangerous and unappealing simplicity of mind. But as a voice expressing shifts in the conceptualization of communism as a power-seizing formula, his is an *auténtico*. He shared with Fidel a distaste for ideological stricture and careless appraisal of the ideological traditions with which the Cuban regime became associated through the party influences upon it. Thus, he could share with him, too, an abiding faith in the effectiveness of guerrilla organization as a mode of acquiring power independent of party. Guerrilla organization as a power-seizing instrument returned to "will" a capacity for shaping environment that was not inhibited by the "timing" of action according to historical "law." This latter was relegated to a merely post hoc justification for an accomplished deed and did not impose a presence in the power struggle itself. Guerrilla organization thus succeeded party organization, as will fully succeeded law, as an instrument of gaining power. It thus created alternatives to party-centered Communist revolution that are potentially competitive with it (except where the mollifying effects of "alliance" are fully exploited and appreciated).

Regis Debray has synthesized this entire development into a new ideology of Communist revolution and has given it the "system" it was lacking in the minds of "men of action" like Castro and Guevara. His is a bold effort, which consciously sweeps away "law," "party" and "history" as obstructions to power seizure, and is likely to enjoy considerable popularity among Communists tiring of "reading" the signs of history into policy and anxious to commit themselves to effective deeds.

Debray (1967, p. 19) is clear that from the beginning "the socialist revolution is the result of an armed struggle against the armed power of the bourgeois state." Failure to gasp this "beginning" has plagued Communist parties still living in the idealized world of the accidents of 1917. Each party, in each succeeding period, has been living parasitically off a victorious predecessor and has been saddled with its pet theories about seizing power. This is not true of the Cuban Revolution. The Cuban leaders started with the point, the *foco,* of armed struggle as the basis for revolutionary policy formulation. They were not oppressed by costly party dogmas. Only late in the revolution did they discover the writings of Mao (Debray, 1967, p. 20), and then their tactics were already so well defined they could not be led to fruitless imitation. To their everlasting advantage, they were able to read Mao Tse-tung from a specifically Cuban standpoint and escape the ruinous devotion to party he counseled. Cuba can thus stand proudly as a model for the Latin American continent, for it displays the wisdom and courage of following no dogmas. By its antidogmatic character it emerges as a "model." Moreover, Cuba demonstrated the value of starting with arms and generalizing only in the course of battle. The new revolutionary model is an "antimodel," and thus a perfect model. We need only be satisfied with one initial commitment, that of conceiving revolution against the bourgeoisie as a matter of picking up a gun. All else will follow according to the conditions revolutionaries find in their own context of operation. Since the world is ready for "total class warfare" and total showdown, theories about who is who according to historical law are inhibitions on what must be done. The task is simple: Aim for total class war, and do not surrender until victory; find theories, generalizations and guiding ideas from the battle situations themselves. Older Communist parties are leavings of a "political age," when the class struggle was still fully or partially a matter of political struggle for political advantages. That time is past. Fight now until victory. Fight to the death. Action in the "streets," for compromises and coalitions—all that is fading into the Communist past (Debray, 1967, p. 27).

The new context for struggle is set by the massive weaponry of bourgeois nations and the exhaustion of old communist techniques (Debray, 1967, p. 28). It must even be faced that the intellectual per se fails to illuminate our understanding of what has happened. He is, by nature, conservative, *not* revolutionary. He is always aware of precedents, a past, other strategies and high abstractions. These are useless. What is valuable is "data," tactical data, drawn from battle experience. The seasoned guerrilla knows this. The intellectual thinks he knows this, but he does not. He knows only his own *political* experience. This is not transferable to a battlefield where outcomes are determined. Even a guerrilla not so beset by intellectual illusions, Guevara, could rattle on about the need for guerrilla bases after the manner of Mao. This is outmoded. It is necessary to strike and run, always. To rest, to worry about "liberating areas" and settling down to governing them, is to risk destruction (Debray, 1967, p. 62). This only serves to show how pervasive the intellectual's influence is. We must always guard against the outmoded knowledge he represents.

Illustrations of the Communist intellectual's conservatism abound. He believes that the politics of the city is the center of revolutionary action. The countryside is supplementary to and dependent upon city politics, as it is for everything else. He thus counsels guerrillas to make contact with the city, to coordinate action with Communist party planning there. Fidel suffered from this illusion for a while. He nearly lost the revolutionary initiative because of it. Contact with the city party makes location and destruction of the guerrilla organization easier. At all costs contact with the city must be avoided. Better to kidnap a country doctor to help the wounded than to go to the city for medical aid (Debray, 1967, p. 69). Any dependence upon the city is corrupting. Who there can understand the life and death significance that a piece of cloth can have for the fighting guerrilla? Such things are always replaceable in a city, and the party intellectual located there will always give advice that is insensitive to this desperate need. He can always find himself a piece of cloth. He does not know what to tell a guerrilla who may not be so blessed in the wilds of the country. His advice is corrupted by his own situation. Better not to deal with or rely upon him all. All of these important ideas were not learned by the Cuban insurgents in a day. But they were learned. The fact that they were, accounts for victory. And all of this validates the importance of the guerrilla organization in the countryside as the true instrument of revolutionary science, not plagued by the intellectual's vanity, corruption, conservatism and obsession with historical nonsense and law. Fidel proved this, but slowly, shedding only bit by bit the city's and the intellectual's influence upon him. Not these influences, but the "shedding" process is what is so illuminating about the Cuban experience.

Debray is careful to say that military operations must have a political object, must aim at political goals. Political and military goals are "inseparable." But no party should be responsible for setting the political goals of the guerrilla organization (although Debray cannot articulate what these might be aside from "total" confrontation with a bourgeoisie). All parties, including the Communist party, are obsessed with "commissions, congresses, conferences, plenary sessions, meetings, and assemblies at all levels, national, provincial, regional and local" (Debray, 1967, p. 102). This leads it to dwell on problems of its own internal cohesion. It socializes members into the going system by failing to direct energies toward seizing government power (Debray, 1967, p. 103). It is an unfit instrument for power seizure. At best, its value is assistance in governance. Power seizure is inherently a military operation and requires an organizational apparatus suited to this end. Military discipline over a group of committed and armed men is what is needed, not party discipline suited to party needs. Political experience and its acquisition cannot justify party dominance in revolutionary affairs. Political experience can always be acquired. Military experience is what is so hard to acquire, and this is what must be deliberately sought. A military body can always gain in political experience on ascension to power (more easily said than done, Debray forgets). Thus, a vanguard military organization is more easily a ruling party in embryo than a party can be an effective military organization (Debray, 1967, p. 106). And the triumph of the guerrilla military outfit is made complete with this arch lesson of the Cuban Revolution.

The Cuban Revolution emerged from a set of circumstances in which a militant band of pragmatic revolutionaries initiated armed action against city strongholds of government. Uncommitted to any given source outside themselves, they pursued the apparently fruitful pattern that involved independence from the Communist party, ignoring "history" and communist propriety. But alliance, being mutually useful, was effected between the Castro and the communist forces. The elements of the two organizations showed mutual influence, especially as the Castro regime is committed to open communism. But his insurrection stands as a model of independence and the triumph of will over law, the triumph of initiative over the dogma-bound party model. Communists everywhere are able to consider another available line of action open to them without involving the surrender of their communist convictions, that of outfitting an exclusively military (however "popular") organization for power seizure. History calls, not for a reading of its latest manifestations, but for total showdown and the exertion of initiative and armed will. To abandon the wearisome politics of the Communist party can now connote, not betrayal of Marxism-Leninism, but the fitting of revolutionary aims to a modern context. Not only the party of the communists may be freely discarded (except as allies when they are powerful enough in a given context), but the political form itself may be set aside for later considerations.

We have moved from the politicalization of socialism in the Russian Revolution to the militarization of communism in the Cuban Revolution. The Soviet case called forth a party with a merely embryonic revolutionary military. It did not require its full services. The Chinese model effected an organic union between the military and the political as two well-developed features of revolutionary organization. Still, there was no question about the centrality of the political party head. The Cuban guerrilla victory has been made to show that the guerrilla band is a revolutionary "first cause," and that within it, awaiting orders and uses, is an embryo party. Ultimately, each combination of "law" and "will" in organizational form solved problems of power acquisition by favoring one of these elements in the communist world picture at the expense of the other.

The concept "organization" has undergone major changes when we consider policy outcomes and variations. But each also underwent a process of idealization, of pretensions to exercising a new leadership, based on a more current, more correct version of "success." As a result, each has viewed its immediate predecessor with animosity, as new radicals disdaining old conservatives. For the latter, in the meantime, had acquired a stake in stabilization and self-development of national resources. We must, then, accept something less than harmony among the various segments of the international Communist movement. For all of the nations claiming the faith have idealized their own experience to the point of uncompromising national pride and are competing for international influence by exhorting others to follow their own lead. In the long run, modifications are and will continue to be made. But Communists everywhere have found a rare and possibly dangerous moment of choice between organizational "models" for seizing power.

REFERENCES

Aguero, L. C. (1959) *Cartas del presidio*. Havana: Editorial Lex.

Brandt, C. (1958) *Stalin's Failure in China*. Cambridge, Mass.: Harvard University Press.

Castro, F. (1968) *History Will Absolve Me*. London: Cape.

Debray, R. (1967) *Revolution in the Revolution?* New York: Monthly Review Press.

Debray, R. (1970) *Strategy for Revolution: Essays on Latin America*. New York: Monthly Review Press.

Fainsod, M. (1953) *How Russia is Ruled*. Cambridge, Mass.: Harvard University Press.

Fairbanks, J. K. (1958) *The United States and China*, rev. ed. Cambridge, Mass.: Harvard University Press.

Fischer, L. (1964) *The Life of Lenin*. New York: Harper & Row.

Guevara, E. (1961) *Guerrilla Welfare*. New York: Monthly Review Press.

Horowitz, I. L. (1970) *Cuban Communism*. Chicago: Aldine-Atherton.

Lenin, V. I. (1929) *What Is To Be Done?* in *Collected Works of V. I. Lenin*, trans. T. Fineberg, vol. 4, bk. 2. New York: International Publishers.

Mao Tse-tung (1954–56) *Selected Works*, vols. 1, 2. London: Lawrence and Wishart.

Mao Tse-tung (1962) *An Anthology of His Writings,* ed. A. Fremantle. New York: American Library.

Schwartz, B. (1951) *Chinese Communism and the Rise of Mao.* Cambridge, Mass.: Harvard University Press.

Shapiro, L. (1960) *The Communist Party of the Soviet Union.* New York: Random House and Knopf.

Tang, P., and J. Maloney (1962) *The Chinese Communist Impact on Cuba,* monograph series no. 12. Washington: Research Institute on the Sino-Soviet Bloc.

CHAPTER 11

FASCISM:
A TWENTIETH-CENTURY
MASS MOVEMENT

THEORIES OF THE FASCIST STATE

Fascism came about without design, with no prerequisites that permit a firm characterization of its doctrinal uniformities. It seemed at first to be less a social system than a collective therapy. In a narrowing choice of options after the collapse of bourgeois rule in the post-World War I epoch, fascism seemed painless in comparison to the severe prophecies of bolshevism (See Hamilton, 1971, p. xxiii). A crucial aspect of fascism is that it exhibits cohesion in national practice, yet lacks cohesion at any international level. The national state has been so much the defining characteristic of the fascist system that it has rarely developed international or transnational bases. This tells us a great deal about the relation of nationalism to fascism, and also indicates the organizational weaknesses in the fascist system which caused it serious difficulties in its international relations, difficulties not faced by other social systems in the modern period.

Descriptions of fascism are numerous and varied. For some, fascism is the political activities of the Fascisti in Italy, while German activity during the same period is labeled as Nazism—which is simply an abbreviation for National Socialism. Further distinctions can be drawn between Franco's

Spain and Argentina under Peron. Some have labeled the Tojo-Hirohito period in Japan between 1930 and 1945 as fascistic. The mere fact that five distinctive *national systems* of fascism have just been named underlines the absence of an international fascist prehistory such as that possessed by socialism, or for that matter by liberalism or conservatism. Fascism's ambiguous character in part is due to the fact that it is historically linked to socialist-syndicalist doctrines on the left and capitalist-corporativist doctrines on the right. Fascism is, however, amoebic only in form, not in magnitude.

THE MARXIST THEORY

Various theories of fascism have been fashioned over the years. They are worth examining to see how accurately they represent the fascist system. One of the better defined and better known is the Marxist theory of fascism, which essentially states that fascism is a bourgeois movement of the upper middle classes. These classes are driven to adapt anti-democratic postures in order to mobilize the nation for new colonial markets; theirs is the only expression of imperialism possible in a world already divided among older capitalist empires (Dutt, 1935, p. 35). The burden of the Marxist theory of fascism is to provide a strict class interpretation of national and racial movements; and to declare fascism more virulent and violent because the imperial domains have already been carved up, and hence must be taken by force from powerful adversaries. Earlier forms of capitalism could afford a certain amount of benevolence and equanimity in their treatment of colonial possessions because they were confronting defenseless peoples, whose cooperation in part they required for administrative purposes.

There are difficulties with this theory. First, it is by no means obvious that the bourgeoisie itself was not swallowed up in the fascist movements. It is certainly doubtful that the upper bourgeoisie remained in command positions under fascism to any great extent. Fascist movements may have required and received the acquiescence of the bourgeoisie and the bourgeoisie may have even participated actively in the early periods, but as the military machine developed it became difficult to maintain an independent role for the bourgeoisie. It lost out to other social strata either as an instrumentality or a final cause.

There are also several anomalies surrounding the Marxist theory of fascist imperialism. The fascist imperialist adventures during the period before World War II were much more minimal than one would expect from the theory. Italy did conquer Abyssinia, and Germany did make some economic penetration into Africa. But these adventures did not require a theory of fascism. It is not that the Germans and Italians were not imperialistic in these pursuits, but that they had always been so. Fascism did not alter the imperial process in any overt way, but accelerated the form it was already taking. Furthermore, the object of fascist aggression was more often than not European sovereigns rather than their colonial holdings. One could argue that after Germany overran France and Belgium the colonial possessions would naturally fall prey to German imperial designs, but in fact when the imperial nations fell, their possessions remained remarkably intact. Southeast Asia and Africa did not surrender to Germany, Italy or Japan; indeed, they were enabled to liberate themselves from the old colonial powers after the termination of World War II. Although the Marxist theory of fascism has ancillary insights and, indeed, compels attention to important aspects of the fascist movement at the levels of both national and international stratification, it is neither a necessary nor sufficient explanation of the rise of fascism.

THE LIBERAL THEORY

Sophisticated liberal analysts explain German fascism as a result of the fact that the German bourgeoisie had mismanaged the economy and allowed it to reach a point of incredible inflation. Hence, the German system under the Weimar Republic was subject to an extreme pressure from the masses as a result of the chaos created by middle and upper economic management. The German economy did not so much require foreign bases as it required internal reorganization: Therefore, what the Nazis promised and were able to deliver was a system of elite organization, which instead of displacing the bourgeoisie, augmented it with organized cadres. By militarizing the society, the Nazis were able to control inflation, stop unemployment, and in general organize the society in relatively efficient ways (Ebenstein, 1943, 1945).

As an ancillary theory, this makes a good deal of sense. It is true that the fascist movement in Germany was able to create internal stability where the bourgeoisie had left only confusion, doubt and incredible unemployment. What remains to be explained is the severity of this organizational restructuring. Indeed, the reorganization was far harsher than that which took place anywhere else in the world. There were many other ways the society could have been restructured, but none of these was taken despite a history of nineteenth-century liberalism. The question then becomes why fascism was institutionalized in Germany and Italy; but not elsewhere in the industrial West. Fascism provided internal stability, but the same stability was achieved in the United States and England with far less pain and difficulty. Gregor (1969) has recently provided an interesting explanation of what has always befuddled classical bourgeois theorists about the selective rise of fascism.

> Fascism was, in fact, a political phenomenon characteristic of the partially industrialized nations of Europe. It was strongest and succeeded to power in the Latin countries of Europe where the gross national product and

the per capita income were lowest, and in countries marginally industrialized like Spain, Portugal, Romania, and Hungary. . . . Only the appearance of National Socialism in industrialized Germany seems to resist such analysis and yet the traumatic experience of Germany after World War I, its reduction to a second class power at the moment it had every promise of becoming a world power of first rank, suggests that gross status deprivation might aid in explaining its identification with the aspiring revolutionary powers of the continent with whom it had so little in common. (Gregor, 1969, p. xiv)

The difficulty with this thesis is that other marginally developed countries of Europe, which suffered similar status deprivation, managed to avoid the fascist option. Further, the theory of status deprivation, however intriguing as an ancillary explanation, fails to explain why the very countries that did move toward fascism had a period after World War I in which the Communist option was close to being adopted, if not adopted outright—such as German countries under the Spartacists and Hungary under the Bela Kun interregnum. Indeed, it might well be that the status deprivation theory explains the discontent of central Europe with classical capitalism, more than it does the rise of fascism.

THE PSYCHOANALYTIC THEORY

What might be called the psychoanalytic theory of fascism was made popular by Erich Fromm (1941). In its essence the theory claims that as the twentieth century becomes highly anomic, people develop abstract relations with one another; life becomes extraordinarily depersonalized. As a leading industrial nation of the twentieth century, Germany, for example, had the most advanced cast of a generalized alienation. The attraction of the fascist movement can be explained as the need of mass alienated man to identify with a concrete object, a need for relevance within an irrelevant kind of society. There are suggestions in Fromm that the state symbolizes the father figure and the restoration of authority.

In general, this view has the advantage of hindsight. However, when an attempt is made to convert hindsight into a general analysis of society, the psychoanalytic view does not hold up well. It is dangerous to interpret a symbol system as necessarily meaning one thing. It might very well be true that Hitler represents a father figure, but then what did Eva Peron represent? The Virgin Mary? Such thinking, for all of its provocative features, can generate incredible abstraction so that the generalizability of the theory is severely minimized. The argument by analogy, while intriguing, simply omits from consideration all those cases where similar psychological types did not generate fascist political institutions.

Generalizations about the effects of industrialism or urbanization upon the individual have merit, but fail to explain fascism satisfactorily, since in point of fact, fascism has arisen in both advanced and backward industrial contexts.

THE POLITICAL-SOCIOLOGICAL THEORY

The political-sociological explanation of fascism best explains its different varieties and strains. The theory states that the efforts of fascism and its leadership are no longer centered upon the economy, but the state. The objects of fascist energies are thus outside of the economic realm, and are not directed toward a reconstitution of the economy. Indeed, the shabbiest aspect of the fascist doctrine is generally its economic theory. The fascists have one peculiarity in common throughout the world—they have no fully evolved doctrine, and scant expression of an economic strategy.

> In the six years that elapsed between the Fascist victory and the outbreak of war, Nazism erected a system of production, distribution, and consumption which defies classification in any of the usual categories. It was not capitalism in the traditional sense; the autonomous market mechanism so characteristic of capitalism during the last two centuries had all but disappeared. It was not State capitalism; the government disclaimed any desire to own the means of production, and, in fact, took steps to denationalize them. It was not socialism or communism; private property and private profit still existed. It was, rather, a combination of some of the characteristics of capitalism and a highly planned economy. Without in any way destroying its class character, a comprehensive planning mechanism was imposed on an economy in which private property was not expropriated, in which the distribution of national income remained fundamentally unchanged, and in which private entrepreneurs retained some of the prerogatives and responsibilities which were theirs under traditional capitalism. This was done in a society which was dominated by a ruthless political dictatorship. (Nathan, 1944, p. 367)

Marxists assert that this is prima facie evidence that fascism simply employed the existing bourgeois economy. But this is not confirmed by the actions of the fascists. The fascist concerns primarily were with the state; the economy, its regulation and operations, all economic functions were seen as a by-product of the state (Stolper, 1940). The theory of economy always reflected the theory of state power. Thus, fascism required no developed economic theory, but only an elaborate doctrine of state power. The greatest strength of the fascist movement since the thirties has been that of the major doctrines of political power, it alone accepts the fact that the base is the state and the superstructure, the economy. Liberals, conservatives, socialists, Communists and capitalists all talk and argue as if the economy is basic; all make assumptions about some kind of long-range economic determinism in the affairs of men. The fascists do not have this concern with economic metaphysics. They alone of the modern revolutionary forces grasp the essence of the century in terms of the state; perhaps they are the only true Hegelians. The Marxists were so concerned with the dialectical form of Hegel that they forgot his empirical content, the role of state power. The core of fascist strength is that they understand that those who control the state control the economy. The successes of the Italian

Fascisti and of the Nazis were no accidental, were not aberrations, were not exaggerations; they were inevitable in the sense that they uniquely understood the role of the state. This appreciation permitted fascism to make all sorts of blunders in strategy and tactics and yet retain the allegiance of the masses and the active participation of the elites.

Both capitalist and socialist theorists argue that under conditions of modern systems of production it is irrational to assert the primacy of politics, unless the political order can act as a trustee of a homogenous series of social needs and interests. But the fact is that politics has become central, and the fascist model is the prototype of this orientation.

> In Germany it became the function of National Socialism to create a new social and economic compromise, a new public consensus, in fact a new general representation of the people, by political means, and in the context of 1933 that necessarily meant the open use of force. The "primacy of politics," which was undeniably there in 1933—the creation of a dictatorship, terrorism, political and cultural Gleichschaltung, was the result of a social disintegration which it was the function of National Socialism to repair. (Mason, 1968, p. 172)

THE SOCIAL BASIS OF FASCISM

Nineteenth-century doctrines that carried over into the present century explain the social basis of fascism in terms of the classes that they saw themselves in historic conflict with. The Marxists interpreted it in terms of the bourgeoisie. The capitalists interpreted it in terms of a working class run amuck. But classical analysis has omitted discussion of the rise of the new class, the bureaucratic class, a class which in Germany had grown disproportionate to the other classes; its rate of growth was much more rapid than that of the working class, for example. The bourgeoisie, for its part, was consolidated and becoming more powerful rather than more extensive. The only viable growing class in Central Europe and the largest uncommitted sector in the first half of the present century has been the bureaucratic class. It is not incidental that the bureaucracy was linked directly to the state apparatus, for it became natural to think of the seizure of state power as the way to define the bureaucracy's new situation.

Class interests are basic in European history: Thus, we must study the class interests of the bureaucracy. Like the working class and the bourgeoisie, the bureaucracy has independent interests, and as it grew large enough to challenge the working classes in size, it began to exhibit certain special features: (1) The bureaucracy was directly related to the tasks and to the apparatus of the state; therefore, it developed a statist ideology. (2) The bureaucracy was concerned with managing the economy and the society. (3) The bureaucracy had definite interests apart from other class formations, which could only be realized by their monopoly of power. If the bureaucracy in Germany is considered to include the military caste, which was also directly linked to state authority, one can appreciate how the fascists represented a formidable social force; if not a majority at the outset, a substantial minority.

This analysis accounts not only for the social bases and the ideological content of the fascist movement but also for its strictly national character, because a national bureaucracy cannot raise internationalist slogans. A national bureaucracy manages the internal affairs of nationhood; the bourgeoisie on the other hand, has an international base, and one can therefore speak of an international bourgeoisie in spite of the amorphous world capitalist market. Likewise, there remains a notion of the fusion and union of all working classes, as exhibited in all sorts of international working-class agencies. But the bureaucracy has never managed more than the nation nor has it advanced ideological tenets that would enable it to overcome its localism. Consequently, the bureaucracy has been a national factor rather than an international factor, and its characteristics have been as much shaped by the nation as it has been the shaper of the national destiny. The characteristics of the bureaucracy generally have become more or less the dominant features of the fascist regime's hatreds and loathings as well as their approbations and desires.

In Germany, the bureaucratic class was that sector of the society relatively uncontaminated by the Jews. The bourgeoisie included many Jews; the proletariat had many Jews; the proletariat leadership was composed of Jews. The anti-Jewish element of the bureaucratic sector, which is so often ridiculed ideologically, was thus rational from the point of view of the bureaucratic group seeking its place in the sun. If the German bureaucracy was indeed a class, and if their demands for entrance into political power were legitimate, then the attacks on their competitors—Jews, the bourgeoisie and the proletariat—make good sense. Thus, too, the apparent contradiction between an advanced economy and backward social attitudes is also comprehensible.

The bureaucracy generally demands formulas for action, not simply an esoteric importation from pragmatism but as the basic requirement of bureaucratic functioning. They are not concerned with the complexities of ideas. This particular stratum of society holds certain conservative attitudes toward marriage, women, religion and a host of other phenomena. As a result, the bureaucratic stratum is generally more conservative than other social groups.

What forms did this bureaucratic ideology take in Italy and Germany? Traditionalism toward women, toward religion, toward the values of property and the mythology of the state prevailed. All of these were seen as best exemplified in the bureaucratic sector—which uniquely linked nationalism, patriotism and a peculiarly political, rather than economic, view of life. Both fascist systems were permeated with notions of legitimized rites of passage whereby one advanced in definite and precise ways. These were not so much fitted to the German or Italian "national character" as to bureaucratic modes of performing operations—to notions of impersonal advancement, of getting things done, of traditional verities in general.

While the *system* of fascism rested on the bourgeoisie, the *support base* rested on the working classes. The labor laws enacted in 1934 in Germany were intended to unionize every worker in Germany. Support for the fascist movement was generated from both the working classes and the bourgeoisie, but neither was powerful enough to exercise its own will. For example, during the late stages of Nazism, it was necessary to expropriate directly from many of the middle echelons in Germany. Commodity production for the bourgeoisie actually decreased. The middle echelon of the bourgeoisie paid for the privilege of existence. This pattern, in even a more labor oriented form, existed between 1921 and 1939 in Italy, where the syndicalist tradition was well entrenched.

The major difference between fascism and other political systems is not merely that it is a system of class management, but rather that it has social by-products in the realm of ideas, culture and the relations between people. The sociological domain could become a vast exercise in distinguishing between revolutions of the Bolshevik variety and a capitalist revolution, such as fascism. Fascism has to do with elitism and with managing classes. Bolshevism was concerned with smashing rather than managing social classes. There is no bourgeoisie in Russia, there is no stock exchange in Moscow, and they could not be restored. The difference between Bolshevism and fascism lies also in the strategies of "above" and "below," in the movement of ordinary citizens through the political system to change the economy or reroute all economic arrangements, and that of the elites' expert management of economies. The state's main role in modern society is to control the economy. What the state does to or for its class structure determines whether the system is fascist or nonfascist, whether one is smashing classes like the Communists or mending classes like the fascists.

THE POLITICAL SYNTHESIS OF FASCISM

Fascism as a political structure is a socialist heresy whose successes stem from the failure of socialist techniques to achieve state power. For, generally, socialist attempts to politicize the working class and internationalize its class interests led to unionization rather than politicalization. The breakdown of the socialist effort in Italy in 1911 with respect to the Turks, in France in 1914 with respect to the Germans, in Germany in the same year with respect to the French and so forth, created the basis of a new right-wing socialist movement. Fascism differs from socialism in its tactics rather than its principles. It emphasizes economic conditions of the laboring classes and above all, makes an appeal to their nationalist sentiments. This double formula of nationalism and economism in displacement of internationalism and politization distinguished fascism from socialism after the World War I debacle.

In his recent work on fascism, James A. Gregor (1969) has caught both the mass and nationalist aspects of fascism very well, for he points out how nationalism displaced internationalism as a twentieth-century organizing principle.

> Revolutionary mass movements in our own time have, in fact, a prevailing tendency to make their appeals to the people—the category to which nationalism must make final recourse. Totalitarian movements, like Fascism and National Socialism, which develop in environments where there are well-articulated classes, must make such an appeal at the very commencement of their enterprise if they seriously aspire to mass membership. Given their clear intentions they cannot advance themselves as class movements. . . . Nationalism, which classical Marxism had dismissed as an anachronism, has proven itself to be one of the most potent political forces in the socialist nations. Socialist nations have in the past, and continue in the present, to pursue national interests with as much, if not more, dedication than non-socialist nations. There is little, in fact, to distinguish the nationalism and internationalism of contemporary socialism from that of paradigmatic Fascism. The internationalism of both ideologies was, in fact, equally diaphanous. Nationalism alone was vital. (Gregor, 1969, pp. 363, 357)

Related to this is an equally suppressed fact: the mass character of fascism. Fascism is the only authentic mass movement unique to the twentieth century that has proven successful. The socialist movement never really developed beyond an elite cadre and rarely, if ever, strayed from party politics of a relatively orthodox variety. In part, this was due to the democratic traditions of socialism, and in part, to a disbelief in the capacity of the masses to rule equitably. It is true that the Soviet Revolution was a mass movement, but its successes were due, in the main, to disillusionment over the defeat of Russian national ambitions in World War I; it too, in the form of Leninism, had to accommodate the national question; and it had to take into profound consideration economic rather than political interests. Nonetheless, it can be stated that throughout Europe, fascism represented a unique combination of mass sentiment and elitist manipulation that enabled the existing capitalist social structure to survive, if not always flourish.

Fascism has two main historical pivots: The first is fascism in Italy—which represented an attempt to synthesize the syndicates and the corporations; the second is National Socialism, or Nazism, in Germany, which similarly represented a synthesis, albeit with far different weightings. But what united fascism as a doctrine is the theory of the state as a balance wheel, harmonizing the interests of capital and labor, proletariat and bourgeoisie. The social origins, even of leadership in Italy and Germany were, however, startlingly different—most of the Italian leadership was drawn from the socialist movement; whereas most of the Nazi leadership was drawn from the military Junkers and the old Prussian aristocracy.

Before probing into major differences between the two chief tendencies of fascism in Italy and Germany, it is important to appreciate the role of values distinguishing fascism from socialism. The goal of fascism was to fuse class interests—or at least to dampen class conflict by means of the state. The socialist impulse was to exacerbate the class conflict by means of the revolutionary vanguard party, and also to attempt to overthrow the very state that the fascists used for their ends. Thus, one might say that at the analytic level—at the level of explaining the crisis of traditional bourgeois democracy and classical capitalist economics—there was much less difference between socialism and fascism than there was at the level of correctives. The tensions within fascism were stimulated by the imperfect fusion of class interests. The tensions within socialism were a consequence of the attempt to destroy the old order of things.

> Fascism, unlike socialist orthodoxy, did not exclude the cult of the individual provided that the individual could be seen as the executor of some organic national force. The "new man" whom fascism wished to create symbolized the new society. He had released within himself the creative forces of his own soul and through strength of will would usher in a new world. Intellectuals had a special mission in transforming the old into the new man, for education played a vital part in this process and education was a traditional field of activity for intellectuals. (Mosse, 1970, p. 163)

Within the framework of fascist doctrine, however, there are overriding unities that deserve special attention. First, is the primacy of politics over economics; that is, both the right and the duty of the party apparatus manipulated by the state to direct the economy rather than accept the socialist doctrine of an economic base with a political superstructure. In fact, the doctrine of a military-industrial complex managed by the state is a direct result of this fascist reorientation.

Second, the fascists hold to the primacy of the party over the government. That is to say, the fascist theory of legitimacy is lodged in the party apparatus and not the government structure. Indeed a near perfect isomorphism between structure and party leadership serves to underscore the unique role of party affiliation in the life of the nation. Fascism emphasizes not just the primacy of the party over the government, but the primacy of the single party of the people over and against pluralistic party systems, representing different interest groups. The fascist party presumably incorporates and translates the will of the people into action—and does so without the supposed sham of multiparty structures.

Third, there is a primacy of the leadership over the rank and file. That is, the elitist aspects surface in fascism in terms of criteria of leadership as people are chosen not necessarily from the proletarian class, but rather for their special ability as charismatic as well as efficient leaders. This aspect of fascism caused perhaps the greatest difficulty, both in Italy and Germany, since it underlined a direct contradiction between the mass movement and its elite core, between a system whose mode of force were the masses and whose organizational structure was separated from these masses by rank and status. This tendency toward elitism was even more pronounced in Germany than in Italy, because of the military source of much Nazi power. And it might be argued that it was the traditional aristocratic features of fascism rather than its inherent ideological constraints that moved it toward elitism and away from the masses.

In terms of the economy, it must be said that fascist doctrine simply was an extension of the pragmatic force of twentieth-century theory. Fascism assumed that only a powerful state could rationalize economic production and only a rational economic production and only a rational state could, in fact, preserve the bourgeoisie from its own self-serving interests.

While it is difficult to extrapolate an explicit theory of economics from fascist doctrine, certain features of this doctrine are notable for their extremism rather than for their novelty. First was the elimination of corporate secrecy; second was the elimination of corporate competition; third, the elimination of boom and bust cycles through price and wage controls; and fourth, the elimination of mass unemployment through public works. In order to bring this rationalization about, the old bourgeois state not only became transformed into the new fascist state, but also, in fact, relinquished its power, at least at the level of political authority. The fascist theory of economics, in effect, reduced the power of the bourgeoisie—not as profoundly as it reduced the power of the proletariat but nonetheless enough to assume the success of state planning. The state became important, not just as an adjunct to the old ruling class, but precisely because it was able, for the first time, to create a new ruling class separate from the bureaucracy and the military, and beholden neither to the factory owners or to the factory workers. Thus, the rationalization of the economy meant, in effect, the reduction of the capacity of old ruling elites to influence the political and social course of the fascist state. This delimitation of influence was certainly a major factor in the anti-Semitic pogroms—or at least their extensive character.

When examining the military, we find that the fascists provided a masterful exercise in innovation, which directly linked militarism to the functions of an advanced technology, and harnessed the production apparatus to military ends. To make the cycle complete, the fascists became extraordinarily aggressive with respect to the rest of the world, but did succeed in achieving a military-industrial fusion that underwrote the economy and sustained the military.

The fascists created a network whereby they were able to use the professional military for various political ends and economic goals. Given the unique condition of Europe in the post-World War I era, a Europe which had already divided up the overseas colonial possessions, the fascists made their military the most sophisticated in all of the world. They did so because they had to confront the advanced colonial powers—France, Belgium, Holland, England—and ultimately the Soviet Union. In other words, an advanced military-industrial complex was made necessary by the tasks of a vigorous, politicized military apparatus, and at the same time, was to prove extremely serviceable in the further rationalization of the economy.

Nazism, in particular, understood the double role of the military system: that is, its role in international political conquests and national economic recovery. And it was the Nazis who perfected a system of military aggrandizement that serviced their ends so well. In other words, Nazism understood militarism as a critical mass in the new imperialism, because it well understood that Germany would not confront Africans with spears, but Europeans with airplanes.

At the level of social systems, the fascists created a level of governance that proved to be eminently satisfactory and feasible. In the main, fascism elevated the concept of the social bond over that of social conflict. This was an extension of the old principle—in which the nation-state was viewed as an analogue to the human organism, with all the parts of the system functioning in unison to keep the body alive and healthy. The social bond, therefore, became by extension necessary to the physical health of the nation. But not all of the values of the social bond were ultimately reducible to such forms of physical health.

Both Fascisti and Nazis, therefore, emphasized the importance of the work life and the sex life as part of a traditional ethic that helped to cement highly technological goals. The social bond thus re-created the feudal *Gemeinschaft,* or the feudal community of fate, as part of a highly technological network.

This notion of the social bond along feudal lines rationalized all managerial aspects of capitalism and all trade union aspects within the working class. It served to do away with "extensive individualism," laissez faire culture and all of the aspects of traditional bourgeois democracy that could be peeled away from the capitalist crust. In other words, the fascists were able to show that a very old-fashioned and old ethic was compatible with the technological tradition of the new. As a result, the fascist social system emphasized traditional values while at the same time encouraging the technological spirit. Let us now turn more precisely to the special features of Italian fascism and German Nazism.

First, there is a strong emphasis on the socialist aspects of fascism within Italy. The preeminence of the trade union movement within the fascist regime and the very coming to power of fascism as a result of a general strike and the attendant march on Rome, indicated an importance to labor that was never really present in the German case. In other words, the seizure of power in Italy came about as a result of mass participation and mobilization, whereas in Germany, power came about through a series of electoral maneuvers and manipulations.

Second, Italian fascism, because of its sensitive relationship to Catholicism—which was housed in the bosom of Italy, in the Vatican—tended to be quite benign to the religious life of its citizenry. Count Ciano, one of the leaders of Italy and indeed its prime minister, was very favorable to the cause of the Jews. And, in fact, Italy strangely became a haven, until 1938 at least, from the anti-Semitic repressions which took place elsewhere in Europe. Whether the position of the Italian Fascisti was favorable toward the Jews remains a disputable and debatable point; but what is not in dispute is that the Jews and other ethnic minorities were hardly distinguished from the Italians. and the assimilation was so complete that the possibility of antireligious and antiethnic attacks were well-nigh impossible, and indeed when they did take place as a result of Nazi pressure, they proved artificial and ineffectual.

Third, there was a good deal more experimentalism and a good deal less traditionalism in the Italian model than in the German model of fascism. Futurism in art and in architecture was strongly encouraged, and Italian fascism properly viewed itself as far more innovative than did the German Nazi regime.

> National socialism never emphasized the thrust toward revolution which Italian fascism inscribed on its banners after the First World War. Mussolini himself may not have taken this radical vocabulary seriously, but the dynamic "open endedness" which many earlier fascists had prized was more deeply embedded in the Italian than in the German movement. (Mosse, 1970, p. 165)

That part of this esthetic had to do with the grandeur of Rome and with the restoration of an ancient giganticism is, no doubt, true. Nonetheless, here, too. whether fascist esthetics or culture were innovative or worthwhile is less important than the relatively benign and nonrepressive features of the regime in relation to the whole world of the cultural superstructure.

Fourth, one might find that the entire history of Italian nationhood involved an antimilitary spirit and anti-Protestant work ethic in general—an anticollectivized approach toward problems of family and society. As a result, the attempt to mobilize and regiment the Italian population was in large measure unsuccessful. Even if it were true that Mussolini made the trains run on time, he never quite succeeded in making the people move on time. As a result, there was a certain continuation of traditional political and social forms of behavior long after the regime itself had hardened into antidemocratic forms.

Finally, one would have to say that the main characteristic of fascism in Italy was its bias in favor of the working class. The powerful organizational class of the proletariat allowed the bourgeoisie to continue, but never allowed it to capture the leadership of the fascist movement. As Ledeen (1971, p. 108) recently noted:

While fascism represented a new form of politics, it also embodied much of the kind of activity which had been carried on by the radical parties of the past. This vigorous support of a dynamic proletarian movement within the ranks of fascism added to the already substantial anxiety of the Italian industrialists who had supported Mussolini hoping to block this sort of working class agitation. With fascist syndicalism flexing its muscles, Mussolini had to act to calm the nerves of the leaders of the Confindustria.

Here again, economism and nationalism were viable goals of the working class. Fascism was successful in Italy. It became unsuccessful only at the point that the Germans, in effect, became rulers of Italy—thus doing away with the national flavor. And when the Italian economy was rendered helpless and hopeless by the allied war effort, Italy became one of the allies' main military targets. In short, Italian fascism remained far closer to traditional bourgeois forms of rule and even traditional socialist conceptions than did its German counterpart.

The special features of German Nazism are better known, primarily the success of German fascism in creating a viable military-industrial complex which satisfied basic mass needs and at the same time stabilized the bourgeois class. The stabilization necessitated a shrinking of profits and a wide acceptance of state monopolization; yet it did manage to curb inflation and preserve class hegemony.

> In the Third Reich, due to the intensive efforts at rearmament, monopoly capitalism developed into a monopolistic state war capitalism. Goods were no longer produced for an open market, but solely on orders given by the state. The state distributed its orders to the manufacturers, decided what was to be produced in the interest of the war effort, and what lines were to be dropped so as to conserve the available raw materials, machinery, and manpower for the production of armament material. The state also doled out raw materials, machinery, and manpower among the various producers, and placed them where they were most needed. . . . The management of business by the state, in which the representatives of business take a hand, and the elimination of the open market, in whose stead the state appears as the only purchaser, have made the competitive struggle of capitalist business superfluous. (Seydewitz, 1945, pp. 412–413)

Second of the special features of German Nazism was the open assault on the colonial powers—that is, the direct attempt to smash the imperialist powers of France, England and the United States, and establish Germany as exclusive international imperial praetor. But even the Nazi movement could not pursue its imperial goals without firm class support. And this Wilhelm Reich articulated well.

> In its first successful onset, the National Socialist movement relied upon the broad layers of the so-called middle classes, i.e., the millions of private and pubic officials, middle class merchants, and lower and middle class

farmers. From the point of view of its social basis, National Socialism was a lower middle class movement, and this was the case wherever it appeared, whether in Italy, Hungary, Argentina, or Norway. . . . That a fascist movement exists at all is doubtlessly the social expression of nationalistic imperialism. However, that this fascist movement could become a mass movement, indeed, could seize power (only then fulfilling its imperialistic function), is to be ascribed to the full backing it received from the middle classes. (Reich, 1970, pp. 40–41, 44)

The third significant feature of German fascism is that it was directed externally, with a fervor at least equal to that displayed with the first two objectives, to demolishing the socialists of the Soviet Union. This was, in part, a consequence of Nazi foreign policy, but even more, of a feeling of ideological competition with the one other mass movement that had been successful. Given the fact that the Nazi movement turned more heavily toward the bourgeoisie than toward the proletariat, the fervor of the military resistance to the Bolsheviks is perhaps understandable.

A fourth special internal feature of Nazism was its policy of systematic anti-Semitism and the destruction of the once powerful Jewish communities in the German-speaking areas under its control. This had the effect of (1) eliminating bourgeois competition from within, thus paralleling the effect of getting rid of bourgeois competition externally, and (2) destroying the socialist and communist apparatus, which was largely in the leadership hands of the Jewish community (Niewyk, 1971, pp. 95–120). These actions were, of course, paralleled by its foreign policy effort directed against the Soviet Union. Therefore, it might be understood that the policy of anti-Semitism was the internalized national expression of a Nazi foreign policy of aggrandizement and suppression. In this way, anti-Semitism functioned not as a religious aberration, but as a continuation of fascist foreign policy by domestic means.

Fifth, the role of the armed forces in Germany was a critical feature not present in Italy's defeated military after World War I. The German armed forces became highly professionalized during the Weimar period and at this time, forged links with the political and industrial communities of the reich.

The military rather than being broken as a result of defeat, became professionalized. And in this, the formal characteristics were far more severe in Germany than in Italy, which retained largely civilian rule during its early fascist stage. The military apparatus must be seen as part of the general rise of the bureaucratic class in Germany. The emergence of the national bureaucracy to a place of primacy was a crucial factor, since the bureaucracy had an allegiance only to the state and neither to the bourgeoisie nor to the proletariat—neither to those who were desirous of high profits nor to those desirous of high wages. Therefore, the antibourgeois and antiunion spirit of the bureaucratic sector became manifest and ultimately dominant in the ethos of German fascism. The class struggle that the Nazi party went out to suppress continued, only to be shifted into the party apparatus (Stolper, 1940, p. 234).

We can observe that the special features of fascism, while extremely important, were indeed a response to local and parochial conditions of the more general features of the fascist system of organization and ideology. To imagine that fascism can be of those multifaceted roots and antidemocratic tendencies, that it is less of an intellectual system than either socialism or liberalism, is a profound error, one that has proven costly in the past and could well prove costly in the future. Fascism is not an aberration, it is indeed an advanced stage of industrial capitalism—a stage in which the proletariat shows far more importance than any classical theory of capitalist control would consider tolerable. Beyond that, fascism is a stage in which class factors in themselves become less significant than the overall bureaucratization and technification of society. That is why fascism is no simple European aberration, but a constant possibility in any society whose political goals are blocked by democracy and whose economic priorities are frustrated by the market network.

FASCISM AND AMERICANISM

Why then did fascism fail to develop in the United States? The United States also had an enormous bureaucracy which was relatively independent of the other social classes; it had depressions and discontent; it was also a latecomer in the imperialist race; and it was highly industrialized. I am suggesting that to explain how a system comes to be the way it is is only half the problem: Equally important is why some systems fail to materialize when a similitude of circumstances obtain. In part, the answer in the case of the United State is that it did have a neofascist regime during the New Deal; the essence of state management went into effect with the New Deal, but because it was a liberal fascism and lacked an anti-Semitic character, it has not been considered fascistic. Except for the disastrous internment of Japanese and Americans of Japanese descent after the outbreak of World War II, there was no visible persecution of minorities in the United States —therefore no fascism. Of course, this equation leaves out of the reckoning the function of racism as an American equivalent to anti-Semitism. Because there were few visible brutalities in the American context, its fascism seemed different from what was taking place in Europe.

But what accounts for the past failures of fascism in the United States? One answer might be that the contradictions between fascist tendencies in the United States and the fascist system in Germany reached such a peak that the resulting antagonisms between the two were enough to mitigate, if not completely halt, the development of fascism in the United States for quite some time. Another explanation is that fascism in the United States never succeeded in coopting the other classes, or that the other classes were still relatively underdeveloped in comparison to Germany and Italy. The bourgeoisie in the United States still had a great deal of vitality and the working class during the period 1934–1940 had only reached the degree of organizational sophistication that Germany experienced forty years earlier. Organizations like the Congress of Industrial Organizations acted to prevent working class cooptation by maintaining a class rather than a national posture. In effect, the state acted the role of mediator between the bourgeoisie and the working classes. However, it had to do so in a recessive way, since both the bourgeoisie and the proletariat were in an expansive period in the decade after the depression.

Fascist trends in the United States were, and remain, juridical in character, not military, largely because of the virility of the nonbureaucratic classes. In Germany, fascism took a military form because the bourgeoisie and the working class had exhausted themselves. In the United States, fascism was a stage in the development and evolution of a class system. The fact that several classes were contending for power prevented any real hardening along fascist lines, but the bureaucracy's intent and mood in the United States during those years were far more in the direction of a fascist solution than in the direction of a socialist solution. The idea that classes can be managed without a revolution is the essence of fascism. Managerialism, or the manipulation of multiple classes and interests in a juridical fashion, is the essential content of civilian fascism. To think that fascism comes only in military forms is to mistake the trappings of a system for its essence, which is that when social classes can no longer manage themselves, the political state will do the job and do it in nonrevolutionary fashion— without overthrowing the class structure.

The depression in the United States was resolved through managerial expertise, without the expense or the sacrifice of any social class and without either overt or covert signs of revolution. The idea of the loss of autonomy by the classes is less difficult to accept now than it was then. Today, as the number of people involved in the control apparatus of a society declines with the advent of automation, the possibility of direct control by small cliques becomes a constant problem. For this reason, the question of fascism, far from being historically obsolete, is perpetually on the agenda in the postindustrial world.

Fascism, contrary to a great deal of earlier scholarly literature on the subject, is a well-articulated, well-developed doctrine. It is sophisticated, and should not be viewed as a simple aberration, an exaggeration, a moment of history that has passed, but as a vital and still powerful, if opportunistic force. To take any other view of fascism is to risk accepting it as a phenomenon beyond explanation. Since the fascist view is from the perspective of state control, the numbers that are involved in the institutionalization of a fascist regime may be far fewer and rely less on political enfranchisement than on professional expertise. The ultimate push and drive of the state is for technocratic expertise and hard data, hence appointive office replaces elective office as the key influence upon contemporary politics. To think that fascists can never be elected, or that the two-party system can never be broken, is simply to ignore the fact that fascism's power historically has not been beholden to classical party politics, and it may therefore function just as effectively within as without the multiparty system.

In recent years, attention to the problems and prospects of fascism in America has notably increased. While the approach of fascism has always been a leitmotif among radical political groups, it is becoming an issue of central interest to social scientists (See Weiss, 1967). Clearly, recent years have witnessed an increasing congruence between military and industrial institutions. And just as clearly, government management of the economy is more widespread, irrespective of the particular economic philosophies of the executive heads of state. Yet, whether such factors are in and of themselves sufficient to define a situation as fascist or neofascist remains hotly contested. As Corliss Lamont has recently noted:

> The capitalist class in the United States does not need a fascist regime in order to maintain its dominance. The radical and revolutionary movements are weak and disunited. A large majority of the trade unionists are conservative, and are actually part of the Establishment. We shall always no doubt have with us crackpot rightist and superpatriotic groups yelling about "Communist conspiracy," but I do not see in the offing any constellation of forces that could put fascism across here. (Lamont, 1971, p. 13)

However, the possibility of a rightist swing in America is a persistent thought. The basic position emerging seems to be that articulated by Bertram Gross (1970, pp. 44–52). His view is that any directly repressive regime would have to be accompanied by the sophisticated development of indirect mechanisms of control and domination. He indicates four main elements that would have to be present in such a "neofascism"—apart from the main aspects of European fascism.

Basically, the combination is not military-industrial, but rather a warfare-welfare complex. The success of such a fascism would depend on the government becoming the balance wheel for both an economy geared to full national employment, no matter what the international price would be, and for a welfare establishment that links its political mobilization to nationalist ambitions. Thus, the proletariat in the first instance, and the lumpenproletriat in the second instance, would become harnessed to federally sponsored projects. The difficulty thus far is that the welfare groups have tended, with their full array of racial and ethnic minorities, to thwart national integration by demanding parity with other social forces in the United States. The fact that the supply of money to reward all interest groups is obviously limited, has the effect of frustrating any pattern of an integrated fascism. On the other hand, fascism in its traditional guise, as repressive bureaucratic administration, remains a distinct possibility, however remote.

The decline of federalism in the United States and the failure of representative government to represent, have indeed created a crisis of confidence, but just what the outcomes of this current crisis in governance will be remains hard to determine. The fact is that as long as the economy can reinforce and respond to interest group demands, the likelihood of fascism seems remote, but in the event that government, which has indeed become the central factor in economic stability, fails to satisfy basic demands, to that degree political polarization will be heightened. And in the absence of an organized and coherent radical or socialist response, the possibility of mass demands for law, order and morality might well indeed take a strong turn to a new fascism.

REFERENCES

Dutt, R. P. (1935) *Fascism and Social Revolution.* New York: International Press.

Ebenstein, W. (1943) *The Nazi State.* New York: Holt, Rinehart & Winston.

Ebenstein, W. (1945) *The German Record.* New York: Holt, Rinehart & Winston.

Fromm, E. (1941) *Escape from Freedom.* New York: Holt, Rinehart & Winston.

Gregor, J. A. (1969) *The Ideology of Fascism: The Rationale of Totalitarianism.* New York: Free Press.

Gross, B. (1970) "Friendly Fascism: A Model for America," *Social Policy,* vol. 1, no. 4 (November-December), pp. 44–53.

Hamilton, A. (1971) *The Appeal of Fascism: A Study of Intellectuals and Fascism.* New York: Macmillan.

Lamont, C. (1971) "Will Fascism Arise in America?" *Current,* whole no. 132 (September), pp. 11–13.

Ledeen, M. A. (1971) "Fascist Social Policy," in I. L. Horowitz, ed., *The Use and Abuse of Social Science,* New Brunswick, N.J.: Transaction Books; distributed by Dutton.

Mason, T. W. (1968) "The Primacy of Politics—Politics and Economics in National Socialist Germany," in S. J. Woolfe, ed., *The Nature of Fascism.* New York: Random House.

Mosse, G. L. (1970) *Germans and Jews: The Right, the Left, and the Search for a "Third Force" in Pre-Nazi Germany.* New York: Howard Fertig.

Nathan, O. (1944) *The Nazi Economic System: Germany's Mobilization for War.* Durham, N. C.: Duke University Press.

Niewyk, D. L. (1971) *Socialist, Anti-Semite, and Jew: German Social Democracy confronts the Problem of Anti-Semitism.* Baton Rouge, La.: Louisiana State University.

Reich, W. (1970) *The Mass Psychology of Fascism,* trans. Vincent J. Carfagno. New York: Farrar, Straus & Giroux.

Seydewitz, M. (1945) *Civil Life in Wartime Germany: The Story of the Home Front.* New York: Viking Press.

Stolper, G. (1940) *German Economy—1870–1940: Issues and Trends.* New York: Harcourt Brace Jovanovich.

Weiss, J. (1967) *The Fascist Tradition.* New York: Harper & Row.

CHANGES

CHAPTER 12

THE MORPHOLOGY OF MODERN REVOLUTION

The term *revolution* can mean almost anything, and definitions have ranged all the way from "simple change" to "international holocaust." Nonetheless, a body of literature has emerged that attempts to formulate some working models for how changes called revolutionary take place, and under what conditions (Hopper, 1950; Horowitz, 1964, pp. 313-330, Gross and Hopper, 1959, pp. 21–86). If this same literature does not deal seriously with why revolutions occur, this is because social scientists have focused too exclusively on consensual and functional patterns of interaction, and not nearly enough on conflictual and dysfunctional patterns. But our concern will be to understand what a revolution is in its morphological sense, rather than to explicate why a revolution takes place in its more abstract sense.

TYPES OF REVOLUTIONS

It is best to begin with the basic available models. It is preferable to see them as models rather than theories, for what is offered has little, if any, predictive value and is useful, rather, in getting at the structural components of revolution. The work of Lasswell and Kaplan (1950, p. 252) provides a categorization: (1) palace revolutions, (2) political revolutions, and (3) social revolutions. More recently, this trichotomy was reintroduced by Rosenau (1964, pp. 45–91), who described internal wars as being fought over changes in personnel, changes in the systems of authority and, finally, changes in the structures of economy, education and political direction.

This typology was elaborated and extended by other political scientists to include more limited types of revolutionary activity. Thus, scholars like Huntington (1962, pp. 17–50) have operationalized their models into the following: mass revolutions having high participation, of long duration, with high violence, seeking fundamental changes in the socioeconomic system; revolutionary coups having low participation, of short to moderate duration, with little violence, oriented more to changes in political directorates than in social systems; reform coups, much like revolutionary coups, only revealing less ambitious changes in the political order; and finally, palace revolutions, with hardly any participation, that change leaderships rather than social structures. There are many variations on the typology, but its essential theme is the recognition that revolution implies selective participation—and that definitions are feasible precisely in terms of how many people are actually involved in revolution making rather than in the rhetoric of revolutionary goals.

If this typology helps us appreciate different *types* of revolutionary efforts, we must arrive at a comparable understanding of *forms* of revolutionary activity. The work of Chalmers Johnson (1964) is significant at this level. He defines revolution and types of revolution in terms of four variables: "(1) targets of revolutionary activity; (2) identity of the revolutionaries (masses, elites leading masses, and elites); (3) revolutionary goals or 'ideology'; and (4) whether or not the revolution is spontaneous or calculated" (Johnson, 1964, pp. 27–28). On this basis he distinguishes six types of "revolutions": the *jacquerie* (government-oriented, masses, status quo oriented, and spontaneous); the *millennarian rebellion* (effectively— that is, in practice—regime-oriented, elites leading masses, otherworldly, and spontaneous); the *anarchistic rebellion* (government- or regime-oriented, flexible participation, utopian-reactionary, and spontaneous); the *Jacobin communist revolution* (community oriented, elites leading masses, nationalist-new integrative myth, and calculated); the *conspiratorial coup d'état* (unclear—either regime or community, elites, elitist or tutelary, and calculated); and the *militarized mass insurrection* (elites leading masses, nationalistic, and calculated).

The first three of Johnson's types of "revolutions" are not revolutions at all. None of these types are aimed at the "community" and thus, even if successful, would leave untouched much, if not most, of the essential features of the "prerevolutionary" society. They do not represent truly *fundamental* change. Further, none of these types has an ideology or integrative myth significantly different from that already in existence. The millennarian rebellion is an ambiguous case, but by rendering unto Caesar that which is Caesar's and unto God that which is God's, Caesar's realm ought to undergo only slight change. Given this line of reasoning, it is possible to eliminate the criteria of calculation-spontaneity from consideration, since all of the remaining types represent *planned* actions. Similarly, the elimination of the first three categories leaves all revolutions with the characteristic of being either *elite* or *elite-dominated* movements. This is in accord with the idea of calculation.

There are further similarities. All revolutions are aimed at the community level. Even if the community has changed nonviolently, the revolution itself has a community orientation because it seeks to overthrow political arrangements designed to support and sanction a now-outmoded conception of community and to introduce and to institutionalize a political structure (that is, regime) synchronous with the realities of the political community. But more basically, there is an implication throughout Johnson's discussion that the community is defined by how much the population is socially and politically *mobilized*—that is, who are no longer essentially parochial. This carries with it, by implication, the assumption that those who do not have a parochial political orientation must have at least a subject orientation to the political system—and are, therefore, a part of the political community.

A more pragmatic notion, in this context, is that of Karl Deutsch (1954, pp. 98–103) to the effect that social mobilization involves two distinct phases: mobilization *out* of traditional patterns; and integration *into* new roles, structures and values. The first does not by any means imply the second. Given this, it is quite possible that revolutionaries may attempt to alter the nature of the political community in order to incorporate groups who were formerly excluded—but mobilized. According to the somewhat formalistic conception presented by Johnson, this would not constitute a change in the community (because such groups must have been "subjects" beforehand and thus were already included). Furthermore, and equally telling, a significant alteration in the relative positions of groups in the community ought to constitute as much a change in the nature of that community as does the incorporation of new members. What constitutes a "significant alteration" is ambiguous, but this is directly analogous to— indeed, is the occurence of—reform shading off into revolution.

A characteristic of the mass militarized insurrection (that is, a revolutionary strategy of guerrilla war) is, in fact, an attempted alteration of the nature of the community. A defining characteristic of revolution is an attack upon and an attempted major alteration of the nature of the political network. This has a necessary corollary: A conspiratorial coup d'état can be considered revolutionary only if the conspirators intend to institute changes throughout the social and political system, including the level of the political community. All revolutions involve the creation and attempted institutionalization of a new integrating social myth. The alteration of the community must have some rationale, some justification. It is through the spread of the revolutionary ideology (which may be ad hoc and/or ex post facto, as is the glorification of ethnic minorities or outcast groups in the Third World that the changes instituted by the new elite are legitimized.

There are three essential features of revolution: (1) It is elite dominated; whatever the role of the masses may be, it can be stated with certainty that they will never be in control of the revolutionary movement—they may provide support, cannon fodder and a cause, but they will never provide the direction for and leadership of the movement, (2) it is aimed at the radical alteration of the political community; and, directly related to this, (3) it presents a new integrating mythology, a revolutionary ideology. As a consequence of these features, it is also possible to state that revolutions will not occur spontaneously; although tactical maneuvers, including even the actual outbreak of fighting, may be heavily influenced by chance occurrences, no revolution will achieve power without achieving organization.

This is not a matter of excluding the possibility of spontaneity by arbitrary definition. Rather, it is based upon the consideration that a revolution is a concerted attack upon an ongoing, even if weak, political system. Resistance must be expected, both in the form of the organized enforcement arm of the state while the old regime is in power and in the form of ad hoc counterrevolutionary efforts by the displaced elite and its allies after the old regime has fallen. The revolutionaries must be capable of (1) protecting themselves from the coercive power of the state before the revolution; (2) overcoming in some way the state's initial monopoly over the means of organized violence; and (3) maintaining control once the old regime has been overthrown. For all of these tasks organization is necessary. Thus, another characteristic of revolution: Revolution consists, in part, of a struggle for domination of control over the system-wide monopoly of coercion and, hence, necessarily involves violence and organization.

CONDITIONS FOR REVOLUTION

Rather than deal with what might be labeled basic dysfunctional aspects of the political system—such as a lack of circulation of elites, exploitation of various classes and changes in class structure and/or technology—this analysis will be limited to precipitants of revolution. A thorough understanding of the nature of revolutionary situations will be possible only after regional variations have been systematically taken into account and after the integration of political development with theorizing on revolution. Any society that has undergone a revolution had, previous to that revolution, either a revolutionary situation or conditions that insurgents could utilize in order to create a revolutionary situation. This does not imply that societies that have not undergone revolution cannot "suffer" from revolutionary conditions; indeed, one advantage of focusing initially upon "precipitants" is that by establishing when revolutionary conditions are present—even if no revolution ultimately occurs—the number of cases appropriate for the study of "ultimate causes" may be appreciably increased. Accordingly, this assumption by no means should be taken as a value judgment to the effect that societies where revolutions have not occurred are, ipso facto, societies in which revoltuion *ought not* to occur.

The discussion based upon a model of revolution predates the tactic of systematic guerrilla warfare, of revolutionary wars of attrition. There is likely to be a very significant difference in the abilities, determination, sophistication and class makeup of about-to-be-overthrown governments, and the problems faced by each type of regime in preventing the revolution are quite different. While this position has considerable force, a discussion of the preconditions is relevant to pointing out conditions that indicate that the collapse of the regime is imminent.

The time period of revolution extends roughly from the initiation of significant and widespread antiregime activities (indicated by the beginning of an insurgency—in the Eastern or Asian context; of politically motivated antigovernment violence; of radical resistance to governmental policies and/or laws; and of presentation of demands for major reform and basic policy changes—all in the Western case), and lasts until the collapse or overthrow of the regime. Brinton (1957) finds a number of similarities among his four European and American case studies during this period. These may be listed as follows: (1) governmental financial difficulties; (2) ineffective governmental reform efforts; (3) desertion of the intellectuals; and, concomitantly, (4) the development of a revolutionary (integrating) myth; (5) division within the ranks of an inept ruling class; (6) an increase in class antagonisms; (7) an increase, throughout the period, of antigovernment activity; (8) an accelerator, such as resistance to increased tax levies and collection; and (9) revolutionaries. Chalmers Johnson (1966), in *Revolutionary Change,* presents three essential characteristics: (1) the occurrence of a "power deflation"—that is, increased reliance upon force as the means of maintaining the coherence of and order in the society; (2) the "loss of authority" by the system elite—that is, the popular withdrawal of legitimacy from the elite's use of force and also the popular loss of confidence in the ability of the elite (and, perhaps, of the system) to survive the present crisis; (3) an accelerator; that is, an event or phenomenon that either deprives the elite of its ability to use the coercive apparatus of the state and/or convinces the revolutionaries that such force will no longer be effective against them. A fourth characteristic, elite intransigence, he considers to be an indirect cause of revolution.

It is possible to synthesize from these works four major operational categories of revolutionary precipitants (see Stone, 1966). Although other conditions may well be important and frequently present, it would seem that the following features are *essential* for the overthrow of the old regime:

(1) loss of effective coercive power by the government; (2) disintegration of ruling elite unity; (3) rise of a new integrative myth; and (4) the widespread loss of legitimacy by the regime.

There are a number of ways in which a government may lose its coercive capability. Defeat by a superior armed force is frequently cited. Usually this refers to defeat in a foreign war, which may cause a significant reduction in armed strength, in organizational efficiency and in morale. Disorganization and loss of morale would likely be unimportant only in the case of an unusually effective guerrilla war. Otherwise, even this revolutionary strategy is likely to work only after the psychological and organizational effects of a long war of attrition have reduced the combat capabilities of governmental forces. Therefore, it is generally argued, the cause of a decline in effective military power is most often due to internal decay within either the ranks of the officer corps or of the political elite proper. The issue becomes one not so much of the relative strength of the would-be revolutionaries, but more of the ability and determination of the government to use effectively the force that it possesses.

A large part of the explanation for this loss of coercive potential must be sought in the disintegration of the unity of the ruling elite (which may well include members of the armed services). Although it is difficult to establish general rules to account for this lack of cohesiveness, a number of factors can be suggested: (1) fear of eventual governmental collapse combined with a desire to "make the best of a bad situation"; (2) policy differences stemming from the adoption of either a reformist attitude or, even, acceptance of the revolutionary ideology—as well as the maintenance of conservative or reactionary policies (elite intransigence); (3) conflicting interests within the elite; and (4) general disaffection due to the government's inability to control the situation. Whatever the reasons, the important item is that such disintegration does occur and that it significantly reduces the government's ability to resist the revolutionaries.

Another factor is the rise of a new integrative myth, a revolutionary ideology. It is not necessary that these goals be widely accepted. What is important, however, is that they be accepted by a politically active segment of the population—by a group that has the capabilities to organize in order to press for the institutionalization of such goals, to spread and to popularize their position and to act rapidly with a high degree of political sophistication and coherence, especially in a time of confusion and disorder. There are, commonly, only three "segments" of the population that meet these criteria: the officer corps of the military, a Leninist political party and, at a more general level, the intelligentsia. If in a revolutionary situation the military, or important segments of it, adopts the revolutionary ideology, then a revolutionary—or Nasserist—coup is quite likely. But, more frequently, the armed forces represent an obstacle to the revolution. The party, properly speaking, ought not to be considered here. It represents an organizational structure rather than a social group. I have mentioned it simply to indicate that any group, if properly organized and sufficiently astute—and powerful —can play an important role in forcing the enactment of the new goals. However, even if workers or, in some contexts, peasants make up the bulk of the party, the leadership is still likely to be drawn from among the intellectuals (Kautsky, 1962). Thus, it is most likely to be the intellectuals who push for the "radicalization of the revolution." For this reason, the widespread "desertion of the intellectuals" may be taken as an important condition for revolution and, more importantly, as a sign of the growth of a new integrating myth.

The final necessary ingredient is a widespread loss of governmental and, to a lesser degree, regime legitimacy. If a revolution is to occur, regime legitimacy must be low among all politically relevant elements of the population. Two things must be noted here: The preceding statement refers to *groups,* not to individuals; and it indicates modal tendencies. To say that a "low level" is needed does not mean either that there exists some quantifiable, absolute level that may be taken as a cutoff point or that the political consequences of a given level of legitimacy are constant across groups. Rather, the essential feature of this argument is that the degree of support for present political structures (even in the event of minor reformist changes) must be low enough within the various groups that there exists no viable coalition that could seize control of the government and stabilize the situation short of radical change. The "art" of making a revolution in the Western model consists of preventing such a status quo or reformist coalition from thwarting revolution.

Withdrawal of legitimacy—as well as military defeat or stalemate— can be considered to be both a cause and a consequence of the demoralization and disorganization of the military. The same argument can be made in reference to the internal decay of the ruling elite and to the readiness of intellectuals to adopt a new integrating ideology. As Brinton (1957, pp. 44–51, 56) points out, moreover, in none of these groups must the withdrawal be total; the condition will be satisfied if a significant and prominent minority follows this path.

The reasons for this reduction in legitimacy must be found in the interaction of political, social and economic factors affecting such individual group, that is, in concrete, situationally specific events. However, it is possible to make some general theoretical remarks regarding the nature of legitimacy that can provide a guide to the type of process that should be looked for—remembering, all the while, that the focus is upon precipitants, not long-run preconditions. Lipset (1959, pp. 69–105) focuses upon long-term behavior and interactions and "democratic" systems.

> The stability of a given democratic system depends not only on the system's efficiency in modernization, but also upon the *effectiveness* and *legitimacy* of the political system. By effectiveness is meant the actual performance of a political system, the extent to which it satisfies the basic functions of

government as defined by the expectations of most members of a society, and the expectations of powerful groups within it which might threaten the system, such as the armed forces. . . . Legitimacy involves the capacity of a political system to engender and maintain the belief that existing political institutions are the most appropriate or proper ones for the society. The extent to which contemporary democratic political systems are legitimate depends in large measure upon the ways in which the key issues which have historically divided the society have been resolved. . . . the degree of legitimacy of a democratic system may affect its capacity to survive the crises of effectiveness.

Stability is dependent upon effectiveness and legitimacy, while legitimacy, in turn, is to a degree dependent upon effectiveness. A decline in governmental effectiveness, then, can be expected to be deleterious for political stability both directly—by increasing policy dissatisfactions—and indirectly—by decreasing the regime's legitimacy. In accordance with Lipset's model, a reasonable level of effectiveness can be expected to contribute to immediate, concrete satisfaction and to a gradual increase in legitimacy. And finally, a high level of legitimacy can be expected to provide the regime with a safety margin by buffering the impact of dissatisfactions growing out of governmental ineffectiveness.

Lipset is concerned with long-term historical trends and with major societal cleavages and changes. His discussion is relevant when dealing with revolutionary preconditions, but it applies less convincingly when the focus is on causal determinants. It must be assumed that the "health" of the polity has already undergone a process of historical deterioration, that many of the basic political and social values have been weakened or undermined to the point where their continued existence in a dominant position is problematical. This does not mean that their collapse is inevitable or that legitimacy is everywhere low and dissatisfaction high. Rather, it means that the society is faced with a crisis situation, one in which the government's reserves of propriety, good faith and ability to cope have been exhausted. Under these conditions, it is reasonable to expect that the "stability–legitimacy–effectiveness" relationship will hold in the short run and will reflect changes induced by pressures and policies far less significant than the key issues that have historically divided the society.

There exists a huge number of *specific* policies and events that can contribute to a loss of legitimacy; yet only a few categories are required as illustrations. Brinton reported that common to all of the revolutions that he investigated were the facts that the governments of the old regimes were confronted with severe financial difficulties and that they made unsuccessful attempts at political and social reforms. Three elements of this situation are of great importance. First, the governments lacked the resources, skills and/or motivation to deal adequately with the problems they face. If and when they enacted reforms, such programs tended to be inadequate to the task. Second, the potentially ameliorative effects of these policies were undermined by the fact that reformist measures were often applied in an inconsistent and vacillating manner—that is, they were enacted, rescinded and replaced eventually by additional programs, which only suffered the same fate. Probably the most important long-range effect of such vacillation was not an increase in popular demands and expectations (as the frustration–aggression approach might lead one to expect), but rather the spread of the belief that, whatever the policies the government might enact, the regime was incapable of providing relief. Both factors are related to the contribution of "effectiveness" (or lack thereof) to stability. A third factor, also related to effectiveness, which is especially important in the Eastern revolutionary context, is the government's demonstration of military weakness through its inability to eliminate active and significant guerrilla bands. In effect, the continued presence of guerrilla activity may be expected to establish a positive, that is, amplifying, feedback effect. Lack of effectiveness against such revolutionaries is likely to lower the morale of the armed forces and of government supporters, thereby lessening the state's military capacity and encouraging desertions from its side; and at the same time, a bandwagon effect further weakening the government may be produced by the apparent successes of the insurgents in both the military and political fields. Such pressures will develop most strongly when and if the guerrillas are capable of mounting an effective offensive against the government. But it may also be present, albeit to a somewhat lesser degree, if the insurgents are able to hold their own against the government attacks, if they are able to gain clear control over a substantial territory and, importantly, if at the same time they are able to publicize widely and focus attention upon their achievement.

Effectiveness is related to legitimacy. The development of the conditions enumerated above will thus have impact in both areas. But there are also two categories of governmental actions that influence "legitimacy" directly. The first category is the abrogation of the normal judical and political processes (whether by legal or illegal means) and the total violation of political norms and institutions, as might be the case in the event of a palace coup. It is important to note that the amount of withdrawal of legitimacy that such actions will incur is likely to be directly related to (1) the degree to which an individual has already withdrawn legitimacy from the regime (an individual who dislikes the government is apt to dislike its "illegitimate" efforts to ensure its survival); (2) the degree to which an individual feels that such actions are likely to produce an increased threat to his own well-being (that is, he sees the reasonable likelihood of such measures being used against him); and (3) there is likely to be no reduction in legitimacy if the individual feels that such actions are necessary and/or reasonable, given the severity of the threat against the regime to which he owes loyalty.

The second category of governmental actions related directly to legitimacy refers to the use of coercion. More appropriate in this context are the terms "terror," "counterterror" or "repression" because they effectively remove the discussion from the realm of vigorous and efficient, even if heavy-handed, law enforcement. Widespread use of terror by the government is likely to produce a substantial lowering of legitimacy. It has been argued by frustration–aggression theorists that a high level of coercion blocks aggression on the part of insurgents. Most plausible is the argument that, while extensive coercion does raise the risks of antigovernment activity, it achieves its major impact by physically *eliminating* insurgent leaders and organizers (Ekstein, 1965). Thus, their findings do not actually contradict the hypothesis offered here. Selected repression is ambiguous in its consequences. Although it will still operate to reduce the regime's legitimacy among those groups affected, since these are the insurgents it may well be a productive strategy for the government to follow: further reduction in the legitimacy levels from their already low point can be more than offset by the systematic elimination of these individuals and by the fact that dead men and prisoners are usually unable to assist the spread of their ideology. The ambiguity enters if the repression is not effective. Widespread use of terror is worse than inefficient selective terror from the standpoint of the government since it will undoubtedly create more enemies and neutrals than it will eliminate. Furthermore, the use of the police and military in such tasks may well contributte to their demoralization. Populations can be terrorized into silence and passivity. Indeed, for most realistic purposes, no matter how low the general popular level of legitimacy may be, a successful revolution is impossible while the government maintains effective control over its coercive apparatus.

STAGES OF REVOLUTION

In the Western model, the old regime, suffering from all the weaknesses indicated in the previous section, eventually loses its coercive ability and topples easily with only minimal prodding by the revolutionaries. The revolution then goes through five stages: (1) the honeymoon; (2) the rule of the moderates; (3) the rule of the extremists; (4) a reign of terror; and finally, (5) the Thermidor. The honeymoon period is short. It lasts from the collapse of the old regime to the initial stabilization of power and the assumption of control over the remaining parts of the governmental apparatus by a united, but noncohesive, revolutionary front. The "revolutionaries" are united, essentially, only by the fact that they had all been in opposition to the *ancien régime*. Policy differences and incompatibilities become apparent almost as soon as the actual process of governing is undertaken, and this brings the honeymoon to a close.

Moderates tend to assume control of the government upon the demise of the informal unity of the first stage. "They represented the richer, better known, and higher placed of the old opposition to the government, and it is only to be expected that they should take over from that government. Indeed, their assumption of responsibility is almost a spontaneous act" (Brinton, 1957, pp. 128–129). In effect, Brinton is arguing that these men, due to their political prominence, prestige and visibility under the previous government, are the natural figures of authority and symbols of social stability and governmental effectiveness to the population as a whole. As such, they are the natural leaders because their presence will be taken as a reassuring sign that there is, in fact, somebody in charge. That such attributes attain to these men is quite likely the case; however, there are more compelling reasons for their initial accession to the leadership positions.

Moderate politicians suffer from a number of weaknesses. First, they are divided among themselves as to ultimate goals, general policies and specific tactics. Second, they face strong demands for the enactment of increasingly revolutionary policies—demands coming from the radical elements to whom they are likely to feel a debt of gratitude and of "revolutionary solidarity" stemming from their mutual struggle and cooperation during the opposition and honeymoon periods. Third, even the enactment of minimal revolutionary or reformist measures is likely to provoke attempts by the old elite and their allies to bring about a counterrevolution. Thus, the new government is often faced with the problem of civil war. And finally, because the moderates typically attempt to work through existing governmental institutions and wish to act "responsibly" while slowly and legally enacting reforms, they soon find themselves becoming identified by the masses with many of the faults of the old regime as well as those produced by their own slow and indecisive policies.

The difficulties of moderates are intensified by the existence of "dual sovereignty." The moderates' control of the official government is more than counterbalanced by the radicals' development of an "illegal government." The latter consists of an efficient and tightly controlled organizational network penetrating all major politically significant groups. From this base, the revolutionaries (the moderates are essentially reformers) are able to attack and to undermine the legal government and the power and legitimacy of the moderates.

The insurrection that ushers in the rule of extremists is typically a coup d'état. For the reasons indicated above, the moderates have become too weak to offer strong resistance. But at least as important, if not more so, is the fact that the radicals, during the period of "dual sovereignty," have gained control over all of the major organizations of the society. The triumph of the extremists, who are few in number but extremely well organized and effective due to their intense discipline and total devotion to their cause, brings an end to the radicalization of the revolution. It also brings to an end the respect for civil liberties, individual rights, due process and limited government. The "reign of terror and virtue" is established in an attempt, perhaps not fully conscious, to tear the population away from its old patterns and norms and to inculcate the quasi-religious revolutionary mythology. Eventually, exhaustion sets in, and the revolutionary process comes to its final stage with the development of the Thermidor. At this point, there is a return to "normalcy," a reconciliation of the various groups in the society and the achievement of a synthesis of elements from both the old and the revolutionary regimes.

The strongest elements of Brinton's analysis are those relating to the conditions of the old regime, the problems of the moderates and the factors facilitating the rise of the extremists. The discussion of processes after the extremists achieve power is substantially weaker (with the exception of his powerful argument as to the quasi-religious nature of the new integrating myths). This weakness is due to the divergence of his four cases; only the most general and superficial "uniformities" could be abstracted from the concrete instances.

The course of the Chinese mass revolution is quite different from that of the Western variety. In the latter, the old regime, suffering from internal disorganization and lack of cohesiveness, collapses after only minimal direct efforts by the "revolutionaries." The revolution, then, actually takes place as the revolutionaries succeed in driving the conservatives, moderates and liberal reformers from political power. In the Eastern model, however, when the government finally falls to the insurgents, the revolutionaries immediately assume the positions of authority and are able to begin the implementation of their program.

The most readily observable feature of the Chinese or Asian model of revolution is the prominent place given to direct military struggle. These are "protracted wars" which place great importance upon guerrilla and mobile warfare. Since the "classic" works dealing with this form of struggle tend to emphasize the military component over the political, in the following discussion the process is outlined in terms of stages of the armed struggle and, afterwards, its political implications (See Mao Tse-tung, 1960, 1967; Giap, 1962).

Although there are important differences among the major theoreticians of revolutionary guerrilla war, there is general agreement that the struggle may be conceived of as progressing through three stages, defined by the tactics and the relative military strength of the contending sides. In the first stage of combat, the revolutionary forces suffer from grave military weakness. As a result, they must engage in essentially, that is, strategically, defensive operations. Beyond simply staying alive, the revolutionaries have one major goal: to establish and consolidate a base area, or a number of them, within which they will be secure and from which they will be able to expand. A base area, according to Mao Tse-tung, should be distinguished from a guerrilla zone. The latter is merely an area within which guerrilla forces can operate with some hope of success, while the former is an area within which they are secure from attack. To establish a base area, three things are necessary. First of all, the guerrilla force itself must be developed, that is, trained, enlarged and combat hardened. Second, the enemy forces must be soundly defeated; the area must be so securely held by the guerrillas that the government will be unable and unwilling to penetrate it. Third, the population within the area must be mobilized in support of the guerrillas and their cause. Mobilization of political support is an essential characteristic of this phase of the war, although it continues throughout the struggle. In addition to establishing mass support for the revolutionary cause, it provides the insurgents with combatants and reinforcements, with funds, supplies and intelligence, and it denies the government access to rapid and reliable information as to the whereabouts and activities of the guerrillas themselves. Once base areas are established, an effort is made to increase their extent, to expand the size of the guerrilla bands and the geographic range of their activity and, eventually, to establish new zones and base areas.

Throughout the first stage combat takes the basic form of hit-and-run and harassment tactics. The second stage opens when the guerrillas are numerous and powerful enough to carry the fight to the enemy in a more aggressive fashion.

> From the strategic point of view, guerrilla warfare, causing many difficulties and losses to the enemy, wears him out. To annihilate big enemy manpower and liberate land, guerrilla warfare has to move gradually to *mobile warfare*. . . . Through guerrilla activities, our troops were gradually formed, fighting first with small units then with bigger ones, moving from scattered fighting to more concentrated fighting. Guerrilla warfare gradually developed to mobile warfare—a form of fighting in which principles of regular warfare gradually appear and increasingly develop but still bear a guerrilla character. Its task was to annihilate a bigger and bigger number of enemy forces in order to develop our own, while the task of guerrilla warfare was to wear out and destroy the enemy reserves. (Giap, 1968, pp. 218–219)

As the quotation from Giap indicates, mobile warfare is plausible and feasible because of the increasing strength of the guerrilla forces. There is some dispute or confusion between Mao and Giap over the relative importance of guerrilla versus mobile warfare in the second stage. Mao appears to place greater emphasis upon the expansion of the guerrilla campaign. But this may be essentially a terminological difference since the distinction between the two (as well as between mobile and regular warfare) is at least as much qualitative as quantitative.

The second stage is initially one of equilibrium or stalemate. The government troops, having failed to eliminate the guerrilla base areas, attempt to consolidate their hold over their own territory and to prevent further revolutionary inroads. Coordinated guerrilla attacks (which may be described either as guerrilla or mobile warfare) upon exposed or outlying government positions as well as continued pure guerrilla actions eventually weaken the regular military and force it to pull back to major, well-fortified and defended locations such as the cities and communication lines, that is, roads and railroads. At the close of this phase of the war, then, the insurgents control almost the entire countryside, and the government possesses the urban areas. With the expansion of insurgent-held territory goes an expansion of the program of mobilization and, in the most secure areas, the establishment of revolutionary governmental and organizational networks.

By the time the third and final stage of the war starts, the revolutionaries are substantially stronger, militarily, than the government. However, as the government's forces are consolidated and entrenched in relatively small and well-prepared areas of their own choosing, guerrilla tactics are no longer effective against them. The attackers must now adopt conventional tactics and fight positional battles. While Mao maintains that, even at this point, positional warfare is secondary to mobile tactics, the progression to ever-larger troop concentrations and to an increasing acceptance of long, pitched battles is apparent in his writings as well as those of Giap. The "classic" guerrilla war thus ends with the final defeat of the government at the hands of an essentially conventional military force, although variations, such as urban uprisings or infiltration of strategic groups in a temporary coalition government, are occasionally introduced.

TASKS CONFRONTING INSURGENTS

While there are vast tactical differences between the Western and Eastern forms of revolution, these should not be given such priority that they obscure the essential similarity of the problems facing the revolutionaries and the general processes by which these problems are overcome. In both cases, the insurgents face the task of weakening and/or overthrowing the old regime and the separate task of organizing a political base from which to seize power; the differences, while important, are merely ones of timing and tactics and, as such, should not be construed as basic procedural differences.

The overthrow of the state under the conditions of the Western model tends to be less the result of direct, forceful insurgent activity and more the product of internal governmental weakness than is true for mass militarized insurrections. But there appears to be agreement that revolutionary conditions are existent only when similar conditions are met. In an argument quite similar to the earlier discussion of the weaknesses of the old regime, Lenin (1965, p. 86) states as "the fundamental law of revolution" that

> it is not enough for revolution that the exploited and oppressed masses should understand the impossibility of living in the old way and demand changes; it is essential for revolution that the exploiters should not be able to live and rule in the old way. Only when the *"lower classes"* do not want the old way, and when the "upper classes" *cannot carry on in the old way*—only then can revolution triumph. This truth may be expressed in other words: revolution is impossible without a nation-wide crisis

(affecting both the exploited and the exploiters). It follows that for revolution it is essential, first, that a majority of the workers (or at least a majority of the class-conscious, thinking, politically active workers) should fully understand that revolution is necessary and be ready to sacrifice their lives for it; secondly, that the ruling classes should be passing through a governmental crisis, which draws even the most backward masses into politics (a symptom of every real revolution is a rapid, tenfold and even hundredfold increase in the number of members of the toiling and oppressed masses—hitherto apathetic—who are capable of waging the political struggle), weakens the government and makes it possible for the revolutionaries to overthrow it rapidly.

One of the major appeals to revolutionaries of the Eastern model is that "it is not necessary to wait until all conditions for making revolution exist; the insurrection can create them" (Guevara, 1967, p. 1). Emphasis should be placed upon the word "create." It is not the military struggle, per se, but the *political efforts* carried out during the war as well as the *political* and military *consequences* of insurgent victories that bring down the old regime and allow the revolutionaries to seize power. Therefore, even when dealing with the Eastern model, it is necessary to pay particular attention to the political process during the *ancien régime*.

The second task confronting revolutionaries, that of developing a powerful base of political support, is carried out differently both in terms of the time it is accomplished and, usually, the social groups utilized; but conceptually it involves similar processes of social mobilization and political organization. These differences are due to *tactical* problems and are not the products of a basic theoretical divergence of the two types of revolution. Essentially the choice of the countryside over the cities for the base of the revolution is tactically rather than theoretically conditioned, reflecting the inability of the insurgents to win directly in the urban areas. Once the insurgents are forced into the countryside, they have no choice but to mobilize the peasantry as their political base. The weaknesses inherent in this position—the difficulties of effectively and militantly organizing the peasantry and of bringing the weight of the amorphous and scattered peasant masses to bear on urban political elements—are offset because the nature of such a revolution allows, in fact demands, the creation of a large and well-organized armed force. If the military (and political) weakness of the *ancien régime* permits an early insurgent victory, the ensuing power struggle between the radicals and the moderates will take place in an essentially urban context. In this case, the revolutionaries must focus their attention upon urban elements, such as workers and students, who can be relatively quickly organized and whose weight can be immediately and effectively demonstrated. To go off into the countryside in order to gain peasant support would be highly unprofitable given the necessity for rapid and decisive action to prevent the moderates from consolidating their political position. Although the peasantry may become a source of counterrevolutionary manpower in such a situation, the attempt by conservatives to use them in this manner is likely to be hampered by the same obstacles to mobilization and organization (although to a somewhat lesser degree given the force of peasant traditionalism). Successful urban revolutionaries desirous of promoting agrarian change can make a rural "revolution from above" through the use of political and economic appeals and/or coercion. The need for structural economic change in the countryside and the existence of an underdeveloped economy and large rural population do *not* necessitate the use of guerrilla warfare as a revolutionary tactic; the presence of a significant coercive capacity by the government does. If the former conditions were determinant, it might be noted, neither the French nor the Russian revolutions could have occurred as they did.

A society is composed of a limited number of social groups. The government consists of a coalition of groups, each with a specified degree of representation. The degree to which a group is represented in the decision-making process (that is, the coalition) indicates only its present political power. This is likely to reflect a combination of factors such as size, wealth, organization, political sophistication and coercive potential, but the consequences of a specific mix for a group are indeterminate in the abstract, since political power is a relative rather than an absolute term. It may be assumed that the more a group is represented in government circles, the more likely it is to find its interests served by the government and, hence, the more it can be expected to resist changes in the regime. Groups that are not significantly represented may also find satisfaction in governmental policies, but they can be expected to support coalition changes that would provide them with greater access to the decision-making process and, concomitantly, greater payoffs. Then, too, groups may support a government because they fear that any rearrangement of the coalition is likely to leave them worse off than previously, because they consider the regime to be legitimate (legitimacy, as defined previously, has both normative and interest components) or, as if often the case among the peasantry, because they consider it to be traditionally sanctioned (that is, legitimacy based solely upon the normative component). Before returning to the main topic, it is necessary to mention one last detail. Under the terms of this model, a revolution can be said to have occurred when a rapid, violent and substantial alteration of the *class* of the groups comprising the governing coalition has taken place and become finalized, which is to say, when the potential for counterrevolution has been eliminated.

The first problem facing the insurgents, both moderates and revolutionaries, is that of creating conditions under which governmental change will come about. In general, insurgent activities, at least as compared with those used in the Eastern model, are minimal. In a sense, their policy consists of waiting for the "contradictions" of the system to grow so immense that the government topples "of its own weight." In practice, however, it is somewhat more active. The major process during the period of decay of the *ancien régime* is the spread of *discontent* among all groups and especially among the supporters of the regime. Although the most compelling basis for the creation of general dissatisfaction is the overall economic and political crisis that brought on the deterioration in the first place, the revolutionaries can intensify and speed up the development of the "contradictions," they can hasten the process of "polarization." There are basically two ways in which this can be done. First, by creating disorder, disruption and damage to property and occasionally persons (although such terror is often counterproductive), the revolutionaries can promote increased dissatisfaction with the government, which, in effect, is shown to be incapable of maintaining order and of protecting the interests of its constituents. Second, such actions may provoke the government to "overreact," to embark upon a policy of widespread repression which is likely to alienate those liberals and moderates who suddenly perceive, accurately or not, that the lives and security of themselves and their families and friends are threatened unnecessarily. But, it must be noted, such policies are *only* viable in an environment of a broad, amorphous united-front coalition. If "terrorist" activities begin before there is widespread disaffection from the government, potential supporters of political change are likely to be driven, out of fear, into support for the status quo. If they begin later, however, it is quite possible that many people will be able to maintain that there is a need for governmental change both because the government is ineffective and, perhaps, reactionary, and because only with such change will it be possible to isolate the extremists.

What is needed for the collapse of the old regime is that the government should be forced to rely upon an ever-narrower base of support. The expansion of the antigovernment forces will permit an interplay of interests and provide the basis for a new governmental coalition—composed to a large degree, it should be noted, of the centrist groups that formerly supported the government. The moderate character of this alternative government is an important factor in the collapse of the old regime. Since it would appear that the change will be either at the regime or government levels, but definitely not at the level of the political community, that is, *not* revolutionary, and since such change apparently affords the opportunity to solve some of the societal problems and to reestablish law and order, many moderate and conservative elements may well prefer this option to the alternative of siding with the unpopular and insecure incumbent government. If the military forces of the government have not been neutralized by infiltration, demoralization or defeat, this is a highly likely time for a conservative or reform coup de'état. But if a coup is not possible, there are a number of important factors that give the revolutionaries an opportunity to move the political change from reform to revolution. First of all, even if the nucleus of the new coalition is moderate and composed of many of the same elements that were prominent under the former government, there will still be some expansion of the scope of the coalition, which will give the revolutionaries some access. Such an expansion is necessary; hence, it takes wider support to institute and secure a new government than it does to maintain one in existence. Legitimacy, apathy, self-interest, fear of the risks of change and, often, traditional values—all operate to support an incumbent government, but during a state of flux only self-interest, in the form of promises and anticipations rather than past performances, is likely to bring about support for a potential government. Since each group is likely to bring only a small amount of support to the coalition, there is a need to incorporate a larger number of groups in order to "insure" stability.

At the same time, given the insecurity of the new government and the fact that it is faced with substantially the same problems that brought down its predecessor, the moderates must include radical elements in the hope of bringing an end to their disruptive activities. This is all the more true if the extremists have demonstrated a significant capacity for anti-government action. A final factor working to advance the revolution is that not all possible coalitions are viable. To the extent that radical and conservative groups have major policy conflicts, it will be impossible to give them each substantial representation. Due both to the revolutionaries' proven disruptive capabilities and to the moderates' general policy of "no enemies to the left," it is likely to be the more conservative groups that are excluded. This is much less likely to be the case if the new government came about through a military coup, since then the radicals' coercive tactics could be countered by repressive measures.

There is an additional point adduced: Revolutionaries must not be solely programmatic. To advance a clear, radical program and to try to mobilize support on the basis of a revolutionary ideology is self-defeating at this stage in the process. The program and ideology, if they are truly revolutionary, are likely to cause the radicals to be excluded from the governing coalition because the moderate and conservative groups which would be hurt by the enactment of revolutionary measures will still have sufficient power, unity and motivation to take a strong stand against their clearly visible enemy. Indeed, if the revolutionary threat is substantial and obvious enough, it would be to their interest to support the old regime and to back harsh repressive measures rather than to risk the possibility of the radical forces growing in strength during a period of governmental change.

While it is true that the moderates are the natural heirs to the fallen government, Brinton's argument that this is due to their wealth, prestige and previous political prominence is only partially correct and misses a far more important reason. Moderates initially assume control in the Western model because the balance of contending political forces, composed essentially of those groups that were fairly well organized and relatively comfortably situated under the old regime, is on the whole moderate. A further implication of his argument is that the reason for the decline in the strength of the moderates is basically that they suffer a loss of prestige due to their use of the old governmental forms and institutions and that they are confronted with the same problems that caused the collapse of the previous government. Again these arguments of Brinton are important but secondary. Of greater significance is the fact, which he underrates, that radicals through organization and social mobilization substantially increase both their political power and their ability to disrupt the government.

Revolutionaries are motivated by their ideology to develop a political base upon social groups or classes that have been excluded from or minimally incorporated into the political system. It is not simply the addition of new groups to the political process that constitutes the revolution. Also implied is the idea that these groups come to occupy such a prominent political position that many of the previously important elements must be excluded from the decision-making centers. Furthermore, the interests and goals of the new groups (and of society in general) are defined by the revolutionary organizations which thoroughly penetrate them and which act in accordance with the new integrating mythology. These developments constitute, in effect, a transformation of the political community.

Since activities leading toward such a state of affairs will not be acceptable to the initial moderate coalition, it is necessary that they be carried out in a covert or at least inconspicuous manner. Hence even after the fall of the old regime and the institution of the moderate-controlled government, it is necessary that the revolutionaries not give the appearance of being extremely radical. As they develop their mass power base and spread and strengthen their organizations, they will be able to "move" to a more extreme position. This greater freedom is due to three factors. First, their increased strength gives them a greater disruptive capability. Second, the governing coalition, in addition to being subject to a Left blindspot, faces a realistic political problem: The revolutionaries' ability to disrupt or bring down the still insecure government has increased, and the "easiest" way to avoid this is to attempt to coopt them, to give them larger representation in the coalition. Such an approach is logical, also, because the efficient, mass radical apparatus can guarantee and deliver support more effectively than almost any other group. And finally, to attempt ruthlessly to root out and destroy the revolutionary organization would result not only in a betrayal of the principles for which the moderates are likely to stand, as Brinton mentions, but also would plunge the country into a seemingly avoidable (since alternative policies exist) civil war. Whatever the danger of close alliance with extremists, moderates must also face the fact that they are unlikely to be able to command a dependable military force, since the old armed services were unable to defend the previous government, and, if a new organization is being developed, it is still untried—and perhaps infiltrated by extremists. Thus, moderates have many reasons to be responsive to radical elements.

To make matters more difficult for the centrists, increased responsiveness to radicals and to their increasingly militant demands inevitably produce increased disaffection on the part of the more conservative elements.

Conservatives are unable to duplicate radical strategy since to engage in policies of competitive social mobilization and political appeals would undermine the position that they are attempting to conserve. With political negotiation ruled out, their only option is the use of force. Here they have two possibilities: foreign military aid and/or intervention and the mobilization of the peasantry on the basis of traditional appeals, such as traditional bonds of loyalty and religious faith, or simply on the basis of anticipated war booty. Both of these are dangerous tactics. Foreign intervention is likely to rally the population to the moderate and revolutionary sides so that, unless overwhelming force is applied, it is unlikely to lead to the desired result. The mobilization of the peasantry not only might get "out of control," that is, develop revolutionary potential, but also is unlikely to be effective without thorough preparation and organization. Furthermore, since this type of revolution is an urban phenomenon, transportation difficulties may render such attempts ineffective. But again, from the government point of view, the serious danger of conflict in either of these forms will tend to make reliance upon the efficiently organized, and perhaps paramilitary, revolutionary forces more of a necessity.

As the revolutionaries grow in strength and militancy, the government becomes more responsive to them, thus encouraging further growth. At the same time, as the revolutionaries gain increased representation in the governing coalition, the conservatives lose power and become increasingly dissatisfied with the regime. Since their opposition raises the possibility of civil war, the moderates must enter into an even closer alliance with the radicals in order to be able to use their mass organizations to protect the state should conflict break out and also to minimize disunity in time of crisis. This further alienates the conservatives and increases the risk of war. At some point in this cycle, the revolutionaries find that they are the dominant group in the coalition or that they have a sufficient political and coercive base that they can organize a simple *coup d'état,* exclude the moderates and take over the government.

Revolutionaries do not reach this point through political manipulation alone. Rather they have been able to organize a mass following and to threaten or bring to bear a significant coercive potential. Spontaneity, luck, political appeals, charisma and political genius may have been important at various moments in their rise to power, but the essential ingredient in the revolutionaries' success is superior *organization.* If the revolutionaries are to triumph, they must organize an apparatus that consistently and rapidly can deliver the threats and promises, both violent and nonviolent, that the leadership needs in order to achieve the political weight necessary to drive out the conservatives and overwhelm the moderates in the governmental coalition.

The apparatus provides the basis for the organization of political processes and for the enforcement of the laws in the revolutionary state. After the radicals seize complete power, their control over the instruments of coercion is used for two special and immediate problems. The "terror," as Brinton emphasizes, is a result of the desire of the revolutionaries forcefully and almost messianically to institutionalize the new integrating myth. However, he gives scant attention to the fact that the revolutionary governments is in a precarious position. Although it possesses a dedicated, militant army and the most efficient and well-organized political structure since, at least, the collapse of the old regime, it also possesses one of the narrowest political coalitions since that time. All conservatives and most of the moderates are in substantial opposition to the government. And as the coalition attempts to enact its radical program, it will for some time continue to create more dedicated opponents. Terror may be seen basically as an effort to eliminate—through exile, death and imprisonment—to disorganize and to disorient all potential opposition forces.

While the much greater importance of the military struggle clearly distinguishes the Eastern from the Western model of revolution, the two forms also have certain differences in their political processes. There are essentially two major differences: First, the "classic" Eastern revolution cannot be won without a prolonged military effort, while in the Western case the old regime is sufficiently weak that armed confrontation does not play a highly noticeable role; and second, given the extended period of conflict under the old regime in the Eastern model, the revolutionaries are able to emerge sufficiently strong, both in coercive capacity and political organization, that they do not have to contend with an interim period of rule by a moderate coalition. Politically, then, the Eastern revolution goes through only one stage, but in that stage the revolutionaries must (1) militarily and politically defeat the old regime; (2) develop a political base through social and political mobilization; (3) organize the final, narrow revolutionary coalition and necessary political and coercive apparatus; and (4) prevent the rise of a moderate coalition which, in this case, might seize power from the old regime and neutralize the revolutionaries' political appeal.

The major political base of the revolutionaries lies in the peasantry. Yet, this group is typically weak and ineffective politically, being fairly scattered, of low cohesiveness and removed from the normal centers of political activity. These facts seemed to have been recognized in the most important instances of Eastern revolution, since in both China and Vietnam the strategy of protracted guerrilla warfare was adopted only after military disaster in the urban areas. In overcoming these initial handicaps, the insurgents are aided by two factors. First, before the development of guerrilla bands, or simultaneously with their initial weak appearance, there is a period of intense organizational work by the *existing* revolutionary party. The goal of this work is to build up throughout the countryside both peasant backing for the guerrillas, their cause and struggle, and a supportive organizational network. The people who carry out these tasks are not, it should be noted, the locally recruited guerrillas themselves, but rather party members

and special military elite cadres. Even though the decisive fighting throughout most of the war takes place in the countryside, the enemy- or govern-
ment-held urban areas are also penetrated by a revolutionary apparatus
that is in close touch with the rural organization. "While the working class
(i.e., the Party) is in the class leading the revolution, the peasantry is the
main force of the revolution, full of anti-imperialist and anti-feudal spirit"
(Giap, 1968, p. 212). The initial work of mobilization and organization,
which is necessary to prepare a receptive environment for the guerrillas,
takes time. Here the second factor aiding the insurgents becomes evident:
In the classic guerrilla situation, there exists either substantial territory
outside the control of government forces or nearby foreign territory where
the initial organizational and military cadres can receive training, equipment and security (Mao Tse-tung, 1967, p. 65). Thus, considerable effort
can be expended on propaganda and organizational matters before the
government becomes aware of the existence of an insurgency.

The efforts of revolutionaries to build their political base among the
peasant population has both military and political dimensions. Politically,
the revolutionary ideology is spread throughout the countryside by the party
apparatus or the party cadres within the guerrilla army. Self-conscious,
intensive and multipronged propaganda campaigns are carried out in in-
surgent-controlled or dominated areas (Mao Tse-tung, 1967, pp. 60–61).
Thus, the extent of their political support is, in part, a function of the
extent of their guerrilla operations. Furthermore, efforts at political persuasion are bolstered by two additional policies. Within base areas, as has
been indicated earlier, revolutionary governments are established, which,
to the extent practicable during the period of struggle, enact and enforce
the revolutionary program. During the period of "dual sovereignty," the
population gains experience and familiarity with many features of the revolutionary code and organization. To a substantially greater degree than
occurs during the "rule of the moderates" in Western revolutions, the population undergoes a process of resocialization. Another policy supporting the
new integrating myth is the implemenation of what is often called "armed
propaganda." Especially in effectively secured areas, the revolutionary position is not only argued for, it is also *enforced*. This involves not merely the
enactment of specific proposals such as land reform, but also the elimination of active opponents and, often, of prestigious but nonsupportive local
figures—for instance, the use of selective terror and assassination. While
it is difficult to evaluate the relative efficacy of the carrot as opposed to
the stick, it is clear that they both contribute significantly to the winning of
support for, or at least acceptance of, the insurgent position.

An important consequence of these policies is that by the time the
revolutionaries take power officially, they have already eliminated many of
the most likely and prominent rural counterrevolutionaries and have cowed
or coopted most of the neutrals who might otherwise have rallied to the
antirevolutionary cause. In effect, the period of revolutionary terror comes

before the insurgents seize the government, not after, as in the Western model. Thus, the combination of propaganda, indoctrination and armed propaganda operates to increase the size and intensity of the revolutionaries' political base and to weaken the ability of the moderates to create a large antiinsurgent coalition.

The creation of a strong, well-disciplined military and political organization, whether separate as in the case of a party and an army or combined as in the case of a political elite corps within the army itself, is intended to provide the revolutionaries with the apparatus necessary to defeat the government militarily and to mobilize the political potential of the scattered and amorphous peasant masses. This can be seen in Mao Tse-tung's (1967, p. 49) statement:

> The mobilization of the common people throughout the country will create a vast sea in which to drown the enemy, create the conditions that will make up for our inferiority in arms and other things, and create the prerequisites for overcoming every difficulty in the war. To win victory, we must persevere in the War of Resistance, in the united front and in the protracted war. But all these are inseparable from the mobilization of the common people. . . . What does political mobilization mean? First, it means telling the army and the people about the political aim of the war.

Despite his concern with peasant mobilization and the military struggle, Mao does not neglect more general political appeals and notes the importance of a united-front policy. This point is brought out more clearly by Giap (1968, p. 209):

> Our party led the people . . . to wage a resistance war against the French colonialists. To spearhead all the forces at the principal enemy, the party carried out the line of winning more friends and creating less enemies, endeavored to widen the national united front . . . united all forces which could be united, neutralized all those which could be neutralized, and differentiated between forces which could be differentiated.

If the Maoist revolution were simply the military victory of a revolutionary army and its peasant supporters, this concern with the development of a broadly based coalition would be inexplicable or at least superfluous. One of the major advantages of the coalition approach is that it provides an explanation of the need for united-front policies.

In the context of the modern nation–state, the locus of political power is the city. Without control over the urban areas it is almost impossible to control fiscal and communications resources and to possess the security necessary to make policy for the nation. If a group is capable of sustaining itself in power in the urban areas against military and political threats from the countryside, it will be able to continue to govern and is likely eventually to be able to overcome the rural danger. Asymmetrical relationships in regard to attack and defense, communication, organization, effectiveness of political coercion, recruitment and training of personnel and financial base —all favor the urban political forces over the long run. Even in the short run, if the urban groups are able to maintain a fairly high degree of cohesiveness, they are unlikely to be overthrown by an indigenous, rurally based, funded and recruited military–political force.

As the tactics of political revolution change in the postnuclear epoch, so, too, has the terrain. The most successful revolutions have taken place in rural environments, underdeveloped areas, and where the risks were visibly low and the rewards potentially high. Certainly, the Maoist insistence on winning the broad masses, on enlisting and maintaining peasant support, and finally, on surrounding the urban regions, reveals a keen appreciation of the special difficulties involved in guerrilla insurrections. But as the terrain of struggle has increasingly shifted to urban environments, even capital cities, the rate of success has gone down noticeably, and the amount of mass suffering has gone way up. Whether we take the Paris Commune of 1871, the Warsaw ghetto uprising of 1943, the Prague rebellion of 1968, or the Hong Kong uprisings against the British of 1968, the results have been uniformly harsh and severe for the revolutionary factions. And when guerrilla violence was crowned with success in the city environment, the reasons were usually unrelated to the exercise of mass violence (Oppenheimer, 1969, pp. 73–101).

Another, more recent, commentator on the subject of guerrilla revolution has offered some cogent explanations for why revolutions by insurrectionary foci come upon such hard times in the cities.

> It is more difficult to win the support of the city dwellers than of rural folk because the urban environment makes people much more dependent upon the efficient functioning of the public services. The peasant is initially difficult to win over because he has an ingrained attitude of respect for authority—for the landlord and the government. If this attitude can be broken down, then he is likely to swing completely over to the guerrillas. If they induce him to throw off the hold of the landlord, then at once he has a tangible gain: his own plot of land. He then discovers that he is dependent on nobody. He grows his own food, and the few goods he needs can be furnished locally. The police only symbolize repression, and he has little need for other public services—the mails, trains and buses, etc. The situation of the city dweller is quite the reverse. He will have no natural respect for authority: he will reject "the Establishment," but he is totally dependent on the public system. If water supplies and electricity are cut off, he cannot survive. If sewage and rubbish disposal services collapse, his whole environment becomes polluted. In desperation, he will appeal to the regime to restore normality. (Tinker, 1971, pp. 54–55)

Given the fact the industrial heartland is located in the urban regions, and that it is such regions that define the source of power in advanced nations, the prospects for minority revolutions continue to look bleak.

Two factors must be taken into account when evaluating the relative strengths of urban and rural groups. First, to the extent that the rural forces receive funds, supplies and training from outside the country, they will have a better chance of conquering the cities—this is especially important if the ruling urban groups fail to receive external support. Second, it is a presupposition of this argument that many or most of the groups in the dominant urban coalition are relatively independent of the countryside. For example, a coalition composed of urban or internationally oriented businessmen and/or urban workers would be able to continue many of their normal financial activities and thus maintain their political strength even if the countryside were controlled by hostile forces. This would not be the case, however, if the dominant urban group were absentee landlords who would have their source of income cut off by an effective rural rebellion.

There are three important consequences of this position. First, in its pure form the Asian revolutionary model is applicable only to situations of fairly low political and economic development. As economic development proceeds, the political weight of rural-based elites tends to decrease relative to urban groups, and, therefore, the ability of the cities to withstand an agrarian insurrection is increased. Second, since a direct assault upon urban bastions will be difficult under the "best" of conditions, it is important to consider those factors that will weaken the ability of the government to maintain itself and to make use of the long-term asymmetries in its favor. In other words, even in the case of the mass militarized insurrection it is useful to focus attention upon the loss of cohesiveness of the old regime. And third, it is necessary to understand how the insurgents are able to prevent the moderates from seizing power and preventing the expansion of the revolution into the urban centers. Thus, the description of signs of decay of the old regime is essentially similar in the Western and Eastern contexts, with the obvious addition that military failures are much more important in the latter case.

The initial position of the moderates is much weaker in the Eastern as opposed to the Western revolutionary situation. The fact that the urban population of these countries is always quite small, 20 or 30 percent, is important but does not appear to be decisive, since it is about the same in the "classic" revolutions of both types. Rather, this may be taken as a sign that revolution is a byproduct of political development. As the nation becomes increasingly urbanized, revolution, should it occur, will be more likely to fit the Western mold. This is only in part a function of the size of the urban moderate groups, the national bourgeoisie. Their political role within the context of the status quo is of far greater significance. If previous to the revolutionary outbreak they have achieved a substantial degree of power, have developed fairly strong political institutions and/or have a sizable interest in the continuation of the social system with, at most, only reformist alterations, then a successful Eastern revolution will be highly unlikely. And all of these conditions are more likely to obtain when the urban population—and economy—is large. The moderate groups must be sufficiently weak that (1) they would prefer an alliance with a powerful *revolutionary* force to the alternatives of standing alone or allying themselves with the old regime, and (2) they lack sufficient political skill, cohesion and sophistication to organize themselves independently of and in opposition to the revolutionary groups. This, rather than size, would appear to be the major characteristic differentiating moderate groups in Eastern and Western revolutions. It must be reiterated that under most conditions a politically united urban coalition is unlikely to be overthrown by rural armed forces.

Even relatively weak moderate groups, however, must be neutralized by the revolutionaries. This appears to be accomplished through cooptation and infiltration, or, in Giap's phrase, policies by which the revolutionaries "united all forces which could be united, neutralized all those which could be neutralized, and differentiated between forces which could be differentiated" (Giap, 1968, p. 210). Basic to the success of this technique is the fact that the announced program of the revolutionaries is typically minimal. Since the vast majority of the population is peasant and since land is everywhere distributed unequally, one of the basic appeals will be land reform. It ought to be noted that, even if the revolutionaries' long-range goal is the socialization of the agricultural system, in keeping with the overall strategy of developing the broadest possible coalition and focusing that coalition against the incumbent government, such programs will not be immediately carried out. Rather than risk losing peasant support by introducing new forms of agricultural organization, the general policy is one of "land to the tiller" in order to satisfy the peasant's desire for control over and ownership of his plot of land. Similarly, in dealing with urban groups, where the revolutionaries desire to make structural changes in the normal social and economic patters, the specific and often even the general features of these alterations will remain the knowledge only of those in the party, and will be kept from the masses.

The other common rallying point is nationalism which, according to the circumstances, is likely to be either specifically anticolonial or generally antiimperialist. In either case, the foreign "they" and their immediate supporters are apt to be the only clear targets of the movement. If no further programmatic content is elaborated publicly, it is only the *large* landowners, the colonizers and a few members of the small native political, economic and social elite who have anything to fear should the revolution be successful. The situation becomes blurred the more the nationalist banner assumes an antiimperialist tinge. The "we–they" distinction is far less sharp when the ruling elite is native to the country. When the differentiation between "good guys" and "bad guys" is based upon economic activity, the opposition forces may swell as numerous individuals either feel themselves to be implicated or feel that the breaking of the economic ties with the imperialist country will endanger their livelihood. Furthermore, simply the use of the term "imperialism," with its implications of economic analysis, may drive some groups into opposition out of fear that the revolutionary movement is actually radical, that is, communist, and will bring with it socialism, the dictatorship of the proletariat and the domination of the Soviet Union. The point is not whether they perceive the situation correctly, but rather the fact that the use of certain slogans, even when undefined, is likely to promote stiffer resistance to the revolution by encouraging the moderates to side with the government. Coincidentally, it might be noted, both the Vietnamese and the Chinese revolutions, the "classic" examples of this type, were carried out against colonial occupation either entirely or during the crucial years, covering the development of guerrilla warfare into the predominantly mobile form. Given the wide base for support that remains after these few elements have been excluded, the strategy that is followed is the formation of a large and diverse united front, incorporating all or most of the politically organized and significant urban groups.

The creation of the united front and its constituent organizations are made easier by the fact that the revolutionaries are likely to have an efficient and extensive urban underground apparatus already in existence, left over from the days of their urban struggle. The creation of the "front" serves a number of purposes. It keeps the moderates weak and divided and prevents their effective opposition to the revolutionaries. The infiltration of civilian groups and governmental institutions will render them weak and unable to resist efficiently the revolutionary forces should direct military victory prove unattainable and a negotiated settlement and "coalition government" be the only way to gain access to the urban strongholds. One further advantage of an apparently moderate-dominated front is that it may tend to attract international assistance which might otherwise go to the government. High visibility for weak moderate forces may serve the propaganda aims of the revolutionaries by making it easier to portray the government coalition as reactionary and undeserving of local or foreign support. Overall, this argument is in accord with the spirit if not the language of Douglas Pike (1968, pp. 40–42) on guerrilla organizational tactics.

> Don't try for too much; don't smash the existing social system, use it; don't destroy opposition organizations, take them over. Use the amorphous united front to attack opposition political forces too large or too powerful for you to take over; then fragment their leadership, using terror if necessary, and drown their followers in the front organization. At all times appear outwardly reasonable about the matter of sharing power with rival organizations although secretly working by every means to eliminate them. . . . Divide your organization rigidly into overt and covert sections and minimize traffic between the two. The overt group's chief task is to generate broad public support; the covert group seeks to accumulate and manipulate political power. . . . Don't antagonize anyone if it can be helped; this forestalls the formation of rival blocs. Blend the proper

mixture of the materialistic appeals of communism [*sic*] and the endemic feelings of nationalism. . . . Plan to win in the end not as Communists but as nationalists.

The united front in many ways is the Asian equivalent to the broad coalition of moderate and revolutionary groups that represents the opposition to the old regime in the Western model. In both cases, antigovernment forces grow at the expense of the ruling coalition (which is not strictly the case in regard to increasing peasant support of the revolutionaries); the narrowing of the coalition is likely to be due to the growth of discontent, the adoption of the revolutionary ideology and governmental ineffectiveness; the process is likely to be intensified by elite intransigence and general repressive measures; and the cooperation between moderate and revolutionary forces lessens the hostility of the reformers and their ability to combat the radicals.

The different consequences of the broad front are due to the facts that (1) moderates in the Eastern context are initially weak, politically, socially and economically, relative to their Western counterparts; (2) revolutionaries are capable of infiltrating and manipulating moderate organizations in order to prevent them from becoming an effective force, whereas in the Western context the revolutionaries must divide a poorly coordinated ruling coalition; (3) by the time the Eastern old regime falls, the revolutionaries have control over the dominant sources of coercion, have a mass following and have a large, efficient militant organization, rather than having to create these important assets in the face of a new and initially popular, moderate government; and finally, (4) prolonged military struggle in the Asian world has given revolutionaries the opportunity to neutralize or eliminate most of their potential opposition. This combination of historical factors is probably why Maoism and its varieties have become the dominant style of revolution making even in higher industrialized societies.

REFERENCES

Brinton, C. C. (1957) *The Anatomy of Revolution*, rev. ed. New York: Vintage Books.

Deutsch, K. W. (1954) *Political Community at the International Level*. New York: Random House.

Ekstein, H. (1965) "On the Etiology of Internal War," *History and Theory*, vol. 4, no. 2, pp. 133–163.

Giap, V. N. (1962) *People's War, People's Army*. New York: Praeger.

Giap, V. N. (1968) "The Resistance War Against French Imperialism," in W. Pemeroy, ed., *Guerrilla Warfare and Marxism*. New York: International Publishers.

Gross, F., and R. D. Hopper (1959) *Un Siglo de Revolución*. Mexico: Biblioteca de Ensayos Sociologicos-Instituto de Investigaciones Sociales.

Guevara, E. (1967) *Guerrilla Warfare.* New York: Random House, Vintage Press.

Hopper, R. D. (1950) "The Revolutionary Process," *Social Forces,* 28 (March), pp. 270–279.

Horowitz, I. L., ed. (1964) *The New Sociology.* New York: Oxford University Press.

Huntington, S., ed. (1962) *Changing Patterns of Military Politics.* New York: Free Press.

Johnson, C. (1964) *Revolution and the Social System,* Hoover Institution Studies, no. 3. Stanford: Stanford University Press.

Johnson, C. (1966) *Revolutionary Change.* Boston: Little, Brown.

Kautsky, J. (1962) *Political Change in Underdeveloped Countries.* New York: John Wiley.

Lasswell, H., and A. Kaplan (1950) *Power and Society.* New Haven: Yale University Press.

Lenin, V. I. (1965) *"Left-Wing" Communism, an Infantile Disorder.* Peking: Foreign Languages Press.

Lipset, S. M. (1959) "Some Social Requisites of Democracy," *American Political Science Review,* vol. 53 (March), pp. 69–105.

Mao Tse-tung (1960) *Strategic Problems in the Anti-Japanese Guerrilla War.* Peking: Foreign Languages Press.

Mao Tse-tung (1967) *On Protracted War.* Peking: Foreign Languages Press.

Oppenheimer, M. (1969) *The Urban Guerrilla.* Chicago: Quadrangle Books.

Pike, D. (1968) *Viet Cong.* Cambridge, Mass.: M.I.T. Press.

Rosenau, J., ed. (1964) *International Aspects of Civil Strife.* Princeton: Princeton University Press.

Stone, L. (1966) "Theories of Revolution," *World Politics,* vol. 18, no. 2 (January), pp. 159–176.

Tinker, H. (1971) "Can Urban Guerrilla Warfare Succeed?" *Current,* whole no. 129 (May), pp. 52–57.

CHAPTER 13

THE MORPHOLOGY OF COUNTERREVOLUTION

GUERRILLA WARFARE: AN OVERVIEW

Guerrilla warfare has become the most common form of military conflict since World War II, mostly because the threat of mutual nuclear annihilation makes a conventional warfare between major powers counterproductive. Guerrilla warfare enables major powers to engage in indirect limited wars, with limited objectives, without risking nuclear escalation. At the same time, and perhaps more important, guerrilla warfare makes military conflict possible in situations where only political conflict previously occurred—between Third World nations and major powers, or poorly armed dissident groups and well-armed government forces. Guerrilla warfare, or unconventional warfare, neutralizes the effects of conventional military strength to a large extent. A militarily inferior insurgent force can, therefore, engage superior forces with a reasonable chance of success.

In terms of both theory and practice, most of the experience with insurgency and counterinsurgency has been in the Third World; guerrilla wars have been fought between national liberation movements and colonial powers, as in Indochina and Algeria, or between revolutionary movements and governing powers, as in Cuba.

Guerrilla insurgency has proved to be a remarkably effective strategy for political groups without conventional military strength. Highly visible victories against technologically superior opponents were registered in China, Indochina, Cuba, Algeria and now Vietnam. This is not to say that guerrilla insurgencies are invincible, for they are not. There have been many less visible and less striking defeats. Guerrilla insurgency does not insure victory. It simply makes military conflict possible and reasonable by insuring some prospect of success. Like any other form of warfare, it is a gamble. The insurgent can either win or lose, but that is precisely the same prospect that the counterinsurgent faces. Under those conditions, war is possible.

Given the prospect of success, the ideology and strategy of guerrilla insurgency has spread throughout the Third World and even to political minorities within advanced industrial societies. In the United States, for example, guerrilla insurgency is viewed as a means of liberation by some black people, who are beginning to define themselves as a colony within the mother country; as a means of destroying an imperialist military apparatus from within by radical whites, or white mother-country radicals; and as a means of preventing a left-wing takeover, by the radical Right.

At least in terms of ideology, many American radicals are beginning to identify with the struggle of Third World peoples for liberation, and to view themselves as the American contingent of an international guerrilla army, as participants in a worldwide insurgency against American rule. At the same time, the radical Right is preparing for the possibility that the government will be unable to defeat such an insurgency. Should such a contingency arise, they, like the European settlers in South Africa, Rhodesia and Algeria, hope to function as a vigilante counterinsurgency force.

The important point is that guerrilla warfare provides a model for *military* conflict where none existed before. Where political goals cannot be attained by political means in the political arena, for whatever reasons, conflict can now be escalated to the military arena. The credo has become: "War is politics with violence; and politics is war without violence."

To a large extent, it is erroneous to talk about purely political conflict. The use of official violence by the state is an accepted characteristic of traditional political conflict—police and domestic military agencies intervene in political matters, such as demonstrations and strikes. What guerrilla warfare really makes possible, then, is escalation from one-sided military conflict to two-sided military conflict. In this sense, it is a response to the use of official violence in political conflicts.

In any event, guerrilla warfare has come to America, if only ideologically. It is possible, indeed likely, that guerrilla warfare would take a fundamentally different form in a technological society such as the United States than it has in the Third World. In the past, for example, there have been significant differences between guerrilla wars fought in rural settings and those fought in urban areas. Since our major concern is with violence in America, and therefore with the particular form that counterinsurgency would take in the United States, we shall have to learn what we can from the Third World experience—which is the only available body of knowledge —while at the same time recognizing that it cannot be applied without revision to the American situation. Should guerrilla warfare occur in America, its particular form will be created out of experiences that insurgents and counterinsurgents will have. It will reflect the pragmatic needs of the struggle. It is, however, possible to speculate somewhat about the patterns of violence that might possibly emerge.

THEORY OF INSURGENCY

The most important question posed by guerrilla insurgency is how a small band of poorly armed revolutionaries can defeat a large, well-equipped, modern army. The answer, according to Lt. Col. T. N. Greene, USMC (1962, p. 13), is that guerrilla warfare is designed to defeat military strength with political strength: "Although Mao never states it quite this way, the basic premise of his theory is that political mobilization may be substituted for industrial mobilization with a successful military outcome." Put differently, political mobilization becomes a military weapon, offsetting the impact of conventional military strength or industrial mobilization. This process is the main dynamic of insurgency.

In guerrilla warfare, military strength and political strength are interchangeable. Political strength can be converted into military strength, and military strength into political strength. In these terms, actual political strength can be viewed as potential military strength, and actual military strength as potential political strength. The art of successful insurgency, and counterinsurgency as well, lies in converting useless potential strength, whether it be political or military, into appropriate actual strength at every stage of the conflict.

It is generally agreed that insurgency follows a three-stage model: (1) a political stage, (2) an unconventional warfare stage, and (3) a conventional warfare stage. Each of these stages builds the strength required for the following stage, just as each gear in a car builds the speed and momentum necessary for the following gears. The first stage is designed to develop political strength, which is the insurgents' only initial asset. In the second stage, that political strength is converted into unconventional military strength; and in the final stage, unconventional military strength is converted into conventional military strength. It is not possible to move directly from political strength to conventional military strength, just as it is not generally possible to shift from first gear to third gear in a car. In this sense, the unconventional military stage can be viewed as an intermediary stage of transition. It is the stage that makes possible conversion from political strength to conventional military strength. Conversion from political strength to conventional military strength is the ultimate objective of guerrilla insurgency. In a sense, armed insurgency is a strategy for creating conventional military strength where none existed.

Guerrilla movements generally begin without any significant military strength. Their only initial asset is political—a cause that can mobilize the population, and which the government cannot adopt with any credibility. This initial political capital asset can be converted into military capital during later stages or can be invested in ways that will increase the total politicomilitary capital available to the insurgency. However, revolution is not possible unless the guerrillas have at least a minimal political working capital at the outset. A certain minimal level of political strength is required for the conversion process to occur.

In the first stage, which is primarily, if not totally, political, priority is given to forming political coalitions, united fronts and, ultimately, a revolutionary political party. The objective of this stage is to develop the political strength needed for conversion to unconventional military strength. In practice, this means increasing opposition to the government and exhausting all legitimate means of creating needed changes. The goal is to create a demand for change and demonstrate that it cannot be brought about through legitimate political channels.

The revolutionary movement has a difficult task at this stage. It must convince the people that revolution is needed and that viable reform is not possible. To do this, the insurgents must present a political program that meets two major criteria: (1) the government cannot satisfy it by reform, and (2) it must generate widespread and active popular support. If it fails to meet either criterion—if it is not sufficiently radical, or if it is too radical—the revolutionary movement will isolate itself from its political base of support.

During the initial political stage, it is difficult to distinguish an incipient guerrilla insurgency from conventional political opposition, to predict whether political opposition will escalate to military conflict or remain within the political arena.

The crucial question here is how escalation from purely political conflict to unconventional military conflict occurs—how transition from the stage of political mobilization to the stage of unconventional warfare occurs. Although this is by no means the only dynamic involved, in many cases insurgency seems to be a response to government attempts to violently suppress legitimate political resistance; it is a response to official violence.

It is inaccurate to speak of purely political conflict in the Third World. Most Third World governments are dictatorships, and they respond to political demands for change with military and police repression. Politics in the Third World can more accurately be described as one-sided military conflict. Guerrilla warfare makes escalation to two-sided armed conflict possible. Therefore, where demand for change is blocked at the political level, where all legitimate channels are exhausted in an attempt to bring about change and the government uses official violence against political opposition groups, escalation to unconventional warfare is likely to occur.

According to one authority, Samuel B. Griffith (1961, p. 27), the stage of political mobilization is central in the process of insurgency; guerrilla wars are won or lost in the political stage, before military operations begin: "Historical experience suggests that there is very little hope of destroying a revolutionary guerrilla movement *after it has survived the first phase and has acquired the sympathetic support of a significant segment of the population.*" Translated into the three-stage model, this means that it is difficult to defeat a guerrilla movement once it has successfully entered the stage of unconventional warfare, that it is easier to defeat an insurgency in the political stage, before conventional military strength is developed.

How does political mobilization contribute in a military sense to insurgency? Why is political mobilization essential to the success of an insurgency, and why would unconventional warfare be impossible without popular support? Certain conditions must exist for an unconventional military force to defeat a technologically superior conventional military force. Popular support is essential for the creation of these conditions.

Unconventional warfare attempts to maintain a military presence— that is, pose a military *threat*—while at the same time avoiding conventional military conflict with superior government forces. This is the strategy of the "war of attrition" or "war of the flea": to inflict damage through many small engagements while at the same time carefully avoiding contact with the superior enemy military units. Lt. Col. William R. Corson, USMC, Ret. (1968, pp. 147–148), who served as a combat officer in Vietnam, describes how this process works:

> No one who has opposed the Vietcong will deny that they fight extremely well. The Communists would like us to believe the entire reason for their success is based solely on "egalitarianism" and comradeship, but this is not correct. The reason, aside from the romanticism of the movement and the perverse effect on morale attributable to adversity, is their ability to limit their troops' exposure to combat. The Vietcong concept of protracted war enables them to fight well. To illustrate the meaning of this proposition it is necessary to look at General Westmoreland's attritional strategy. The idea of "steady unremitting pressure" conjures up an image of American forces flitting here, there, and everywhere in helicopter chariots as if they were riding to the hounds. Too often the bugle call to "go get the little red bastards" produces a sound and fury signifying nothing but frustration. Less than 2 per cent of all U.S. offensive operations produce any contact whatsoever with the Vietcong. The significant fact is that the enemy retains the capability to fight at a place and time of his own choosing.
>
> Truong did not complain about the Vietcong's protracted view of the war. He was required to mount only one large-scale (company or larger) attack each quarter along with a greater number of small-scale attacks. By adopting this tactic, the Vietcong are able to plan their operations

thoroughly and use their forces selectively. Superficially this appears to be a series of random attacks; however, the real result to our forces throughout all of South Vietnam is like the Chinese torture of a thousand cuts. No single cut can kill, but the cumulative effect is disastrous. The Vietcong believe they can draw off enough blood in this manner to make the war intolerable for the U.S. forces. My own study confirmed Truong's statement that main force units (company and larger) engage in offensive operations for only approximately three or four days in a twelve-week period.

Colonial naval victories during the American Revolution are a perfect example of this strategy. The almost nonexistent colonial navy was remarkably successful against the vastly superior British fleet, primarily because colonial captains could choose whether to fight or run while British captains were ordered to engage any enemy ships they could locate. Thus, colonial captains would flee from superior British ships, while British ships fought superior colonial vessels. The colonial navy fought only when sure of victory, while the British navy fought in situations that would almost certainly bring defeat.

The ability to choose the time and place of battle—to fight when it is advantageous and avoid battle when expedient—is central to unconventional warfare. An insurgent force can be easily defeated if it cannot maintain this ability.

Posing a military threat by terrorism is not really difficult. Terrorist raids can be launched against any number of important and relatively undefended targets. While insurgents choose the targets they will attack, the government must defend every potential target. This gives the insurgents an important advantage, as Galula (1964, p. 11) so aptly points out:

> Disorder—the normal state of nature—is cheap to create and very costly to prevent. The insurgent blows up a bridge, so every bridge has to be guarded; he throws a grenade in a movie theater, so every person entering a public place has to be searched. . . . Merely by making anonymous phone calls warning of bombs planted in luggage, the insurgent can disrupt civilian schedules and scare away tourists.

The government has a complex social, political and economic system to defend. The insurgents have nothing to defend; they present no target for government troops. In turn, guerrillas can carefully locate the weak spots in the social, economic and political system and then attack those strategic and vulnerable points. In this case, the advantage lies with the offensive force.

The military threat posed by insurgents is often greater than the actual military damage they inflict, or even the military potential they possess. Even in nonrevolutionary situations, a similar problem exists with respect to crime. Hysteria over rising crime—fear of a "crime wave"—and political demands for law and order occur even though the actual incidence of crime is low and most people will never be victims of crime. Thus, the political impact of insurgents is far greater than their actual military strength. During the Mau Mau uprising in Kenya, for example, the actual number of deaths was surprisingly small, and European deaths almost nonexistent. Yet the Mau Mau movement created an "emergency" situation and eventually attained Kenyan independence.

It should be pointed out that a certain level of terrorism, like a certain level of crime, can be tolerated by a political system. The system can adapt to a degree of private political violence and begin to treat it as normative, as a hidden cost of operation. Unless the level of terrorism is greater than this tolerance level, the process of insurgency will be arrested and an equilibrium reached.

Conventional warfare is waged primarily between competing armies. That is not true of unconventional warfare, where the civilian population and the social, political and economic structure are the major target. The object of guerrilla warfare is to attack these targets directly without openly confronting the military, to bypass the military while attacking and destroying the targets it is supposed to defend.

Guerrilla terrorism can destroy confidence in the government's ability to maintain order. Demands are placed upon the government to destroy the insurgent movement and restore domestic peace. If it cannot restore order, it will fail to perform its most essential function, and it will lose its legitimacy. In this situation, people will look to the guerrilla movement, which offers a parallel political structure, for leadership. "When the insurgent burns a farm, all the farmers clamor for protection; if they do not receive it, they may be tempted to deal privately with the insurgent" (Galula, 1964, p. 11).

The insurgent movement will have established itself as a political alternative to the government in power. Once it shatters the government's monopoly over the means of violence, the insurgent movement can claim to be the legitimate ruling power. By this point, it will have a well-developed parallel structure—tax collectors, land reform programs, judicial system, elected officials, perhaps even its own money. If successful, this structure can immediately replace the defeated government.

Guerrillas aim for a long, costly war of attrition rather than a speedy victory. Since they cannot defeat the superior government forces at the outset, guerrillas try to drain the government—both materially and in terms of political support—by inflicting as much damage over as long a period of time as possible. Time is on the side of the insurgency. Each day that disorder continues and the government proves itself incapable of destroying the revolutionary movement, the legitimacy of the ruling government is reduced and the insurgent movement gains more support. If the process continues long enough, a condition of military parity may eventually come about.

Waging a war of attrition is not a simple military operation; certain basic conditions are necessary. First, the insurgents must operate in favorable terrain with which they are thoroughly familiar. Second, the insurgents must have an elaborate and accurate intelligence network, to inform them, in advance, of government operations. Third, they must have access to food and medical supplies. And fourth, there must be people who will hide them when necessary. These are all basic military requirements of unconventional warfare.

Anonymity is the key to guerrilla survival and success. The hard-core revolution cadre is small and has negligible conventional military strength. It could be easily destroyed *if* the government could identify and locate it. The ability of an insurgent force to avoid detection, while at the same time engaging in small but secure operations, is a prerequisite of success.

Most insurgency movements have operated out of impenetrable mountain or jungle terrain, in remote rural areas. Government presence, which in most Third World nations is generally confined to urban areas, is often minimal in remote rural areas. Guerrilla movements can thus remain uncontested while they develop sufficient political strength to begin military operations.

Once the guerrillas become familiar with the terrain, they can turn it to their advantage against invading government troops, who are forced to fight in unknown and unfavorable territory. Under these conditions, guerrillas can set ambushes, engage in small encounters and escape without being followed. They can set up base camps, networks of tunnels, booby traps and storage places for food, medicine and ammunition.[1] For example, Burchett (1965) describes how the Vietminh and the National Liberation Front (NLF) build elaborate networks of bunkers and tunnels that enable them to set surprise ambushes and escape from government troops. In short, this kind of terrain provides insurgents with a significant military advantage if they use it properly. At the same time, this terrain places government troops at a distinct disadvantage. This is the natural setting for guerrilla warfare, for the "war of the flea." The government's conventional military advantage is considerably reduced by the impenetrable character of the terrain, while the insurgents' unconventional advantage is enhanced.

The advantage of favorable terrain depends to some extent on the technological level of the government forces. For example, during the American Revolution, colonial ships could avoid superior British vessels only because visibility was limited to crude telescopes. With the development of radar, sonar and other detection systems, the ocean surface has ceased to be a favorable terrain for unconventional warfare. During World War I, submarines provided an unconventional warfare capability—they

---

[1] For an example of how guerrillas familiarize themselves with terrain and increase its natural military benefits, see Scheer (1968) and Burchett (1965).

could strike at their own choosing and avoid detection. The development of sophisticated underwater detection devices has eliminated this capability to a large extent.

Technology can play an important role in guerrilla warfare as well. There are reports that the Bolivian guerrillas led by Che Guevara were located, at least in part, by infrared sensing devices (*Guardian,* November 1968). If technology can deprive guerrillas of shelter in dense forests and mountain areas, just as it has deprived submarines of underwater shelter, the complexion of guerrilla warfare would be changed considerably.

Popular support is the second major condition needed for unconventional warfare, a fact of which Che Guevara (1961, pp. 6–7) was acutely aware:

> Popular support is indispensable. Let us consider the example of robber bands that roam a certain region. They possess all the characteristics of a guerrilla band—homogeneity, respect for their leaders, familiarity with the terrain, and frequently even thorough understanding of tactics. They lack only one thing: the support of the people. And inevitably, these bands are caught and wiped out by police forces.

This is the heart of the matter: how political mobilization contributes to the military success of unconventional warfare, and how political strength is converted into military strength.

Where guerrillas have a popular base of support, they can avoid identification or detection by remaining anonymous. It is difficult to distinguish guerrillas from the people among whom they live: They wear no uniforms and carry no flags. Outwardly, there is nothing to distinguish them from the population they are trying to mobilize. The problem that guerrillas pose for the government is therefore, more a police problem than a military problem—to locate and identify insurgents and insurgent supporters, and to distinguish them from the noninsurgent population. Once this police problem is solved, the military problem of destroying them is simple.

But police cannot identify guerrillas, political cadres or guerrilla sympathizers without informants. Preventing access to informants is a major factor in guerrilla success. There really is no other way to penetrate a well-organized guerrilla structure.

Lacking any real military capability, insurgents rely on mobility and intelligence for survival. They have to know about government operations in advance. At the same time, they have to keep the government from knowing about their activities. According to Burchett, the National Liberation Front has developed a very sophisticated and effective intelligence system. Couriers would often appear in prearranged locations at precisely specified times with detailed information about government operations. Popular support is the key to an effective intelligence and counterintelligence system.

Further, insurgents have to get food and medical supplies without becoming visible targets. Most of this clandestine quartermaster function must be performed by the civilian population, by a popular base of support. Of course, insurgents require a recruitment system, both to replace guerrillas who are killed, wounded or defect and to increase their military strength to the point at which it approaches parity with the government. Recruitment is essential for the transition from unconventional warfare to conventional warfare.

In a successful insurgency, where guerrillas derive active support from the population, many people are involved in important support functions. The police task of isolating the guerrillas from the population—identifying and locating the insurgent political and miltary cadres—is extremely difficult under these conditions. "In a guerrilla area, every person without exception must be considered an agent—old men and women, boys driving ox carts, girls tending goats, farm laborers, storekeepers, schoolteachers, priests, boatment, scavengers" (Griffith, 1961, p. 22). It becomes a war of the government against the people, instead of a war against a small guerrilla band: Government attempts to crush the guerrilla movement are likely to lead to generalized repression, in which innocent people, as well as guerrillas or guerrilla sympathizers, are arrested, tortured and killed in an effort to locate and identify guerrillas. One of the objectives of counterinsurgents is to identify guerrillas, yet minimize generalized repression; at the same time, guerrillas try to create conditions where government repression will be maximized.

Guerrilla warfare poses this dilemma for the government: to locate and destroy the revolutionary cadre, they must risk alienating the population. This is a calculated risk. If it works, if the guerrillas can be effectively deprived of essential support functions like intelligence and food supplies, and if the government can get the information it needs to locate and identify revolutionary cadres, the guerrilla movement can be quickly and easily crushed. If not, the generalized repression could generate widespread political support for the guerrillas, making likely a long and costly war of attrition. This is the object of unconventional warfare—to create a situation in which the government must resort to overt repression, thereby alienating the population and losing its legitimacy.

It should be clear that the basic strategy of unconventional warfare, a war of attrition, in which guerrillas inflict many small wounds, none of which are fatal, cannot by itself topple the government and lead to victory. The question then becomes, how can a revolutionary guerrilla movement win? What, indeed, does victory mean in guerrilla warfare?

A successful war of attrition may destroy the will of the government to continue, and gain a political victory, even when military victory remains impossible. "The purpose of the war of national liberation, pitting the feeble resources of a small and primitive nation against the strength of a great, industrial power is not to conquer or terrorize, but to create an intolerable situation for the occupying power or its puppet government" (Taber, 1965,

p. 102). Thus, military victory, in the traditional sense used in conventional warfare, is not essential for final victory in a war of attrition.

> In the end, it will be a question of whether the government falls before the military is destroyed in the field, or whether the destruction of the military brings about the final desposition of the political regime. The two processes are complementary. Social and political dissolution bleeds the military, and the protracted and futile campaign in the field contributes to the process of social and political dissolution, creating what I have elsewhere called the "climate of collapse."
>
>   This is the grand strategy of the guerrilla: to create the "climate of collapse." It may be taken as the key to everything he does. (Taber, 1965, p. 29)

This "climate of collapse" describes the process of transition from the stage of unconventional warfare to the stage of conventional warfare, and the dynamics of ultimate politico-military victory.

If the counterinsurgent force consists only of native government troops, political mobilization may cause loss of morale and desertion in the army. Thus, political mobilization can deplete the military strength of the government while at the same time increase that of the insurgency by means of higher recruitment rates.

Third World governments often rely on external support for survival. For example, the present South Vietnamese government probably could not exist without American military and economic support. Guerrillas can win a political victory by cutting the government off from external aid, either because of domestic political pressure generated within the great-power nation over the cost of the war of attrition or because of political protest in the international arena.

Political mobilization, in terms of paralyzing general strikes, political assassinations and terrorist raids on targets previously considered invulnerable, can have impact far beyond the actual military capability of the insurgent movement.

This, then, is the design for guerrilla victory—a gradual process in which the government strength is slowly but surely dissipated and the guerrilla strength is slowly but surely increased. Guerrillas can win even though they are suffering military defeat, if they can destroy the will of the government, or of the great powers that support the government, to continue the war.

This is an important principle. The ability to win a war is different from the will to win it. The cost of winning a war may be greater than the government is willing to pay for the purpose of gaining a political victory. That, for example, is how the American Revolution was won. The British could certainly have defeated the American colonies, if they had been willing to allocate the necessary resources, but they were not.

The concept of victory in guerrilla warfare poses a real paradox.

Escalation to military insurgency occurs because groups cannot achieve their goals through political means. At the same time, it should be clear that an insurgency cannot achieve its goals solely through military means either. However, the strategy of guerrilla warfare makes it possible for them to achieve by politico-military conflict, by combining political and military operations in an overall strategy of guerrilla warfare, what they could not achieve by either traditional political conflict or conventional military conflict.

This is the strategy that counterinsurgency is designed to combat. To be successful, guerrillas must gain widespread popular support, build tightly knit, well-disciplined organizations and successfully attack widely dispersed, vulnerable targets. Unless all of these requirements are met, guerrillas will probably not be successful.

INSURGENCY IN AMERICA

Given the history of insurgency in the Third World, what are the prospects for insurgency in America, and what form would it take? Some of the necessary conditions for an insurgency exist in America: a large radical movement that has failed to gain its objectives through legitimate political means, increasing political repression and widespread access to guerrilla ideology and tactics. For this reason, the possibility of insurgency must be taken seriously.

It is difficult to predict in advance whether an insurgency situation will actually develop. It is possible, however, to say that the necessary conditions for an insurgency are present, and it is possible to describe the present stage of political protest. Political opposition in America clearly lies within the first stage of insurgency, that of political mobilization. This means that while most protest is political, some indicators of unconventional warfare exist.

To some degree, there is a militarization of conflict. While the process is severely limited at present, there are scattered examples of political violence, in the form of terrorism or unconventional warfare. This is not yet prevalent enough to form a pattern, but there certainly is a precedent for political violence.

Certain processes that are essential for escalation to guerrilla warfare are also present. For example, there is a process of delegitimation: The legitimacy of the government, and the political system itself, is being challenged, if only by political activists. This is reflected in a trend toward a style of illegitimacy in political protest and the emergence of increasingly illegitimate forms of political action. In short, there is an escalation in the direction of what might be called the militarization of conflict and away from legitimate political forms of conflict. The question is whether this escalation will proceed far enough to transform an essentially political conflict into a military conflict.

Despite the emergence of riots as a common form of protest, conflict in America remains essentially political. For the most part, riots are not a form of unconventional warfare: They are spontaneous; they lack ongoing and effective organization; they lack ideological content or direction; and, most important, they lack active popular support, an essential prerequisite for insurgency. There can be no doubt, for example, that black revolutionaries do not have the level of support, even in the black community, that the NLF has in Vietnam; for example, there is not yet a consensus on the need or desirability of armed rebellion among black Americans. Creation of that consensus is the objective of the stage of political mobilization. Until this objective has been achieved, transition from political mobilization to unconventional warfare will probably not occur.

Riots are, however, the last stage of political mobilization; they are the last step before transition to unconventional warfare either occurs or fails to occur. In a sense, they define the boundary between political opposition and military resistance.

The process of delegitimation, in which the legitimacy of the government and the political system comes into question, facilitates the transition from political to military conflict. To a large extent, delegitimation reflects disillusionment with the system of law, based on the use of legal institutions to prevent change. This involves a growing awareness of the *political* function of law—the way courts and police are used to prevent political and economic change. It is a response to the use of illegitimate official violence by the government to prevent political change. Given the use of legal institutions to suppress political protest, there are grounds for defining conflict in this country as a one-sided military system rather than a political conflict system. When there is a consensus that conflict is resolved in a one-sided military system, escalation to armed insurgency, or a two-sided military system, becomes very likely. If successful, political mobilization will create this consensus.

At the present time, the process of delegitimation is limited to the radical faction of the protest movement. It has not yet spread to the population in general, or even to the entire protest movement. But it has begun. When enough people question the legitimacy of the political system and accept the need for illegitimate, that is, military means, insurgency becomes likely. That point occurs when the demand for change becomes irrepressible and the belief that change is not possible through the existing political structure becomes widespread. That point has not yet been reached, but the trend seems to be in that direction. This process is purely political; the destruction of governmental legitimacy is the function of political mobilization. When this function has been successfully completed, unconventional warfare can be initiated.

The trend toward increasing illegitimacy of tactics has been evident in both the civil rights movement and the antiwar movement. Not all elements in these movements have undergone this transition, nor have they become convinced that change is impossible through legitimate political means. But it is undeniable that the tone of both movements, their public image, is less legitimate now than it was a few years ago. The radical pole has shifted considerably toward illegitimacy—the range of political action has been expanded considerably to include illegitimate actions.

The civil rights movement began as a religious, nonviolent movement, in which equal emphasis was placed on means and ends. Indeed, means and ends were seen as inseparable—a peaceful society could be created only by peaceful means. The goal was to destroy inhumanity by creating a living example of humanity, to demonstrate the ends by the means.

Transition from nonviolence as a way of life to nonviolence as a tactic occurred early in the southern desegregation and voter registration movement. At that point, the change was ideological rather than behavioral. Demonstrations continued to be nonviolent, but now they were justified as a useful weapon rather than a way of life, as a political expedient rather than a moral obligation.

Given this change in ideology, it became possible to challenge nonviolence on tactical grounds. In this climate, Robert Williams developed the ideology and tactics of self-defense. The choice between nonviolence and self-defense was made by most on empirical grounds: Which is more effective? While nonviolence as a way of life remained, it became a minority position. The ideology of self-defense was expanded by the Student Nonviolent Coordinating Committee and the Black Panther party, while the Revolutionary Action Movement (RAM) moved to the stage of advocating guerrilla warfare. In terms of ideology, then, there was escalation from nonviolence as a way of life to guerrilla warfare; although this in turn provoked considerable controversy.

In terms of tactics, there was an escalation from nonviolent civil disobedience, to disruptive civil disobedience, to unorganized riots and ultimately to scattered acts of organized political violence. In Philadelphia, for example, police contended that militants planned to poison the food that police and the National Guard would use during riots. In Cleveland, black nationalists ambushed a small unit of police. While specific details remain unknown, gun battles have been fought between police and the Black Panthers in California and black militants in East St. Louis and Chicago. In many cities, small organized groups have conducted bombing raids against white-owned stores in black communities, and continuous sniping has occurred in several cities.

The same pattern of escalation exists within the antiwar movement: (1) traditional nonviolent demonstrations, often combined with small-scale civil disobedience; (2) mobilization of electoral opposition to the war, especially through local referendums; (3) resistance to the draft by refusing induction or burning draft cards; (4) disruption of war-related activities, such as stopping troop trains in Oakland and preventing military-industrial recruiters from conducting interviews on campuses; (5) disruption of speakers; (6) occupation of university buildings to protest business recruitment and to protest university complicity with the Selective Service System and ROTC programs; (7) attempted disruption of Selective Service Centers by sit-ins, as in New York City and Oakland; (8) bombing of ROTC buildings, Selective Service Centers or other war-related buildings; and (9) destroying draft files to prevent the operation of the Selective Service System, as in Baltimore, Catonsville, Boston and Milwaukee.

The last set of tactics—bombing buildings or destroying draft files—resembles guerrilla operations in many important respects. It had more than symbolic value. The burning of draft files temporarily frustrated the induction process, in addition to having focused public attention on the war and the draft. Symbolic action was replaced by action that had tactical consequences. Perhaps more important, these actions required many skills necessary for unconventional warfare: demolitions, breaking and entering, intelligence and a quasi-military organization.

This escalation of tactics had been matched by an escalation of ideology. Originally, opposition to the Vietnam War reflected traditional pacifist sentiments by people who are opposed to war in any form. Antiwar feeling soon spread to people in the civil rights movement. Their experience in trying to initiate domestic change led them to perceive the federal government as an enemy. In addition, they opposed the cuts in domestic spending that rising military expenditures necessitated, and they soon began to identify with the Vietnamese as a nonwhite people. It spread even further to young men who were subject to the draft. They had to take sides; the draft made neutrality impossible. There was escalation from traditional pacifist opposition to specific opposition to the Vietnam War. This change is clear in the Call to Resist Illegitimate Authority (Horowitz, 1970, pp. 24–47). On an ideological level, radicals came to believe that the government had not acted legitimately with respect to the Vietnam War and that all laws concerning the draft and the pursuit of military operations were therefore illegitimate and should be violated. Following the precedent of the Nuremberg Trials, many radicals felt they had an obligation to oppose the war, indeed to impede the war effort, by any available means, A major thrust of the ideological escalation was the identification of the United States as an imperialist power. At this stage, some American radicals identified with the guerrilla movement in Vietnam and hoped for an NLF victory.

Despite these escalations, despite the large number of bombings that have occurred throughout the country and the large number of riots, opposition in America at this point remained in the stage of political mobilization.

One of the most crucial questions, of course, is whether insurgency is possible in a highly industrialized and urbanized society like the United States. Do the conditions that were necessary for insurgency in the Third World exist in America? Beyond that, are there any additional conditions that would make insurgency possible in an urban-industrial situation, or that would prevent such insurgency from occurring?

Terrain. Favorable terrain is an important precondition. Terrain must give an advantage to the side that knows the area best. In the Third World, this meant rough, impenetrable terrain such as mountains, jungles or rice paddies. This kind of terrain obviously does not exist in an urban-industrial environment; therefore, the traditional advantage provided by terrain does not exist.

What then is likely to be the impact of terrain on the prospects for insurgency in the United States? Urban terrain may provide insurgents with one important advantage. Unless the insurgency or potential insurgency population can by physically isolated from the noninsurgent population— the Germans were able to do this successfully in the Warsaw ghetto and the French in the Algiers Casbah—the government's ability to use its conventional military superiority will be seriously curtailed. If isolation cannot be achieved, the government cannot destroy the insurgent population without at the same time destroying the noninsurgent population and the physical plant, in terms of buildings, roads, factories and public utilities, which is the *raison d'être* of an urban–industrial society. That is, if it uses its conventional superiority, it cannot destroy the insurgents without destroying itself. In this situation, its conventional capability is substantially neutralized.

An urban environment can be converted into a favorable terrain by guerrillas. The Warsaw ghetto uprising, which was completely crushed by the Nazis, provides an excellent example of this potential. Underground bunkers were built, hiding places were constructed in houses, and sewer systems were used for military purposes. The Algiers experience was similar.

Why then did the Warsaw uprising fail? The primary factor was the willingness of the Nazis to completely destroy the ghetto, to engage in genocide. They avoided the problem of distinguishing between insurgents and noninsurgents by destroying the entire population. If, for example, the United States were willing to destroy the entire Vietnamese population, it could easily defeat the NLF. Under these conditions, guerrillas are deprived of their primary advantage—anonymity—and the counterinsurgents eliminate their greatest problem—locating and identifying guerrillas who live among a noninsurgent population.

A second reason for the failure of the Warsaw uprising was that the potentially insurgent population was small and distinguishable. It could easily be separated from the rest of the population. It got no external support, even from the Polish Resistance. The parallels between this situation and that of blacks in America should be clear, except that the American government may be less willing to completely destroy the potential insurgent population than were the Nazis.

Popular Support. A second major condition for a successful insurgency, active popular support, does not yet exist in the United States. Until active support can be developed, insurgents will not have access to a viable intelligence network, to food and medical supplies or to security from informants. Further, there will be no broad-based political opposition to widespread police and military repression. Without these support functions, a successful insurgency would not be possible.

What are the prospects for developing an active support base in this country, and what are the laws or dynamics governing that development? In this regard, government policy is fully as important as insurgent strategy. The emergence of an active guerrilla support base depends to a large extent on whether United States militarism, poverty and racial inequality are ended and whether the side effects of these problems—particularly in terms of private violence and official violence, or lawlessness and repression—are minimized. Accomplishing this is the major political objective of counterinsurgency—to deprive insurgents of a political climate in which armed insurgency is likely to occur.

Government counterinsurgency. Two other considerations affect the possibility of insurgency in America: the level of technology available to the government; and the morale of government troops and the will of the government to wage a war of attrition to completion. Since successful insurgencies are generally ended by political settlements rather than military settlements, the will to wage a war of attrition is particularly important.

On both these counts, the prospects for successful revolution in America are significantly lower than in Third World nations. The technological level of the United States is, of course, far superior to that of any Third World nation. Its willingness to allocate resources for research and development of counterinsurgent technology would be far greater in a domestic guerrilla war than a foreign one. There is a very simple principle involved here. The will of a nation to fight—in terms of the morale of troops, the allocation of resources for military development and the will to continue the war to a victorious conclusion regardless of the costs involved—varies with the importance of the interests it has at stake. The United States military would be more effective fighting in their own country for the direct interests of their own country than it has been in Vietnam. In addition, a domestic guerrilla war would probably be pursued to a military conclusion. A political settlement or an insurgent political victory would be out of the question unless revolutionary demands were minimal and could be met without sacrificing important interests.

Nevertheless, the possibility of unconventional warfare is very real; there are, as I have pointed out, many indications of movement in that direction. More important, there is room for considerable escalation beyond the level of political opposition that exists now. If an insurgency should occur, it would not simply mean a continuation of the present level of conflict—unorganized riots combined with occasional acts of organized political violence. It would mean a qualitative, as well as quantitative, change in patterns of political opposition.

An insurgency movement in America might have one important advantage that is not available to Third World guerrilla movements: the accessibility of a large number of indefensible and strategically important targets. America's complex social, economic and political structure provides guerrillas with a wide range of vulnerable targets: transportation and communication facilities, power sources and entertainment centers. The interdependence of the system makes it possible to create significant damage by destroying relatively minor targets. For example, a power failure that cut off electricity to most of the East Coast in 1968 was caused by the failure of one tiny electrical component. If any subunit of a complex interdependent system can be destroyed, the entire system is affected. A slowup in one part of an assembly line can tie up the entire production. The very complexity of America makes it impossible to defend or guard all the possible targets.

Above all else, guerrilla warfare relies for success on an ability to prevent life as usual from going on. There exist many kinds of targets for guerrilla attack in the United States. For example, every New Year's Eve, hundreds of thousands of New Yorkers pack themselves into Times Square so tightly that it is virtually impossible for them to move. They present a perfect target for a damaging guerrilla attack. Or the traditional Army-Navy football game, where the entire cadet corps of West Point and Annapolis, the future officer corps of this country, are located in a small area. Or almost any baseball or football game, any airport or train station during peak hours. Or reservoirs or electric power stations or factories. The list is endless. There is no absence of targets. To defend these targets would require a garrison state; even then, many weak points would remain.

An affluent, urban industrial society is a perfect target for a guerrilla insurgency. That is one of the hidden costs of affluence. Most of these targets could be attacked and severely damaged by dedicated and well-trained units of very small size. A decentralized guerrilla organization is an ideal structure for attacking a complex interdependent urban system.

There are many options between the poles of political mobilization and armed insurgency. Escalation of many different forms could occur. Political violence need not follow the traditional pattern of armed insurgency in order to pose a serious problem; The effects of sporadic and unorganized riots clearly demonstrate this. The question, in its simplest form, is what level of political violence is our society willing to accept or tolerate in order to pursue certain policies and interests, and what level of political violence can dissidents generate?

Beyond this is a question of greater concern. What will be the effects of changing patterns of private political violence on the pattern of official violence? What level of official violence is our society willing to tolerate in order to pursue policies or interests?

THEORY OF COUNTERINSURGENCY

Most of the historical experience with counterinsurgency has been that meted out by the colonial powers in the Third World: France in Indochina and Algeria; Britain in Malaya and Palestine; and the United States in Latin America, the Philippines and, of course, Vietnam. A body of counterinsurgency theory has developed out of these experiences.

The form that counterinsurgency takes in America will reflect both the prior Third World experience and the unique American situation. To get a realistic view of how the patterns of official violence are likely to change in an insurgency situation, both these factors must be taken into consideration.

What then is counterinsurgency? That question is not so simple as might first appear. The scope of counterinsurgency ranges all the way from primarily political programs like pacification to primarily military programs like search and destroy or counterinfiltration surveillance.

There are two distinct types of counterinsurgency: what might be termed political counterinsurgency and military counterinsurgency. The objective of the first is to prevent political conflicts from escalating into military conflicts and to deprive guerrillas of active popular support by employing political means. Should escalation occur, the objective of the second is to defeat insurgencies that have reached the military stage by employing military means—to develop military tactics appropriate for unconventional warfare.

In the first case, counterinsurgency consists of tactics developed to combat the political dimensions of insurgency; in the second, tactics to combat the unconventional military strategy of armed insurgency. They proceed from fundamentally different views of insurgency: One maintains that it is a political phenomenon; the other, a military phenomenon. This split reflects the complexity of guerrilla insurgency, which, being a politico-military strategy, incorporates both political and military components. While the goal of insurgency is to weld political and military measures into a unified and inseparable whole, many people, including most counterinsurgents, view it as being essentially *either* political *or* military in nature; they feel that an insurgency can most strategically be attacked and defeated either by political or military means. This belief is indicative of a failure to develop a unified politico-military theory and practice of counterinsurgency. In practice, most counterinsurgents emphasize either political measures or military tactics at the expense of the other.

There is a theme common to both types of tactics, however. In both, the main thrust is to deprive insurgents of an active base of popular support, thereby denying them the military advantage it provides—to cut them off from intelligence, food and medical supplies and recruitment. There is a common recognition that active popular support is the primary ingredient of successful insurgency. Both schools of counterinsurgency recognize the need to destroy the revolutionary political infrastructure; they acknowledge that destroying the military arm, while leaving the political arm intact, is an ineffectual response to guerrilla insurgency. Sir Robert Thompson (1966, pp. 55–56), a counterinsurgency theorist who served as a civilian official in Malaya and Vietnam, contends that this is a basic principle of counterinsurgency:

> The government must give priority to defeating the political subversion, not the guerrillas. . . . Unless the communist subversive political organization in the towns and villages is broken and eliminated, the insurgent guerrilla units will not be defeated. If the guerrillas can be isolated from the population, i.e., the "little fishes" removed from "the water," then their eventual destruction becomes automatic.

Despite this broad agreement about the need to isolate insurgents from their support base and to destroy the political structure, there is serious disagreement about how to do it: Should emphasis be placed on political or military action? Should illegitimate repression, such as torture, be employed or eliminated? Both schools agree on the need to destroy the political infrastructure. They differ on whether political or military means should be used to accomplish this objective.

These tactical differences reflect divergent views about how insurgents gain popular support and, therefore, how the government could best neutralize the insurgents' political advantage and build its own base of support. According to one view, guerrillas gain support because they are acting in the interests of the people. This kind of support is voluntary. The insurgents and the people are common allies in a war against an oppressive government. According to the other view, support is gained by terror. Col. Roger Trinquier (1964, p. 8), a commander of French paratroops in Indochina and Algeria, is an advocate of this position:

> We know that the *sine qua non* of victory in *modern warfare* is the unconditional support of a population. According to Mao Tse-tung, it is as essential to the combatant as water to the fish. Such support may be spontaneous, although that is quite rare and probably a temporary condition. If it doesn't exist, it must be secured by every possible means, the most effective of which is *terrorism*.

This kind of support is based on coercion. According to this position, the people are either neutral and apathetic, simply wanting to be left alone, or government supporters. Thompson (1966, p. 62) states this principle well:

> While the insurgent strength both in armed units and in active supporters may be one percent or less of the population, the hard core on which the government can definitely rely is also likely to be quite a small percentage of the population, perhaps 10 percent and probably never more than 20 percent. The remaining 80 or 90 percent of the population is neutral or near neutral as between the government and the insurgents.

In either case, they are forced to support the guerrilla movement against their will.

Corson (1968, p. 61) suggests that these two schools of counterinsurgency may be mutually exclusive, that military counterinsurgency measures may, in fact, impede political programs: "The pursuit of victory in Vietnam through the so-called strategy of escalation has conspired with a variety of other forces to literally make the other war unwinnable." Another example is the efforts to win over the people of a village by economic development programs, which may be frustrated by enforced relocation programs. Thus, these two major thrusts of pacification may be logically inconsistent. The goal is to move people away from their villages into strategic hamlets, where they can be isolated from the guerrilla movement and/or defended against guerrilla terrorism, and then win them over with social, economic and political development programs. Meanwhile escalation continues apace. This indicates a failure to coordinate political and military measures into a unified politico-military strategy in which political actions and military actions complement each other. The two types of counterinsurgency may be incompatible and may actually work at cross-purposes; military actions may make it impossible to conduct effective political programs.

This dilemma is complicated by disagreement about goals and objectives. On the surface, the question of goals is simple: the goal of counterinsurgency is obviously to prevent or destroy an insurgency. In practice, however, it is far more complicated. For example, is the goal of counterinsurgency to prevent only *armed* insurgency, while permitting or even supporting change by legitimate political means? Is it to maintain the existing government and prevent any kind of change? Or is it to prevent takeover of the county by another major power. Should counterinsurgency be a modernizing force or a force to prevent change? Should it determine the rules by which change occurs or determine which changes can be made? Should it *create* the conditions for peaceful change or maintain the existing order completely?

This is not a matter of semantics. In practice, there are serious differences involving leading to substantially different programs. For example, the United States has several different objectives in Vietnam. One is to contain expansion by Communist nations, particularly China. Another is to support the present Saigon regime, as an anti-Communist ally, or to support any anti-Communist government. Another is to help the Vietnamese people by promoting needed changes, even if they are opposed by the present government. If this is the objective, we have to determine which Vietnamese people we want to help, because what is in the interests of some Vietnamese is clearly detrimental to others. For example, the interests of the landowners and peasants clearly conflict. Is the goal to prevent an NLF victory because they seek change by violence or because they are Communist? If a third party that is non-Communist, but not anti-Communist, would seek the same changes as the NLF, such as land reform, but by peaceful means, what would our position be then? These are by no means simple questions, and the ambiguity of American objectives in Vietnam has been reflected in the failure and inconsistency of American policy there.

W. R. Corson, who was in charge of a highly effective counter-insurgency program in Vietnam, gives an excellent example of the ambiguities and contradictions involved in our present counterinsurgency program. Its objective is to maintain and strengthen the present South Vietnamese government. This objective is not precisely the same as opposing the National Liberation Front. The NLF could effectively be opposed without necessarily supporting the present regime, or even a different government that supports the same interests as the present one. The question of whom to support is separate from the question of whom to oppose. Corson thus suggests an alternative to the present policy: The United States should oppose *both* the National Liberation Front *and* the present Saigon government. In his opinion, neither force represents the interests of the Vietnamese people. Indeed, he defines an effective counterinsurgency program as one that enables the people to defend themselves against anyone who exploits and oppresses.

> In conclusion, the pacification goal I selected for Phong Bac was basically accomplished by and through the joint efforts of the people and the Marines. The goal chosen was not the official one of "paving the way for the GVN to assert its control over Phong Bac and to engender the support of the people for the GVN" but rather to make Phong Bac strong enough to resist the encroachments of *both* the GVN and the Vietcong against the rights of the people. Today neither the GVN nor the Vietcong can claim Phong Bac for its own. The people of Phong Bac are in control of their own destiny and are willing to resist equally the efforts of the Vietcong or the GVN to deprive them of what is rightfully theirs. (Corson, 1968, p. 173)

This position, with the counterinsurgents acting as a third force, greatly expands the range of alternatives. The choice need not be between withdrawal and continuing the present policy and objectives, if the legitimacy of pursuing a program of counterinsurgency in Vietnam is accepted. The range of options available to the counterinsurgent in terms of goals as well as tactics, is far greater than has been realized.

Counterinsurgents can choose what they are fighting for as well as what they are fighting against, what they are going to build as well as what they will prevent the insurgents from building. Unfortunately, counterinsurgency has been traditionally defined only in terms of what it is fighting against. What it is fighting for has always been taken for granted. That limited view is no longer possible.

Counterinsurgency, thus, means many things to many people. It is nothing more or less than a program designed to defeat insurgencies. Several different such programs have been developed. They differ not only in their tactics but also in their definition of what insurgency is and in their objectives. It is not possible to discuss counterinsurgency without taking these differences into consideration and specifying what type of counterinsurgency is involved.

Counterinsurgency attempts to engage the guerrilla movement during the initial political stage, before it can build a popular support base and accumulate the political capital needed to initiate unconventional military operations. Conventional warfare often disregarded the stage of political mobilization and engaged the guerrilla movement only after military insurgency was begun. It is now generally recognized that the sooner counterinsurgent operations are begun, the greater the chance of success. This basic principle was emphasized in the U.S. Army (1963, p. 20) field manual on counterguerrilla operations: "Preventing the formation of a resistance movement is easier than dealing with one after it is formed. Likewise, destroying such a movement is much easier during its early stages than when it has reached more advanced stages of development." Trinquier (1964, p. 27) also emphasizes the importance of this doctrine:

> The fact that *modern warfare* is not officially declared, that a state of war is not generally proclaimed, permits the adversary to continue to take advantage of peacetime legislation, to pursue his activities both openly and secretly. He will strive by every means to preserve the fiction of peace, which is so essential to the pursuit of his design. . . . Therefore, the surest means of unveiling the adversary is to declare a state of war at the earliest moment, at the very latest when the first symptoms of the struggle are revealed in political assassinations, terrorism, guerrilla activities, etc.

This principle of counterinsurgency is based on an iceberg view of guerrilla warfare: that unconventional military operations, which are visible above the surface, constitute only a small portion of revolutionary warfare; that the major portion, which is political, lies submerged beneath the surface. Counterinsurgents recognize that military insurgency is not possible without political mobilization, and that destroying the guerrilla military arm while leaving the political arm intact is not enough. The object is to destroy the political infrastructure that forms the base of the revolution.

Many crucial counterinsurgency battles are fought during the stage of political organization, *before* any visible military threat exists. During each stage of a guerrilla war, combating the political arm of the revolution is a primary objective. Put differently, one characteristic of counterinsurgency is a recognition of the primacy of politics in the process of insurgency. For the counterinsurgent, a guerrilla war begins during the stage of political mobilization. For the conventional military force, it does not begin until unconventional warfare occurs.

If there is one governing principle of counterinsurgency, it is to defeat the guerrilla at his own game: "A governing power can defeat any revolutionary movement if it adopts the revolutionary strategy and principles and applies them in reverse to defeat the revolutionaries with their own weapons in their own battlefield" (McCuen, 1966, p. 28). Since there is disagreement about the nature of revolutionary principles, strategies and weapons, especially about whether guerrillas gain active popular support by their political program or by terrorism, there is disagreement about the nature of counterinsurgency.

There is, however, basic agreement on two points: (1) the need to isolate guerrillas from their base of active popular support; and (2) the need to turn revolutionary strategies and weapons against insurgents. It is generally recognized that guerrillas must be met and defeated on their own terms. That is what counterinsurgency is all about. But within this broad context of agreement, there is serious tactical disagreement on how to isolate insurgents from popular support. This has led to the growth of two major schools of counterinsurgency: military counterinsurgency and political counterinsurgency. Each school employs both military and political techniques. The difference between them is a matter of emphasis, priority and control. In one, military means are primary and political means secondary. The first is designed to defeat an insurgency by engaging guerrilla military forces directly or by crushing the political infrastructure through repression. The second seeks to destroy an insurgency by eliminating the support base. It assumes that an insurgency cannot survive without active popular support and that military repression is counterproductive.

MILITARY COUNTERINSURGENCY

Guerrilla warfare presents peculiar military problems. Conventional military operations have not proved effective in this situation. Unconventional military tactics and strategies have been developed to fill this gap. This is the essence of military counterinsurgency.

Military counterinsurgents are faced with a police problem more than a military problem. Destroying guerrilla military units, which is a military problem, presents no real difficulties; locating and identifying guerrillas, a police problem, presents serious difficulties. Therefore, identification and location is a major objective of military counterinsurgency.

From a military viewpoint, counterinsurgency was developed primarily to eliminate the failures of conventional military strategy. These failures were of three major types: (1) failure to isolate the civilian population from the guerrillas; (2) failure to adapt to the unconventional tactics of guerrilla forces and defeat them on the battlefield; and (3) failure to locate and destroy the insurgent political structure. Military counterinsurgency is designed to accomplish these objectives.

The strategic hamlet program and forced relocation programs are the major counterinsurgency strategies for isolating guerrillas from their base of popular support. These programs are justified in two different ways:

(1) They prevent guerrilla sympathizers from aiding the insurgency; and (2) they protect the civilian population from guerrilla terrorism. The first position recognizes a certain degree of voluntary popular support for the guerrilla movement. This creates a category of "guerrilla sympathizer." The second justification, however, entails no recognition of voluntary support for the guerrilla movement. The problem, according to this position, is to keep the guerrillas out, to prevent terrorism, rather than to keep the population in. Either way, the operation of the program is similar.

Most Third World nations are decentralized; people are scattered in many small, semiautonomous villages or hamlets. Communication among these villages is tenuous. This situation is ideal for small guerrilla politico-military teams which operate with little interference, since government presence is limited in outlying villages and hamlets. These teams have the primary responsibility for gaining and maintaining popular support—they collect taxes, distribute land, establish intelligence networks, recruit armed guerrillas and provide food and shelter to insurgent military units. It is the job of the armed political teams to establish the necessary support base, to establish a political, social and economic structure parallel to the official governmental structure. If the revolution is successful, this parallel structure will become the new political structure. Decentralization benefits the guerrillas. It enables them to build popular support while avoiding confrontation with the government forces.

In conventional military operations, government troops are centrally located in forts or other base camps. They are assigned to defend territory rather than population units such as villages. While government troops control a region in theory, in practice guerrillas are free to control the area between forts. The insurgent cadres are assigned to population units rather than territorial areas. Armed revolutionary political teams live in hamlets. The guerrilla structure is sufficiently decentralized to adapt to the reality of the situation, to correspond to the actual distribution of people. For this reason, the guerrillas are able to wage their war unopposed; government troops seldom initiated conflict with guerrilla forces.

Counterinsurgency units are designed to rectify this problem by actively engaging the guerrilla forces on the semiautonomous hamlet level. This objective can be accomplished either by centralizing the hamlet structure or by decentralizing military operations. The strategic hamlet program follows the first approach—centralizing the social, political and economic structure by converting many small, semiautonomous hamlets into larger strategic hamlets.

Forced relocation makes it possible to concentrate government troops in a few large hamlets, where they can engage in rigorous population control measures: Such hamlets are surrounded by barbed wire, all residents are required to carry identification papers, and people can leave the hamlet and return only at specified times. In this way, the counterinsurgents hope to prevent contact between the guerrillas and the people, either to keep the people from voluntarily aiding the revolution or to prevent the guerrillas from coercing support by terrorism. In either case, the objective is to build a wall between the insurgent units and the populace.

Most evidence suggests that the strategic hamlets have been a failure. For the most part, this is because forced relocation alienates the people involved and increases, rather than reduces, the likelihood that they will support the guerrilla movement. In many Third World nations, primary allegiance is to small units like the family, tribe or hamlet rather than the nation. Often, families have lived in a hamlet and worked the same land for generations. Forced relocation and resettlement into strategic hamlets breaks this important bond. Corson (1968, pp. 70–71) gives an excellent firsthand description of forced relocation in Vietnam:

> The first groan resulted from the peasants' fear that they were to be turned into paupers and stripped of their dignity as productive human beings. The second groan is a little hard for an American to understand fully because of our frontier heritage of migration. The truth of the matter from the Vietnamese peasants' point of view was that a trip of twenty miles was more fearful than the trek of Steinbeck's "Okies" to California during the 1930s. Over 90 percent of the residents of Trung Luong had never travelled farther than ten kilometers (about six miles) from their homes. They feared that Cam Lo would not be "California" but rather a point of no return. Furthermore, the natives of Trung Luong were Buddhists who because of their religious beliefs were greatly concerned about dying in a strange place. They believe quite strongly in the necessity of being buried in their own family burial plots in order to achieve the Buddhist version of heaven.

Such policies create guerrillas, or guerrilla sympathizers, out of people who may previously have supported the government or at least been neutral.

Since guerrillas rely so heavily on support by the people, it becomes difficult to fight insurgents without at the same time fighting the people, to distinguish between guerrillas, guerrilla sympathizers, neutralists and government loyalists. If these distinctions cannot be accurately made, however, military repression becomes generalized. If the guerrillas are successful, they will make it impossible for the government to direct repressive measures against them without at the same time engaging in generalized repression of the entire populace. For example, in search-and-destroy missions in Vietnam, any guerrilla fire from a village made that entire village a target for return fire. Even in the normal operation of strategic hamlets, every resident was treated as a potential guerrilla or guerrilla supporter.

Other attempts to deprive guerrillas of food and shelter are even more disastrous. Chemical herbicides deprive insurgents of food and jungle hiding areas by destroying vegetation. However, the destruction of crops affects all the people in that area, regardless of their political ideology.

The second alternative, that of decentralizing government troops, does not present the same problems. Corson suggests that armed counterinsurgent political teams, patterned after armed insurgent political teams, be assigned to live and operate in hamlets and villages. These teams would be self-contained—they would have the size and firepower to withstand anything but large-scale attacks and would be able to perform the necessary political functions. At the same time, however, this proposal poses certain new problems. To the extent that government forces are decentralized, centralized conventional military strength would be reduced. To some degree, then, this approach involves a heavier emphasis on political counterinsurgency at some expense to military counterinsurgency.

As presently constituted, pacification teams are too small to defend themselves against armed insurgent cadres. They cannot survive without the protection of regular troops. Since the troops are not quartered in the villages, they are unable to provide the permanent protection that pacification teams require. To a large extent, the failure of pacification lies in the inability of presently constituted teams to live in the villages: They perform their political function by day and retire to the safety of the nearest fort by night, leaving revolutionary cadres uncontested. In effect, Corson's proposal was an attempt to duplicate the politico-military organizational structure of the guerrilla movement in Vietnam, to create a situation in which counterinsurgent and insurgent forces will come into direct conflict with each other and to deny the insurgents uncontested access to rural villages and hamlets.[2]

Armed political teams would have six primary objectives: (1) to prevent recruitment in the village by insurgents; (2) to prevent acquisition of food and supplies from the village by guerrillas; (3) to combat guerrilla units in the area and defend the village; (4) to provide security for the hamlet political, social and economic structure; (5) to organize intelligence networks; and (6) to establish an effective civic action program.

The Combined Action Platoons perform one highly important military function: They provide security from terrorism. Most counterinsurgent theorists contend that guerrillas derive most of their support through terrorism rather than political consensus. According to this view, the population can be divided into three categories: (1) a small minority that supports the guerrilla movement; (2) a small minority that supports the government; and (3) the vast majority that is neutral and relatively uninvolved in the conflict between the revolutionaries and the government. The battles of insurgency and counterinsurgency are waged for the support of this neutral majority. Given this definition of the situation, government policy has two main objectives: (1) to prevent the guerrillas from gaining support from the neutral majority; and (2) to minimize government actions that might alienate the neutral majority and lead them to support the guerrilla move-

[2] For a description of Combined Action Platoons, see Corson (1968, pp. 180–188).

ment. If it is assumed that guerrillas derive support by terrorism and intimidation, then first priority must be given to providing security against insurgent terrorism. If people are secure from intimidation, it is felt, they are less likely to provide aid to the guerrilla movement.

According to this position, peasants are forced to give guerrillas food and other supplies, pay taxes to the revolutionary movement, give information to the guerrillas and withhold information from the government. Trinquier's (1964, p. 15) description of the Algerian revolution is an excellent example of this view:

> When one or several members of the council wanted to install themselves in a house in the Casbah, they first sent a team of masons to construct a hiding place there. The masons immediately gathered together the people in the building and told them, in substance: "You are soon to receive important personages. You will be responsible for their security with your lives." And sometimes, to indicate that this was no idle threat, a burst of gunfire cut down on the spot residents who seemed to them most suspect. From then on, the movements of the residents were strictly controlled; never could more than half of them be outside at a time. The secret was well kept.

This view that counterinsurgents have of insurgency contradicts the body of guerrilla strategy developed by revolutionaries—that guerrilla military units should at all times respect the persons and property of the people and pay for everything they take. In his Bolivian diary, Che Guevara repeatedly talks of paying peasants lavishly for food or their assistance as guides in difficult terrain (see Scheer, 1968). Indeed, the evidence in Che's diary is that active support was bought rather than gained by political consensus.

It is probable that guerrillas engage in acts and terrorism. Without doubt, terrorism has been practiced against government officials and village chiefs who support the government. It is even likely that terrorism has, on some occasions, been waged against entire villages. At the same time, terrorism is not the sole or even primary vehicle for gaining and maintaining popular support. Guerrillas could not maintain the kind of active support they need by coercion. Popular support is maintained primarily by voluntaristic means, whether it be payment for services or political consensus. For example, when guerrillas occupy a region, they ordinarily institute a land reform program. Land that was owned by large landholders is distributed among the peasants. This gives the peasants a vested interest in a guerrilla victory.

If counterinsurgency is based on the assumption that guerrillas maintain popular support by terrorism, its main thrust will be counterterrorism —terrorizing the population until they fear the government more than they fear the guerrillas.

Counterterrorism emerged as the main thrust of French counterinsurgency in Algeria. In this school of counterinsurgency, torture is viewed as an indispensable tactic, an integral component of counterinsurgency. It is seen as the most effective, if not only, way to obtain essential information about the clandestine revolutionary organization.

> What the forces of order who have arrested him are seeking is not to punish a crime, for which he is otherwise not personally responsible, but, as in any war, the destruction of the enemy army or its surrender. Therefore he is not asked details about himself or about attacks that he may or may not have committed and that are not of immediate interest, but rather for precise information about his organization. In particular, each man has a superior whom he knows; he will first have to give the name of this person, along with his address, so that it will be possible to proceed with the arrest without delay. . . . No lawyer is present for such an interrogation. If the prisoner gives the information requested, the examination is quickly terminated; if not, specialists must force his secret from him. Then, as a soldier, he must face the suffering, and perhaps the death, he has heretofore managed to avoid. The terrorist must accept this as a condition inherent in his trade and in the methods of warfare that, with full knowledge, his superiors and he himself have chosen. (Trinquier, 1964, pp. 21–22)

The legitimacy of torture is defended on the grounds of pragmatic necessity —the human cost of torture must be weighed against the human cost of what the guerrillas will do if torture is not used to locate them and the human cost of less effective counterinsurgency measures.

> The interrogators must always strive not to injure the physical and moral integrity of individuals. Science can easily place at the army's disposition the means for obtaining what is sought. . . . But we must not trifle with our responsibilities. It is deceitful to permit artillery or aviation to bomb villages and slaughter women and children, while the real enemy usually escapes, and to refuse interrogation specialists the right to seize the truly guilty terrorist and spare the innocent. (Trinquier, 1964, p. 23)

There is major disagreement among counterinsurgents on this point. While one school employs counterterrorism, seeking to excel the insurgents in the realm of terrorism, the other major school seeks to minimize repression. This position is based on the assumption that government-sponsored repression is an important, if not essential, ingredient of revolution; at the least, repression accelerates revolution, and at the most, it is a necessary condition. This philosophy is ably expressed by Thompson (1966, p. 52):

> The government must function in accordance with the law. There is a very strong temptation in dealing both with terrorism and with guerrilla actions for government forces to act outside the law, the excuses being that the processes of law are too cumbersome, that the normal safeguards

in the law for the individual are not designed for an insurgency and that a terrorist deserves to be treated as an outlaw anyway. Not only is this morally wrong, but, over a period, it will create many more practical difficulties for a government than it solves.

The main thrust of this approach is the development of "nonlethal" weapons and the use of technological means, such as lie detectors, to replace coercive methods like torture in obtaining information. This school is more advanced with respect to domestic counterinsurgency in America than it is with respect to counterinsurgency in the Third World.

Counterterrorism and the reduction of repression operate on conflicting assumptions about the dynamics of insurgency. They work at cross-purposes to each other. To the extent that an overall counterinsurgency program contains elements of both approaches, it will possess severe internal contradictions. The presence of internal contradiction and ambivalence is a central characteristic of counterinsurgency. The tension between military counterinsurgency and political counterinsurgency heightens this contradiction considerably.

The main thrust of counterinsurgency is an attempt to resolve this contradiction and combine both elements. As advocated by McCuen (1966, p. 57), it accepts the premise that terrorism is central to insurgency but denies that counterterrorism is either legitimate or effective:

> Force and sanctions—not torture or terrorism—may be the quickest and most humane methods of neutralizing fear of the terrorists, breaking the rebel organization, destroying revolutionary control and isolating the population from further pressure. By force and sanctions, we are talking about stringent curfews, control of movements, regroupment of people and villages, rationing food, martial law and maximum penalties for aiding revolutionaries or carrying weapons.

There is fairly widespread consensus among counterinsurgent theorists about the essential characteristics of this approach (See Momboisse, 1967; U.S. Army, 1963; U.S. House of Representatives, 1968): (1) control of movement; (2) strict curfews; (3) registration of all civilians; (4) inspection of identification papers; (5) roadblocks and checkpoints; (6) patrols and block surveillance; (7) control of transportation and communication; (8) suspension of civil liberties; (9) prevention of illegal political meetings and rallies; (10) arrest of guerrilla sympathizers; and (11) censorship of communications media. This broad program of population control, which is the single best description of military counterinsurgency, is supplemented by the creation of comprehensive intelligence networks. Police agencies recruit potentially sympathetic people to provide them with information. "Such strategically located persons as school teachers, community workers, ministers, transportation employees, housing directors and social workers can usually be persuaded to work in conjunction with officials from the police department to gather comprehensive and important information as to tension and possible development" (Momboisse, 1967, p. 51). Through this intelligence system, the police apparatus thus permeates the entire society. Everyone becomes a potential informer, just as everyone is a potential guerrilla. Just as there are categories of guerrilla and guerrilla sympathizer, there are now categories of counterinsurgent and counterinsurgent sympathizer. The conflict is broadened to incorporate more people. Neutrality becomes even more difficult. Every major social institution becomes an arm of counterinsurgency, an arm of the police system.

While this approach makes the internal contradiction less visible, it does little to eliminate it. In practice, the program of population control, which is the main thrust of counterinsurgency, is repressive. While it is not so blatantly repressive as the use of torture, a program of population control affects far more people. The repression, while less intense, is more generalized. For this reason, the basic dilemma remains: On the one hand, counterinsurgency attempts to use repressive measures to cut the guerrilla movement off from popular support; on the other, it recognizes that repression is counterproductive and attempts to minimize it.

POLITICAL COUNTERINSURGENCY

Political counterinsurgency is faced with the task of developing new political responses to the chronic social, political and economic problems that form the context of revolution. It is based, as McCuen (1966, p. 56) notes, on the assumption that ultimately the government can only defeat an insurgency by political means: "for the governing authorities to win, they must not only defeat the revolutionary attempts to mobilize the people, but mobilize the people themselves. To limit themselves to any effort less than their adversaries will be to invite disaster." Since the basic strength of revolutionary movements is political, the objective is to confront guerrillas directly at their strength.

This strategy raises several important questions: Are there political measures that could effectively defeat an insurgency? If such political measures exist, does the government have access to them? Can the government compete on equal terms with guerrillas in the political arena?

Political counterinsurgency poses a serious dilemma for the government. Revolutions are waged to bring about certain changes. To the extent that the government must itself initiate those changes in order to destroy the insurgency, effective political counterinsurgency may bring a de facto guerrilla victory and government defeat. "To deprive the insurgent of a good cause amounts to solving the country's basic problems. If this is possible, well and good, but we know now that a good cause for the insurgent is one that his opponent cannot adopt without losing his power in the process" (Galula, 1964, p. 67). Where important political issues are involved and real interests are at stake, the ability of the government to employ political counterinsurgent measures that threaten its own interests may be severely limited; the government does not, therefore, have access to the entire range of available political responses.

Not all insurgent movements launch revolutionary wars for the same purposes, and not all governments oppose them for the same reasons. It is necessary to understand the political context in which a given guerrilla war occurs: What major interests are involved in the conflict between the revolutionaries and the government? What are the objectives of the guerrillas and the counterguerrillas?

Galula (1964, p. 101) has identified three main political configurations that an insurgency can assume: (1) the guerrilla has no real ideological or political cause; (2) the guerrilla has a political cause that the government can espouse without losing power or sacrificing important interests; and (3) the guerrilla has a monopoly of viable political causes, and the government cannot accede to demands for change without losing power. The possibilities for political counterinsurgency differ significantly for each of these configurations. For that reason, it is important to determine which case is most typical of insurgency situations.

At issues here is the role of politics in guerrilla insurgency. Do insurgents use, or even manufacture, political issues in order to take power and overthrow the government, or are they sincerely interested in creating necessary change? Is their goal social change, whether or not revolution is the only possible vehicle for change, or is it the takeover of power by revolution in any way possible? The answer to this determines to a large extent the course of political counterinsurgency. In the first instance, a government-sponsored program of basic changes would be more likely to succeed than in the second.

The prospects for political counterinsurgency are obviously best when the guerrillas have no real cause. In this situation, counterinsurgents need only neutralize revolutionary propaganda and demonstrate that there is no need for that basic change—to prevent the guerrillas from *creating* a demand for change. In this kind of propaganda war, the government has at least equal access to the weapons of political warfare.

Political counterinsurgency can be effective when the guerrillas have a real cause that the government can also endorse and implement. In this instance, the counterinsurgents must develop an effective government-sponsored program of change that will meet the needs of the people, without threatening important government interests.

The prospects for political counterinsurgency are worst in the third case, where there is a real need and demand for change that the government cannot meet without losing power. In this situation, which is the ideal context for revolution, the possibilities for political counterinsurgency are severely limited. The government will not be able to compete equally with guerrillas in the political arena.

The main program of political counterinsurgency is civic action in which police or military units undertake reform programs such as building schools, wells, hospitals or roads. The purpose is twofold: to initiate reform measures that will hopefully satisfy the demand for change, and to identify the police and military as a force for reform and modernization rather than repression. Identification of the police and military as a repressive force is a major factor in the process of revolution. Civic action is an attempt to neutralize that factor, by replacing the repressive image with a benevolent one. Black and Lake (1967, pp. 668–669) contend that American police should adopt the role of civic action as a solution to antipolice sentiment.

> Although no invading army destroyed the housing, the economy, and the well-being of the inhabitants of high-crime areas, still all these conditions exist there. If the police wish to pacify enemy territory and to separate the criminal from the noncriminal, they will have to undertake a significant portion of the helping function. The time has come for some police department to develop imaginative social programs and to implement them under available legislation.

Civic action describes a broad range of political reform programs, ranging from those that are primarily symbolic to those that bring substantial change. Civic action, like political counterinsurgency in general, can be initiated for several different reasons: to create only the minimum change required to neutralize the revolutionary political advantage, or to satisfy the legitimate demand for change by creating substantial change. The object in the first case is to prevent change whenever possible, and to grudgingly initiate change when it cannot possibly be avoided. The second case is based on a belief that nothing but substantial change can effectively combat a revolution. The object is not to prevent change, but to prevent the takeover of power by a revolutionary party. In any event, it is important to determine the specific political content of a counterinsurgency program—what interest it is designed to protect, and what goals it is intended to achieve.

Corson describes an effective civic action program that he initiated in Vietnam. He assumed that the guerrrillas have an important political advantage at the outset. The program was specifically designed to neutralize their advantage by political means.

> The Vietcong had, by and large, not offered material rewards to the peasant but nevertheless were able to engender both tacit and overt support. This support was not achieved by terrorizing the bulk of the peasant population but rather sprang from the empathy the peasant had with the Vietcong. . . . Since this was the fundamental obstacle to overcome in initiating a pacification program, it was necessary to determine an alternative to the ideological appeal of the National Liberation Front, and in order to do so certain fundamental elements of the NFL ideology had to be understood. (Corson, 1968, pp. 160–161)

The strategy was to focus on concrete and visible practical change instead of confronting the NLF ideologically. Ideological conflict—convincing the people that capitalism is a better system than communism and that democracy is better than totalitarianism—has been the traditional emphasis in political counterinsurgency. Corson worked on the explicit assumption that the influence of ideology can be minimized if a program of material change is implemented.

> Furthermore, the thing Mao understood—and we miss—is that a population's peasant element is largely indifferent to the ideologies of the contending forces. The peasant in Vietnam cares as little about the ideology of the VC as he does about the ideology of the GVN. This fact in itself provides the ARVN with as great an opportunity to build up popular nonideological support as the VC, and nonideological support is essential for victory; even more important, it is essential for the troops' own survival. (Corson, 1968, pp. 96–97)

The program assumes that economic problems are central to peasants, that hunger and poor housing are the main issues with which they are concerned. If economic progress can be provided, ideological issues like nationalism would become less important. "Lenin is reported to have said, 'If you scratch a peasant you will find a petit bourgeois.' We scratched the Vietnamese peasant and found this to be true. The mechanics of creating the cash prize was deceptively simple. It was necessary to use the resources in the area and to achieve simple capital accumulation without significant United States assistance" (Corson, 1968, p. 170). The objective is to implement a modernization program that brings tangible benefits to a village.

First, the marines developed rapport with the people by playing *co tuong,* a form of chess that is played by most Vietnamese peasants. The second step was to demonstrate visibly the possibility of economic progress. The marines hired several fishermen and their boats, paying extremely high wages in return. Then, using demolitions charges, they caught several hundreds pounds of fish. Following this, they hired peasants to carry the fish to market and sold it for less than half the regular price. Even at that price, they made a profit which was given to the hamlet chief to begin the "hamlet fund." During the Christmas truce, the marines publicly challenged the NLF to debate what each side could tangibly do for the people of the hamlet. After this first success, a pig-breeding operation was begun, with part of the profits going to the peasants involved and part going to the hamlet fund. The income of some of the peasants involved was increased tenfold. Other projects were soon started, and before long almost 50 families were involved in new enterprises. This broke the landowners' monopoly over employment, and land values began to drop in accordance with the law of supply and demand. Average rents were reduced by 50 percent (See Corson, 1968, pp. 165–173). The objective of creating a viable economy was accomplished.

> More than a year later the pleasing epilogue to the pacification program in Phong Bac is its "thriving" economy. For example, there is a drive-in/walk-in nightly movie with an attendance of about 2,000 persons, numerous new shops ranging from a cobbler to a blacksmith, two new schools built by the people with teachers paid for by the people, an active self-run dispensary, and a hamlet self-defense force. The original capitalistic ventures are all continuing—without any U.S. assistance. The pig farm netted some $10,000 U.S. dollars in its first year of operation, and the beekeeping and fishing enterprises continue to provide additional profits and capital for other business ventures. The business council is active and has established several cooperative credit unions to help finance new enterprises and to underwrite the peasant's purchase of his own land. The farmer's cooperative has more than six hundred members and is rapidly upgrading the methods of farming used in the area. (Corson, 1968, p. 173)

The similarity between this program and effective antipoverty programs in the United States is obvious. Equally obvious is the conclusion that effective political counterinsurgency is possible, that the programs necessary to defeat an insurgency do exist. More properly, the programs exist that are required to channel conflict away from the military arena into the constructive political arena.

The significant point, however, is that they are not being used. Despite the success of the pacification program in Phong Bac, it has not become a model for the United States counterinsurgency effort in Vietnam. This raises the obvious but nonetheless important question: Why has the blatant success of this program been overlooked while far less effective programs, whose failure is adequately documented, have continued to form the main thrust of political counterinsurgency?

The answer is that counterinsurgency is a tool of foreign or domestic policy. Its purpose is to achieve the objectives of that policy; it is a means to an end and not an end in itself. Goals and objectives are determined *for* counterinsurgents by political bodies. The range of options available to counterinsurgents is limited by broader political decisions. For this reason, counterinsurgents may be prevented from using effective political tactics because they conflict with the broader policy considerations. This is simply to say that counterinsurgency, like insurgency, cannot be isolated from the political context in which it occurs.

Our current foreign policy is designed to keep in power the present South Vietnamese government, or a government with the same ideology and interests. It is based on the assumption that the interests of the United States and the interests of the South Vietnamese government are the same. Corson (1968, p. 16) questions the validity of that assumption:

A fallacy from the beginning of our involvement was the assumption that the goals of the United States and South Vietnam were the same. The results accruing from our actions categorically refute this assumption. It may be said that the GVN wanted to resist aggression, but unfortunately they wanted to resist aggression in their own way for their own purposes. The people of Vietnam may have wanted to achieve a democratic representative government, but not for the purposes we wanted. The Army of the Republic of Vietnam (ARVN) may have wanted to fight the Vietcong and the North Vietnamese Army (NVA), but not for the purposes we desired. The obverse of each of these factors is that our government, our military, and our bureaucracy all wanted things for Vietnam, but not for the same purposes that the corresponding elements in Vietnamese society wanted them.

Thus, for whatever reasons, American foreign policy has tied the interests of the United States to the interests of certain groups and classes in Vietnam. In general, these classes are anticommunist as well as against basic change in almost any form. In many cases, American foreign policy has tied the counterinsurgency efforts to those classes that have traditionally oppressed the Vietnamese peasants. In this situation, liberation from the NLF actually means the return of oppression. *"In many areas pacification has not only brought American troops, but also meant the return of the absentee landlords,* who made use of the peasants' gullibility and fear of authority to equate the power of U.S. forces with the authority to enforce collection of illegal land rents" (Corson, 1968, p. 162). At present, the policy is to oppose, or at least not support, those groups or classes that are anti-Communist but at the same time seek basic change or reform and oppose any United States' presence in Vietnam. In practice, this means that the American counterinsurgency program is designed to defeat the NFL without creating any change or eliminating the oppression and exploitation that created the revolutionary situation.

The pacification program Corson implemented was intentionally designed to prevent this oppression and exploitation by reducing the power of the classes that American foreign policy supports. For that reason, it represents a set of counterinsurgency measures that are, in practice, not available to counterinsurgents in Vietnam, and that will not be available until the fundamental basis of American foreign policy is altered. Thus, while counterinsurgents could theoretically compete on equal terms with revolutionaries in the political arena, in practice they are prevented from using the necessary tactics.

If effective programs of change are not implemented, it is to the counterinsurgent's advantage to remove the conflict from the political arena, where the guerrilla's strength lies, to the military arena, where his own strength lies. To some extent, the importance of political issues diminishes, nd the guerrilla's political advantage is at last partially neutralized, once military operations are begun. "The possibility is that only one cause exists. If the insurgent has pre-empted it, then the force of ideology works for him and not for the counterinsurgent. However, this is true largely in the early parts of the conflict. Later on, as the war develops, war itself becomes the paramount issue, and the original cause loses some of its importance" (Galula, 1964, p. 14). The implications are clear: It is the counter-insurgent, rather than the insurgent, who benefits from waging a military rather than political conflict. The process of militarization is initiated primarily by the government.

Counterinsurgency is thus based on the assumption that the importance of politics decreases as the militarization of conflict escalates.

> It has been asserted that a counterinsurgent confronted by a dynamic insurgent ideology is bound to meet defeat, that no amount of tactics and techniques can compensate for his ideological handicap. This is not necessarily so because the population's attitude in the middle stage of the war is dictated not so much by the relative popularity and merits of the opponents as by the more primitive concern for safety. Which side gives the best protection, which one threatens the most, which one is likely to win, these are the criteria governing the population's stand. (Galula, 1964, p. 14)

One major political objective of counterinsurgency is to depoliticize guerrilla warfare, to remove politics as a significant factor in guerrilla warfare and to make the conflict, as much as possible, purely military.

This strategy is only partially successful, since the effects of political factors can be reduced, but not completely eliminated. The counterinsurgent is still left with the problem of cutting off the strategic military aid that the guerrillas receive from the populace. In most cases, for the reasons already cited, the government will not be able to accomplish this objective by espousing a popular political cause or by initiating a popular political program. Given this limitation, the major thrust of political counterinsurgency is the building of highly structured political organizations that are devoid of any political content geared toward fundamental change. It is an attempt to create new political structures or extend already existing structures without creating new political programs. Trinquier (1964, p. 30) describes such an organization:

> First, we designate an energetic and intelligent man in each city who will, with one or more reliable assistants, build the projected organization with a minimum of help from the authorities. . . . The principle is very simple. The designated leader divides the city into districts, at the head of each of which he places a chief and two or three assistants. These, in turn, divide the district into sub-districts and designate a chief and several assistants for each of them. Finally, each building or group receives a chief and two or three assistants who will be in direct contact with the populace.

The object is to make the presence of the government felt in the remotest regions of the society, where it is not now felt, on the hamlet and village level. The objective is to provide intelligence information on revolutionary activity, taking a census of the entire population, providing the populace with identification cards and preventing all forms of aid to the guerrillas.

In a sense, this form of organization is administrative rather than political. Its function is to extend the political system against which the revolution is directed, without any attempts to meet the demands for change, to increase the efficiency of the administrative government apparatus without changing the political content. It is based on the assumption that political factors are negligible, and that the government need not initiate any political changes in order to combat the guerrillas. In this sense, it is an apolitical response—it does not take into account the political context of revolution and counterrevolution. "This organization will require the governing authorities to foster all sorts of classes, associations, clubs, groups, and societies. They may be designed for social, vocational, sports, agricultural, educational, medical, religious, military or other suitable activities" (McCuen, 1966, p. 58).

The main thrust of political counterinsurgency, then, seems to be the elimination of politics as a major factor, in the belief that the government can more easily win a purely military conflict. Beyond this, it is to increase the efficiency of the government bureaucratic apparatus. The development of new political programs, or programs for modernization or change, is rare. In other words, there is, for the most part, no viable political response to the revolutionary political program or to the chronic problems that make revolutions possible.

COUNTERINSURGENCY IN AMERICA

The main thrust of military counterinsurgency in America is the development of nonlethal weapons and the reduction of generalized and indiscriminate repression. Acting on the theory that police repression is a major factor in revolution, Janowitz (1968, pp. 23–24) argues that repression should be carefully restricted. In pursuit of this objective, he has recommended that (1) the National Guard be integrated; (2) the use of bayonets, police dogs and other provocative weapons be eliminated; (3) only the minimum amount of necessary force be used; and (4) trained antisniper units, rather than undisciplined mass firing, be used against snipers during riots.

Rex Applegate, the foremost American authority on riot control, argues that the absence of a viable counterinsurgency strategy leads American police to use more force than is either necessary or productive: "Americans know so little about riots. Most parts of the world live with them and have learned to treat them as everyday matters—look at Hong Kong, and France, and South American countries. Here, we don't know what to do at each stage of a riot's growth. We wait till it gets out of hand, then roll in the machine guns" (Wills, 1968, p. 56).

Overt police repression and brutality have been a major factor in the growth of a radical political movement in this country. To a large extent, it is responsible for the escalation of both demands and tactics. For example, the use of police dogs in Birmingham, Alabama, served an important function in the escalation of the civil rights movement. Similarly, the use of fire hoses against peaceful demonstrators and the use of cattle prods increased the militancy of protest. The use of tear gas and nightsticks on university campuses like Berkeley, Wisconsin and Columbia was an important ingredient in the escalation of conflict between university students and police, administrators and, in some cases, state politicians. The radical movement in America has relied to a considerable extent on officially sanctioned police violence for its momentum; it is possible that a more rational policy of police intervention would reverse this process and lead to de-escalation.

That possibility is the basis of counterinsurgency in America. For the most part, it is an attempt to reduce or eliminate counterproductive police violence. There is considerable evidence that police and National Guard units have engaged in indiscriminate violence during riots. For example, sniper fire is frequently returned with heavy machine-gun fire, often because National Guardsmen are not equipped with smaller caliber arms. Proposals to create specially trained antisniper units are designed to eliminate this particular form of counterproductive force. "In Philadelphia, Commissioner Rizzo has 125 trained sharpshooters manning his seven S-Cars (S for Stakeout). They have rifles and shotguns in the cars. . . . They are now working on antisniper tactics, learning to shoot from heights, from ladders; testing heavier guns and body armor" (Wills, 1968, p. 80). The development and use of nonlethal weapons are a significant part of this counterinsurgency strategy. Applegate's argument in favor of nonlethal weapons, such as Chemical Mace, is a perfect example of the main objective of American counterinsurgency—efficiency.

> As far as self-defense goes, they would be better off with the Mace than with a stick. You don't need training to use the Mace, and it will subdue a prisoner better than any club, without making the marshal look like a brute. There is a dare, a challenge to combat, in facing a man with a stick. But with Mace there is no test of strength, no struggle; and shedding tears does not make a martyr, the way shedding blood does. The thing to do with agitators is destroy their romantic image. (Wills, 1968, p. 69)

In this sense, counterinsurgency lies very directly in the tradition of realpolitik. It is used because it works: If martyrs contribute to revolution, then deprive revolutionaries of martyrs. The basic principle is that simple.

This approach to counterinsurgency avoids the political questions entirely. Goals and objectives are taken as given; the only question is efficiency of implementation. To some extent, this reflects an explicit assumption that political factors are not primary in the revolutionary situation. Janowitz' (1968, p. 71) perception of riots is a good example of this position: "Social tensions generated by discrimination, prejudice and poverty offer essential but only partial explanations of Negro mass rioting in the urban centers of the United States." The implicit assumption is that insofar as political factors like prejudice and poverty offer only partial explanations, the elimination of these conditions offers only a partial solution to riots. What, then, are the significant factors? "Along elements that account for the outbreak of mass rioting are both (a) the organizational weaknesses and professional limitations of law enforcement agencies, and (b) a moral and social climate that encourages violence" (Janowitz, 1968, p. 71). Although not explicitly stated, the implication is clear: The second set of factors, which can be described as administrative or apolitical, is primary, while the first set, which is political in nature, is secondary in importance. This perception has policy implications. Based on this orientation, Janowitz recommends increasing the professionalization of police forces, thereby reducing unnecessary and counterproductive violence, and eliminating the moral climate that encourages violence by controlling the content of mass media. He offers no proposals for eliminating poverty or discrimination, nor does he propose any basic change in the role of police. His perspective is that riots can be controlled and eliminated without the need for basic change *if* more efficient police-military procedures are implemented. He clearly places primacy on military counterinsurgency over political counterinsurgency.

Counterinsurgency programs are an alternative to conventional military repression. For example, police departments in many major cities are beginning to purchase military-type weapons—authomatic rifles, high-powered Stoner rifles and armored vehicles. At this point, the future role of police is not determined: There is a conflict between advocates of both forms of counterinsurgency and proponents of conventional military-police approaches for control of domestic policy, a conflict which has not yet been resolved.

There is, at the same time, a highly developed program of political counterinsurgency, although it is not explicitly defined as such. Whether by intention or not, programs like the War Against Poverty and the Model Cities Program perform an important counterinsurgency function. The antipoverty program was originally intended to reduce juvenile crime and violence, which at that point was not yet political in nature. To the extent that violence by marginal groups has now become political, these programs have become counterinsurgent in nature.

There are important local differences and variations in the War Against Poverty and the Model Cities Program. Some local programs attempt to create basic change while others do not. Some are explicitly designed to prevent fundamental change. The central government has imperfect control over local organizations, and local variation is therefore common.

At the same time that it is important to recognize local differences, in general the effect of the antipoverty and Model Cities programs is to permit, or even facilitate, minor changes in order to prevent major change. The definition of what is minor and what is major is constantly being reviewed. For example, there had been considerable resistance to programs for integration—equal employment, school integration and fair housing. With the advent of black power and the separatist threat it posed, integration became an acceptable change for most Americans and for the federal government. When compared with militant separatism, there was a recognition that integration does not really threaten major interests. For instance, most large corporate employers do not really care whether they employ blacks or whites. They are, however, concerned with wage scales, levels of union demands and production.

To some extent, these programs are symbolic. They promise far more than they are able to produce given the resources that are allocated and the programmatic limitations that are preserved. They demonstrate a concern, they indicate an intention to do something, and they illuminate problems, but they are unable really to create the kinds of changes that are needed. Even in this symbolic form, however, these programs are fighting for their survival. Conservative members of Congress are attempting to eliminate them entirely.

These programs are counterproductive from the perspective of their architects: They create a sense of hope and raise the level of expectation among impoverished Americans. When they are unable to fulfill the hopes they have raised, the level of frustration is increased, and the possibility of revolution becomes more real. The possibility that the programs could be completely ended makes this problem even more acute.

In general, political counterinsurgency in America is designed to create the image of basic change without the reality, to use the rhetoric of change without the implementation. Its objective is to permit the minimum amount of change that is necessary to prevent an insurgency. This, of course, is a very difficult calculation—how much change is necessary to avoid revolution, and to what extent can fundamental change be prevented without generating a revolutionary situation? Given that such calculations involve rough estimates, in what direction is it better to miscalculate—too much change or too little? These are the political decisions that determine the characteristics of the overall counterinsurgency program.

The concept of black capitalism was really the culmination of the American counterinsurgency effort. It converted the general direction of the black power movement, which was a potential force for basic change, into a conservative force to channel such change. Black people are gaining access to economic rewards, which gives them a vested interest in preserving the social, economic and political system in its present form. The process is simple: Meet those demands that do not threaten important interests at an early stage in order to prevent the escalation of demands. Changes like the integration of schools, equal employment for black people or the creation of black studies programs can be implemented without substantially affecting the basic structure of American society or its major institutions.

With respect to university rebellions, counterinsurgency is designed to permit marginal changes and create or support liberal student groups as an alternative to the radical groups that now form the leadership of campus movements. Such programs were implemented in the aftermath of the Columbia University rebellion with considerable success. Insofar as the administration was willing to concede some demands and negotiated only with liberal student groups, allowing them to take credit for the change, radicals could be isolated from the popular support they needed.

Counterinsurgency is by no means the major response to political protest in America at the present time. There is a tension between counterinsurgency and conventional military repression on the one hand and political counterinsurgency and military counterinsurgency on the other. These different strategies often work at cross-purposes to each other. In Chicago, for example, the Woodlawn Organization (TWO) got a federal grant to work with the Blackstone Rangers. Police raided the first meeting between the two groups and arrested Blackstone Ranger leaders. Similarly, overt repression of the kind that occurred during the Democratic National Convention in Chicago offsets whatever may be gained by political counterinsurgency.

THE WEAKNESSES OF COUNTERINSURGENCY

Counterinsurgency is intended as an alternative to conventional warfare and traditional politics. What precisely does it offer that is new? It offers a reduction of indiscriminate and generalized repression; it offers civic action; and finally, it offers an efficient administrative political structure. It does not, however, offer a real response to the political demands of the revolution, and it offers no program to meet demands for change.

Counterinsurgency is justified primarily in terms of efficiency: It offers a viable means of opposing a guerrilla insurgency. In these terms, one question that must be asked is whether it can, in fact, perform that function. Given the proper conditions for counterinsurgency and a guerrilla force that has a strong base of popular support, can a program that does not offer an alternative program of social, political and economic change combat an insurgency?

A second question is what cost even successful counterinsurgency entails. And third, assuming that guerrilla movements desire change and that they are not solely interested in wresting power from the government, are the demands for change legitimate? If the changes are desirable, and, in the long run, beneficial, is not counterinsurgency destructive precisely to the extent that it is successful? The question of whether change can be prevented is quite separate from the question of whether it should be prevented. To some extent, riots and revolutions are symptoms of a need for change. If counterinsurgency suppresses the symptoms without curing the illness— creating the necessary change—it may be counterproductive, unless, of course, its objectives are defined in terms of the special interests of certain classes.

In terms of costs, counterinsurgency often entails the creation of a police state: curfews, identification papers, roadblocks, military patrols, appointment of political officials, censorship of media, control of travel and prevention of opposition political meetings. This cost must be weighed against the advantages to be gained from destroying the insurgency. Since there is no precise beginning or end to a guerrilla war, this police state apparatus becomes a semipermanent part of the social structure; since the threat of armed insurgency exists even in the purely political stage, before military operations begin, and continues after the military threat has been temporarily thwarted, the police state must be maintained as long as the *political* conditions for revolution prevail. "If we prepare ourselves in peacetime to face *modern warfare,* if we provide the people with a means of defending themselves, if we take precautions to be informed at all times of the preparations and intentions of our adversaries, then we will have no difficulty in quickly taking the necessary action when the time comes to reduce our adversaries to impotence" (Trinquier, 1964, p. 39).

Is there an alternative to a permanent police state apparatus? In theory, counterinsurgents recognize the necessity of dealing with the political challenge posed by insurgency. In practice, they often ignore political considerations. The only reasonably certain alternative to a costly war of attrition lies in political settlement. This means making some basic political, social and economic changes. This approach, however, lies outside the main direction of counterinsurgency. For example, none of the major recommendations of the President's Commission on Civil Disorders has been implemented. Even such token measures as the War Against Poverty and the Model Cities Program are fighting for their survival. As long as the political climate remains like this, counterinsurgency does not provide an alternative to a war of attrition; it remains only a weapon that offers some hope of winning such a war.

The key assumption of counterinsurgency is that the revolutionary political program can be defeated by minor reforms, propaganda and psychological warfare—the government does not have to deal seriously with the revolutionary political demands. This avoids the important questions: Are the demands for change legitimate? Is basic change necessary? Is a more efficient means of preventing change desirable?

The goals of counterinsurgency can be defined in several different ways. Its success depends upon the goals and objectives used. In theory, these are to prevent armed revolution, to prevent change by violent means, while permitting change by peaceful political means to occur. Counterinsurgency attempts to prevent escalation from political conflict to military conflict. In practice, however, it is often designed to prevent escalation from one-sided military conflict, in which the state has a monopoly over the means of violence and maintains power by force, to two-sided military conflict. Ultimately, the efficiency of counterinsurgency makes it more difficult for societies to deal with the question of the kind and amount of change that is needed. To the extent that it is used to prevent needed change, it is repressive in nature, and it prevents the resolution of conflict by political means.

REFERENCES

Black, H., and M. J. Lake (1967) "Guerrilla Warfare: An Analogy to Police–Criminal Interactions, *American Journal of Orthopsychiatry,* vol. 37, no. 4 (July), pp. 666–670.

Burchett, W. (1965) *Vietnam: Inside Story of the Guerrilla War.* New York: International Publishers.

Corson, W. R. (1968) *The Betrayal.* New York: Ace Books.

Galula, D. (1964) *Counter-Insurgency Warfare: Theory and Practice.* New York: Praeger.

Greene, T. N., ed. (1962) *The Guerrilla and How to Fight Him.* New York: Praeger.

Griffith, S. B., ed. (1961) *Mao Tse-tung on Guerrilla Warfare.* New York: Praeger.

Guevara, E. (1961) *Guerrilla Warfare.* New York: Monthly Review Press.

Horowitz, I. L. (1970) *The Struggle Is the Message: The Organization and Ideology of the Anti-War Movement.* Berkeley: The Glendessary Press.

Janowitz, M. (1968) *Social Control of Escalated Riots.* Chicago: University of Chicago Center for Policy Study.

McCuen, J. J. (1966) *The Art of Counter-Revolutionary War: The Strategy of Counterinsurgency.* Harrisburg, Pa.: Stackpole Books.

Momboisse, R. M. (1967) *Riots, Revolts and Insurrections.* Springfield, Ill.: C. C Thomas.

Scheer, R., ed. (1968) *The Diary of Che Guevara; Bolivia: November 7, 1966–October 7, 1967.* New York: Bantam.

Taber, R. (1965) *The War of the Flea.* New York: Lyle Stuart.

Thompson, R. G. K. (1966) *Defeating Communist Insurgency: Experiences from Malaya and Vietnam.* New York: Praeger.

Trinquier, R. (1964) *Modern Warfare: A French View of Counterinsurgency.* New York: Praeger.

U.S. Army (1963) *Department of the Army Field Manual, FM31-16, Counterguerrilla Operations* (February). Washington, D.C.: Department of the Army.

U.S. House Committee on Un-American Activities (1968) *Guerrilla Warfare Advocates in the United States,* 90th Cong., 2nd sess., pub. no. 85-008 (May 6). Washington, D.C.: Government Printing Office.

Wills, G. (1968) *The Second Civil War: Arming for Armageddon.* New York: New American Library.

CHAPTER 14

MILITARIZATION, MODERNIZATION AND MOBILIZATION

MILITARY POWER AND STATE POWER

Military power exists in its relation to state power. It is geared to defend a well-defined geographic terrain and a certain body of people having a common set of economic, psychological and linguistic elements within this terrain. The main function of the armed forces at the outset of nation-building is to preserve and make visible national sovereignty. They "defend" and "project" the national entity into the international arena. And once actual sovereignty is obtained, they acquire a critical role with respect to the internal affairs of the state. The military revolutionists may come to power against colonialists, but they maintain their power against internal threats, especially by preventing political infighting among the ruling groups (Meister, 1968, p. 261).

The relationship between government and the military is no less intimate than the connection between the control of power and the control of violence at the more general level. But whatever the main role of the armed forces at any given moment, whether the maintenance of the state against external enemies or against internal terrorists, the military leadership alone is assigned the right to use physical violence. Such a right does not, however, extend to legal authorization. The ambiguity in civil–military relations often resides in the separation of the permission to use violence (a legal-social function) from the actual conduct of violence (a military function). Such exercise of violence in the absence of complete legitimation also remains a constant source of tension between the military and the civil apparatus. The military, when functioning properly, quickly acquires a sense of the nation and becomes sensitized toward vested interests and factional enclaves that break down the egalitarian consensus of the revolutionary period. Of course, there are many cases in which the military itself becomes a vested interest and serves to unbalance equitable arrangements that may have been made during the early revolutionary period. Furthermore, when various factions of the military cleave and adopt different ideologies toward national goals, a period of protracted civil strife usually follows. This was certainly a prime factor in both the Congolese and Nigerian civil wars. While there is no automatic rule which insures the military maintenance of a postrevolutionary equilibrium, the military will assume such a role when no other social factor does so.

One way the military is able to serve national interests with relative equality is related to its methods of recruitment. The military gains membership from disparate groups and classes within the society. By minimizing the class base of membership through a heterogenous recruitment policy, the armed forces can function as an important socializing agency (La Palombara, 1963, pp. 31–32). This transclass role can be performed despite the relatively pronounced class base of military leadership. In Middle Eastern states and nations such as Egypt and Iran, where the class formations remain relatively diffuse and weak, the corresponding importance of the army as a national and even a class-welding agency becomes manifest (Halpern, 1963; Kirk, 1963).

Unlike the experience in either the United States or the Soviet Union, the armed forces in the newly emergent nations are not absorbed into the civilian society, but instead become partners with the society. One of the hallmarks of George Washington's Administration was that it made the military subject to political control (Lipset, 1963, pp. 16–45; Chambers, 1963, pp. 21–27). After the Russian Revolution, despite urgings of the permanent revolutionists, the military was placed under the rule of the political elites (Werner, 1939, p. 36). In the United States, civilian control had democratic consequences and in the Soviet Union autocratic consequences, but in neither case did it make much difference in terms of the functional efficiency of the armed forces. In both the United States and the Soviet Union the military served as a professional source of political strength and orientations toward economic development rather than as a ruling directorate. The same cannot be said for most Third World nations, where, as a matter of fact, the political functions are oftentimes militarized from the onset of independence. Due to this early identification with the national cause, the military is transformed from a symbolic badge of sovereignty into a decisive partner in the composition of the state.

The function of the military establishment as the mark of sovereignty is well exemplified by postliberation India. Given its strong traditional bias against force and violence, India represents a good test case. Under the reign of Nehru, the Gandhian approach to pacifism was severely modified in the name of expediency. According to Gandhi, the key to real victory is the doctrine of *Satyagraha*—the force that is born of truth and love, rather than error and hatred. Nonmilitary, nonviolent social action was pitted against all enemies (Bondurant, 1958; Erikson, 1969, pp. 364–392; Horowitz, 1957, pp. 89–106; Naess, 1965). But the actual conduct of foreign policy after the British left compelled a quick and uneven modification of this policy. With reference to the early stages of the Kashmir dispute, Nehru (1957, p. 357) considered it his "misfortune that we even have to keep an army, a navy, and an air force. In the world one is compelled to take these precautions." While the rhetoric remains pacifist, the actual chore of strengthening the military was well under way no more than two years after independence. And, by the end of the 1950s, Nehru (1957, p. 211) had abandoned even the pacifist rhetoric. He noted that "none of us would dare, in the present state of the world, to do away with the instruments of organized violence. We keep armies both to defend ourselves against aggression from without and to meet trouble from within." India responded to the increased military determinism of all worldly situations. It was not so much that Gandhism was a dead letter in India by Independence Day, but rather that nationalism proved to be more compelling than ideology in shaping Indian society. The bitter controversy over Pakistani independence in the 1950s, the equally dangerous rift with China in the 1960s, and now its participation in the Bangla Desh struggles in the 1970s, moved India into a much more conventional statist posture than it was in its origins. But at the same time, it became more nearly a national power and lost a good deal of its claim to be an international moral authority.

The increase in military spending in India has kept pace with the general militarization of the Third World. From 1960 to 1964 alone, the increase in military allocations was nearly threefold (Ministry of Information and Broadcasting, 1962, pp. 72–74; 1963, pp. 21, 64, 180). India's defense appropriations went from 6 percent of the gross national product (GNP) in 1961 to 17 percent in 1964, and enrollment in the national military cadet corps, India's "West Point," rose from 150,000 in 1958 to 300,000 in 1964. Slowly also, the military mix of army, navy, and air force grew steadily at the expense of the other branches. And with the increasing military hardware sent in by both the Soviet Union and the United States, India was transformed from a Third World leader to a buffer zone.

The military buildup is continuing. The rise of Communist opposition to Congress Party rule in Kerala and elsewhere and the pressures from

China and Pakistan only partly explain this increase. For, as in the other Third World nations, national greatness is becoming ever more linked to military grandeur. And no Third World country, even one conscientiously dedicated to pacifism, has been able to withstand this formula of a civil-military partnership; what can be controlled is the degree of military involvement (as in some parts of Africa) but no longer the fact of involvement.

THE POLITICIZED MILITARY

The capacity of the military in Third World nations to help establish a political system depends upon three main factors: its control of the instruments of violence, its ethos of public service and national identity instead of private interest and class identity, and its representation as an articulate and expert group (Janowitz, 1964, pp. 27–28). In the Third World the military alone combines these factors, which may be generalized as technical skills combined with an ethic of national purpose.

These factors also help to explain why the elite of the armed forces no longer confine their allegiance to traditional upper classes. The rise of the middle class, as well as of the working class, in many portions of the Third World has forced the military to become more nearly representative of the nation as a whole than its own vested interests or natural proclivities might have indicated. As long as the military maintained such alignments with the aristocracy and with religious groups, it was difficult, if not impossible, for the nation to become developmentally oriented or for the military to perform in terms of public service or its technical or professional skills. This shift has been most pronounced in those nations where the military underwent a transformation from within, especially in Asian and Sub-Sahara Africa where the inherited military establishment had to break with this oligarchical notion of service to the upper classes in order to function as a redeemer of the popular will.

The military becomes concerned with internal security when a national revolution becomes a class revolution. Since most Third World societies are highly stratified according to class, race, caste or area, the possibilities, even inevitabilities, of class conflict persist. Thus the military establishment, whether it so desires or not, is compelled to align itself with either traditional social classes or modern social classes. In a concrete sense, the role of the military in maintaining internal security is impaired by the very existence of class forces, for it is subject to pressure from both sides. It is possible to overthrow military establishments as part of a general upheaval against traditional class. At the same time, if the military is identified too closely with the popular classes, it tends to bring about an oligarchically inspired counterrevolution.

The role of the military is impaled upon the horns of a structural dilemma. In the very act of serving as an instrument of national redemption, it finds itself aligned against traditional class forces that have a great deal to lose in terms of wealth as well as prestige. At the same time, the use of the military as an instrument of suppression for riot control and secret police action has the effect of aligning the military against the popular class forces it is ostensibly serving. This problem is more acute in the Middle East and in Latin America than in most parts of Asia or Africa, where the military has not been replaced in the course of revolutionary action so much as it has found its roles transformed in the course of the developmental process (Rustow, 1963, p. 11; Vatikiotis, 1961). Interestingly, these former areas also contain nations where there is high tension and low stability.

There is an obvious tension between the function of military systems in the Third World that move toward socialism and populism and those that move toward more traditionalist economies and polities. The military clearly stands closer to the class and sector that actually wield power; and only when such classes and sectors are in a condition of impotence or cleavage does the military perform overt leadership tasks. One might say that within the "iron law of militarism" the choice is to be made between the military defense of national interests or the military definition of what these interests are. This is a more realistic goal than nonmilitary solutions in nations and cultures in which politics has been and continues to be militarized. The case of the Arab nations in this connection is most significant. The analysis by Avneri (1970, pp. 31–44) of militarism in North Africa deserves serious attention: "Within the Arab context, the emergence of military regimes has not signified a breakthrough to modernization, but a reversion to the traditional, legitimate form of government accepted and revered by the Arabs and by Islam for the past fifteen hundred years." Avneri (1970, p. 33) concludes the point by noting that "within the political culture of Arab society, military power equals political legitimacy, and for this reason military leaders have had very little difficulty establishing their authority in Arab countries" (See also Perlmutter, 1967).

The political leadership in the Third World tends to be drawn from the military corps. Therefore, in the "Egyptian socialism" of Nasser, or in the "guided democracy" of Sukarno, there was extreme emphasis on providing adequate policy-making roles for the armed forces. The tendency of political leadership in the Third World to stimulate military models, and at times to adopt even the dress, manners and bureaucratic norms of the military establishment, underscores the close kinship and partnership between military and civilian elements.

The military often functions as a counterweight to the party apparatus on the one hand and the bureaucratic apparatus on the other. These two major forces of domination in the Third World are often kept harnessed and even bridled by the military acting in this adjudicatory role. The military acts to insure a partnership between party and bureaucracy, so that if the conversion from colonial rule to independence is not particularly constitutional, it is at least orderly. Involvement by the military in the political system and in the bureaucratic system can take place by promoting developmental programs or by consolidating or stabilizing popular revolution. But, whatever the mechanism, the fact of its involvement in the maintenance of the social structure is clear.

The strength of the military is often in inverse proportion to the absence of strength on the part of the middle or working classes. This is particularly true in the new nations. When the popular classes are too ineffectual in changing obviously bankrupt social relations, the elite of the armed forces perceive themselves as capable of filling a social vacuum. The army, by virtue of its national liberation character, may not have the capacity to crush opposition, but it may prevent any attempts to restore the old regime. It is remarkable how few counterrevolutionary or restorationist regimes have been successful in the Third World despite the large number of *coups d'état*. For although there has been an enormous amount of turmoil and transformation within the single party states during the postcolonial era, these have not led either to the restoration of colonial rule anywhere in the Third World, or to a particularly more advanced stage of social revolution once the nationalist phase has been achieved. However, in such multiparty states as the Congo, where there are no fewer than two hundred political parties and theree different military directorates, there is far more instability than in the one-party political-military condition. Many leaders who were in charge when independence was attained in Africa remained heads of state or of the party a decade and even two decades later. Among these are Nyerere, Toure, Kenyatta, Senghor and Banda. Even when this original leadership collapsed, as in Algeria and Ghana, the new leaders were chosen from an alternative faction of the original revolutionary group —usually from the military faction of that early leadership. This indicates how ably strains in the social system are managed by the present power hierarchy.

The military in the new nations can oftentimes exercise international power. The Egyptian and the Algerian military see themselves very much concerned with problems of the unification of all North Africa, including the sporadic support of Palestinian Arabs urging the reconquest of Israel. The same kind of regional pattern is to be found with Indonesia in Southeast Asia, where it too hopes to function as a homogenizing force in the whole of the area, especially in the Malaysian peninsula. But thus far, the international role is more regional than truly worldwide. The internal role predominates.

Nevertheless, the search for regional, if not international roles cannot simply be dismissed as artificial. The annual regional meetings within the Third World provide a show of force no less than a show of political principles. The collective military might of the Third World determines its strength in relation to the First and Second Worlds. At the same time, the individual might of each nation within the Third World determines its position in relation to the other nations within that world. Even nations that are debtors before the International Monetary Fund may act as creditor nations within regional blocs. Thus, a nation like Egypt may be a borrower of funds, but it is a distributor of arms to other Middle Eastern nations. As long as the First World and Second World were organized against each other for the purpose of making nuclear exchanges, the Third World could not be considered militarily significant. With the widespread acceptance of war as a game, the rise of insurgency and counterinsurgency, and the nuclear standoff created by First and Second World competition, the conventional military hardware of the Third World has come to function as a more significant variable in international geopolitics than it did a decade ago.

When there is a balance of nuclear terror between the First and Second Worlds, relatively powerless Third World countries can become influential. However, one must be cautious on this point, since in fact such a perfect balance rarely exists. What does exist is a modernized version of the sphere of influence doctrine that still leaves the Third World in a relatively powerless position, at least with respect to exercising a role in foreign affairs. For example, when the Soviet Union decided to crack down on the revisionist regime of Czechoslovakia in the late 1960s, or equally when the United States decided to break the back of radicalism in the Dominican Republic a few years earlier, they were able to do so with impunity in part as a consequence of the unwritten sphere of influence doctrine established between the United States and the Soviet Union during the 1960s. Conversely, the prestige of the Third World, at least as a homogeneous military unit, has been seriously undercut, for example, by the failure of the Organization of African Unity (OAU) to be able to resolve civil war in Nigeria, white rule in Rhodesia, or the continued colonial domination of Mozambique. The same situation obtains with other regional Third World clusters, such as the Organization of American States (OAS), which was virtually powerless during the Dominican crisis to affect United States foreign policy. In other words, when there is, in fact, a delicate equilibrium between the First and Second Worlds, then the military of the Third World can be important. Otherwise, it tends to be far less significant than, in fact, it would like to become (Haas, 1969, pp. 151–158).

The character of the military of the Third World is often shaped, symbolically at least, by the military power or powers that trained or occupied the territory during the colonial period. Thus, in Indonesia, one finds a Japanese and Dutch combination; in Egypt, there are English and German types of models; in many parts of Latin America, there is a combination of French and German as well as United States prototypes. In other words, the actual organizational charts which describe these military organizations are based upon prototypes brought over from the former imperial power.

Even though the military in the Third World may think of itself as distinct and distinctively nationalistic, it still carries on the traditions of the old colonial armies. This is not just a cultural inheritance but a consequence of the complex nature of modern warfare, especially the complicated technology of advanced combat and the problem of training human forces so that they become a significant military asset. Thus, there is rising tension between the need for autonomy and the necessity for seeking out models and materials from the advanced blocs. One way Third World nations attempt to overcome this contradiction is by the process of "spin-off," by relying on one major power for technological and military hardware and on another for its military organization charts. Many African nations, for example, Ghana, Nigeria, and Sierra Leone, which exhibited total military dependence on the British style at the outset of the independence period, have moved to counteract this by arrangements with advanced countries as disparate as West Germany, France, and Czechoslovakia. At this point, a three-person rather than a two-person game model comes into its own. The First and Second Worlds increasingly must respond to Third World pressures, and not just the other way around. For example, Great Britain must provide arms to Nigeria in order to forestall the Soviet Union in the area, and France must refuse to deliver aircraft to Israel in order to maintain Arab support and also Arab oil supplies. However, as in the three-person game model itself, the outcomes can often be frighteningly unpredictable, and, as in the case of the Nigerian civil war or in the Indian-Pakistan war, gruesome (Horowitz, 1972).

Another reason for the diversification of military programming derives from local factors. Thus, the strength of Ethiopia compels Somalia to accept Russian military missions. Pressure from China leads India to diversify its forces by using both Soviet and U.S. tactical and strategic weapons. A limiting factor is that the debtor nation faces the same problems in military terms that it does in economic terms. The credit line is not irrevocable. This serves to place an economic impediment and limit to the problem of political management in the Third World. Military assistance becomes a focal point in maintaining exclusive relations with the former imperial power. For example, the fact that France remains the exclusive distributor of military hardware to most of its former African colonies can undermine the purpose of independence as much as it is undermined by exclusive trade arrangements (Gutteridge, 1965, pp. 117–129).

There is less apparent ambiguity in the military's role on the international level than in its role as an internal agency. Military organizations directly influence social structure by their allocation and distribution of power. The military decides how much violence should be used in any internal situation. Not only is the military reluctant to compete with civilian authority, but also positive factors contribute to this situation. First, institutions subject to comparison, such as an army, are tested against other armies. The army can never be wholly judged in terms of maintaining internal security. The military thrust cannot completely avoid international considerations. Second, because of the long-range aspect of foreign affairs, armed forces are immune to pragmatic tests of economic efficiency. They are not subject to the pressures of private enterprise or to the rules of business and investment. They can function as a planning agency even within a "free enterprise" social order. Third, an armed force generally has a style of its own. It is not subject to or limited by ordinary standards of behavior or legal canons (Pye, 1959, pp. 12–13).

These distinctive features also have negative by-products. The role of the army as an international agency now requires a highly professional group of men, capable of making and rendering decisions on strategic issues, whereas an armed force concerned with internal security requires a much more politicalized orientation in which considerations of bureaucratic efficiency or separation may be secondary. Hence, the multiplicity of roles for military establishments in the Third World may involve structural incompatibilities. As Andrezejewski (1954, pp. 83–84) indicates, "Modern military technique produced two contrary effects. On the one hand, it strengthened the centripetal forces by making subjugation of distinct regions easier; but on the other hand, it fostered a disintegration of multi-nation empires, because universal conscript became an unavoidable condition of military strength, and armies raised in this way were of little value unless permeated by patriotism."

DEMOCRACY AND DEVELOPMENT

A continuing source of concern for those working in the area of comparative international development is the ever-widening disparity between political democracy and economic development. This disparity has been dealt with usually in what might be termed a "necessitarian" framework by scholars like Heilbroner (1963) who assert that a choice has to be made between political democracy and economic development. In point of fact, what is really being claimed is that no choice exists at all. Economic growth is a necessity, whereas political mobilization is declared to be a luxury. The mark of sovereignty, the mark of growth is, in fact, developmental, and therefore, is said to offer no real volition and no viable option.

On the other hand, there are economists and sociologists like Hoselitz (1960) and Moore (1967) who have taken what might be called a "libertarian" point of view. They claim that the disparity between democracy and development is real enough but that the costs of development remain uniformly too high in the developing regions; and therefore, it is more important to preserve and enhance democracy than any irrational assumptions that development is either a singular mark of sovereignty of the necessary road to economic development. Underlying such thinking is a political determinism no less dogmatic, albeit far neater to advocate them the economic determinism under attack.

By now this argument of the 1960s has a somewhat arid ring. The assumptions are either that development is necessary and we can do nothing about the costs involved, or that democracy is a categorical imperative and we must curb whatever developmental propensities we have to preserve this supreme good. Rather than penetrate the debate at this level, since the premises are either well known or well worn by this time, we should perhaps turn the matter around and inquire what has, in fact, been the relationship between political democracy and social and economic development over the past decade; and what are the dynamics in this Third World network of interrelationships?

The first observation that has to be made is that the process of comparative development includes a wide and real disparity between democracy and development. There exists a relatively high congruence between coercion and even terrorism and development, and a far lower congruence between consensus and development. In part, our problem is that middle-class spokesmen of the Western World have often tended to identify a model of consensus with a model of democracy, and both become systematically linked to what has taken place in North America and western Europe in the last 150 to 200 years: that is, a model of congruence in which political democracy and economic growth move toward the future in common unison. The very phrase "political economy of growth" gives substance to this "bourgeois" model of development. When faced with the necessity of playing a role in the Third World and performing certain activities economically, politically, and socially in terms of the inherited model, what is retained in the rhetoric no longer can be sustained in performance. What one is left with, and why it has been difficult to confront so much theorizing on development, is a democratic model at the rhetorical level that is different from the capitalist model at the functional level. Further, there is a strong propensity, once this ambiguous model is accepted, to avoid coming to grips with the role of high coercion in achieving high development.

If we examine the available data, and here I shall restrict myself to the nonsocialist sector, in part, because there is a problem of data reliability, and also, because socialist systems have their own peculiar dynamic in relation to development and democracy, which requires a different set of parameters to explain relationships. Further, since there is a bias already established which links socialist systems to a high degree of political coercion, it is instructive to see how capitalist systems stand up to such coercive strains. Developmentalists are already prone to employ a Stalinist model as the basic type of socialist option. Thus, there is no problem in conceptualizing the relationship between coercion and development as a natural one when it comes to the socialist sector. However, when we turn systems around and look at the Western or capitalist sector of the developmental orbit, which reveals an absence of the same kind of coercive model, there are great problems in conceptualizing Third World tendencies.

When the word *democracy* is herein referred to it will be defined in terms of: (1) multiparty operations (2) under civilian regimes. Those two variables are key. There is no point in cluttering matters up with rhetorical theorizing about nice people who do good deeds. Simply put, democracy refers to multiparty control of politics on one hand, and civilian bureaucratic administrative control on the other. This definition is bare-boned and obviously subject to refinement. However, when talking about a military leadership or a military regime, we can be equally simple (hopefully not simple-minded). Military government ranges from outright rule of the armed forces without any civilian participation to co-participation by civilians under military domination and control. It will usually signify a single party structure, rather than a multiparty structure in the legal-superstructural aspects of political life.

The data herein examined is drawn from reports issued by the Organization for Economic Cooperation and Development (Martin, 1969). It concerns growth rates of the total and per capita GNP output between 1960 and 1967 on average per annum; and per capita GNP in 1968 for selected developing countries. The information, although provided randomly, does break down into three large clusters. (1) There are those countries that are single party, under military rule, that have high developmental outputs and a high GNP rate over the decade. (2) There are, at the opposite end of the spectrum, those countries that are democratic (or relatively democratic) and have low GNP levels. (3) There is a clustering in the middle of approximately twenty nations that do not reveal any consistent pattern in terms of problems of conflict and consensus in development. It is not that they violate any model construction, but that they remain undecided—significantly uncommitted at economic levels and in political techniques for generating socioeconomic change.

MILITARISM AND DEVELOPMENT

Let me outline three national clusterings and see what the results are at the factual level. Such material is a useful place to start in this most dismal science called development (Martin, 1969, pp. 5–12).

In the high developmental, high militarization cluster, there are the following nations: Israel, Libya, Spain, Greece, Panama, Nicaragua, Iraq, Iran, Taiwan, the Ivory Coast, Jordan, Bolivia, Thailand and South Korea. Even a surface inspection indicates that this is hardly a line-up of democratic states. Let us directly examine the GNP figures, so that some sense of the extent of the aforementioned correlation can be gauged. On an annual percent increase over the decade, the percentile figures are as follows: Israel, 7.6; Libya, 19.2 (there are some special circumstances related to oil deposits in Libya, but, nonetheless, the figure is impressive); Spain, 5.9 (an interesting example because it is a long-militarized European mainland country); Greece, 7.5 (with no slow-up in sight under its present military regime); Nicaragua, 7.5 (one of the most "backward" countries in Latin America from a "democratic" point of view); Iraq, 6.9; Iran, 7.9; Taiwan, 10.0 (a growth figure which even the Soviets have recently marveled at); Ivory Coast, 7.5 (by all odds, one of the most conservative regimes in Africa and boasting the highest growth rate on the continent in the sub-Sahara region); Jordan, 8.8; Bolivia, 4.9 (a long way from the old socialist days of high foreign subvention); Thailand, 7.1; South Korea, 7.6. This is a most interesting line-up. One would have to say that those with democratic proclivities and propensities must face the fact that high development correlates well with high authoritarianism. Whether this is because authoritarianism quickens production, limits consumption, or frustrates redistribution is not at issue. The potential for growth under militarism remains an ineluctable fact.

Let us turn to the other end of the spectrum. These are relatively low GNP units: Venezuela, Argentina, Uruguay, Honduras, Ghana, Guatemala, Brazil, Dominican Republic, Senegal, Ecuador, Tunisia, Paraguay, Morocco, Ceylon, Kenya, Nigeria, Sudan, Uganda, India, Tanzania. Within a Third World context and without gilding the lily, and admitting that there are exceptions in this list like Paraguay, this second cluster in the main represents a far less militarized group of nations than the first list presented. It is instructive to list their GNP per capital annual percent increase: Venezuela, 1.0; Argentina, 1.2; Uruguay, —1.0 (which is one of the most democratic, one of the most liberal countries in South America); Honduras, 1.8; Columbia, 1.2; Ghana, which exhibits no percentile change over time in the whole decade; Guatemala, 1.9; Brazil, 1.2 (increasing, however, under military rule since 1964); Dominican Republic, —0.7; Senegal, 1.2; Ecuador, 1.1; Tunisia, 1.5; Paraguay, 1.0; Morocco, 0.3; The Philippines, 1.0; Ceylon, 1.3; Kenya, 0.3; Nigeria, 1.6; Sudan, 1.2; Uganda, 1.2; India, 1.5; Tanzania, 1.2. The data plainly yields that the low rate of development intersects with the nonmilitary character of political mobilization in this second group of nations. Low militarization and low development are only slightly less isomorphic than high militarization and high development.

There is a most important middle group of nations not subject to this correlation coefficient. They do not share the same series of extensive polarities in GNP that vary in opposite directions in a perfectly consistent linear fashion. Further, they exhibit different kinds of transitory patterns of political systems. Chile, for example, has 2.4; Jamaica, 2.1; Mexico, 2.8; Gabon, 3.2; Costa Rica, 2.4.; Peru, 3.2; Turkey, 2.7.; Malaysia, 2.5; Salvador, 2.7; Egypt, 2.1; Pakistan, 3.1; Ethiopia, 2.7. Many of those nations have relatively stable GNP figures over time and do not easily fit the description of being depressed or accelerated in GNP rates. They are also the most experimental politically—at least during the 1960s. Certainly, experimentation (both by design and accident) characterize countries like Pakistan, Egypt, Costa Rica and Chile. It is not entirely clear what this middle cluster of nations represents, or whether these trends are politically significant. Yet, they do represent a separate tertiary group and should be seen apart from the other two clusters of nations.

The critical level of GNP seems to be where levels of growth are under 2 percent, and where there is high population growth rate which more or less offsets the GNP. Under such circumstances, it is extremely difficult to achieve basic social services for a population, or maintain social equilibrium. For example, in India, if there is a 1.5 level of growth of GNP and a 2.4 level of population growth per annum, there is an actual decline in real growth rate. This is how economists usually deal with the measurement of development. It may by faulty reasoning to accept *ex cathedra* this economic variable as exclusive; yet this measure is so widely used that the GNP provides a good starting point in our evaluation.

The correlations at the lower end of the model are not as good as at the upper end. Statistically, it is necessary to point out that militarized societies like Argentina and Brazil are not doing all that well economically. However, Latin America has a kind of "benign" militarism; a genteel quality that comes with the normalization of political illegitimacy. Thus, Latin American military regimes, in contrast to their African and Asian counterparts, have many exceptional features that account for why the fit of the model is better at the upper end of the GNP than at the lower end.

Before interpreting such information further, the possibility that many nations clustering in the middle also seem to be the carriers of such experimental political forms as single-party socialism, communal living, socialized medicine and the like. The "ambiguous" nations also reveal an impressive movement toward some kind of democratic socialism that somehow eludes electoral definitions. In other words, the experimental forms seemed to be clustered in that middle grouping, whereas the nonexperimental nations tend to be polarized, just as the GNP itself is polarized.

The most important single conclusion is that the political structure of coercion is a far more decisive factor in explaining GNP than the economic character of production in any Third World system per se. Without becoming involved in a model of military determinism, the amount of explained variance that the military factor yields *vis à vis* the economic factor is much higher than the classical literature allows for. If we had comparable data for the socialist countries, and if we were to do an analysis of the Soviet Union over time, then we would see that there is a functional correlation between the coercive mechanisms that a state can bring to bear on its citizenry and the ability to produce high economic development, however development be defined, and ignoring the special problems involved in definitions based upon the GNP. For example, one problem in GNP is the development of a cost-accounting mechanism whereby education is evaluated only by cost factors in input rather than output, whereas in goods and commodities you tend to have a profit margin built into the GNP figure. But such variations are true across the board; therefore, special problems involved in using the GNP formula are cancelled out in the larger picture. But the main point is that the element of coercion is itself directly linked to the character of military domination, while the specific form of the economy is less important than that relationship between military coercion and economic development.

Those critics in the West who celebrate progress as if it were only a matter of GNP cannot then turn around and inquire about the "quality of life" elsewhere (Hunt, 1966, pp. 134–156). Developmentalists cannot demand of foreign societies what they are unwilling to expect from their own society. Too many theorists of modernization ask questions of the quality of life of countries that themselves ask questions about the quality of life. The military is the one sector, in most parts of the Third World, that is not absorbed in consumerism and commodity fetishism. The military is not a *modernizing* sector, but rather a developmental sector. Insofar as the military is autonomous, its concern is nation building: highway construction, national communication networks, and so forth. It creates goals that are not based on the going norms of commodities that characterize the urban sectors of most parts of the developing regions. The functional value of this model is that the linkage between the military and the economy is unique. The military is the sector that dampens consumerism and modernization and promotes, instead, forms of developmentalism that may move toward heavy industry and even heavy agriculture. This is a critical decision in nearly every part of the Third World. Because the military most often will make its decision on behalf of industrialism rather than modernism, it generates considerable support among nationalists and revolutionists alike. This is a big factor in explaining the continuing strength of the military in the Third World.

The data clear up a number of points. They help explain why many regimes in the Third World seem to have such a murky formula for their own economy or polity. For example, despite the brilliance of Julius Nyerere (1968, pp. 9–32) it is exceedingly difficult to determine the political economy of Tanzania. One reason for this is that there is a powerful military apparatus in nearly every expanding nation of the Third World. And this military structure, if it does not share in national rule directly, is directly plugged into the nation as an adjudicating voice between the political revolutionary element and the bureaucratic cadre.

To appreciate the role of the military in developing nations, we must go beyond the kind of economic definitions that have been employed either in Western Europe or in the United States. The murkiness of the Third World at the level of economics is, in fact, a function of the lack of clearly defined class boundaries and class formations. A critical factor is not so much social structure as social process. There is stability over time in these regimes. The political regime, the civilianized political regime, tends to be much less stable than the military regime. This is slightly obscured by the fact that in many of these nations there are *coups* within the *coup*—that is, *inner coups* within the military structure that function to de-legitimize civilian rule altogether. But these processes do not obscure the main fact that the military character and the military definition are not altered. For this reason, the relationship between military determinism and high economic growth tends to be stable over time; precisely to the degree that civilian mechanisms are found wanting.

Cutright and Wiley (1969–70) came to this conclusion through an entirely circuitous and different route. They examined a mass of information on health, welfare, and security and found that the contents of the national political system usually become stabilized at that point in time when basic socioeconomic needs are satisfied. Further, there is no mass mobilization beyond such a point in time. If socioeconomic needs are satisfied within a socialist regime, then the Soviet system is stabilized. If such social needs are satisfied during a capitalist regime, then the capitalist system becomes permanent. If they are satisfied during an outright military dictatorship, then outright military dictatorship becomes normative and durable. In other words, the satisfaction of basic social services and economic wants is a critical factor beyond which masses do not carry on active political struggle. This quantitative support for the Hobbesian thesis on social order in the Leviathan has not been lost on the leadership of Third World nations, who continue to see the military as a stabilizing factor in economic development.

POLITICAL STABILITY
AND DEVELOPMENT

If this foregoing analysis is correct, and if the military is able to solve these outstanding problems at the level of the GNP, we should be able to predict its continued stability. Since basic social services will be resolved at the particular level of military rule, political struggles will cease to assume a revolutionary character in much of the Third World. In point of fact, the character of socialist politics does not determine the strength of political behavior, but rather the other way around. The critical point in the Soviet regime comes at a time of Stalinist consolidation. During the 1930s, the Soviet regime achieved internal stability. The contours of Socialism in Russia were thus fixed, some might say atrophied, at this specific historical juncture. True, certain adjustments have had to be made, certain safety valves have had to be opened to prevent friction or crisis. The Soviet Union has exhibited a move from totalitarianism to authoritarianism. However, basically the political organization is set and defined. There are no opposition movements in the Soviet Union, since there are no mass movements at the level of social discontent.

Similarly, in the United States, the point of resolution was when the political democracy became operational. Therefore, it continues to be relatively operational two hundred years later, even though great pressures have been brought to bear on the federalist system in recent times. Many Third World areas are stabilized at that point when military intervention occurs.

When the initial revolutionary leadership vanishes (or is displaced) and when the bureaucracy and the polity are both bridled and yet oriented toward common tasks, at that point the military becomes powerful. This is also the moment when economic growth charts start rocketing upward. Therefore, it is no accident that this is also a moment at which fervor for political experimentation declines. What we are confronted with is not simply transitional social forms, but permanent social forms.

The trouble with most general theories of development is that they postulate conditions in the Third World as transitional when they fail to coincide with preconceived models. We are told, in effect, that military regimes in the Third World are a necessary transition of "political economy" (Ilchman and Uphoff, 1969, pp. 3–48). Socialist doctrines of development often employ the same teleological model of politics for explaining away uncomfortable situations. Marxists declare that everything is in transition until achieving the height of socialism. Everything else is either an aberration, deviation or a transition. The difficulty with teleological explanations is that they work from the future back to the present, instead of taking seriously the present Third World social structures and political systems.

From an empirical perspective, social science determines what is meant by stability over time in terms of survival rates. Therefore, on the basis of this kind of measurement, the kind of network that exists in the Third World is, in point of fact, stable. What we are dealing with in many Third World clusterings are not permutations, or the grafting on of parts of other social systems. Third World systems are not transitional or derivational. They have worked out a modality of their own. Let us proceed one step further in the characterization of militarism and modernism. Going over the basic data presented, we can observe that what has happened is that the Third World, on the whole, and in particular those nations that exhibit a pattern of high economic growth during military rule, have accepted a Leninist theory of the state, while at the same time having rejected a Marxist theory of economics. That is to say, they accept the need for political coercion as a central feature of Third World existence, but at the same time deny socialist principles of economic organization.

The military state model is invariably a one-party model. Interparty struggle and interparty discipline vanishes. The party apparatus becomes cloudy as to its gubernatorial, bureaucratic and even political functions. The Leninist model is decisively emulated. The party serves the nation, but with a new dimension: The party also serves the military. The traditional Leninist model has the military politicized to the point of serving the ruling party. In the Third World variation, the political elites become militarized to the point of serving the ruling junta. And this role reversal of military and political groups is a decisive characteristic of the Third World today.

The economic consequences of this sort of Third World neo-Leninism is an acceptance of some kind of market economy based on a neocapitalist model. This process might be called: one step forward, and two steps backward. Any series of national advertisements will point out the low-wages, obedient-worker syndrome of many new nations. The model being sold to overseas investors by Third World rulers is, in large measure (whatever the rhetoric socialism may dictate), a model built on production for the market, private consumption, private profit, and a network that in some sense encourages the development of differential class patterns within Third World nations. But to gain such capitalist ends, what seemingly is rejected is the political participatory and congressional model common in northern and western Europe and the United States. There is no reason why this sort of system is transitional. On the contrary, given the conditions and background of underdevelopment, the kind of revolution made, the historical time of these revolutions and the rivalry between contending power blocs, this neo-Leninist polity, linked as it is to a neocapitalist economy, is a highly efficacious, functional and exacting model of the way most societies in the Third World have evolved in terms of political economy.

It might well be that with a greater amount of accurate data, this theory of the militarization of modernization will require modification, or even abandonment. However, the *prima facie* evidence would seem to indicate otherwise. More countries in the Third World have taken a more sharply military turn than anyone had a right to predict on the basis of prerevolutionary ideology or postrevolutionary democratic fervor. Therefore, the overwhelming trend toward militarism (either of a left wing or right wing variety) must itself be considered a primary starting point in the study of the Third World as it is, rather than how analysts might want it to become.

This is not a matter of either celebrating or criticizing the good society, or how Third World nations have fallen short of their own ideals. Few of us are entirely happy with any available system of society. Being critical of systems of society is a professional and occupational hazard. It is, however, not something that one would simply use as a proof that the system is unworkable. Indeed, if anything is revealed by the foregoing analysis, it is that the Third World has evolved a highly stable social system, a model of development without tears that forcefully draws our attention to the possibility that the Third World, far from disappearing, far from being transitional, far from being buffeted about, is becoming stronger, more resilient, and more adaptive over time. The widespread formula of military adjudication of political and bureaucratic strains within the emerging society is an efficacious model for getting the kind of mobilization out of "backward" populations that at least makes possible real economic development. It might well be that the strains in this military stage of development become too great, and the resolution itself too costly, to sustain real socioeconomic stability. However, at that point in the future, the Hobbesian laws of struggle against an unworkable state will once more appear and we shall know the realities of the situation by the renewed cries of revolution: This time against internal militarists rather than external colonialists.

REFERENCES

Andrezejewski, S. (1954) *Military Organization and Society.* London: Routledge & Kegan Paul.

Avneri, S. (1970) "The Palestinians and Israel," *Commentary,* vol. 49 (June), pp. 31–44.

Bondurant, J. V. (1958) *Conquest of Violence.* Princeton, N.J.: Princeton University Press.

Chambers, W. N. (1963) *Political Parties in a New Nation.* New York: Oxford University Press.

Cutright, P., and J. A. Wiley (1969–70) "Modernization and Political Representation: 1927–1966." *Studies in Comparative International Development,* 5 (Winter), 23–44.

Erikson, E. H. (1969) *Gandhi's Truth: On the Origins of Militant Nonviolence.* New York: Norton.

Gutteridge, W. (1965) *Military Institutions and Power in the New States.* New York: Praeger.

Haas, E. B. (1969) *Tangle of Hopes: American Commitments and World Order.* Englewood Cliffs, N.J.: Prentice-Hall.

Halpern, M. (1963) *The Politics of Social Change in the Middle East and North Africa.* Princeton, N.J.: Princeton University Press.

Heilbroner, R. (1963) *The Great Ascent.* New York: Harper & Row.

Horowitz, I. L. (1957) *The Idea of War and Peace in Contemporary Philosophy.* New York: Paine-Whitman.

Horowitz, I. L. (1972) *Three Worlds of Development: The Theory and Practice of International Stratification.* New York and London: Oxford University Press.

Hoselitz, B. (1960) *Sociological Aspects of Economic Growth.* New York: Free Press.

Hunt, C. L. (1966) *Social Aspects of Economic Development.* New York: McGraw-Hill.

Ilchman, W. F., and N. T. Uphoff (1969) *The Political Economy of Change.* Berkeley: University of California Press.

Janowitz, M. (1964) *The Military in the Political Development of New Nations.* Chicago: University of Chicago Press.

Kirk, E. (1963) "The Rise of the Military in Society: and Government: Egypt," in S. N. Fisher, ed., *The Military and the Middle East.* Columbus: Ohio State University Press.

Kirk, M. (1964) *The Military in the Political Development of New Nations.* Chicago: University of Chicago Press.

La Palombara, J. (1963) *Bureaucracy and Political Development.* Princeton, N.J.: Princeton University Press.

Lipset, S. M. (1963) *The First New Nation: The United States in Historical and Comparative Perspective.* New York: Basic Books.

Martin, E. M. (1969) "Development Aid: Successes and Failures," *The OECD Observer,* no. 43 (December), pp. 5–12.

Meister, A. (1968) *East Africa: The Past in Chains, the Future in Pawn.* New York: Walker.

Ministry of Information and Broadcasting (1962) *India, 1962.* New Delhi; Government of India, Publications Division.

Ministry of Information and Broadcasting (1963) *India, 1963.* New Delhi: Government of India, Publications Division.

Moore, W. E. (1967) *Order and Change: Essays in Comparative Sociology.* New York: John Wiley.

Naess, A. (1965) *Gandhi and the Nuclear Age.* Totowa, N.J.: The Bedminster Press.

Nehru, J. (1957) *Speeches: 1949–1953.* New Delhi: Government of India, Ministry of Information and Broadcasting, Publications Division.

Nyerere, J. K. (1968) *Freedom and Socialism* [Uhuru na Ujamaa]. London and New York: Oxford University Press.

Perlmutter, A. (1967) "Egypt and the Myth of the New Middle Class," *Comparative Studies in Society and History,* vol. 19 (October), pp. 46–65.

Pye, L. (1959) *Armies in the Process of Political Modernization.* Cambridge, Mass.: M.I.T. Press.

Rustow, D. A. (1963) "The Military in Middle Eastern Society and Politics," in S. N. Fisher, ed., *The Military in the Middle East.* Columbus, Ohio: Ohio State University Press.

Vatikiotis, P. J. (1961) *The Egyptian Army in Politics.* Bloomington, Ind.: University of Indiana Press.

Werner, M. (1939) *The Military Strength of the Powers.* London: Gollancz; quoted from Klementi Voroshilov, *Fifteen Years of the Red Army.* Moscow, 1933.

CHAPTER 15

SOCIAL DEVIANCE AND POLITICAL MARGINALITY

THE WELFARE MODEL
OF SOCIAL PROBLEMS

The study of social deviance within American sociology has traditionally been based on a model that consigns delinquent behavior to the instruments of social welfare. This model has sought to liberalize the visible agencies of social control (the police, judiciary, and welfare agents) by converting them for punitive instruments into rehabilitative instruments. This underlying premise that punishment and rehabilitation are the only two possible responses to deviance yields the conventional tendency to evaluate deviant behavior in *therapeutic* rather than *political* terms (Nettler, 1958–59, pp. 203–212).

The rehabilitation model seeks a more human redefinition of the moral code as its long-range goal. Its short-range goal is to indicate the superordinate role that agencies of social control adopt in ascribing subordinate status to deviants. Coser (1965, p. 145) recognized this role conflict in the welfare orientation to poverty when he indicated that "in the very process of being helped and assisted, the poor are assigned to a special career that impairs their identity and becomes a stigma which marks their intercourse with others."

However serviceable this model has been in the past, and notwithstanding its use in resisting encroachments on the civil liberties of accused deviants, the social welfare model does not exhaust present options—either on logical or on pragmatic grounds. A relationship among equals is possible only in democratic politics, where conflicts are resolved by power rather than a priori considerations of ascribed status. Only in such politics can deviants attain the status of legitimate combatants in social conflict.

POLITICAL REQUISITES
OF SOCIAL PROBLEMS

In the traditional welfare model, deviant behavior is defined as a social problem. This definition implies several important assumptions about the nature of deviance. First, it takes for granted that deviance is a problem about which something should be done. Second, it assumes that deviance is a *public* problem, which means that social agencies have the right to intervene. Finally, deviance is treated as a social problem in contradistinction to a political issue. Thus, decisions concerning it are relegated to administrative policy rather than to the political arena. As a result, deviance is handled by experts instead of being debated by the very publics who are supposedly menaced.

These beliefs about the nature of deviance have scant empirical justification. They derive from no intrinsic characteristics of deviance. Rather, they are normative statements about how deviant behavior should be treated. Bernard (1958–59, pp. 212, 215) has shown a singular appreciation of this.

> Values are inherent in the very concept of social problems. The conditions that are viewed as social problems are evaluated by the decision-maker as bad, as requiring change or reform. Something must be done about them. The reason for coming to the conclusion may be humanitarian, utilitarian, or functional. In any case, a system of values is always implicit, and usually quite explicit.

In this framework, identifying the values of the decision-makers is crucial. As Becker indicates (1963, p. 7), if we take the above seriously, the selection of decision-makers who define deviance as a social problem is a *political* process, not just a value problem:

> The question of what the purpose or goal (function) of a group is, and, consequently, what things will help or hinder the achievement of that purpose, is very often a political question. Factions within the group disagree and maneuver to have their own definition of the group's function accepted. The function of the group or organization, then, is decided in political conflict, not given in the nature of the organization. If this is true, then it is likewise true that the questions of what rules are to be enforced,

what behavior regarded as deviant and what people labeled as outsiders must also be regarded as political.

The decision to treat deviance as a social problem is itself a political decision. It represents the political ability of one group of decision-makers to impose its value sentiments on decisions concerning deviance. The anomaly is that although the political decision has been to treat deviance as a nonpolitical problem, deviance persists as a political problem. A comprehensive analysis of deviance must include political factors by determining which decision-makers define deviance as a social problem, and indicating why they consider deviance a problem. Lemert (1951, p. 4) was almost alone among the sociologists of the past decade in contending that deviance does not pose an objectively serious problem:

> In studying the problem-defining reactions of a community, it can be shown that public consciousness of "problems" and aggregate moral reactions frequently center around forms of behavior which on closer analysis often prove to be of minor importance in the social system. Conversely, community members not infrequently ignore behavior which is a major disruptive influence on their lives. We are all too familiar with the way in which populations in various cities and states have been aroused to frenzied punitive action against sex offenders. Nevertheless, in these same areas the people as a whole often are indifferent toward crimes committed by businessmen or corporations—crimes which affect far more people and which may be far more serious over a period of time.

A CONFLICT MODEL OF DEVIANCE

Deviance is a conflict between at least two parties: superordinates who make and enforce rules, and subordinates whose behavior violates those rules. Lemert (1967, p. v) noted the implications of this conflict for understanding the sources of deviance: "Their common concern is with social control and its consequences for deviance. This is a large turn away from older sociology which tended to rest heavily upon the idea that deviance leads to social control. I have come to believe that the reverse idea, *i.e.,* social control leads to deviance, is equally tenable and the potentially richer premise for studying deviance in modern society."

The conflict model implies alternative formulations of deviance as a problem: the deviant behavior itself, and the actions of rule-makers to prevent such behavior. The political climate prescribes both the conflicts that will occur between deviants and nondeviants, and the rules by which such conflicts will be resolved. The struggle of groups for legitimation thus constitutes an integral part of deviant behavior.

Deviance has been studied by employing a consensus welfare model rather than a conflict model because, for the most part, decision making concerning deviance has been one-sided: The superordinate parties who regulate deviance have developed measures of control, while the subordinate parties, the deviants themselves, have not entered the political arena. The conflict, though existent, has remained hidden. As Becker (1967, pp. 240–241) correctly notes, this leads to a nonpolitical treatment of deviance. Becker has duly noted:

> It is a situation in which, while conflict and tension exist in the hierarchy, the conflict has not become openly political. The conflicting segments or ranks are not organized for conflict; no one attempts to alter the shape of the hierarchy. While subordinates may complain about the treatment they receive from those above them, they do not propose to move to a position of equality with them, or to reverse positions in the hierarchy. Thus, no one proposes that addicts should make and enforce laws for policemen, that patients should prescribe for doctors, or that adolescents should give orders to adults. We call this the *apolitical* case.

As the politicalization of deviance develops, this apolitical case will become atypical—the hidden conflict will become visible, and deviants can be expected to demand changes in the configuration of the social hierarchy.

Although there has been scattered intellectual opposition to asylums in the past, patients have never been organized to eliminate or radically alter mental hospitals; or addicts to legalize drug use; or criminals to abolish prisons. Synanon, a center formed by addicts to treat drug addiction, is a striking exception to this pattern. Staffed completely by former addicts, it has no professional therapists. Thus, it represents an insistence that deviants themselves are best able to define their own problems and deal with them. Ironically, while Synanon challenges both the right and competency of professional therapists to intervene in the lives of addicts, it has not discarded the value premises of an adjustment therapy. Nonetheless, as Yablonsky (1965, p. 368) indicates, this marks a departure from the conventional welfare model:

> Over the past fifty years, the treatment of social problems has been dropped into the professional lap and has been held onto tightly. The propaganda about the professional's exclusive right to treat social problems has reached its high mark. The professionals, the public, and even patients are firmly convinced that the only "bona fide" treatments and "cures" available come from "legitimate professionals" with the right set of degrees.

Even where deviant social movements have become powerful, they have avoided political participation as special interest groups. For instance, Synanon has acted politically only when new zoning codes threatened its very existence. The politicalization of deviance is occurring, as groups like homosexuals and drug addicts pioneer the development of organizational responses to harassment. A broad base for the legitimation of deviant behavior will increasingly be made.

The political questions inherent in a conflict model of deviance focus on the use of social control in society. What behavior is forbidden? How is this behavior controlled? At issue is a conflict between individual freedom and social restraint, with social disorder (anarchy) and authoritarian social control (Leviathan) as the polar expressions. The resolution of this conflict entails a political decision about how much social disorder will be tolerated at the expense of how much social control. This choice can not be confronted as long as deviance is relegated to the arena of administrative policy making. For example, public schools are perceived as a repressive institution by many black youths, yet there is no political option of refusing to attend or racially altering them. This problem is now being raised by Black Power advocates who demand indigenous control over schools in black ghettoes despite the citywide taxation network.

POLITICAL MARGINALITY AND SOCIAL DEVIANCE: AN OBSOLETE DISTINCTION

Conventional wisdom about deviance is reinforced by the highly formalistic vision of politics held by many social workers and sociological theorists. This view confines politics to the formal juridical aspects of social life, such as the electoral process, and to the maintenance of a party apparatus through procedural norms. In this view, only behavior within the electoral process is defined as political in character, thus excluding acts of social deviance from the area of legitimacy (Campbell et al., 1960; Key, 1961; Lipset, 1960; Lubell, 1952).

In its liberal form—the form most readily adopted by social pathologists—the majoritarian formulation of politics prevails. This is a framework limited to the political strategies available to majorities or to powerful minorities having access to elite groups (Mills, 1963, pp. 525–552). The strategies available to disenfranchised minorities are largely ignored, and thus the politics of deviance also goes unexamined. The behavior of rule makers and law enforcers is treated as a policy decision rather than as a political phenomenon, while a needlessly severe distinction is made between law and politics. Analyses of political reality at the level of electoral results help foster this limited conception of politics. Consequently, the shared inheritance of sociology has placed the study of deviant behavior at one end of the spectrum and the study of political behavior at the other.

Conventional nonpolitical responses on the part of sociology were possible largely because the political world itself has encouraged this kind of crisp differentiation between personal deviance and public dissent. Political deviance is a concept rarely invoked by politicians because the notion of politics itself implies the right of dissension. Lemert points out that this has not always been true for radical political deviants (Lemert, 1951, pp. 203–209). There is a history of punitive response to political deviants in this country, involving repression of anarchists, communists, socialists and labor organizers. This has spread at times to a persecution of liberal groups as well. What characterized the "McCarthy Era" was not the hunt for radicals, but rather a broadening of the definition of radicals to include all sorts of mild dissenters. Only on rare occasions has political deviance been defined as a major social problem requiring severe repression. Thus, with the possible exception of anarchists, communists and socialists (and sometimes even including these groups in the political spectrum normally defined as legitimate), there is no way of dealing with political life as a deviant area. The nature of American political pluralism itself promotes dissent, at least in the ideal version of the American political system. The onus of responsibility in the castigation of a political victim is upon the victimizer. Rights and guarantees are often marshaled on behalf of a widening of the political dialogue. Indeed, the definition of American democracy has often been in terms of minority supports rather than majority victories.

The area of deviance is not covered by the same set of norms governing minority political life. The source of responsibility for deviant behavior, whether it be drug addiction, homosexuality, alcoholism or prostitution, is not borne by the person making the charges, but rather is absorbed by the victims of such charges. The widespread recognition of the juridical shakiness of the deviant's position serves to privatize the deviant and embolden those who press for the legal prosecution of deviance. While the right to dissent politically is guaranteed (within certain limits), the right to dissent socially is almost totally denied those without high social status.

One simple test might be the perceived reactions toward political radicalism in contrast to social deviance. If a person is accused of being an anarchist, there may actually occur a certain "halo effect." Perhaps a charge of naïvete or ignorance will be made against the politically marginal man, but not a censorious response demanding nonpolitical behavior.

In the area of deviance, if there is a self-proclamation of drug addiction or alcoholism, the demand for therapeutic or punitive action follows very quickly. If one admits to being a drug addict, there is an attempt to remove the curse from everyday life by the incarceration of the "patient" into a total institution, so that at least the visibility of deviance is diminished.

The line between the social deviant and the political marginal is fading. It is rapidly becoming an obsolete distinction. As this happens, political dissent by deviant means will become subject to the types of repression that have been a traditional response to social deviance. This development compels social scientists to reconsider their definitions of the entire range of social phenomena—from deviance to politics. Wolfgang and Ferracuti have taken an important first step toward an interdisciplinary study of social violence (Wolfgang and Ferracuti, 1967, pp. 1–14).

For the social science, this implies a new connection between social problems and political action. The old division between the two can no longer be sustained. In terms of theory, the new conditions throw into doubt the entire history of political science as an examination of the electoral situation, and of social problems research as a study of personal welfare. If politics is amplified to incorporate all forms of pressure, whether by deviants or orthodox pressure groups, to change the established social order, and if sociology is redefined to include pressure by deviants to re-design the social system so that they can be accepted by the general society on their own terms, then there is a common fusion, a common drive, and a common necessity between sociology and political science, not only on the level of empirical facts, but also on the level of scientific interpretation.

Some sociologists have already adapted to this new situation. Cloward's work in organizing welfare recipients is a particularly striking effort, which is an outrageous idea to both the classical capitalist and socialist doctrines (Cloward and Elman, 1966, pp. 27–35). This marks the first time that a sociologist has been involved in organizing welfare recipients. This enlarge-ment of roles demonstrates that changes are occurring in what constitutes political life and social work.

There are several other important directions that applied sociologists might follow: drug addicts might be organized to alter laws concerning drug use, students might be organized to change the character of schools, and mental patients might be organized to change the way they are treated. In each of these cases, change would be initiated from below by members of subordinate marginal groups. This would be in sharp contrast to the conventional elitist pattern of politics, where decisions are made from above by members of the prevailing majority. This is the primary distinction between the existing political party style and the political outsider style that is currently emerging.

THE POLITICIZED SOCIAL DEVIANT

A serious dilemma for many deviant and marginal groups alike is their failure to perceive any main-line organizations (either overtly political or social) as providing the sort of universal legitimation that governed an earlier, more tranquil period in American history. All formal and informal organizations seems arrayed against the kind of deviant particularisms ex-pressed by freaks, Hell's Angels, or druggies. Thus, the subgroups, whether of deviant lower-class origins or marginal middle-class origins, begin to align themselves with each other and against the mainstream of American life per se. A new set of cultural heroes, dance forms, and art forms coalesce to define not just a classical generational revolt for the rage to live, but a particularistic expression of immediate personal liberation as a prelude to distant public egalitarianism.

The key demonstration effect that such particularistic responses may prove extremely effective, even if they involve small numbers, is the rise of guerrilla insurgency as a military style in the underdeveloped areas. If "colored people" can conduct protracted struggles in Asia and in Africa, why can't the same sorts of struggles be conducted from the rooftops of

Watts and Newark? Indeed, the expanding internationalization of the deviant and marginal groups can best be appreciated in cultural heroes such as Franz Fanon, Malcolm X, and others connected with the demimonde of the Black Power movement. The seeds of this were long ago raised in the works of Padmore and DuBois, who urged precisely such ideological linkages with revolutionary forces elsewhere in the world—particularly in Pan-Africanism. What was absent before was the mechanism for success. In the guerrilla style, this mechanism, this critical missing ingredient, was finally supplied—and the linkage made complete.

The area of black struggles is a particularly fertile source for reevaluating the relationship between deviance and politics. Originally, there was a clear distinction between vandalism for personal gain and acts of organization for political gain. When the political life of blacks was circumscribed by the NAACP, it was clear that political life entailed normative behavior within the formal civic culture. Similarly, it was clear that acts of personal deviance fell outside the realm of politics. Indeed, there was little contact between black deviants and participants in the civil rights protest.

The rise of civil disobedience as a mass strategy has blurred this distinction. Such disobedience entails personal deviance to attain political ends. Regardless of the political goals involved, it is a conscious violation of the law. The treatment of civil disobedience in the courts has therefore been marked by ambiguity. It is difficult to predict whether it will be treated as a political act of insurrection or a simple personal violation of the law. Many law enforcement officials see no distinction between civil disobedience and crime, and blame the ideology of lawbreaking inherent in civil disobedience for rising crime rates and the occurrence of race riots (Lieberson, 1966, pp. 371–378).

In turn, these officials may be responding to the large-scale denial by blacks of the traditional role of the police as keepers of social order. This can perhaps best be gauged not only directly, in the expressed attitudes of political leaders from governors down to sheriffs, but indirectly as well—that is, by the inability of local gendarmeries to cope with black mass rioting. The Watts riots of August 1965, were, in this connection, prototypical of the current breakdown in traditional forms of police legitimacy. In that riot, which lasted four days, caused 34 deaths and 1,032 injuries, and ended in 4,000 arrests being made, the key fact was the role of the National Guard in quelling the riot. The Los Angeles police were thoroughly unable to cope with a situation once it achieved paramilitary proportions. This lesson has clearly not been lost on black ghetto communities elsewhere in the United States.

Confining ourselves to the cluster of race riots which took place in June and July of 1967, we can see how Watts heralded a new stage in the relationship between deviance and politics. In the main riot areas of Chicago, Detroit, Cleveland, Cincinnati, Buffalo and Newark (we will disregard for present purposes the satellitic riots which took place in the smaller centers of Plainfield, Louisville, Hartford, Prattville, and Jackson) the following characteristics were prevalent in each community during the duration of the riot.

1. Each city requested and received National Guardsmen to restore social order. Correspondingly, in each city, the police proved ineffectual in coping with the riots once the shield of legitimation was removed.
2. In each city, there were deaths and serious injuries not only to the rioters but to the established police and invading guardsmen.
3. In each city, the riots lasted more than one day, the duration being from two to seven days, which indicates the guerrilla-like nature of the struggle.
4. In each case, the triggering mechanism for the riot was an altercation involving police officials (usually traffic patrolmen) and blacks accused of reckless driving, driving without a license, or driving under the influence of alcohol.
5. In each case, the major rioting took place during summer months, when the normal load of black male unemployed is swelled by students and teenage former students not yet relocated.
6. In each city, property damage was extensive, with the sort of sniper tactics and "scorched earth" policies usually associated with so-called wars of national liberation.
7. In each case, the major rioting seemed to lack official civil rights organization sponsorship; however, participation in the protests did not take place on an individual basis.

Table 15.1 gives some indication of the character and extent to which the conflict model dominates current black deviance marginality. The parallel with what Eckstein has termed internal violence (Eckstein, 1964; Black and Labes, 1967, pp. 666–670) and with what is more customarily referred to as guerrilla warfare (Horowitz, 1967) is clear.

TABLE 15.1 Major Negro Riots in Urban Ghettos, 1965–67

Date	Place	Casualties			National Guard[a]	Riot Duration (days)	Property Damages (thousands of dollars)
		Killed	Injured	Arrested			
8/65	Watts (Los Angeles)	35	1,000+	4,000+	14,000	5	$ 50,000+
6/67	Buffalo	0	68	182	500	4	100+
6/67	Cincinnati	1	50	300	1,100	2	2,000
7/67	Cleveland	4	55	275	n.d.[c]	5	4,000+
7/67	Chicago	2	100+	500+	4,200	4	n.a.[d]
7/67	Newark	24	1,150	1,600+	3,375	6	15,000+
7/67	Detroit	36	1,500+	2,665+	13,000[b]	5	500,000+

SOURCE: Compiled from *New York Times Index.*
[a] National Guard figures exclude city police.
[b] Includes 8,000 National Guard and 5,000 federal troops.
[c] n.d. = no data.   [d] n.a. = not available.

What this amounts to is a military rather than a civil definition of the situation in racial ghettos. The essential deterrent was the raw fire power of the combatants rather than the legitimated authority of the police uniform. Under such circumstances, the established welfare distinction between juvenile delinquency and guerrilla warfare means very little.

The rapidly rising crime rates indicate a further ambiguity in the traditional formulation of social deviance. It is of decreasing *sociological* importance whether "crime" is perceived as an act of politics or deviance. The consequences are the same in either case: Cities are becoming increasingly unsafe for whites, and white-owned businesses are suffering mounting losses. Whether it is political insurgency or traditional crime, the consequences remain the same—a disruption in the legitimation system of American society.

THE DEVIANT POLITICAL MARGINAL

At the opposite pole—minoritarian politics—a similar set of ambiguities plagues those in search of precise boundary lines. An example is the behavioral pattern of the left wing. Among the radical youth of the 1930s certain characteristics clearly emerged: a relatively straitlaced "puritan" ethos concerning sexual mores; a clear priority of politics over personal life—what might be called the ascetic purification of self; and a concern for a relatively well-defined ideology, combined with the encouragement for all to participate in the life of the working classes. The radical Left of an earlier generation shared with the dominant cultural milieu a distinct, even an intense, disafiliation from deviant patterns. Indeed, the old Left pointed to social deviance as illustrative of the moral degeneration of bourgeois society. The need for social revolution came about precisely because the existing social order was considered incapable of controlling social deviance. Thus, the demands of the traditional Left with respect to social deviance were not very different from Establishment demands.

This contrasts markedly with the position of the New Left on conventional indicators of deviance. First, they exhibit substantial positive affect toward an extreme and libertarian ethos replacing puritanism. Second, there is an identification with deviant forms, stemming from a continued affiliation with the "beatnik" movement of the 1950s. There was a considerable absorption of the Beat generation of the 1950s into the activist generation of the 1960s. The ideology of the New Left, insofar as it has clear guidelines, is based on freedom from repression. It has both political and social components: freedom for the black from the effects of racial discrimination; freedom for the student from the constraints of university regulations; freedom for the young generation from the demands of their elders; and freedom of politically powerless groups from the growing authority of the centralized state. In this sense, Freud feeds the ideology of the New Left at least as much as Marx defined the ideology of the old Left.

The traditional notion of a noble affiliation of radical youth with the working class has already dissolved in favor of a highly positive response to deviant and marginal groups in American society. There is a relative unconcern for the traditional class formations engaged in the struggle for upward mobility. If there is a hero, it is the alienated man who understands what is wrong and seeks escape. Often, escape takes the form of social deviance, which is considered no worse than the forms of behavior traditionally defined as normative. The traditional hero has been supplanted by the antihero, who wins and attains heroic proportions by not getting involved in the political process. This antihero is defined by what he is against as much as by what he is for; he is for a world of his own, free from outside constraints, in which he is free to experiment and experience.

What this means operationally is that the line between left-wing political behavior and personal deviance has been largely obliterated. Nowhere has this been more obvious than in the student protest movement, where it is impossible to separate the deviant student subculture from the substantive demands of the student revolt. Spence (1965, p. 217) accurately describes the significance of this student movement at the University of California at Berkeley:

> This was the first successful student strike at a major university in the United States. But more important, this was the first significant white-collar rebellion of our time. These sons and daughters of the middle class demonstrated and walked picket lines, not behind the moral banner of the oppressed Negro, but on the basis of their own grievances against a system that had deprived them of their rights of responsibility and self-expression.

The student rebellion underlies a major thesis herein proposed, since it led not to organized political responses of a conventional variety, but rather to a celebration of deviance itself as the ultimate response to orthodox politics. Stopping "the operation of the machine," which for Mario Savio "becomes so odious, makes you so sick at heart that you can't take part; can't even tactically take part," led to only one conclusion: "The machine must be prevented from running at all" (Newfield, 1966, p. 27; Horowitz, 1965, pp. 15–18).

It is interesting that victory was not defined as taking over the operations of the machine, not the classical capture of organized political power, but rather in nonparticipation and in nonacceptance. Savio himself, as if in conscious defiance of Michels' "iron law of oligarchies" governing the performance of organizations, simply refused to participate in any leadership functions in the Berkeley postrebellion period. The definition of victory, then, is in the ability of marginal groups to disrupt the operations of political power either in its direct parliamentary form or in surrogate forms.

Among young members of the New Left, draft evasion has become an important form of deviance. The number of people who adopt the traditional political path by refusing to serve and going to jail as political prisoners is small compared with the number who adopt the deviant path, using mental illness, homosexuality, or drug addiction (whether these be real or feigned) to avoid serving. In effect, they are taking advantage of the prevailing established norms toward deviants. However, this path is made much more accessible with the merger of leftist politics and social deviance, since only politics can transform private desires into public principles.

An important social characteristic of the New Left is its self-definition as culturally *avant garde,* or conversely, not being left behind the times. This new definition of leftism is also a central definition of the deviant subculture. So it is that Berkeley and Watts became the symbols of the twin arms of radical politics: the university campus and the black ghetto. Even in terms of social psychological definitions of friends and foes, the line between the political Left and social deviance is now largely transcended. Thus, there is a deep distrust of formal politics and of the people who operate within the bureaucratic channels of the political apparatus. This definition of friends and foes is obvious at Berkeley, where many student feel that they cannot trust their elders.

The right-wing movement in America also illustrates this perspective. The old Right was characterized by extreme antipathy for any kind of promiscuous or overtly immoral behavior. The American Right viewed with alarm attacks upon law-enforcement officials. The old Right perceived itself conventionally as a paragon of law enforcement. This is the core around which the right wing has traditionally been established. But a phenomenon such as the Minutemen reveals a spin-off from law-abiding to direct-action approaches to politics. The Minutemen, for example, are encouraged to acquire possession of fully automatic weapons, even though many such weapons are forbidden to individuals by law. They are urged to join the National Rifle Association to become eligible for rifles and handguns at cost as well as free ammunition. The Minutemen *Handbook* contains lessons on such subjects as "Booby Traps," "Anti-Vehicular Mines," and "Incendiary Weapons Composition." The self-made saboteur is encouraged to improvise lethal weapons. Espionage and infiltration of established political groupings are also encouraged. A subunit called the Minuteman Intelligence Organization is in possession of a fairly sophisticated organization, not unlike those of paramilitary units (Turner, 1967, p. 69–76).

Breakaway segments of the New Right, like their opposite numbers in the New Left, are concerned with redefining the relationship of the person to the legal code in very loose terms. The appeals to youth are in terms of training in weaponry rather than in law. When confronted by the law, the Minutemen dissolved their public leadership and created a new underground leadership. This phenomenon could be an extreme situation in American life, precisely because so many armed forces veterans may be attracted to such a combination of politics and deviance. At the same time, similar military experiences may take a Left turn, as with disillusioned veterans returning from Vietnam. A situation is arising where the line between the deviant act of gun-toting in an undisciplined way for personal (or political) ends, and the use of "hardware" for the purpose of maintaining law and order, is largely dissolved. Political conflict may become marked by opposing marginal political groups confronting each other in armed conflict, with the legitimated state agencies of power the enemy of both.

THE POLITICS OF DEVIANT VIOLENCE

Attention should now be drawn to the growing Latinization of black riots and student revolts in the present period. This is done in terms of rough macroscopic data. Here we wish to underscore this point by taking closer note of the workings of the new style of subculture in America. The largest black gang in Chicago during the 1960s was the Blackstone Rangers. This quasi-political organization represented a clear example of the breakdown in the distinction between crime and marginal politics, as well as the course the politics of marginality is likely to follow. The Rangers acted as an autonomous group, in conflict with both local residents and politics. The gang entered into negotiations with the Chicago police, and reached a satisfactory (if temporary) settlement: They agreed to surrender their weapons and stop fighting other gangs if the police would drop certain charges against their leaders and disarm a rival gang. The negotiations thus served to "keep the peace," but only at the expense of enhancing the credibility of the gang networks.

Negotiation of this sort is a major strategy of international politics, although it has seldom been used to resolve conflicts involving marginal domestic groups. The negotiation process itself entails the recognition that marginal groups represent legitimate political interests. So far, the art of negotiation has not been adequately developed for dealing with such situations, just as it has not been adequately developed for dealing with unconventional international conflicts.

The problem posed by marginal groups like the Rangers is not yet viewed as a political problem to be solved by political strategies. When police violated the negotiated settlement, the Blackstone Rangers planned to file suit in the federal courts to prohibit a pattern of harassment. It is novel for such deviant groups to engage in political conflict with legitimate agencies like the police, but it does indicate a step beyond the "good bad boy" approach of social welfare.

There is a growing impulse to develop political means of resolving conflicts that involve marginal groups, as an alternative to the military means that have thus far prevailed. The Woodlawn Organization, composed of local residents, received a federal grant of $927,341 to work with gangs like the Rangers and the Disciples. The Chicago police raided the first meeting between the gang leaders and leaders of The Woodlawn Organization, demonstrating a conflict between advocates of a political solution and proponents of what amounts to a military solution to the gang problem (Evans and Novak, 1967). In the absence of acceptable political solutions, it is probable that increasing reliance upon domestic military solutions will be sought—just as the failure of political solutions internationally often leads to pressing for quick military solutions.

This trend toward marginal politics reflects a rejection of conventional political styles that have proven unsuited to the needs of marginal groups. In the past, the powerless had recourse to two choices for political action: legitimate means, to which they do not have sufficient access to be influential; or accessible but ineffective illegitimate means that bring little structural change. Marginal minorities are now searching for the development of political means that are both accessible and effective. It is probable that these new styles will be illegitimate rather than legitimate, and that the distinction between social deviance and political insurgency will be further reduced.

Race riots differ from both orthodox politics and personal delinquency. They offer some important insights into these new styles. Race riots have an ideological core, while many other forms of collective behavior do not. They are avowedly political, organized and purposeful. Typically, deviant acts such as theft, assault and homicide have none of these attributes. For these reasons, race riots may be closer to organized unconventional warfare than they are to conventional crime. Once perceived in this way, they constitute a powerful if latent political weapon.

At present, in most American cities a relatively small police force can effectively control the populace. But this is true only as long as police are accorded legitimacy. When conflicts are defined totally in terms of power and force rather than authority and legitimacy, as during race riots, the police cannot effectively maintain control. For this reason, riots constitute a major departure from established patterns of interaction between police and deviants. Deviants are not organized to battle police, and they have no ideology that labels police as enemies to be attacked and destroyed. Police have legitimacy as long as deviants avoid rather than attack them. However, police traditionally mount an organized collective effort against deviants, who typically respond only as unorganized individuals. The existing conflict is a one-sided war. The emergence of a bilateral conflict situation promises to be a major development in the link between politics and deviance. Race riots are the first indication of this change (Cray, 1967, p. 121).

This conflict can take several alternative forms: On a *minimax* scale, there could be de-escalation to the English system, in which both black militants (or deviants in general) and police would not carry arms; at the other end, there could be escalation to race riots, which are sporadic and constitute a relatively unorganized set of events. Beyond sporadic racial strife lies the possibility of sustained conventional war. This is most closely approximated in American history by the Indian Wars and the Civil War. Presently, unconventional warfare is coming into focus. The latter two possibilities indicate how social deviance could spill over into insurrection-ary politics, given both the peculiar racial division that exists in American society and the consistent exclusion of marginal groups from political and social legitimacy.

This marginal style of politics is being adopted by groups of all "extreme" ideological persuasions. Marginals of both the Left and Right fear the growing power of the centralized government, which they feel will be used to repress them, and are opposed to the consolidation of power by the majority. This commonality is demonstrated by the high amount of social interaction that occurs, in places like Greenwich Village and Berkeley, between politically opposed deviant groups. Even such political opposites as the Hell's Angels and the opponents of the Vietnam War shared a common social network in California. Their political enmity was balanced by their similar enjoyment of deviant social patterns (Thompson, 1966, pp. 231–257).

The clearest example of this movement toward violence, and one easily overlooked, is the reappearance of assassination as a political style, coupled with the inability to know whether "Left," "Right," or "Deviant" is spear-heading this style. It is almost impossible to say whether the assassination of John F. Kennedy, Malcolm X or Martin Luther King was a deviant act or a political act. No group took responsibility for the assassinations as overt political acts, and the assassins did not link the deaths to ideological demands. Without into account the breakdown in the distinction between politics and deviance, the meaningfulness of both sociology and political science is seriously compromised.

MARGINAL SECTORS
AND DEVIANT VALUES

Applied social science must take account of this new view of marginality in American life. If any group has emerged as the human carrier of the breakdown between political and private deviance, it has been the lum-penproletariat, or the nonworking class. This group has replaced the estab-lished working and middle classes as the deciding political force in America. Lang and Lang (1961, p. 18) point out in their discussion of collective dynamics that this is precisely the condition that breeds collective deviance. Ordinarily the cleavages within a society are between clearly constituted social strata or between parties whose special interests seek recognition within a broader framework of order. When cleavages occur between con-stituted authority and those who do not accept it, or between those who feel unable to share in the established authority systems, we can refer to the condition as one of widespread and general alienation.

The army of marginally employed comprises a significant segment of *both* politically radical and socially deviant cultures. If in Western Europe the bureaucracy grew disproportionately to all other classes, the disproportionate rise of the marginally employed characterizes contemporary America. This group, rather than disappearing or, as Marx would have it, becoming a social scum to be wiped out by revolution, grows even larger. At a practical level, there is now a new and powerful intermediary class that performs vital roles in the authoritarian political system, while at the same time it sets the style for a new libertarian morality.

The boundaries of American politics reflect the growing affluence that typifies the American social structure. However, a significant minority of disaffected marginals exists in the midst of this affluence. It is becoming increasingly clear that these marginals threaten to destroy the fruits of general affluence, and, indeed, to disrupt the entire situation. Race riots are a more serious indicator of the inability of the political system to maintain an equilibrium despite the general affluence.

The overlap of deviance and marginality is well captured in a book on the Hell's Angels (Thompson, 1966). The Hell's Angels—with the Swastika, German helmet and Iron Cross as their main symbols—differ but slightly from the pseudo-Maoist organizations of the Left. Without wishing to equate Maoists with either Minutemen or Hell's Angels, it is clear that each of these groups is marginal and deviant with respect to established political norms. Further, it is even difficult to give conventional definitions to those holding a gun in one hand and a flower in the other.

> The Angels have given up hope that the world is going to change for them. They assume, on good evidence, that the people who run the social machinery have little use for outlaw motorcyclists, and they are reconciled to being losers. But instead of losing quietly, one by one, they have banded together with a mindless kind of loyalty and moved outside the framework, for good or ill. They may not have the answer; but at least they are still on their feet. It is safe to say that no Hell's Angel has ever heard of Joe Hill or would know a Wobbly from a bushmaster, but there is something very similar about their attitudes. The Industrial Workers of the World had serious blueprints for society, while the Hell's Angels mean only to defy the social machinery. There is no talk among the Angels of building a better world, yet their reactions to the world they live in are rooted in the same kind of anarchic, para-legal sense of conviction that brought the armed wrath of the Establishment down on the Wobblies. There is the same kind of suicidal loyalty, the same kind of in-group rituals and nicknames, and above all, the same feelings of constant warfare with an unjust world. (Thompson, 1966, pp. 265–266)

The policy response to this dilemma has been the Welfare State—an attempt to "cool out" the marginal underclass and minimize the potential danger it poses. It is an attempt to avoid the consequences of large-scale marginality without making any social structural changes. Schatzman and Strauss (1966, p. 12) contend that this welfare style deals with the problem by avoiding its political implications:

America pours its wealth into vast numbers of opportunity programs to achieve its goals and names almost any conceivable group, event, or thing a social problem if it can be seen as threatening the achievement of these goals. Hence its concern for the culturally deprived, the under-achievers, the school dropouts, the job displaced, the aged, the ill, the retarded, and the mentally disturbed. This concern goes beyond that of the nineteenth-century humanitarians who involved themselves with the underprivileged outgroups on moral grounds. Now all these aggregates are seen as special groups whose conditions are intolerable to society, if not actually threatening, in light of today's social and economic requirements.

This attempt to depoliticize a highly political problem has proved inadequate. The welfare solution has not erased the consequences of having a growing number of disaffected people in the midst of general affluence. Indeed, the very existence of affluence on so wide a scale creates demands that parallel those made by the "poor nations" on the "rich nations." Because of this, a political attempt to solve the problem is bound to emerge. If this attempt is not initiated from above within the legitimate political or electoral apparatus, it will be generated from below and probably take illegitimate paramilitary forms.

The implicit exchange system which formerly existed between the very poor and the very rich in American society was simple: "Don't bother us and we won't bother you." In exchange for the poor not disturbing the rich, the wealthy provided just enough money for the poor to live at Ricardian subsistence levels. This exchange has been the basis of American social work, and continues to define the boundaries of the welfare system. The rich have only vaguely appreciated the magnitude of the poor's potential power and their ability to disrupt the entire system. For their part, the poor only vaguely appreciate the power at the disposal of the rich, which accounts for the suicidal characteristics of many race riots.

This interchange system is now being threatened. The poor are gradually developing an appreciation of their own power, while at the same time they have a greater appreciation of the power held by the rich. For their part, the rich are becoming more aware of the power available to the poor, as seen in the generalized fear created by rising crime rates and race riots. In short, there is a greater polarization of conflict between the two classes.

The primary political problem of deviance can be framed as a Hobbesian dilemma. Hobbes sought the creation of the state as a solution to the problem of social disorder, in which individuals war with each other in pursuit of their individual interests. The dilemma is that the creation of the state creates a problem of social control. The solution to the problem of chaos, or the Anarch, is the Leviathan. But the Leviathan is the *totalitarian* state. Indeed, totalitarianism is the perfect solution to the problem of disorder. The dilemma for those who consider social problems obstacles to be overcome is that any true overcoming of social problems implies a perfect social system. And this entails several goals: first, the total institutionalization of all people; second, the thoroughgoing equilibrium between the parts of a system with respect to their functioning and the functioning of other sectors; and third, the elimination of social change as either a fact or value. Thus, the resolution of social problems from the point of view of the social system would signify the totalitarian resolution of social life.

The political problem posed by deviance is how to avoid social disorder while at the same time avoiding the problem of total social control. It is a dilemma precisely because of the impossibility of solving both problems simultaneously. Political decisions about deviance must reflect judgments about the relative dangers of these two problems, and must constitute a weighing process based on ethical no less than on empirical considerations.

Connections between deviance and politics take place most often when a society does not satisfactorily manage its affairs. For better or worse, a well-ordered society is one that can impose a distinction between responses to deviance and responses to marginality. Antecedents for the linkage of deviance and marginality exist in two "conflict societies." In the 1890s in Russia, the *Narodnik* movement was directly linked to the movement toward personal liberation. In Germany of the 1920s, the "underground" movement, aptly summed up by the Brecht theater, nihilism and amoralism, gave rise to both Nazi and Bolshevik political tendencies. The merger of the Beat generation and the radical student movements reveals this same pattern of connecting political revolution with demands for personal liberation.

These examples indicate how the fusion between deviant behavior and political processes is a prelude to radical change. If the fusion of politics and deviance is the herald of revolution, or at least indicates a high degree of disassociation and disorganization within the society, then radical changes in the structure of American social and political life are imminent.

What takes place in personal life has major political ramifications in contemporary society. Until now, American life has been resilient enough to forestall a crisis in treating marginality. This is a testimonial to the flexibility of the American system of political legitimation. But it might well be that the extent of deviance in the past was not sufficient to cause more than a ripple in the political system (Hopper, 1964, pp. 313–330). In the emerging system, with automation and cybernation creating greater dislocation and marginal employment, personal deviance may generate a distinct transformation in normal political functions; it marks the point at which the political system cannot cope with deviant expressions of discontent.

A political description of this condition begins with the inability of American society to resolve political problems that are important to *marginal* people. Almost one-third of the potential voting population does not vote and is therefore without even the most minimal political representation. The fact that these disenfranchised people have important problems in common that cannot be managed within existing arrangements creates a volatile situation (Schattschneider, 1960).

Political styles evolve that are now presently labeled as political behavior, much as race riots are not now generally considered as political behavior. These new styles are characterized, first, by a rejection of the legitimacy of the existing political system (the challenge to the rules by which the game is now played); second, by a rejection of compromise as a political style; and third, by a willingness to oppose established authority with illicit power in order to change not merely the rules but the game itself. Ends will attain a primacy over means, whereas a concern with the legitimacy of means has traditionally characterized American politics. Direct expressions of power might assume a more important role than legitimate authority in resolving important conflicts.

Political legitimacy is itself subject to change in order to meet the demands of a society in which social deviants and political marginals have become more, rather than less, important in determining the structure of American society.

REFERENCES

Becker, H. S. (1963) *The Outsiders.* New York: Free Press.

Becker, H. S. (1967) "Whose Side Are We On?" *Social Problems,* vol. 14, no. 3 (Winter), pp. 239–247.

Bernard J. (1958–59) "Social Problems as Problems of Decision," *Social Problems,* vol. 6, no. 3 (Winter), pp. 204–213.

Black, H., and M. J. Labes (1967) "Guerrilla Warfare: An Analogy to Police–Criminal Interaction," *American Journal of Orthopsychiatry,* vol. 37 (July), pp. 666–670.

Campbell, A., *et al.* (1960) *The American Voter.* New York: John Wiley.

Cloward, R. A., and R. M. Elman (1966) "Advocacy in the Ghetto," *trans*action, vol. 4 (December), pp. 27–35.

Coser, L. A. (1965) "The Sociology of Poverty," *Social Problems,* vol. 13, no. 2 (Fall), pp. 140–148.

Cray, E. (1967) *The Big Blue Line: Police Power vs. Human Rights.* New York: Coward-McCann.

Eckstein, H. (1964) *Internal War.* New York: Free Press.

Evans, R., and R. Novak (1967) "The Ghetto Gangs," *Herald Tribune* (International Edition), July 5.

Hopper, R. (1964) "Cybernation, Marginality, and Revolution," in I. L. Horowitz, ed., *The New Sociology.* New York: Oxford University Press.

Horowitz, I. L. (1965) "Radicalism and Contemporary American Society," *Liberation,* vol. 10 (May), 15–18.

Horowitz, I. L. (1967) "The Military Elite," in S. M. Lipset and A. Solari, eds. *Elites of Latin America.* New York: Oxford University Press.

Key, V. O., Jr. (1961) *Public Opinion and American Democracy.* New York: Knopf.

Lang, K., and G. E. Lang (1961) *Collective Dynamics.* New York: T. Y. Crowell.

Lemert, E. M. (1951) *Social Pathology.* New York: McGraw-Hill.

Lemert, E. M. (1967) *Human Deviance, Social Problems, and Social Control.* Englewood Cliffs, N.J.: Prentice-Hall.

Lieberson, S. (1966) "The Meaning of Race Riots." *Race,* vol. 7, no. 4, pp. 371–378.

Lipset, S. M. (1960) *Political Man.* Garden City, N.Y.: Doubleday.

Lubell, S. (1952) *The Future of American Politics.* New York: Harper & Row.

Mills, C. W. (1963) "The Professional Ideology of Social Pathologists," in I. L. Horowitz, ed., *Power, Politics and People.* New York: Oxford University Press.

Nettler, G. (1958–59) "Ideology and Welfare Policy," *Social Problems,* vol. 6 (Winter), pp. 203–212.

Newfield, J. (1966) *A Prophetic Minority.* New York: New American Library.

Schattschneider, E. E. (1960) *The Semi-Sovereign People.* New York: Holt, Rinehart & Winston.

Schatzman, L., and A. Strauss (1966) "A Sociology of Psychiatry," *Social Problems,* vol. 14, no. 1 (Summer), pp. 3–15.

Spence, L. D. (1965) "Berkeley: What It Demonstrates," in Michael V. Miller and Susan Gilmore, eds., *Revolution at Berkeley.* New York: Dell.

Thompson, H. S. (1966) *Hell's Angels: The Strange and Terrible Saga of the Outlaw Motorcycle Gangs.* New York: Random House.

Turner, W. W. (1967) "The Minutemen: The Spirit of '66," *Ramparts,* vol. 5 (January), pp. 69–76.

Wolfgang, M. E., and F. Ferracuti (1967) *The Subculture of Violence.* London and New York: Tavistock Publications.

Yablonsky, L. (1965) *The Tunnel Back: Synanon.* New York: Macmillan.

POLICIES

CHAPTER 16

SOCIAL SCIENCE
AND PUBLIC POLICY

Economics, sociology, psychology and the other social sciences have in recent times begun to play a new and problematic role with respect to national and international policy. The problem of social policy has become acute precisely to the extent to which social science has become exact. Legitimation of policy recommendations from social scientists emerges in this period, and not in previous periods, because of a demonstrable feasibility of putting social science and social theory into a framework of political action. Demand for operations research analysts, tactical data systems, war-gaming and simulation experts now rivals the search for basic engineering personnel. There is a paucity of exact information on how this transvaluation took place, due in part to the novelty of the situation and in part to the novelty of self-examination in the social sciences. What is at stake as a result of this newly acquired influence is not the feasibility of social science, but the credibility of social scientists.

Any discussion of villains and values, which inevitably is what the study of social science and public policy boils down to, involves two distinct areas. One is the empirics of present relationships between social science and public policy, its formation and its execution. The other is the question of what the relationship between social science and public policy should be. In connection with both what it is and what it should be, there are two variables. The first is the utilization of social science in the formation of public policy; the second involves the *relation* between social scientists and policy-makers. The fact that an ever-increasing number of individuals can with some legitimacy claim both scientific and policy-making status tends to blur the lines between these issues.

THREE STYLES
OF POLITICAL EXHORTATION

The first problem we come upon concerns the factual issues in the character of the relationship between social scientists and the policy-makers, that is, how this relationship differs in various social structures. What is the relationship of sociologists to society in a totalitarian state? Or in a welfare state? Or in a laissez faire state or system? What are the stresses and strains upon the social scientists and policy-makers in each type of national system?

Most social science disciplines require open-ended conditions for their functioning. Invariably and almost necessarily, established dogmas about society must be challenged. In this sense, sociology has been as much a problem for the socialist ideology as astronomy was for seventeenth-century Roman Catholicism. For example, do women go to church more often than men in the Soviet Union? From the point of view of Marxism, this is a ridiculous question. Men and women are equal by definition. Only historical antecedents are considered in accounting for differential sexual responses to religious practices in a socialist nation. Therefore, the sexual variable itself tends to be suppressed as a legitimate area of inquiry for Soviet researchers despite the noticeable difference in church attendance between male and female, not only in the Soviet Union but also in many countries displaying similar political structures and levels of industrialization.

This discrepancy between fact and theory leads to the conclusion that in a pure command structure the relationship of social science to public policy is not much of a problem because the social sciences, aside from their technical vocabularies, are suppressed. The ideology of science is harnessed to the ideology of the state. This is done by celebrating only the "pure" and the "natural" sciences. Applied social sciences may exist, but what does not exist is an analysis of the whole society. To the extent that meaningful data contradict the established order, the social sciences are suspect. Not accidentally, the more exaggerated the totalitarian system, the less available for public inspection is the social scientists' information. The degree to which the development of the social sciences is permitted within a nation operates as a twentieth-century index of freedom. And the extent to which the development of an independent social science is stifled provides a measure of political stagnation. Allowing myself an *ex cathedra* judgment, I do not think anyone can participate in social research and fail to see a high correlation between good social science and a good society.

The evidence provided by the Soviet Union on this score is illustrative. While the research and academic personnel in the U.S.S.R. engaged in the "arts, humanities and social sciences" continues to grow numerically— from 625,000 in 1956 to 740,000 in 1960—this represents a downward trend with respect to the physical and engineering sciences—from 27.9 to 24.0 percent. If this figure is broken down further, it is found that only 3.9 percent of the scientific personnel are engaged in what would in the West be called social sciences—and these are gathered in the fields of economics and planning (See De Witt, 1955; 1965, pp. 303–321). Undoubtedly, what occurs is a widespread infiltration of social science findings through "alien" fields such as pedagogy, geography, jurisprudence and even such refined areas as mathematical statistics. More recently, this subterranean approach has been replaced by an opening up of the social sciences at least to include sociology and psychology (the latter has always been available as part of the medical and biological sciences and now is being thought of as a social science). This indicates a distinct movement in the Soviet Union from totalitarian to authoritarian modalities. That is to say, there is a distinct tendency away from political dominance and surveillance of all scientific products to a political exclusivity that demands relevance rather than conformity in the products of social research (Kassof, 1965; Simirenko, 1966; Parsons, 1965).

In a welfare system, in contrast to a command system, the social sciences tend to have exceptionally close ties with policy-oriented sectors of the society. The two are joined functionally by the ministries of science such as those in England, France and Germany. Policy-makers, for their part, often think of the social sciences as a rationale required for any projected change estimated to be in the social interest. Before a major piece of legislation is introduced into the English Parliament, for example, the likelihood is that a survey has already been conducted providing a form of social science legitimation. Thus, in England, while investment in social science is relatively smaller than in the United States, there is a high payoff for social science information (See Horowitz, 1964a, pp. 43–47). The social scientist is not only listened to, his advice is fervently sought. Social science has become a recognized aspect of national investment. The welfare system has been a tremendous source for social science growth, and in turn, the social sciences have reinforced the "socialist" tendencies within the societies in which they operate.

The character of the social science practiced in the welfare system tends to be of a strongly applied nature. England no longer produces the great theories about society; rather, it paves the way for practices intended to reshape social policy.[1] Empiricism extends deep in the marrow of the policy orientation. Both the opportunities and the payoff are in such a direction. Furthermore, "pure" social science research involves a study and evolution of fundamental theories about man, and neither the pragmatism of the twentieth-century British party system nor the empiricism of the educational system places much faith in "fundamentals."

The linkage between the British political and educational systems may have delayed the evolution of an independent social science curriculum at the more traditional places of learning, but when the penetration did take place (by economics in the eighteenth century, administration in the nineteenth century and political science in the present century), the situation was ready-made for the close operation between social science and social policy. And with the defeat of ideological Toryism (based as it was, on "classical studies") by the close of World War II, the last shreds of opposition to social science vanished.[2] The impulses of British social science to welfare projects dovetailed neatly with the welfare projects outlined by the political apparatus. And the mutual suspicions of scientists and policy-makers characteristic of an earlier epoch in British history dissolved into mutual reinforcement and even joint celebration.

In laissez faire consensus systems, the social sciences are compelled to compete with directly involved policy agencies. For example, in the United States, executive policy-makers have traditionally consulted those with training in diplomacy, law and administration. But until well into the present century, little attention was given any of the so-called hard social sciences—psychology, economics and sociology. Furthermore, not until the establishment of bureaucratic modes of social science performance have the social sciences been granted the kind of hearing they enjoy in the welfare state. The extent to which the laissez faire system becomes permeated with welfare elements, concerning itself with protecting and caring for the citizenry, to that degree is there a high penetration of the social sciences into the area of government policy.

There appear to be three distinctive factors accounting for the special role of social science in the formation of American policy. They explain not only the significance of social science in policy making but also the dependence of American social science on policy agencies.

First, a strong social reform tendency developed early in opposition to general theories of change and revolution. American social science has been consciously, almost self-consciously, dedicated to issues of practical reform: elimination of poverty, integration of ethnic minorities, immigration

---

[1] A series of articles on "reshaping social policy" appearing in the English publication *New Society* is indicative of this trend. The articles deal with population pressures, urban design, professional practices and immigration, all as they relate to England. See *New Society*, vol. 7, nos. 179-181 (March 1966).

[2] For a general outline, see Cardwell (1957). For a more specific essay, see Ashby (1966, pp. 13–26).

and population issues, urban redevelopment schemes and so forth. This has led major foundations and philanthropic agencies to lose interest in the direct alleviation of social problems through charity and to invest heavily in indirect means of alleviation: social science programs.

Second, development of a pluralistic educational system made room for many and diverse social scientific activities. This gainful employment in teaching, while it prevented some of the worst excesses of the German university system from being repeated in the United States—chauvinism, nationalism, anti-Semitism—weakened the status system in American higher education. Status tended to be conferred from the outside, especially from federal and private agencies that drew upon educational expertise as the only sources of nonpolitical opinion. This permitted the American social scientist to retain an independence from government, and the policy-maker to reserve judgment on the worth of the social sciences.

Third, an entrepreneurial spirit developed in American social science to accommodate growing government needs. Bureaucratic organizations served to mediate the claims of educational and political establishments, safeguarding both from detriment or disrepute. Social science middlemen emerged in all forms. Bureaus of social research blossomed at the major universities. Independent, nonuniversity agencies sprang up: the RAND Corporation, the Institute for Defense Analysis, the Aerospace Corporation and the Peace Research Institute. Organizations geared to marketing research and national opinion surveys proliferated. These entrepreneurial responses to government needs meant the institutionalization of a buying and selling arrangement. And, as is customary in such arrangements, the buyers perform superordinate and the sellers subordinate roles, except in unusual circumstances.

Table 16.1 indicates the network of private military research agencies and their base of military support.

The laissez faire consensus system is not an exact description of American society. The system of social science evolved in the special circumstances of United States political and economic history. In effect, its political rhetoric remains steeped in consensus, while its economic characteristics have increasingly been subject to welfare elements. This is one central reason for the "schizophrenia" in applied social research.

As an overall characterization it could be said that:

1. In a command society, policy dictates both the character and the activities of the social sciences. Social science loses control over both the instruments and purposes of research. The operational aspects become so important with respect to what policy dictates that the social sciences can do little but "plug into" the going political system and hope for enlightened outcomes. To the extent that the sciences do so satisfactorily, they survive.
2. In a welfare system, policy and social sciences interact, but without any sense of tension or contradiction between scientific propositions

TABLE 16.1   Private Military Research Agencies

Supported Military	Contract Holdings (millions of dollars)[a]
Air Force	
Aerospace Corporation	$76.2
Systems Development Corporation	51.6
Mitre Corporation	34.4
RAND Corporation	11.4
Analytic Services, Inc.	1.3
Navy	
Applied Physics Laboratory (Johns Hopkins)	54.9
Franklin Institute (Center for Naval Analysis)	11.5
Army	
Research Analysis Corporation	9.3
Defense Department	
Institute for Defense Analysis	2.1
Logistics Management Institute	1.0
Created at suggestion of military (Major Institutions)	
Lincoln Laboratory (M.I.T.)	49.4
Instrumentation Laboratory (M.I.T.)	47.0

SOURCE: Defense Department.
[a] Net value of prime contract award, fiscal 1964.

and the therapeutic orientations. The integration is so complete that there is a loss of identity at both the scientific and political poles. Spillover between scientific propositions and therapeutic prescriptions is tremendous; all functions of social science are funneled into a social problems orientation. The result is a decline of interest in the larger analysis of social systems or social forces.

3. In a laissez faire system, the social sciences tend to be independent and autonomous of political policy. However, to the degree they remain in this pristine condition, they are also weak in power and status. What takes place typically is an exchange system based on a reciprocal transference of information for money. But this reduces the amount of social science autonomy, which leads to a tradeoff of high status for maximum power. This, in its turn, creates a source of inner tension within the social sciences as to the appropriate role of the social scientist in the forging of public policy.

SOCIALIZATION INTO SECRECY

Until now, we have considered the training of social scientists as a given. Here we must take note of their training as policy consultants or advisers. While most officials in government have a series of checks and balances to guide their behavior, few forms of anticipatory socialization apply to social scientists who advise government agencies. Because such social science advisers are asked for operational guidance on sensitive issues, they are often shielded from the consequences of their policy utterances. The anomaly arises that the more sensitive the policy question, the less subject it is to public scrutiny.

Secrecy has been maintained about government scientists that is practiced elsewhere in Washington only on behalf of CIA agents. As one commentator has recently pointed out:

> Not only are the names of some two hundred P-SAC consultants kept secret, but so are those of other paid scientific advisers to government. Spokesmen for both the Air Force and the Arms Control and Disarmament Agency recently refused to divulge the identity of certain of their scientific advisers on the grounds that to do so would (1) expose them to pressure, (2) ensure that they would receive unwanted mail, and (3) put them under public scrutiny, which was exactly where they did not want to be. (Greenfield, 1965, pp. 415–429)

Yet, since the purpose of research may have an effect on the judgment of social scientists, why should secrecy be either prized or praised?

The question of secrecy is intimately connected with that of policy because it is a standing assumption of policy-makers never to reveal themselves entirely. No government in the game of international politics feel that its policies can be placed on the table for full public review. Therefore operational research done in connection with policy considerations is bound by the canons of privacy. In its most basic form, the dilemma is as follows: Social scientists have a fetish for publicizing their information. However, policy branches of society have as their fetish, as their essential method, private documents and privileged information. How else does one gain in the game of one-upsmanship without privacy, without knowing something that the other side does not know? Therefore, a premium is placed not simply on gaining information but on maintaining silence about such information. A reversal of premiums and a transvaluation of values arises, leading to extreme tension. What often reduces such tension is the sacrifice of the social sciences, their yielding to considerations of policy.

Social scientists yield on such issues not simply because of a power imbalance between buyer and seller of ideas, but because they prefer a secondary role. Social scientists may enjoy the idea of partaking of a secret order of things. There is something tremendously fascinating about being "in" and not being "out." The cost of this "inside dopester" role may be a heavy one—the institutionalization of a subordinate position. But in being privy to things of secrecy, the feeling of powerlessness is largely eliminated; the subordinate role with respect to political authorities may be more than counterbalanced by a superordinate feeling with respect to other social scientists.

One critical factor reinforcing the common acceptance of the norm of secrecy is the allocation of most government research funds for military or semimilitary purposes. As Table 16.2 indicates, approximately 70 percent of such funds have either a directly military or semimilitary basis. Under such circumstances, the real wonder is not the existence of a norm of secrecy, but the relative availability of information.

TABLE 16.2   Federal R & D Expenditure, Fiscal 1965, by Program Area

Program Area	Estimated Expenditure (millions of dollars)
Space research[a]	$6,700
Military research	5,200
Medical research[a]	1,300
Nuclear research[a]	1,200
Agricultural research	179
Oceanographic research[a]	138
Meteorological research[a]	108
Water and transportation research[a]	129
Education research	24
Vocational rehabilitation research	19
Welfare administration research	7
Other (not allocable)	87
Total	$15,091

SOURCE: 1965 Federal Budget.
[a] Program estimate by Bureau of the Budget. Other items estimated by author.

Social scientists involved with research defined as secret or confidential can easily develop a self-definition of importance derived from their connection rather than the intrinsic merits or demerits of their work (See Price, 1954; Hagstrom, 1965.) They come to desire secrecy as much as their superordinates because they want to be shielded from public scrutiny of their work. Being publicly called to account in congressional committee hearings, for example, has a demeaning effect on status. If an economist or political scientist working for the Central Intelligence Agency filed a report to the government so erroneous that it helped pave the way for policy disasters, public availability of the report would reflect negatively on his standing in the academic community. Thus, secrecy is a mutual advantage in the event of failure even more than in successful ventures. In this protected environment, the social science advisory competence becomes an unknown quantity. About the only surety available to the hiring federal agencies is to choose from the elite corps of social scientists and to offer financial rewards high enough to attract such an elite.[3]

[3] This was clearly done in the case of Project Camelot. The consultants were drawn from the more eminent members of the social science community. See U.S. House, Committee on Foreign Affairs (1965a, 1965b).

The widespread acceptance of the canons of secrecy, no less than the commitment to policy as such, makes it extremely difficult to separate science from patriotism and hence to question the research design itself. The acceptance of the first stage, the right of the government to secrecy, often carries with it acquiescence in the last stage, the necessity for silence on the part of social scientists. The demand for secrecy has its most telling impact on the methodology of the social sciences. Presumably, policy personnel hire or employ social scientists because this group represents objectivity and honesty. The social scientists represent a wall of truth, off which the policy-makers can bounce their premises and practices. The social scientist is thought to provide information that public opinion is not able (or willing) to supply. To some degree, social scientists are hired because they will say things that may be unpopular but nonetheless significant. For example, that the Chinese Communist system is viable and will not collapse is a difficult position to assert, made far less so by the backing of social science experts. Then such a statement can be made with relative impunity—even before a Senate Foreign Relations Committee hearing.

Social scientists think they have a good commodity for sale or for hire, and at least one large sector of society shares this estimate. Avid consumers of social science products such as government policy-makers may come into direct competition for services with equally concerned but less affluent consumers of social science. There are people who think highly of social science information and others who think poorly of it. However, even those with a high opinion are not always in a position to pay for social science services. Thus, as can be seen in Table 16.3, funds for research are, for all practical purposes, restricted to government, industry and university sources.

Given the complex nature of social science activities and their increasing costs—both for human and machine labor—the government becomes the most widespread buyer. Government policy-makers get the first yield

TABLE 16.3 Sources of Funds Used for Research and Development, by Sector, 1953–62 (millions of dollars)

Year	Total	Federal Government	Industry	Colleges and Universities	Other Nonprofit Institutions
1953–54	$ 5,150	$2,740	$2,240	$130	$ 40
1954–55	5,620	3,070	2,365	140	45
1955–56	6,390	3,670	2,510	155	55
1956–57	8,670	5,095	3,325	180	70
1957–58	10,100	6,390	3,450	190	70
1958–59	11,130	7,170	3,680	190	90
1959–60	12,680	8,320	4,060	200	100
1960–61	13,890	9,010	4,550	210	120
1961–62	14,740	9,650	4,705	230	155

SOURCE: National Science Foundation.

also because they claim a maximum need. Private pressure groups representing corporate interests are the next highest buyer of social science services. The bureaus of social research vaguely attached to universities service most nonfederal research needs. The role of foundations and universities is ambiguous. Theoretically, they ought to be encouraging pure research, particularly if government agencies encourage applied research. In fact, rarely are they interested in pure research. If anything, they tend to be as concerned with applied problems as the public and business agencies, since they are concerned with justifying their worth precisely to business donors and government agencies. Further, big foundations and major universities are often policy extensions of federal agencies—if not directly, then through special laws and rules governing the taxation of philanthropic agencies and universities. The source of funds for research tend to be exclusively concentrated in the upper classes. The fact that the President can indirectly participate in the selection process of major foundations indicates the intimacy that exists between federal and private controllers of wealth despite legal niceties. This fusion of government and corporate wealth makes it difficult to bring about a countervailing pluralistic system of power with respect to social science funding.[4]

There is a direct relationship between ability to pay and belief in the utility of the social sciences. Who are the high users? The federal government, some state governments, basic industries, marketing industries. Who are the low users? Farmer-labor groups, the poor in general, minority groups (with the exception of highly sophisticated groups such as affluent religious organizations that spill over into the high-users category). In the main, racial and ethnic groups do not place much value on the uses of social science. Perhaps the use of social science research is itself a suave reflection of wealth. Those who wish to use social science agencies extensively are wealthy enough to afford them; those who disparage social science groups are often rationalizing their own lack of affluence.

The image of social science tends to be far less flattering among the poorer classes than among the wealthier classes. Ultimately, the social scientists, to the extent that they become involved with policy-making agencies, become committed to an elitist ideology. They come to accept as basic the idea that men who really change things are at the top. Thus, the closer to the top one can get, the more likely he will be able to bring about intended changes (See Presthus, 1964, esp. pp. 3–63).

Two flies can be found in this particular ointment. First, there is slender evidence that information bought and paid for is made the basis of policy in critical times. Indeed, there is just as much evidence for the conclusion that information is used when it suits policy-makers and discarded when it does not "fit" political plans. Second, there is no evidence that the

---

[4] For a defense and an acknowledgment of this, see Lazarsfeld (1959). For a critique, see Horowitz (1963).

elitist model is uniquely cast to solve problems of social change. The model of elites changing the world is itself controversial. It may be flattering to think that involvement with elites enables one to determine the course of society. But if a Marxian or mass model is used, what happens to the relationship of the policy-maker to the social scientist? The whole situation must then be perceived in terms of social forces. By minimizing any other historically derived model, such as a mass model, the social scientist leaves unexplored the variables that ought to be examined and tested for their significance; these variables simply become heuristically manipulated as part of the ongoing ethos of social life.

An aspect of the norm of secrecy often alluded to informally, but rarely publicly, is: How is exact information obtained about potentially enemy or alien groups? In situations of relative insularity or isolation, whose judgments concerning the intentions of other nations, races or groups can be relied upon? The character of the informants no less than the quality of the information itself has become a central problem in decision making. Nor is this merely a problem for foreign affairs. For example, in estimating the potential for mass violence of American blacks, how valuable is information supplied by major institutionalized black associations? If the leadership of the Urban League is asked about the possibility of mass racial violence, will it provide the same kind of response as the Black Muslims or an opinion survey of the unorganized blacks? The tendency has been to rely upon institutionalized expressions for information concerning "spontaneous" crowd behavior, but reliance upon established organizations may easily distort our vision of a situation. There is a judgmental issue to be settled even before any sampling is undertaken. How serious this can be is reflected in the fact that at the very height of the black revolution, studies of crowd behavior and mass movements in the United States have practically faded from the work done by behavioral scientists (Lazarsfeld, 1963, p. 187).

Even more complicated is the evaluation of foreign affairs. How are the military intentions of the People's Republic of China to be estimated? Are studies made in Hong Kong or information supplied by Taiwanese army officers to be relied upon? Yet, if there is no direct access to the "enemy," whoever it may be at any time, how is exact information to be derived? The alternative to partisan bias would be to accept the rhetoric of the enemy society at face value. However, reading reports for major political and military figures of the enemy society from afar may create an approach akin to inspirational divinations of biblical passages. Recent examples of multiple and conflicting interpretations abound. Consider the Chinese addresses that have been monitored concerning the politicalization of military cadres in North Vietnam. These remarks have been "interpreted" as indicating Chinese support for the war effort, Chinese distance and even withdrawal from the war effort, Chinese pleasure (and displeasure) with the National Liberation Front. Interpretation too easily becomes a function of policy perspectives rather than an objective study of foreign power intentions.

The filtering process, based as it is on the secrecy norm, leads to an abuse of what can be considered legitimate scientific inquiry. It minimizes possibilities of empirical and ethnographic surveys. Knowing what the "other side" is doing or planning in the main areas of government policy is absolutely necessary for the establishment of informational parity. But this runs squarely against policy rulings having to do with overseas travel, having to do with definition of the enemy and sometimes having to do with attitudes toward people considered to be less than human. The needs of policy are difficult to square with the needs of the social sciences. Policy may dictate de jure nonrecognition of a foreign power, but it is impossible for the social scientists to accept such policy recommendations as a de facto basis for research. He has to find a way of violating nonrecognition in order to serve in a scholarly capacity.

This unanticipated contradiction between science and policy cannot easily be resolved without redefining the enemy in nonpartisan terms or accepting the idea of partisanship as an institutionalized limit to scientific inquiry. But to do so would require a general redefinition of the role of social science in a democratic culture. What results in situations of high policy stress is low quality research. Conversely, when there is a low stress situation there can be high yield information. Democracy is linked to social visibility; hence we know a great deal about England and its society. But England poses no immediate threat, and therefore social scientists working in the area of English affairs are less than vital with respect to policy. The more important the subject, the less likely is there to be access to critical information. As long as the political situation is defined exclusively in terms of policy needs, the possibility of a social science of operational worth remains seriously impaired.

The proud announcement in the early fifties of the policy sciences has given way to a profound skepticism of such a concept in the sixties. Perhaps the notion of a policy science is a contradiction in terms, not previously recognized as such only because of the enormity of federal and commercial needs for exact information in an age when mass participatory democracy has sharply declined. There can never be a policy science from the point of view of the polity, because its needs have to do with sovereignty and with the protection of its citizens even if this involves secrecy, war and deceitful forms of defense or attack; whereas from the point of view of the social scientist, the same concept of policy science must be challenged, because in the final analysis the scientific community can never accept an exclusively therapeutic definition of social life. Social science can never take for granted the things that make for political sovereignty. Perhaps this contradiction is a creative tension. But I am not so optimistic. My own feeling is that this is a degenerative relationship. The negative features implied both for policy and for science cancel the pragmatic worth of a concept of policy science.

The value-free doctrine has been examined at too great a length to require additional commentary. Yet there is an aspect of the fact–value issue that deserves deeper analysis here, since it involves the connection of social science to public policy in a direct way. When translated into a personal ideological expression, this fact–value dualism can provide a rationale for selling information to the highest bidder. It can become a way of saying that facts are for public sale, while values are for private sensibilities.

Quite conceivably, the classical disjunction between fact and value may turn out to be a greater problem for distributors of "hard" science than for those who traffic in "soft" science. For if the doctrine of value irrelevance is taken seriously, it becomes a mandate for any values. Hence, the complete separation of fact and value can jeopardize tough policy scientists quite thoroughly. Conventionally, advocates of the value-free doctrine have considered it to be a functional instrument safeguarding against any ideological infiltration of the social sciences. However, it is becoming uncomfortably plain that the notion of selling information to the highest bidder is not at all inconsistent with people who have no "higher" values at all, and not only those who refuse to express value preference in their social research.

The more expensive an originating research design turns out to be, the more differential access to the findings is demanded as the price for an initial expenditure of risk capital.[5] The policy-sector demand for differential access may take various forms: (1) the policy agency will insist upon a defined period of lead time before release of findings to the public; (2) the results can be made immediately available only if they are initially cleared by the sponsoring agency so that no information of a "delicate" nature is revealed; (3) this last often leads to a more formal situation, in which the publication of an esoteric document is allowed, while a more complete esoteric document serves as a special payoff to the agency; or (4) by insisting that all research done under contract is private, the sponsoring agency settles all "problems" of publication. Often the distinction between "liberal" and "conservative" agencies is made on the basis of data released and hás no general political moorings.

None of these four types of processing data represents a classical model of social scientific behavior with respect to publication. But the bureaucratic style has become increasingly generalized. New elements have entered into the policy game even at the level of publication. One sensitive issue, for example, is what constitutes publication. Is a mimeographed report an authentic publication? Reports in such nontypographical form

[5] On this question, see the contribution by Barber (1966, pp. 91–108).

appear regularly and have peculiar qualities. They are not available for public consumption. They are not copyrighted and hence not subject to public review. Even "official-looking" mimeographed reports released in bound form remain private documents. This raises questions not only of differential access but of arbitrary limits to access. It is not only who but how many people are in a position to read such a document. The norm of secrecy has become so much a part of the character of social science publications that the general risks to unlimited diffusion of information have greatly increased.

The issues can be divided into sponsorship problems and ideological problems. At one level, the policy issue is who sponsors the research, rather than the character of the research. At the other end of the spectrum, the scientific issue is the goal sought from any given research. More profoundly, as I have already suggested, the issue is the nature of sovereignty and the nature of privacy.

Nations are not often thought to be private entities. Rather, we think of them as macroscopic, and publicly available to investigation. However, sovereignty carries with it, if not explicitly then surely implicitly, a notion of restricted public access, that is, privacy. Sovereignty is a statement of the rights of citizens, and such rights impose restrictions upon noncitizens. Therefore, a sovereign, whether in its universalistic national form or a person, has a private side, a private self.

This might best be seen in legal terms of juror performance and jury-room wiretapping. From the point of view of social science, the phenomenology of decision making in a closed setting represents a fascinating problem. How do people interact within "alien," restricted confines? Do the decisions they reach rest upon rational or irrational indicators? What is the character of personal interaction in a jury room? From the point of view of the sovereign, the elements of jury decision making require secrecy for their realization. The sovereign assumes that people in private interaction, untouched by public pressure, are in a position to make decisions that are more truthful and hence more useful than publicly debated decisions. This is an example of competing needs. The political requirement is different from the scientific requirement. Who is right? Would it be right to implant a microphone in a jury room for the sake of social science, running the risk ultimately of destroying the confidence of jurors and potential jurors in a democratic legal system? Or is it right to preserve an irrational system of decision-making, which may well be what the jury system is about, simply to maintain the myth of democratic processes?

There is no ready-made answer to this kind of dilemma. But raising this sort of problem gives an indication of the anxieties and disturbances felt by sovereign powers in the realm of foreign area research. For what is being tested by one nation studying another nation's inner workings is nothing short of the right to remain private. The justification of such privacy may be quite shaky, based on custom and myth. At the moment, however, the problem is not the *origins* of sovereignty, but rather the *rights* of sovereignty. From this point of view, anxieties concerning foreign area research have to be appreciated, irrespective of social scientific or policy claims.

The sponsoring agent of research may not be as important for the sovereign under scrutiny as for the individual engaging in a field of investigation. Whether sponsorship of foreign area research is under the aegis of the Department of Health, Education, and Welfare or the Department of Defense may dwindle in significance with respect to how such research is perceived by the foreign government. But from either the public or the private viewpoint, visibility of research funds is significant. It may well be that openness of sponsorship is a determining element in how far access to a foreign sovereign may be pushed. To put matters directly: The reaction of the sovereign to an investigatory body in some measure depends on the premises and purposes of the investigatory body. This, in turn, may require a fresh look at the norm of secrecy—and understanding that such a norm affects sovereignty as well as science.

UNIVERSITY BUREAUCRACIES
AND VALUE SYSTEMS

The social ecology of where various activities are performed leaves an imprint on the nature of the findings. Social scientific activities usually take place within a university context. The university, viewed as a social force, has strong feudalistic elements. Some people mistake this feudal ancestry for humanism, possibly because of the historical distance between our epoch and the founding of the university system nearly 800 years ago. The feudal core of university life is that a stratum of people is employed to engage in activities that may not be practical. They are paid to be non-functional. The function of a university is to absorb the welter of non-pragmatic activities that go on within any viable society. University activities may or may not relate to the betterment of man, but pragmatic goals do not exhaust the scholarly role as such. This traditional nonfunctionality has begun to crumble under the impact of courses in basket weaving and jewelry making on one side and war gaming and system designing on the other. Still, the great thrust of university life in America through the mid-fifties has been to keep the university a place of general theory and statements of fundamentals, to retain the European notion of *universitas*.

Policy-making activities, however, usually take place in a nonacademic or bureaucratic context. Policy as distinct from politics as such is a modern innovation, beginning as a mass enterprise in the industrial era. True, there was a species of policy connected to political classes in ancient or medieval times, where political structure was directly and organically related to class interests. However, policy making as an autonomous activity, linked to appointment based on expertise, is a twentieth-century

TABLE 16.4 Select Behavioral Science Contracts Related to Foreign Areas and Foreign Populations

Title	Location	Description
1963 American Mount Everest Expedition	Berkeley Institute of Psychological Research	Psychological aspects of stress behavior
Changing values in Japanese, Americans and Japanese-Americans	Institute of Advanced Projects, University of Hawaii	Analysis of how Japanese change their values as they come in contact with American culture
International conflict (Israel and Egypt)	Stanford University	Analysis of relationship of opinions and writings of decision-makers and the actual actions that took place
Foreign research symposia	Social Science Research Council	Meetings of American and foreign scholars in Europe in social psychology
Persuasive communications in the international field	University of Wisconsin	How foreign nationalities react to various kinds of American communications
Sociopolitical precursors to insurgency	Pennsylvania State College	Study of insurgency and causes related to it in order to determine role the navy plays
Nationalism and the perception of international crises	University of Texas	Perceptions that people have of international crises and their relationship to the persons' psychology
Group factors influencing creativity	University of Illinois	Discovering how a heterogeneous group establishes a common effective communication system where the group is composed of individuals of different languages and cultural backgrounds
Group equilibrium	Rutgers University	Replication in Japan of studies made in U.S. on small-group effectiveness
Role theory	University of Missouri	Theory of role structure—work being done with collaborators in Australia and England
Cross-cultural investigation of some factors in persuasion and attitude change	University of Maryland	Structure and mechanics of attitude-change methods—research replicated with Japanese subjects to determine generality of findings

SOURCE: U.S. House, Committee on Foreign Affairs, Subcommittee on International Organizations and Movements, *Behavioral Sciences and the National Security*, report no. 4 (Washington, D.C.: Government Printing Office, 1965).

phenomenon. The style of policy is antifeudal. It is based on premises converting theory into immediate practice. This differs radically from the traditional university bias toward separation and even suspicion of a ready conversion of theory into action.

The invasion of policy making into university life, in the form of direct capital expenditures no less than through contractual arrangements for specific purposes, transforms this traditional feudal–industrial dichotomy. Indeed, it undermines even the long-standing ties between university life and the business community that arose earlier in this century. Table 16.4 on behavioral science contracts for the study of foreign areas is simply one miniscule indicator of the degree to which the social sciences have furthered an interpenetration of social sciences and policy formation. The investigators are, for the overwhelming part, professors, and they are located at major university centers. This serves not only to pragmatize university research projects but also to supply financial support for graduate instruction, administrative and office personnel and new and improved buildings and equipment.

The Air Force Office of Scientific Research, the Office of Naval Research and the Special Operations Research Office of the United States Army each maintain separate funding arms. These are in addition to standard funding agencies such as the National Science Foundation and National Institutes of Health. Federal funding to universities has become so extensive and sophisticated that subcontracting is now commonplace. A government agency may provide a cover-all grant to the Smithsonian Institution or the Social Science Research Council, which in turn may parcel out the funds to private agencies and individuals. In 1965, the total amount spent by the Department of Defense establishment alone came to $27,300,000 (see Table 16.5). It is abundantly evident that these funds are usually distributed indirectly, through university agencies, and only infrequently directly, through subagencies having direct responsibility to the government. And it is apparent to students of the sociology of science that universities are now faced with the alternatives of either maximizing or holding constant such government allocations of research contracts.

This is a problem not of universities in general, but of social science in particular. For to the extent that the social sciences are connected to university styles, to that extent are they concerned with issues beyond those of policy. Bureaucratic mechanisms and institutes to funnel and channelize social science activities, while they have become increasingly important, still do not represent more than a distinct minority of social science staffing in the United States. For the most part, teaching remains the core occupation.[6] It is worth considering the degree to which the strain between social

---

[6] See National Register of Scientific and Technical Personnel (1966) and Committee on the National Science Foundation Report on the Economics Profession (1965).

TABLE 16.5 1965 Budgeted Behavioral and Social Sciences Research Funds
(thousands of dollars)

	Military Departments			Total		Grand Total
	Contract	In-house	ARPA[a] Contract	Contract	In-house	
Selection and classification	$ 730	$1,900		$ 730	$1,900	$ 2,630
Training and education	4,150	1,480	$ 60	4,210	1,480	5,690
Job design	300	620		300	620	920
Human performance, engineering and proficiency management	2,230	2,620	470	2,700	2,620	5,320
Manpower management (assignment, retention, etc.)	520	430		520	430	950
Group effectiveness	1,270		240	1,510		1,510
Psychophysiology and stress	1,650	470		1,650	470	2,120
Support of policy planning and strategic concepts	820		210	1,030		1,030
Studies of foreign countries, counterinsurgency and unconventional warfare	1,790		3,070	4,860		4,860
Information in foreign areas	870		250	1,120		1,120
Psychological operations and weapons	380			380		380
Military assistance and civic action	400			400		400
Decision-making in military operations	110	260		110	260	370
Total	$15,220	$7,780	$4,300	$19,520	$7,780	$27,300
Percentage	66	29	5	71	29	

SOURCE: U.S. House, Committee on Foreign Affairs, Subcommittee on International Organizations and Movements, *Behavioral Sciences and the National Security*, report no. 4 (Washington, D.C.: Government Printing Office, 1965).
[a] Advanced Research Projects Agency.

scientific activities and policy-making activities ought to be viewed as a conflict of roles between feudal, university-based institutions and modern, state-based institutions. Recognizing the different origins and locales of the distinctive work styles inherent in science and policy will help account for present discrepancies. The strains that exist are not just transient or temporary, not reducible to financial allocations; they are basic differences in the way objects are studied, as well as in what is considered worthy of study.

In examining contract social science research, two problems have to be distinguished: (1) the sponsorship involved in any kind of research and (2) the nature and purposes of the research design. Both problems simultaneously involve methodological and moral dimensions. Methodological guidelines can do everything but answer the question "Why study a field?" That is why the moral base of social science is directly involved in the nature of the investigatory proceedings.

Let us restrict ourselves to an issue raised, but not resolved, in the previous section of this chapter—the issue of sovereignty. Sovereignty is an ultimate politically, but not scientifically. The investigation of another nation is no more but no less legitimate than the study of another person, for the problem of magnitude is not one of morals. It is hard to envision a situation in the immediate future when national studies, so long a part of social science, will vanish. The whole of the nineteenth century was taken up by Europeans studying the United States, from Alexis de Tocqueville to Harriet Martineau. The tradition has persisted into this century. Many of the so-called classics of the social sciences have a national character, including the work of men like Ostrogorskii and Weber. Indeed, anthropologists have made the nation a basic measure. They have been accused of engaging in unfriendly acts, or in secular missionary roles, but they were not denied access to data.

The question is: Why has this traditional situation of tolerance not prevailed? First, in the past, social scientists were not working for a government. Therefore, they were without special interest in bringing to light the private aspects of another sovereignty. Second, the issue of sponsorship has become particularly acute at the present time because to define research in operational terms is necessarily to arouse a considerable amount of fear and trepidation. Operational or instrumental research has a goal beyond the research itself. Such latent political goals elicit fear and even hostility on the part of a "host" sovereign to the social science "vendors." Third, the problem has become acute because sovereigns of superordinate nations are interested not so much in the public side of life in the subordinate nations they study, but in their private side. The subordinate nations are viewed not as objects of disinterested inquiry, but as objects of instrumental or operational worth.

AUTONOMY AND RELEVANCE
IN SOCIAL SCIENCE

Let us now turn to the connection that the social scientist should maintain with policy-making bodies. Should the policy-maker continue to be a separate entity with a separate professional identity, or should he be a social scientist in government? Is it the role played or the functions performed that divide policy-maker from social scientist? Before attempting to answer questions of advantages or disadvantages in various relationships of social scientists to policy-making bodies, we ought to look more carefully into the lines of relationships that presently obtain.

Dividing the "world" into four parts—basic social sciences and applied social sciences on one side, executive and legislative branches of government on the other—reveals interesting relations. The basic social sciences (anthropology, political science, economics, psychology and sociology) have government connections different from the applied social sciences (administrative sciences, education, law, planning and social work). Let us divide the federal government into the presidential or executive government

(White House staff and the cabinet-level officials) and the permanent or legislative government (career federal executives, Congress and the federal judiciary).

The State Department and the Defense Department and the various cabinet level executives are the ones who make the highest use of basic social sciences. The State Department, through its diplomatic functions, has long been associated with political science and anthropology. The White House, for its part, is directly linked to the economics profession through the Council of Economic Advisers. The State of the Union Address institutionalizes the relation of the executive branch of government to economics as a social science. The Defense Department, perhaps because its own power is of more recent derivation, relies heavily upon the younger social sciences, especially psychology and, to a somewhat lesser degree, sociology. In sum, the basic social sciences are used primarily by the presidential staff and by the executive branch of government as a whole.

The area of applied social science is more often called upon by the congressional and legislative branches. Education, administrative sciences, social work and particularly law are themselves areas of professional competence for many congressmen. Thus, the legislative relationship to applied social science fields is not only utilitarian but also organic. The pragmatic base of enacting legislation having to do with changing relations between men insures a continuing demand for applied researches among legislators.

The gap between applied and basic models of social science that obtains in most American universities is paralleled by lines of influence in the government.[7] Policy making cannot be considered a unified science or a unified role. Quite the contrary, the tendency is for policy-making groups within the executive branch to be related to the social sciences differently from policy-making bodies within the congressional sphere. While it is true that definitions of "basic" and "applied" social sciences vary, there is enough consistency to reveal this differential policy pattern.

What then are the supposed advantages of fusing social science and social policy? The basic advantage is said to be a higher sense of responsibility for the social sciences, and a greater degree of training for policy-oriented personnel. This has, at any rate, been the classical rationale for a tighter linkage between policy making and social science.

What has prevented this amalgamation from occurring is not simple negligence or sloth. On the contrary, to judge by the amount of federal funds dedicated to bringing about such a union—de facto if not de jure—

---

[7] The judiciary itself makes little direct use of social science findings. If it employs such findings at all, it is through the law journals and periodicals relating to the legal profession. Insofar as social science permeates law journals, to that degree the judiciary reacts to trends in social science. This may be one factor in the length of time it takes for judicial decision concerning black–white relations. The access system between the judiciary and social sciences is often so blocked that important social science issues escape the attention of the judiciary for a longer span than any other federal group.

the wonder is how slight the steps toward amalgamation have been. The reason is that it is quite impossible to think of therapeutics being the same as science. In order to get a fusion of social science and policy, there would have to be a complete disruption of the present notion of social science as sharply different from reform therapy. While applied social science may be the expression of practical reason in the twentieth century, an applied social science cannot dictate the character of social science findings. The notion of basic science requires a distinct separation of its functions from policy-making functions. That high-level policy implies a recognition of this distinction can be seen by the extensive use made of "basic" findings and theories. However, the more practical the level of policy making (legislative activities are typical), the more closely it is linked to applied researches. The realities of the situation are such that the utility of the social sciences to policy-making bodies depends upon some maintenance of the separation of the social sciences from the policy situation.

Essential to understanding the present dilemmas about the relationship of science to policy are the radically different conceptions that government officials and social scientists have of that relationship. What concerns social scientists is making available not only the most important findings for "intelligence" needs but also the methods by which the policy process gets put into motion and the results of the study of policy for general scientific theory. What concerns government policy-makers is not so much social science but social engineering. The ready-to-hand bureaucratic research institutions set up at major universities and in the giant corporations provide both the institutional and the ideological props with which to pursue these engineering "systems" ends with great vigor (See Boguslaw, 1965).

The government in the present period has sought to resolve its staffing problems on key agencies and committees by attracting people whose conception of social science extends to construction but not to criticism. In contrast to the types of men solicited for marginal advisory roles, decision-makers have been chosen from the fields of business administration and urban planning rather than from the "hard" social sciences.

The "constructive" policy-science approach was actually begun in the Administration of Herbert Hoover and continued at an accelerated rate by Franklin Delano Roosevelt. Hoover had a deep engineering commitment. In fact, his image of the presidency often bordered on that of the great engineer, the social engineer. The President's Research Committee on Social Trends (1930–32), which Hoover created, inaugurated the difficult relationships between social science and social policy that have now come to plague American policy. The degree to which this early effort was a mutually felt need is reflected in the fact that the Social Science Research Council, with its support stemming from the Rockefeller-dominated Spelman Fund, underwrote the President's Research Committee on Social Trends. The demands of social science professionalization coincided with the crisis in the American economy—a crisis profound enough to generate demands from within the policy-making elite to seek out support from previously ignored, if not feared, intellectual currents.

Given the enormous significance of the "generation of the thirties" in founding relations between public officials and social scientists, it might be instructive to single out three important intellectual figures who assisted in the creation of these relations: Charles Merriam, Luther Gulick and Louis Brownlow. Merriam, a founder of the American Political Science Association and of the Social Science Research Council, was the only one of the three who qualified as an academic figure. Even he had stronger ties to government officials, regional planners and managers than to other social scientists. Brownlow was Merriam's closest associate at the University of Chicago; his main contribution was as director of the Public Administration Clearing House. He was, in effect, the chief manager of the nation's city managers. Brownlow had been a city manager in Washington, D.C., Knoxville and Petersburg, Va., long before he came to join Merriam at Chicago. Gulick was a different kettle of fish. Like the Dulles, Kennan and Davies families, he came out of the milieu of the American (Congregation) Foreign Mission Society. John Foster Dulles was, in fact, an aide to Gulick's father. He entered government planning service not by way of the social sciences but through the auspices of the New York Bureau of Municipal Research, which also had the support of large capital (the Harriman banking interests).

These were the men who comprised the Committee on Administrative Management under Franklin Delano Roosevelt and before that, under Herbert Hoover. They provided government officials with an early indication of what was to become the dominant "policy-making style," that is, an unconcern with politics as a mass activity (with which the policy-making social scientists were unconcerned) and policy as an elite activity (with which they were intimately concerned) (See Karl, 1963).

Their highest achievement was to draft the Executive Reorganization Act of 1939, which foreshadowed many of the changes that took place in the postwar executive regimes of Truman, Eisenhower and Kennedy. The Council of Economic Advisers, for instance, was an early fruit of this reorganization plan. This, in turn, led to the Council of Scientific Advisers. The men who established the institutional and organizational patterns by which social science became social policy were by training and inclination engineers, managers and planners. When they did link up to a social science, it was invariably to political science—a field that in its successful attempt at rapid professionalization chose alignment with federal interests rather than criticism of such interests as its high road to success.

The dominant view of the relationship of social science to social policy was consequently that social science should fulfill an ancillary function to social engineering—no less, but certainly no more. The policy-makers sought to answer the question "Knowledge for what?" in a pragmatic and direct way: Harold Lasswell sought to answer Robert Lynd's defiant stance by asserting the need of knowledge for augmentation and operationalization of federal policies in the areas of health, welfare and war. During the period between 1930 and 1945, the growth of social science organizations was fused to their increasing acceptance of a professional ideology. This combination of organizational advancement in the social sciences and ideological commitment to the political system served to cement the relations with policy-making branches of government by removing the last vestiges of ideological mistrust.

These new developments deeply affected the autonomous character and growth of the social sciences. Standards of methodological precision were raised, a wider set of people from diverse class and ethnic backgrounds began to permeate the social sciences, and professionalism itself served both to unite and distinguish between tasks confronting social science and those of government. The very growth of work styles in the social sciences that were both accessible and amenable to policy-makers also served to raise anew the doubts as to the worth of such a fusion (See Lipset and Schwartz, 1966, pp. 299–309; Horowitz, 1964b).

This brings us face to face with the relationship of autonomy to involvement, an issue especially significant in the light of the large number of government contracts and policy-making demands upon the time, energies and capabilities of social scientists. This is not simply a contrast of citizen responsibility and professional roles, but a question of the nature of the discipline itself—over and beyond the way in which the social scientist perceives institutional affiliations. The autonomy of the social sciences was rarely doubted until the present. The same cannot be said for the autonomy of policy-making sectors of government. Since the latter are openly involved in operational research, they make slender pretenses to autonomy.

The problem now arises on two fronts in the federally supported research situation. What are the lines of independence, and what are the lines of responsibility, from the "vendors" to the "funding agency"? The autonomy of a social science is directly linked to the very existence of each field. The most powerful argument for the maintenance of a distinction between public policy and social science is that without such a distinction the very concept is severely jeopardized. Admitting the risk of inviting dilettantism of "idle speculation" to transform all research into command performances is far riskier. There is no science that does not have an element of autonomous growth. Indeed, a great deal of time and energy in any social science is spent arguing and worrying, not about the social world in general, but about people occupying critical roles or command positions in the world of social science. Nor is such self-reflection and constant autoexamination to be lightly dismissed, since it accounts precisely for the sorts of improvements in the functioning of a scientific theory that provide operational worth to begin with. In other words, the autonomous realm is not incidental either to the formation of the social scientist or to that which makes him truly scientific in his behavior.

The great failing of a policy-science approach is that it has not recognized that the price of rapid professionalization and integration is high. By raising the banner of "the policy sciences of democracy," this approach minimizes the autonomous and critical aspects of social scientific development (See, for example, Lasswell, 1951, pp. 3–15). Without this autonomic aspect to science, one cannot really speak either of a profession or of an occupation. There are standards in a social science, and levels of performance within each science, that link its practitioners together apart from their actions or reactions to policy questions. When a breakdown of autonomy occurs, when policy questions or ideological requirements prevail, the deterioration in the quality of the social science is a certain consequence. Policy places a premium on involvement and influence; science places a premium on investigation and ideas. The issue is not so much what is studied, or even the way an inquiry is conducted, but the auspices and the purposes of a study.

Finally, the discussion of the relationship of social science to public policy as a question reflects first and foremost the belief (at least among the practitioners of social science) in the efficacy and the feasibility of scientific activities in social life. It is no longer either fashionable or particularly profound to ask, "Are the social sciences really sciences?" This as a naïve question, a meaningless question. The efficacy of social science is firmly established. Precisely at that point in scientific history where efficacy is established beyond any doubt in the minds of both policy personnel and social scientists, the question of the aims of social science looms large. This issue of purpose was not raised when the social sciences were really little else than a species of literature or belles lettres. When an individual pontificates about the nature of the world or the nature of man in society, one man's platitudes may be another man's poison. But when someone offers a plan for redesigning the world, and proceeds to do so in a more or less anticipated way, he can be ridiculed and reviled, but not easily ignored. The recognition of this has been so widespread that the value demands upon the social sciences have become central, with decisions as to the performance of the science becoming directly linked to the goals set for the society.

What we witness in the present generation from the point of view of the social sciences is the breakup of the functionalist ideology with its value-free orientation. Because the peculiar autonomous aspects of each social science generate a special internal history, the breakup occurs differently in each discipline (Demerath and Peterson, 1966).

From the point of view of policy-makers, the breakup of the old way of doing things has been equally profound. Perhaps the largest shock that they have undergone is the recognition that there is probably no such animal as a policy scientist. There has been no definition of a policy-maker that can legitimate his role as a social scientist—basic or applied. Policy-makers in one agency have slender connection with policy-makers in other branches of government. Increasingly, the policy-maker is being confronted with the fact that he is not so much an applied social scientist as he is a representative of the State Department or a representative of Health, Education, and Welfare. In other words, what defines his role is not the policy-making activities but rather the requirements of the agency for which he works. In effect, what he is engaged in is ideology, not policy (See Horowitz, 1965; Silvert, 1965). Therefore, unless one is willing to speak of the science of ideology, which is a contradiction in terms, it is not possible to deal legitimately with the social sciences exclusively from a policy point of view.

The social sciences are challenged and tested as never before by their involvements with policy organs. This association increases the chances for meaningful research and knowledge scientists may acquire about the workings of the world. It also makes possible the corruption of social science on a scale hitherto unimagined—through the submerging of tasks of inquiry into contract fulfillments. The drive shaft of government agencies' demands upon social scientists is ideological, and yet the larger needs of such agencies are, as never before, a wider understanding of the shape of societies around the world. Perhaps the main problem, therefore, is not so much the relation of policy to science—a common challenge for social scientists and policy-makers—but how each can maintain its respective autonomy when so many integrating pressures exist. And the question of how involvement and autonomy link up becomes the next great challenge in this newest claimant to the passions and energies of the social intelligentsia.

REFERENCES

Ashby, E. (1966) "Science and Public Policy: Some Institutional Patterns Outside America," in B. R. Keenan, ed., *Science and the University*. New York: Columbia University Press.

Barber, R. J. (1966) *The Politics of Research*. Washington, D.C.: Public Affairs Press.

Boguslaw, R. (1965) *The New Utopians: A Study of System Design and Social Change*. Englewood Cliffs, N.J.: Prentice-Hall.

Cardwell, D. S. L. (1957) *The Organization of Science in England: A Retrospect*. London: Heinemann.

Committee on the National Science Foundation Report on the Economics Profession (1965) "The Structure of Economists' Employment and Salaries, 1964," *American Economic Review*, vol. 55, no. 4 (December), pt. 2, supplement.

Demerath, N. J., III, and R. A. Peterson, eds. (1966) *System, Change and Conflict: Functionalists and Their Critics*. New York: Free Press.

DeWitt, N. (1955) *Soviet Professional Manpower: Its Education, Training and Supply*. Washington, D.C.: U. S. National Science Foundation.

DeWitt, N. (1965) "Reorganization of Science and Research in the U.S.S.R.," in N. Kaplan, ed., *Science and Society*. Stokie, Ill.: Rand McNally.

Greenfield, M. (1965) "Science Goes to Washington," in N. Kaplan, ed., *Science and Society*. Stokie, Ill.: Rand McNally.

394 POLICIES

Hagstrom, W. O. (1965) *The Scientific Community.* New York: Basic Books.

Horowitz, I. L. (1963) "Establishment Sociology: The Value of Being Value Free," *Inquiry: An Interdisciplinary Journal of Philosophy and the Social Sciences,* vol. 6, no. 2 (Spring), pp. 129–139.

Horowitz, I. L. (1964a) *The New Sociology.* New York: Oxford University Press.

Horowitz, I. L. (1964b) "Professionalism and Disciplinarianism," *Philosophy of Science,* vol. 31, no. 3 (July), pp. 275–281.

Horowitz, I. L. (1965) "The Life and Death of Project Camelot," *transaction,* vol. 3, no. 1 (November–December), pp. 3–7, 44–47.

Karl, B. D. (1963) *Executive Reorganization and Reform in the New Deal: The Genesis of Administrative Management, 1900–1939.* Cambridge, Mass.: Harvard University Press.

Kassof, A. (1965) "American Sociology Through Soviet Eyes," *American Sociological Review,* vol. 30, no. 1 (February), pp. 114–124.

Lasswell, H. D. (1951) "The Policy Orientation," in D. Lerner and H. D. Lasswell, eds., *The Policy Sciences.* Stanford, Calif.: Stanford University Press.

Lazarsfeld, P. F. (1959) "Reflections on Business," *American Journal of Sociology,* vol. 65, no. 1 (July), pp. 1–26.

Lazarsfeld, P. F. (1963) "Political Behavior and Public Opinion," in B. Berelson, ed., *The Behavioral Sciences Today.* New York: Basic Books.

Lipset, S. M., and M. A. Schwartz (1966) "The Politics of Professionals," in H. W. Vollmer and D. L. Mills, eds., *Professionalization.* Englewood Cliffs, N.J.: Prentice-Hall

National Register of Scientific and Technical Personnel (1966) *Summary of American Science Manpower, 1964.* Washington, D.C.: National Science Foundation.

Parsons, T. (1965) "An American Impression of Sociology in the Soviet Union," *American Sociological Review,* vol. 30, no. 1 (February), pp. 114–124.

Presthus, R. (1964) *Men at the Top: A Study in Community Power.* New York: Oxford University Press.

Price, D. K. (1954) *Government and Science: Their Dynamic Relation in American Democracy.* New York: New York University Press.

Silvert, K. H. (1965) "American Academic Ethics and Social Research Abroad: The Lesson of Project Camelot," *American Universities Field Staff Reports* (West Coast South American Series), vol. 12, no. 3 (July).

Simirenko, A. (1966) *Soviet Sociology.* Chicago: Quadrangle Books.

U.S. House, Committee on Foreign Affairs (1965a) *Behavioral Sciences and the National Security,* report no. 4. Washington, D.C.: Government Printing Office.

U.S. House, Committee on Foreign Affairs (1965b) "Hearings on Winning the Cold War: The U.S. Ideological Offensive," p. 9. Washington, D.C.: Government Printing Office.

CHAPTER 17

THE ACADEMY
AND THE POLITY

This chapter is generally concerned with the operations of those government agencies of the United States (such as the Department of Defense and the Department of State) having the most to do with international relations and military affairs, and how they intersect with the operations of those university extensions (such as Stanford Research Institute and Cornell Aeronautical Laboratories) set up to deal with the same sorts of problems. It is an effort at ethnography, at summarizing what I have seen and heard discussed at all echelons of government and in all sectors of the university. The model that emerges makes no claim to inclusiveness, only to accuracy—an immodest enough statement given the scope of our subject.

The area we enter into is the sociology of political mobilization, that is, how academics view politicians and how politicians view academics. The problem is to locate either the mutuality or incompatibility of interests involved in any interaction between the academy and the polity.

To construct a satisfactory framework, we should focus on problem areas that are decisive for both groups: initially, how the interaction is perceived by the social scientists, to be followed by a presentation of problem areas perceived by political men. Apart from the interaction itself, there is the shadowy area of their consequences on the network of proposals and responses following from the relationship between the two contracting parties. For social scientists and politicians not only interact with one another, but the professional ideologies they arrive at and the norms they establish also guide present and future interactions.

One of the most serious, and at the same time difficult to resolve, aspects of the relationships of academics to politicians is determining at what point normative behavior leaves off and conflictual behavior starts. Only with the latter sort of interaction does a true problem-solving situation exist. For example, the norm of secrecy that guides bureaucratic behavior contrasts markedly with the norm of publicity governing most forms of academic behavior. There is little question that this normative distinction leads to a considerable amount of exacerbated sentiment. Yet, the differences between the two groups at this level seem intrinsic to the nature of sovereignty (for politicians) and to the nature of science (for academics). Such differences can hardly be "ironed out" or "smoothed over" simply because we would have a nicer world if they were. Thus, at best, an explication of the issues can permit an intellectual and ideological climate to unfold in which differences may be appreciated and in this way come to be lived with. This must be started explicitly. Those who expect a set of recommendations for the governance of relations between academics and politicians should be dissuaded from the advisability of such an approach, lest we find ourselves manufacturing perfect doctrinal formulas and juridical restraints that prove far worse than the initial problem being considered.

PROBLEM AREAS PERCEIVED BY THE ACADEMICIANS

MONEY

The initial and perhaps most immediate experience that social scientists have with politicians or their counterparts on various federal granting agencies relates to the financial structure of contracts and grants. But first, the difference between contracts and grants should be explained. As an operational definition we can speak of contracts as those agreements made with social scientists that originate in a federal bureaucracy. Most research on Thailand and Southeast Asia or on Pax Americana is contract work. Grants can be considered as those projects that are initiated by the social scientists.

Nonetheless, the distinction between contracts and grants should not be drawn too sharply, since in fact, if not in law, many contracts do originate with social scientists. Such agreements may be structured broadly to give the researcher a vast range of freedom, or they may be narrowly conceived to get a project tailored to an agency's "needs." The entrepreneurial spirit of social scientists, particularly those working in nonacademic research centers, makes them ingeniously adept at discovering what a government administrator is ready to pay for. Thus, while a *de jure* distinction between contracts and grants is useful, it is limited on *de facto* grounds by the inability to track down who originates a proposal and also who really shapes the final project.

Perhaps more important than the formal distinction between contracts and grants is the disproportionate funds made available by various federal agencies for social scientific purposes. The Department of Defense in the fiscal year 1967 budgeted 21.7 percent of its research funds for the social sciences. The Department of State budgeted only 1.6 percent of its funds for the social sciences—and most of this was in the separately administered Agency for International Development. This disparity indicates that the "modern" Department of Defense is far readier to make use of social science results than is the "traditional" Department of State.

A related complaint is that most contracts issued, in contrast to grants awarded by agencies such as the Department of Health, Education, and Welfare (HEW) or the National Institutes of Health (NIH), allocate little money for free-floating research. Funds are targeted so directly and budgeted so carefully that, with the exception of the overhead portion which is controlled by administrators rather than scholars, little elasticity is permitted for work that may be allied to but not directly connected with the specific purpose of the contract itself. This contrasts markedly with contracts made with many physical scientists and even with researchers in the field of mental health, who are often able to set aside a portion of their funds for innovative purposes. Even so-called kept organizations, such as IDA (Institute for Defense Analysis), SDC (System Development Corporation) or RAND (Rand Corporation), enjoy more latitude in developing their work programs than the usual "free" university researchers.

Related to this matter of financial reward for "hardware" and "high payoff" research is the funding available for social science research as a whole. Social scientists often claim that the funding structure is irrational. Government funds are available in large sums for big-team research, but little spillover is available for individual scholarly efforts. The government reinforces big-team research by encouraging large-scale grants administered by agencies and institutes and by its stubborn unwillingness to contribute to individual scholarly enterprise.

The assumption is made that big-scale ideas can be executed only by big-scale spending—a fallacy in logic, if not in plain fact. Large-scale grants are also made because they minimize bureaucratic opposition within the government and eliminate specific responsibility for research failures. But at the same time, this approach contributes to the dilemma of the scholar who is concerned with research at modest, "retail" levels which may be far more limited than the grant proposal itself indicates. The present contract structure encourages a degree of entrepreneurial hypocrisy that is often alien to the spirit of the individual researcher and costly to the purchaser of ideas and plans. And while individual agency efforts, notably by the National Science Foundation (NSF) have moved counter to this bureaucratic trend, the bulk of funds continues to be made available without much regard for the persons actually engaged in the researches.

SECRECY

Social scientists have become increasingly critical of the government's established norms of secrecy. The professional orientation of social scientists has normally been directed toward publicity rather than secrecy. The polity places a premium not only on acquiring vital information but also on maintaining silence about such information precisely in the degree that the data might be of high decisional value. This norm leads to differing premiums—and tensions—between analysts and policy-makers.

Terms of research and conditions of work tend to demand an initial compromise with social science methodology. The social scientist is placed in a cognitive bind. He is conditioned not to reveal maximum information lest he become victimized by the federal agencies that employ his services. Yet he is employed precisely because of his presumed thoroughness, impartiality and candor. The social scientist who survives in government service becomes "gingerly," or learns to play the game. His value to social science becomes seriously jeopardized. At the same time, however, if he should raise these considerations, his usefulness to the policy-making sector is likewise jeopardized.

Social scientists complain that the norm of secrecy often demands that they sacrifice their own essential work premises. A critical factor reinforcing the unwilling acceptance of the norm of secrecy by social scientists is that a great many government research funds are allocated for military or semimilitary purposes. United States Senate testimony has shown that approximately 50 percent of federal funds targeted for the social sciences are subject to some sort of federal review check.

The real wonder turns out to be not the existence of restrictions on the use of social science findings, but the relative availability of large chunks of information. Indeed, the classification of materials is so inept that documents (such as the Pax Americana research) designated as confidential or secret by one agency may often be made available as a "public service" by another agency. There are also occasions when documents that sponsoring government agencies place in a classified category can be secured without charge from the private research institute doing the work.

Social scientists believe that openness involves more than meeting formal requirements of scientific canons; it also requires that information be made universally available. The norm of secrecy encourages selective presentation of data. In this area, the social scientist is opposed by the policy-maker because of conflicting notions of the significance of data and their general need to be replicated elsewhere and by others. The policy-maker who demands differential access to findings considers this a normal price extracted for the initial expenditure of risk capital. The academic social scientist has a general attitude that sponsorship of research does not entitle any one sector to benefit unduly from the findings; he believes that sponsorship by federal agencies ought not to place limits on the use of work done any more than when research is sponsored by private agencies or by universities.

LOYALTY

The third major area that deeply concerns the social scientist is that of dual allegiance. The social scientist often expresses the charge that government work has such specific requirements and goal-oriented tasks that it intrudes upon his autonomy. He is compelled to choose between full participation in the world of the federal bureaucracy and his more familiar academic confines. He does not, however, want the former to create isolation in the latter. He thus often criticizes the federal bureaucracy's unwillingness to recognize his basic needs: (1) the need to teach and retain a full academic identity; (2) the need to publicize information; and above all, (3) the need to place scientific responsibility above the call of patriotic obligation—when they may happen to clash. In short, he does not want to be plagued by dual or competing allegiances.

The norm of secrecy exacerbates this problem. While many of the social scientists who became involved with federal research are intrigued by the opportunity to address important issues, they are confronted by bureaucracies which often do not share their passion for resolving *social* problems. For example, federal obligations commit the bureaucracy to assign high priority to items having *military* potential and effectiveness and low priorities to many idealistic themes in which social scientists are interested.

Those social scientists connected to the government as employees or as consultants are hamstrung by federal agencies which are, in turn, limited by political circumstances beyond their control. A federal bureaucracy must manage cumbersome, overgrown committees and data-gathering agencies. Federal agencies often protect a status quo merely for the sake of rational functioning. They must conceive of the academic in their midst as a standard bureaucratic type entitled to rise to certain federal ranks. Federal agencies limit innovating concepts simply to what is immediately useful, not out of choice, and certainly not out of resentment of the social sciences, but from what is deemed as impersonal necessity. This has the effect of reducing the social scientist's role in the government to that of ally or advocate rather than that of innovator or designer. Social scientists, particularly those with strong academic allegiances, begin to feel that their enthusiasm for rapid change is unrealistic considering how little can be done by the government bureaucracy. And they come to resent the involvement in theoryless application to immediacy foisted on them by the "New Utopians," along with surrender of the value of confronting men with the wide range of possible choices of action. The schism between autonomy and involvement is, in its own way, as thorough as that between secrecy and publicity, for it cuts to the quick, well-intentioned pretensions at human engineering.

The problem of competing allegiances is not made simpler by the fact that many high-ranking federal bureaucrats have strongly nationalistic and conservative political ideologies, in marked contrast with those of the social scientist. The social scientist comes to the nation's capital not only believing in the primacy of science over nationalism but defining what is patriotic in a more open-ended and consciously liberal manner than that of most appointed officials. Hence, he often perceives that the conflict involves more than research design and social applicability; it is a consequence of the incompatible ideologies held respectively by the social scientists and entrenched Washington bureaucrats. He comes to resent the "proprietary" attitude of the bureaucrat toward "his" government processes. He is likely to conclude that his social science biases are a necessary buffer against the federal bureaucracy.

IDEOLOGY

A question arising with greater frequency now that many social scientists are doing federally sponsored research concerns the relationship between heuristic and valuative aspects of work. Put plainly, should the social scientist not only supply an operational framework of information but also assist in the creation of a viable ideological framework? Does he have the right to discuss, examine and prescribe the goals of social research for social science? Whether social scientists in government service ever raise such issues is less important than the fact that some might refuse any connection with the federal bureaucracy for this reason.

Many social scientists, especially those working on foreign area research, bitterly complain that government policy-makers envision social science to be limited to heuristics, to supplying operational codebooks and facts about our own and other societies, and that the social scientist is supposed to perform maintenance services for military missions. Social scientists, however, also consider their work in terms of its normative function, in terms of the principles and goals of foreign and domestic policy. But given their small tolerance for error, policy-makers cannot absorb mistaken evaluations. This inhibits the social scientist's long-range evaluations and renders empiricism the common denominator of investigation. Factual presentations become not only "value-free" but "trouble-free."

This is not so much indicative of a choice between pure and applied social research as a consequence of differing perspectives on the character of application. Social scientists working for the political establishment realize that applied research is clearly here to stay. They are the first to announce that it is probably the most novel element in American—in contrast to European—social science. But federal bureaucrats operate with a concept of application that often removes theoretical considerations from research. Designing the future out of present-day hard facts, rather than analyzing types of action and interest and their relations in the present, comes to stand for a limited administrative utopianism and creates the illusion that demands for theory and candid ideological commitment have been met.

The social world is constructed like a behavioral field, the dynamics and manipulation of which are reserved for policy-makers' efforts to design futures. But social scientists are aware that "interests" and their representative values are contending for influence on that field, and that social planning is often a matter of choosing among these values for the sake of political goals. Thus, tension arises between social scientists, who consider their work set in highly political terms, and federal bureaucrats, who prefer to consider the work of the social scientists in nonpolitical terms. Indeed, federal administrators particularly go out of their way to depoliticize the results of potentially volatile social research so as to render it a better legitimizing device for their own bureaucratic activities. Social scientists come to suspect that their work is weighed for efficiency and applicability to an immediate and limited situation. The ability of the social system to confront large-scale and long-standing problems is left out of reckoning.

REWARD

Federal bureaucrats measure the rewards of social science involvement in the government in terms of payoffs generated. These are conceived to be the result of "big-team" research involving heavy funding (like the Model Cities Program). Moreover, the high status of individuals is appreciated when they are at the center rather than the periphery of policy performance, having an opportunity to influence policy at high levels, to secure valuable information and to give prestige to projects in which they participate. And, it might be added, many social scientists who contract research from the government seek just such power rewards.

Even those social scientists most involved with the government—as employees rather than as marginal consultants—express profound reservations about the reward system. First, as we have noted, social scientists operate under various degrees of secrecy which stifle their urge toward publicity for the work they do. Recognition goes instead to the men they work for. Second, social scientists must share responsibility for policy mistakes. Thus, they may be targeted for public criticism under difficult conditions more frequently than praised when they perform their duties well. Finally, those social scientists closest to policy agencies are most subject to congressional inquiry and to forms of harassment and investigation unlike anything that may befall strictly academic men.

The government-employed social scientist runs risks to which his colleagues at universities are not subject. He often contends that these risks are not properly understood by academics or rewarded by policy-makers (salary scales, for example, are adequate in federal work but not noticeably higher than academic salaries). Marginal payoffs resulting from publication are often denied the federally sponsored social scientists. Publication is a sensitive area for other reasons. Social scientists' fears concerning their removal from channels of professional respectability and visibility seem to increase proportionately to their distance from the academy. Few of those in federal work receive recognition from their own professional societies, and few gain influential positions within these professional establishments. The marginality produced by federal work means that scholars willing to be funded through government agencies, or even to accept consultantships, will reject primary association with a federal administration. For this reason, the list of high-quality social scientists who choose to remain in the government as professional civil servants remains low.

While outsiders may accuse federally sponsored social scientists of "selling out," the latter defend themselves by pointing out that they make sacrifices for the sake of positively influencing social change. This self-defense, however, is often received skeptically by their colleagues in the academic arena (as well as by their would-be supporters in the federal bureaucracy), who regard such hypersensitive moralism with suspicion. The upshot of this matter of "rewards" is, then, that status derived from proximity to sources of power is offset by isolation from the actual wielders of power—academic no less than political.

PROBLEM AREAS PERCEIVED
BY THE POLITICIANS

Social scientists' complaints about their difficulties with government-sponsored research have received more attention than administrative complaints against social scientists simply because social scientists tend to be more articulate in examining their feelings and in registering their complaints about the work they do. Also, the relationship of the social scientist to the bureaucrat has a greater import for the social scientist than for the bureaucrat. It is small wonder that government complaints about social scientists have been poorly understood.

Federal agencies and their bureaucratic leaderships remain skeptical about the necessity of employing basic social science data in their own formulations. Among traditionally appointed officials, the local lawyer or party worker is the key means for transmitting information upward. For many sectors of the military, expertise comes mainly from military personnel performing military functions and does not require outside social science validation. As we witnessed in the military response to the Department of Defense "Whiz Kids," outside efforts may be considered intrusions. High military brass (as well as a number of politicians) sounded off hotly against the Defense Department and echoed in their critiques a traditional posture which pits military intuition and empirical proximity to the real world against mathematical techniques and ivory tower orientations.

When social scientists attempt to combat these doubts and suspicions by preparing memorandums and documents that prove the efficacy of social science for direct political and military use, they may do more to reinforce negative sentiments than to overcome them. When the academy responds that way to the polity (as it did in its recommendations to the Defense Science Board),[1] then it underwrites its own lack of autonomy, if not its own ineptitude. It cannot prove its worth by moral declarations and public offerings to bureaucratic agencies. The total service orientation of social research, in contrast with the independent "feudal" academic orientation, is one that breeds contempt for the performer of such services and a lack of faith in his results. This helps to explain the resentment for social science research extending from the Joint Chiefs of Staff to the Senate Foreign Relations Committee. Suppliers of intellectual labor are well paid if they have a powerful union or guild—as many social sciences have—but they hardly command high status in a political atmosphere that strains toward quick and inexpensive solutions.

WASTE

The first and perhaps most significant criticism made by administrators against the academy is that social scientists make excessive demands for funds and special treatment while working on projects that frequently have little tactical value. This is translated into a charge of impracticality. Typical is the critique made by the General Accounting Office against the Hudson Institute, headed by defense strategist Herman Kahn. Underlining charges made by the Office of Civil Defense, the work of the Hudson Institute in the area of the behavioral sciences was scored for being "less useful than had been expected," and cited as unacceptable without "major revision." Various social science reports, particularly those prepared by semiprivate agencies, have been criticized for their superficiality, for their "tired" thinking, for their sensationalism and, above all, for their lack of immediate relevance.

In response, social researchers claim that the purpose of a good report is imaginative effort rather than practical settlement of all outstanding issues. Government agencies should not expect a high rate of success on every research attempt, they argue. One reason for the persistence of this line of criticism is how rarely demands for high-payoff utilitarian research are ever contested. The questionable practicality of much social science research remains a sore point in the relationship, which cannot be resolved until and unless social scientists themselves work out a comfortable formula governing the worth of relevance in contrast with the demand for relevance.

[1] *The Report of the Panel on Defense Social and Behavioral Sciences* urged increased effort and funding for research on manpower in all its aspects: for research on organization studies, for research on decision making, for increased intervention research on foreign areas and for research on man and his physical environment. For an analysis of this report, see Horowitz (1968).

INUTILITY

Another criticism leveled at academics by federal sponsors issues from the first—namely, that there are no systems for ensuring that results obtained in research are usable. A gap exists between the proposal and fulfillment stages of a research undertaking, and there is an equally wide gap between the *results* obtained and the *process* involved in grappling with problems. Proposals that are handsomely drawn up and attractively packaged often have disappointing results. And while many sophisticated agencies, such as NIH, NSF or OEO (Office of Economic Opportunity), are aware of the need for permissiveness in research design, those agencies more firmly rooted in hard science and engineering traditions are not so tolerant of such experimentation.

Moreover, it is charged that academics engaged in government research "overconservatize" their responses to placate a federal bureaucracy. This may come, however, at the very point when the administrator is trying to establish some liberal policy departures. The chore of the federal agency becomes much more difficult, since it must cope not only with bureaucratic sloth and the conservative bias of top officials but also with reinforcements for it in research reports by the social scientists from whom more liberal formulations might have been expected. Thus, not only is there a gap between proposal stage and fulfillment stage in the research enterprise, but also some reports may structure conservative biases into the programs assigned to the federal bureaucracy by congressional committees or by executive branch leadership.

The charge of inutility is often related to a differential intellectual style or culture. The government-versus-academy cleavage is largely a consequence of intellectual specialization of a kind that makes it difficult for the typical bureaucrat to talk meaningfully with the typical "modern" behavioral scientist. Most government officers in the Department of State, for example, are trained either in history or in a political science of a normative sort. International relations taught in the descriptive traditions of the twenties or, at the least, in the style of a Morgenthau or a Schuman, continue to prevail. Whatever difficulties may exist between the academy and the polity at the level of role performance, these can at least be overcome by those who share a common intellectual formation. But often communication cannot be achieved with those behaviorists whose vocabulary, methods and even concepts seem esoteric, irrelevant, occasionally trivial and not rarely fraudulent. Thus, at the root of the charge of inutility is a conflict of intellectual cultures that negatively affects the relations between the academics and the politicians.

ELITISM

Federal administrators point out that academic men often demand deferential treatment, contrary to the norms that govern other federal employees. They charge that social science personnel do not really accept their role as government employees, but rather see themselves as transiently or marginally connected to the government. Particularly in areas of foreign affairs, the academic appears to want the advantages of being privy to all kinds of quasi-secret information and of being involved in decision making, and yet to avoid normal responsibilities accepted by other government employees.

Such attitudes smack of elitism to federal officials—an elitism built into the structure of social scientific thinking. Trained to analyze problems rather than to convince constituencies, social scientists become impatient with the vagaries of politics, preferring the challenge of policy. One reason adduced by elected officials for preferring legal rather than scientific advisers is that the former have a far keener appreciation of mechanisms for governing people and being governed by them. The legal culture breeds a respect for the "popular will" rarely found among social scientists attached to government agencies. Indeed, the resentment expressed by many House and Senate committees against Defense Department and State Department social scientists is a direct response to the elitist streak that seems to characterize social scientists in government.

This is the reverse side of the "involvement–autonomy" debate. The government pushes for total involvement and participation, while the social scientist presses for autonomy and limited responsibility in decisions directly affecting policy. Elitism rationalizes the performance of important services while enabling the social scientist to maintain the appearance of detachment.

ACCESS

Although social scientists view their own federal involvement as marginal, at the same time they demand access to top elites so that they may be assured that their recommendations will be implemented or at least seriously considered. But access at this level entails bypassing the standard bureaucratic channels through which other federal employees must go.

The social scientist's demand for elite accessibility, though said to be inspired by noble purpose, tends to set the social scientist apart from other employees of the federal government. He sees himself as an advising expert, not an employee. The social scientist takes himself seriously as an appointed official playing a political role in a way that most other federal workers do not. But the federal bureaucracy finds the social scientist has come to Washington to "set the world on fire," and finds that a presumptuous intention, one unmindful of the flame that also burns in the heart of the staff administrator.

The question of ready access to leadership rests on notions of the superior wisdom of the social scientist; however, it is precisely this claim that is most sharply contested by federal administrators. Reflecting popular biases, administrators claim that the easy admission of social scientists to the halls of power presumes a correctness in their policy judgments not supported by historical events and not warranted by mass support from popular sectors. The separation of science and citizen roles often justifies lack of citizen participation. The scientific ethos thus comes to serve as a basis for admission into a system of power by circumventing the civic culture. This is precisely why federal bureaucrats feel that they are defending their political constituencies (and not, incidentally, their own bailiwicks) by limiting social science participation in the decision-making process.

MARGINALITY

If social scientists chafe at being outside the mainstream of academic life during their period of involvement with the political system, the federal bureaucrats are themselves highly piqued by the degree of supplemental employment enjoyed and desired by the social scientists. Also, in clear contrast with other federal governmental personnel, social scientists are able to locate supplemental positions in the Washington, D.C., area. They work as teachers and professors; they do writing on the side for newspapers and magazines; they edit books and monographs; they offer themselves as specialist consultants capitalizing on their government involvement. They become active in self-promotion to a degree far beyond the reasons for their being hired.

In the more loosely structured world of the academy, such self-promotion not only goes uncriticized but is rewarded. Royalty payments for textbook writing, involvement with publishing firms in editorial capacities, *honoraria* connected with membership in granting agencies and payments for lectures on American campuses are all highly respected forms of supplemental "employment." But federal government employment involves 12 months a year and 24 hours a day. This condition and its demands are far different from the nine months a year and fluid scheduling endemic to most social scientist relations with academic institutions.

Federal agencies disdain the marginal aspects of the academics' involvement in political life, and their awareness that men involved in government effort are often enough *not* representative of the most outstanding talent available in the social sciences also disturbs them, particularly because they traffic in the status spinoff of both the academy and the polity. The anomaly exists that men who may not have been especially successful in academic life make demands upon the federal bureaucracy as if, in fact, they were the most outstanding representatives of their fields. The same problems might well arise in connection with outstanding representatives from the social sciences, but the situation becomes exacerbated precisely because the federal bureaucrats know they are dealing with—at least in many instances—second- and even third-echelon federally employed social scientists.

IMPROVING INTERACTION

In this profile the academics and federal administrators alike have been presented as more uniform in their response to each other than is actually the case. It should not be imagined that the two groups spend all their time in bickering criticism of each other, for then certainly no stable relationship worth speaking of could exist. Still, the roles acted out by both parties make it clear that we are in a period of extensive redefinition. The criticism that academics and politicos have of each other often has a mirror-image effect, each side sharply focusing on the least commendable features of the other.

Significantly, the political context and content of this issue has, in the main, been unconsciously suppressed by both sides. The academics have preferred to emphasize their scientific activities in objective and neutral terminology, while the politicos have expressed their interests in organizational and bureaucratic terms. The strangest aspect of this interaction, then, is that in the world of politics it seems that nothing is more embarrassing than political analysis and synthesis. As if by common consent, social scientists and policy-makers have agreed to conduct their relations by a code of genteel disdain rather than open confrontation. The gulf between the two groups requires political distance as an operational equivalent to the social distance between competing tribal villagers.

THE CONTRACT STATE

There may be cause for concern that federal government sponsorship corrupts the character of social science output because it emphasizes big money, an overly practical orientation and limited dissemination of information, and because it fails to accept the possibility that any research may be potentially subversive. But ironically, timid or opportunistic social scientific personnel are not recruited by the government. Most often the social scientist seeks the federal sponsor and becomes overly ambitious in the process of pressing exaggerated claims for unique research designs and high-payoff promises. The chief danger for the academic who has come to depend on the federal bureaucracy for research funds and its variety of career satisfactions is not more financial dependence; rather, it is that he may begin to develop the loyalties and cautionary temperament of the opportunistic civil servant per se.

Many interlocking appointments between the academy and the polity have occurred at the organizational level without resolving persistent questions as to what constitutes legitimate interaction between the academy and the polity. This indicates that the line between the academy and the polity is blurred enough to require precise determination of exactly who is stimulating what kinds of research and under what conditions. As it becomes increasingly clear that academics are the stimulants and administrators the respondents in a majority of instances, it becomes obvious also that criticism must be leveled at social science participation rather than at federal practice.

To understand fully the sources of tension in the interaction between academics and administrators, it is necessary to illuminate the range of attitudes toward connection between the government and the academy, which extends from advocating complete integration between administrators and academics to calling for complete rupture between the two groups. A spectrum of positions is presented on this matter.

POLICY-SCIENCE APPROACH

The quarter of a century period from 1943 to 1968 witnessed a range of attitudes from complete integration to complete rupture. From World War II, and even prior to that, during the era of the New Deal, optimism prevailed about an integrated relationship between academics and administrators. This was perhaps best expressed by the "policy-science" approach frequently associated with the work of Harold Lasswell (1951, pp. 3–15).

In his view, the relationship between the academic and the political networks would be an internal affair, with political men involved in academic affairs just as frequently and as fully as academic men would be involved in political affairs. The policy-science approach was a noble effort to redefine familiar departmental division of labor. Sociology, political science, economics and the other social sciences would be absorbed by a *unified policy science* which involved a common methodological core. The problem with his exchange network, as Lasswell himself well understood in later years, is the federal administrators spoke with the presumed authority of the "garrison state," while academics (even those temporarily in government service) spoke with the presumed impracticality of the "ivory tower."

The policy-science approach did, in fact, have direct policy consequences. The end of World War II and the fifties saw the rise of new forms of institutional arrangements for housing social science. But more than organization was involved. A new emphasis cut across disciplinary boundaries. Area studies emerged in every major university. Communism was studied as part of the more general problem of the role of ideology in social change. This was followed by centers for urban studies and the study of industrial and labor relations. But despite the rise of institutionalized methods for uniting specialties, university department structures had a strange way of persisting, not just as lingering fossils but as expanding spheres of influence.

It soon became apparent that in the struggle to influence the graduate-student world and to decide who shall or shall not be appointed and promoted in university positions, the "department" held final authority. The separate departments of social sciences enabled the disciplines to retain their vitality. At the same time that the policy-science approach was confronting departmentalism, disciplinary specialization was increasing. During the postwar period, anthropology insisted on departmental arrangements distinguishing it from sociology and theology, while other areas such as political science and social work became more sharply delineated than ever before. The policy-science approach was able to institutionalize all sorts of aggressive and at times even progressive reorderings of available *information,* but failed to establish the existence of a policy-science *organization.* And this proved fatal to its claims for operational primacy.

The policy-science approach was supplanted by the "handmaiden" approach of the early fifties, in which the academy was to supply the necessary ingredients to make the political world function smoothly. The reasoning was that the social sciences were uniquely qualified to instill styles in federal decision making based on confirmed data. But this was not to entail complete integration of services and functions. This handmaiden approach was considered more suitable to the nature of both the sciences and the policy-making aspects of government and was materially assisted by a rising emphasis on applied social research. The new emphasis on application and on large-scale research provided the theoretical rationale for janitorial "mop-up" services. Applied research was to make the search for the big news, for the vital thrust; participation in this intimate consensual arrangement would not deprive the social sciences of their freedom, but would guarantee relevance. The "theoryless" service approach was thus wedded to an action orientation.

Advocates of the handmaiden approach such as Ithiel de Sola Pool (1967, pp. 267–280) vigorously defended social scientists' obligation to do meaningful research for government. It was noted that an organization such as the Department of Defense has manifold needs for the tools of social science analysis as a means for better understanding its world. It was pointed out that the intelligence test had been an operational instrument in manpower management since World War I, and that the Defense Department and other federal agencies had become major users of social psychology in military and sensitive areas. As the world's largest training and educational institution, the United States government had to acquire exact knowledge for the selection and training of an enormous number of human subjects. Equally significant was the federal government's needs for exact foreign area information. This thirst for knowledge of the particular cultural values and social and political structures of foreign countries increased as the world was carved up into potential enemies or potential allies of the United States.

The ironic aspect of this support for useful research is that although the handmaiden approach ostensibly left social science autonomy intact, it reduced that autonomy in fact by establishing criteria for federal rather than social science "payoff." High-yield research areas uniformly involved what the social sciences could do for the political structures and not necessarily the other way around. Thus, while the policy-science approach gave way to the service-industry orientation of the handmaiden approach, the latter, too, was not based on any real parity between the academy and the polity.

SELECTIVE PARTICIPATION APPROACH

A new approach, considerably removed from both the policy-science and handmaiden approaches, has been finely articulated by David B. Truman (1968). As theory, it expresses a renewed sense of equity and parity between social scientists and administrators. Under Truman's arrangement, there would be frequent but largely unplanned interchanges between federal bureaucratic positions and university positions. This exchange of roles would prove valuable and could eventually be explored and encouraged on a systematic basis. Meanwhile, the selective participation approach advocates minimal formal structure in the system.

The most important aspect of the selective participation approach is that it is based upon a norm of reciprocity. A partial interchange of personnel could be accomplished primarily through regular seminars and conferences mutually attended by social scientists and government administrators, each cluster of men representing carefully designed combinations. Another method might be alternating presentation of scientific development and policy problems at these meetings. Unlike the normal consultant relationship of the handmaiden style, this would guarantee some kind of equity between the academy and the polity. Selective participation would include securing grants and promoting federal research for multidisciplinary teams of academics working on political problems, instead of the usual outright political employment of individual social scientists or academic talent. This, it was hoped, would provide a flexible arrangement of specialties that would fill the gap between scientific knowledge and public purpose without detriment either to social scientists or political policy-makers. Operationally, it meant a greater flow of funds from government agencies to research institutes housed on university campuses—a not inconsequential change over the policy-science approach, which projected a much more intimate ecological, network.

FORMS OF NONPARTICIPATION

The dilemma was that the selective participation approach implicitly assumed an exchange network with a parity of strength between political decision-makers and academics. The approach failed to demonstrate that the academic would be on a par with the administrator, for the latter had financial inputs while the former had the information outputs. In point of fact, the government agency still does the hiring, even in the selective participation approach and the academic participates in a policy-making role without much expectancy of a payoff for social science theory or methodology.

This has given rise to what might be called the principle of "nonparticipation," which is increasingly being adopted. Social scientists continue to write and publish in areas of foreign research or in sectors vital to the national political arena, but do not do so under government contract or as a direct response to a federal agency. It was felt that if the autonomy of the social sciences means anything at all, uses and findings legitimately arrived at will be incorporated into federal policy making whether or not social scientists participate actively or critically.

The principle of nonparticipation tended to be adopted by many conservative as well as radical social scientists who saw in the growth of federal social research a threat to the standard forms of status advancement in the professions and also a movement toward applied social planning that violated their own feelings for the generalizing nature of social science. On organizational and intellectual grounds, the principle of nonparticipation served as an effective response to the policy-science approach. The underlying assumption of the notion of nonparticipation is that the federal government has more to gain than does the social scientist by the interaction between them. Although interaction would be maintained, the order of priorities would be changed so that social scientists no longer would have the onerous task of providing high-payoff research for others with low yields to themselves.

In many ways, the principle of nonparticipation suggested that the university department remain the primary agency in the organization of social science instead of the federal research bureau. The nonparticipant in federal programs often found himself to be the critic of bureaucratic research in general, and of bureaucratic agencies attached to universities in particular. He did not want to have his research controlled by federal decision making and, more important, he did not want a federal agency to usurp what was properly a judgment in the domain of a university department.

At the same time, the principle of nonparticipation spilled over into the principle of active opposition. This opposition was registered in the main by younger scholars in areas such as history and by graduate students in the social sciences, that is, among those often involved in student protest movements. From their point of view, the matter could not be resolved on the essentially conservative grounds of selective use by the government of the best of social science. A conscious attempt must be made to utilize scholarship for partisan or revolutionary goals that could under no circumstances be employed by the establishments linked to government agencies. As Hans Morgenthau indicated, this represented a movement away from the belief that the social scientist and the federal administrator inhabited mutually exclusive institutions, to a belief in a more active opposition because they occupied mutually hostile positions with antithetical goals.

In one sense, the radical posture accepts the policy-science appraisal of a political world dominated by the "garrison state," but rejects its remedy of social science immersion to reorient government away from its predatory world missions. The policy-science view assumed the educability of military-minded rulers. The antiparticipation view assumes the reverse, namely, the ease with which social scientists become incorporated into the military and political goals of men of power.

Radical critics like John McDermott assert that in practice the goals of the academy and the polity have become antithetical. Furthermore, they say, theoretically, they ought to be antithetical. A transformation of the dream of action into the nightmare of federal participation has been brought about, in which the academy has become, in effect, an adjunct of the federal establishment. Academic social scientists' dream of position and prestige has in some sense been realized by their transformation into men of action: Academic men have become high priests of social change. The desire for social change has, in effect, overwhelmed the goals toward which such change was directed.

The move toward active opposition is a critique of the way in which the university, no less than the government, is structured. Those who moved away from federal participation simultaneously turned their energies on the university system. They hold that the academy itself, as beneficiary of federal funds, has become the political party of the academic man. The rash of student attacks against the university must be considered, in part at least, symbolic attacks against the notion of integration of policy making and academic performance.

SURROGATE POLITICS

The most well-guarded nonsecret of the present era of university relationships to the government, at least insofar as these ties bear upon the notion of active opposition, concerns the general political and ideological climate that now prevails.

During the 1941–45 period, when the United States was engaged in a world conflict in which the overwhelming number of citizens felt involved in the very survival of civilization itself, there were no pained expressions about government recruiting on campuses. There was no resentment toward the retooling of universities to satisfy military research needs and psychological warfare, propaganda research or conventional bombing surveys. Nor were any scholarly panels held at professional meetings concerning the propriety of social scientists who accepted appointments under the Roosevelt Administration in the Office of War Information or in the Office of Strategic Services, such as those panels that now discuss the propriety of relationships between social scientists and the Federal Bureau of Investigation or the Central Intelligence Agency.

The present level of controversy about the relationship between the academy and the polity has spilled over into a series of surrogate discussions of the legitimacy of the war in Vietnam, Latin American self-determination and civil strife in American ghettos. Unable to address such issues directly and unprepared to design structures for future alleviation of such world and national pressures, social scientists exaggerate the politics of inner organizational life. Professional societies engage in mimetic reproduction of central social concerns on a low-risk and probably a low-yield basis.

Organizational struggles also receive the encouragement and support of corresponding professional men and societies from the Third World and from minority groups. It is no accident that federal projects that had Latin American targets have come under particularly severe assault. The existence of a counter-social science establishment in countries such as Mexico, Chile, Argentina and Brazil provides vocal support for domestic United States academic opposition, and for firming up such opposition by posing the threat of total isolation from foreign area research for a failure to heed the dangers of certain kinds of political research. Increasingly, black militants in this country have adopted a similar posture of nonparticipation in social science projects without clearly stating preconditions of protection of the "rights" of the subjects or sovereigns.

The risks to both social science and public policy from the predetermination of research designs will not be discussed here. Suffice it to say that surrogate politics has now become a rooted pattern in American academic affairs, partly because academics come to politics by way of moral concern, while politicians come to moral concern by way of political participation. Surrogate politics is also a reflex action of the expanding articulate but impotent social sectors against what have become the dominant political trends of the United States at this time.

Surrogate politics has its place in national affairs. Indeed, the question of the relationship between the academy and the polity is precisely a question of surrogate politics. A common undercurrent of moral revulsion for professional hucksterism and amateur gamesmanship had forced the present review of the status between social scientists and policy-makers. This same reexamination should have taken place a quarter of a century ago, despite the difficulties of the situation. But precisely because of the optimal consensus that existed in the past concerning the political climate, the issues now being discussed were considered improper topics for social scientists in pursuit of truth.

REFERENCES

de Sola Pool, I. (1967) "The Necessity for Social Scientists Doing Research for Governments," in I. L. Horowitz, ed., *The Rise and Fall of Project Camelot: Studies in the Relationship Between Social Science and Practical Politics.* Cambridge, Mass.: M.I.T. Press.

Horowitz, I. L. (1968) "Social Science Yogis and Military Commissars," *transaction*, vol. 5, no. 6 (May), pp. 29–38.

Lasswell, H. D. (1951) "The Policy Orientation," in D. Lerner and H. D. Lasswell, eds., *The Policy Sciences.* Stanford, Calif.: Stanford University Press.

Truman, D. B. (1968) "The Social Sciences and Public Policy," *Science,* vol. 160, no. 3827 (May 3), pp. 508–512.

CHAPTER 18

SOCIAL SCIENCE MANDARINS

There is a myth prevalent among social scientists and even their critics to the Left and Right. It has many variations, but its theme is simple enough. The scenario goes something like this: The government, or one of its major agencies, has "a need to know." It realizes that a vacuum exists in its knowledge and thus seeks to narrow the "information gap." This is done by contracting or granting awards to outside knowledge factories—located either in private firms or in university adjunct bureaus. Next comes the "bid" on the given project, followed by the actual research reports generated by the winning bidder. When the topic is "hot," more than one contract might be let for the same topic of investigation—ostensibly for the purpose of checking results and insuring useful applications. After the project is completed, the results are turned over to policy-makers, or their agency representatives; this information in then sifted, routed, evaluated and finally channelized for prompt or delayed action (Lasswell, 1951).

The casual sequence just outlined, and assumed as the gospel truth by a myriad of "investigators," "contractors" and "information purchasers," is rarely used and often abused. The fuss and the fury surrounding the uses of social science for evil purposes largely misses its target. It is not that social scientists engaged in governmental work, either as a main or peripheral activity, are beyond criticism, but rather that what they are being criticized for is wide of the mark. Criticism is often made to appear idiosyncratic and misanthropic, such as when a group of patriotic social scientists are holding the fort for America against their critics ranging from the Vietniks to the superpatriots. The truth of the matter is less theatrical or melodramatic and, indeed, less attractive than either the ideologists or counterideologists of social science care to admit.

The model that I believe is more nearly empirically verifiable goes as follows: (1) policies are decided upon by some department of the legislative or executive branch of government; (2) these policies are arrived at through assumption of the needs of some mass or elite constituency externally; and (3) the need for any new Administration or ambitious member of the House or Senate to define their uniqueness in the political heavens leads them to search out what Gaetano Mosca long ago called the political formula, that is, "the New Frontier," "the War on Poverty," "black capitalism" and so on, ad infinitum; (4) once the political course is set, *then* there is a frantic search for precedent in the past, justification in the present and rationalization in the future; (5) in order to justify decisions made without any reference to the empirical world, social scientists are called in to do "feasibility studies," "demonstration effects" and "simulation analyses" that prove beyond a shadow of a doubt the legitimacy of the course of decision making decided upon in some political backroom or congressional cloakroom, or even in some presidential "state of the nation" report.

Social scientists engaged in governmental work are committed to an advocacy model defined by politicians. For the most part, they do not *establish* or even verify policy—only *legitimize* policy. They are, in effect, the great mandarins of the present era. They proclaim a position, more than prove its efficacy or necessity. They operate within a teleological model, rather than a causal model. They enter at the termination, not the beginning, of the policy-making process. If they are going to be judged, let it be for their role as mandarins, not as logicians; for their adaptation to problems of political advocacy, rather than their unique capacity to predict and operationalize the future.

Why do social scientists willingly perform such a role as legitimizers, and why are they asked (and paid so well) to do so? The answers are linked more to the nature of American political life than to any inner propensities of social scientists. America has now entered a period of great transformation in the decision-making process—a move from politics to policies. In human terms, this represents a move from politicians making decisions in response to popular wishes to policy-makers making decisions on the bases of the "logic" of political interest groups.

It is nonsense to assume, on the basis of dubious voting data, that the Democratic Party is partial to social science (because more social scientists are Democratic Party voters) and the Republican Party less partial to social science (because fewer social scientists vote Republican). There is no evidence of such professional distribution. Polls indicate that on select issues, such as the Vietnam War and crime in the streets, academics seem to cleave along lines common to the public as a whole. And even if there are more Democratic voters than Republican voters among social scientists, this is plainly irrelevant, because the determination of social science use is by policy-makers who are themselves effectively depoliticized through the bureaucratic process and not just politicians. Just as Presidents Kennedy and Johnson had their social science "advisers"—Walt W. Rostow, Walter Heller and Daniel P. Moynihan—so does Nixon have his—Paul Mc-Cracken, Henry Kissinger and the same Daniel P. Moynihan. On close inspection, one is led to the conclusion that Nixon's social scientists are both more "liberal" and more numerous than Johnson's (Weidenbaum, 1969). Also, as in the case of Kissinger and Moynihan, social scientists "proved" their value neutrality by serving different leaders of different parties without any serious qualms.

This move from politics to policy represents a crisis in federalism. It is a move from simple government to complex government, from a trust lodged in the peoples' representatives to the trust lodged in computer representatives. The shift from legislative to executive decision making, especially in the area of foreign policy, is linked to the belief that the world is too complicated and decisions have to be made too quickly to permit constant parliamentary debate on every issue as it arises. The role of the expert is therefore to advise the policy-maker. The result is a hard bureaucratic core of hundreds of thousands of people involved in nitty-gritty activities on a daily basis, and who either hire, or are themselves, social scientists whose purpose it is to legitimize their activities.

That this condition is encouraged, much less permitted, is due to the rise of genteel fascism in America, or for the fainthearted, a modernized Platonism, in which every man knows his "place," and in which information is held to be equivalent to wisdom. The mystique of science has spilled over into a belief in social science along the same lines. Social scientists have done little to discourage this halo effect because they are endlessly involved in the process of simulating and incorporating scientific instruments, not to mention physical science programming, to justify their own activities and claim for wider support. Thus, the public comes to believe in the sanctifying wisdom of social science and in its ability to predict future events. A policy announced as having scientific support is far easier to install than one that does not have such legitimation. The reassuring sight of Henry Kissinger or Daniel Moynihan at the President's side on a trip to Europe or Asia, or on an inspection of poverty programs in the nation's capital, inspires confidence of a sort not rendered to ordinary politicians. It is easier to believe the nonpartisan image of a social scientist than of a representative of a political party organization—no matter how capable the latter may, in fact, be. The doctrine of value-free social science continues to have an enormous payoff in the public image of the social scientist as an honest broker. In the absence of a sophisticated and informed public, who is to say that the social scientist will not function more democratically than the elected constituency. In moments of national crisis, it is presumed easier to trust the judgment of experts than that of *vox populi*. This is, of course, the classic conservative argument against democracy come to life, but in the form of the much hated social scientist, who no more cares for conservatism than he does for radicalism.

Social science as a legitimizing device performs necessary ideological services for a society that has already announced the end of ideology as a populist activity. The end of ideology masks the end of politics as a significant mass activity, and its displacement by the rise of policy making as the mainspring of political control. In the absence of mass legitimation through the electoral process or through the indirect authority of the people, politicians must seek legitimacy through the analytical process or through the will of Platonic social scientists. If the world does not seem to be improving with this influx of new types into the political spectrum, the economic and social lot of the social scientist has improved. With the exception of the opposition and disdain from some grumpy poor white trash on the Right, and even more surly (because more articulate) affluent intellectuals on the Left, the new political formula for governing America seems to be widely accepted, if not openly acknowledged to exist.

Why are social scientists, if they have this Olympian role in government as Great Legitimizers, nonetheless coming under increasingly sharp criticism? Social scientists tend to adopt innovative stances with respect to social structures. They must somehow show that things are not perfect, and when things are perfect, they tend to justify their high fees. This confronts them with conservative elements that equate planning, tinkering, budgeting and the like with creeping socialism, or even worse, subversion of basic patriotic values. Lacking as they do an independent constituency, the social science legitimizers are subject to frequent attack from right-wing elements. These attacks usually are not made directly on the social scientists, but rather on their sponsoring agencies, especially those foundations and think tanks that provide the government with basic research and survey reports (Cf. Horowitz and Horowitz, 1970).

This criticism from the Right (and from the Left, too) hurts the social science legitimizers, who believe that the performance of their role demonstrates a fealty to the sacred canons of Americanism and an unquestioning assumption of the workability of the system. If they call for anything short of revolution, then the Left declares social scientists to be copouts, unwilling to examine the "root problems" of American society. Lacking their own source of independent legitimation, social scientists become subject to assaults from the political poles without much room for maneuver. While they are needed by the ongoing political system, they are more like ordinary monks than mandarins. Once they get out on a limb, and subject to rank-

and-file criticism, the social scientists find they have few friends, and even fewer defenders. The pay is good, but the work risky.

Now we shall turn to various illustrations of social scientists in action —or, how the Great Legitimizer does his job. Because there are different users of social science, for different political ends, we shall try to draw upon a wide number of examples from different fields.

BROWN v. BOARD OF EDUCATION

The classic example cited in support of the role of social science in government is the Supreme Court desegregation rulings of 1954 (*Brown* v. *Board of Education* 374 U.S. 483). It is said that without the evidence provided by the social sciences, this decision could not have been reached, at least not with such unanimity. While it is true that certain precedents in social science research were brought to bear, there are several dubious aspects of this argument. First, social science information on the biological equality of races has been with us for many years—even during years that the Supreme Court either ignored the inequality of the black and minority groups or declined to consider a broadening interpretation of judicial responsibility. Second, the Supreme Court merely used available information; on its own it made no effort to convene a special commission to draw upon as a source for rendering its decision. It simply took a random sampling of information to justify a decision it was bound to make on more prosaic grounds of rising black militance and postwar discontent of the educated liberal sectors of white America. Third, there is no indication that the Supreme Court use of social science data was systematic, not even to the point of evaluating existing information. Many important figures are left out of consideration while many minor figures are cited, reinforcing the opinion of the random use of technical data. Fourth, there is no evidence that the decision to desegregate southern school systems follows from social science data. The debate between geneticists and environmentalists for example, between Arthur Jensen and J. McVicker Hunt, is compatible with desegregation. The belief in maximizing opportunity rests not on the technical status feasibility of intelligence testing, but on the fundamental concern for equity within American society. Fifth, and finally, the quality of evidence marshaled in the Supreme Court rulings could barely pass as a college term paper. This heightens the suspicion that social science information was at most ancillary to the judicial decision-making process.

Even Kenneth B. Clark, who believed in the crucial role of social science in Supreme Court deliberations, was recently forced to conclude that the Court accepted the findings of social scientists in a most selective and unconvincing fashion:

> The social scientists testified concerning the damage inherent in the total pattern of segregation on the human personality. On the basis of their

testimony, the Court held that separate educational facilities are inherently unequal by virtue of being separate. By providing such evidence, the social scientists made it possible to avoid the need to obtain proof of individual damage and to avoid assessment of the equality of facilities in each individual school situation. The assumption of inequality could now be made wherever segregation existed. In this regard it must now be stated that in doing so the Court, which appeared to rely on the findings of the social scientists in the 1954 decision, rejected the findings in handing down the 1955 implementation decision. An empirical study of various forms and techniques of desegregation suggested that the gradual approach to desegregation did not increase its chances of success or effectiveness. The findings further suggested that forthright, direct desegregation within the minimum time required for the necessary administrative changes tended to facilitate the process. Gradualism or any form of ambiguity and equivocation on the part of those with the power of decision is interpreted by the segregationists as indecision and provides them with the basis for increasing resistance, as well as giving them time to organize, intensify, and prolong their opposition. In this regard, it is relevant to note that the pattern of massive resistance and sporadic, violent opposition to desegregation occurred after the 1955 decision. There is no evidence that a more direct, specific, and concrete implementation decree would have resulted in any more tension, procrastination, or evasion than the seemingly rational, statesmanlike deliberate speed decision of the Court. It does not seem likely that the pace of public school desegregation could have been slower. (Clark, 1969, pp. xxxvii)

The quotation from Clark is indicative of the ambiguous legacy the social sciences provide even in relation to this celebrated case of educational desegregation. Just as social science data were employed one year, they were ignored with impunity the next year. At the same time, the Supreme Court has demanded an accelerated program of desegregation in the South, the counterattack by racist forms of social science has intensified. The work of Ralph Gilbert Ross and Ernest van den Haag (1957), Arthur Jensen (1969) and Edmond Cahn (1961) is not likely to bring about a shift in Court sentiment. This leads to the suspicion that confusion of social science do not in any way affect the judicial review of major test cases. Therefore, we must assert the unlikely status of social science as a cause for egalitarian decision making by the courts.

Social science *has* had a role in providing an objective rationale for equality of opportunity in education. However, it is clear from the record that the United States Supreme Court had a number of pending cases (such as *Brown* v. *Board of Education* and *Bolling* v. *Sharpe*) that were going to be decided against the historic "separate but equal" doctrine outlined in *Plessy* v. *Ferguson*. The Court's unanimous declaration that "in the field of public education the doctrine of 'separate but equal' has no place" was a decision that made use of social science, but did not breathlessly await such information to make its decision. It might even be argued that the courts ignored sophisticated social scientists' warnings that the quest for racial equality through law had come too late to affect militancy and "separate but equal" claims from the aggrieved side—from the black people.

The contributions of men like Kenneth B. Clark, Guy Johnson, Hylan Lewis, Tobin Williams, Howard Odum and J. Milton Yinger, among others, must be noted. But as it is clear in Harry S. Ashmore's (1954) *The Negro and the Schools,* which stated the position of the Ford Foundation and its subsidiary, the Fund for the Advancement of Education, "The Fund will not undertake to argue the case for or against segregation in public education, and in no sense will it become involved as an advocate on either side of the issue before the Supreme Court." The other two clauses in the charge to the Ashmore Commission underscore the fact that social scientists were aware that a decision on desegregation was pending, and that they were in the position to supply intellectual ammunition; and that at the same time—the early fifties—social science was far less certain about its policy commitments than it was in the decade of the sixties.

Had a more honest admission of advocacy roles by social scientists been forthcoming in 1954 around the desegregation issue, there would have been greater clarity possible in 1964 around the counterinsurgency issue. But the fact remains that, "good or bad," social science was the effect and not the cause of a major transformation in American political life.

The sort of advocacy model employed by Thurgood Marshall in arguing before the Supreme Court desegregation hearings is perfectly respectable, and in accord with the nature of judicial review. But the same advocacy model that is celebrated in black–white relations is categorically suppressed in relation to counterinsurgency affairs abroad. While the Supreme Court ruling offered exemplar evidence for the worth of value-free social science, everyone winked his collective eye at the flaws in the argument because it rested ultimately on the values of egalitarianism. But if there has been a notable cooling off toward the same doctrine of value-free social science, it is because the celebration of the United States counterinsurgency does not afford the comfort of a moral goal shared by large numbers of social scientists. In other words, "ethical neutrality" can work in social science only as long as there is a presupposed ethical consensus among the powers.

PROJECT CLEAR

The position of the black soldier in the United States Army provides an especially rich and impressive field for study. The work of men like Leo Bogart and Elmo C. Wilson has recorded this American military dilemma: a vicious circle of racist attitudes built up from the post-Revolutionary War to the post-World War II period on one side, and a constant need for manpower to fight the war and defend the flag on the other—

particularly in times of an utter breakdown of any notion of a common foe and feelings of mutual interdependence.

The black soldier has been in the anomalous position of being over-represented on the battlefields and underrespresented in the decision-making sectors, of being the champion of democracy and equality in an institution built upon a total institutional pattern of loyalty and duty. Several factors exist that have made the army especially vulnerable to demands for equality —whether that term be defined in either integrational or separatist terms. These factors can be listed (without ranking in terms of importance) as follows:

1. The realization that black political strength was a national, political and economic factor, and hence the necessity for the army simply to obey the dictates of the post-World War II epoch.
2. The avant garde portion of the federal civil service, particularly those branches linked to policy activities and image-building wings of the government. Given the increasing internationalization of American political and military commitments, the need for desegregating the armed forces became apparent.
3. The long-standing political power of the Democratic Party. Given the fact that the blacks established a new power base in that Party, the drive toward equality in those areas under political supervision became emphatic.
4. The army's desperate need for combat manpower and its utter despair over the poor combat performance of artificially segregated black units. Remobilization during the Korean War and high manpower skills worked to accelerate desegregation.
5. The army provided many black youths, in an era not yet dominated by political militance, with upward mobility through well-defined bureaucratic channels. Whatever was wrong with the army, it at least made crystal clear how advancement in rank occurs, and who benefits from such advancement. Additionally, the high unemployment among black youth during this period was alleviated easily and directly be participation in a mass army apparatus.

There are without a doubt other factors in the desegregation rulings that were crystallized in the military regulations published by the army in January 1950 that established a policy of equality of treatment and opportunity for all persons in the army without regard to race, color, religion or national origin. But above all, this process of conflict resolution took place largely without benefit of social science advisers.

However, by 1950, an outstanding team of social scientists became involved with the Operations Research Office (ORO) "to initiate a project to determine how best to utilize Negro personnel within the Army." The work done under the label "Project Clear" was stated by one high ORO official as: "The Army wants to know what to do with all their niggers."

The "research staff" was then called into existence after and not before desegregation became the undeclared policy of the United States Army.

The social sciences were once again (this time on the side of the "good") being used as a legitimizing agency. The social scientists were to provide operational data on utilization of manpower resources rather than on the desirability or feasibility of segregation or integration; which had already been widely acknowledged by the military men. Indeed, Leo Bogart (1969, pp. 1–41) in his summation of social science and public policy on this matter said:

> The Army's desegregation was willed by historical necessity, not by research. It would have come about without *Project Clear,* and perhaps not very differently or very much later. Social research was conducted on a large scale and at substantial expense in the process of arriving at the decision and in working out the procedure for implementing and enforcing it. This means that both the major decision and all of the subsidiary decisions cannot really be divorced from the influence of the studies.

Project Clear reported four main findings on the "integration experience": (1) strong hierarchical structures like the army have been able to desegregate more efficiently than institutions depending upon voluntary action; (2) black Americans in and out of the army resent enforced segregation; (3) many black officers and noncoms hold positions of rank and privilege to which they could not return if the armed forces desegregation were to cease immediately; (4) there is a de facto segregation in the army despite the de jure bans against such segregation.

These sorts of "results," while obviously motivated by the best intentions of liberalism and the best traditions of survey research, only reinforce the mandarin tradition. For it is the failure to ask questions that go beyond the legitimizing tasks of Project Clear that makes it poor science. The researchers might have inquired into the social structure of the army as such—and how any "absolute'" notion of equality is made impossible within the military institutional context. They might also have explained how a theory of equality in the armed forces could be linked up to the larger purposes of the Korean War. They might have explained whether the black troops desired equality within the army or whether equality was a general social goal that could be frustrated by military service.

In all fairness, the introductory statement to Project Clear, written nearly two decades after the actual research was conducted, does make some sort of effort to come to grips with the aforementioned issues. The two original field reports do not, and these formed the basis of the findings and were the source of revenue, not the belated introduction. Again, this is not an assertion of the intrinsic inability of social science to perform critical and critically needed tasks, but rather an assertion that mandarinism is just as much a part of the liberal wing of sociology as of its conservative wing.

The quality of social science independence, not political ideology, is really at stake.

PROJECT CAMELOT

The case of the ill-famed Project Camelot is typical of what happens in the absence of consensus about the goals of research. This $5 million project for the

> measurement of internal war potential, and estimation of reaction effects did not initiate United States policy toward revolution in underdeveloped areas. Quite the contrary, it was the outcome of the failures of United States counterinsurgency missions in places as far apart as Cuba and Vietnam. The civic action programs and aid of the United States to military regimes of its own choosing took place long before the mid-sixties. There is some suspicion that the impulse behind Project Camelot is the extraordinary failures in counterinsurgency activities that characterized the earlier part of the sixties. (Horowitz, 1967, pp. 41–44)

Without wishing to reexamine the meaning of Project Camelot, certain simple facts, such as the asymmetry of the research design, make it plain that it was a consequence and not the cause of our foreign policy. There was no study of how revolutionary change is to be induced, only how it is to be frustrated and inhibited.

Eclecticism damaged the scientific aims of the Camelot research. What took place is that the four research associates of the working group presented a four-part outline, in a manner that by no means made it evident that unified results were either anticipated or even plausibly to be expected. Had the four sets of working papers been presented as just that—four sets of papers—instead of a "unified front" of ideas and attitudes, the scientific character would have been enhanced, and the policy-oriented aspects could have been placed in a larger perspective of social science scholarship. Also, the many people who had the opportunity to make criticism were reticent to express themselves. The Project Camelot working groups, when they did make criticisms, found a ready response from the project directors. But their roles as legitimizers rather than innovators limited such criticisms to technical rather than ethical levels.

There was a tendency toward the use of sanitized language in the descriptions of the project. We are told about a "precipitant" of internal war as being an "event which actually starts the war," whereas "preconditions" are "circumstances which make it possible for the precipitants to bring about political violence." Obviously, "events" never started wars, only *people* do. "Precipitants" never bring about political violence, only *participants* do.

There is a general critique of social science for failing to deal with social conflict and social control. And while this in itself represents an admirable recognition, the tenor and context of the design make it plain that a "stable society" is the considered norm no less than the desired outcome. The "breakdown of social order" is spoken of accusingly. Stabilizing agencies in developing areas are not so much criticized as presumed to be absent. A critique of United States Army policy is absent because the army is presumed to be a stabilizing agency engaged in legitimate tasks: "If the U.S. Army is to perform effectively its part in the U.S. mission of counterinsurgency, it must recognize that insurgency represents a breakdown of social order." Such a proposition has never been doubted—by army officials or anyone else. The issue is whether such breakdowns are in the nature of the existing system or a product of conspiratorial movements. Here hygienic language disguises antirevolutionary assumptions under a cloud of powder-puff declarations.

Sanitary terminology is also evident in descriptions of political regimes and in evaluations of nations to be studied. Paraguay is recommended "because trends in this situation (the Stroessner regime) may also render it 'unique' when analyzed in terms of the transition from 'dictatorship' to political stability." What "transition"? Since when have social scientists perceived dictatorship and political stability as occupying the same level of meaning? No dictatorship has ever been more "stable" than Hitlerism. One might speak of the transition from dictatorship to democracy or from totalitarianism to authoritarianism. But to speak about changes from dictatorship to stability is an obvious rubric. In this case, it is a tactic to disguise the fact that Paraguay is one of the most vicious, undemocratic (*and stable*) societies in the Western Hemisphere.

These typify the sorts of hygienic sociological premises that have extrascientific purposes. They illustrate the confusion of commitments among Project Camelot spokesmen. The absence of ideological terms such as "revolutionary masses," "communism," "socialism," "capitalism" and so forth intensifies the discomfort one feels on examination, since the abstract vocabulary disguises rather than resolves the problems of international revolution. It does not proceed beyond United States Army vocabulary, not because this vocabulary is superior to the revolutionary vocabulary, but simply because it is the language of the donor. To have used clearly political rather than military language would not "justify" governmental support. Furthermore, shabby assumptions of academic respectability replaced innovative orientations. By adopting a systems approach, the problematic, open-ended and practical aspects of the study of revolutions were largely omitted, and the design of the system became an oppressive curb on the contents of the problems inspected.

This points up a critical implication of the Camelot affair. The importance of the subject being researched does not uniquely determine the importance of the project per se. A sociology of large-scale relevance and reference is all to the good. It is important that scholars be willing to risk something of their reputations in helping to resolve major world social problems. But it is no less important that in the process of addressing their attention to major international problems the autonomous character of the social science disciplines, their own criteria of worthwhile scholarship, not be abandoned. The ambiguity, asymmetry, eclecticism and fragmented and programmatic nature of even the most advanced documents circulated by Project Camelot lost sight of this autonomous social science character in the pursuit of the larger demands of society.

The Camelot directorship never inquired into the changes and desirability for successful revolution. This is just as solid a line of inquiry as that which was emphasized, namely, under what conditions will revolutionary movements be able to overthrow a government? Furthermore, they did not inquire into the role of the United States in these countries. This points up the asymmetry. The problem should have been phrased to include the study of "us" as well as "them." A social scientific analysis of a situation must take into account the role of the different people and major groups involved. There was no room in the Camelot design for such contingency analysis— which is the weakness of legitimizing models.

This one-sidedness is not unusual. As a result, shortcomings in this approach were not readily apparant to any of the key participants in the project. Camelot did not seem sufficiently different from ordinary sociological practices to warrant any special precautionary measures. And the precedents relied upon were indeed of a reassuring variety.

An early example was industrial sociology, where many people worked for many years on essentially managerial problems. But there were some sociologists with an affinity for labor who saw through the business bias and began to complain about a sociology that simply performed the dirty work of industrial management. A better example is medical sociology. In that field, almost everyone took (and still takes) for granted the proposition that what the doctors want and think is good for everyone. Until the publication of *Boys in White,* it never occurred to anyone to ask how things might be from the patient's point of view (Becker, 1961). Later, there were other exceptions, research that insisted on treating doctors just like anyone else.

Many sociologists ask their questions improperly simply because to do so may serve legitimizing ends in a marketable way. When they are presented with the opportunity to influence policy-makers as in the case of Project Camelot, they can do little better than puff up stale methodological forms for new use. There are also the primitive substantive guidelines used. The Enlightenment assumption that people in power need only to be shown the truth in order to do the right thing is unacceptable. Some well-intentioned people have accepted elitism as an exclusive framework. They need to be reminded that this is by no means the only possible position.

The nature of the asymmetry in Project Camelot is twofold. First, it failed to ask *all* the questions that needed to be asked. Second, it did not open to investigation the motives and biases of the sponsoring agencies.

No fundamental change in counterinsurgency programs has taken place either as a result of or in defense of Project Camelot. The project simply went out of business when the heat became intense and the political fallout within the government intensified. There was not a single defender of Project Camelot from either the executive staff, the State Department under Rusk or the Defense Department under McNamara. All agreed that the project was "unfortunate," and few were willing to declare that it was even abstractly worthwhile.

THE MOYNIHAN REPORT

A fourth example of how social science is reputed to have influenced national policy is the famed Moynihan Report on *The Negro Family: The Case for National Action* (Moynihan, 1965). Here, too, there was at least as large an outcry at the national level as the Camelot project elicited at an international level. But here, too, it is impossible to declare that the report either stimulated or provoked a new course of political action. Indeed, like Camelot, it tended to reinforce stereotypes about black life, and to confirm the welfare measures proposed by the Johnson Administration. The Moynihan Report contained nothing new about black family life, but instead enshrined Democratic Party policies on matters of health, welfare and education.

One of the most frequent criticisms of the report was that its author spoke of "the Negro family" and thus did injustice to those blacks whose lives were not characterized by the kind of instability and pathology with which he dealt. Yet at two points in the report Moynihan indicated that the black community contained two broad groupings—an increasingly successful middle class and an increasingly disorganized lower class. Even so, those who wished to emphasize the source of strength within the black community or who wished to preserve the "good name" of black families were highly displeased with Moynihan's characterizations (Cf. Rainwater and Yancy, 1967).

To social scientists with a professional interest in the situation of black Americans, the report offered little that was new. Rather, it presented in a dramatic and policy-oriented way a well-established, though not universally supported, view of the afflictions of black Americans. The basic paradigm of black life that Moynihan's report reflected had been laid down by the great black sociologist E. Franklin Frazier (1962) over thirty years before. The most direct contemporary source for the thinking in the report probably lay in the work of Kenneth Clark (1965) whose book *Dark Ghetto* was published at about the time the report was sent to the White House. Moynihan's work took the form of testing the accuracy of and then restating Frazier's predictions about the intertwining effects of socioeconomic deprivation and family disorganization on the situation of black Americans as they migrated to the cities. Further, he sought to show that Clark's work in Harlem, initially published as a 1964 report of the HARYOU project entitled *Youth in the Ghetto,* described a process that could be said to apply generally in the black sections of America cities. The report provided data indicating the situation of blacks over the past fifteen years, particularly in relation to government labor and welfare programs.

The Moynihan Report was intended to legitimize the new guidelines established by President Johnson, over and against the Kennedy period. It was meant to consecrate a shift of emphasis from the two main lines of attack during the Kennedy years—community action programs and welfare services—and place instead a greater emphasis on employment, income maintenance and educational opportunity. This was the direction that establishment black leaders wanted, and it seems clear in retrospect that President Johnson shared this emphasis—as evidenced by his support for OEO programs for maximum feasible participation. Why then did this exercise in legitimation meet with the disastrous fate that befell Project Camelot and other such efforts and social science benediction?

Black power and black nationalist thinking which had been slowly growing among black civil rights activists, and which played a subdued and mostly unnoticed role in the Moynihan controversy, catapulted into the spotlight of the national media, much to the consternation of more conservative civil rights leaders and to the mixed gratification and endorsement of younger, more radical activists. As a national issue, the black problem was now defined by concerns with black power, black autonomy and black secession from white-dominated structures.

Then, in response to Martin Luther King's first excursion into the northern ghettos, Chicago and Cicero whites showed their "southern" face by responding violently to blacks' assertion of their right to decent housing. For anyone who had forgotten it, the television screen brought home the fact that the deepest of prejudices sustained patterns of housing discrimination and segregation. These whites would "put their bodies on the line" to deny equal housing opportunity to blacks; they certainly would not support programs for equality.

As summer wore on, the frustration and rage engendered by ghetto living spawned a series of small-scale riots across the country, and fear and the desire to contain them came to dominate the thinking of those in government and in the white community. By the fall of 1966, governmental attention in the area of civil rights was turned to the effects of black power, the riots and the white "backlash" on the November elections. The watered-down open housing legislation that was before Congress during the summer of 1966 was never truly pushed by the White House, as had been predicted by some of our informants at the beginning of the year. Even though the delegates to the White House Conference had insisted that this bill be both strengthened and passed, the President made little more than public gestures in support of it. As Everett Dirksen indicated to a reporter after a visit with Johnson, "The President said he wanted the bill passed, but he didn't say it very strongly."

After the White House Conference, the central civil rights problem in the White House was "how to stop the riots, without doing too much." To allow the riots to continue would mean white backlash and increased support for Republicans in the November election. Implementing social and economic change in northern ghettos, which was required to prevent riots, would also result in additional Republican votes.

The shooting of James Meredith, the subsequent rise of black power, the white racism that was exhibited in the Chicago and Cicero marches, the increased fear of additional backlash in the November elections and escalation in Vietnam resulted in the Johnson Administration's moving still further away from the policy-action lines indicated in the Howard University speech.

One additional casualty of the turn to the Right presaged by these events seemed likely to be the war on poverty and its bureaucratic embodiment, the Office of Economic Opportunity. From the spring of 1966 on, authoritative sources were predicting the demise of OEO as its programs were absorbed into other agencies or allowed to die on the vine. Efforts like Moynihan's to shift the direction of the war on poverty were becoming overshadowed by the question of whether there were to be any meaningfully financed antipoverty programs.

The Republican victories of 1966 resulted in further stagnation of governmental action in the areas of poverty and civil rights. Whether these victories could be attributed to white backlash, the rising cost of living or increased concern over the Vietnam War, the watered-down housing bill that failed to get through the 89th Congress would doubtless have an even more difficult time in the 90th Congress. The chances of implementation of existing programs, much less the establishment of new ones, grew slimmer. And Moynihan himself became disenchanted with his own role as an administration legitimizer (Moynihan, 1969).

The Moynihan Report and the government's use of it were in response to a situation in which the government sought to be venturesome instead of reactive to the civil rights movement. The administration felt politically prepared to implement new policies. From the point of view of independent governmental action, the issues raised by the Moynihan Report were dead. The Randolph Freedom Budget, an effort to describe in some detail the kind of program that Moynihan's efforts pointed toward, made its public appearance in the same week that the Republican-southern coalition regained its congressional hegemony. The conditions of life in the northern ghettos remain, and the need for broad social and economic changes remains. It is not likely that the civil rights movement or the increasing aspirations and demands of the black American will decline.

Whatever political turns were taken by President Johnson on the treatment of the black question hinged little on Moynihan or the social sciences. The report aroused enormous hostility among black leaders of all sorts and their white supporters. It was issued at a point of the swing to the Right in 1966. Thus, while the report was suppressed, it had little bearing on the actual course of policy. It is interesting that in his role of adviser on urban affairs to President Nixon, Moynihan has made no effort to re-create or reintroduce the report or to implement its findings.

I introduce these four case studies—the Supreme Court's use of social science, the United States Army's attitudes toward segregation, the Defense Department's Project Camelot, and the Department of Labor's use of social science with respect to black employment—because they provide clear evidence of social science in action. There are other reputed and reported uses: the use of decision making and game theory in the Cuban missile crisis of 1962 and the use of behavioral research in stimulating as well as formulating the fallout shelter programs in 1960–61 (Kahn, 1960). How-ever, the complete collapse of the fallout shelter program leads one to suspect that this is a simple case of heuristic rather than scientific use of a social science report. Finally, the work of Ithiel de Sola Pool and the Simulmatics group in studying Vietcong captives in 1969 has neither precip-itated, altered nor diminished the American commitment in Vietnam.

It is not my purpose to establish whether domestic or foreign policy would be better or worse by making wider use of social science, but only to show that the reputed utilization is so often post facto, and made with the purpose of forecasting or evaluating such policies. I know of very few social science evaluations that have been used to initiate and institute a policy. What appears as cause is actually effect; it appears as cause because it serves the purpose of policy-makers to have social science legitimizers, while it serves the purpose of social science legitimizers to go along with presumptions of authority because this enhances their own opportunity for future participation and funds.

REFERENCES

Ashmore, H. S. (1954) *The Negro and the Schools.* Chapel Hill, N.C.: University of North Carolina Press.

Becker, H. S. (1961) *Boys in White: Student Culture in Medical School.* Chicago: University of Chicago Press.

Bogart, L., ed. (1969) *Social Research and the Desegregation of the U.S. Army.* Chicago: Markham.

Cahn, E. (1961) *The Predicament of Democratic Man.* New York: Mac-millan.

Clark, K. B. (1965) *Dark Ghetto: Dilemmas of Social Power.* New York: Harper & Row.

Clark, K. B. (1969) "The Social Scientists, the Brown Decision and Con-temporary Confusion," in L. Friedman, ed., *Argument: The Oral Argument*

Before the Supreme Court in Brown v. *Board of Education of Topeka, 1952–55.* New York: Chelsea House.

Frazier, E. F. (1962) *Black Bourgeoisie.* New York: Macmillan (Collier Books).

Horowitz, I. L. (1967) *The Rise and Fall of Project Camelot: Studies in the Relationship Between Social Science and Practical Politics.* Cambridge, Mass.: M.I.T. Press.

Horowitz, I. L., and R. L. Horowitz (1970) "Tax-Exempt Foundations," *Science,* vol. 168 (10 April), pp. 220–228.

Jensen, A. (1969) "How Much Can We Boost I.Q. and Scholastic Achievement?" *Harvard Educational Review,* vol. 39 (Winter), pp. 18–61.

Kahn, H. (1960) *On Thermonuclear War.* Princeton, N.J.: Princeton University Press.

Lasswell, H. D. (1951) "The Policy Orientation," in D. Lerner and H. D. Lasswell, eds., *The Policy Sciences.* Stanford, Calif.: Stanford University Press.

Moynihan, D. P. (1965) *The Negro Family: The Case for National Action.* Washington, D.C.: Office of Policy Planning and Research, U.S. Department of Labor.

Moynihan, D. P. (1969) *Maximum Feasible Misunderstanding: Community Action in the War on Poverty.* New York: Free Press.

Rainwater, L., and W. L. Yancey (1967) *The Moynihan Report and the Politics of Controversy.* Cambridge, Mass.: M.I.T. Press.

Ross, R. G., and E. van den Haag (1957) *The Fabric of Society: An Introduction to the Social Sciences.* New York: Harcourt Brace Jovanovich.

Weidenbaum, M. (1969) "The Use of Social Science Research in the Federal Administration," Conference on Social Science and National Policy, Rutgers University, November 1969 (mimeograph).

CHAPTER 19

NATIONAL POLICY AND PRIVATE AGENCY RESEARCH

The large tax-exempt foundation is a child of private enterprise. Foundations have acquired a unique role which is not readily describable in terms of "public" or "private" sector. The purpose of this chapter is to examine the impact of tax-exempt foundations upon public policy in the United States and to show that their "third-sector" character makes it difficult for them to secure acceptance of their activities or an economic base for charting new directions.

The term "foundations" designates organizations that have grown during the twentieth century (most often in the form of corporations or trusts) and that have broadly defined charitable purposes, substantial capital assets and income derived from gifts, bequests and capital investments. They are granted tax-exempt status by section 501-c-3 of the Internal Revenue Code. The code also allows income, gift and estate tax deductions for contributions to foundations. Organizations supported by government funds are not foundations, nor are formal educational or church institutions, organizations testing and experimenting on behalf of the public interest or certain non-tax-exempt trusts that set aside some funds for charity.[1]

---

[1] For the distinction between foundations and other public welfare-oriented organizations, see U.S. Department of the Treasury (1965, pp. 9–10).

LONGITUDINAL PROFILE OF
FOUNDATIONS AND GOVERNMENT

Big foundations became rooted in the United States at the beginning of this century and are a unique product of affluent industrialism. Organizations of such scale could hardly exist without the vast surplus of wealth that was accumulated in the United States during the twentieth century. However, they grow out of charitable organizations which flourished in earlier American history.[2] These were endorsed, to an extent unparalleled anywhere else, by cultural influences that strongly favored "charity" as a mode of ameliorating social problems.

1. A dominant Protestantism propagated the idea that men achieved salvation by "good works" rather than religious rituals. Money could be spent to accomplish good works; individuals with sufficient funds used them in this way to assure themselves a life in the hereafter and, more especially, to give the pursuit of profit a higher status and meaning.

2. As a young nation, the United States was basically a loose collection of dispersed and diverse communities relying more on ethical bonds than on a strong national government as a source of unity. Charitable donation was a means of strengthening the moral firmness of individuals and, indirectly, of the nation. Philanthropy was seen as encouraging the social development of the donor and improving the character of the recipient. Expenditure of money for moral ends enabled the rich and the poor to live in harmony, and thus money could be a force for social cohesion.

3. Charitable organizations were favored by a tradition of improving social conditions through voluntary associations, all the more so because this was seen as a form of "moral," as distinct from interest-group, pressure. The great Fundamentalist awakenings of the nineteenth century widely popularized this idea.

4. In a laissez faire culture, where government was regarded as a special contrivance for settling social disputes and not as a dispenser of welfare, charitable organizations assumed welfare-dispensing functions almost by fiat.

5. Of equal importance, businessmen acquired political leadership along with vast fortunes. And as long as Americans identified business as the source of all good things, the populace looked to businessmen to discharge welfare responsibilities to communities. The federal government encouraged this by granting tax allowances for charitable contributions. And since the tax system is itself a product of this century, the special relationship between foundations and government received a basic economic impetus.

[2] For a historical account, see Bremner (1960).

The advent of big foundations coincided with the era of muckraking, trust-busting, left-wing populism and growing militance on the part of labor. This had the effect of casting deep suspicion upon business and, by association, upon business-generated charities or foundations. The charge that philanthropic money was "tainted" became widespread. Between 1914 and 1915, an Industrial Relations Commission set up by a number of United States senators to explore causes of social unrest extended its investigation to foundation affairs.[3] The result was that the foundations were censured because of the size of their fortunes and the nature of their special privileges. They were perceived as dangerous extensions of business power, since not only did businessmen endow them but also men with business backgrounds administered them.

Investigation and suspicion notwithstanding, foundations grew as business grew. They were organized mainly as corporations and, to a lesser extent, as trusts.[4] The procedures for establishing a charitable trust are similar to those involving the transfer of wealth from a private donor to a corporate recipient. By defining the recipient as "the public," transfer of private wealth to the community at large is possible. The trust is a device for disposing of property in cases where legal title and managerial duties are given over to a trustee charged with overseeing the property and using it on behalf of beneficiaries specified by the donor. In the case of charitable trusts, the "beneficiary" is the public. The trust provides a ready form in which administration of a property or funds may be efficiently established according to existing statute, and thus it was applied to the establishment of foundations.

THE PRIVATE ENTERPRISE MODEL
OF PUBLIC FOUNDATIONS

The corporate device is more frequently used in creating foundations because the corporate form pervades modern American business—the main source of foundation funding—and the creators of foundations are familiar with it. The corporation was widely adopted in this country because it provided that means whereby large amounts of capital could be raised from investors whose ownership would be separable from managerial responsibilities and from liability for debt of the business enterprise. The right to exist as a corporation is granted by an act of state, although state laws regarding nonprofit corporations vary so greatly that it is difficult to enumerate the rules for the formation of corporate foundations.[5]

---

[3] See the report, issued by Senator Manly, submitted to Congress by the Commission on Industrial Relations (U.S. Senate, 1916).

[4] See Fremont-Smith (1965, especially chaps. 1 and 2) for a discussion of the historical roots of the laws relating to charities. Other chapters in this book give an extremely clear account of the trust and corporate bases of the foundations.

[5] See Fremont-Smith (1965, pp. 479–490) for a state-by-state summary.

The executives of a foundation trust or corporation are involved in a fiduciary relationship that legally applies where one individual is duty bound to act for the benefit of another party according to the terms within which the relation was established. This duty involves three parts: loyalty to the beneficiary's interest, avoidance of excessive delegation of administrative obligations and rendering of accounts to the beneficiary. Foundation administrators are subject to legal sanctions if it can be demonstrated that they have violated this fiduciary relationship.

My concern here is not with the legal bases, as such, for establishing foundations. Rather, my purpose is to demonstrate how the emulation of business forms for establishing foundations as *independent* entities led them to be associated with the profit-making sphere of the economy. This caused foundations public embarrassment early in this century and established a precedent for congressional inquiry into their ethical integrity and financial affairs.[6] It was charged that, if foundations serve a "public welfare" function while businessmen circumvent costly taxes by contributing to them, the nonprofit sector exists to serve the profit motives of businessmen and not the commonweal. Thus, because of their peculiar nonprofit status, foundations, for all their privileges, lost the moral connotations of the earlier charities, and hence lost a certain degree of legitimacy in the eyes of the public. This problem of the "real" purposes of foundations was further compounded when big government—especially in the New Deal period— made great incursions into their traditional area of activity by acquiring welfare functions and sponsoring a wide variety of civic projects, as well as research in the physical and social sciences. Although this development did not decrease foundation activities, it pressed the foundations to try to justify their existence. The ways in which they did so only rendered them more vulnerable to congressional suspicion.

The greatest amount of congressional inquiry into foundation affairs has occurred in the post-World War II period. One reason for this is the fact that 1940–60 was the period of accelerated foundation growth in American history. The data of Table 19.1, drawn from a Treasury Department study conducted in 1964 and published in 1965, show this growth. The foundations established since 1950 are smaller than those established

---

[6] Congressional investigation has not been directed at all philanthropic foundations. There are a number of types; for a good description of them, see Harrison and Andrews (1946). These authors refer to four main types: (1) the "name only" type, usually of a nongranting, soliciting variety with no capital funds; (2) the "marginal type," supported by fees or foundation grants, having highly restricted purposes; (3) the "community-trust type," set up to enable a number of small donors to pool their resources; and (4) the big general philanthropic foundation, the type discussed in this chapter and the type most subject to congressional inquiry. Within the fourth type, Harrison and Andrews make a distinction between "operating" and "nonoperating" foundations, the former being those that maintain their own research staffs and the latter those that make grants to outside researchers. Also, a number of "general" philanthropic foundations are a blend of "operating" and "nonoperating" varieties.

TABLE 19.1   The Period of Establishment of 5,050 Foundations, by Decades after 1900 and by Latest Asset Classes[a]

| | | | Latest Asset Class | | | | | |
| | | | $10 Million or More | | $1 Million to $10 Million | | Less than $1 Million | |
Period	Number	Per-centage	N	%	N	%	N	%
Before 1900	18	_[b]	1	1	9	1	8	_[b]
1900–09	18	_[b]	8	5	5	1	5	_[b]
1910–19	76	2	14	8	36	4	26	1
1920–29	173	3	27	15	65	8	81	2
1930–39	288	6	45	26	100	12	143	3
1940–49	1,638	32	54	31	299	38	1,285	32
1950–59[c]	2,839	56	26	15	286	36	2,527	62
Total	5,050	100	175	100	800	100	4,075	100

SOURCE: *Treasury Department Report on Private Foundations* (Washington, D.C.: Government Printing Office, 1965).

[a] The 5,050 foundations tabulated by the Treasury Department are those that had at least $100,000 in assets in 1962 and were thus included in the *Foundation Directory*, hence providing information to the Foundation Library Center as to date of organization.

[b] Less than 0.5 percent.

[c] Record incomplete; also, the fragmentary 1960 record (45 foundations) is not included here.

before that date, but the study indicates that this is due simply to the fact that the younger foundations responded to the Treasury Department's questionnaire, and therefore generalizations from the data of Table 19.1 are tentative. But no data from other sources exist to support or refute these findings.[7]

The Treasury report indicates that the rapid growth of foundations relative to the rest of the economy in the 1930s and 1940s can be associated in part with the "adoption of increased progressivity in estate and income taxes" during the early 1930s—this in addition to the deduction for charitable contributions allowed under each tax. Furthermore, since 1950, the total wealth of foundations has grown faster than the rest of the economy. This is thought to be due to the fact that the foundations' principal assets

[7] See F. Andrews in Russell Sage Foundation (1964, pp. 15–16). Andrews shows, in keeping with the Treasury Department's observation, that less than 0.5 percent of the foundations listed the second edition of *The Foundation Directory* were organized before 1900. During the first decade of the twentieth century, the growth rate was less than 2 per year (although 2 of those established in that decade now have assets of more than $25 million). For the decade 1910-19, the rate increased to more than 7 per year, for a total of 76, including three giants: Rockefeller Funds, the Carnegie Corporation of New York and the Commonwealth Fund. This is the decade in which the community-trust type of foundation became important. In the 1920s, the rate of growth more than doubled, to 17 a year, 12 of those established in that decade being in the large-asset range. Though the depression slowed the rate of growth, it still increased to nearly 30 a year. In the 1940s, more than six times as many foundations were established as in the 1930s, and in the 1950s, growth reached an all-time high.

and corporate stocks have been increasing in value more rapidly than other assets; the amount of shares owned by the foundations has been quite stable. gives aggregate foundation income. Table 19.2, adopted from the Treasury Department study, gives comparisons made at the end of 1961 between the book value of foundation assets and their market value and net worth. Table 19.3 adapted from the same study, gives aggregate foundation income.

We are accustomed to associating high industrialism with increases in government expenditure. This association is valid. The world depression of 1929, the devastation of World War II and the demands of those who had not benefited from improved conditions and economic support, among other events and factors, led the public sector to increase taxation in order to assume these burdens. The consequences involved increases in government wealth, personnel and power. Moreover, advanced industrial societies sustain their high economic levels by increases in research and development (R&D) activities.

One of the most important stimulants to R&D activities in the United States has been the Department of Defense. This situation arose for the obvious reason that the United States was engaged in an arms race with the Soviet Union and was wedded to the idea that a dangerous and expensive weapons arsenal was essential to its security. Thus, concern with defense- and security-related R&D resulted in enlargement of the operations and power of the government sector, and this, in turn, dramatically altered the role, if not the structure, of American foundations.[8]

FOUNDATION LIBERALISM

Despite this customary association between a well-defined public sector and an advanced industrial economy, the nonprofit sector in the United States had increased its activities at a fast pace along with economic and industrial advances. This is striking in view of a general belief that increased government spending on research and civic welfare programs diminishes the number of societal areas in which foundations can operate. No such diminishment has occurred (although the possibility contributed greatly to the unease of the foundations). For this there are many reasons. First, increases in the complexity of higher education and industry have produced a great number of trained researchers and a great demand for their skills. More people of ability are going into research. There is need for many public and private sources of support. Second, the demand for welfare and com-

---

[8] The importance of defense-related, rather than welfare-related, R&D to government sector operations is illustrated by the fact the research in the areas of health, education and welfare receives only a small portion of funds compared to defense-related R&D; the figure for defense-related R&D is in the billions. Defense R&D jumped from $1.183 billion in 1954 to $7.551 billion in 1968 (See issues of *Congressional Quarterly Almanac* for the years 1954 to 1968).

TABLE 19.2 Assets, Liabilities and Market Values at Beginning of Tax Year 1962, and Donor-Related Influence over Investment Policy

	Assets, Liabilities and Market Values for Foundations of Various Sizes[a] (millions of dollars)					Donor-Related Influence over Investment Policy (percentage)				
	Total (N= 14,865)	Very large (N= 175)	Large (N= 800)	Medium (N= 4,910)	Small (N= 8,980)	50% or more (N= 11,000)	Over 33%, not over 50% (N=810)	Over 20%, not over 33% (N=100)	Not over 20% (N=2,430)	Unclassified (N= 525)
Assets: Ledger Values, End of Year										
Cash	$ 443	$ 110	$ 124	$ 166	$ 43	268	31	21	109	14
Accounts receivable	50	12	9	25	4	32	1	_b	14	4
Notes receivable	189	118	30	35	6	117	32	32	21	_b
Mortgage loans	149	63	61	19	6	60	13	_b	77	1
Corporation stock	6,529	4,409	1,237	783	100	2,620	488	249	3,072	103
Other assets[c]	5,119	3,174	1,095	744	106	1,728	351	266	2,737	35
Total assets	11,648	7,583	2,332	1,527	206	4,348	839	515	5,809	138
Liabilities										
Accounts payable	$ 17	$ 8	$ 6	$ 3	$ _b	8	1	1	7	1
Grants payable	524	488	31	5	_b	75	10	20	419	_b
Bonds, etc., payable	137	73	32	27	5	101	4	11	22	_b
Other liabilities	114	53	42	15	4	44	3	2	64	1
Net worth	10,856	6,961	2,221	1,477	197	4,120	821	481	5,297	136
Market Values, End of Year										
Corporation stock	$10,896	$ 8,050	$1,783	$ 955	$108	3,880	860	668	5,331	159
Total assets	16,262	11,331	2,940	1,773	218	5,666	1,270	945	8,180	201
Net worth	15,470	10,709	2,829	1,723	209	5,438	1,252	911	7,668	199

SOURCE: Treasury Department survey of private foundations, 1964.

[a] Foundations are broken down into the following categories: Very large, more than $10 million; Large, $1 million to $10 million; Medium, $100,000 to $1 million; Small, less than $100,000.

[b] Less than 0.5 percent.   [c] Almost entirely in bonds.

TABLE 19.3 Aggregate Income of Foundations and Donor-Related Influence over Investment Policy

	Receipts and Grants for Foundations of Various Sizes[a] (millions of dollars)					Donor-Related Influence over Investment Policy (percentage)				
	Total (N= 14,865)	Very large (N= 175)	Large (N= 800)	Medium (N= 4,910)	Small (N= 8,980)	50% or more (N= 11,000)	Over 33%, not over 50% (N=810)	Over 20%, not over 33% (N=100)	Not over 20% (N=2,430)	Unclassified[b] (N= 525)
Receipts										
Gross profit from business activities[c]	$ 8	$ 3	$ 3	$ 1	$ 1.7	1	1	1	6	n.d.[d]
Interest	159	104	35	18	2.1	47	12	8	91	1
Dividends	374	268	67	36	3.1	125	28	18	197	6
Rents	43	21	16	5	0.7	18	1	9	14	n.d.
Other ordinary income	57	39	5	12	1.2	30	5	3	20	1
Less expenses earning gross income	62	35	13	11	2.6	28	5	8	20	1
Net ordinary income	580	400	113	61	6.2	194	42	31	307	6
Gains from sales of assets, exclusive of inventory	$ 484	$ 434	$ 33	$ 15	$ 1.0	45	14	3	419	2
Total net ordinary income plus gains	1,065	834	146	76	7.2	239	56	34	726	10
Contributions received	833	290	251	235	57.4	536	30	18	238	13
Total receipts	1,898	1,124	397	311	64.6	775	86	52	964	23
Grants from Income										
Net	$ 693	$ 478	$ 139	$ 68	$ 8.1	233	40	30	381	8
Cost of distribution	64	36	16	11	0.8	20	4	2	38	1
Gross	757	514	155	79	8.9	253	44	32	419	9
Grants from Principal										
Net	$ 239	$ 32	$ 68	$111	$28.1	174	11	6	41	8
Cost of distribution	16	1	5	7	2.5	4	2	3	5	5
Gross	255	33	73	118	30.6	178	12	8	46	13
Total grants	1,012	547	228	197	29.5	431	56	40	464	21

SOURCE: Treasury Department survey of private foundations, 1964.

[a] Foundations are broken down into the following categories: Very large, more than $10 million; Large, $1 million to $10 million; Medium, $100,000 to $1 million; Small, less than $100,000.

[b] Less than $500,000.   [c] Gross sales or receipts from related and unrelated business activities less cost of goods sold or of operations.   [d] n.d. = no data.

munity services outran the supply made available by government, particularly because of the government's military expenditures. Foundations were able to expand in this area. Third, efforts to promote international contact and cooperation after World War II revealed needs and opened opportunities for travel and research in foreign countries, for the encouragement of travel and study in the United States by foreign nationals and for expansion of the "charity" concept to include "good works" on behalf of international cooperation. Thus, the foundations expanded in this area as well.

In view of this rapid increase in the nonprofit sector, we may properly conclude that one effect the big foundations have had on public policy has been that of multiplying its sources of support. The area for research directed toward something other than the promotion of particular industries or the supplementing of defense-policy concerns is greatly enlarged. The fact that great sums are being made available for international studies, community services and civic uses strengthens the possibility of the government's circumventing political obstacles to engage in such activities. The increased range of these activities, over time, establishes their value and enhances possibilities for their wider public acceptance. Indirectly, the foundations have a liberalizing effect upon public policy. This effect is complex and needs explanation, especially because it is one of the main grounds for criticism of the foundations, as well as a source of strength.

The liberalizing effect upon public policy is the outcome of two factors: (1) the liberal outlook of the major foundations and their promotion of liberal programs and (2) government reliance (especially on the part of executive agencies) upon the experiments of liberal foundations. Thus the federal government can promote liberal policies with a minimum of obstacles by virtue of the prior acceptance these policies may have gained under foundation sponsorship. As one foundation spokesman put it to some skeptics who questioned the value of cooperation between government and foundations, "foundations can be valuable to society by probing and supporting risky or highly experimental projects in fields in which a government impact sooner or later will be necessary" (Magat, 1969).

In referring to the liberal outlook of major foundations, we are not denying that liberalism is multifaceted and complicated by historical mutations. But here we need only say that foundations are mainly associated with a liberal constituency—with academic intellectuals holding attitudes that have been opposed by political groups showing markedly right- or left-wing characteristics. For example, the foundations favor United States involvement with foreign nations on the grounds that all parts of the world are interdependent, that wealthy nations like the United States have responsibilities to the rest of the world and that contact between the United States and other nations provides an opportunity for benevolent exchange. The foundations disdain the nationalistic isolationism of the Right, as well as left-wing suspicion of American motives and behavior abroad. Moreover, they strongly favor social science research as an approach to social problems.

Such research suggests to them no echoes of "socialism," as it does to the Right, and no threat of the "dehumanization" by statistic and computers feared by the Left.

The major foundations favor community projects that experiment with expanded citizen participation, and they disdain substitution of a policy of moralizing for one of participation. This means that they allocate funds to implement participation and do not promote the traditional view that all citizens should be tested in the competitive process. Nor do foundations encourage citizen participation through confrontation, a mode currently favored by the Left. The foundations publicly commit themselves to fostering racial equality and, in general, to encouraging the realization of democratic goals. They have kept an open attitude toward social criticism, especially in view of its present rising tide. Yet they defend their business origins and financial sources and will not join in criticism of "big organization." Big business brings more money. Big government may pose problems of seeking out spheres in which to establish foundation activities. The foundations see their own bigness as primarily a consequence of surplus wealth and of rising demands for responsible research, and they view it as wholly an advantage because it enables them to bring more resources to the investigation of problems. Moreover, foundation executives view the fact that they confer with government and business personnel as only a natural outcome of shared concerns and experiences, not as a sign, as the Left generally views it, of interlocking elite structures.

The liberalism of the foundations is more than an attitude fostered by their associations or activities. It is a function of their precarious social and political location between government and business. It enables them to look upon their third-sector status as a contribution to pluralism (U.S. House, 1969, pp. 81–82, 84–85). It gives them a "vocabulary" for introducing innovation into their programming, and innovation is something they require in order to survive huge government incursions without hostility, speaking the language of cooperation, for they can ill afford to tempt government to revoke their tax privileges. In short, the foundation's liberalism is at present linked to its survival. This is the big foundation's way of steering a difficult course toward public acceptance. Some years ago, a congressional representative apprehensively noted this liberal tendency and its sources in necessity when he said that foundations were being forced "to enter these controversial fields which many people object to as being too far to the left" (U.S. House, 1952, p. 52).

The Ford Foundation occupies a unique position in the world of foundations. Thus, any generalizations about foundations and liberalism that are based exclusively, or even primarily, on data drawn from the Ford Foundation can easily provide a less-than-accurate picture of the whole. Yet Ford does uniquely illustrate a number of the major, as well as minor, points presented here (See Ford Foundation, 1969a).

1. Ford went into the "business" of assisting developing nations over-

seas at precisely that point in history when the United States recognized that it must fact up to a Third World ideology as something valid and not a subtle form of pseudocommunism. This recognition followed the collapse, at home, of McCarthyism in the mid-1950s; the crystallization of nationalist tendencies in the Third World only underscored the need for a liberal option. Governmental aid to Latin America and Asia began in the early 1950s, and aid to Africa began in the late 1950s. Foundation studies of the benefits of such aid quickly followed.

2. Invariably, this assistance strengthened the liberal tendencies within the Third World, just as it strengthened these same tendencies in domestic programming. The aid to agriculture, education, economic planning and public administration invariably followed lines that made it impossible for a "neutral" American government to support the projects financially, and yet the United States was anxious to support them through private or quasi-public channels.

3. The dramatic shift to foreign support, to the internationalization of foundations, is further reflected in the fact that what began in 1958 —namely, a systematic program for international grants—only ten years later, in 1968, accounted for $480 million of the $3.37 billion granted by the Ford Foundation. These grants invariably involved pivotal nations in the East–West confrontation—a confrontation that the United States could hope to win or resolve in its favor only by putting its most liberal foot forward.

POLITICAL POLICY AND FOUNDATION LIBERALISM

Under the impact of social upheavals in the United States over the last few years, foundations have shown a more vigorous liberalism than they could a decade ago, in Senator Joseph McCarthy's heyday. For example, the Council on Foundations (1968, p. 5). states:

In a year marked by dissension and violence in important areas of our society, the philanthropic scene provided several constructive developments, three of which deserve special mention: cooperation among foundations to make better use of funds and staff; increased attention to investment portfolios, including consideration of program-related investments as an adjunct to grant making; *and recognition of the need to involve citizens in decisions affecting their communities* [italics mine].

The Council states, in addition (Council on Foundations, 1968, p. 7):

The demand for more effective community participation in many areas of decision-making became an increasingly important factor in foundation programs . . . in city planning, urban renewal, economic development and public education. In the last-named field, the Ford Foundation's support of the New York City Board of Education's experimental decentralization projects was sharply criticized by the president of the United Federation of Teachers, Albert Shanker, and stoutly defended by the foundation's president McGeorge Bundy, who stated his case succinctly: "A Foundation should not shrink from important issues even if they become controversial, and we do not intend to back away from this one."

The Council on Foundations (1968, p. 7) also states:

The Foundation is increasingly taking the risk of providing funds and offers of expertise if asked to by community organizations within the Black Ghetto. The Foundation is disciplining itself to sit back and let Black leaders utilize the resources as they see fit. We see no other alternative to the Black Conditions in the Urban Crisis.

The Ford Foundation (1968, p. 3) has shown a similar tendency.

In a major departure from past policy, the Foundation this year began using part of its investment portfolio directly for social purposes. In the past, the Foundation has worked mainly through outright grants to non-profit institutions. It will now also devote to civic or research organizations part of its investment portfolio, through such devices as guarantees, profit-making as well as non-profit if necessary.

On May 8, 1969, the Ford Foundation (1969d) announced grants of $2.45 million to five universities for research, teaching and training in urban problems. In response to the "student revolution," the foundation announced the award of funds for student-directed research on poverty in the ghettos of New England and in the Appalachian South, on state and local tax reform and on universities and local government (Ford Foundation, 1969e). Many other programs that display a strongly liberal orientation have been continued or initiated (Ford Foundation, 1968, p. 3).

The Danforth Foundation, long interested in educational affairs, has recently shown a marked interest in urban affairs.[9] It defends this change of emphasis in terms that appeal strongly to those of a liberal turn of mind (Danforth Foundation, 1969, pp. 12–13).

Foundations are not properly engaged in popularity contests. At times of their tallest stature in American life they have taken stands on issues of public concern. They play the role of actor, not merely reactor. . . . To oppose special privilege in any of its forms is inevitably to run the risk of controversy. But special privilege is what the urban unrest is all about. It is not just low wages, poor plumbing and no grass. It is the denial of equal status, of a voice in civic decisions, of the fullness of human dignity. We

[9] See the differences in Danforth Foundation annual reports for 1964–65 and 1967–68.

believe that all citizens must be free to participate fully in community life and in decision-making processes. Giving up privileges is hard; giving up authority is even harder. Yet these things must happen if our cities are to survive and prosper.

This new awareness of the foundation as a liberal corporate conscience is also expressed by Dana S. Creel (1969), president of the Rockefeller Brothers Fund, who defends even direct political involvement for foundations:

> Minor excursions on the part of a few foundations affecting the legislative process have added considerable fuel to Congressional fire. Foundation grants to voter regisration projects are the most notable example. . . . This type of activity strikes a politically sensitive nerve and hits close to home for elected officials who are the lawmakers. These voter registration projects with their general objective of broadening the franchise—which is a commonly accepted objective in a democracy—have been viewed as upsetting traditional voter patterns and therefore not legitimate activities for foundations but rather political activities which, if not already prohibited under present law, should definitely be prohibited by more restrictive legislation. I am tempted to ask what might have been the outcry had the voter registration projects tended to reinforce the traditional voting patterns.

Foundations also see themselves as fostering development of a cooperative, yet individualist, liberal model for association between nations. They envision an association between partners rather than conflict between competitors for power or the relationship of a rich and benevolent patron and its dependent: "The image of foundation assistance that emerges is not simply that of a benevolent patron; ideally, it is that of a partner with resources and competences, but one who also makes exactions and is attentive to the performance of others" (Sutton, 1968, pp. 7–8).

Foundations are in a better position than government to embrace liberal ideals, for government is often rendered conservative by its constituencies and by considerations of power and frugality. Further, foundations are not constrained by the sharp tests of national loyalty that are required of recipients of federal funds (Sutton, 1968).

Statements on the liberalism of foundations are borne out by the allocation of funds. The two areas in which charitable "good works" have received increased support from foundations have been civic welfare and international activities. Tables 19.4 and 19.5, containing data drawn from *The Foundation Directory,* show the increases in welfare spending, by subcategory, from 1960 to 1966. However, one should view the totals with some reservation because, in the data for 1960 and for 1962, family- and company-sponsored foundations are underrepresented.

The $20 million in grants for different kinds of civic welfare, reported for 1960 and 1962, from 67 and 110 foundations, respectively (Tables

TABLE 19.4 Reported Grants for Welfare, 1960

	Number of Foundations	Major Support Area	Amount (thousands of dollars)	Social Welfare Grants (percentage)
Aged	24	0	$ 1,273	6
Child welfare	37	2	3,073	14
Community funds	39	3	4,791	22
Delinquency and crime	19	0	806	4
Family service	27	1	1,584	7
Handicapped	35	1	1,654	8
Housing	9	0	163	1
Industrial relations	5	0	108	
Intercultural relations	12	1	1,006	5
Legal aid	14	0	328	2
Relief	18	1	626	3
Social research	20	1	965	4
Youth agencies	16	3	5,345	24
Other	1	0	18	
Total	67		$21,740	100

SOURCE: *The Foundation Directory*, 1st ed. (New York: Russell Sage Foundation, 1960).

19.4 and 19.5), probably represents less than half the total amount for grants in this field, since it is to civic welfare that frequent contributions were made by small foundations that did not report the sums to the *Directory*.

For some time, welfare, like health services, had been a declining area for foundation grants because of the expansion of social security and because of private health insurance and retirement plans and increased government involvement in similar fields. But in 1962, community-planning innovations received one-third of the total welfare funds. This suggests that the foundations were innovating civic welfare policy and striking out on new paths. This could be a major factor in the substantial increases between the welfare grant figures for 1962, reported in the second edition of the *Directory*, and those for 1966, reported in the third edition (See Table 19.5). The amount increased from roughly $20 million to $80.5 million.

At the same time, the number of grants increased from 269 to 1,928. One contributing factor is the increase in the number of foundations reporting, from 110 in 1962, to 832 in 1966. But this does not account for the entire increase, since an increased number of foundations reporting in 1964, not represented in Table 19.5, showed a declining rate of allocation to welfare. Thus, the 1966 figures do represent a genuine tendency toward growth in the welfare field. Moreover, the striking climb of allocations to "interracial relations," from about a quarter of a million in 1962 (*Directory*, 2nd ed.) to $5.8 million (23 times as much) in 1966 (3rd ed.) is no mere reflection of improved coverage. As stated in the third edition (Russell Sage Foundation, 1967, p. 50), "examination of the grants indicates many

TABLE 19.5 Reported Grants for Welfare, 1962[a] and 1966

	Number of Foundations		Number of Grants		Amount (thousands of dollars)		Welfare Grants (percentage)	
	1962	1966	1962	1966	1962	1966	1962	1966
Community planning	23	44	34	62	$ 6,163	$10,800	31	13
Youth agencies	33	266	57	373	3,651	14,019	18	17
Aged	15	57	20	65	2,513	2,454	13	3
Delinquency and crime	6	13	10	14	1,734	351	9	1
Recreation	24	55	29	63	1,495	1,827	8	2
Children	18	82	28	117	1,426	3,100	7	4
Relief-social agencies	27	107	36	144	1,073	6,214	5	8
Community funds[b]	22	610	22	838	1,044	30,795	5	38
Handicapped	17	95	21	113	589	3,749	3	5
Interracial relations	7	40	8	94	253	5,767	1	7
Transportation and safety	3	15	3	24	55	690	—[c]	1
General	n.d.[d]	15	n.d.	21	n.d.	746	n.d.	1
Total	110	832	268	1,928	19,996	80,512	100	100

SOURCE: *The Foundation Directory*, 2nd and 3rd eds. (New York: Russell Sage Foundation, 1964 and 1967).
[a] The 1962 totals should be accepted with reservation because family- and company-sponsored foundations are not adequately represented.
[b] This category jumped to first place because more family foundations were included and these often made one grant to local community chest-type organizations.
[c] Less than 0.5 percent.
[d] n.d. = no data.

TABLE 19.6 Reported Grants for International Affairs, 1960, 1962 and 1966

	Number of Foundations			Number of Grants			Amount (thousands of dollars)			International Affairs Grants (percentage)		
	1960	1962	1966	1960	1962	1966	1960	1962	1966	1960	1962	1966
Economic aid	4	n.d.^a	n.d.	n.d.	n.d.	n.d.	$ 1,496	n.d.	n.d.	8	n.d.	n.d.
Exchange of persons	15	9	16	n.d.	21	22	4,459	$ 1,988	$ 2,539	24	4	2
International studies	17	13	8	n.d.	81	47	6,632	20,308	50,800	36	39	36
Peace and international cooperation	5	10	15	n.d.	17	33	405	1,146	4,563	2	2	3
Relief and refugees	8	2	15	n.d.	2	16	385	30	661	2	_b	_b
Technical assistance	8	7	25	n.d.	61	131	5,303	8,778	26,535	28	17	19
Education	n.d.	13	58	n.d.	110	139	n.d.	11,520	40,513	n.d.	22	29
Health and medicine	n.d.	15	38	n.d.	108	134	n.d.	7,240	11,280	n.d.	14	8
Cultural relations	n.d.	6	32	n.d.	18	53	n.d.	1,288	3,069	_b	2	2
Other	1	n.d.	13	n.d.	n.d.	21	9	n.d.	1,272	n.d.	n.d.	1
Total	29	33	152	n.d.	418	596	$18,689	$52,298	$141,232	100	100	100

SOURCE: *The Foundation Directory*, 1st, 2nd and 3rd eds. (New York: Russell Sage Foundation, 1960, 1964 and 1967).
^a n.d. = no data.
^b Less than 0.5 percent.

new programs on the part of foundations not previously concerned with this field."

The largest foundations have also sought to establish more liberalizing programs in the field of international activity. For example, Ford is committed to the "partnership" relation as a guide in the conduct of activity (Ford Foundation, 1968).

> The International Division is the Foundation's largest. Our commitment here is deep, long-standing, and long range. We are trying to use our relatively modest resources and our relatively extensive experience to help where a private American nonprofit organization can help best in the social and economic growth of societies in Latin America, Africa, the Middle East and Asia. Our primary method has been that of developing a flexible capacity to respond to the needs of responsible leaders as they perceive them: we try not to give unwanted help.

Bundy recently took the opportunity, in explaining Ford's international programs, to decry the insensitivity of the American Congress to foreign aid. He noted that government is obstructed by the attitude of Congress (Ford Foundation, 1968). Elsewhere (Ford Foundation, 1969b and 1969c), he calls the United States' foreign aid position a "national disgrace," thereby implying that the international programs of the foundations are a liberal corrective to congressional conservatism. Moreover, the concern for racial equality is not to be excluded even in the international field. On April 30, 1969, Ford announced major grants for research on racial problems outside the United States: to the Institute of Race Relations, London, concerned with race problems on an international scale, $350,000; to the Minority Rights Group, London, $72,000; to the South Africa Institute of Race Relations, Johannesburg, $200,000 (Ford Foundation, 1969c).

The Carnegie Foundation has been oriented toward international studies, international peace and the promotion of international contact between scholars and students for so long that it shows little interest in presenting ideological rationales for its programs. For example, in a comparison of the Carnegie Foundation's annual reports for 1964, 1966 and 1968, little shift in interest or in political vocabulary is evident. An examination of other foundation reports shows shifting emphasis in styles and fields of research in the international field. From 1964 to 1966, interest focused on development, trade, population and food supply problems. From 1966 to 1968, the focus was on fostering international communication between scholars, on quantitative studies in international relations and on visiting research scholarships, "world order" studies and technical assistance to underdeveloped countries.

The data of Table 19.6 indicate an over-all increase in grants in the international field, the most startling increase being between 1962 and 1966. In this field, an increase in the number of foundations sampled would not change the picture because the additions to the sample would all be small foundations, which have little interest in international activities. Two other points should be noted: (1) the Ford, Rockefeller and Carnegie foundations make the largest contribution; and yet (2) much foundation funding does not go directly abroad, but rather, to American universities for studies of foreign areas.

Other foundations have recently been concerning themselves with the life sciences and their relation to social policy. Most notable of these is the Russell Sage Foundation (See Russell Sage Foundation, 1968, pp. 10–20). Although it is less likely that these activities are directly motivated by liberal idealism, a certain bias toward aiding "the disadvantaged" suggests itself in some programs of the Russell Sage Foundation (1968, p. 28):

> Foundation interest in the socialization of special groups in American society has gradually been gaining momentum during the last five years. This year . . . the Foundation's efforts in this area will contribute to the understanding of the problems of such sub-groups: racial minorities, women of high ability, the blind, the aging, and professionals. Last year the Foundation announced its support of a six-month exploratory study of Negro executives in the white business world.

None of the above should be construed as meaning that *all* foundations reflect a liberal bias. Some speak exclusively in the apolitical terms of specialized professionalism. The Wenner-Gren Foundation for Anthropological Research, for example, is so closely oriented to professional anthropological studies that its programs seemingly bear no relationship to the American political environment. Even if one considers professionalism to be a special kind of ideological justification, it would be difficult to relate it to the Right-Center-Left framework that we have been employing in discussing the foundations.

Indeed, just as there are foundations with a Left-liberal orientation, so too there are large foundations that overtly promote right-wing activities (the organizations funded by H. L. Hunt) or that devote their resources to "traditional" charity and the promotion of "conservative values." The Indiana-based Lilly Endowment reflects all the remnants of traditional philanthropy. It has a strongly religious interest, sponsors anti-Communist educational projects, promotes little or no social science research and emphasizes charitable giving to foster the development of self-reliant individuals loyal to the United States (Lilly Endowment, 1964).[10] Thus the liberal orientation of big foundations toward racial equality and increased aid to developing nations is by no means unchallenged in the foundation world.

The foundations' relationship with government, especially over the last two decades, has been a particularly important stimulant of liberal attitudes. For one thing, the foundation is often confused by the expansion of gov-

[10] See also the reports for 1965, 1966 and 1967.

ernment-sponsored research. The Danforth Foundation (1967, pp. 10–11) expresses this confusion forthrightly:

> American philanthropy has never been healthier or more puzzled. This is especially true for foundations working in the field of education. On the one hand, the calls for support from schools and colleges are more urgent than ever before, and the foundations are responding in ever-increasing measure. On the other hand, the complexities and uncertainties of education and the millions of new government money cause the foundations to wonder what they should do; and they seem to spend more time in pondering their role in general, and perhaps their particular grants, than was once their custom.

This concern for the continuing redefinition of foundation roles is widespread.[11] Nevertheless, confusion had led to a formula for adaptation and cooperation. This is well expressed in the Danforth Foundation report (1967, pp. 10–11):

> The Danforth Foundation has decided not to abandon those interests that touch upon the areas of Federal activity, but to adopt a policy of parallel action and, where feasible, collaboration. . . . Federal money, like foundation money, is automatically neither an ogre nor an angel. We must learn to live with it creatively and to combine it with other resources to the benefit of all education.

The result is that foundations have been driven into collaboration with government, or, as foundation spokesmen say, into a partnership. But a partnership still leaves the problem of what role foundations will play. They cannot duplicate government efforts; they can only complement them according to government need. Thus arises the innovative role of the foundation, in contrast to the more established role of government—the "cautious partner." The foundations are in a position to innovate. Public regard for foundations depends on it. Moreover, complementing government research efforts means taking risks government cannot afford politically and sometimes financially. The partnership thus involves the foundation in both practical collaboration and innovative political risk-taking. A number of statements are available indicating both the fact and the acceptance, by both partners, of this collaboration. In addition to joint ventures, there is collaboration on the personnel level.

> Foundation staff members and governmental officials do move back and forth between each other's vineyards, sometimes for a stretch of years, sometimes on ad hoc assignments, the most elementary answer is that of the patriotic obligation. Our government should get talented people where

[11] For some recent examples, see M. Bundy in Ford Foundation (1968) and Creel (1969).

it can find them, and members of foundation staffs have no less an obligation to respond than university professors or business executives. But patriotism . . . is not the only basis for the interchange. To remain alert and informed, both foundations and government need the infusion of talented and specialized outsiders. . . . Foundations can be the source of support for disinterested evaluation of government activities. It is no reflection on the Congressional right and competence to evaluate government activity to suggest that judgments from this source are not always free of political implications. Congress itself and the Executive Branch have acknowledged the importance of independent, non-government appraisal of government, and where else are the evaluators of government social and economic programs to obtain non-governmental support but (from) the foundations? (Magat, 1969, pp. 7–8)

Magat (1969, p. 6) emphasizes the practical value of collaboration for foundations:

The partnership may be conducted through joint ventures with local, state, or national governments. Participation affords government direct experience in the venture, so that it does not have to rely on second-hand or after-the-fact observations and it enhances the prospects of continuing interest and financing after the foundation's role is concluded. Collaboration sometimes is also indicated for the simple reason that the undertaking may be too costly for foundations alone.

Collaboration extends down to local government, and extends to sensitive issues. (U.S. House, 1969, p. 430).

Collaboration and risk taking by foundations have become so firm a trend that a Commission on Foundations and Private Philanthropy has been formed to give it systematic attention. The commission will consider, among other things, "new roles for foundations as the government invests unprecedented amounts in traditional areas of welfare and philanthropy," and "guidelines to help determine the proper role of private philanthropy to controversial public policy issues and the political process" (Peterson, 1969).

While the subject of the responses of the federal government to foundation activities is a subject for study in itself, it is evident that recent investigations of the Patman subcommittee (United States House of Representatives) and ensuing congressional activities designed to make foundations subject to new tax reform measures are directly aimed at the third-force liberalism of the foundations. According to the hearings before the House Committee on Ways and Means held in 1969 and presided over by Congressman Wright Patman, a tax surcharge of 100 percent would be levied on any foundation making an investment "which jeopardizes the carrying out of its exempt purposes." This provision seems especially aimed at discouraging foundation support for measures such as voter registration drives and black ghetto self-help programs. The section of the bill entitled

"Taxes and Taxable Expenditures" is emphatic in citing termination of tax-exempt status to penalize efforts "to carry out propaganda or otherwise influence legislation," or "to influence the outcome of any public election" (Walsh, 1969, pp. 678–679). Aside from some vague references to travel and study, there is little in the bill to indicate real concern about manifestations of foundation liberalism in activities overseas. It is clear, then, that it is in the area of domestic politics that the real thrust and the real concerns exist.

The foundations have proved singularly inept at lobbying in support of their causes. Aside from some recent action on the part of foundation officials and aside from sporadic congressional support, there has been remarkably little defense of the foundations from those individuals and political institutions that benefit from their existence. One might argue that this refutes the idea of a monolithic establishment acting as a mighty phalanx to delay social justice and economic change.

The main problem seems to be that the corporate model for public trusts is an unwieldy one, at least for generating mass support, or even the support of particular elite groups. Cut off from a major national constituency, foundations are buffeted by those "below," whom they seek to serve, and no less by those "above," who determine the operational framework of foundation activities and policies. This explains the rather conventional commitment to liberal ideologies and causes, and also explains a good deal of the resentment concerning foundation activities from both right-wing crusader and left-wing critics.

While foundation responses to criticism have been both cautious and vigorously self-defensive, the foundations' peculiar position between business and government has left them vulnerable and searching for formulas for survival. A liberal orientation and collaboration with government agencies to liberalize policy have helped them. But these trends have led to more criticism from both the Right and the Left. A major increase in the impact of either type of critic would precipitate a crisis.

REFERENCES

Bremner, R. H. (1960) *American Philanthropy*. Chicago: University of Chicago Press.

Council on Foundations (1968) *Council on Foundations Annual Report, 1967–1968*.

Creel, D. S. (1969) "The Role of the Foundations in Today's Society," address presented May 20, 1969, before the Ninth Biennial Conference on Charitable Foundations, New York University.

Danforth Foundation (1967) *Danforth Foundation Annual Report, 1965–1966*, St. Louis.

Danforth Foundation (1969) *Danforth Foundation Annual Report, 1967–1968*, St. Louis.

Ford Foundation (1968) *Ford Foundation Annual Report, 1967–1968,* New York.

Ford Foundation (1969a) *Ford Foundation in East and Central Africa.* New York: Ford Foundation Office of Reports.

Ford Foundation (1969b) *News from Ford Foundation* (March 2).

Ford Foundation 1969c) *News from Ford Foundation* (April 30).

Ford Foundation (1969d) *News from Ford Foundation* (May 8).

Ford Foundation (1969e) *News from Ford Foundation* (June 19).

Fremont-Smith, M. R. (1965) *Foundations and Government.* New York: Russell Sage Foundation.

Harrison, S., and F. E. Andrews (1946) *American Foundations for Social Welfare.* New York: Russell Sage Foundation.

Lilly Endowment (1964) *Lilly Endowment Report for 1964,* Boston.

Magat, R. (1969) "Foundation Reporting," address presented May 19, 1969, before the Ninth Biennial Conference on Charitable Foundations, New York University.

Peterson, P. G. (1969) Press release, April 23, 1969, Bell and Howell Company.

Russell Sage Foundation (1964) *The Foundation Directory,* 2d ed., New York.

Russell Sage Foundation (1967) *The Foundation Directory,* 3d. ed., New York.

Russell Sage Foundation (1968) *Russell Sage Foundation Annual Report, 1967–68,* New York.

Sutton, F. X. (1968) *American Foundations and U.S. Public Diplomacy.* New York: Ford Foundation; reprinted from an address delivered before the Symposium on the Future of U.S. Public Diplomacy, submitted to the U.S. House Committee on Foreign Affairs Subcommittee on International Organizations and Movements.

U. S. Department of the Treasury (1965) *Treasury Department Report on Private Foundations,* vol. 1. Washington, D.C.: Government Printing Office.

U. S. House (1952) *Hearings Before the Select Committee to Investigate Tax-Exempt Foundations and Comparable Organizations,* 82nd Cong., 2nd sess. Washington, D.C.: Government Printing Office.

U. S. House (1969) *Hearings Before the Committee on Ways and Means, Tax Reform,* 91st Cong., 1st sess. Washington, D.C.: Government Printing Office.

U. S. Senate (1916) *Final Report and Testimony,* 64th Cong., 1st sess., Senate Document No. 415. Washington, D.C.: Government Printing Office.

Walsh, J. (1969) "Tax Reform: House Bill Holds Penalties for Foundations," *Science,* vol. 165 (March 20), pp. 678–679.

CHAPTER 20

DETERRENCE POLICIES: FROM ACADEMIC CASEBOOK TO MILITARY CODEBOOK

The outrage traditional scholars exhibit at the work done by war game strategists, be they of civilian or military affiliation, is closer to the anguish of men concerned with professional status than to that of men compromised by poor social science. In part, this chapter is an attempt to redress this set of concerns. This is the problem: No amount of theoretical assault on war gaming as a strategy has discouraged raising the use of this technique of analysis to the level of theory. Perhaps one solution is to look more soberly and seriously at the consequences such a strategy has in the real world and for actual men.

First, I shall examine the social structural components entailed in war game strategies that facilitate its use by military leaders. Second, I shall examine the theory of war gaming in the light of military practice. Only by examining empirical events that claim to have employed game strategies to advantage can we move beyond the arguments over the actual worth of the theory. If I eschew the usual criticisms of war game theory, it is not because of ignorance of them—indeed, I feel partially responsible for having collated these arguments in the first place (Horowitz, 1962 and 1963)— but simply because the test of any theory must ultimately be its use. One unnerving missile crisis may not constitute a definitive rebuke, but at least it opens up the possibility of counterfactualizing statements in an area thus far held sacrosanct by at least some portion of the social scientific community connected to military decision making.

War game theorists' reactions, when confronted by the military use of their findings, customarily vary from amusement to disaffiliation. Some maintain that the work of war gamers is of great therapeutic value in replacing old-fashioned horror stories, but that it has no more and no less validity. Others claim that war game concepts are radically distinct from and even contradictory to basic game theorems derived from probability theory. My own belief is that these disclaimers are much like the one made by the original founding members of the Royal Academy of Science when they discovered that atheists and agnostics were attempting to obtain membership on the basis of the principles of mechanics: to reaffirm, against all empirical information, that the principles of mechanics demonstrably prove the existence of Providential Will and, therefore, that nothing but good can come of such principles.

The assumption herein made is that however proximate or distant the relationship between war games and other games, there is such a connection. Further, however amusing or frightening these games are to participants or victims, game theory represents genuine empirical as well as metaphorical elements which, translated into operational terms through federal agencies, become part of the foreign policy of the United States.

This chapter is not to be a history or a chronicle of the relationship between war games and federal policy, but rather an attempt to understand the most general relations between national policy and military behavior by testing a specific theory about the influence of strategy expertise in policy matters, using deterrence theory as a model and testing it against the Cuban missile crisis as an empirical event of major consequence. In its specifics, this is an attempt to understand some of the general relations between politics and militarism through a test of a specific theory about the influence of war game theory on United States foreign policy.

THE GAME OF DETERRENCE:
A MILITARY CODEBOOK

The theory of military deterrence through games of strategy is contained in an article by Colonel Wesley Posvar, former chairman of the Air Force Academy Political Science Department, entitled "The Impact of Strategy Expertise on the National Security Policy of the United States." His theory begins with a definition of strategy:

> In the present context strategy pertains to the systematic development and employment of national power, particularly military power, to secure national aims. The constituents of national power which are relevant . . . include military power and other instruments to the extent that they are

closely linked to military power, including economic (foreign assistance, trade, discrimination), psychological (propaganda, terror), and in limited degree, ideological and political. (Posvar, 1964, p. 38)

This definition is one that is generally accepted by the strategy experts and is suitable to this context, so I see no reason not to accept it.

Part of Posvar's theory concerns how strategic policy is created: "Policy is formulated not only in the way usually understood, that is, by a body at the center of government, drawing the information it needs." Strategy is also formed by the cumulative action of subordinate and outlying elements, "in the sense that the weapons chosen for development today determine national strategy ten years from now. . . . Although the making of strategy is a function of government . . . it is possible for this function to be performed to a great extent completely outside the structure of government" (Posvar, 1964, pp. 39–40). Here he is describing a process that many others have observed—policy by lack of decision, by default. Insofar as decisions could be made but are not, Posvar feels that decisive influence (he would not use the word "power") passes to the strategy experts, because they invent or define available options.

Posvar next describes the system of games of strategy: "Strategy expertise is the product of men, organizations, and methods." It is not the product of a statistical aggregate, for the strategy experts make up a community "with a degree of coherence that seems to exceed the bonds of common organization and shared technique" (Posvar, 1964, p. 43). Strategy expertise is produced in two organizational contexts: research corporations and university research centers (Cf. Lyons and Morton, 1965). The most highly organized strategy expertise is concentrated in half a dozen research corporations: RAND (working primarily for the air force), Research Analysis Corporation (successor to ORO [Operations Research Office] working mostly for the army), the Institute for Defense Analysis (performing contract studies for the Department of Defense at large), the Hudson Institute, the Operations Evaluation Group (working for the navy) and the Stanford Research Institute (working for industry as well as government).

Strategy expertise is produced by distinctive methods of analysis such as economic theory—for example, mathematical models of war used for computer simulation, or informal games of decision-makers in conflict situations simulated by individual role playing. It also includes, of course, that amalgamation of everything (which is therefore, particularly attractive to some social scientists), systems analysis—the "result of associating experts from various disciplines together under favorable circumstance of organization and communication, experts who share attention to common tasks" (Posvar, 1964, p. 52). Posvar's description of the organization and methods of the system of game strategy is brief but fairly accurate, though the coherence he ascribes to it has implications far beyond his own considerations.

Posvar finally describes several ways in which game strategy can be implemented in actual policy. One way is "the reverse of the dispersal of the strategy-making function . . . the problem of assembling and using the output of the system. . . . This step involves the whole decision-making process of the U.S. government. So we are forced to limit our present observations to the difficulties which are encountered in attempting to place recommendations and studies in the right hands" (Posvar, 1964, pp. 56–57). Here Posvar observes that in order to maintain their institutional autonomy, the game strategy experts try to maintain the principle of non-advocacy. This factor, combined with the position of the experts outside the government, tends "to obstruct the entry of important ideas and findings into the decision-making process." What happens to the specific policy recommendations once they are in the proper hands is a separate question that Posvar (1964, pp. 56–57) does not consider.

> The pattern of influence works another way, too, as strategic analysis is solicited by high government offices for specific tasks. There is little wonder that the "celibate mistress" (i.e., the RAND Corporation, kept but ignored by the Air Force) has become the object of flirtation by the Office of the Secretary of Defense, which now includes former members of the strategic community who fully appreciate her charms.

His theory provides another way in which strategic analysis has influence on policy; of greater importance is the direct and objective influence upon the whole policy echelon provided by a massive outpouring of scholarship. The system provides an ever-larger volume of published works plus myriad briefings of policy officials and staff officers. This is the process by which game strategy experts are able to influence the decisions in the subordinate and outlying elements.

Such is the foundation of Posvar's theory of game strategy. However, he raises other important issues which it is necessary to consider. First, there is the question of an evaluation of the system. At this point, Posvar's theory turns into celebration: "RAND appears to be one of the best investments the United States government has made since the Louisiana Purchase. Secretary McNamara, who is not prone to make such extravagant statements as this, does acknowledge that the Air Force gets 'ten times the value' of the cost of the RAND contract." Posvar illustrates this evaluation with seven examples in which strategic analysis was implemented successfully, but presents no examples of failure. He explains:

> We are unable to perceive a failure in a weapon system, so long as the goals of policy are being adequately served. Who can say now whether our decision to rely on the B-47 plus aerial tanker force, and on the B-36 force before it, were the best decisions? Who, indeed, cares? The presumption is in favor of success inasmuch as the policy of deterrence of general war was fulfilled. (Posvar, 1965, pp. 61, 64–65)

This explanation has the same sophistication as that of the compulsive urbanite when asked why he continually snaps his fingers: "To keep the elephants away. Works pretty well, doesn't it?" Be that as it may, Posvar's theory of how the system works can be judged independently of his evaluation of the system.

A second issue is the relationship of civilian strategy experts to military professionals. Some people feel that the strategy experts undermine that older military professions by preempting their essential functions. Posvar feels that "this complaint masks a need for further strengthening the professional bureaucracy itself" by learning the methods and techniques of strategy expertise so that the military can better judge and use it.

A third issue is whether strategy experts constitute a power elite, whether they are part of the military-industrial-academic complex. Posvar considers this question just long enough to dismiss it, though it crops up again later in a different form:

> We may therefore state the basis of our concern explicitly as a displacement of power relative to responsibility. We refer to the power (or authority) to make or decisively to influence strategic decisions, and the responsibility (or accountability) to a superior political object for the consequences of those decisions. They should reside in the same place. (Posvar, 1964, p. 65)

Posvar feels that the solution is clear: "The dissociation of power and responsibility which is a deficiency of the strategy-making process could be largely remedied by raising the qualifications of professional bureaucrats, both military and civilian" (Posvar, 1964, pp. 63–64). The military in this country has long had an ideology of being professional and apolitical. Military professionalism, of course, puts an emphasis on expert judgment. Posvar is a military man, and he seems to assume that the professional quality of game strategy, or its "scientific" status, assures its pervasive implementation at all levels of government. When management fails to put into effect the research findings it contracts for, Posvar thinks it is a failure of understanding, to be corrected by education. To think that this can be changed through education is to fail to perceive political reality. Expert judgment may be correct, but correctness alone is not enough. There is also the question of interests, of who benefits.

Finally, Posvar specifically mentions the Cuban missile crisis. He writes:

> There is a new awareness of the utility and also the limitations of strategic striking power in situations involving limited national objectives, like Cuba. Herman Kahn's Type II Deterrent [which "guards against major aggression against a vital area other than the U.S. (e.g., Europe) by the threat of retaliation directly against the U.S.S.R."], and Thomas Schelling's Threat That Leaves Something to Chance [which "deters lower scale actions by

the danger that somebody might inadvertently start a big war"], have contributed to this awareness. When one reflects on these new perceptions in strategic thought, and the likelihood that a president would be familiar with them as President Kennedy evidently was in the Cuba crisis, the conclusion is inescapable that the strategists have made a vital contribution. (Posvar, 1964, pp. 66–67)

The difficulty is the failure to note whether the Kahn–Schelling framework was as "familiar" to either Castro or Khrushchev—those directly involved and in power at that time. This is said only partially in jest. In point of fact, both Kahn and Schelling imply an explicit level of mutual rationality in order for the deterrent and threat mechanisms to be made operational. In a sense, too, this is the Achilles' heel of such gaming strategies, since if shared rationality is a requirement for the conduct of politics by military means, there is no way of avoiding the counterproposal: the conduct of military activities by political means. However, the reason this logical equivalent is not developed by Posvar and his fellow new civilian militarists is that if such a high degree of rationality can be assumed in the pursuit of self-interest, one should be able to claim, in good Adam Smithian terms, that this same rationality would point up the futility of brinksmanship games to begin with, and hence reinforce the notion of settlement through accommodation rather than victory through fear.

THE GAME OF DETERRENCE:
AN ORGANIZATIONAL NETWORK

Doubtless, the Cuban missile crisis fits Posvar's definition of war game strategy. The United States government had at the time of the missile crisis (and still has) three basic national aims with respect to Cuba. These main goals were to prevent the spread of communism, to overthrow the Castro government and to crush communism in Cuba. These sentiments were expressed in a joint resolution of Congress passed on September 20 and 26, 1962:

The United States is determined: (a) to prevent by whatever means may be necessary, including the use of arms, the Marxist-Leninist regime in Cuba from extending, by force or by the threat of force, its aggressive or subversive activities to any part of this hemisphere; (b) to prevent in Cuba the creation or use of an externally supported military capability endangering the security of the United States; and (c) to work with the Organization of American States and with freedom-loving Cubans to support the aspirations of the Cuban people for self-determination. (Pachter, 1963, p. 179)

By military power and by other instruments of national power such as trade discrimination. Cuba was to be isolated, to make the maintenance of communism in Cuba costly to the Soviet Union (McNamara, 1963, p. 274). Since it fits his definition, the missile crisis is a test case relevant to Posvar's theory.

The next question is how game strategy policy was formulated in the Cuban case. In formal terms, the answer is simple. An executive committee of the National Security Council, appointed *ad hoc* by President Kennedy, formulated and recommended a course of action, and the President approved it. But the real issue is how game strategy came to be implemented, if it was, in the actual policy followed. This is the crux of the problem and a much more difficult question to answer.

There are several modes of influence to be considered. First is the assembly and use of specific recommendations or studies dealing with the introduction of offensive weapons into Cuba. Whether the analysis is solicited by higher or lower government offices makes a difference only after the recommendations exist; the first problem is to establish their existence. Bruce Smith (1966, p. 231) pointed out, however, that the effective advisory group usually goes to great pains to conceal its impact on policy. For example, the RAND strategic bases study, *Selection and Use of Strategic Air Bases,* R-266, was put into effect in 1953, but remained classified until 1962, nine years later. In establishing his case for the influence of this study over air force policy, Smith relied extensively on personal interviews, which might have been difficult to obtain if his dissertation adviser had not been a member of RAND's board of trustees. (Smith's study was a Ph.D. dissertion. His faculty adviser, Don K. Price, was both a Harvard dean and a RAND trustee.) The RAND Corporation made a number of studies after the crisis, but if any studies were made before the crisis they are still classified (Cf. Graham and Brease, 1967). Because any such study would be extremely politically sensitive in nature, it would be unlikely to be declassified in the near future. Second, specific policy recommendations are atypical; most RAND strategy analysis deals with more abstract questions. Information analysis directed toward specific policy is the responsibility of the intelligence branch. Although on the Cuban question the theoretical distinction between research and intelligence fades, the institutional distinction remains clear—research and intelligence functions are performed by different bureaus. By all accounts, only the intelligence experts were involved in the executive committee council of war. According to Wohlstetter (1965), no one thought the Cubans and Russians would install the missiles. One must infer, lacking any other evidence, that no specific policy recommendations relating to the Cuban situation were produced by the RAND Corporation. Since RAND's influence seems out of the question in this case, there is no point in speculating about methodological problems such as communication and distortion of policy recommendations or the merits of systems analysis.

The other mode of influence is the pervasive frame of reference contained in the "massive outpouring of scholarship" in support of the new politics based on behavioral psychology. The early sixties were characterized by the emergence of war game theory as the basic form of macroscopic social science. This occurred in part as a metaphorical displacement of the "historical" orientations of previous periods characterized by the writings of such men as Hans Margenthau and Arnold J. Toynbee, and in part as a commonly held belief that the results of experimental psychology, particularly of reinforcement, exchange and balance theories, could be extended to cover political behavior between nations. The concurrence of circumstance, that is, the emergence of a group of war gamers such as Alain Enthoven and Adam Yarmolinsky in positions of advisory power, the professional demands by men like Bernard Brodie and Itheil de Sola Pool to "test" behaviorist assumptions in a broadened context, the coalescence of "systems" designers with engineering backgrounds such as Seymour J. Deitchman and "social" designers with behavioral backgrounds such as Henry J. Kissinger—all of these factors served as a fulcrum for organizing a new view of "relevance," a new faith in a social science of political "meaning."

At the same time that the inner organizational requisites of war game theory were being met, the outer political requisites of real conflict were also being met in the Cuban missile crisis. This crisis had the perfect scenario dimensions: (1) It was a simple two-person struggle between major powers (or so it seemed to the protagonists at the time); (2) it had a stage setting of showdown proportions that revealed relatively clear-cut and unambiguous dimensions; and (3) it was a situation in which victor and vanquished would be readily determined by the behavior shown. That all of these assumptions were radically in error was either disbelieved or discounted at the time. It was not a simple two-person struggle, but one interpreted by Cuba—and much of the Third World—as a struggle between big powers acting arrogantly and a small power acting with principles to preserve its autonomy and sovereignty. There was nothing unambiguous about the showdown, since, in fact, the resolution was such as to convince all combatants and parties to the dispute that they had, in fact, been the winner. It was a showdown without losers, in fact. Indeed, this really made peace possible under the circumstances because no one was willing to accept responsibilities for any defeat, or any outcome perceived by each people as a defeat.

According to the *New York Times'* (1962) account of the committee's October 19 meeting, there were some second thoughts about the blockade, some renewed interest in an air attack: "The reason was what the group called a 'scenario' [a phrase originating in the strategy community]—a paper indicating in detail all the possible consequences of an action." Elie Abel (1966, p. 86) pointed out that "Bundy prepared the air-strike argument; and Alexis Johnson with Paul Nitze's assistance, drafted what came to be called the blockade scenario," indicating that the frame of reference of the executive committee was game strategy analysis.

Bruce Smith (1966, p. 112) noted that "gaming and simulation had important uses as a training device for government officials to help them understand what kinds of behavior to be prepared for in various crisis situations. Crisis games became widely used by high State and Defense Department officials early in the Kennedy Administration." In addition, many high-level civilian executives were formerly members of the game strategy community: Charles Hitch, Assistant Secretary of Defense (comptroller), Henry Rowen and Alain Enthoven, Deputy Assistant Secretaries of Defense, Walt W. Rostow, Assistant Secretary of State, and Paul Nitze, Secretary of the Navy (Posvar, 1964, p. 48). At the time of the crisis, Paul Nitze was Assistant Secretary of Defense for International Security Affairs and a member of Kennedy's ad hoc crisis committee.

Political gaming as a special subfunction of military policy is a procedure for the study of foreign affairs that the RAND Corporation began developing in 1954. A RAND report, referring to the State Department's interest in gaming, noted that "Even before the first four games had been completed RAND began to receive requests for information about its political gaming procedures, and staff members have by now taken part in a substantial number of discussions about it" (Speier and Goldhammer, 1959, p. 80). As witness to this interest, "three senior Foreign Service officers from the Department of State participated in the fourth political game, along with specialists from RAND's Social Science, Economics, and Physics Divisions" (Speier and Goldhammer, 1959, p. 74).

There is scant doubt that gaming and simulation were widely used by the President's executive committee. Nearly all higher echelon figures knew immediately what games were referred to. Although State Department officers like George W. Ball may have doubted that political games were of greater value than a similar amount of involvement in ordinary reading and study, many senior officers even of the "traditional" State Department no less than the "modern" Defense Department participated in the fourth round. Although only a minority of Kennedy's war council came from the Departments of State and Defense, the rest were seemingly also familiar with strategy analysis.

The chilling degree to which a game of showdown proportions had been around the Cuban missile crisis is reported by Schlesinger (1965, p. 830): "Saturday night was almost the blackest of all. Unless Khrushchev came through in a few hours, the meeting of the Executive Committee on Sunday night might well face the most terrible decisions." In a revealing metaphor, Schlesinger then notes, "At nine in the morning Khrushchev's answer began to come in. By the fifth sentence it was clear that he had thrown in the hand." And it is finally clear that this unwillingness to risk all-out war on the Soviet Union's part came "barely in time." Schlesinger concludes by drawing out the option: "If word had not come that Sunday, if work had continued on the bases, the United States would have had no real choice but to take action against Cuba the next week. No one could discern what lay darkly beyond an air strike or invasion, what measures and countermeasures, actions and reactions, might have driven the hapless world to the ghastly consummation." It should be noted that this account is made not simply from a writer but from a member of the President's inner group of advisers, and that the differences between hard-liners and soft-liners over the missile crisis concerned the character of the response, not the necessity for playing the game of showdown poker. Thus, at a critical point in United States foreign policy, traditional methods of accommodations were abandoned in favor of a military definition of the situation —a definition made intellectually palatable by the "science" of game theory.

Game strategy analysis also played an influential role through the Joint Chiefs of Staff. Although Senator Sparkman (1962, p. 75) of Alabama, in the September hearings, remembered "General LeMay, Chief of Staff of the Air Force, stating that there would be no difficulty in knocking out those missile sites," only the chairman of the Joint Chiefs, Maxwell Taylor, actually sat on the executive committee. When Kennedy met separately with the Joint Chiefs, they would not guarantee that a so-called surgical strike—one that would destroy all the missiles and bombers, yet inflict few casualties on the general population—was feasible (Cf. Sorenson, 1965). In any case, such feasibility studies are the proper responsibility of the military profession and are not farmed out to research corporations. Posvar's argument about the influence of strategy analysis thus has little value. The final executive committee recommendations actually emerged from a political bargaining process that involved not only the military factors and strategic analysis but also considerations of morality (for example, Robert F. Kennedy argued against the air strike position, saying it would be another Pearl Harbor) and international political consequences.

Many questions arise to make even the hardiest political man uneasy over this concept of "surgical strike." For people like Wohlstetter and Kahn, the problem of defense begins with the military issues surrounding a first strike strategy and proceeds to conditions for a second strike situation. The uses of war game theory thus serve to limit options and deepen ambiguity in the military situation as well. Under such circumstances, it is small wonder that even those who in the past were close to the systems design would raise serious questions as to the efficacy of war gaming. The following remarks by Robert Boguslaw (1967, p. 57) well illustrate the source of much fear that arose both during and after the Cuban missile crisis.

To what extent does the Wohlstetter solution introduce more uncertainty into the international situation and thereby increase the probability of a first strike? To what extent does the effort to confuse an enemy so that he can "never be sure" about the destination of a flight of American bombers serve to make his radar crews and "first strike" forces more jumpy? What are the implications of the analyses and the fail-safe procedures for increasing the probability of unintended nuclear war? Where are the spectacles to correct the consumer-oriented analytic myopia of contemporary systems analysis?

The fact that neither Posvar nor any of his colleagues at RAND addressed themselves to these issues means that a basic aspect in a true gaming situation is constantly violated—namely, the existence of sufficient equilibrium in the situation to prevent an artificial resolution of the problem, or a termination of the game due to bias and misinformation. Yet, it was precisely the increase in ambiguity that decreased rather than increased chances for making accurate predictions as to the outcome of the Cuban missile crisis. It ultimately came down to the "rationality" of the "other player," rather than a science of game theory, since all moves of the United States had been telegraphed well in advance, whereas only the Soviet response remained truly problematic (Cf. Brodie, 1964, p. 53; Horelick, 1963, p. 26).

DETERRENCE GAMES:
THE POLITICAL CONTEXT

The military emphasis on how a game strategy system molds future decisions outside the government ignores the political aspects of decisions made inside the government. According to such a view, no central body tries to "understand" problems of government; instead, a number of partially conflicting factions try to promote particular interpretations and emphases favorable to their own interests. There are at least three interest groups in government: the top civilian officeholders of the national security apparatus, the military professionals of the various armed services and the civilian strategy experts.

Interservice rivalry is an important aspect of this political context. Interservice competition is a post-World War II phenomenon resulting from new technology of war—atomic bombs and missiles—and the changed military requirements of the cold war balance of power.

> The transition from civilian-service controversy to inter-service controversy as the main focus of service political activity was graphically illustrated in the struggle over Universal Military Training between 1945 and 1948. The lines of battle were initially drawn between the Army and certain patriotic and veterans groups on the one hand, and various civilian educational, religious, pacifist, and farm groups on the other. (Huntington, 1965, p. 453)

This issue was resolved by the convergence of two factors: the relative persuasiveness of air force versus army strategy doctrine and the relative political costs of an $822 million hardware appropriation versus universal conscription. This provides only one illustration of how political forces on the congressional battlefield are deployed.

The military services can mobilize several kinds of political forces. The first of these is voluntary associations such as the Navy League or the Association of the U.S. Army. These can engage in political tactics and activities traditionally denied to active servicemen by the restraint of civilian control and the prohibition of military politics. Patriotic groups still support the military generally, but not always the viewpoint of one service over another. In cultivating grass-roots support, the services face a difficult problem:

> Unlike many private associations and a fair number of governmental agencies, the services could not easily mobilize sentiment across the country in support of a national program. The problem which they faced was not dissimilar from that confronted by the large industrial corporations. Both the corporation and the services are national and highly centralized institutions. Political power in America, however, is to a large extent channeled through local organs. Individual political influence depends on prolonged local residence and participation; the employees of the corporation and the service are continually on the move. On the one hand, the economic health of the local community may depend upon decisions by a General Staff in Washington or a board of directors in New York. On the other hand, the small community normally possesses direct access to state and local governing bodies, and frequently to Congress, in a way that is denied to the national organization. (Huntington, 1965, pp. 463–464)

Since national organizations cannot guarantee serving local *interests,* they try to influence local power through appealing to local *values.* The corporations play upon their ideology of free enterprise; the military services emphasize their ideology of anticommunism. The cold war has made it possible to outmaneuver the traditional antimilitarism of isolationists, pacifists and religious and educational groups by playing upon their fear of Communist subversion and aggression.

Political support is also available for industry. The air force used to be able to rely on the aircraft industry and the navy on the shipbuilding industry for political lobbying and support, but the shift of demand to missiles and electronics—often manufactured by companies holding contracts with two or more services—means that industrial interests no longer take sides in interservice competition.

A final type of political support is provided by doctrine. Productive enterprise needs no justification save its product; military expenditures are wasteful and thus require intellectual rationale. The armed services explicitly justify all their activities as essential for the achievement of national goals. The bureaucratic rigidity of the military made it incapable of doctrinal innovation so it hired outside consultants to rethink strategy. Because technical questions about what strategies best serve national ends have political consequences for the military, game strategy experts became part of the fray.

> It is a rare man in Washington who does not suffer from the "Edifice Complex," a tendency which directs his work toward building up his own agency or service whenever possible. Thus, experts associated with the Army or the Navy have developed arguments supporting stabilized deterrence combined with a buildup of conventional forces. Air Force-linked experts have countered with a strategy based on overwhelming superiority in missiles and bombers, buttressed with schemes such as civil defense and studies that prove that *under certain conditions,* we could win a thermonuclear war without destroying our society. (Maccoby, 1963, p. 106)

The class of civilian strategy experts originated when the air force set up the RAND Corporation. At this time, "the mission of the Air Force was almost equivalent to the whole of the national defense effort. The Air Force was secure in its possession of the atomic bomb and the means of its delivery, and had little reason to fear either foreign enemies or a competing sister service" (Smith, 1966, p. 49). In the early days of the RAND Corporation, loyalties to the theory of scientific strategy and to doctrine supporting the air force position coincided perfectly; game strategy experts felt they could work for a single service without sacrificing their scholarly autonomy. As the other services obtained bombs and missiles of their own, this confidence changed. RAND began to diversify its sponsorship contracts and strategic theory as it elaborated and took cognizance of the international and interservice strategic situation. Thus, RAND deviated from its support of air force interests. The air force attempted to bring RAND back into line. "It was the cumulative effect of various RAND-Air Force difference that led to RAND's budget preparation" (Smith, 1966, p. 134). The RAND management acknowledged that its primary loyalties lay with the air force and agreed that air force sources should supply most of its research funds. This political resolution was not without scientific cost. RAND had "the problem of continuing to attract first-rate staff at a time when Air Force concerns no longer [were] the central focus of the nation's defense policies" (Smith, 1966, p. 138). The strategy community's ambiguity on policy questions is a political strategy of self-preservation that only half succeeds.

Top civilian officeholders are in a quite different position. As the bureaucratic superordinates of the professional military men, they are limited only by what political pressures the military can indirectly bring to bear upon them through Congress.

> They have assigned themselves the task of presiding over a vast military bureaucracy—and its supporting institutions—in a period in which changes in technology have forced revolutionary changes in the military art. They

generally lack military training and yet somehow must try to maintain direction over the efforts of their always restive military technicians. Under such circumstances they have become the most ideological of men. Without the presumed superiority of an almost infallible conception of the National Interest they could not hope to force grudging acquiescence from their more technically skilled military subordinates.

John McDermott's (1967, p. 5) description of the "crisis managers" ignores the role of the civilian strategy experts and overestimates the military bureaucracy's ability to adjust to the revolutionary developments in war technology. In founding the RAND Corporation, the air force admitted its own inflexibility. It could neither pay high enough salaries nor provide enough intellectual freedom to attract to its own ranks men capable of coping theoretically with the new technology. The civilian managers, realizing that the services bought their expertise from the civilian strategy experts, did likewise. When RAND wanted to diversify its sponsorship, the Defense Department was ready. "The Air Force, seeing RAND develop an intimate advisory relationship with the agencies at the level of the Office of the Secretary of Defense, had second thoughts about its confidential lawyer-client tie with RAND" (Smith, 1966, p. 129). In addition, the Defense Department is in a position to monitor all research. In April 1962, the Secretary of Defense directed the Secretaries of the Air Force, Army and Navy to forward to his office copies of each study received from RAND, ORO and the other advisory corporations (Horowitz, 1968, pp. 695–749). And while such periodic reviews of research are no proof that such research is actually used, the distinct impression was instilled—in part, as a consequence of Kahn's inordinate influence on many presidential advisers —that game theory was the operational codebook, and not just an intellectual curiosity, of the new Administration.

THE GAME OF DETERRENCE:
A CUBAN CASEBOOK

Given the general context of the political situation of the defense establishment, it is time to examine the Cuban missile crisis in its specifics. The services and the Defense Department expressed different strategic interpretations of the Cuban crisis in the congressional appropriations hearings in 1965. General Curtis LeMay (1963, pp. 888–896), Air Force Chief of Staff, expressed the air force position:

We must maintain a credible general war force so that lesser options may be exercised under the protection of this general war deterrent. It is the general war strength of aircraft and missile forces which place an upper limit on the risks an aggressor is willing to take, and which deter escalation into an all-out conflict. In the Cuban crisis, this limit was tested. . . .

I am convinced that superior U.S. strategic power, coupled with obvious will and ability to apply this power, was the major factor that forced the Soviets to back down. Under the shelter of strategic power, which the Soviets did not dare challenge, the other elements of military power were free to exercise their full potential.

This version of strategic theory is clearly beneficial to the long-run interests of the air force. The air force answer to the problem of how to deter minor "aggression" is to play "chicken" with the air-force-delivered general war force. Posvar's comments on the Cuban crisis, given above, though brief, seem quite consonant with their force position. General Earle Wheeler (1963, p. 507), Army Chief of Staff, expressed the army position in his statement:

> In my opinion, the major lesson for the Army in the Cuban situation lies in the demonstrated value of maintaining ready Army forces at a high state of alert in order to equip national security policy with the military power to permit a direct confrontation of Soviet power. As Secretary McNamara pointed out to the NATO ministers recently, ". . . the forces that were the cutting edge of the action were the nonnuclear ones. Nuclear force was not irrelevant, but it was in the background. Nonnuclear forces were our sword, our nuclear forces were our shield." I wholeheartedly agree with this statement. In the Cuban situation, the Army forces were alerted, brought up to strength in personnel and equipment, moved and made ready for the operations as part of the largest U.S. invasion force prepared since World War II.

The air force interpreted limited war and limited "aggression" as capable of being deterred by strategic nuclear forces and the credibility of its threatened use, while the army viewed strategic nuclear forces alone as insufficient.

A circumstantial argument for the influence of strategy expertise could be made if the position of the RAND Corporation coincided with the strategic interpretation of the air force, its sponsor. A staff-initiated RAND study, however, as early as 1957 noted that "in the case of a sharply limited war in Europe, tactical forces have renewed utility, with strategic air forces complementing tactical forces as the necessary enforcers of weapons limitations" (Hoag, 1957, p. 13, and 1961, p. 26). In at least a dozen other studies of limited war before the crisis, the RAND Corporation developed the same theme. Because of the strategic balance of power, "neither side could expect to use its strategic capabilities to enforce a level of violence in the local area favorable to itself." A limited war capability was needed because "we shall not be able to rely on our strategic forces to deal with limited aggressions" (DeWeerd, 1961, p. 17). These studies clearly supported the army doctrine on limited warfare and contributed to the above-mentioned estrangement of RAND and the air force. The Defense Department, however, became quite interested:

> In early 1962, a large contract was consummated between the RAND Corporation and the Office of the Assistant Secretary of Defense for International Security Affairs (ISA). The ISA contract involved analytic studies of a variety of defense problems, including counterinsurgency and limited war questions, and the annual funding under the ISA contract for a two-year period amounted to over $1,000,000. The ISA contract frightened the Air Force . . . because many Air Force officers felt that some of the civilians in the ISA were contemptuous of military professionalism. (Smith, 1966, p. 127)

The standard interpretation of this complaint by the new civilian militarists (NCM) is the masking of a lack of understanding and competence in strategic theory. However, the air force officers correctly perceived a threat to their position in the defense establishment—a more plausible explanation. The NCM theory would similarly attribute the air force's failure to implement the RAND-generated expertise on limited war to a lack of understanding. This theory would not explain why bureaucratic incompetence was limited to the air force, and was not also a fault of the army or Defense Department. The NCM theory of expertise equates lack of enthusiasm with ignorance and incompetence. One might argue that the air force neglected RAND's contribution because they did not know about it; Smith's account of the implementation of the strategic bases study shows that the communication of research findings is a long and complicated process. Furthermore, this NCM objection does not explain how the army and the Defense Department positions coincided with the RAND position —they knew about RAND's work. The air force refused to understand because RAND's expert judgment benefited the army to the detriment of the air force.

Implementation of policy depends not only on the validity of game theory but also on the question of who benefits. The above emphasis on conflicts within the defense establishment neglects the consensus on two articles of faith: ideological anticommunism which divides the world into Communists and anti-Communists and coercion as the only mode of intercourse between the two.

The careful perusal of the military definition of game theory reveals that gaming strategy is the "science" of coercion. Anything that is not coercive is irrational from a strategic frame of reference. Anticommunism, too, if deeply rooted in strategic analysis. A RAND study notes that if limited wars occur, "they should be looked at as a local and limited manifestation of the global struggle between Communism and the Non-Communist World" (DeWeerd, 1961, p. 17). These two articles of faith pervade not only the strategy community and the defense establishment but also the rest of the government involved in the crisis, so that even if the strategy community had no influence over anyone else, it is questionable whether there would be any substantial difference in policy (Cf. Commager, 1968).

While this analysis has emphasized the political and sociological aspects of gaming analogies, experts themselves often emphasize the truth and rationality of war games. As de Sola Pool (1967, p. 268) puts matters: "That is essentially policy based on social science." Traditional political concerns vanish in this hygienic version of social science. The claim of truth is a powerful way to legitimate authority, but it is also an exclusive way. The claim to social science expertise illegitimates other decision criteria. The illegitimation inherent in the recommendations is a function of ignorance and bureaucratic incompetence. Further, the claim that the failure to perceive the role of expertise as a weapon in the political conflict within the defense establishment and between the defense establishment and civilian groups against militarism weakens the United States military "posture" abroad. Thus, game theory serves as an organizational weapon of military terror—even when its strategies may go awry—as in the Cuban missile crisis.

One might conclude by noting that the United States used war game strategies, while the Soviet Union used conventional rhetoric of Marxism—and yet the latter managed to walk away with at the very least a stalemate, and in some interpretations the full victory. In exchange for the withdrawal of long-range missiles, the Soviet Union guaranteed the long-range survival of Cuba's socialist regime and, no less, a long-term Soviet presence in the Western Hemisphere. It might be argued that conventional diplomacy might have netted the United States far greater results: the maintenance of diplomatic ties between Cuba and the United States. Direct negotiations with Castro rather than negotiations with the Soviets about Castro would have prevented the Soviets from maintaining a long-range presence and would not have strengthened Cuba's sense of sovereignty any more than it already is. But, of course, this would make the military subject to pressures of a historical, geographic and cultural variety that they reject almost instinctively. War game theory is a model of simplicity. It supplies a two-person situation, even if it does sometimes select the wrong players. It structures outcomes, even if it does leave out of the reckoning the optimal sort of outcome. It resolves problems, even if it does so by raising the ante of the problem beyond its initial worth.

The sociological explanation of the functional role of war game theory for the military is still in its infancy (Cf. Green, 1966; Horowitz, 1967, pp. 339–376). Only a final word needs to be said about the symbol role of war game theory, namely, the comfort provided by a world of psychological neatness—a world in which the behavior of large-scale nations is reducible to the decisions of a single man or small group of men. In this sense, war game theory is the ultimate expression, not only of the military ethic but also of the elitist and *etatist* mentality. But it remains the case that the management of political crisis is made more complex, not more simple, by the new military technology. The danger is that military leaders have chosen to ignore this and respond simplistically, precisely as the world of politics and ideology grows more problematic and complicated.

It is important to appreciate the fact that we have been describing a conventional war game built on coercion and threat, and not a model of a game premised on a mechanism of positivist reinforcement built on consensus and compromise. Nor am I prepared to argue the merits of the claim that, ultimately, consensual game models reduce to conflictual models anyhow, thus eliminating the need to study "milder" forms of game theory. Indeed, one might point out that the consensual models only seem to penetrate the literature when some sort of stable equilibrium was, in fact, reached between the Soviet Union and the United States in the post-missile crisis period. Hence, war game theory is not so much an independent input in decision making as it is a sophisticated rationalization of decisions already taken.

Beyond the clear sets of objections other analysts of war game theory and I have pointed out over the years, there is one that has seemingly escaped everyone's attention in the past (including my own), namely, the role of war game theory as a legitimation device for whatever crude military strategy has been decided upon. A tautological aspect thus emerges: If the decision to blockade Cuba is taken, war game theory is appealed to as ultimate arbiter; if the decision to lift the blockade is taken, the same appeal to war gaming is made; and since any complete holocaust would "terminate the game" and "eliminate the players," there is no real possibility of disconfirming the "theory on which the decision is ostensibly reached."

Under such a wonderful protective covering of post hoc legitimation, and with every strategic decision confirming anew the worth of war game theory, it is extremely difficult to reach any final estimate of the theory as such. For this reason, the examination of real events—particularly military retaliations—may be the clearest way open to analysts for evaluating the potency, or as is more usually the case, the paucity, of war game strategies.

In part, what has been described in this chapter belongs to history rather than to politics. And this is as it should be, because when a particular strategy becomes elevated to the level of military theology, the clear and present danger to human survival soon becomes apparent. And in the shock surrounding the Cuban missile crisis—the delayed awareness that the world stood still for a week while games of strategy were permitted to run their course—war game theory had its proudest moment and yet its last moment.

It was not long after the Great Missile Crisis that the "game of chicken" was abandoned in favor of conventional forms of political accommodation. This came about through the mutual realization of the Soviet Union and the United States (especially the latter) that Cuba was not a pawn or an ace-in-the-hole, but a sovereign power in its own right. The Castro Revolution was both national and hemispheric; it evolved its own brand of socialism to meet the challenges of a single-crop island economy. Thus, the Cuban regime was a system that had to be dealt with in traditional political terms of how sovereign states with differing social structures relate to each other. When this dawning took place, the Cuban "crisis" was really solved, precisely by surrendering the notion that this was a behavioral situation reducible to the moves and countermoves of the world's two big military powers. Yet, as long as such repudiation of strategic thinking remains informal and unthinking, the dangers in a repetition of such forms of crisis management through games of change remain ever present. And what first appeared as tragedy may return not so much as comedy, but rather as absurdity—in this instance, the absurdity of total mutual annihilation.

REFERENCES

Abel, E. (1966) *The Missile Crisis.* New York: Bantam Books.

Boguslaw, R. (1967) "RAND in Retrospect," *trans*action, vol. 4, no. 5 (April), pp. 56–57.

Brodie, B. (1964) "The American Scientific Strategists," RAND Corporation, p-2979 (October).

Commager, H. S. (1968) "Can We Limit Presidential Power?" *New Republic,* 158 (February), 15–18.

de Sola Pool, I. (1967) "The Necessity for Social Scientists Doing Research for Government," in I. L. Horowitz, ed., (1967).

DeWeerd, H. A. (1961) "Concepts of Limited War: An Historical Approach," RAND Corporation, p-2352 (November).

Graham, I. C. C., and E. Brease (1967) "Publications of the Social Science Department," RAND Corporation, RM-3600-4 (May).

Green, P. (1966) *Deadly Logic: The Theory of Nuclear Deterrence.* Columbus, Ohio: Ohio State University Press.

Hoag, M. W. (1957) "NATO Deterrent vs. Shield," RAND Corporation, RM-1926-RC (June).

Hoag, M. W. (1961) "On Local War Doctrine," RAND Corporation, p-2433 (August).

Horelick, A. L. (1963) "The Cuban Missile Crisis: An Analysis of Soviet Calculations and Behavior," RAND Corporation, p-2433 (August).

Horowitz, I. L. (1962) *Games, Strategies and Peace.* Philadelphia: American Friends Service Committee.

Horowitz, I. L. (1963) *The War Game: Studies of the New Civilian Militarists.* New York: Ballantine.

Horowitz, I. L., ed. (1967) *The Rise and Fall of Project Camelot: Studies in the Relationship between Social Science and Practical Politics.* Cambridge, Mass.: M.I.T. Press.

Horowitz, I. L. (1968) "America as a Conflict Society," in H. S. Becker, ed., *Social Problems: A Modern Approach.* New York: John Wiley.

Huntington, S. P. (1965) "Inter-Service Competition and the Political Roles of the Armed Services," in H. Kissinger, ed., *Problems of National Strategy.* New York: Praeger.

LeMay, C. (1963) *Hearings Before the Committee on Armed Services,* U.S. Senate, 88th Cong., 1st sess. Washington, D.C.: Government Printing Office.

Lyons, G. M., and L. Morton (1965) *Schools for Strategy: Education and Research in National Security Affairs.* New York: Praeger.

Maccoby, M. (1963) "Social Scientists on War and Peace: An Essay Review," *Social Problems,* vol. 11, no. 1 (Summer), pp. 106–116.

McDermott, J. (1967) "Crisis Managers," *New York Review of Books* (September 14), pp. 4–10.

McNamara, R. S. (1963) *Hearings on Military Posture, Committee on Armed Services,* U.S. House, 88th Cong., 1st sess. Washington, D.C.: Government Printing Office.

New York Times (1962) "Cuban Crisis: A Step-by-Step Review" (November 13).

Pachter, H. (1963) *Collision Course: The Cuban Missile Crisis and Co-existence.* New York: Praeger.

Posvar, W. W. (1964) "The Impact of Strategy Expertise on the National Security Policy of the United States," in J. Montgomery and A. Smithies, eds., *Public Policy 13.* Cambridge, Mass.: Harvard School of Public Administration.

Schlesinger, A. M., Jr. (1965) *A Thousand Days: John F. Kennedy in the White House.* Boston: Houghton Mifflin.

Smith, B. (1966) *The RAND Corporation: Case Study of a Non-Profit Advisory Corporation.* Cambridge, Mass.: Harvard University Press.

Sorenson, T. (1965) *Kennedy.* New York: Harper & Row.

Sparkman, J. (1962) *Situation in Cuba: Hearings Before the Committee on Foreign Relations and the Committee on Armed Services,* U.S. Senate, 87th Cong., 2nd sess., September. Washington, D.C.: Government Printing Office.

Speier, H., and H. Goldhammer (1959) "Some Observations on Political Gaming," RAND Corporation, RM-1679-RC (June); reprinted in *World Politics,* 12 (1960).

Wheeler, E. (1963) *Hearings Before the Committee on Armed Services,* U.S. Senate, 88th Cong., 1st sess. Washington, D.C.: Government Printing Office.

Wohlstetter, A. (1965) "Cuba and Pearl Harbor: Hindsight and Foresight," RAND Corporation, RM-4320-ISA (April).

INTERESTS

CHAPTER 21

POWER
AS THE MEASURE
OF POLITICAL MAN

POWER ELITES AND POWER PLURALITIES

The liveliest issue that occupies political science is the status of pluralism with respect to power concentration theories. This may very well turn out to be not so much an argument within political science itself as a surrogate debate between political scientists and sociologists. Sociologists have generally tended to underestimate or (in the eyes of political scientists at any rate) undervalue the worth of the idea of pluralism because they have undervalued the notion of political party apparatus. Conversely, the position of many sociologists has been that political scientists have tended, for their part, to overestimate the role of the party system and the role of the politician and to underestimate the role of the mass group. In effect, the theory of power elites starts with the social group, whereas the pluralist theory assumes the priority of the political party. Beneath the shadowboxing there is the gap between political science and general sociology as professions with different constituencies. It might be that this difference between political sociology and political socialization (or sociological politicalization) hinges precisely on this internal "professional" pivot, rather than on any objective claims to causal primacy.

Sociological politics is really a primary concern with the party and its apparatus. The relationship we are discussing, however, seen from a sociological point of view, involves the impact of parties and of politicians on interest groups. Two sound examples—perhaps the clearest illustrations available—of what this difference amounts to and how it manifests itself are contained in the works of C. Wright Mills and Floyd Hunter on one side, and Seymour Martin Lipset and Robert Dahl on the other. They will be taken as symbolic both of the political and professional levels on the debate between those who carve up the world into power elites or into interest groups.

The work of sociologist Hunter (1953) on *Community Power Structure* is a study of Atlanta done early in the 1950s when it was a regional city rather than a national city. The work of political scientist Dahl (1961) in *Who Governs?* is an examination of New Haven as an autonomous community. What is emphasized reveals clearly, perhaps more clearly than in any other writings, what the differences between the two "sister" social sciences amount to. One of the most important assumptions of the Hunter study is exhibited as he notes: "It might be said that this study assumes the existence of two group ideological considerations which help men to shape policy in industrial communities today, namely, capitalism and socialism" (Hunter, 1953, Preface). The significance of that remark becomes very apparent upon examining Dahl's work. Not only does Dahl make no allusions to the world-scale controversy between socialism and capitalism, but also he makes few references to the national position of New Haven— that is to say, New Haven never appears as a way station between New York and Boston.

Consequently, one never understands from Dahl's work that New Haven is not an autonomous center of power; and therefore the fact that he describes a pluralistic distribution of power does not necessarily validate his main underlying thesis concerning pluralism in American society. To do this he would have had to examine pluralism within the power vortex rather than extrapolated from that vortex. Dahl's work exhibits a fundamental difference from the way Hunter conceives of a city. Hunter discusses the city as part of an industrial network, which is one reason why he calls it a regional center servicing a network of other smaller centers— a center which itself is not really autonomous, since its power derives locally. Dahl, however, tends to accept at face value the autonomous nature of the subject under consideration, so that the distinction is made not so much between the pluralistic and polarized theory as between the city as an autonomous unit and as an interdependent region. The version we accept depends ultimately on whether we perceive a city, whether it be like New Haven or Atlanta, as an autonomous district or an interlocking complex.

This is the sociological equivalent of the periodization problem of historians, who must define historical periods in a meaningful way. This question of dependency and autonomy also comes out clearly in the differences between the Dahl and Hunter volumes—for example, the question of the organized community and the individual. Hunter states that the rise of interest groups has brought in its train growing centralization of leadership, and not any further pluralization of authority. Here the question of the social plan as well as the notion of the interest group come into direct contrast with Dahl's approach. Essentially, Dahl claims in rebuttal that this is not an example of ideology as a residual category, but rather an example of ideology as a dominant category, for it takes the ideal, rather than what actually is the nature of the problem. Dahl puts it in slightly different terms. He says that no sooner have observers begun to discuss the extraordinary importance of political parties than we are confronted with the heterodox nature of politics. The competing political parties govern, but they do so with the consent of voters secured by competitive elections. So for Dahl the question of who governs is made equivalent to the question of who rules. For Hunter the question of who governs in the formalistic sense is distinguished from the question of who rules.

One of the great ambiguities concerning C. Wright Mills' (1948, 1956) work also pivots on the question "who governs?" The relationship of power to governing goes back to the Franco-Italian school of political sociology. Men like Roberto Michels and Vilfredo Pareto—the Machiavellian school—were not concerned with who governs, but with who rules, so that for them the notion of the ruling class was not the same as the notion of the governing class. According to their theory, the ruling class assigns a group to control, to take care of the formal judicial apparatus of government, so that the question "Who governs?" does not even come to terms with the question "Who rules?" Arguing that a pluralistic body of men governs, or that men govern in terms of a two-party system in which there is conflict and struggle and a resolution of the party system, fails to come to terms with the fact that a ruling elite may arrange for alternative competing parties in order to have an efficient juridical system for maintaining legislative and executive power. To avoid forthrightly examining the question of authority leads Dahl to assume that New Haven is an autonomous center of power. In short, Dahl deals not with power, but with law—and the dilemma between a theory of law and a theory of power remains unresolved by his unexamined faith in local levels of governance.

Mills' problem is that he never developed a theory of law; he failed to account for the operations of the juridical system. One never feels in Mills' writings the existence of any system of checks to power operating within American society. It is as if the legislative and judicial branches of government dissolve and what remains is executive power or presidential power as the major, if not the sole, aspect of the general system of power. The dilemma for Mills and for the so-called neo-Machiavellian school has always been that it has never taken seriously the exercise of justice, nor has it meaningfully accounted for legislative politics. Mills claimed that the last great senatorial debates were between Clay and Webster. He omits consideration of the legislative branch during the past 100 years by that verbal fiat. His exclusion of discussion of the judiciary is done simply by declaring the judiciary an arm of executive strength. In all fairness, certain phenomena within American life have lent weight to Mills' position; otherwise *The Power Elite* (Mills, 1956) would not be in its nineteenth printing. The basic political phenomenon of the twentieth century has been the expansion of executive power. Power now resides in the Defense Department and agencies of executive power, not in the Congress as it did thirty or forty years ago. So, from the neo-Machiavellian point of view, the problem remains the question of the relationship between who governs and who has power, rather than the legal sources of legitimacy.

The other side of the coin is that the pluralist position, the Dahl position, describes clearly the governing apparatus, but not the power apparatus. There has not yet been a synthetic work in the political sociology of America because there has never been an analysis linking those who have power with those who govern. The network of relationships between the formal political system and the informal power system has been explored far too casually. Both systems have been explored as independent variables but have not been shown to have any relationship to each other. Perhaps Ostrogorski (1964) came closest to this kind of study in his work on party and community.

For Lipset (1950), political sociology is basically a question of the reduction of who has power to the formal apparatus of who votes. His designation of Right, Left and Center is arbitrarily assigned: The only referee is the voting pattern of the social class. If the laboring classes, as they do in Scandinavia, vote more heavily for the reform socialist party than for the so-called conservative party, they are categorized as the Left. If the old-line ownership classes vote for Catholic parties, they are designated the Right. The Center (neither capitalist nor socialist) is designated as liberal. Thus, he already has the triadic association worked out by definition rather than by exploration. The fact that there are three parties, in effect, as there are in many Scandinavian countries, reinforces his theory of legal socialism, which he has held since his work on agrarian socialism. Lipset has made political sociology a study of voting patterns and their relationship to social class origins, but he has not defined the terminology in such a way that Right, Left and Center have any meaning in themselves; furthermore, he has not defined a system of power that would explain Right, Left and Center in nonvoting situations. The effect is a marriage of the ideal type to statistics, and by restricting the analysis to the ideal types (Scandinavia and Canada) political sociology is boiled down to a classical pattern. But in this attempt to fuse a theory of social stratification to a theory of political behavior, he obtains not theories of political behavior, but theories of voting behavior. Although Lipset's formal position may be different and more sophisticated than Dahl's, the analytical resolution is no more fundamental, and once again the questions of governing and rule remain to be answered.

This gap between ruling and governing has become extremely important, precisely because the current thrust of research has been in the quantitative direction, which has led to a series of assumptions that governing is the same as electioneering. This development has led toward a desperate search for voting patterns, as an example of a hard indicator that can be checked; they provide a kind of monetary equivalent for the political sociologist, an indicator that he can test his propositions against. Since the political sociologist shares with both the political scientist and the sociologist a tremendous desire to gain acceptance as a member of a respected professional group, he is driven to use the voting indicator far out of proportion to its actual worth. Thus, in exchange for presumed hard scientific data, the price paid by quantitative analysts has been the failure to develop any theory of power. For the very gap between electoral processes and decision-making processes has served to empty the intellectual content of much political sociology. Yet, it is also evident that power analysis that loses respect for the place of legitimation and authority in advanced societies does not necessarily resolve the problems that it has so ably pointed out.

POINT AND COUNTERPOINT
IN THEORIES OF POWER

Let us go on to some basic distinctions. I shall first present the essential positions of one side, such as those of Floyd Hunter and C. Wright Mills, the neo-Machiavellians, and then contrast them with the propositions of men like Lipset and Dahl, to pinpoint the difficulties with both analytical frameworks.

1. The first issue is the occupational and status position of the power groups. According to the neo-Machiavellians, power groups are completely removed from the ordinary activities of life. They are located in the command posts of major institutional hierarchies and are not subject to the pressures, be they political or sociological, of ordinary men.

2. A second point, in support of this power concentration theory, is that while individuals may be unaware of the full extent of their power, they are, nonetheless, led to act in concert to defend their power in mass conditions. This range of power is, therefore, objectively real and not simply subjectively felt.

3. Power and the concentration of power, because they are objective, can be measured by indicators, unlike subjective phenomena; that is, the amount of power can be variously gauged, unlike, for example, certain kinds of subjectively felt status. It is much harder to measure something one is endowed with by the opinion

of others (as when status is conferred by the outside) than it is to develop a system of power whereby the power is measured according to the energy expended by the power-holder—almost like the physical definition of work. In physics, work is defined by what is moved, not energy expended; the analogy is how many men are pushed around (as Lasswell put it), not simply the amount of shoving that goes on. In a system in which everyone pushes in perfect equilibrium, there is no system of power, only a system of energies expended. What is measured, then, is energy rather than power. But the Millsians point out that the world is not really that way; individuals are in a disequilibrated position, and power, unlike status, can be measured. In order to underscore this, a fourth point is adduced.

4. Despite differences in the sources of power and differences in power intensities, the backgrounds of the powerful reflect striking similarities in status, environment and attendance at certain institutions. These similarities and occupational exigencies lead to formal and informal linkages. The intermarital patterns of the rich are no accident, nor are the kinds of hiring practices for colleges and government and military establishments that develop from the private schools.

5. The advocates of power concentration raise the point that the powerful have relatively complete control over entry to their ranks, and that political mobility is closed, since recruitment is by the men of power. The rites of passage to political power are more sealed than are those to social fortune. The measurement of the difference between political and social mobility therefore defines the extent of power.

6. The decision-making range is vast though exercised by a small number of people. Decisions made by the powers provide for the entire population. This leads to the seventh proposition.

7. The range of decision making is set by three major institutional hierarchies: the state, the corporation and the armed forces. The interrelation and activities of these institutions create the basis of political solidarity in contrast to social solidarity. Their decisions and activities and interdependent skills further link the areas of political control with economic power.

8. Interestingly enough, the higher one rises in this pyramidal system, the more one feels the interrelation of not just skills but of power itself. According to this kind of reasoning, the parts of the whole are interchangeable. One day McGeorge Bundy may be the presidential adviser, the next day, head of the Ford Foundation. Tomorrow he may be the attorney general; the day after, the head of General Motors. He can be plugged into various sectors of power without much worry about his expertise.

No one asks his qualifications; it is assumed that they are interchangeable.

9. The distance the powerful are able to establish between themselves and the mass or the public enables them to function with a relatively high degree of secrecy. Their activities are generally unclear or even unknown to an informed public. They are all college graduates, their names may be unknown—name two directors of the Board of Directors of the Chase Manhattan Bank —but they are men of enormous power. An invisibility factor is involved in the very act of putting distance between the powerful and the public, and the interlocking nature of power relationships requires invisibility for its operation. A man may function as a member of the board of directors of a bank, as a chairman of a board of a university, as the head of a corporate enterprise or network, or hold a seat on the Stock Exchange. All these positions may involve relatively few men at the very pinnacle. An incredibly large number of men have the touch of power; they sense power, can sniff it, can even taste it, but they never have it.

10. Various theories from conservative to radical project a power consensus in terms of cohesive interest, and admit not just the manipulative control of an ownership upper class but oftentimes spill over into doctrines of conspiracy. This has been a very bitterly contested point. The pluralists have discredited such theories by calling every search for conspiracy "the conspiratorial theory," at which point everyone withdraws in fear of being accused of holding a conspiracy theory. Meanwhile, the question is not theoretical, but whether or not conspiracies occur. To say that the conspiratorial theory of history is not a good device for explaining universal history may be true, but it is not the same as saying that there was a conspiracy to kill John F. Kennedy on a given date. This may not require an elaborate theory of history but may, nonetheless, be the case. To rule out a priori is to eliminate the possibility of analysis of a concentration of power precisely in such terms. Mills, for example, was not proposing a defense of conspiracy theory as an explanatory device, but a recognition that there really are conspirators, that there are men at General Electric who are responsible for fixing prices, and that the same sort of men at Chrysler call General Motors and ask how much they are going to raise the prices that year. The mere fact that one cannot frame a theory of history around such conspiracies is not the same as denying that they exist.

The retaliations and the defense of the pluralistic framework also provide a powerful, complete set of documents.

1. The foremost point of the Dahl position, of the old Riesman posi-

tion and generally of the juridical German tradition stemming from Weber, is that a defense of a narrow range of immediate interests oftentimes prevails over provisions for long-range leadership toward ruling-class interests. The men who make decisions do not make them with an eye to history; decisions are made pragmatically. A man does not contemplate his role in the power hierarchy when he has to make a decision; decisions are made on an everyday basis, not on the basis of theory.

2. Other groups institutionalized in the checks and balances system built fragmentation into the political culture and limit the domination of any one group. Self-interests, local interests and the differing kinds of individual interests lead to fragmentation of power, so perhaps the issue is not pluralization so much as fragmentation; and the guarantee, therefore, for local democracy lies precisely in the amount of fragmentation available.

3. Within groups the organization is of a team constituency nature involving delegations of authority that not only provide concentration in a central sense but also impose limits on that central source in order to accomplish things. In any given situation at any given level, people will not require simply a command system; to elicit their support involves an exchange device whereby one obtains certain power by surrendering certain power. The whole of the Dahl system is one in which certain political powers are bartered to get victory in the primaries, or in the election itself. There is no complete victory because every victory is bought by giving away or parceling out some of the power of the victor.

4. Extremely important to this notion of checks and balances is that the context of the exertion of power is amorphous. It does not call forth a response of solidarity. Limits to power are psychologically felt and are accepted by leadership groups as well as mass groups. This whole amorphous quality makes political solidarity extremely difficult to maintain.

5. The vast number of power groups impedes the possibility of any strong leadership and consistent attitudes toward rulings. For instance, the vastness of the banking network in America makes it very difficult for a man to have any say in other banking hierarchies. Interpenetration throughout the vast structure of the United States is difficult, not because power as such is divided, but because the range of possible performance is divided.

6. Political struggle or the struggles of groups serve as a prism for the refraction of distinctive rather than common qualities. This separation is inherent in the competitive character and function of party group formations. The very arrangement of power in parties sets up a gaming device. It builds in competition, and it begins to reinforce the competitive atmosphere even if nothing

underlies it. So pluralistic parties or a multiplicity of parties may serve to diffuse power.

7. Within a developed economic society there is high social mobility. This social mobility impedes any concentration of political power, since the forms of advancement are not limited to political movement. Because it is possible to gain wealth, it is possible to gain access to social sources of strength. This itself delimits the sphere of authority. But many men who have all kinds of economic wealth do not have access to political power. Men who employ 150 people may not have the faintest idea of powerful interests much less access to sources of national strength. Social mobility intensifies the gap between forms of power and acts as a pluralizing device.

8. In this context of plural activities the power system in which the political apparatus operates is a regulatory device, leading ultimately to the idea of the state itself functioning as a regulatory system. What was the New Deal if not a brokerage system regulating management and labor? The New Deal's power derived from a relative equilibrium of other social factors, and therefore called for a different kind of option. In conditions of relative stability, pluralism is high. Disequilibrium has polarized factions.

9. Just as the state apparatus may act as a broker between labor and management, a whole stratum of society reinforces that by being a middleman in middle positions, not between ruling classes and laboring classes. This sector of society tends to become the source of strength of the state apparatus and creates conditions for balancing rather than conditions for domination. The result is that instead of having a ruling class that is at the same time an upper class, the ruling class may be the middle class.

10. According to the pluralists, what determines power are horizontal rather than hierarchical relationships. Power is determined by one's position within the structured group; it is not determined by being at the top of a pyramid. For example, Morris Fishbein was head of the American Medical Association. His power derived from very strictly formal networks within this organization. These gave him power nationally, not direct national power. It is probably true that this kind of professional leader is more powerful than the governor of Nebraska. If so, instead of dealing with concepts of power according to a pyramidal power elite theory, one ought to deal with a horizontal theory of power.

ON DEMOCRACY AND POWER ELITES

These two alternative theories define what political sociology is about at the level of power and politics. My own leanings are toward power concentration theories; however, I do not deny a good deal of cogency in the pluralist position. The problem is how pluralism manifests itself and under what conditions. Pluralism as an ideal is certainly a more pleasant one than a monistic power elite system. The debate may not be a descriptive one, but a problem of social planning. How is a pluralist design built into the social order? These questions have to do with an applied political science no less than sociology, not simply with a description of the world but with the remaking of that world.

The fundamental difference between men like Dahl and Bell on the one hand and Hunter and Mills on the other is that the former believe that we have a democracy now, and the latter believe that we had a democratic system in the nineteenth century. That is really the essence of a grand debate on democracy. The charges against Mills made by the pluralists, in particular have to do with this whole question of nostalgia—that is, they claim that Mills' "democracy" is really an elitist conception not far removed from the Town Hall, which is highly unsuited to any urbanized industrial complex. Indeed, there are moments when one feels that Mills is attacking the urban industrial complex or the lack of democracy in that complex. He has very few good things to say for urbanism. He seems to be more concerned with restorationism. But Mills' charges against the pluralists have been no less acrimonious. His major accusation is that the pluralists are engaging in celebrationism. These men are not giving descriptive analyses; they are celebrating the present, as if the two-party system were ordained by divine providence. Men like Dahl, in Mills' view, are the Hegels of the twentieth century. They describe the perfect case. One never understands after reading Dahl why anyone could ever be upset with American life. The question becomes the relationship between restorationism and celebrationism.

POWER ELITES AND VETO EFFECTS

The Power Elite has been the object of considerable controversy that has hardly abated with time. In the course of critical discussion of Mills' classic study, comment collected around his other leading works, producing intelligent insights into the relevance of *The Power Elite* to Mills' other books. After all, when an American social scientist produces a book that attempts to evaluate the whole of United States society, such an effort is impossible to ignore. What is more, Mills wrote in the morally charged tone of indictment that invites challenge.

The New Sociology (Horowitz, 1964) is an anthology that attempts to evaluate the impact of Mills on his profession, and on social science generally. Contributors made note of and treated various issues "in the spirit" of Mills' leading ideas, while others attempted to analyze the man and his works as a whole. *The New Sociology* contains some of the most sympathetic commentary to be found from many points of view and representing many disciplines.

Ralph Miliband (1964, pp. 76–87) relates *The Power Elite* to Mills' earlier *The New Men of Power* (1948), and it is thus useful to consider Miliband's comments. In *The New Men of Power,* a study of American labor leadership and trade unionism published in 1948, Miliband sees important conceptual clues to *The Power Elite* and to Mills' view of politics generally. Disclaiming a view of Mills as necessarily "representative" of a generation, and considering him as a unique writer, Miliband nevertheless sees Mills as one of the final expressions of the hopes engendered by the Roosevelt era. Those hopes were linked to the faith that the United States would be turned into a progressive society by means of a political alliance between blue collar, white collar and intellectuals. This hope, however faint, remained an ideal for critics and defenders of United States power.

Mills carried over this idea of class alliance from *The New Men of Power* of the 1940s into the 1950s of *The Power Elite*. From the vantage point of the Roosevelt era, Mills became a critic of the "American condition." The appellations often applied to him—radical, ideologist, socialist— were ill-fitting and stemmed from comparisons of United States political styles with those of Europe. Actually, Mills was neither doctrinaire nor apocalyptic enough for such a designation. What rankled him was the nation-state as an object of loyalty. He hoped to attack this "sacred cow" as the larger ideological aim of his observations on specific instances of power. It was partially out of this that his study of the Cuban Revolution, *Listen Yankee,* was written and drew its force. Loyalties were to be extended to values and convictions, rather than objects of worship like the nation-state. Miliband believes that this antinationalism gave Mills a classic liberal independence and provided a sound ideological cast to his work.

Despite the possible nihilism in such a marked negativism, Miliband, among others, has noted Mills' "faith in reason" and use of knowledge by an enlightened public, as a constructive option of decadence. Mills was antibureaucratic, antielitist, antirule-bounded. He draws broadly on classic Western humanism for the elements of protest in his work.

In searching for, or rather inheriting the search for a labor-intellectual alliance fulfilling the classic liberalism of the "enlightened public," Mills' concern with the labor movement in *The New Men of Power* expanded into a study of power as such. He reflects no trace of utopian labor doctrine; indeed, he found this distasteful. But from such a source, as well as from students and intellectuals everywhere, Mills gave some concrete meaning to the "public" that would countervail an irresponsible elite. In this sense, *The New Men of Power* reveals lines of continuity with *The Power Elite*.

Anatol Rapoport (1964 pp. 94–107) has considered "The Scientific Relevance of C. Wright Mills." This innovative giant in his own right also appreciates the humanist strain in Mills' analysis of power in *The Power Elite*. But he sees in Mills confirmation of its scientific relevance; that is, he considers Mills' work to be illustrative of a scientifically informed humanist. In the critique of sociological "trivialization," Mills demonstrated his loyalties to and capacity for embodying this relationship in his work. He bridged the gap between "macroscopic" and "microscopic" social inquiry. He helped to focus sociology on the tasks of relating "findings" with socially pressing and meaningful questions. He was repelled more by the ritualism of microscopic methodologies and the unreality of grand, other-worldly theorizing, and sought to unite concreteness and large concern in a scientifically and socially relevant sociological discourse on questions of power.

Critics and essayists have pointed repeatedly to Mills' moral commitment and loyalty to the Enlightenment faith in informed publics as well as to his disgust with the intellectual default in acquiescence with ritualistic, respectable and flabby realism. The radical effect of *The Power Elite* was not in founding schools of power theory, but rather in giving a moral force to sociological thinking on large-scale social questions. The book performed a unique role in restoring consciousness of scientific uses of value theory and thereby pierced the *wertfrei* sociological postures. In his own literary example, he sought to overcome the "modern malaise" of alienation and powerlessness.

Andrew Hacker (1964, pp. 134–146) begins by noting the critics' complaint of vagueness and ambiguity in Mills' argument in *The Power Elite*. Everyone was perplexed by the fact that Mills did not stipulate or designate the "big decisions" that were supposed to be central to the formation of a power elite. Hacker defends Mills by addressing himself to this doubt. He grants that Mills left some "unfinished business." He grants the genuineness of democracy in America and the public pride in it. In fact, policy-makers know that they must accommodate this public sentiment.

Top elite policy-makers, however, are not particularly hampered by democracy nor angered by it. In fact, it is much safer for the public to "blow off steam." The public must have images to distract it from facts. In this way, Hacker says, the business of government can be concluded at the top without great danger of interference. The conventional view disclaims freedom of action at the elite level. Businessmen, corporate leaders, the President, all will claim that they are "hemmed in" on all sides. The point is whether the restrictions that make the elite feel hamstrung are of real significance compared to the areas in which they exercise relatively unrestricted authority.

Large corporations do not go bankrupt even if they are inefficient. Mergers, reorganization, and now government loans, keep them going when necessary. But they are autonomous in price-setting despite occasional outcries from the White House. They need not submit plans for approval to any government agency. They push to the outer limit of the market and then some. Stockholders get only a modest portion of profits and this is generally passed on to them without discussion. Wages are subject to collective bargaining, but this helps the workingman to keep the status quo. The relative share of corporation profits that goes to wages remains stable.

Executive life styles and salaries are the models of aspiration for mass society.

The corporate elite decides what kind of jobs, and how many are to be available. They decide where they will locate their plants, the size of investment, stimulation of sales, withholding of products. The allocation of capital or investment remains the most important decision made by the corporate elite. Its decisions set the order of priorities for the nation, and ultimately the values and behavior of the society. It is free to decide when power at its disposal shall not be used. They have been indifferent to matters of civil and political rights. There is little "broader statesmanship" or social leadership.

Hacker insists that Mills's rejection of conspiracy theories is clear and unambiguous. This was registered through a common set of associations and interests that the elite established as its public image. However, the elite was not viewed as a class either. Even the term "capitalist" is not applicable in its traditional sense the way Mills uses such terms. Hacker bemoans that America is going down a road it has not consented to travel —Mills understood this—and no alternative appears at present.

Mills has critics as well as crusaders. We shall be able to take up only the more stimulating and interesting of these "higher" critics. Daniel Bell, Robert Lynd, Talcott Parsons and Robert A. Dahl have made important criticisms of *The Power Elite*. And each will now be briefly stated.

Writing in *The End of Ideology* (1965), Bell considers that *The Power Elite* is not a description of a specific instance of power allocation but a scheme for power analysis. For him, Mills is dealing with one aspect of the "comedy of morals." He holds that Mills writes in "vivid metaphor" surrounded by statistics, that he appears guided by Balzac's moral that "behind every fortune there is a crime." Bell sees *The Power Elite* as static and ahistorical because of Mills' disregard for the influence of ideology in shaping men's sociopolitical behavior in their own time. *The Power Elite*, then, is a hierarchy of "orders," rather than power organization in time. It is a "model," rather than a historical analysis.

Bell holds that Mills improperly interchanges terms such as *institutions* and *domains* and confuses these for sectors, or orders. Therefore, to speak of a priority of certain orders over others says little. It ignores how and why such a dominance of priorities is maintained, the belief systems that perpetuate it and influence its historical course.

What is more, according to Bell, Mills lacks a working definition of power. For Mills, it is nothing more than domination, but he fails to take up the norms, values, traditions, matters of legitimacy and leadership in relation to power, which would give it concrete substance in the present context.

The notion of a power elite at the command posts of institutions is a perfect example of argument by metaphor. These institutions are set up like granite blocks, with heads. There are no identities or ideas. Even if these are not of primary value their significance is still misunderstood. It is what people *do* and *think* that gives them access to power, even within the major institutions. To locate a top stratum does not come to terms with the actual distribution of power. Bell complains of Mills' vagueness on what the "big decisions" are, or on their meaning. Mills comes close, though he disclaims it, to a conspiracy theory of history, and by implication, the idea of perfect ruling-class cohesion. Mills is said not to describe what unites or disunifies the elite, since he does not include or appreciate the role of ideas and issues in their interaction. And ideas and issues for Bell are the "stuff" of politics. Thus, Mills fails to see conflict of interests, and provides no explanation about how centralization withstands disunifying tendencies.

Because Mills fails to distinguish prestige and power from honor and violence, he cannot trace the consequences of the former to the leading beliefs and patterns that produce the latter. He does not tell us what constitutes honor, or why power will spill over into violence. He merely indicates where prestige derives from within the institutional hierarchy. This does not explain why some values are brutally fought over and why others are limited to political gaming.

Mills' "big decisions" reduce themselves, according to Bell, to foreign policy and war decisions, rather than policies applied to domestic institutions, where more levels of decision making are involved. These decisions are linked to violence. Mills is accused of failing to recognize that to prevent a military elite from dominating top decisions, the American power structure centers war decisions on the presidential office, checked even in this power by Congress. These big decisions are vested in the presidncy by constitutional authority. Presidential reliance on expert military personnel is hence not the equivalent of the "military ascendancy," especially because decisions on violence are grounded on a world situation and not merely on military expertise informing present-day foreign policy making. Mills takes the fact that leaders are responsible for decisions, and converts the obvious into a sensational discovery to suit a popular resentment of power. By avoiding everyday issues, he gives his work an exotic European appeal. His general neglect of the concrete American experience leads to "obsessive oversimplification."

According to Bell, "power elite" is a slippery phrase that allows the social scientist to ignore the basic character of a social system. Thus there is little in Mills to differentiate the United States and the U.S.S.R. The Supreme Court in its vital role of upholding or defeating a legal embodiment and reading of what constitutes national and other interest is ignored by Mills. Bell points out that the Supreme Court has been of absolutely vital importance in this respect. For Bell, *The Power Elite* is merely "a polemic" against those who say that in the United States decisions are democratically arrived at.

Critics, of course, have points of view in common, and there is likely to be considerable overlap in criticism. Robert Lynd (1956) simply and clearly raises the question of where the book was intended to go and then proceeds to a criticism of Mills that in some respects parallels the position of Bell—but without his vitriol.

Lynd has been occupied with the matter of developing a theory of power in democracy since the days of *Middletown* (Lynd and Lynd, 1929). For him, power is a social resource absolutely necessary for the operation of society. Like physical energy, it can be consciously harnessed for human welfare or corrupted by misuse. A determination of democratic goals and tasks for a given social operation and its enhancement of a democratic national life is therefore a responsibility of all power theorists. Like Mills, Lynd is concerned with the proper uses and applications of power, which he also has found much abused by elite groups. Yet he chides Mills for failing to undertake an analysis of power that extends its meaning, especially for democracy. A tone of moral indictment is not sufficient. As a result, the chief task for the observer of power is developing a theory of power for a given society. This was not, according to Lynd, what Mills aimed at. While Lynd is in basic sympathy with Mills' view of American institutional life, he is out of sympathy with Mills' lack of commitment to a liberal democratic ethos and consequently finds that his ambiguous "expose" lacks concreteness as well as meaningful goals.

Lynd also finds elite analysis in social science generally limited, if not distasteful, because it obscures or ignores the basic characteristics of a given nation and social system. It breeds a careless or superficial "hit and run" type analysis that amounts to a way out of dealing with capitalism, socialism and class structure. For Lynd, the pragmatism of Mills is far less attractive when seen as a poor stand-in for Marxist analysis.

Because Mills concentrated exclusively on differences between the present power setup and the past, Lynd claims he overlooks the important continuities between present-day and nineteenth-century American capitalism. This is said to stem from his lack of systematic analysis of the American economy. By focusing on "great changes," he fails to account for property as a power base. Yet this is the chief characteristic of the *system,* and not this or that institution within the social order. Hence the capitalist character of United States economic institutions is treated by Mills as if it were a mere entry to the elite rather than the defining quality of economic life in the United States from the very outset of the Revolution.

Talcott Parsons has raised meaningful criticisms of Mills from a more conservative framework (1960, 199–225). He grants considerable importance to *The Power Elite* because it is one of the few works by an American social scientist that attempts a major interpretation of the entire American society. Parsons begins by taking issue with Mills' usage of terms —for example the economic meaning ascribed to "class," the vagueness of the "higher immorality," and the like. He considers that Mills is vague on relations between the power elite and other high prestige elements in the elite structure. But his doubts are more fundamental than this.

Parsons questions whether the recruitment of the "very rich" has shown a sharper increase through inheritance than through self-earning. He argues that Mills ascribes to them more decision-making influence than they actually enjoy, and emphasizes, out of proportion to reality, the role of property in accounting for the influence of owning groups. For this reason, too, Parsons holds that Mills erroneously fuses the "very rich" to the "corporate rich," making it appear as if they comprise a solid corporate hierarchy, when, in fact, they are distinct groups. Parsons also argues that Mill's treatment of the "political directorate" is weak because he made it appear that it is infiltrated by business, thus leaving it little or no policy-making independence. Mills allows independence only to the military, but on grounds that could just as easily admit the autonomy of the polity.

Parsons claims that the increase in government influence is great and very real. Hence its influence has considerable autonomy. It is not directed by business interests, however related decisions may be to the latter from time to time. This governmental influence makes the "political directorate" highly independent. Precisely its independence is the product of the United States' world position and its corresponding industrial maturation. But this seems pronounced, only because of the nonpolitical life of nineteenth-century America. This was enhanced by a cultural emphasis on economic values—an activist sense of enterprise and production—which its unimpeded development further reinforced.

Mills is said to look nostalgically back at Jeffersonianism, a doctrine that was incompatible with industrialization; and Jeffersonianism, however much it may have preserved decentralization, would have impeded industrialization. The local family elite, the family unit, even if it preserved the "scatter of power," and thus preserved competitive values, would also have impeded advanced industrialization. The Jeffersonian economy and the locally based family do not allow for differentiation of economic production from other functions in specialized organization. Instead, they provide a production unit that is at the same time a kinship unit and a unit of community citizenship.

Development has brought specialization and structural differentiation. Leadership becomes more specialized as a social function. The growth of a nationwide industrial network is the result of specialization and industrial maturity. There is specialization at three levels: (1) in organizations of economic production, (2) in functions within the economy, and (3) in class differentiation within the society.

Concentration is linked to the need to administer efficient production units while allowing fully for the numerous special tasks and skills needed to carry on production in a mature industrial economy. The real question that Parsons insists that Mills should have raised is whether this concentration has gone too far because of factors extraneous to development. Mills assumes that concentration exceeds the limits of efficiency. Parsons claims that Mills has provided no evidence and has contented himself with noting the fact of concentration. Parsons further notes that the relative share of profits for the largest firms has been stable and the same for more than a generation. This points to an equilibrium rather than to an excess. Parsons asks whether the power of managerial and executive classes has increased inordinately, and places the burden upon Mills to demonstrate this.

Parsons, unlike Mills, separates the fortune-holders (very rich) from the executives (corporate rich). Family fortunes are still largely gathered through property. The larger corporation is still more the exception than the rule. For the most part, executives do not acquire the fortunes in corporate life that raise their status and position. They are advanced by promotion rather than by property, and decision-making control is in their hands rather than centered in family ownership.

The original "captains of industry" failed to achieve or exercise cumulative advantages to consolidate control of their enterprises. There were factors operating against cumulative advantage. The main pressure was to link executive responsibility with competence in such a way that the ascriptive rights of property ownership give way to the occupational functions of "professionals." There are two ways in which Mills obscures this shift, according to Parsons.

Mills continues to speak of power *within* the economy as based on property. While this is often legally true, since legal control rests with stockholders, it is not substantively true. In old-style family enterprise, still predominant in the small business sector, functions of management and ownership are fused in the same people. In the larger enterprise, they have by and large become differentiated. Bonuses and large executive salaries should not be twisted to mean control through property ownership. Business relations to the power structure have been altered through the specialization process, not through control of property.

Unlike Mills' contention, the process of recruitment into the upper reaches of the economy operates almost entirely through appointment, although this is relatively structured. Mills insists that qualifications have little to do with this process. But the absence of formal entry procedures does not prove his contention. While it is true that "cumulative advantage" has a lot to do with the high level of remuneration of high executive groups, this is different from fortune building within the power structure.

Given the nature of industrial society, Parsons indicates that a well-defined elite or leadership in business should be expected to develop. Power cannot be diffused equally in small units as small business ideology would have it. The business elite is no longer one of property ownership. The center of gravity has shifted over to professional management. However, Mills is right in showing that recruitment does derive largely from upper-class groups. The problems of an elite within the economy must be differentiated from an elite over the whole society. "Eliteness" is used by Mills to mean "rule" over society. Parsons claims that Mills should have separated professions of high prestige within the upper classes from those who have power, instead of lumping them into one category.

In a complex society, the main locus of power lies in its political system. The early United States power system lagged behind its economic system. Since the end of the nineteenth century, the mechanisms of political control have grown to control the economic sector. Parsons accuses Mills of mistakenly implying that this process is reversed; he says Mills fails to understand the role of political organizations such as political parties in the power structure. With the American system, the presidential office is the prize of party politics. It integrates the political system and provides a focus for it. For the executive branch to have extraordinary prestige as well as great powers is natural and necessary for political integration at a national level. Thus, it is without foundation for Mills to regard this as inordinate power, or to imply that it is a part of a political directorate manipulated by business or military interests.

Parsons insists that Mills exaggerates the importance of the military. While Mills sees the military as filling a decision-making vacuum, he is said to ignore crucial instances when the military have been overruled. This is meant to illustrate Mills' tendency to take short-term trends and generalize them into essential features of the society. Mills further misunderstands the role of the courts and lawyers in interpreting, legitimizing and translating the legal embodiments of power into the terms by which the members of the community agree to live. His conception of power is a "zero-sum" game—power above others. Power is not simply a facility for the performance of a function, but a basic social resource.

As a result, Mills is insensitive to what binds people to their positions, to their leadership, to their tasks—inequities aside. He focuses exclusively on distributive aspects: who has power, what interests are served. He ignores how it comes to be generated and what communal functions are served. The result is a partial and selective treatment. Mills foreshortens social processes, and the outcome is that short-run effects are taken for long-term factors. He also tends to think of power as "presumptively" illegitimate. Out of one of three types of philosophical uptopianisms schematized by Parsons, Mills is said to share a socialist mistrust of private interest and a utopian notion of public control.

Although criticisms of Mills' *The Power Elite* have had a wide hearing, empirically based studies have been conducted which implicitly or explicitly have sought to answer or broaden Mills' leading ideas. The most notable of these has been *Who Governs?* (Dahl, 1961).

This study, while implying that *The Power Elite* is at least oversimplified, stands Mills on his head by reversing the conclusions reached in Mills' work. Actually, neither Mills nor Dahl is specifically concerned with the *nature* of power and its relation to socioeconomic systems. Both focus on the *distribution* of power in a modern (rather than specifically socialist or capitalist) context. Both are concerned with the effectiveness of restraining norms on the exercise of political power. Yet it is as if Dahl had deliberately decided that if Mills is right in the larger context it will be borne out in any community study. And this is precisely what Mills' premises do not require. To reach the "nodal point" where decision-making power passes into the hands of a power elite, the range must be directly national in scope and ramification. To isolate the parts of the larger system is to focus on what is isolatable and not necessarily on what is essential.

Dahl draws richly on the history of the city and the backgrounds of its leading people. He begins with the premise that historically the exercise of power has moved from a ruling oligarchy in a relatively simple and undifferentiated social context, toward a pluralistic-democratic community in a complicated and highly specialized context. This movement occurred first as part of the growing complications and fragmentations imposed by an industrial society; and second, through yielding to pressures for dominance by advantaged ethnic, business, middle- and lower-class groups. The breakdown of oligarchy was insured by specialization and mass pressure. The small, aristocratically oriented ruling group could not, and finally would not, resist these democratizing tendencies.

A proliferation of new claims was imposed on government. A fragmentation of areas of influence ensured. Politics could no longer be contained in the practices of narrow and small upper classes. As ever, the lower classes remain without adequate resources or high motivation to press their influence upon government, and hence, political machinery is largely manipulated by many middle-range groups whose various overlapping interests have brought about a political style of variously patterned coalitions. What is more, power and influence are primarily, if not entirely, centered in politics, which does not operate through a guiding or covert directorate outside of government machinery.

Due to the dispersion of advantages and resources for middle-class groups and disadvantage for lower-class groups, politics is an interaction system with pockets of intense influence, gradually shading off outward. Influence crystallizes on issues rather than class lines, and the various interests an issue calls forth give a pragmatic coalition style to politics. This takes place in a context in which widely believed-in democratic norms impose limits on excessive concentration of power.

Dahl shares with Mills a feeling for the ambiguity of sources and intensity of power. But aside from a few superficial resemblances, the similarity ends there. Dahl develops an elaborate structure, replete with detailed charts, on the nature of the public. This public is far from excluded from major decisions, and its removal from major issues is virtually self-willed rather than engineered "from above." From a set of interesting hypotheses, Dahl finds that this public is always courted as an electorate, and its temper and different interests are nurtured, appealed to, and cautiously accounted for in higher policy. Insofar as the public is ignorant or disinterested, this is a natural outcome of differences in leisure, resources, advantages, education, motivation, and interests. Opportunities are presumably always available to the elites, but, as in all societies, there are numerous other pursuits and interests that impose limits to participation and attitudes toward participation. Consequently, it is only to be expected that a concentration of political resources and influence will be in the hands of those who fully apply themselves to political practice whether out of interest or personal suitability.

Dahl's shrewd analysis, in its community focus, is not unlike sociological analyses of the 1940s, which also considered the problem of class definition from the standpoint of pluralism. This is the crux of the matter— the area of focus. By exclusive concentration on political machinery and the ideology and composition of one city, whether typical or not, other matters are sacrificed. For example, a "Millsian" approach would have pursued the obvious economic ties of a middle-sized city like New Haven to its neighboring giants, New York City or Boston. Furthermore, Mills would not deny, nor did he deny, popular effectiveness in local government on local issues. His argument rested on the extent to which this unit of power can suffice for the larger national picture. For example, he would have attempted to gauge the extent to which any New Haven mayor could achieve a significant political voice outside of his immediate electorate. For Dahl, this is not a serious question, for he is examining fluid interaction in one of its "eddies"—New Haven. For Mills, this is an all-important question, since access to power is based on acquisition of office in a hierarchy. Lower offices are steppingstones to higher ones, entry into which is the achievement of significant power. Mills would have examined, not New Haven to gauge the mayor's power, but the "mayoralty" in a national context.

Two different starting points, and not merely points of view, account heavily for the widest differences between Dahl and Mills. Thus, far from providing an "answer" to *The Power Elite,* the "community" point of view must be weighed against a "national" approach to political sociology.

MILLS AND HIS CRITICS: A SUMMATION

While Mills' critics are shrewd and knowing, and clarify many issues important to a discussion of the nature, function and division of power at a given time, they do not explain the enduring character of *The Power Elite.* This is a work that was addressed to dangerous power tendencies at a time in the United States when few seriously thought to plunge with moral commitment into the examination of power. The United States was emerging from crippling McCarthyism. One of its effects was to create a facade of government power that was unmistakably oppressive. Furthermore, a critical evaluation of a great American celebration of its own power after World War II was needed as an antiseptic effect upon national conceit and to provide warning that the possibilities of such power could lead to a reversal of some of the best traditions in the American past.

To sneer that Mills merely represented some popular mistrust of power is to underestimate the extent to which the populace has been given good reason to do so. World War II, the rise of the Soviet Union and China, among others, has given drastic illustration that power does not merely "balance out" in performance of social functions. To regard an immediately oppressive condition as one that becomes benevolent in time is not an appreciation of long-term factors. It is a failure to see and appreciate changes in a system that go unmarked because they are not overtly brought about through a dramatic act. They are profound changes nonetheless. Just such new American experiences were being ignored in the 1950s when *The Power Elite* made its succesful appearance. It warned that modern history might be making the United States instead of the other way around.

REFERENCES

Bell, D. (1958) "The Power Elite—Reconsidered," *American Journal of Sociology,* vol. 65 (November), pp. 238–250.

Bell, D. (1965) *The End of Ideology: On the Exhaustion of Political Ideas in the Fifties,* rev. ed. New York: Free Press.

Dahl, R. (1961) *Who Governs? Democracy and Power in an American City.* New Haven, Conn.: Yale University Press.

Hacker, A. (1964) "Power To Do What?" in I. L. Horowitz, ed. (1964).

Horowitz, I. L., ed. (1964) *The New Sociology.* New York: Oxford University Press.

Hunter, F. (1953) *Community Power Structure: A Study of Decision Makers.* Chapel Hill: University of North Carolina Press.

Lipset, S. M. (1950) *Agrarian Socialism.* Berkeley: University of California Press.

Lynd, R. S. (1956) "Power in the United States," *The Nation,* vol. 182 (May 12), pp. 408–411.

Lynd, R. S., and H. M. Lynd (1929) *Middletown.* New York: Harcourt Brace Jovanovich.

Miliband, R. (1964) "Mills and Politics," in I. L. Horowitz, ed. (1964).

Mills, C. W. (1948) *The New Men of Power: America's Labor Leaders.* New York: Harcourt Brace Jovanovich.

Mills, C. W. (1956) *The Power Elite.* New York: Oxford University Press.

Ostrogorski, M. (1964) *Democracy and the Organization of Political Parties,* abridged ed. Garden City, N.Y.: Anchor Books [written in 1902].

Parsons, R. (1960) "The Destruction of Power in American Society," in *Structure and Process in Modern Societies.* New York: Free Press.

Rapoport, A. (1964) "The Scientific Relevance of C. Wright Mills," in I. L. Horowitz, ed. (1964).

CHAPTER 22

POLITICAL REALISM: THE PRIMACY OF INTERESTS OVER VALUES

Political realists give the concept of the national interest a central importance in the conduct of contemporary international affairs. As "political realism" and the "national interest" are sufficiently overburdened terms, I will not add to the definitional freight they already bear, but rather seek to clarify the implications of defining the latter according to the former. More specifically, this is an inquiry into the use of the concept of the national interest as a representative symbol and the difficulties arising from uncritical acceptance of this usage.

Political realism is as much an insight as it is a theory—an insight into the dilemma of explaining power and security within a single framework. It represents an overriding concern with the seeming irreconcilability of interests and policies in the modern society, and the inevitability of the struggle for controlling the mechanisms of power (and therefore security) in the larger society. On the theoretical side, political realism is an outgrowth of European conflict theory of the "bourgeois" sort—that is, Simmel, Sorel, Gumplowicz and Mosca—while on the practical side, it has a strong antibourgeois property, since it is an outgrowth of the failure of political reforms and doctrines of consensus either to create or improve society. Indeed, the claim of political realism is that existing approaches do not have the capacity to oust basic social evils (Cf. Moon, 1968, esp. chap. 3). Political realism therefore insists upon the primacy of conflict among individuals and groups for dominance over their respective state, class and community units. And these take place at all levels of the "public philosophy" as they do within the "private psychology" of individuals. What unites the entire package called "society" is the state. This marks the political realists as a group more interested in security than in welfare, and in well-defined power rather than amorphous forms of social authority. In other words, they are linked to the "Continental tradition" stemming from Hegel, in contrast to the Anglo-American tradition stemming from Locke and Jefferson.

Political realism is a broad term for some commonalities shared by otherwise diverse political thinkers. It refers to those who consider politics to be based in the nature of men to exercise all the energy and influence they can toward maximizing individual and group interests. Political realists consider the pursuit of self-interest and the exercise of power to be *the* fundamental elements of politics. For them, to suppress these as "evils" is to deny the realities of political life which, in fact, impose a contrary responsibility, that of constructively and artfully formulating the means whereby the potential of self-interest and power for liberty and order may be utilized. Thus, "political realists" are distinct from "political idealists," who see men in a state of aspiration toward norms of harmony and selflessness, as yet unrealized but allegedly superior standards by which people may be inspired to correct their "destructive" propensity toward self-interest and power accumulations. To idealists, realists answer that the pursuit of ideal norms can result only in hypocrisy, failure and the attempted purge of man's very essence in order that some unworkable scheme for improving the human condition be upheld (Morgenthau, 1962, pp. 80–81).

The realists' severance of politics from the ideal is not the equivalent of a preference for amoral politics. For it is clear to all of their most intelligent representatives (Morgenthau, Kennan and Niebuhr) that among the many interests of men are their preferences, desires or needs for some things over others. Indeed, they recall that politics is all about value choices, the worth of favoring one interest claim over another, one course of action toward some end over another. For men achieve even their capacity for regular social interaction in the process of sharing, contending over and creating a rank order of interests, that is, a body of evaluations about priorities. Doing so is a natural extension of the processes of thinking about the human interest in survival. Political realism does not contrast morality to politics. Rather it seeks to derive morality from the traditions of politics, as one seeks guides to the future from the way men have behaved in the past. This mode of thinking about politics has provided political realism with a long-range perspective on the "national interest."

What, according to political realists, unites the various contending interests within a national society around acceptance of a national interest as pursued, and even defined, by a national government? The answer is the process of identification.[1] How does it happen that masses of self-interested men in a national society, primarily concerned with the gratification and promotion of "self," identify with the power and foreign policies of their nation, and do so with an intensity that surpasses their own individual aspirations to increased influence? Here, the answer is given that most people are unable to satisfy their desire for power within the national community and lack even more the ability to secure their goods and persons against collectivities outside the nation. Unable to find full satisfaction of their desire for power within the national boundaries, they project these unsatisfied aspirations onto the international scene through a national leadership (Morgenthau, 1960, pp. 102–103). Then, too, as men need protection against the collective power of others, as they need security and safety, they entrust the task to a leadership along with sufficient powers to carry out this function. Moreover, many men have a stake in advancing their interests abroad. Thus, protection of a national interest through "foreign policy" also involves securing the safety and interests of nationals in their dealings with foreign communities (Kennan, 1954, pp. 5–6). Another vital consideration is the fact that the self-interested rivalry that exists within a nation must be civilized by some standard of limitation, a higher "national interest," so that some men do not crush others and so that all interests existent in a society are guaranteed at least their survival if not their advancement. Thus, a national center becomes both legally and psychologically entrusted with the task of limiting domestic competition and advancing the whole in dealing with other nations (Niebuhr, 1953, pp. 134–137).

The individual's need for safety, survival and supplements to his personal limitations enables him to find meaning in national identity, to entrust a national leadership with the task of securing these and to uphold national belonging as a value sufficiently strong to be felt as a personal interest. Whatever the material wealth of a society, it must invest a portion of its resources abroad, not so much because of economic gain but rather for national security and the maintenance of a maximum national status and strength for the benefit of the cosmopolitan center. This is true however much the objects of foreign policy may shift from time to time. And so, to pursue the national interest on behalf of men who have internalized the value of national belonging brings interest contention to the international arena as a natural outgrowth of individual self-interest. Since the pursuit

---

[1] This is explicitly stated by Morgenthau (1960, p. 511). It is only implied in various writings of George Kennan and Reinhold Niebuhr. Arnold Wolfers (1962), however, has not taken the "identification process" as a given and strongly maintains the need to analyze the various "levels" in a society for their relevance to a given formulation or implementation of given policies.

of interest is natural, the pursuit of a communist interest as its extension is natural, and thus, in the era of the nation-state community, the pursuit of national interest is natural. Suppression of the national interests of nations can only result in their reappearance in indirect but highly aggressive and dangerous forms. As interest competition at group or individual levels is resolved, or at least contained, by mutual exchanges and commitments to survival, that is, by bargaining within agreed upon limits, so at the international level the preservation of national interests can be attained by bargaining within agreed upon limits (that is, limits on destructive action to which nations will go to gain an advantage). The "balance-of-power" model is a virtual ideal type, for realists, of the frank realization of interest in international affairs, of the natural tendency of men to compete for advantage and exert power toward this end and as a mode of limiting these elements by bargaining within limits without aiming at the impossible, that of outlawing them. And political realism has become bound up with exhortations urging the retention, revival or reformulation of balance-of-power theories for international politics.

Even the value of international associations is taken to rest only on their capacity to smooth rather than abolish competitive international relations. At best they further civilize nations by reinforcing habits of bargaining that only occasionally resort to force (and then in a limited way for short periods and for specific ends). When properly instituted they merely facilitate negotiation and heighten efforts at national self-control in conflict situations. When, however, these are conceived as a means to totally outlaw arms, rivalry and interest, international organizations fall into disuse out of ineffectuality. Even when one nation adopts the idea that its treaties and agreements with other nations will "outlaw" the competitive interests between them on behalf of commonly held principles against a major common enemy, and that nation attempts to emulate or institute a universalistic internationalist morality for a region or group of nations, that nation will be driven to hypocrisy or abandonment of its sought-after principle. For interests will assert themselves along with rivalry, and some party to the agreement, less advantaged than the others by its terms, will violate it by committing some act aimed at throwing off its intolerable restraints. This party will probably, but improperly, be regarded as lacking in civility and high principle, a self-centered outlaw. The adhering nation, or nations, will find themselves compelled either to punish the outlaw by force or to change the agreement to accord with reality. If the choice is made to punish the offender with force, the punishment cannot be limited, for its end is nothing less than the surrender or destruction of the violator. It is not undertaken for the specific terms of a treaty designed for specific ends, but for the maintenance of agreement "in principle," an ideal goal impossible to realize. Nations guided by such universalism are driven to nothing less, in the end, than forcing principles upon other nations, formulating ideas for the governance of their internal life—a hopeless task full of arrogance and danger, and impossible to achieve in the long run.[2] In fact, the realists contend, nations can only determine for themselves alone what their interests and principles are. All nations, and international organizations devoted to world peace, must remain humble before this fact and limit treaties and laws to the regulation of specific interests, and not exceed these limits to enforce universalistic principles. Even when one, such as Hans Morgenthau, has carried justification of the autonomy of the national interest from moralistic restraint very far, to the point of polarizing them, so far that he must accept internationalist schemes and organizations as transcendental absolutes necessary to curb human excesses, he, as a realist, will really mean that this "absolute" is only ameliorative and not transforming in its effects upon national behavior. For while "moral rules do not permit certain policies to be considered at all from the point of view of expediency," still they cannot obliterate the competitive nature of men and nations and can merely limit the *means* to which they may resort in order to realize an end (Morgenthau, 1960, pp. 212–214).

Realists such as George Kennan (1954) and Reinhold Niebuhr (1941–42, 1953) have also taken national interest to be a thing civilized by some intuitive adherence of men to the idea of survival. Kennan's relativism assumes that each nation contains some system of restrained bargaining embodied in its culture traditions and respected by its leaders. As each nation has its own code in this respect, some agents, policy-makers or officers of an international organization, such as the United Nations, must find where the commonalities between them lie for restraining the extent of interest-based conflict on behalf of mutual survival. Morgenthau's polarizing mentality, as we have noted, has set national interest and moral restraint far apart from one another, but he also sees their point of contact created by similar purposes. Niebuhr has attuned interest and moral restraint more continuously and finely toward one another by suggesting that at every level of society there operates a delicate interplay between them, with a final result that a national leadership is aware of and socialized by both practices and may formulate a national interest bearing both elements at once. For Niebuhr perceives egotistical interests to be seeking restraint in order to guarantee survival, and this pattern characterizes every level of mature societies, ultimately correcting, in the process of cultural growth, the excesses of national self-centeredness. While interests reveal the incompleteness, the imperfection of men, for Niebuhr, limiting them to a merely partial view of the world as a result, they are also liberating, for at least they en-

---

[2] George Kennan is renowned for this position, although he has seen it mainly as applying to the foreign policy of the United States (1956). Arnold Wolfers (1962) realistically has seen it as one emergent style among European nations, including Britain (the great balance-of-power advocate) and France, and the implication is that this is a consequence of the entry into international politics of popular opinion as a force.

courage the development of autonomous "selves." But cultural or religious, especially Christian, teachings round out the self by engendering a principle of connection between selves, that of "love." Thus, tolerant love is a corrective to interest at every level of social life, from the family to the state. It cultivates an awareness in people that "our toleration of truths opposed to those which we confess is an expression of the spirit of forgiveness in the realm of culture" and meliorates all of the interest-centered aspects of social life (Niebuhr, 1941-42, p. 234).

In sum, whether civilizing the ambitions of nation-states is held to be due to custom, religion or international organizational conveniences, realists contend that it is the maximum possible and that schemes for obliterating rivalry at the international level can only result in disaster either out of their ineffectuality or tyrannical application. Therefore, consensus can never be an adequate response to conflict. A basic realist claim is that the force of national identity and interest has been so powerful that both imperial as well as internationalizing designs have been forced to accommodate them. These have, on historic occasions, even surpassed all rational bounds and unleashed salvationary crusades upon the world. In order to come to terms with their persistence, while curbing their irrationalities, realists have called attention to their ineradicable, elemental character, in an era when men were prepared to stifle them, and to their potential for rational international politics when translated into the terms of interest theory. But worthy as this effort has been, realist national interest advocates have gone far toward conceiving national interests not merely as the fundamental but as the sole factors in international politics, losing sight of the human beings both by whom and for whom a national interest is formulated and pursued.

Attempts have been made to correct this excessive tendency to abstract the national interest and the nation-state from the persons who compose them. The "decision-making" approach is one such effort to "humanize" the abstract national body by making an analytical entrance into the motives and actions of policy formulators. Other approaches have traced the influences of organized interest groups and "public opinion" upon foreign policy makers. In short, some people have tried to conceive of the national interests of nations as the result of specific kinds of interactions entered into by specific persons and groups. These efforts have surely concretized political analysis and have been as valuable in their way as the national interest advocate has been in his. A major problem, however, remains not only unresolved but barely considered. Of the realists, only Arnold Wolfers (1962, p. 7) shows an intuitive sensitivity about what it might be and where it might lead. In 1959 he noted:

> One wonders today . . . whether the bulk of the population in countries facing the risks of nuclear war will long continue to regard as vital . . . all the state interests they were once ready to place in this category. Signs

point up to the likelihood that the masses, who have gained greater influence as behind-the-scenes actors, will push for greater restraints upon the pursuit of those state interests—such as national security or prestige—that are seen to conflict with private welfare needs.

Few will disagree that recent years have borne out the value of Wolfers' observation. He struck at one of the larger and more embarrasing ambiguities in the national interest concept, at least as it has been employed to date. For it has been endowed by realists with a representative quality, that is, a capacity to stand for the interests and aspirations of substantial national majorities. However, these populations show important signs of either suspecting or denying this idea (by disinterest, passivity or protest). Wolfers' comment implies that the national interest of the policy-maker's creation will have to be coordinated with the felt needs of men in a national community if it is to serve as nothing less than a fundament for international relations. At the worst, there is the insinuation that the "popular interest" has drifted far from the "national interest" and that a potential antagonism may be arising or is already irreconcilable between them.

Perhaps this drift, if we agree with Wolfers that it is there, is the product of the vast technological and organizational networks engulfing modern mature nations, whicn defeat ready popular understanding of or participation in national interest formulation. Perhaps the "neither peace nor war" state of the cold war years has exhausted people who now seek some new means of resolving matters one way or another. Perhaps the various crises in the domestic lives of industrialized nations (like urban enlargement and breakdown) have produced new and uncompromising demands for attention. And perhaps it is only that "the people" are conservative in matters of foreign policy, and this shows itself more than ever because foreign policy is more than ever available to their influence. But even if we dispute these possibilities, we may be sure that the "national interest" resists the ready equation with the "majority" interest made by national interest advocates, and that it is something more than stark "realism" to insist that it be that way.

If, however, their touching faith in the national interest as a foundation for world politics unites the realists, so does their recalcitrance toward any popular criticism that mitigates it. There is no end of proclaiming that the tragedy of the powerful, but democratic, nations is the albatross of popular opinion they must bear. Realists agree, implicitly or explicitly, that the "mass" should play no significant role in the formulation of the national interest in foreign policy. Walter Lippmann (1955, p. 20) speaks for many others when he writes that

the unhapply truth is that the prevailing public opinion has been destructively wrong at the critical junctures. The people have imposed a veto upon the judgments of informed and responsible officials. They have compelled the governments, which usually knew what would have been wiser, or was necessary, or was more expedient, to be too late with too little, or too long with too much, too pacifist in peace, too bellicose in war, too neutralist or appeasing in negotiation or too intransigent. Mass opinion has acquired mounting power in this century. It has shown itself to be a dangerous master of decisions.

Morgenthau (1960, p. 512) is more lenient, but of a similar mind on this question. He would prefer that the gap between elite expertise and mass immaturity be bridged through a leadership effort really to lead and educate the masses, whose support can only be expected then, for they are otherwise incapable of translating or implementing the national interest. This process is supposed to satisfy the Democratic requirement while not diminishing an elite principle in foreign policy making. If leadership adopts this educational function it is rendered open to criticism, yet not so indulgent as to allow popular groups to alter policy. Kennan (1954, pp. 54–55) has decried the emotionalism that gathers around national interest issues. He noted the extent to which popular influences are responsible. But he did not pursue the matter with determination. And it is difficult to say that Niebuhr has approached it at all, for his prime concerns have been with interest reconciliation, but not specifically in terms of the political apparatus or the specific popular relations to it.

Of this realist group, it is Wolfers who admits that the "nation-state" and its "interest" is an "ideal type" from which there are in reality numerous deviations. Populace and government are in a state of highest accord, that is, approaching "the ideal," under conditions in which extreme fear has been generated by an external foe. But otherwise, popular and government elements must be differentiated; "all events occurring in the national arena must be conceived of and understood from two angles simultaneously: one calling for concentration on the behavior of states as organized bodies of men, the other calling for concentration on human beings upon whose psychological reactions the behavior credited to states ultimately rests" (Wolfers, 1962, p. 9). Wolfers' point, however, was meant only to concretize political analysis (he is often absorbed by this concern and that of reconciling grand theorizers with empiricists in order to effect it). Yet not even he pursues either the ideologies or methodologies as means with which the national and the popular interest have been made to coincide, or the feasibility of their coincidence.

The question remains: Does a national population find itself "represented" in government formulations of a foreign policy based upon what government through appointed officials takes to be the "national interest," as realists have assumed it does? Now most observers of popular opinion on foreign policy have found that the majority of men are both apathetic and ill-informed about foreign policy. They show, even if they do not always explicitly state, that it is popular passivity rather than active commitment that is taken as popular support for any given foreign policy. Can ignorance or indifference be "represented" in foreign policy? The classic study by Almond (1960) varies from, but essentially verifies, this general idea. He indicates that popular thinking about national policy abroad at most provides nothing more clear than a permissive or nonpermissive "mood" as a context for the pursuit of foreign policy. The populace is not found to be an articulate, or even interested, public in this area of concern. Further support for this trend of thought may be found, indirectly stated, in a work by Bernard Cohen (1957) who has shown that a foreign policy issue draws the concern or participation of a few highly informed groups and individuals capable of disinterested understanding, in addition to "interest groups" made active by a direct material stake in it.

It appears that these and many other public opinion analysts find substantial national majorities too limited or distracted by immediate concerns to be conscious of whether they are represented by the "national interest." A few select individuals are rightfully obliged, then, to bear the burden of its formulation on behalf of the rest of the nation.

Others are prepared to challenge this seemingly safe and infinitely "verified" assumption. Pranger (1968, pp. 60–71) has held that popular passivity toward foreign policy issues is unique to that area alone, domestic issues showing a much higher degree of popular awareness and sense of felt interest (indeed, this is a widely held assumption as well). Surely "urban crime," the educational system, wages, prices and profits, medical plans, welfare programs and civil rights are not such "simple" issues as to be more readily available to the understanding of the majority of the nation. Perhaps, it is argued, popular groups, and the electorate generally, are granted more of a role in determining their course, and this fact explains the deeper popular interest in domestic affairs. If this is correct, then we may indeed inquire as to the validity of passing off a "national interest" and accompanying foreign policy, formulated by a comparatively small number of individuals, as a representative act.

It is possible that the popular passivity, indifference or ignorance about the national interest and foreign affairs of which the realists complain is a function of the distance at which foreign policy is maintained to preserve it from maximum popular influence. If publics are called on to do less on foreign policy issues, which after all affect their lives and purses as vitally as any other, they will, quite reasonably, feel marginal to them, and if reacting to them at all, will do so awkwardly and "emotionally." This is borne out, rather than refuted, by extreme situations where a popular movement mounts drastically around the "national interest abroad," for this is regularly and historically associated with policies that have drawn the nation into war and where the person is likely to feel capable of increased influence by militant acceptance or rejection of military obligations. It is fair to inquire, then, of our realist proponents of national interest whether the practice of concretizing it at high government levels can also stand for national consensus upon it. The question is, in effect, Can the "national interest," considered so basic to the conduct of international politics, be democratically "representative" of a national majority without maximizing procedures for popular participation in formulating or approving it?

The traditional procedure for legitimizing the representative character of decisions taken on domestic issues has been the electoral process (either through election of officials or issue referenda). But the realists object to applying such a practice to the higher personnel and questions involved in foreign policy decision-making out of their fear that popular influence in this area would be disastrous. The prevailing belief among them is that here the populace is capable of showing the bestial passions it does not exhibit, at least often, over domestic issues. But we have seen that this is a value-laden view and hardly an established fact. Can we then maintain, as they do, that the national interest as a base for foreign policy is "representative" in the way that we can about national consensus achieved on domestic issues? And can we sanction, as they do, limiting the popular influence in order that specially trained persons be enabled to more efficiently represent the nation?

This is a difficult problem, one for which no swift remedies are now available. For even if we could persuade the realists that better coordination between felt interest at the popular level and the national interest at a high decision-making level was both desirable and possible by electoral means, the question would, perhaps very justifiably, remain for them as to whether this was a luxury that could be afforded in a world where fast decisions need to be taken against efficient enemies neither so fastidious about nor hampered by their own national majorities. Indeed, as we have noted earlier, realists have held that the popular influence is already too powerful an element in modifying foreign policy, and its strength is considered partly responsible for policy failures against menacing protagonists. No mere words or sentiments will dispel the seriousness of this problem. But it is necessary to point out that considerable dangers also attend a government that cannot adjust to rising pressures for just such coordination. The alienation or passivity of national populations lacking in powers of influence over foreign policy will diminish, in any event, government capacity to sustain policies, especially those dependent upon strong popular loyalties. This is in addition to the possibilities latent in alienation for hostility, protest and, under extreme conditions, revolution. And so to assume that a population can or even does identify with a national interest policy pursued in the international arena merely because the policy is "there" and superior men have formulated it, and merely because the population may not actively oppose it, is, to say the least, an oversimplification unbefitting the realist tradition. And to decry what research has shown to be, after all, the quite limited claims of public opinion upon foreign policy, is a display of insensitivity unbefitting the democratic tradition.

There is throughout Western society a train of thought that favors the idea that a small collection of especially prepared individuals may act to represent the whole while supporting a democratic order. It has always obscured the matter of defining the national interest so that it accords with a democratic society. In 1934, for example, Charles Beard (1934, p. 406) stated that "objective criteria appear to be lacking, both for the interpretation and testing of moral obligation, and for determining the 'true' national interest." This train of thought is both individualist and consensualist. It is clear that our realists rest serenely, if unconsciously, upon it and do not appear to be strongly aware of the challenges that have shaken its traditional appeal.

In this tradition it was early assumed that men once dwelt randomly, as disconnected by self-interested entities in an original chaos, but were drawn into community when sufficient rational development occurred which permitted them insight into the benefits of mutuality and social organization. Community (whatever its type—"city-state," "ecclesia" or "nation") was thus the outcome of an original, voluntary individual commitment and was thereafter, in all its forms, an aggregate of unique, egocentric "selves" nevertheless able to cooperate socially out of a felt need for mutual aid. Cohesion in society could then come to be seen as the outcome of the fact that all particular self-bound interests intersected at a vital point, the one where resolution of difference promised enhancement of survival or gain, creating a least common denominator among men, and was thereafter sustained by a periodic show of public affirmation. (Voting is one variation, individual partaking of sacraments for the sake of combination into a spiritual community is another; many others, obviously, exist and coexist.) This public affirmation of community belonging, permissible because men may discover the point at which agreement between contending individuals is possible, constitutes the "objectification" of a "common," "public" or, later, "national" interest. That Western man has seen himself in atomistic terms, that his social ties are thus voluntaristic, that he affirms their value by public acts he codifies in law, that he does so because reason informs him that survival and enrichment are protected in this way and that his differences are thus balanced by an area of commonality have given him a habit of mind that lends itself to the idea that a public or national interest exists that can be considered a "whole" and a real sum of parts.

There have been suppositions that this state of affairs arose in gradual stages, first within a nuclear family fostering human sociality and then reaching for cooperative ties between families toward a village life, followed by the interconnection of villages and the higher tasks of social management in the "polity" (Aristotle). Later assumptions posit a natural will to aggression and competition in a mythic "state of nature" where man finally acquires, through experience with brutality and fear, reason enough to desire protection and peace. He thus "contracts" with his fellows toward this end (Hobbes). However, the compact can be seen to have rationally extended and organized man's instinctive social sympathies (Locke). Still further, particular adaptations to natural conditions breed commonalities, the basis for community, and are validated and extended by successive generational experience, rendering man, originally disparate, united by a cultural core (Burke). Variations on this theme touch otherwise highly distinct theories. But whatever the scheme by which disunited men become one community unit, and in whatever manner they are seen publicly to affirm their formula for unity, its content is filled by issues of survival and gain over which disunited and self-interested men have contended, found sufficient rationality to fix an area of commonality and performed a public act, collectively but voluntarily, to validate it. And so, a Western social atomism and an individualistic conception of interest have fostered the concept of a "common interest" as a product of human maturation, and it reaches down to the concept of "national interest."

Along with this habit of mind there also developed the idea that various communities of men grew in internal complexity, either within themselves or as one community type gave way to another, and that this condition involved individuals not only in affirmation of community but in complicated arrangements for preserving it. Preserving the individualistic content but complicated forms of community is supposed to have brought men to devise consensus-building schemes like "representative government," a means by which conflicting individual interests, public affirmation of community interest and the specialized requirements of governance could simultaneously be serviced. And so, individuals empowered by others to act for the whole could be seen as bearers of a public interest. This mode of thought could be readily transferred to the national interest. But a penchant went with it for analyzing leadership actions and motivations from which it was supposed that the common interest could be understood because of an assumed equivalence taken to exist between leadership and those they represented. Thus, the idea of voluntaristic community proceeded together with one about complex community and ideas about the special requirements of social management. Identifying the managers with the managed (even if the former are seen as endowed with superior qualities and others in the social order do not possess sufficient prerequisites for being represented out of their subhuman or dependent state upon superiors) also led to a habit of scrutinizing the former's actions as if the latter were embodied in them. This neglected the possibilities that groups among the rulers, and others among the ruled, had distinct, even antagonistic, interests. The facts and fortunes of communities could be made to unfold as the story of princes, presidents, their advisers within and adversaries outside the political system. Western history shows the predominance of this view in periods where rights to represent or be represented, to "citizenship," were bound to independent land ownership, and where the quantity of relevant actors in the political system was quite small compared with the present.

Distinctions between the leaders and the led were eventually interpreted in a variety of schemes stressing their antagonisms. "Community interest" ideas came, especially in the nineteenth century, to be seen as rationalizations useful for covering up the schism. For far from standing in accord with the community, rulers serviced merely themselves or the most powerful, politicized and advantaged elements of the community, the latter even being capable of reducing government to mere instruments of their own interests. They did these things by deception, ideological rationalization or physical coercion, and their moral pretensions to representation of the whole community, or nation, functioned only to secure them against exposure.

Under the Darwinist impact emphasizing competitive struggle, on the one hand, and a long-standing process of capitalist competition, class conflict, industrial specialization, population growth, and ideologies of egalitarianism favoring the inclusion of rights of representation of the formerly excluded, on the other hand, men could more easily be seen as bound in groups, attaining individual identities through group (class) experiences, acquiring group skills and consequent rankings according to *skill* and money income in the social order, engaging in interest conflicts as groups, and in this manner laying claim to varieties of popular rights. Individualist-consensualist habits of mind were modified by the growing tendency to conceptualize society as a collection of contending "groups," bargaining and competing for advantages by political pressure, and the governing apparatus as an instrument of group conflict, up for capture by the most powerful and bureaucratic sectors.

A "group conflict" body of theorizing grew in importance and popularity and provided political observers with another framework within which to analyze the national interest, as a temporary product of the shifting coalitions between conflicting groups, established through pressure upon or from within the government in order to realize the particular interests of groups and persons. Because the vocabulary of antagonistic groups rather than common interests has proven so serviceable for popular causes seeking to establish or enlarge their rights and privileges, it is one that will not vanish in order to ease the irritations of realists. Indeed, it may even be surprising that so many relinquish the use of it on behalf of a common interest in safety and order.

This discussion of contrasting politic.¹ "thought styles" allows us to conclude that, at the least, men in Western society have contrasting vocabularies for discussing their interests, however inchoate or unconscious the level of that discussion may be. It behooves those who defend the national interest as a common interest, and those who dissect it for its social class content, to be clear that they stand one way or the other. The need for research is pointed up in order to determine the extent to which the consensus or conflict idiom prevails at the level of "public opinion," among "interest groups" and decision-makers high and low with respect to this area of the national interest and foreign policy. This would assist in determining the extent to which coordination between government and public opinion is possible in the prevailing terms of political communication.

In the general pressure toward idealistic schemes for the suppression of international conflict that followed World War II, and considering the demands a new nuclear technology placed upon powerful countries for cooperation, there were some, like the realists, who were wisely critical of those organizational plans that bore the dangers of ignoring and thus compounding conflicts in international affairs. But they had proposed a restoration of the national interest that largely ignored or disdained the popular majorities it was supposed to represent by rejecting the validity of a popular role in appraising it. In view of recent politics, and considering the scholarly findings that the public is generally distant or alienated from foreign affairs, we should be recalling, however, that national leaders may disdain popular alienation, disinterest or active pressure only at their peril. Yet the realist proponents of the national interest have not deeply probed this dilemma, to the detriment of both "realism" and the "national interest."

REFERENCES

Almond, G. A. (1960) *The American People and Foreign Policy.* New York: Praeger.

Beard, C. A. (1934) *The Idea of National Interest.* New York: Macmillan.

Cohen, B. (1957) *The Political Process and Foreign Policy: The Making of the Japanese Peace Settlement.* Princeton, N.J.: Princeton University Press.

Kennan, G. F. (1954) *Realities of American Foreign Policy.* Princeton, N.J.: Princeton University Press.

Kennan, G. F. (1956) *Soviet-American Relations, 1917–1920.* Princeton, N.J.: Princeton University Press.

Lippmann, W. (1955) *The Public Philosophy.* Boston: Little, Brown.

Moon, S. E. (1968) "The Anti-Science Position: The Thesis against Positivist Political Science in Contemporary Political Writings" (mimeograph).

Morgenthau, H. J. (1960) *Politics Among Nations,* 3rd ed. New York: Knopf.

Morgenthau, H. J. (1962) *The Decline of Democratic Polities: Politics in the Twentieth Century,* vol. 1. Chicago: University of Chicago Press.

Niebuhr, R. (1941–42) *Human Destiny.* New York: Scribner.

Niebuhr, R. (1953) *Christian Realism and Political Problems.* New York: Scribner.

Pranger, R. J. (1968) *The Eclipse of Citizenship.* New York: Holt, Rinehart & Winston.

Wolfers, A. (1962) *Discord and Collaboration: Essays on International Politics.* Baltimore, Md.: Johns Hopkins Press.

CHAPTER 23

THE WORKING CLASS AS INTEREST GROUP

Even a casual perusal of the socialist and radical literature on the contemporary condition of the working class and the prospects of its making a revolution reveals a situation of towering confusion. The workers have become a veritable inkblot test, confirming the faith of "classicists" in their vision of a vanguard workers' movement and, equally, confirming the belief of "revisionists" in their vision of workers as authoritarian. And there is a whole cluster of academics uncertain of the workers' political ideology but nonetheless convinced that workers are better off unorganized lest they enlarge the size and scope of the fascist thrust. In such circumstances it is perhaps easier to understand, if not appreciate, the reticence of social scientists to express themselves on the condition of the working class in the United States.

THREE THEORIES OF THE WORKING CLASS

Illustrative of the orthodox tendency is the work of Ernest Mandel. He claims that "if we examine the long term trend, there is no doubt that the basic process is one of growing homogeneity and not of growing heterogeneity of the proletariat" (Mandel, 1968, p. 165). Mandel still argues that there is a "working-class vanguard" and that said vanguard was betrayed by a degenerate "classical labor movement" which "stopped inculcating the working-class vanguard in any consistent manner against the poison of bourgeois ideas" (pp. 168–169). But despite this pharmaceutical description of betrayal from within and the pernicious force of mass communications and bourgeois ideology from without, we are assured that the contradictions grow sharper, and that the very character of labor union organization stimulated proletarian revolution (p. 169).

The difficulty is that when confronted by the need to present evidence for this classical position, Mandel is reduced to the student movement in France. To be even remotely convincing in his argument, Mandel must convert the students into an arm of the proletariat. Further, although Mandel is apparently elated at the size of the 1968 "May revolution" in France, claiming it to be larger than past historic proletarian movements, he does not discuss why, given such numbers, the revolution petered out and the workers returned to Gaullist normality within a week. Only two years later, the analysis reads like a sorry piece of black humor.

It is also necessary to raise forcefully, without shame or trepidation, the "American exceptionalism" thesis. The polarization of class and race in the United States, with its attendant movement of the unionized working class to the Right, makes it hard to maintain the doctrine of "Trahison." The working class has not been betrayed, it has done much of the betraying—and the failure of industrial unions like construction and steel to integrate the races, would indicate that labor conservatism is not the exclusive hallmark of craft unionism but characterizes proletarian trends as a whole. But the point is not to criticize Mandel, since he illustrates only one tendency in contemporary neoradical thinking. Let us turn to his opposite number, Seymour Martin Lipset, for another view.

According to Lipset, the rise in literacy and formal education should have brought about a lessening of working-class authoritarianism. In point of fact, using his own measures, a very different outcome occurred: The working classes have actively supported political candidates from Robert Kennedy to George Wallace. In short, they support precisely those candidates who support them on economic issues. The working class becomes neither more democratic nor more reactionary, but, instead, less political in general. Another major conceptual problem in Lipset's work is that he makes little serious effort to distinguish between working class and lower class. With the exception of those distinctions which the data collected by others forces upon him, he makes no real distinction between types of working-class activities that might more readily account for variations in attitudes than conventional variables drawn from Weberian notions of social status.

At the time Lipset formulated his authoritarian hypothesis in the late 1950s, it was clearly intended as a buffer against a Communist interpretation of working-class behavior. It is also clear, as the steady stream of references to Marx, Engels and Lenin reveals, that Lipset conceived of this essay, as Theodore Adorno before him had, as an exercise in revisionist Marxism, and not anything resembling a Weberian formula for studying the masses. Lipset conceded that his data present problems—activitists can turn into retreatists overnight and authoritarianism in one situation does not necessarily lead to an authoritarian personality-type, as Adorno (1950) postulated. Nonetheless, the same problems that befell Mandel, earlier had befallen Lipset—problems that arise from the assumption of an historic world mission for the proletariat and the requirement that the proletariat not, under any conditions, break faith with the masses.

If the proletariat is authoritarian and the middle class is the carrier of the libertarian faith, where does that leave the Marxist concept of working class revolution? It is precisely this problem in Marxism, and not the problems of the proletariat, that informs Lipset's vision. Like Lenin, he must make the condition of the working class a cause for profound concern in the postrevolutionary period. But we have yet to compare the working class and the middle class in terms of revolution, marriage making and home building. Crude measures of voter identification prove very little, since political parties in the West usually contain both authoritarian and democratic tendencies.

Lipset's position is more subtle and complex than his critics are usually willing to admit. In the first place, he draws a sharp distinction between economic and noneconomic issues; he declares that the poorer strata are everywhere more liberal or leftist on such economic issues as state support, graduated income taxes and support of unionism. However, "when liberalism is defined in noneconomic terms—as support of civil liberties, internationalism, etc.—the correlation is reversed. The more well-to-do are more liberal, the poorer are more intolerant" (Lipset, 1960, p. 169).

Lipset adduces a number of variables to prove his contention about authoritarian predispositions in lower-class individuals. Among them are fundamentalist religious beliefs, low education, low participation in political or voluntary organizations, little reading, isolated occupations, economic insecurity and authoritarian family patterns. A major difficulty is that the data, drawn from Stouffer's work (1955), actually show very small political differences between well-defined manual workers and white collar workers. Indeed, education seems to be a more important variable than class in determining "authoritarianism." Lipset is thus forced to equate, at least implicitly, know-nothingism and working-class authoritarianism. Furthermore, it is far from self-evident that the new working class is as inextricably committed to a Leninist notion of "economism" as Lipset believes.

In a recent article on new currents in labor, Bogdain Denitch (1970, p. 353) made the intriguing observation that in

France in 1968 and Italy in 1970, the most militant strikers came from areas with the most advanced technology and the highest proportion of highly skilled or educated workers in electronics, chemistry, auto, aircraft, as well as from previously passive "middle class" professions-teaching and journalism. Characteristic of these strikes is a stress on democracy at the point of production rather than mere traditional wage demands.

In other words, the newer and more specialized elements in the working class, far from increasing authoritarian pressures, have raised anew the classic democratic issues. At the very least, this lends support to those who still maintain a certain faith in the open-endedness of working-class ideologies.

The difficulties in Lipset's appraisal are more apparent in retrospect. And while this evaluation is by no means intended to minimize the importance of his great insights, a catalog of the problems inherent in his perspective is necessary to move beyond them. First, he operates with an unstated, and I daresay, unexamined code of union democracy that is more typical of some old-fashioned craft unions than new-fashioned industrial unions, and this is because craft unions approximate the professional standard of nonlaboring elites. Second, he operates with a theory of authoritarianism that fails to appreciate adequately the special nonpolitical characteristics of labor organization and labor ideology among the American working class. And third, he operates with a theory of status deprivation rather than one of class consciousness; hence, he better explains the behavior of a smaller militant wing of labor than he does the general labor force as such. The large bulk of labor remains committed to liberal ideology and electoral politics. The notion of working class authoritarianism cannot help but disguise this ongoing central fact of American society.

Above all, Lipset has the same problem as Mandel: a problem of evidence. He must prove that the mainline behavior of the middle class is somehow more democratic than that of any other sector. Since all definitions of authoritarian and democratic political behavior are relative, the question is, Authoritarian in relation to whom? At that point it becomes quite apparent that the working class is neither more nor less authoritarian but increasingly like the middle class in its political ideology and voting patterns.

Labor is wedded to the ideology of American society and that means the politics of interest groups and the economics of state manipulation (if not state intervention). One might say, therefore, that labor has become pragmatically antirevolutionary, or at least antisocialist. But such developments, onerous as they may appear to advocates of socialism, are a far cry from authoritarianism. One gets the impression that Lipset, like Mandel, is deeply troubled by a labor movement that does not conform to socialist goals. Rather than accept this fact, Lipset labels the working class authoritarian, when in point of fact, this is simply a euphemism for the working class's rejection of European socialism.

In a sense, the work of John Leggett (1968), and before him, Ely Chinoy (1955) and Robert Blauner (1964), represents efforts to preserve the Marxist kernel, without falling into cliché-ridden ideas either of the Left or of the Right. Interestingly enough, each of these three researchers did his work among industrial workers and, in particular, automobile workers. Their work represents an effort to link Marxism to sophisticated survey research and field techniques of investigation. Using Leggett as a prototype, we can say that the sociological Marxists have gone far beyond the abstracted empiricism of a Lipset or the grand theory of a Mandel.

Leggett's position is that two variables—uprootedness and ethnic-racial background—scored highest in explaining class consciousness. Those workers uprooted and fragmented by the Depression and its lengthy aftermath still harbor strong tendencies toward a class definition of reality, and ethnic groups consistently show greater class consciousness than long-assimilated groups. Leggett tries to indicate that workers engaged in marginal activities, such as the California farm workers, reveal a higher degree of working-class identification than others. The same is true for other marginal sectors which, unorganized in unions, tend to show a pattern of demand and identification sharply distinct from that of unionized laboring groups.

Counter to Mandel's claims, Leggett indicates that there is a growing heterogeneity in the working class. He discovered that the mainstream working class does not constitute a homogeneous mass of workmen undifferentiated in ethnic background and opinions on class matters. Ethnic subcultures exist and in certain ways reflect their class composition (Leggett, 1968, pp. 62–75). But this heterogeneity may represent new forms of coalition politics having progressive payoffs—for instance, labor-black coalitions—and does not necessarily lead to simple fragmentation.

In some strange sense, although Leggett's research is consciously, almost self-consciously, "anti-Lipset," it probably does more damage to such orthodox Marxist notions of class as Mandel's than to the Lipset framework, since the latter already clearly demarcated a realm of analysis which granted the continuing force of "progressive" ideas in the economic arena but documented the continuing impulse to democracy among unionists. Nevertheless, Leggett's data do not reveal any particularly strong authoritarian tendencies even in the more general questioning he engaged in. Quite the contrary, the workers tend to reveal not just a class consciousness but a relatively democratic value orientation as well.

What seems particularly relevant is the underlying implication in Leggett's work: The working class is basically a large-scale interest group, which may overlap at times with neighborhood organizations based on racial or ethnic interests and which has at its core the advancement of the needs and position of the working class in American society. Insofar as these needs and demands represent a vanguard frame of reference, socially and politically, no less than economically, the interest patterns exhibited retain their progressive vitality. Leggett does grant the growing tendency toward violence that may vitiate and cancel older forms of nonviolent voting responses to political affairs. This does not necessarily represent authoritarianism, but rather a simple change of tactics necessitated by the continuing failure of American society to provide for the basic needs of workingmen—black and white, organized and unorganized.

While Leggett has gone far in providing serious measures of working-class consciousness, like all speculation about labor's unique role, his work is burdened with notions of the ultimate destiny of American labor. Since labor is very much like other groups in the United States and is becoming more so annually, a defense of its special democratic nature seems at least as difficult to sustain as Lipset's argument concerning its special authoritarian nature. Legett is reduced to saying that some interest groups are really better and more progressive than others. This certainly may be the case, but it is a far cry from the higher promises of revolutionary action and ultimate democratic commitment. I therefore find Leggett's argument persuasive but his conclusions somewhat less than encouraging—at least from the standpoint of revolution making.

FROM CLASS POLITICS
TO INTEREST GROUP ECONOMICS

I have fewer objections to Leggett's approach than to the rigidity of a Mandel or a Lipset. And my objections rest upon a belief that Leggett's stratum of Detroit auto workers may be atypical, rather than typical, of certain national and international trends. After all, "Reuther's union" remained one of the few honest efforts to raise radical and liberal alternatives, and the auto union constantly worked to integrate black workers—particularly in the wake of the 1943 Detroit riots. Even so fertile an acorn as Leggett's studies is not by any means the whole forest. But before proceeding to trees and forests, it is instructive to take up one point implicitly rather than explicitly stated in Leggett's argument: namely, that interest-determined demands of the working class are somehow instinctively and intuitively more progressive than those of other sectors. In a sense, any large-scale disaffiliation on the part of the workers, Southerners, blacks and so forth, creates a basis for undermining confidence in the United States; but it is really hard to see why labor is in a unique historical position on this score or why "militancy" is somehow galvanized toward left-oriented mass politics. Indeed, the Wallace phenomenon occurred precisely after the death of Robert Kennedy—so that the formal designations of Right or Left seem less important than the central importance of interest demands among the working class. And it is hard to determine that working class demands are peculiarly more noble or more radical than other demands. Further, Leggett fails to investigate the possibility that labor demands may actually conflict with black demands, that coalition efforts may not occur. Indeed the developments in such working class cities as Gary and Cleveland indicate a rising polarization, rather than pluralization, and a distinction between kinds of consciousness, so that *black consciousness* becomes a veiled euphemism for "antihonky" attitudes and *union consciousness* a reference to racist attitudes among whites. Thus, heterogeneity ought not to be confused with democracy, any more than homogeneity was confused with consciousness by Mandel.

Certain microscopic observations must be made if the subject of labor is to be discussed intelligently and if we are finally to get to some appreciation of the scientific rather than the emotive aspects of the Marxist tradition. Because for so long we have been accustomed—in the social sciences at least—to speak of workers in terms of upper, middle and lower sectors of the working class, we have forgotten that this designation is based on considerations of status rather than considerations of class. Also, since most of our statistics are in the form of occupations, the data we have on the labor force in the United States is limited to considerations of income and work performance, with little data on intraclass factors.

There is a whole range of factors with which present types of statistics are unable to cope satisfactorily. Among the most prominent of these is the distinction between skilled workers and unskilled workers. Only a hairline separates managers from technicians, but a veritable millennium separates both from day laborers and more traditional types of factory labor. In a sense, we now have a portion of the labor movement which is not so much bourgeoisified as it is professionalized, with very high notions of craft and skills. I daresay there is at least as much pride in specialized knowledge among locksmiths as there is among lawyers, and this development, along with its attendant conferences, seminars, schools, congresses, and so forth, provides a new basis of security and safety for the working classes. Increasingly, working-class consciousness is not so much a matter of political activity, as of professional skills.

It might be argued that this does not touch the problem of the assembly line workers or manual laborers but, in point of fact, it touches it very directly since it is precisely this kind of labor that is increasingly automated and increasingly subject to obsolescence. In other words, that portion of the labor movement which conforms most closely to socialist imagery is losing its capacity for large-scale political clout.

It is also the case that among unskilled workers are found the sharpest group identifications in the United States. That is to say, the ranks of the unskilled laborers are filled with white ethnic Americans and black Americans who have only a vague and distant affiliation with trade union ideology, so that working together simply reinforces ethnic and racial distinctions rather than builds any sense of common labor identity. In this respect, the American experience sharply diverges from the European, since in Europe one can count on a high degree of ethnic and national homogeneity, whereas in the United States these forms of identification become factors in minority self-consciousness.

Beyond that, the nature of work itself has changed. It is not that work is less important than it was in the past. This is a kind of holy myth held by technologists and hippies alike who somehow have the mistaken and misanthropic notion that we work less because we are more technological in orientation and skill. What has occurred is not a lessening of the work pattern—sometimes it is the work itself that has expanded rather than that the nature of the work process has changed, and work requirements have become extraordinarily complicated. This again is related to the rise of the skilled workers and once more clearly separates the categories of labor from each other. There can be no common struggle unless there is a commonly felt need to struggle and this is precisely what we do not have in the United States. It is therefore absurd to expect a classical type of working class to emerge in American society. But, parenthetically, the rise of extreme right-wing groups is also unlikely, since professionalism is not so much anti-Left or anti-Right, as it is antipolitical and antiideological as such.

What we are witnessing is a phenomenon quite common in American history: the decline of a social class. We have seen an agrarian class shrivel in less than 70 years, from 60 percent to 6.5 percent of the American population. At the same time we need and grow more food than ever before. The same phenomenon is occurring in the ranks of the proletariat. The fact that workers are becoming proportionately fewer in numbers and at the same time more productive in their output produces the problems of a declining class and the fear and trembling attendant to such a decline. The muscular show of force on the part of the "hard hats" is not so much the energized outburst of a revolutionary class as it is the fear-stricken response of a group dimly aware of the ebbing of its own importance, while it must witness the emergence of an educated subclass which always seems victorious despite its supposed effetenes.

We now have the rise of a Hobbesian working class; that is to say, a class that calls for law and order and demands that the bourgeoisie behave itself and mind its manners, not to mention its morals. The political impact of this conservative response to American mobility and innovation has been vitiated by the rise of specialization and professionalization, by absorption of the working classes into the ranks of mainstream America. Such parallel processes mitigate political sentiment among the working class and make them neither authoritarian nor democratic, neither fish nor fowl, but, like most Americans, concerned for their economic well-being and devoted to maximizing their own portion of the finite pie on which the whole system rests.

A remarkable illustration of this turn from politics and toward economics is contained in the recent interview of AFL-CIO president, George Meany. His assault on the leftist sectors in the Democratic party, on the

New Left directly and, no less, on the Wallace rightist movement, add up to a disengagement from politics as such. His belief that the Democratic party is in "desperate shape," in a "shambles," echoes the belief of many elements in the white working class who see the political apparatus as such slipping out of their control and becoming the voice for other interest groups, particularly the black people. Meany's ideology is not classically conservative and hardly authoritarian, but rather status quo, pure and simple: "the more a person has of the world's goods, you know what I mean—for himself and his family—the more conservative he becomes in the sense that if he is moving along and he sees chances of moving further along, he doesn't want to upset the machinery. . . . I think he is going to fight for a greater share and that he is going to do it through the same instrumentalities that he used in the past" (Meany, 1970).

Raising the question, Whither labor? is basically to ask if labor will rise again in a swell of more or less leftist militancy to give moral leadership to the "disadvantaged." It is clear that I do not believe a resurgence of the militant-moralistic unionism of the Left is likely in the foreseeable future. Indeed, given present tendencies, even should a massive economic depression occur, the shape of labor organization is more likely to move it even further to the Right than to the Left—for a number of reasons.

First, American labor, at least after 1880, was not, in the main, of the Left in any classically socialist sense of the term. A Left orientation has always been modest, if not peripheral, and thus has not suffered such a dramatic decline as is often made out. Since there is more continuity between past and present labor attitudes than is usually appreciated, it is not likely that leftist rejuvenation will be dramatic.

Second, the acceptance of unionism has been too widespread and publicly legitimated by national legislation, especially since 1932, for the issue of union recognition to incite labor agitation. Earlier periods of militancy were chiefly the result of employer or government (though mainly the former) hostility to recognition of trade unions, to principles of collective bargaining and certainly to recognition of trade unions as collective bargaining representatives for the rest of the working class. Recognition, quite established now, cannot presently or in the near future stir labor unrest.

Third, organized labor is only a small minority of the U.S. population and considers itself dependent upon public sympathy, congressional benevolence and, for various reasons too involved to go into here, the Democratic party's good offices. It has, for this reason, always hesitated to press itself politically through building an independent labor party because such a party could not sustain a broad coalition of interests and labor suspected that in the long run it would wind up isolated, alone and a mere political sect. (There are many other reasons, of course, for resistance to an independent radical labor party but fear of isolation is a chief one.) This was not true in England and elsewhere, where the laboring class was a much larger portion of the population. The minority status of organized labor in the United States, combined with the fact that technological change did not multiply at a great enough rate the kind of jobs that could have vastly enlarged a labor constituency, makes it unlikely that labor would initiate "third" or radical party building. So, in addition to the fact that labor is not likely to revive moralistic union building in the name of industrial democracy, it is also not likely to build any labor or radical independent party in the name of political democracy (at least not unless all kinds of industrial jobs are "deprofessionalized" and become subject to union domain, thereby enlarging the organized labor force).

Fourth, the organized worker is no longer likely to be a European immigrant struggling for citizenship as well as union status. He is "Americanized" and better integrated into U.S. society. He has fewer motives for indignation at exclusion and mistreatment. Moreover, there are more legal channels through which he can act (such as labor relation boards), and, because he is no foreigner but a "native American," he is more aware of them and feels entitled to resort to them.

Fifth, his children are not learning about his trade. Instead, they are escaping, at his own insistence, to colleges and elsewhere, and the family no longer engenders militant union values.

Sixth, widespread publicity has been given to corrupt union practices, and so few intellectuals or youth look to unions as models of popular democracy. The worker has lost many of his ardent admirers and apologists and is in no position to entertain himself with illusions about the breadth and quality of public support he could rely on if he were to get up, stretch his radical muscles and carry on a bit. A favorable "climate of opinion" would have to be created to encourage him to think boldly and no such radical trends are in the offing.

All this should now be obvious. Like other people, workers suffer disadvantages and, at some point in time and in response to certain stimuli, they devise strategies for overcoming them. Once they have overcome the major part of their distress, they deal with other grievances and problems by reliance on incremental adjustment; they organize to protect gains won and settle into the society to behave like other interest groups.

However, it would be a mistake to contrive an argument with this as its sum and substance no matter how elaborately stated. The implication is that once material gains are achieved, discontent generally simmers down. In fact, in the past, when workers' demands were met or limited objectives realized, they were often emboldened to define and press for new benefits. Therefore, precisely because workers' goals (union recognition, control of job dispensing, wage and material benefits, shorter hours, improved health and safety conditions on the job) were finally formulated in legislation, one could reasonably have expected that this success would have created the very preconditions today for demanding more, socially as well as economically.

The question, then, is why workers have not carried the struggle further?

There are several reasons in addition to those mentioned at the outset. A demand for reconstitution of economic and political relationships to allow disadvantaged groups a high degree of control in public decision making is not a claim or demand timid men can make. Where could workers derive such a conception today? Socialists are sometimes interesting critics but unconvincing analysts of American society, or preoccupied with concerns not closely related to industrial affairs. Moreover, creating a sense of being entitled to full "industrial citizenship," or even outright industrial control, is dependent on higher levels of education and technological ability, promoting a sense of competence among men who feel capable of wielding greater power and will not tolerate being deprived of it.

But worker technological and educational growth have not kept pace with industrial change and growth. Workers do not feel able to govern. In previous periods, their skills inspired them to demand recognition and bargaining power. Workers were especially emboldened by the fact that employee and employer expertise often approximated each other in business and technological matters. The workingman, especially the craft worker (who frequently had supervisory or shop-owning experience in the late nineteenth century) had an idea of exactly what duties were involved in the greater role he sought. Nevertheless, he did not demand industrial control because even then industrial complexity was beginning to surpass his knowledge.

FROM INTEREST GROUP
TO PROFESSIONAL CASTE

If late nineteenth-century industry was beginning to elude worker expertise, how much truer is this today. Today the workingman would need massive doses of scientific, technological and investment policy-training in order to think in grand terms, as a competitor for industrial control. Moreover, the workingman is often too ill-equipped, without training in the rudiments of law and economics, to rise in union ranks; he is not likely to replace present union leadership with a more militant voice. In fact, as Chinoy demonstrates, the worker's comparatively diminished "expertise" destroys his interest in industrial affairs and causes him to dream of escaping from industrial discipline to a little farm or small business of his own, living as a consumer rather than as a producer. He fears groups like blacks or students who show signs of gaining sufficient political importance to outstrip his influence in society altogether. Pushed aside, peripheral, he is more likely to follow the blandishments of the Wallaces than those of the radicals. Burnham has pointed out that when men belong to class or ideological parties, they are much more "immunized" from political challenges than when they do not. In the United States, neither Democrats nor Republicans are receptive to political ideology or class; they are thus less inhibited from moving to the Right. The American worker, not immunized by membership in a socialist or labor party, is more likely to drift to the Right when the society makes him particularly uncomfortable or diminishes his importance. The union leadership, preying on workers' fears of loss of welfare benefits, is all that has stood between cementing an alliance of the workers and Wallace's movement.

A leftist labor movement can only rise again (if, indeed, it can be said that it ever existed in the United States) among new workers in the labor movement—recent students and blacks; that is, among sectors of the population already radicalized. The former's educational attainments enable them to compete for industrial control, and the blacks have motivations not unlike those of the old immigrants (granting all kinds of differences). But neither of these groups are flocking to industry.

Without fresh recruits the labor movement loses its "movement" character and settles for interest group status—incremental adjustment of economic demands and grievances—and rests uneasily in a politically polarizing environment, trying to make such economic gains as it can protect in lieu of an increase in participatory or decision-making rights. And while blacks are becoming a crucial factor in some industries, such as auto and rubber, they remain marginal to the general network of power in labor organizations.

It might be argued that it does not really matter if today's worker and the present labor movement are not likely to surge to the Left. What if the labor movement should "rise" and go so far as to dominate every industrial enterprise in sight? Is it not technology, and not "interests," which determines decisions? Not entirely! Does construction of low-, middle- or high-income housing arise from technological necessity? Does it make a difference that military rather than civilian resources developed atomic energy and an "atomic technology"? It is true that state-owned enterprise allocates funds for cultivating certain technologies and not others, recognizing, of course, that domestic national arrangements are not the only framework within which technologies are developed. This does not mean that technology does not make demands on men for rationalization of production, accounting and distribution methods. It does. It also does not mean that men are free to push technological evolution in any direction they please. They are not. But it does mean that technology and governance are related affairs. Technology is a bundle of possibilities at any given time. The direction any one of its parts takes in the course of time is, as much as it is anything else, a reflection of value choices, social needs, policy arrangements. To rearrange industrial governance by changing the industrial governors, a change in priorities within a nation must be made, and this will find its technological reflection in the United States as a whole.

This does not negate the fact that, to a degree, labor must adjust to the character of technology. However, if men can consciously make something as elusive as "history," they can also consciously direct something as concrete as technology, although not strictly according to their own will. In a word, technology is not bound by "iron laws." If workers could press for industrial control and achieve it, technological development could be altered in important enough ways to make a difference.

The constant search for labor's Archimedian lever usually takes the form of coalition demands: Will it be a coalition of black people, students and intellectuals that will pave the way for the future of labor? Blacks are clearly into a pattern of upward mobility leading to professional roles rather than union activities. The students are perhaps a radical wing of their own and perhaps form a class unto themselves. While they may emulate and even absorb many trade union features in the years to come, the fact that students perform head work rather than hand work and perform such activities in relatively nonprivate enterprise, makes the possibility of unity between the working class and student class remote.

Although labor intellectuals still exist in the ranks of the working class (indeed they have begun new efforts at developing labor colleges and research projects geared to the historical, sociological efforts of labor), they have really lost out in any meaningful sense. After the fiasco of the 1948 CIO Political Action Committee and with the further fragmentation of all pre-World War II coalitions, any chance of a Left-led intellectual faction within labor or between the labor movement as a whole and the intellectuals has just about vanished.

This is not to say that coalitions cannot occur or will not take place among all of these groups. It is to say that the very subject of coalition illustrates the dilemma of the working class. It seems uniquely incapable any longer of functioning as a class in itself, much less for itself; thus the politics of interest group behavior take over. It is important to take into account the fact that interest groups do not require massive size and massive mobilization. Labor does not require coalition of any kind because it does not, in fact, have ultimate demands to make upon society but rather ameliorative demands, which are being met.

The failure of labor politics in the United States largely flows from the new forms of work, which increasingly revolve around the peculiar cross fertilization of labor and management or, at the very least, of technical labor and professional occupations. As we move beyond the present era, we may well experience a renewed and vigorous critique of the bourgeoisie as a class of owners who neither work in management nor work in production but simply absorb profits. A portion of the managerial class may join the ranks of organized labor in a renewed assault on the economic and moral opprobrium of ownership without operational control and without consent, thereby diminishing external dominion.

If, in fact, managerial sectors move into labor and provoke corporate reaction, a left-wing thrust is more than possible. On the other hand, if labor cannot generate sufficient autonomy to provide dynamic leadership and must join the managerial ranks to gain any of its ends, it is likely that the thrust of labor will be toward some kind of industrial quasi-fascism in which technology and managerialism rule.

If such realignments and polarizations seem somewhat distant, they do represent very real, if limited, options available to the working class. And if we are able to begin to think in these terms, we will be in a position to discard what is obviously dead in socialist rhetoric about labor and perhaps to preserve its kernel of empirical and moral truth: Men who work also deserve to be men who rule.

REFERENCES

Adorno, T. N. (1950) *The Authoritarian Personality: Studies in Prejudice.* New York: Harper & Row.

Blauner, R. (1964) *Alienation and Freedom.* Chicago: University of Chicago Press.

Burnham, W. D. (1970) "Political Immunization and Political Confessionalism: Some Comparative Inquiries" (mimeograph).

Chinoy, E. (1955) *Automobile Workers and the American Dream.* Garden City, N. Y.: Doubleday.

Denitch, B. (1970) "Is There a 'New Working Class'?" *Dissent,* vol. 17, no. 40, (July/August), pp. 351–355.

Hill, H. (1965) "Racial Practices of Organized Labor," *New Politics,* whole no. 14, vol. 4, no. 2 (Spring), pp. 26–46.

Hill, H. (1969) "Black Protest and the Struggle for Union Democracy," *Issues in Industrial Society,* vol. 1, no. 1 (Spring), pp. 19–29.

Horowitz, I. L. (1970) "The Trade-Unionization of the Student Seventies," *New Society* (July), pp. 70–71.

Jacobson, J. ed. (1968) Special issue on "The American Labor Movement," *New Politics,* whole no. 27, vol. 7, no. 3 (Summer).

Laslett, J. H. M. (1970) *Labor and the Left: A Study of Socialist and Radical Influences in the American Labor Movement, 1881–1924.* New York: Basic Books.

Leggett, J. C. (1968) *Class, Race and Labor: Working Class Consciousness in Detroit.* New York: Oxford University Press.

Lipset, S. M. (1960) *Political Man: The Social Bases of Politics.* Garden City, N. Y.: Doubleday.

Mandel, E. (1968) "Workers Under Neo-Capitalism," *International Socialist Review* (November-December); reprinted in David Mermelstein, ed. (1970) *Economics: Mainstream Readings and Radical Critiques.* New York: Random House.

Meany, G. (1970) Interview with Neil Gilbride of the Associated Press. *The Washington Post,* August 31.

Oppenheimer, M. (1970) "White Collar Revisited: The Making of a New York Class," *Social Policy,* vol. 1, no. 2 (July-August), pp. 27–32.

Stouffer, S. A. (1955) *Communism, Conformity and Civil Liberties.* New York: Doubleday.

CHAPTER 24

RACE, CLASS
AND ETHNICITY

The recent attitudes and behavior of working-class Americans, some-times called "ethnics" for short, have deeply shocked and bewildered many acute commentators. The supposed return to militant self-identification has led one radical to claim that "the working-class white man is actually in revolt against taxes, joyless work, the double standards and short memories of professional politicians, hypocrisy and what he considers the debasement of the American dream" (Hamill, 1969). The same display of muscular working-class behavior has led an equally radical critic to assert that "the hard-hat labor unionists, and they are by no means limited to the building trades, have joined with the military elite and their political spokesmen. This suggests the great danger of the rise of a proto-fascist workers move-ment in the United States. Whatever social and cultural forces may be in-voked to explain this development, it is already manifesting itself in a variety of ways. The racist hard-hats from many unions are the potential street fighters of American fascism" (Hill, 1971). From the foregoing statements it is hard to know who is in greater need of depolarization—the working class or its intellectual respondents.

WHO IS AN ETHNIC?

Whatever actual evidence we have is considerably more bland and nondescript than either projections for an ethnic-based fascism or for an ethnic-based new politics. At the level of attitudes, several facts are clear: (1) It would appear that working-class ethnics for the most part are neither more nor less prejudiced against the black community than the wealthier classes (Hamilton, 1971, p. 135). (2) It would also appear that classical aspirations of upward mobility and geographical relocation along class rather than ethnic lines still permeate working-class ambitions (Campbell, 1971, pp. 43-44). (3) Traditional class allegiances to the party system remain essentially as fluid or as fixed as they have been for other classes (Reiter, 1971, pp. 101-128). Further, it has been questioned whether feelings of alienation and anomie have effected the working class any more than other social sectors. The working class continues to favor government welfare and income maintenance programs—especially those affecting them in particular (Greeley, 1969, pp. 45-55).

In a recent prestigious colloquium, it was asserted that there remains no clear definition of the working class; no clear statement, even at a statistical level, of any special economic squeeze against the working class; and finally, there remains the highest doubt that a problem specific to blue collar workers or to white ethnics as such even exists. Problems seem universal, affecting blue collar and white collar people alike, affecting ethnics and blacks alike, and affecting different nationalities and religious groups alike. In short, the problems are endemic to the United States of America, and the class and ethnic aspects of these problems are simply expressions of such universal dilemmas (Levitan, 1971, pp. xiii-xx).

Whether or not the foregoing interpretation is correct, the rise of a new literature on blue collar ethnics does herald something novel in the social sciences. At the very least, analyses based on the end of class interests, class ideologies and class politics have receded to the point of either a memory or a whisper, only to be replaced by a verbal celebration of ethnic interests, ethnic ideologies and ethnic politics.

Any attempt to define ethnicity raises at least three sociological problems: (1) who is an ethnic; (2) how can ethnicity be distinguished from other social variables and character traits; and (3) what can ethnicity predict—what are its behavioral consequences? Before coming to terms with the current ideological and political uses of ethnicity, it becomes necessary to describe the ideological sources of the current celebration of ethnicity.

The general characterizations of ethnics in the social science literature can be presented from negative as well as positive points of view.

1. It is frequently claimed that ethnics are neither very rich nor very poor, and they are often identified with either the blue collar working class or the lower-middle class.

2. The current literature presents highly selective definitions of eth-

nicity. Jews and Japanese are excluded by intellectual fiat from the ethnic category on the basis of their middle or upper-middle class position and on the basis of their upward mobility through education.

3. Ethnicity *within* lower-class groups or racial groups such as blacks seems to be excluded from discussion. Thus, for example, distinctions and differences between East African blacks and Jamaican blacks are very rarely spoken of by those defining or employing the term "ethnicity."

4. There is a strong tendency to think of ethnics in terms of whites living in the urban complex or in the inner city, in contrast to whites living in suburban or nonurban regions.

5. A distinction is often made between nativists and ethnics, that is, between people who have Protestant and English-speaking backgrounds and those with Catholic and non-English speaking backgrounds, although in some cases (for instance, the Irish) ethnics may be identified solely on the basis of religion.

6. Ethnics have in common a vocational orientation toward education in contrast to a liberal arts or humanities orientation. They tend to be nonacademic, antiintellectual and highly pragmatic. Interestingly, although blacks are perhaps the best illustration of a vocationally oriented subculture, they are not generally catagorized as ethnics.

7. Ethnics are usually said to possess characteristics and attitudes identified with those on the political Right: strong patriotic fervor, religious fundamentalism, authoritarian family patterns and so forth. Indeed, characterizations of ethnicity and conservatism show such a profound overlap that the only difference would appear to be the currently positive attitude toward such behavior on the part of learned observers (See, for example, Codes, 1971).

In sum, determining who is an ethnic has more to do with the sentiment of sociologists than with the science of sociology. The concept defines a new, positive attitude toward those who fit in the model. One now hears "them" spoken of as middle class, lower-middle class or working class in contrast to lower class. They are said to be part of a great new wave of struggle, the struggle against opulence on one hand and welfare on the other. As such, the concept of ethnicity claims a middle ground. It does not celebrate a national consensus nor does it accept the concept of a class struggle. Its ideologists perceive of ethnics as an interest group rather than a social class. In this sense there is something strangely like classical liberalism in the ideology of ethnicity. It promotes the theme of cultural pluralism and cultural difference rather than social change or social action. Perhaps this explains why dedicated civil libertarians have moved their attentions and affections from the black underclass to the white ethnic class (Coles, 1971; Novak, 1971; Cottle, 1971a; and Friedman, 1967).

This tentative definition also indicates that we are dealing primarily with sentiments rather than organizational forms. What was formerly kept in the closet comes into the open. The hidden and covert expressions of racism and anti-Semitism, instead of being whispered about, are openly celebrated or, at the very least, openly presented as virtuous and morally neutral (Novak, 1971, pp. 44-50).

THE IDEOLOGY OF ETHNICITY

Ethnicity refers to a cluster of cultural factors that define the sociogram of the person rather than the racial or class connections of that person. It defines the binding impact of linguistic origins, geographic backgrounds, cultural and culinary tastes and religious homogeneity. Therefore, the concept of ethnicity is not only distinguished from class but in a certain respect must be considered its operational counterpart. It provides the cultural and theological linkages that cut through class lines and form new sources both of tension and definition of inclusionary–exclusionary relationships in an American society grown weary of class perspectives on social reality.

In part, the renewed emphasis upon ethnicity signifies the end of the achievement society and the return to an ascriptive society. Generational success can no longer be measured in terms of job performance or career satisfaction. Therefore, new definitions of group membership are sought in order to generate pride. These often take the form of a celebration of ethnic origins, and a feeling that such origins somehow are more significant to group cohesion than is class.

The notion of ethnicity, like other barometers of disaffection, is indicative of problems in self-definition. Americans have long been known to have weak class identification. Most studies have shown that class identification is weak because class conflict is thought foreign to American society; everyone claims to be a middle-class member. Few see themselves at either end of the class spectrum. As a result, class as a source of status distinction is strong, but as a source of economic mobilization it is weak. In a sense, the concept of ethnicity closely emulates the concept of race; for race, unlike class, is based upon ascription rather than achievement. But ethnicity defines a community of peoples having language, religion and race in common. If it does not imply a commonality of tasks, it does at least imply a commonality of tastes. For example, Poles and Italians share religious similarities, but they are not likely to share ethnic identities. The Church has long recognized ethnicity on the basis of linguistic and national origin rather than simply the universal ministerial claims of Catholicism.

The problem with determining the behavioral consequences of ethnicity is the difficulty of establishing whether there are common political demands or even common economic conditions that all national and linguistic minorities face. Aside from the fact that most ethnics participate in

Democratic party politics there is little evidence that ethnics do in fact share common political goals. There seem to be greater gaps between first- and second-generation Irish and Poles than Irish and Poles of the same generation (Greeley, 1969, pp. 46-48). Hence the actual power of ethnicity as an explanatory variable must be carefully evaluated.

We must face the fact that in large part, the present era represents a new kind of emphasis. The collapse of federalism, the strain on the American national system and the consequent termination of the melting-pot ideology has led to a situation where ethnicity in a sense fulfills the thirst for community—a modest-sized community in which the values of rural America as well as rural Europe could be simulated in the context of a postindustrial world, yet without the critique implied by the radical and youth movements.

In part, disillusionment with the American value systems and America's inability to preserve a universal series of goals has led to a reemergence of community-centered parochial and particularistic doctrines. Indeed, the positive response of the American nation to the historical injustices heaped upon the black people has made it seem that ethnicity could achieve the same results by using a similar model of social protest.

There has been a notable shift of attitudes at the ideological level. What once appeared to be a minority problem with its attendant drives toward integration into the American mainstream has now become an ethnic problem with its attendant drives toward self-determination apart from the American mainstream. To be more precise, there has been an erosion of that mainstream. With the existence of 20 to 30 million first- and second-generation Italian-Americans, 9 million Spanish-speaking Americans, some 13 million Irish-Americans (these often overlapping with 48 million Catholics), who in turn share a country with 6 million Jews and 23 million blacks, the notion of majority status for white Protestant America has been seriously eroded. The notion of the WASP serves to identify a dominant economic group but no longer a uniquely gifted or uniquely destined-to-rule political or cultural group. Thus, ethnicity has served to express a genuine plurality of interests, without necessarily effecting a revolution in life styles or attitudes. Equality increasingly becomes the right to be different and to express such differences in language, customs and habits, rather than a shared position in the white Anglo-Saxon Protestant ethos which dominated the United States up and through the end of World War II and the Cold War period.

Further, ethnicity is an expression of the coming into being of new nations throughout the Third World—African nations, Asian nations, Latin American socialist states, Israel as a Jewish homeland, the reemergence of Irish nationalism. In short, the world trend toward diversified power bases has had domestic repercussions on minority standing in the United States. The external reinforcement of internal minorities have changed the self-image of these internal minorities. The new ethnics are the old minorities in an era of postcolonialism, in an era of imperialism on the defensive at least as a cultural ideal if not as an economic reality. Thus, whether ethnicity takes revolutionary or reactionary forms internally, its rise to conceptual and ideological preeminence is clearly a function of the breakup of the old order in which Anglo-American dominance went uncontested, except by a Bolshevik menace.

RACE, RELIGION AND ETHNICITY

The concept of ethnicity is not only an attempt to simulate the strategy of the blacks for gaining equality through struggle, it also is patterned after the main tactic of the Jews for gaining equality through education. Whether such simulation or imitation will be successful depends on whether ethnicity is an overriding concept or simply a word covering differences of a profound sort between linguistic groups and religious groups. The fact of being Irish may be of binding value, but the fact of being *Protestant* Irish or *Catholic* Irish certainly would take precedence over the ethnic unity. Similarly, being a Ukraine may be a binding value as long as Ukraines are defined exclusively in nonreligious terms. For the Ukranian Jews certainly do not participate in the same ethnic goals despite a shared geographic and linguistic background. Hence, the concept of ethnicity may explain little in the way of behavior unless it can be demonstrated that it forms the basis of social solidarity and political action and is not simply a residual category.

It might well turn out that the new emphasis on ethnicity is distinguishable from the old emphasis on minority groups in the United States primarily because it represents a breakdown in what used to be known as the majority. It is terriblly difficult to have minority studies in a world where the major impulse is weak, nonexistent or defined as another minority. Hence, the rise of ethnicity as a rallying point seems to be in inverse proportion to the decline of white Anglo-Saxon Protestantism as a majority definition. The latter, too, has turned ethnic. Ethnicity has become a relative concept instead of a subordinate concept.

All models are subject to limitations. The call for "Ethnic Power," modeled as it is upon the past decade of civil rights struggles, provides a perfect illustration of this fact; it involves, after all, a blurring of the special circumstances of blacks in the United States. It would not be entirely amiss to recall that the black presence in the United States was largely involuntary whereas the ethnic minority presence was largely voluntary. Moreover, the black experience of America was linked to the plantation as a total institution and connected to their degradation as a people; white immigration (ethnic immigration) involved participation in the building of America and particularly in the building of its industrial life. Thus, while models for ethnic separatism are premised on the black movement, at the same time they display little awareness of the different circumstances of black participation in American affairs throughout the last hundred years.

Few now doubt or even bother to deny that current appeals to ethnicity are directly related to the Great White Hope, to the theme of ethnics preventing blacks from becoming a major power bloc in urban America. As such, ethnicity becomes not just a response to present tension within American society but a response to present superordinate traits of the diminant American sectors. Ethnicity becomes a euphemism for the fight against crime in the streets and for the fight to maintain a white foothold in the major urban centers. And support for the claims of ethnicity must also be viewed as a reaction to the flight of huge sectors of the middle class to suburban America, thus leaving the white working-class ethnics to absorb the impact of black militants and black organizations in the American cities.

In some sense the celebration of ethnicity is not so much a recognition of the special contribution of Europeans to America, as it is the manufacturing of a new myth, the myth of an organized group of white working-class Americans dedicated to the maintenance of their class position. As such, ethnicity becomes yet another hurdle for black Americans to jump in order to gain equity in this society. The open struggle between whites and blacks is intellectually unpalatable; hence ethnicity emerges to defuse racial tension by shifting the struggle to the loftier plane of downtrodden blacks and denigrated ethnics.

At an entirely different level the celebration of ethnicity has brought about strange new alliances or the potential for new coalitions. Most important in this connection has been the renewed effort in the Jewish community to reach an accomodation with ethnic leadership. The informal pact between the Jewish Defense League and the Italian-American Club simply highlights tendencies in current Jewish-American life to accept the current American value system and to reject claims of national or racial separation.

After years of struggle in support of black egalitarianism and in particular black institutions of higher learning, Jews are now being criticized as never before by their black colleagues. Whatever the roots of black nationalism, its first contact is with the Jew as landlord, shopkeeper and realtor. Whether the turn of the Jewish community to ethnics will resolve their problems with blacks is difficult to ascertain. In fact, what is being jeopardized is the special philanthropic relationship which has existed throughout the twentieth century between the black and Jewish communities and which perhaps is epitomized by such established black leaders as the late Martin Luther King and such Jewish leaders as the deceased Rabbi Stephen Wise.

The petty bourgeois character of the alliance between blacks and Jews has long been understood. Its focus on education as the main source of upward mobility a priori ruled out the possibility of revolution. And as young blacks move more conscientiously toward revolutionary goals and as an older generation of Jews move with equal rapidity toward reformist goals, the historic alliance between these two peoples becomes seriously jeopardized. The Jewish model proved less efficacious for the postwar blacks than had been anticipated; as a result, blacks turned toward a Third World model—particularly signified by the Algerian revolution and its cultural hero, Franz Fanon. Be that as it may, declaration of support by the Jewish community, or its self-declared representatives, on behalf of the ethnic urban white working class, has little more than symbolic significance. The class barriers between peoples continue to be clearly more durable than the commonality of race.

Various organizational efforts to sensitize and depolarize, although well intentioned and intellectually sincere, start from a fundamentally erroneous premise; namely, that the key polarity is presently between black America and ethnic America (Levine and Herman, 1971, pp. 3-4). Such a formulation does permit various organizations, especially Jewish middle-class organizations, to perform their historic role of honest broker and friend at both courts. However, the likelihood is that, despite the differences between Poles and blacks in cities like Detroit or Gary, their problems arise from common sources—a lack of steady jobs, poor upgrading procedures, lack of meaningful retraining programs and a breakdown of urban development—all of which should (if the proper conclusions are drawn) create the basis for class solidarity rather than simple ethnic separation along racial or religious lines.

It can be easily understood why the Jewish community would seek rapprochement with ethnic groups. However, since the ethnics themselves often define the Jews as outside ethnicity and since the class formations that separate ethnic America from Jewish America continue unabated, the possibility of alliance seems remote and, when executed, tenuous. It may represent a tactical side bet in a specific community where Jewish–ethnic interaction is high, but little else.

POLITICAL USES OF ETHNICITY

The special tactical relationships between blacks, Jews and ethnics is really the crux of the future of the working class in the United States. Since the United States has become something of a three-track nation, the blacks are identified as being either on the government payroll or on the government dole. The Jews are identified as being the kingpins of entrepreneurial America. The ethnics are seen, or perceive themselves, as the true heirs of the working-class spirit. In a sense, the tendency of Communist parties throughout the world to accept, if not adopt outright, anti-Semitic postures is a very real response to its working-class and black constituencies—which see Jews very much as the exploiters rather than exploited, and likewise see them as elements unwilling to participate in the American way of life by virtue of their alleged dual allegiance to Israel.

Implicit in a great deal of literature on ethnicity is an automatic assumption that ethnicity and working-class membership are axiomatic, while the blacks are identified as lower class, or outside the system of the working class. In a sense, sociologists have oversold the idea of a lower-class culture as distinct from a working-class culture (Rainwater, 1966, pp. 172-216; 1970; pp. 361-397). More to the point, there has been a profound misreading of the actual distribution of the blacks in American society—for if they have a distinctive culture, they nonetheless form an essential human core in the U.S. labor force, particularly in service industries, government work, and heavy-duty labor. They represent between 15 to 16 percent of the labor force, in contrast to 11 percent of the population as a whole. They are becoming unionized at a more rapid rate than their white ethnic colleagues (Brooks, 1970, pp. 169-170; Rustin, 1971, pp. 73-74). They also are a crucial factor in assembly-line activities such as steel and auto. What sets them apart is not that they are lower class while the white ethnics are working class, but that the bulk of black labor (because of its historical marginality and nontechnological characteristics) is nonunionized, while a larger percentage of white ethnic labor (also deriving from historical sources such as emigrant syndicalist backgrounds and specialized craft forms of labor) is and has been for some time largely unionized. Thus, accentuating the gap between lower-class black culture and working-class white ethnicity is a profoundly dangerous misreading of actualities—one that disguises the acute responsibilities of a U.S. labor force sharply divided between the one-fourth which is highly organized, in contrast to the three-fourths which are poorly organized, if organized at all.

This concept of ethnic organization as a precondition for class solidarity is a theme struck by any number of commentators. Richard Krickus (1971, p. 30) has summed up this sentiment with particular force:

> With rising self-awareness, the appearance of vigorous leadership, and the evolution of organizational structures, many black communities can meet the minimum requirement necessary for coalitions. Because similar structures do not exist in most white ethnic communities, a coalition with blacks is not yet feasible. Until the white ethnics, through heightened group identity, generate new leaders and develop new organizational props, the precondition for coalition activities will not materialize in their communities.

But the author of these sentiments makes it clear that the purpose of such organizational pluralism is more ambitious.

> If the white ethnics are to cooperate with and work toward common goals with their nonwhite neighbors, they must acquire the means to articulate their demands in a more effective fashion. Through this process of articulation, a clear view of their own self-interest will surface. This in turn is a precondition to their working together with other groups that share many problems in common with them. (Krickus, 1971, p. 30)

It might well be that such ultimate class identities can become easily blurred by the immediate ethnic pluralities. The rhetoric of racial and ethnic antagonism may be heightened rather than lessened by the assumption that separate organizational forms are now required for both black and ethnic groupings. To define tensions between ethnics and blacks without clearly demarcating the similarity of their class interests, which might also involve an identity of class hostilities, serves to exacerbate rather than eliminate tensions. It is to assume that specialized interest groups and momentary tactical considerations must always prevail over long-run tendencies and trends in the class composition of American society. It is also to assume that Jews as ethnic types have a sameness that also makes them part of this solution based on ethnicity. It might be just as easily the case that Jews too reveal profound antagonism within their numbers based on considerations of class and religion. For example, there remains a considerable spread in the class and occupational ladder among Jews, and perhaps an even wider disparity between orthodox, reformed, conservative, reconstructionist and other varieties of Jewish religious practice. Further, on the very grounds of national and ethnic backgrounds, Jews of East European and Asian or Middle Eastern origins show wide disparities. And of course beyond that are the gulfs of a more political sort, between Zionists, non-Zionists, and even anti-Zionists. To perceive Jews as one unified phalanx is thus to credit them with far greater unity than they in fact possess, and also to assume that the world of Jews, or any ethnic grouping, is necessarily forged by threat mechanisms from outside groups.

The world of ethnicity is filled with premises and strategies based upon models largely derived from other groups. The selective and subjective method of defining membership in an ethnic group permits the concept to be employed in any number of political contexts. It might well be that however flawed the concept of ethnicity may be at the theoretical level, it can nonetheless serve as a rallying cry for those groups who are dismayed and disturbed by the breakup of ethnic communities in American society. The Jews, in particular, castigated for being the first to abandon the urban ship in favor of suburbia. But why ethnicity must, perforce, take an urban rather than a suburban form is rarely examined, much less critically dealt with.

Within the political framework of mass society, it might be that ethnicity functions as a right-wing manifestation against the breakup of community. In substance, although clearly not in form, this is similar to left-wing radical and racial nationalist groups who likewise exhibit tendencies toward communal apartness, and racial and religious efforts at firm exclusionary–inclusionary relationships.

Patterns of disaffiliation have found expression throughout all sectors of American society. Those who identify with the past, like those who trust only in the future, have similar problems with the present system of affluence; but, quite clearly, they have posed different solutions. It is plain that forms of social change will be scarcely less painful in the United States than they have been elsewhere. Such forms involve coalitions and consolidations of a type that may, in the long run, lead to racial harmony and class unity. However, the more likely immediate outcome will be a forging of ethnic sensitivity that will tend to minimize and mitigate against such efforts at unification and national integration.

There are those who look forward to a great day of unification between lower-class blacks and working-class whites; but unification, even on the basis of expediency and political coalition, seems remote. That the concept of ethnicity has created one more large-scale strain in the two-hundred year history of the American society is a reflection of the catastrophe of separatist politics and industrialist economics. The ultimate fruits of a policy of racism have been the emergence of a politics of ethnicity. Both have threatened the survival of the social system and yet neither seems prepared to offer an option for all other peoples living within the United States. In addition to class and race, ethnicity must now be seen as a measure of American sociopolitical cohesion. Indeed, however weak this variable might be, the fact that it has left the sociology texts for the neighborhoods is indicative of the tragic ruptures in a nation unable to overcome the collapse of federalism at home and the shrinkage of imperialism abroad.

Ethnicity is in sum and substance a surrogate concept, an expression of disintegration and deterioration of the national economic system and national social priorities. Like other notions of a particularistic nature, its importance derives more from what and who are excluded than what and who are included. It is a response to a collective anomie, an era in which the halcyon days of confident national priorities and arrogant national goals have become remote. Representative government has turned unrepresentative. Regulatory mechanisms have turned oppressive and bureaucratic. Large factory management and large factory unionism have joined forces to present the ordinary laborer with an unresponsive structure. The drive for economic rationalization has led to the multinational corporation and international cartelization at an accelerated rate. This conglomerate push has underscored the economic impotence of the ordinary person.

In a sense, the rivival of ethnicity as a working-class value is paralleled by the middle-class return to race, sex, property and other definitions for surmounting the vacuity and vapidity of postindustrial capitalist life. The very weakness of the success ethic and the achievement orientation is revealed in middle-class youths' emphasis on rurality, fundamentalism, psychologism and other forms of the Gemeinschaft community of fate that presumably was left behind with the Old World and its feudal relationships. Those groups identified with the blueing of America (See Berger, 1971) are no more content with the progress of this nation than are those who are part of the greening of America (See Reich, 1970). That expressions of discontent should take different forms in different classes is certainly not without precedent, but what is surprising is the *uniformity* of the demand to get beyond the present, the widespread resentment that makes clear that the old sociological consensus and the old political checks and balances are no longer effective mechanisms against disaffection of large portions of American society.

If ethnicity is a surrogate concept, it is nonetheless necessary to make plain what it is a surrogate on behalf of. Politically, it represents a demand for larger participation in the federal bureaucracy; economically, it is a demand for higher rewards for physical "hand" labor, at the expense of mental "head" labor; and culturally, it is a statement of the rights of groups to their distinctive life styles. Beyond that, however, are the historical dimensions: the return to ethnicity, insofar as it is more than an intellectual pipedream, is also a return to a pristine era in American life, before the melting-pot ideology boiled out the impurities of the immigrant generation with a weird mixture of external pressure and internalized guilt.

In this sense, the return to ethnicity is more than a restatement of ascribed values; it harkens back to a period in which family allegiances, patriarchal authority, foreign languages and the meaning of work itself had a certain priority over occupational and monetary achievement. On this point there can be no question that the prime targets are the blacks, who have employed the welfare model in order to gain a measure of influence and even self-respect, and the Jews, especially those of the second and third generations, who have employed the educational model to create the basis for upward mobility. The problem is that the ethnics have a hard time identifying with the former model, and an equally hard time gaining access through the latter model.

By extension, it might be claimed with justification, that the Jews have largely used the concept of social class both to explain the American system and to live within it comfortably. The blacks have generally employed a concept of racial caste to explain why, despite the appearance of wealth, they have been kept out of the advantages of the class network. It is only natural, under the circumstances, that the rise of an ethnic consciousness would lead to a search for why so many people of Catholic faith, Polish-Italian-Irish-Ukrainian ancestry, and working-class membership, seemed to be so inexorably locked into the American system at its lower, but not lowest, points. Ethnicity provides the same sort of explanation without attempting to peddle a working-class analysis to a conservative set of workers, or a race analysis to a set of white people (at least in perception).

Ethnicity is thus a final formula for linking people and classes who would otherwise tend to be more divided than united by matters of religion, country of origin and linguistic affiliation. Whether in fact ethnicity can, in an operational sense, prove to be as potent a factor as class or race, seems somehow to be less important than the fact that the American social science community has moved beyond its old formulas of class, status and power, to a newer formulation of class, race and ethnicity—in which questions of status and power become the "dependent variables" in the larger matrix of primary human associations.

Tendencies toward individualization and privatization are evolving as a counterculture: on the Left are the students, the blacks, the chicanos; while on the Right are the ethnics, the Poles, Catholics, day laborers, and all the whites who have failed to milk or meld into the "system." But whether the response has been Left or Right is less important than the impulse to resist encroachments on the "little people"—the public turned ethnic with a missionary vengeance. The making of the new minorities, whether of the factory proletariat or the student proletariat, nonetheless points up the huge shift in the United States from a nation of workers to a nation of service-oriented personnel. The response, in some measure, whether put in terms of racial politics or ethnic politics, is a demand for real politics, a politics of scale in which the possibility for the control of decision making and policy making would be restored to communities of responsibility. This impulse toward community control is a possible source of new coalitional efforts, whether under the label of populism or welfarism, that might provide some hope for a reinvigorated politics. The rise of ethnicity as a basic concern and a root concept should not be dismissed, nor should it be celebrated. But ethnicity certainly must be charted and ultimately channeled, if this nation is to endure as a republic and as a democracy.

REFERENCES

Berger, P. (1971) "The Blueing of America," *The New Republic,* vol. 164, (April), pp. 20–23.

Brooks, T. R. (1970) "Black Upsurge in the Unions," *Dissent,* whole no. 75, vol. 17 (March-April), pp. 125–138.

Campbell, A. (1971) *White Attitudes Toward Black People.* Ann Arbor: Institute for Social Research, The University of Michigan.

Coles, R. (1971) *The Middle Americans: Proud and Uncertain.* Boston: Little, Brown.

Cottle, T. J. (1971a) "The Non-Elite Student: Billy Kowalski Goes to College," *Change,* vol. 3, no. 2 (March/April), pp. 36–42.

Cottle, T. J. (1971b) *Time's Children, Impressions of Youth.* Boston: Little, Brown.

Friedman, M. (1967) "Kensington, U.S.A.," *La Salle College Magazine,* vol. 11, no. 4 (Fall); reprinted and distributed by the American Jewish Committee.

Greeley, A. M. (1969) *Why Can't They Be Like Us? Facts and Fallacies About Ethnic Differences and Group Conflicts in America.* New York: Institute of Human Relations Press.

Hamill, P. (1969) "The Revolt of the White Lower Middle Class," *New York* (April 14).

Hamilton, R. F. (1971) "Black Demands, White Reactions, and Liberal Alarms," in S. Levitan, ed., *Blue-Collar Workers*. New York: McGraw-Hill.

Hill, H. (1971) "Racism and Organized Labor," *New School Bulletin*, vol. 28, no. 6 (February 8).

Krickus, R. J. (1969) "Forty Million Ethnics Rate More Than Bromides," *The Washington Post* (August 31).

Krickus, R. J. (1971) "The White Ethnics: Who Are They and Where Are They Going?" *City*, vol. 5, no. 3 (May/June), pp. 23–31.

Levine, I. M., and J. M. Herman (1971) "The Ethnic Factor in Blue Collar Life," National Project on Ethnic America, American Jewish Committee (mimeograph).

Levitan, S. (1971) *Blue-Collar Workers: A Symposium on Middle America*. New York: McGraw-Hill.

Novak, M. (1971) "White Ethnic," *Harper's Magazine*, vol. 243 (September), pp. 44–50.

Rainwater, L. (1966) "Crucible of Identity: The Negro Lower Class Family," *Daedalus*, whole no. 95, pp. 172–216.

Rainwater, L. (1970) *Behind Ghetto Walls: Black Family Life in a Federal Slum*. Chicago: Aldine-Atherton.

Reich, C. A. (1970) *The Greening of America: How The Youth Revolution Is Trying to Make America Livable*. New York: Random House.

Rustin, B. (1971) "The Blacks and the Unions," *Harper's Magazine*, vol. 242 (May), pp. 73–81.

OUTCOMES

CHAPTER 25

POLITICAL BIAS
AND
SOCIAL ANALYSIS

The unsettled question of the place of political bias in social analysis has been a major source of irritation since Marx (1939), in *The German Ideology,* implanted the problem of ideological variables and Spencer (1873), in *The Study of Sociology,* attempted the first full-scale resolution. Indeed, from the time of Spencer until the present, the claim has been made that functionalism has settled the issue of the relationship between sociology and the "class bias."[1] The purpose of these remarks is to explore the statement that social theory, to the extent that it employs functionalist canons, is liberated from the long-standing charge that political commitments and prescriptions underline both the conscious theory and the unconscious tendencies of behavioral investigation, especially sociology.

Essentially, this charge (made both by those who are sympathetic as well as hostile to sociology) has been met in contrasting ways. First, there has been the admission that sociology does have to do with political beliefs at some level, whether in originating questions, styles of research or in the

---

[1] Cf. Spencer (1873, pp. 65–74). For a modern variation on this theme, see Mannheim (1936, pp. 97–136).

aims of inquiry, but that this does not impugn the integrity of sociology any more than Keynes' commitment to the welfare state nullifies the importance of his studies in fiscal policy and monetary circulation, or any more than Einstein's concern for world federalism invalidates the theory of relativity. A second way of meeting the challenge has been to deny the premise, by an insistence that sociology is, as a matter of fact, free of value considerations of a political nature. This second approach, usually adopted by the school of structural functional sociologists, further goes on to state that to the extent that a strict separation of facts and values is maintained, sociology is scientific, while insofar as it is not, sociology is tainted and unscientific.[2]

Structural functionalism has, with but rare exceptions, assumed the burden of the second way of meeting the charge that sociology is conditioned by political presuppositions. It is my intention to explore how and in what sense the denial of the connection of sociology to political beliefs achieves the intended goal of purifying sociological research. Simply asserting a link between sociology and politics no more destroys sociological objectivity than the denial of such guarantees objectivity. As Schumpeter (1951) has shown, ideology, those unconscious agencies of interest rationalization and justification, at certain times may serve as a stimulant to the kind of continuing self-evaluation that nourishes the scientific community.

In his study of functionalism as a sociological method, Kingsley Davis (1959) sums up the dilemmas of functionalism in decisive fashion. He introduces four major allegations against its continued use: (1) Professional consensus on even a minimal definition of structural functional analysis does not exist; (2) most work done under the functional label is equivalent to sociological analysis as such, and when divergencies do occur, functionalism shows itself to be social philosophy rather than a unique methodological tool; (3) to debate sociological questions under the guise of evaluating functionalism exhibits teleological qualifications that are not open to scientific evaluation; and (4) terms such as *function, dysfunction* and *eufunction* are semantic artificialities that hinder rather than promote sociological research.

I shall not consider this broadside set of criticisms. To be sure, Davis has independently arrived at a negative view of functionalism earlier made by the philosophers of science, in particular Braithwaite (1953, pp. 319–340), Nagel (1957, pp. 247–283), and Hempel (1959, p. 271–307). What I wish to do here is further develop these aforementioned analyses of functionalism in terms of its effects upon the relationship of sociology to political beliefs.

Specifically, the main contentions that I wish to make and support are as follows: (1) Functionalism, to the extent to which it distinguishes itself from sociology as such, intrinsically entails political commitment, although

[2] Cf. Berger (1961, pp. 37–46). See also Lipset and Smelser (1961).

it does not logically imply any single type of political belief system; (2) functionalism offers no safeguards for the exclusion of political value judgments either in the formation of hypotheses or in the results obtained; (3) where value considerations do not obtain in any form, the term "functionalism" is being employed tautologically, and not as a special research method; and (4) those who have maintained a functionalist orientation generally confuse a historical stratagem for a logical inference. If these four points are correct, then it follows that functionalism, by presenting sociology with the misanthropic enterprise of liquidating political considerations, has blunted the more viable and practically realizable task of studying the place of political beliefs in and for sociological theory and social research.[3]

The classic formulation of the idea that functionalism involves no basic political or ideological commitment is that offered by Merton (1957, p. 39):

> The fact that functional analysis can be seen by some as inherently conservative and by others as inherently radical suggests that it may be inherently neither one nor the other. It suggests that functional analysis may involve no intrinsic ideological commitment, although, like other forms of sociological analysis, it can be infused with any one of a wide range of ideological values.

This suggests that considerations of political ideology are extrinsic to functionalism. It should first be noted that political beliefs and ideological values are not the same. They are as distinct from each other as unconsciously held interest positions differ from consciously adopted value preferences. Thus, even if we grant the claim that functionalism is intrinsically free of ideological elements, it remains a distinct task to examine the extent to which pragmatic criteria of workability entail a series of value perspectives opening wide the floodgates of political commitment.

Even such a formulation grants too much. It is by no means self-evident that the liberation of functionalism from pragmatic assumptions of utility would solve the problem. Insistence on maintaining the strict dochotomization of fact and value, far from offering a satisfactory solution, has only made the functionalist less attentive to political considerations, in general, and the political perspective inherent in specific sociological work, in particular. Emphasis on the words *inherent* and *intrinsic* tends to obfuscate the facts of observation. Functionalists do indeed adopt political frameworks of a more or less explicit nature. Any inventory of sociology textbooks would make that much clear. The question of whether these commitments are intrinsic is thus quite aside from the observed situation. To assert a gulf between political commitment and ideological values is only to make the functionalist attachment to a set of political beliefs more palatable. As a matter of fact, it does not overcome the paradox of asserting, on the one hand, the need for a politically neutral sociology, and the fact

---

[3] For a recent effort to develop a sociological appreciation of values in and for the social scientist, see Edel (1955 and 1961).

of politically conditioned findings, on the other. However tenuous the evidence might be for functionalism as a special methodological adjunct of social research, there is even les evidence that can be adduced for it as an ideologically liberated approach (Cf. Horowitz, 1961, p. 116).

In this connection, it is intriguing to note that Merton himself has exhibited the greatest sort of anxiety over the "neutral" claims of functionalism. He sharply condemns those who would solve problems "by the abdication of moral responsibility" as, in fact, being "no solution at all." The posture of value neutrality "overlooks the crux of the problem: the initial formulation of the scientific investigation has been conditioned by the implied value of the scientist" (Merton, 1947, pp. 187–188). Merton's use of the "narcotizing dysfunction" concept is indeed a direct attempt to shake up the self-satisfied claims of classic functionalism. For it is clear that Merton's urgings not to "mistake *knowing* about problems of the day for *doing* something about them" is a use of dysfunction, not in terms of the social order as such, but in terms of a *democratic* social order (Merton and Lazarsfeld, 1957, p. 464). Given such impressive qualms, it is difficult to fathom the dogmatic insistence on the political neutrality of functionalism as such.

The idea that functionalism, at least in its Parsonian form as a theory of pattern maintenance, is not *intrinsically ideological* tends to avoid an encounter with the primary issue, which is that functionalism is *intrinsically political*. Whereas the emphasis thus far has been on the terms "intrinsic" and "extrinsic" the more realistic emphasis might better be placed on the terms "political" or "politically neutral." The substance of the matter is not whether functionalism evolves out of any single ideological context, but rather the forms in which it serves as a metasociology channelizing research along lines that are deemed compatible with any given political structure. Functionalist advocates speak of need satisfaction as something radically apart from want satisfaction. But in the process of social interaction needs, wants and desires are frequently defined by the same content.

Brotz (1962) has given substance to the problem of functional reduction by taking note of the fact that the level of human association shows differential elements not to be found in the physiological or biological sciences.

> In contrast to the world of human affairs, the heart does not have to plead to be allowed to perform its function, does not have to make a case that it is more important to health and life than other "dispensable" organs, does not have to defend itself by political *action* in the literal meaning of this term. The mechanisms of defense are such only metaphorically. The heart is not a political agent and as such makes no political claims. This is the obverse of the fact that the organs of the body are not ranged in political parties or interest groups with conflicting standards of health. They do their work, without raising the question of relative rights, or the organism as a whole perishes; and if it does they don't even care.

This indicates that even if the language of physiological functions is legitimate within the biological sciences, itself a dubious assertion, this would still not constitute proof for either the sociological relevance or political neutrality of functionalism. The evidence would indicate that functionalism is not only infused with political values but also intrinsically committed to position taking and policy making. What is open is the type of commitment, subject to the political and intellectual moorings of the individual investigator, but not the fact of commitment as such.

One of the difficulties with many criticisms of functionalism is that they have insisted that it leads to only one possible style of polity.[4] If this were, in fact, the case, the myth of functionalism would have been dispelled with the first shafts. The very absence of consensus as to the political implications entailed by functional analysis leads one to assume that the nature of these political commitments is variable, subject to the particular moorings of the investigator. This, however, does not signify the neutrality of the given *ism* known as functionalism.

In his famed work on *The Acquisitive Society,* Tawney (1921, pp. 96–104) has a chapter entitled "The Functional Society." In his view, if we accept the principle of functional requirement, we are led to ask what the purpose is of ground rents, royalties, interest on investments, profits and so forth. Clearly, to pose the problem in this teleological form is to go far in supplying an answer. In Tawney's opinion, capitalist economic relations are organized for the maintenance of *rights* rather than for the performance of socially worthwhile *duties*. Hence this economic order is nonfunctional. Tawney (1921, p. 101) goes on to present a straight functionalist accounting for the "polite ushering out of the State."

> The course of wisdom in the affairs of industry is, after all, what it is in any other department of organized life. It is to consider the end for which economic activity is carried on and then to adopt economic organization to it. It is to pay for service and for service only, and when capital is hired, to make sure that it is hired at the cheapest possible price.

What this involves for Tawney is the liquidation of all nonfuctional aggregates such as private property holdings beyond their actual use, profits extracted from industry that serve that cause of conspicuous consumption and, in general, ownership divorced from production. In short, to achieve a functional society would involve the mass of mankind in a gigantic social upheaval. Tawney's attitude toward functionalism is equivalent to his attitude toward the need for socialism. But whatever socialism is or is not, the desire for a radical overhauling of society is based on a set of political beliefs concerning the worth of an egalitarian economy. It is not in itself neutral in virtue of its being "a functional society."

In an equally familiar work, Alexis Carrel (1935, pp. 233–234) deals

---

[4] Cf. Kolb (1953), and from another perspective, Dahrendorf (1958).

with the "Adaptive Functions" not simply, or even primarily, to show how the chemistry of the human body works, but to evolve a system of "practical significance of adaptive functions," or, as it is put later in the book, "the remaking of man." Involved in this refurbishing process is a theory of the bodily adaptation to the external environment, such as mechanisms of compensation that bring a steady balance into play between biological and mental processes. "These movements of the functional systems express the apprehension by man of the outer reality. They act as a buffer for the material and psychological shocks which he unceasingly receives. They not only permit him to endure, but they also are the agents of his formation and of his progress" (Carrel, 1935, p. 233–234).

But Carrel wishes to carry his brand of adaptive functionalism far beyond the claims of homeostasis. The truly functional view involves a consideration of "natural health;" a knowledge of the "inner mechanisms" responsible for some men being naturally weak and others naturally strong. The entire view of functionalism is thus something that ultimately is said to entail the eugenic purification of the human race. All sorts of overtones emerge in this equation of the *Ubermensch,* biological elites and the cleansing force of genocide: All find a home in this functional view of society. The functionalism of Carrel (1935, pp. 314–315) does not prevent him from advocating an overhauling of civilization no less drastic than that implied by Tawney, although radically different in practical implications to be sure:

> We now have to reestablish, in the fullness of his personality, the human being weakened and standardized by modern life. Sexes have again to be clearly defined. Each individual should be either male or female, and never manifest the sexual tendencies, mental characteristics, and ambitions of the opposite sex. Instead of resembling a machine produced in series, man should, on the contrary, emphasize his uniqueness. In order to reconstruct personality, we must break the frame of the school, factory, and office and reject the very principles of technological civilization.

We do not have to carry further Carrel's design for a *Gemeinschaftliche fascismus* to see that functionalism, in this case, does absolutely nothing to prevent the manipulation of "scientific" information to specific political ends. Indeed, functionalism has meaning for Carrel precisely because it affords a scientific convention by means of which questions of politics can be discussed. Contrary to the claims of its adherents, functionalism has by no means represented to sociology what relativism has meant in the development of physics. A clearer parallel can be drawn between functionalism and the general tendency of modern sociology to place a premium on any heuristic device that held out the promise of being politically noncommital. But this only establishes functionalism as a species of *antipolitique.* It does not guarantee its status as either a method or system of sociology.

While Merton is discomforted by the "motley crew" claiming the functionalist mantle, he nonetheless draws astonishingly positive conclusions about the worth of functional theory for sociology. The very existence of a "motley crew" "suggests anew that agreement on the functional outlook need not imply identity of political or social philosophy" (Merton, 1957, p. 47). True enough, but since it *does,* as a matter of fact, imply *some type* of political commitment, where does that leave the widely repeated claim for the *neutrality* of functionalism? I submit that it entirely nullifies the claim.

It will be objected that the uses of functionalism to support either socialist or fascist claims are few in number and represent only eccentric applications of the doctrine. While this is quite so, the alternative uses of functionalism, while not as politically uncongenial, are nonetheless political in nature. The employment of functionalism by liberal and conservative ideologies constitutes a proof of the intrinsically political nature of the functionalist canons no less than its uses by extreme political doctrines. Indeed, in sociology and anthropology, the ideology of functionalism is in large measure connected with the fusion in the late nineteenth century of the liberal tradition in politics and the secularist tradition in scientific affairs.

We might select as antipodal poles of functionalist accounts, which yet reveal a shared regard to accept liberalism and scientism as the epitome of sound sociology, the work of Durkheim and Malinowski. It will be seen that however "hostile" the Durkheim circle and the followers of Malinowski are to each other, they have a basic ideological frame that derives from a common attitude toward the liberalist implications and meaning of functionalism.

In Durkheim's case, the notion of function as a general social need has its roots in the concept of social solidarity. But the conservative implications of this doctrine seen by later critics were not drawn by Durkheim himself (Cf. Coser, 1960, pp. 211–232). He saw social solidarity as developing in time. The function of social solidarity is to guarantee human fraternity, technological and scientific growth and economic progress. Beyond that, Durkheim (1933, p. 405) plainly looked forward to a universal commonwealth "where war will no longer be the law of international relations, where relations between societies will be pacifically regulated, as those between individuals already are, where all men will collaborate in the same work, and live the same life." Similar sentiments are expressed by Durkheim in nearly all of his major works. The functional society is one in which there is a progressive liberation of the individual from the tyrannies of custom and habit. This is a liberation that, given the social nature of man, must take place through the agencies of society, that is, through organic solidarity and collective thought. To be sure, Durkheim is to sociology what John Dewey is to modern philosophy, the prophet of liberalism through social involvement. "The kingdom of ends and impersonal truths can realize itself only by the cooperation of particular wills" (Durkheim, 1961, p. 494). As a perceptive commentator put matters, Durkheim, "was far from being a radical pessimist in respect to human nature or the condition of society. All his strictures against egotism, his phrases about the necessity of discipline, reveal the bourgeois citizen, the *Dreyfusard,* not the conservative authoritarian" (Richter, 1960, p. 202).

In Malinowski's case, it is even clearer that functionalism operated to enforce the liberal canons of an England caught in the counterclaims of imperialism, nationalism and world war. The functionalism of Malinowski bears a strong resemblance to the kinds of doctrine advocated in an earlier generation by John Stuart Mill and Lionel Hobhouse. Malinowski never failed to use his anthropological and ethnological findings to twit the English bourgeoisie—as if in this way a restoration of the liberal consciousness could be effected. Even Malinowski's emphasis on individual, psychological criteria, rather than upon social solidarity, seems best explicable in terms of his deep abiding faith in the sort of liberal canons of utility commonly associated with the British philosophic tradition. Certainly, there is no more a "functionalist imperative" for Malinowski's individualism than there is for Durkheim's socialism (Cf. Horowitz, 1962).

Malinoski established the "overall functionality" of primitive cultures on grounds quite like those employed by Mill to justify the claims of the minority conscience. In all of his work, Malinowski urges upon us a view of primitive man that takes into account the symbolic regulation of conflict through law and custom rather than through force and coercion. Further, he sees in all primitive groups an established system of mutual obligations involving the recognition that social consensus is integrated with self-interest in a form approximately like Adam Smith's self-regulating laissez faire economy. Other major functional attributes in all going societies are an established system of rewards and punishments judiciously meted out and, above all, a belief that in a functional society every man must count as one and equal, irrespective of racial inheritance, level of economic growth or types of local mores, customs or habits (Cf. Malinowski, 1926, pp. 20–21; 1948, pp. 50–71).

A deeper reading of Malinowski's more general writings only reinforces the impression that his functional imperatives are but liberal political imperatives, dressed up so as to be palatable to a scientific audience. His summary of functionalism contains statements urging an appreciation of the ongoing nature of culture, the dangers of ethnocentrism for both the man of civilization and the man of science, an urging of an evolutionary, progressive view of man (the essence of which is the progressive adaptation of institutions to their functions) and a judgment of the worth of social institutions based on what they do for any specific community and for the numbers of people they do things for (Malinowski, 1957, pp. 519–540). In brief, liberalism is built into the very method of social science that Malinowski was urging upon his colleagues.

The attempt to see Malinowski's use of functionalism as a pathological deviation from a truly scientific functionalism quite misses the point (Radcliffe-Brown, 1949). And the point is simply that all forms of functionalism thus far devised contain political imperatives. Malinowski's form of functionalism has received the widest sort of publicity, not because it is either superior or inferior to other varieties, but rather because of Malinowski's remarkable capacity to sum up the ambitions of the social science researcher to fuse, once and for all, the faith in science *and* liberalism.

The important aspect remains the constancy of political presuppositions in functionalist appraisals. It remains an essential task to uncover and stipulate the prescriptive elements in sociological research as such, and not seek a way out of the *problem* of cognitive status of sociological knowledge by the use of a rubric—by pious declarations of the neutrality of a method that in the main represented the extension of liberal politics to the social sciences. Either sociology recognizes the claims (legitimate and illegitimate) of political prescription upon its efforts or it runs the steady risk of being victimized by an inherited equation of *scientific* social analysis with *functionalist* analysis.

Perhaps the strongest demonstration that functionalist analysis, insofar as it signifies methodological properties other than those usually associated with scientific procedures, has firm political commitments is the earlier work of Kingsley Davis himself. We may here content ourselves with two representative chapters from *Human Society* (Davis, 1949). His analysis of the "Functional Theory of Religion" which is contrasted with "Outmoded Theories of Religion" bears out the apprehensions expressed in Davis' more recent position paper on functionalism. He moves from the necessity of social solidarity for the maintenance of society to the conclusion that only religion seems capable of fulfilling this functional requirement. "Among the societal requirements, the necessity of ideological and sentimental cohesion, or solidarity, is outstanding. One of the functions of religion is to justify, rationalize, and support the sentiments that give cohesion to the society" (Davis, 1949, p. 519).

Now it might be said that Davis is merely pointing out what religion does, without prescribing as to its worth, that is, without making any value judgments. However, in his elaboration upon this functional role of religion, it seems that "religion makes a unique and indispensable contribution to social integration" (Davis, 1949, p. 519). Nowhere in the text does Davis test this proposition of the *unique* functionality of religion, or suggest criteria of measurement, or stipulate conditions for its proof or disproof. Davis does not, as a matter of fact, show what a society cannot live without religion and yet maintain itself intact. Nor does he show that there are any properties that can be designated as uniquely religious. Each of his criteria, from the supposition of supernaturalism, common sentiments and the furnishing of sacred objects to the ultimate source of rewards and punishments, can be readily fulfilled by secular institutions, and indeed is increasingly being so fulfilled by nonchurch institutions. The industrialization process has often exhibited a parallel process of secularization of formerly sacred institutions. To call this "functional compensation" or "dysfunctional" is simply a clumsy admission that a religion is not necessarily functional in the sense of social utility.

Furthermore, it is dubious whether religions the world over entail the sort of commitments to supernaturalism and utilitarianism that Davis says makes a religion functional to begin with. One would have to place a highly restrictive geographical boundary on the meaning of religion to make any sense out of any ethnocentric theory of religion. Thus, rather than show religion to be either indispensable or unique, Davis has only shown that, given the extreme application of functional canons to problems of social solidarity, certain conservative inferences can be axiomatically implied.

Directly conservative political judgments are involved in Davis' functionalist vision of social stratification. Indeed, not since William Sumner's (1934, p. 95) equation of liberty, inequality and the survival of the fittest has a sociologist spoken so decisively in favor of the functional *necessity* of inequality. Sumner's justification of conservatism was made in the name of evolutionism. His position is meritorious in that there is no pretense as to the political neutrality of this brand of sociology. Davis' functionalist account of stratification systems is said to be apart from any such extraneous judgments. Yet it is difficult to fathom how Davis can offer an explanation of social stratification in terms of the "functional necessity of stratification" and then recoil in amazement that this is to be sure a cornerstone of conservative theories of natural law, and not a scientific explanation. Davis' functional necessity turns out to be a defense of the universal necessity of social inequality (See also Davis and Moore, 1945):

> If the rights and prerequisites of different positions in a society must be unequal, then the society must be stratified, because that is precisely what stratification means. Social inequality is thus an unconsciously evolved device by which societies insure that the most important positions are conscientiously filled by the most qualified persons. Hence every society, no matter how simple or complex, must differentiate persons in terms of both prestige and esteem and must therefore possess a certain amount of institutionalized inequality. (Davis, 1949, pp. 367–368)

If Davis desires to speak in defense of Platonic political verities, he certainly has the right (and even necessity) to do so. However, what is not his prerogative is to assert that there is a scientific and sociological mandate for this way of speaking. For it is no more clear that functionalism supplies a mandate to Davis' competitive society than it does for Tawney's cooperative society. The function of social stratification as defined by Davis cannot be empirically studied unless what is understood by "inequality," "stratification," "unconscious devices," "qualified persons" and so forth is made explicit. If no restrictions are placed on these terms, the question of whether a system of social stratification is a "must" is not a factual one, to be decided by empirical examination, but a logical question to be decided by fiat. This is so because Davis' idea that every society necessarily possesses patterns of invariant social relations is taken to be an axiom of the system to be explained. Davis' "functional imperatives" are, like Malinowski's "indispensable ingredients," based upon teleological considerations rather than upon causal explanations. As Nagel (1961, pp. 520–535) indicated, such imagined functional requirements rest on a non sequitur, on "transfer without warrant of the admitted indispensability of *tradition,* to a particular means or instrument that happens to be employed in certain societies for sustaining tradition." In Davis' case, this amounts to a *support* of inequality in the name of functional explanation.

As a matter of fact, and as if to prove the ancient adage that two can play the same game, Tumin (1953) as offered a powerful catalogue of "negative functionality" of stratification systems of the sort advanced by Davis. While the word "function" is retained and repeatedly used, Tumin quite properly offers his counterhypotheses as subject to further empirical study. In Tumin's view, stratification: (1) limits the discovery or use of the full talent of a society; (2) sets arbitrary limits upon the expansion of the productive forces of society; (3) provides the elite with the political power necessary to secure its dominance; (4) distributes favorable self-images unequally throughout a population; (5) encourages hostility, suspicion and mistrust among the various sectors of society; (6) distributes the sense of prestige and status unequally; and (7) distributes loyalty unequally in the population, that is, distributes motivation unequally by making some apathetic and others energetic about their life chances.

The crux of the matter is not simply that functionalism does nothing to prevent the penetration of the sharpest sort of political opposition within its domain, but that this is so for reasons beyond the control of the functionalist method. Sharp differences arise because social systems are in continual interaction with political systems. It is only natural, therefore, to expect sociology to be deeply concerned with questions of political party—either in a manifest form or in a latent form. What has thrown too many sociologists off stride is the equation of neutrality with objectivity. Functionalism presents itself in the linguistic garb of such neutrality, holding out the hope for some sort of methodological superimperative that could once and for all demarcate factual and valuative questions. What has, in fact, occurred is the multiplication of terminology obfuscating rather than explaining basic political loyalties and ambitions. Can it seriously be doubted that Tumin's loyalties are to a social radicalism first and to assumed functional imperatives second to the degree that they support this radicalism? Can it seriously be doubted that Davis' loyalties are to a social conservatism first, with the functional imperatives as such useful to the extent that they provide support for this conservatism? The contrary uses of functionalism are logical contradictions, and hence no proof of the value of functionalism unless, that is, one is willing to brave the logical paradox of assigning scientific importance to tautological statements.

The assumption of political neutrality has too often resulted in an un-reflecting insipidity. The further assumption of a *wertfrei* methodology called functionalism has not had the intended consequences, namely, the reduction (if not the elimination) of political judgments in sociological analysis. The plain fact is that functionalism has neither altered nor modified the basic political commitments of sociologists *qua* sociologists. If from this fact it be deduced that functionalism is free of political implications, then it still must be explained why certain sociologists employ functionalism for very definite political ends. Until a better explanation is provided, we must conclude that functionalism is a strategy (and at times even a posture) that enables the sociologist to make political statements without the necessity of defending these statements in the court of public opinion.

Instead of following through on Weber's clear mandate to distinguish between taking a practical political stand on one side and examining political structures sociologically on the other, the functionalist device has increas-ingly tended to muddy the waters by equating political noncommitment with scientific wisdom. In this connection, Weber's (1946, p. 127) precise formulation should be recalled: "To take a practical stand is one thing, and to analyze political structures and party positions is another. When speaking in a political meeting about democracy, one does not hide one's personal standpoint; indeed, to come out clearly and to take a stand is one's damned duty."

How many sociologists have performed their "damned duty" in this way? Indeed, the myth of functionalism has promoted a concept of the social researcher as a purveyor of puerile information for sale to the highest bidder, while the purveyor himself is said to be protected from the market-place by his magisterial methodology. In place of "here I stand; I can do no other," the functionalist seems to have adopted as his pivotal slogan: "The world is stupid and base, not I" (Weber, 1946, p. 127). Expertise has been improperly preempted as a private possession of the functionalism —a possession that conveniently does away with the need for *either* analy-sis of *or* commitment to any political position. The *antipolitique* of most varieties of functionalism has not led to better sociology, but to puerile sociology. This is not a question of equating the secular with the puerile, for puerility can take many forms, scientific as well as theological. To con-vert a vice into a virtue by an intellectual sleight of hand, by assuming that sociology has "fully matured" because it is now as dismal a science as economic theory is reputed to be, is to shortchange the adventure of science no less than to muddle the tasks of present-day sociology—which I take to include an examination of the conditions under which a society does not work as well as the conditions under which it does. Further, it is to perilously ignore Weber's (1946, p. 153) dictum that "no science is absolutely free from presuppositions, and no science can prove its fundamental value to the man who rejects these presuppositions."

The very completeness with which historical strategy has been accepted as a methodological first principle serves to show how thoroughly functionalism and liberalist politics have been intermeshed in the first half of this century. This does not, however, constitute a scientific proof for the language of functionalism. From a scientific viewpoint the question is not whether functionalism is intrinsically any one kind of political ideology but to what extent it can be distinguished from political ideology as such. A rich tapestry of practical and ultimate political considerations is connected with the generic concept of function. Moreover, since the line between sociology and politics is hardly an impassable barrier, the central issue is not how "liberated" functionalism is of political concerns, but rather the exact line of intersection between functionalism as a political ideology in its own right and functionalism as a rationalization and justification for more conventional division in the political spectrum.

Far from bringing about so euphoric a status as an "end to ideology" in sociology, or a "secularization" of the discipline, or any other gratuitous forms of self-praise, functionalism has only shifted the locus of the ideological dialogue. So clearly is this the case that rather pronounced political differences have come to the foreground in recent discussions of functional sociology. Insofar as functionalism is a political *ism,* it suffers the factional fate of other systems of social analysis that preceded it, such as evolutionism, Marxism, organicism and historicism. To consider ideology as "an irretrievably fallen word" when it continues to inform the writings of even those who speak of its "exhaustion" only serves to show how pernicious the mechanisms of psychic and social self-deception are.[5]

From an analytical as well as from a historical point of view, functionalism has not prevented sociologists from splitting up into competing political camps, not even among those who claim functional doctrine as a protective covering. In large measure, this has been due to its inability to settle the question of the relationship of political beliefs to sociological inquiry—the main question it set for itself since the writings of Spencer. Even if we grant the ability of functionalism to establish its neutrality *vis à vis* radicalism and conservatism, it must still come to terms with a world that is neither black nor white, neither fish nor fowl, but a thousand shades of gray. Only by assuming a bipolarized world of political positions, and by a hidden assumption that liberalism is not a political ideology, has functionalism been able to present itself as a bearer of neutral scientific truths. What happens if such a bipolarization is not assumed is the decomposition of the functionalist canons as some special code by means of which the world of political reality can be safely ignored.

[5] Cf. Bell (1961, pp. 400–401). See also Lipset (1960, pp. 403–417).

REFERENCES

Bell, D. (1961) *The End of Ideology: On the Exhaustion of Political Ideas in the Fifties.* New York: Macmillan (Collier Books).

Berger, B. M. (1961) "Sociology and the Intellectuals: An Analysis of a Stereotype," in S. M. Lipset and N. Smelser, eds., *Sociology, the Progress of a Decade.* Englewood Cliffs, N.J.: Prentice-Hall.

Braithwaite, R. B. (1953) *Scientific Explanation: A Study of the Function of Theory, Probality and Law in Science.* Cambridge: Cambridge University Press.

Brotz, H. (1962) "Functionalism and Conflict Analysis," in I. L. Horowitz, ed., *Conference on Conflict, Consensus and Cooperation.* Geneva: Hobart and William Smith Colleges.

Carrel, A. (1935) "Adaptive Functions," in his *Man, the Unknown.* New York: Harper & Row.

Coser, L. A. (1960) "Durkheim's Conservatism and its Implications for his Sociological Theory," in K. H. Wolff, ed., *Emile Durkheim, 1858–1971.* Columbus: Ohio State University Press.

Dahrendorf, R. (1958) "Out of Utopia: Toward a Reorientation of Sociological Analysis," *American Journal of Sociology,* vol. 64, no. 2 (September), pp. 115–127.

Davis, K. (1949) *Human Society.* New York: Macmillan.

Davis, K. (1959) "The Myth of Functional Analysis as a Special Method in Sociology and Anthropology," *American Sociological Review,* vol. 24 (December), pp. 757–772.

Davis, K., and W. E. Moore (1945) "Some Principles of Stratification," *American Sociological Review,* vol. 10, no. 2 (April), pp. 242–249.

Durkheim, E. (1933) *The Division of Labor in Society,* trans. G. Simpson. New York: Macmillan.

Durkheim, E. (1961) *The Elementary Forms of the Religious Life,* trans. J. W. Swain. New York: Macmillan (Collier Books).

Edel, A. (1955) *Ethical Judgment: The Use of Science in Ethics.* New York: Free Press.

Edel, A. (1961) *Science and the Structure of Ethics.* Chicago: University of Chicago Press.

Hempel, C. G. (1959) "The Logic of Functional Analysis," in L. Gross, ed., *Symposium on Sociological Theory.* New York: Harper & Row.

Horowitz, I. L. (1961) *Philosophy, Science and the Sociology of Knowledge.* Springfield, Ill.: C. C Thomas.

Horowitz, I. L. (1962) "Crime, Custom and Culture: Remarks on the Functionalist Theory of Malinowski," *International Journal of Comparative Sociology,* vol. 3, no. 2 (December), pp. 229–245.

Kolb, W. L. (1953) "Values, Positivism and the Functional Theory of Religion," *Social Forces,* vol. 31, no. 4 (May), pp. 305–311.

Lipset, S. M. (1960) *Political Man: The Social Bases of Politics.* New York: Doubleday.

Lipset, S. M., and N. Smelser (1961) "Change and Controversy in Recent American Sociology," *British Journal of Sociology,* vol. 12, no. 1 (March), pp. 41–51.

Malinowski, B. (1926) *Crime and Custom in Savage Society.* London: Routledge & Kegan Paul.

Malinowski, B. (1948) *Magic, Science and Religion and Other Essays.* New York: Free Press.

Malinowski, B. (1957) "Functionalism in Anthropology," in L. A. Coser and B. Rosenberg, eds., *Sociological Theory: A Book of Readings.* New York: Macmillan.

Mannheim, K. (1936) *Ideology and Utopia.* New York: Harcourt Brace Jovanovich.

Marx, K., and F. Engels (1939) *The German Ideology,* pts. 1, 3. New York: International Publishers.

Merton, R. K. (1947) *Mass Persuasion.* New York: Harper & Row.

Merton, R. K. (1957) *Social Theory and Social Structure.* New York: Free Press.

Merton, R. K., and P. Lazarsfeld (1957) "Mass Communication, Popular Taste and Organized Social Action," in B. Rosenberg and D. M. White, eds., *Mass Culture: The Popular Arts in America.* New York: Free Press.

Nagel, E. (1957) *Logic without Metaphysics, and Other Studies in the Philosophy of Science.* New York: Free Press.

Nagel, E. (1961) *The Structure of Science: Problems in the Logic of Scientific Explanation.* New York: Harcourt Brace Jovanovich.

Radcliffe-Brown, A. R. (1949) "Functionalism: A Protest," *American Anthropologist,* vol. 51, no. 2 (April-June), pp. 320–322.

Richter, M. (1960) "Durkheim's Politics and Political Theory," in K. H. Wolff, ed., *Emile Durkheim, 1858–1917.* Columbus: Ohio State University Press.

Schumpeter, J. (1951) "Science and Ideology," in R. V. Clemence, ed., *Essays of Joseph Schumpeter.* Reading, Mass.: Addison-Wesley.

Spencer, H. (1873) *The Study of Sociology.* New York: Appleton-Century-Crofts.

Sumner, W. G. (1934) "The Challenge of Facts," in A. G. Keller and M. R. Davie, eds., *Essays of William Graham Sumner,* vol. 2. New Haven: Yale University Press.

Tawney, R. H. (1921) *The Acquisitive Society.* London: Bell.

Tumin, M. W. (1953) "Some Principles of Stratification: A Critical Analysis," *American Sociological Review,* vol. 18, no. 4 (August), pp. 387–393.

Weber, M. (1946) *From Max Weber,* H. H. Gerth and C. W. Mills, eds. New York: Oxford University Press.

CHAPTER 26

SOCIAL ALIENATION AND POLITICAL SYSTEMS

ALIENATION IN HISTORY

Despite the incredible degree of confusion that exists about the term *alienation*—a confusion that has caused many influentials in sociology and psychology to try to do without it (e.g., Berelson and Steiner, 1964; Asch, 1952; Merton et al., 1959) there is a danger in a premature scrapping of the term. There are few enough words in the vocabulary of social science having wide generic implications. In some sense, the very confusions about the word *alienation* represent an acute, albeit painful, testimonial to a conceptual complication that exists in consequence of the autonomous development of the social and behavioral sciences. The heavy freight placed on such words as *anomie, aggression, intuition, instinct* and now *alienation* is a burden better met by clarifying the meaning of the term than by urging premature abandonment either on the grounds that any word admitting of multiple different definitions is meaningless, or because of the equally spurious aim of preserving formal symmetry.

The problem with the use of *alienation,* like so many other theoretical issues, is its debt to the philosophical ambiguities of nineteenth-century German realism. Nascent within German philosophical sources were the current schisms and polarization of meanings in this word.

Hegel argued that the true meaning of alienation lay in the separation of the object of cognition from the man of consciousness, the philosopher. Hence, for Hegel the chief way of overcoming alienation is through philosophical understanding, an embrace of the rational world; as if to know the world is somehow to be at one with that world, to become identified with it. To be reasonable is for Hegel the same as being at peace. It was in this problem that the equation of reality with rationality was the resolution of the problem of philosophical alienation; just as the reduction of reason to reasonableness was the resolution of the problem of practical alienation.

In the philosophy of Ludwig Feuerbach, alienation comes to be seen as an anthropological problem. The word *anthropology* was being used as a surrogate for *psychology,* since Feuerbach neither knew of nor really appreciated anthropology in any exact, empirical sense. Feuerbach considered the problem of alienation as a separation out, a parceling out, of human consciousness—one part of man is invested (properly) in the material world, and another to the world of God, the projective ideal world. In effect, the dualism in Feuerbach is almost Platonic. The material world's being dreary and dismal gives rise to a set of projections about a spiritual world of perfection. As long as these two worlds remain separated, there cannot be any resolution of the problem of alienation.

It is a disservice to consider Marx's notion of alienation within a strictly philosophical framework, since Marx insisted upon the necessity of a social scientific resolution of what had up to then been viewed as a metaphysical or humanist dilemma. It was Marx himself who made the clear and decisive break with the philosophical tradition of explaining alienation. No longer was alienation a property of man or of reason; it became a specific property of select classes of men in factory conditions, who were, as a result of these conditions, deprived of its empty universal application; the labor context of alienation itself served as a scientific break with romanticism—a rupture consecrated in the bedrock of political revolution from below.

The word *alienation* implies an intense separation—from objects in a world; from other people; and from ideas about the world held by other people. It might be said that the synonym of alienation is *separation,* while the precise antonym of the word is *integration.* The main difficulty with the philosophical traditions is the assumption that those who are defined as alienated are somehow lacking and that they ought to be integrated. In both Hegel and Feuerbach, therapeutic values are assigned to alienation and to integration, to the distinct disadvantage of the former and to the advantage of the latter. That is how we come to the phrasing of the term *alienated from* as somehow opposite to *integrated with.* This mystic faith in organic union invariably found its way into the work of Hegel and Feuerbach, the mystic organic union being for Hegel *man as idea,* and for Feuerbach *idea as man*. But to the same degree that alienation was seen as a negative concept, the philosophical approach was considered abstract and unreliable in terms of psychological and sociological facts.

The really important break, therefore, which began with Marx, is that in the modern usage of the concept of alienation, there is a distinctive concern for distinguishing therapy from description, and for separating recommendations from actions.

A recent writer, Istvan Meszaros (1970, pp. 63–64) has put the matter bluntly, but accurately.

> The central feature of Marx's theory of alienation is the assertion of the historically necessary supersession of capitalism by socialism freed from all the abstract moral postulates which we can find in the writings of his immediate predecessors. The ground of his assertion was not simply the recognition of the unbearable dehumanizing effects of alienation—though of course subjectively that played a very important part in the formation of Marx's thought—but the profound understanding of the objective ontological foundations of the processes that remained veiled from his predecessors. . . . Thus the historical novelty of Marx's theory of alienation in relation to the conceptions of his predecessors can be summed up in a preliminary way as follows: (1) the terms of reference of his theory are note the categories of *Sollen* (ought), but those of *necessity* (is) inherent in the objective ontological foundations of human life; (2) its point of view is not that of some *utopian partiality* but the *universality* of the critically adopted standpoint of labor; (3) its framework of criticism is not some abstract (Hegelian) speculative totality, but the concrete totality of dynamically developing society perceived from the material basis of the proletariat as a necessarily self-transcending (universal) historical force.

If the language and mode of expression in the Marxian theory of alienation is strained and even archaic, its substance is quite clear and meaningful. There is in the dialectical approach a common belief that alienation, while ontologically and logically no better and no worse than integration (with either doctrine serving positive or destructive ends), in the actual affairs of men alienation provides a basic fuel for social change and political liberation. Alienation is a driveshaft of revolution; and integration is a transitional equilibrium generating new forms of separation from the mainstream—that is, new forms of alienation.

CATEGORIES OF ALIENATION

Let us now examine three fundamental categories of the concept "alienation." First, consider the psychological meanings of alienation. Perhaps the classic definition is that given by Fromm (1955, pp. 120–121): "By alienation is meant a mode of experience in which the person experiences himself as alien. He has become, one might say, estranged from himself." It is important to take note of the fact that Fromm severely modifies the Marxian concept. He gives a definition that converts a "mode of production" into a "mode of experience," while the Marxian proletarian laborer is neatly converted back into the Hegelian abstract person. It is evident in the work of Fromm that he is not concerned with just providing a psychological approach to alienation but also with giving renewed vigor to the older German romantic categorizations.

Alienation is often used as a psychological surrogate in the literature. Instead of being employed as a phenomenon of separation, it is used as a phenomenon of negation, or even of "lessness"—a suffix prefaced by "power-lessness," "norm-lessness," or "meaning-lessness." In this kind of approach, alienation either becomes part of a major body of literature on anomie, or in turn swallows up anomie. The difficulty is that this definition of alienation as negation does not connect up various forms of negation. Further, alienation as anomie tends to describe the social system in terms of an assumed rationality: that which has the power, norms, and meanings, in contrast to the personality system or that which is not a condition of rationality (Seeman, 1964).

At its most elevated form, the psychological definition of alienation is linked to ideology. This, in turn, is fused with the way intellectuals view their roles in a social world. "A great deal of contemporary thought finds a state of alienation precisely in those ideologies that profess to predict with high confidence the outcome of people's behavior. Intellectuals especially find themselves alienated in a world of social determinism; they wish for a world in which the degree of social predictability would be low." In Feuer's (1963) conception, alienation turns out to be much more positive in its potential effects than in almost any other theory. With Feuer, it is almost as if one has to overcome integration, rather than alienation, to arrive at scientific truth. Integration is held to yield precisely the kind of normlessness which is characteristic of an identification with rootlessness and machine-like behavior in general. Feuer thus offers a prototype of what in the literary tradition of Zamyatin, Huxley, and Orwell is the alienated man as an antiutopian—a social realist.

The main contribution of the psychological school of alienation has been to demonstrate the universality of the concept, its connection to the personality structure as well as the social structure, and therefore its existence in socialist societies no less than in capitalist societies (Schaff, 1963). The psychological school holds that the foundation, the reservoir of non-participation in the social system (or even refusal to participate in that system), may be constructive as well as destructive. In this sense, alienation is more akin to deviance than it is to disorganization. It is not a synonym for neurosis or psychosis so much as it is a notion of marginality, which is consciously or unconsciously held. The problem of alienation stems more from a lack of accurate perception of the norms than an active defiance of these norms.

The sociological tradition is perhaps a consequence of this distinction between psychic disorganization and social disorganization. A whole new set of variables is called into force. In this, Marx himself set the tone, since alienation was viewed as the particular response of the workingman to the externality of the product he produced. It was, in effect, a class phenomenon.

> What then, constitutes the alienation of labor? First, the fact that labor is *external* to the worker, *i.e.,* it does not belong to his essential being; that in his work therefore, he does not affirm himself but denies himself, does not feel content but unhappy, does not develop freely his physical and mental energy but mortifies his body and ruins his mind. The worker therefore only feels himself outside his work, and in his work feels outside himself. He is at home when he is not working, and when he is working he is not at home. His labor is therefore not voluntary, but coerced; it is *forced labor.* It is therefore not the satisfaction of a need; it is merely a *means* to satisfy needs external to it. Its alien character emerges clearly in the fact that as soon as no physical or other compulsion exists, labor is shunned like the plague. External labor, labor in which man alienates himself, is labor of self-sacrifice, of mortification. The external character of labor for the worker appears in the fact that it is not his own, but someone else's, that it does not belong to him, that in it he belongs, not to himself, but to another. Just as in religion the spontaneous activity of the human imagination, of the human brain and the human heart, operates independently of the individual—that is, operates on him as an alien, divine or diabolical activity—in the same way the worker's activity is not his spontaneous activity. It belongs to another. It is the loss of his self. (Marx, 1959, pp. 67–84)

Once Marx opened this Pandora's box of the social and cross-cultural locale of alienation, it was just a matter of time before others would see alienation of different social sectors from those Marx had dealt with. Thus, for example, in a modern view of bourgeois society, that held by C. Wright Mills, alienation comes to be understood as a lower middle-class phenomenon, something that debases salesgirls, technicians, and even intellectuals in a similar way. In this Mills (1951, pp. 182–188) provided not only a bridge from one class to another, but even more importantly, a way of viewing alienation as a problem for all nonruling classes, not only the factory-anchored urban proletariat. "In the normal course of her work, because her personality becomes the instrument of an alien purpose, the salesgirl becomes self-alienated. Men are estranged from one another as each secretly tries to make an instrument of the other, and in time a full circle is made: One makes an instrument of himself and is estranged from it also" (Mills, 1951, p. 220).

Most recently we have had the example of alienation as a specific artistic problem, as a problem connected to the marketing of ideas rather than the production of goods. In this sense, alienation is seen to have different functional prerequisites. Moravia (1965–66) has clearly differentiated the alienation of the worker from the alienation of the artist. He offers a clearly defined expression of qualitatively different notions of alienation that are involved in different social sectors. In this approach, there is an attempt to link alienation to specific types of work done, which leads to a fragmentation of the notion of alienation rather than fragmentation of the notion of stratification.

The standard sociological perspective is to see alienation as a phenomenon of a unitary type, with differences being attributed to the stratifiction system. In Moravia, quite to the contrary, we have the unique case of a stratification system giving rise to different forms of alienation. In this we have a more advanced sociological notion of alienation than any thus far given:

> There is no relationship between the alienation of the worker and the alienation of the artist. The worker is alienated because, in the economy of the market, he is a piece of goods like any other and as such he is defrauded of his surplus value, or of what represents his value as a man, whereas the artist creates an object that has no market (or, if it has, it is not that of necessities that always have a market) and no real price in money or kind. The artist receives the price of his work of art in creating it. In other words, when he hands his book over to the publisher, his music to the conductor, or his painting to the art dealer, the artist has already been paid and whatever he receives after that is a bonus. Hence the alienation of the artist consists of the total or partial prevention of his expression, or of his true relationship with society. (Moravia, 1965, p. 66)

The third general variety of alienation theory is based on considering it as part of a general cultural milieu. Within this framework, we find ideology spoken of in national terms, that is, the American ideology, the Soviet ideology, and so forth; whereas Marx, in dealing with the German ideology, dealt with that ideology as if it was a reflection of the ruling class diffused throughout the general society of the times. The newer pluralistic approach emphasizes the mass culture. Boorstin (1961, pp. 3–6) offers a particularly interesting variety of this approach.

> We expect anything and everything. We expect the contradicting and the impossible. We expect compact cars which are spacious; luxurious cars which are economical. We expect to be rich and charitable, powerful and merciful, active and reflective, kind and competitive. We expect to be inspired by mediocre appeals for "excellence," to be made literate by illiterate appeals for literacy. We expect to eat and stay thin, to be constantly on the move and ever more neighborly, to go to a "church of our choice" and yet feel its guiding power over us, to revere God and to be God. Never have a people felt more deceived and disappointed. For never have a people expected so much more than the world could offer.

The culturalist approach is no less critical of alienation as a status than any of the other approaches. Even from the quotation just read, one can see their criticism is severe. What is new and particularly interesting is the assumption of the "national character" from which the concept of alienation flows. The mass cultural school at its peak, with men like Dwight Macdonald and David Riesman (1964) represents an interesting fusion of the psychological and sociological approaches. Alienation comes to be seen as a discrepancy, a measurable discrepancy, between achievements and expectations. At the general sociocultural level, it is a discrepancy between national demands or national purposes and individual demands for an extension of autonomy and pluralism.

One final expression of this cultural style is the tradition of alienation as a religious phenomenon, specifically, alienation as characteristic of marginal religious groupings. This view of alienation, held by men like Karl Barth, Paul Tillich and Martin Buber, has strong ties to Feuerbach. Commentary on the current status of Jews in America is illustrative. As Isaac Rosenfeld once said, "Jews are specialists in alienation." They are alienated from a Diaspora, alienated from a redemptive God, and alienated from nationalism as such (Malin, 1964; for an earlier consideration, see Dubnow, 1961). Of course, alienation as an authentic religious expression has become a major theme for all Western religions.

This view of alienation as marginal has a great deal in common with the sociological view. One can begin to detect a synthesis taking place in present-day expectations of alienation: a systematic linkage of psychological states, sociological classes, and cultural forms.

There is a fourth and final rendering of the alienation concept that, while less in current vogue, has interesting possibilities, since it combines the intensely personal definitions of the term with larger macroscopic political interests. Alienation as a political notion is related to the enlargement or diminuation of participation in the *polis*.

Widespread alienation is reflected in the social and political life of a group by their estrangement from national goals or cultural symbols resulting from the absence of participatory procedures which can make them feel responsible or connected to important national policies. In this sense, alienation is part of the ancient Greek, no less than romantic Germanic, tradition. Perhaps the distance is not quite as great as might first appear; since both traditions assume the total submission of masses to leaders and symbols, or to whatever lies outside the self.

The less historicist and more empirical orientation simply assumes that alienation represents the breakdown of older social structures, accompanied by the inefficient crystallization of new patterns which cause ambivalence, confusion and widespread defeat and withdrawal. The collectivity of these new patterns is then labeled alienation. The political view of alienation generally points to the individualist trends in history—the resultant strains and burdens placed upon a human group half emerged from tribalism and the tutelary system, or the security of a fixed class hierarchy protected by divine law.

Alienation exists then in an individualized environment. It emerges from political or personal failure to resolve the tension imposed by the ideal of autonomy. Thus, a new meaningful identity is linked to responsible self-management, the privacy of men, and the autonomy of nations. As a result, overcoming alienation in its political context signifies a libertarian polity protected by a rational government in which men will have the capacity of at least participating in molding and directing their political contexts. Alienation penetrates social thought when individualistic values permeate the political culture—a culture in which the idealization of the free individual in a free nation, and where the practical conditions for such relations are frustrated by a political agency that depends on quiescent formation of a population and in removing from the citizen responsibility for the management of his own life and the rights of political participation. Thus, alienation is intensified when individual freedom comes to be first idealized and then frustrated. And, of course, the corollary held to be true in alienation is removed when individual freedom is realized within the national polity.

The location of the problem has now decisively shifted. The problem is no longer a fusion of psychological or sociological cultural techniques. The study of alienation is now confronted with a distinction between two modalities of analyses, one formal and the other descriptive. The formal system tends to emphasize the root categories, such as those provided by Seeman in his work, or operationalized definitions capable of survey designs, such as those provided by Nettler (1957, 1945). Descriptive analysis tends to emphasize the weaknesses in the psychological approach by pointing out that the formal modes of analysis are invariably ad hoc. They provide little indication, however, of how the types of alienation or the models built are related to each other or why they should be restricted to three, four or five in number. Descriptive approaches tend to see alienation in a problem-solving context. They have a big problem in settling upon the relation of alienation to deviance, marginality, creativity, and so forth. But they do have the value of being linked to empirical, rather than logical modalities (Scott, 1964).

It might well be that this is simply a social scientific reflex of the ongoing debate concerning the analytical and synthetic modes of argument. Whatever the case may be, it is clear that the literature on alienation has tapped into something extremely meaningful in the emergence of modern social science. Once the various meanings and levels at which the term *alienation* is employed can be properly understood, then social scientists will be better able to employ alienation as a central variable in discussing other features of social structure and process. The task of philosophy in this area might be a clarifying one, to show how various usages of alienation are either synonymous, overlapping or entirely different from one another.

The philosopher might develop some kind of logical or periodic table of alienation. This is what a modern philosophy of science is all about.

REFERENCES

Asch, S. E. (1952) *Social Psychology*. Englewood Cliffs, N.J.: Prentice-Hall.

Berelson, B., and G. A. Steiner, eds. (1964) *Human Behavior: An Inventory of Scientific Findings*. New York: Harcourt Brace Jovanovich.

Boorstin, D. (1961) *The Image*. New York: Atheneum.

Dubnow, S. (1961) *Nationalism and History*. New York: World, Meridian Books.

Feuer, L. (1963) "What is Alienation? The Career of a Concept," in M. Stein and A. Vidich, eds., *Sociology on Trial*. Englewood Cliffs, N.J.: Prentice-Hall.

Fromm, E. (1955) *The Sane Society*. New York: Holt, Rinehart & Winston.

Malin, I. (1965) *Jews and Americans*. Carbondale, Ill.: Southern Illinois University Press.

Marx, K. (1959) *Economic and Philosophical Manuscripts of 1844*. London: Lawrence & Wishart.

Merton, R. K., et al., eds. (1959) *Sociology Today: Problems and Prospects*. New York: Basic Books.

Meszaros, I. (1970) *Marx's Theory of Alienation*. London: Merlin Press.

Mills, C. W. (1951) *White Collar*. New York: Oxford University Press.

Moravia, A. (1965) *Man as an End*. New York: Farrar, Straus & Giroux.

Nettler, G. (1945) "A Test for the Sociology of Knowledge," *American Sociological Review*, vol. 10, no. 3 (June), pp. 393–399.

Nettler, G. (1957) "A Measure of Alienation," *American Sociological Review*, vol. 22 (October), pp. 670–677.

Riesman, D. (1964) *Abundance for What?* Garden City, N.Y.: Doubleday.

Schaff, A. (1963) *Philosophy of Man*. New York: Monthly Review Press.

Scott, M. B. (1964) "The Social Sources of Alienation," in I. L. Horowitz, ed., *The New Sociology*. New York: Oxford University Press.

Seeman, M. (1964) "On the Meaning of Alienation," in L. A. Coser and B. Rosenberg, eds., *Sociological Theory*, 2nd ed. New York: Macmillan.

CHAPTER 27

POLITICAL MARGINALITY AND SOCIAL CLASS IN HISTORICAL PERSPECTIVE

VICTORS AND VANQUISHED IN HISTORY

One problem in studying political life from a longitudinal perspective is that historians, like most other people, tend to ride momentary winners. Their focus of interest is on the victorious; and in the strictest accord with Machiavellianism, it is assumed that victory is to virtue what defeat is to vice. The losers, as part of the secondary tradition, tend to be swallowed up into some tragic footnote to the primary traditions. It may very well be that there is such a thing as a primary tradition of overriding influence. However, it has always seemed more likely to me that a Frenchman of the early nineteenth century lived within the traditions of his own country. For him, it was not a Germanic century simply because Dilthey or Rickert declared the latter to be the case, but just another day in the life of a French village.

There should be historical writing from the point of view of political losers no less than political winners. That may sound odd, but from the truly interactionist viewpoint it is no more odd than writing up events from the point of view of winners. Indeed to do the latter is to reduce political events to the swing and sway of dynasties—secular as well as clerical. Why should one have to write the history of the Russian Revolution from the point of view of Stalin—why not Trotsky? Why write about the French Revolution from the point of view of the revolutionists instead of the monarchists? From an interactionist point of view, the easy answer is—why not write it from both? Why not account for all the pivotal elements in any major sociodrama? The answer is that biases are strong and powerful phenomena. There is an apparent need to make choices when one writes history. For example, if one were completely thoroughgoing about describing political events, history might be written from the point of view of the exile, of the marginal man who watches rather than produces social change. But this is rarely the case. For example, Russian history from the point of view of exiles like Alexander Herzen or Alexander Kerensky might prove most provocative; yet their roles are constantly undervalued. No good book has been written about the Kuomintang, although many Communist leaders returned to lead the 1949 Chinese Revolution; or the role of temporarily defeated exiles like Mohandas Gandhi, who later emerged victorious in India. The only exception to this undervaluation of the exile is the treatment accorded the Jew, and only because he is the perennial exile—and can hardly be written about in terms of standard premises about territorial imperatives (Dubnow, 1958, pp. 336–353).

This distinction between winners and losers is not reducible to a plea for more historical writings on those who fail. There is an abundance of writings by victors on the vanquished dating back to the ancient Greek and Roman historians. Rather, it is a statement of the need for an advocacy model, one that assumes a conscious constituency—and accepts the potentials if not the limitations of that constituency. Historians often fail to take seriously that uses of history for definite social class and political goals. In part, this is a consequence of assuming that historical writing does not serve real people with real interests. But the fact is that as losers become winners they announce this transformation by demanding the rewriting of history—a rewriting made in terms of politics and economics, and not as a plea for greater universality.

There are many ways of analyzing events, and political events in particular. One of the most fruitful, and one we shall pursue, is to write history from the point of view of those who no longer have a history, from the point of view of those who are the losers, or those who are consigned to the dustbins of history by the janitors of society.

One such group, although it is hard to think of them that way, are the French of the early nineteenth-century Restorationist period. Perhaps precisely because of their odd rule they provide interesting insight into modern society. Since they are outside the historical timetable, studying that particular period from their point of view provides a kind of psychological insight that is lacking when we examine the major tradition, which, of course, during the early nineteenth century would be Germanic society. The book I consider the model for this approach is the work of César

Graña (1964). It differs from Jacob Talmon (1960) in its sympathetic treatment of losers rather than winners, reactionaries rather than revolutionaries. I am not advocating reactionary historiography; on the contrary, to understand historical trends is to deal with real protagonists in a meaningful context of social interaction.

The main point that Graña makes is that the nineteenth-century problem was not simply to locate a place for Restorationist politics in France, but rather one of trying to find a combination between tradition and modernity that would strike some happy balance for classes that remained a force, albeit a declining force. France was already an old tired country. It had become exhausted in upheaval, tired of change that seemed to lead nowhere. It sought a tradition that would not violate either the political gains of Robespierre, or the territorial gains of Napoleon. This resolution was found in the person of Louis Philippe of Orleans. What Graña says of him is interesting. He indicates the character of political consolidation in a quiescent postrevolutionary period. Louis Philippe could claim the aura of an ancient house and of the steadfastness of the monarchic principle. But he could also claim for his political ancestry an enlightenment and a new outlook. His father was an ardent camp follower of the intellectual agitation that preceded the Revolution of 1789. He sponsored every daring idea, from liberal British politics to new styles in clothing and philosophy (Graña, 1964, pp. 8–9). In other words, a Restoration period is not a simple-minded reaction. It may often be a period of reconciliation. And as in all periods of reconciliation, the problem is not so much economic progress as it is political survival.

The paradox of the developmental ploy is that a leadership declared that an epoch is no longer a time of class strife but is now a time of national cohesion. As in all periods oriented toward survival rather than progress the argument is really the replacement of struggle by work and the displacement of passion by compassion. Let me parenthetically say that this is just as true in the twentieth-century struggle for development as in the nineteenth-century struggle for progress. A Mexican film called *Back Wind* is development in precisely this way. The working class engages in a struggle against nature. The struggle is not against the bourgeois enemy. The art of the Restorationist period in France is dedicated toward removal of natural rather than social obstacles. There is revealed concern for the idea of development rather than the idea of revolution. The idea of survival as a consequence of men working together displaces men pulling apart. This is not without its violent aspects, but the violence is not so much between men and men as between men and nature. In *Black Wind,* the struggle takes place in Mexican California, in the building of a railroad. Stalinist films like *Cossacks of the Kuban* portrayed the electrification of rural areas as the major struggle. New Deal films like *The Grapes of Wrath* ultimately saw the revolution in clean, new housing rather than continued class animosities. The cultural pattern that emerged in restorationist France was prototypical of this and revealed itself in a developmental art form in contrast to the revolutionary art form. Generally speaking, from a cultural point of view, these were dreary artistic products. Any struggle of man against nature is dreary and tends to be tendentious. The only viable artistic event is struggle between men. This has made great art, from the ancient Greeks and Romans to modern Americans and Russians. That is why periods of prewar class struggle yield more significant cultural gains than postwar class consensus.

Political marginals and deviant outsiders may often be those who produce real history in contrast to those who write official history. This is yet another reason that those defined as losers (either those who once had power or those who thus far have been denied power or those who for a host of reasons can scarcely expect to engage in a struggle for power) can yet effect social processes—at times dramatically. The position outlined by Staughton Lynd (1970, p. 527) in this connection is most noteworthy:

> Most of mankind establishes history in the form of an oral tradition, passed on from the old men of the community to the new generation. Throughout the Third World a history written from written sources would be a history of the conqueror, not of the conquered and the liberated-to-be. Even in advanced industrial societies the people who write and keep copies of their letters, the institutions which preserve extensive records, are for the most part persons and institutions of the governing class. We must explode the fetishistic conception that documents are the most primary indication of human experience. We should overcome the tacit assumption that the written word is by nature precise and definitive when compared to the spoken word.

The oral tradition is to the historian what the ethnographic tradition is to the sociologist: a way to generate empirical information as a shared and felt experience rather than the quantitative transformation of such experiences in secondary and tertiary fashion.

It can scarcely be considered an accident that those scholars who emerge from the secondary tradition of supposed "losers" often provide the best sort of historical documentation and theory. Men like Alain Locke, W. E. B. DuBois and E. Franklin Frazier were, in fact, historians, politicians and sociologists. Their special position permitted them to remain professionally ambiguous precisely because of their marginal racial position in America and society. And on subjects ranging from the transmittal of culture from Africa to America to the social patterns of the black middle classes, these unusual political sociologists created a superior record of real events. Nor is this simply the function of rising classes, of which the black people may be considered a prime example. The same situation is true for French novelists like Balzac, Stendhal, Flaubert, each of whom served as chronicler to the middle of French nineteenth-century society, and each of whom provided a basis of understanding political events that was superior to the court historians who by now are not even names. Thus, one must assume that marginality and the sense of being outside the official currents of society permit rather than prevent the creation of a meaningful record of events.

What we call periods of revolution and periods of great progress are often associated not with the literary tradition but with the scientific tradition; in contrast, the great literary traditions are often connected with decadence. For instance, in Russia the great period was the 1890s, with Dostoyevsky, Turgenev, Gogol, Chekov—all worked in a period of incredible social decay prior to the great industrial takeoff of the twentieth century. As already noted, a period of rapid industrial growth may often be one where there is very little in the way of high-level artistic contribution. But it is important to recognize that development as well as decadence ensues in the postrevolutionary periods. If one can say that present-day Mexico roughly corresponds to early nineteenth-century France in certain respects, it makes perfectly good sense to seek out the artists of the postrevolutionary periods, periods of relative political inactivity, in order to understand the actual history and sociology of a people or a nation.

Another phenomenon that took place in Restorationist France which is highly prototypical of what takes place in later periods and other countries is a decline of politics. It is not so much the end of ideology as the emergence of an independent bureaucracy in a period of political instability (Bottomore, 1964, p. 363). A small cluster of facts might illustrate this point: Half a million people were given the franchise in the French 1789 Revolution. By 1830, under the Orleans monarchy, this had gone down to 100,000; this out of what the French called the "legal nation" of 35 million. In other words, one of the consequences of the post-Revolutionary period was a general lapse of mass politics and a general increase in expertise, in managerial, bureaucratic modes of handling political events and situations. This is prototypical of events in the new nations in their postrevolutionary periods: a sharp falling off in political action combined with a steep incline in economic productivity. To make a revolution requires an ideologist; to carry through a revolution successfully requires a technologist. The ideologist who helps bring about the revolution, the organizer of the revolutionary victories, becomes obsolete at the very point of victory because the new needs are for consolidation and for the expert. The bureaucratic "losers" return to assault the revolutionary "winners"—and in this way return through the back door of history as personnel directors, management consultants, planning agents and ordinary bureaucrats.

Ideology can never be a simple form of justification. That is only one of its roles. It justifies, it reifies, and organizes the mental activities of men. But an ideology also promotes a counterideology, just as utopianisms usher in counterutopias. An ideology is what the state imposes on the whole of society. The counterideology then becomes the expression of marginal groups or the antiestablishment forces. That counterideology is linked to a utopian vision of the future. The ideology is always linked to a counterutopia, to a denial of any expression that the future can be different from the past. Expressions of the future are cast in a dismal, horrible mold—as in Orwell and Huxley. The counterutopian phenomenon is the opposite side of the ideological coin. The future is not only different from what we have, but is viewed as worse than one can imagine, or at least less feasible than what we have.

In a sense the modern Soviets and Americans have an ideology, but that ideology really is in itself not what we commonly call ideology, but rather propaganda. It becomes a form of justification, or rationalizing a present moment. It fails to generate any competition of conflicting ideas. It is self-conscious identification of science with the society, and a linkage of both with the regime. The political leadership are not really ideologists in the classical sense. Ideology as protest is replaced by mass communication as consumer satisfaction. So what appears as the "end of ideology" is actually the bureaucratization of political systems.

The question in some measure becomes: How does a society evolve? The postrevolutionary society is one in a state of near-perfect stagnation. The parts all work toward the maintenance of the system. How does constructive action arise from it? What new problems arise? Ideologies can become divisive because the kinds of ideologies revolutionary leaders advocate are generally conflict ideologies of competition, of struggle, of battle, of mobilizing people in nonlegal activities. But in the postrevolutionary period, problems shift and become linked to "prosaic" issues of construction, output, productivity. Therefore, the ideologists place gets taken by the celebrationist, a lesser breed of political man. Ideologists keenly believe in what they are doing; they are not fabricators or propagandists. The ideologist either degenerates into the propagandist or he loses his role to the court historian. One should not confuse developmental propaganda efforts to mobilize people to greater labor, with a revolutionary ideology that is linked to reorienting the style of life of people by reducing mechanized drudgery. The place of the ideologist is limited; the revolutionary becomes victorians and his ideology becomes dysfunctional within the new society.

This is not an abstract political formula. Rather it seems to be the undulating history of the twentieth century. What happened to the ideologists of the Italian fascist movement? Futurism collapsed as a cultural revolution. Its advocates became educationists; their social roles changed and their ideological fervor vanished. In the Bolshevik Revolution, this same classical form obtained: The ideologists disappeared as persons as well as ideologists. The great names of Russian Marxism were expunged from the Great Soviet Encyclopedia.

A developmental society is not a revolutionary society, and hence even a radical ideology is a divisive force for the historical victors. Instead it focuses on utopianism, a demand that the future be brought into being. The future is good in that all people are mobilized to work for the future.

That is quite different from a radical ideology. Radicals must therefore choose their heroes of the future carefully and limit their villains with equal care, for ideologists come upon hard times in a postrevolutionary situation. Just as the bourgeois were despised for their technological emphasis in prerevolutionary periods, the postrevolutionary period sneers at its ideologists.

This fact was brought home most forcefully in the African revolutions that occurred after World War II. Uniformly the ideologists dissolved, from Algeria to Kenya. To the very extent that the revolution succeeded, the ideologists embraced the state. The ruler spoke as the exclusive ideologist. Technocrats, developmentally inspired, became far safer to deal with than fellow revolutionists (Cf. La Palombara, 1963). The politics of the purge is thus not a nasty, brutish pathological assault by winners against losers, but more nearly a function of redirecting society toward "objective" economic tasks and away from "subjective" political squabbles. Political man is set aside by economic men.

TWO FORMS OF MARGINALITY

We have been dealing, of course, with two distinct forms of marginality: elitist and mass. The marginality of restorationist monarchists is different than of the *sans coullottes*. Indeed, the marginality of disintegrating classes must perforce reveal elitist characteristics that are denied to the poor and the yet-to-becomes. However, the reason for selecting illustrations from what are presumed to be decaying classes highlights the possibilities of working within the theory of political marginality. It is relatively simple to assert the need for history, move from there to emerging social strata, and then celebrate the revolution. The difficulty in asserting the same prerogatives from restorationist sectors comes from a denial of historical inevitability. Yet the continued need to respect the interests of and pay attention to marginal sectors that do not have the pseudolegitimacy of grand historicisms must be asserted by political sociology. It is for this reason that my illustrations of marginality as a function of social change are drawn from declining as well as rising classes. In this way, the theory of social interaction can be easily employed by political sociology.

The process of development makes the need to hear from the losers difficult and yet necessary. The developmental system gives rise to new forms of marginality. The old marginals were the political revolutionists. The new marginals are infinitely larger in number than the old marginals; they are the urban intelligentsia. They inundated and took over cities like Paris and Rome. Even today, it is said in only half jest that Rome is a city where 4,000,000 people live and play and 400,000 work. If that is a characterization of Rome it is also a characterization in some measure of Paris, New York, London and Moscow. Marginality, however limited, comes to be identified with cosmopolitanism and cultivation. These marginal sectors become tremendously instrumental in the transformation of a developmental society into a self-conscious society. Marginal groups move from decadence, disintegration and finally to a new revolutionary society. This is a strange process, because, in part, it converts the virtues of development into vices; it makes work a symbol of obedience rather than of creativity.

What are the virtues of development? Stendahl notes them in fictional form: the notion of the honest man, the virtue of the bourgeois, the person who keeps society going. He is respectable, concerned with legitimate occupational activities. He is involved in the machinery of production whether as artisan or financier and in this sense belongs to people motivated by commercial motivation. He is a dealer in commodities rather than ideas. Since the socialist revolution accepts the same economic standpoint, much of what are held to be bourgeois virtues are in fact industrial virtues, or at least common ground for all modern social classes to establish their power.

Stendahl next takes this same set of virtues and converts them into vices: The bourgeoisie are thing-makers, thing-handlers. Therefore they are inherently disqualified to render decisions in which the higher aims of men are at stake. The paradox is that the same people who are designated the most virtuous in society, are declared morally out of bounds with respect to the promotion of anything new. In this way, French marginal intellectuals in the first half of the nineteenth century condemned those integrated into society, the bourgeois, the workers, and the aristocrats, who had been converted into bankers. They become monsters of the age. They become the diabolical force banalizing art; the promoters of mass culture. They are enemies of progress. The very people who are considered most virtuous with respect to the present are thought to be the most vice-ridden concerning the prospects of the future. The new marginal men were drawn from the antibourgeois ranks. These marginals felt keenly that in order for their own virtues to become manifest, they had to make clear why the middle classes could not possibly carry through any further revolutionary thrust; and why, in fact, more revolution was on the agenda of history.

In the development of a postrevolutionary society there is a huge marginal sector that cannot easily be absorbed in the social system. This huge marginal group oftentimes can be technological as well as ideological; and is not only discontented but acts contrary to the regular mainstream of society. In doing so, marginal men—losers of the moment—create seeds of new revolutions. The revolutions of 1848 were sponsored by precisely this kind of outsider group—the historically obsolete, no less than the historically novel.

French society of the first half of the nineteenth century, German society under Nazism of the early twentieth century, Russian Bolshevism under Stalin, the United States of the orthodox 1960s, all reveal the phenomenon of marginality. The cry of revolution becomes an ideological expression for the rebirth of marginal men. And such marginality is radically different from prerevolutionary situations. Very few men survive the revolution that they make. And very few technologists survive the developmental process they stimulate. In this way, winners and losers are constantly exchanging roles.

What makes this interactionist patter in political history so difficult to appreciate, much less to accept, is the apparent decisiveness of the revolutionary act. Both the United States and the Soviet Union had a revolution, rather than a series of revolutions. They celebrate the continuations of the system, rather than the discontinuations of the political process. This is not to say that revolutions are worthless, or that if winners and losers are constantly interchanging roles, that the purposes of the revolution are obviated. Nothing could be further from the case. What is entailed by such an interactionist network is a foreknowledge that revolutions do not fulfill every ambition of every individual. Those that engage in revolutions, like those who refuse to become involved, or even those who engage in counterrevolution, pay a penalty for their position; and their is no a priori way to determine personal advantages or disadvantages. In a sense, all political participation involves a strong chance that even if the political goals are realized, personal goals may be thwarted and frustrated along the way. That is why marginality is not simply stratification; marginals may be drawn from all strata; and even the "victory of the proletariat" may not necessarily extend to all members of that class. The very victory of a class may result in new-found sources of distinction based on ethnicity and race. Thus, revolution must be seen as giving rise to new forms of distinctions, no less than the removal of old forms of distinctions.

The modern society also gave rise to new social forms, not just to marginality as an abstraction, not just as an ideological category of alienation. It gives rise to gangs. It gives rise to what Marx was to call the lumpenproletariat, the modern deviants. In this development, one can see the nascent birth of new types of modern political groupings. The French counterrevolution had as its aftermath youthful gangs dedicated to cultivation of special passions. Some were aristocratic and they had as their purpose terrorizing Jacobins. Their clothing identification, always a concomitant of youth groups, was expensive and precise: abundant lace, tight trousers, short waistcoat, and artificial beauty marks. The Russian Revolution was marked by young men, dressed in laboring men's clothes, often wearing ill-fitting eyeglasses—indeed, a mode of dress not uncommon among young American revolutionaries today. This legacy, in which marginal groups become dedicated to fomenting revolution, also signifies a turn away from stylistic orthodoxy and toward politics as a basic form of upward mobility. As in the present, so too were past elements of radical society drawn from the disenchanted middle classes rather than the lower classes—from the marginals of choice no less than of necessity.

The transformation of deviance into marginality is a major event. Not only because of size, but because it is a characteristic way in which society gets going "intellectually" in its incipient forms through the "deviant" role of unsanctioned marginal sectors. Oftentimes developmentalists speak of development as a consequence of marginality, but they rarely say what that marginality is comprised of, and they rarely point out that the marginals they speak of are integrated rather than alienated. The new marginals are not just a group of pleasant intellectuals, they can be perverted and as fanatic as any other group. Their importance becomes more and more significant as class decadence rolls along.

The "Unbelievables" wend their way into the Munich beer halls of the 1920s and the *Narodnik* forerunners to Bolshevism in the 1890s. Marginal men become a phenomenon. The picture is not one of alienated men as it was with Rousseau or Diderot or Voltaire, but one of anonymous social forces. There are few durable heroes in the industrial epoch. Intellectual and cultural giants exist; but these are not people who can move the society as a whole. Anonymity becomes a personal characteristic along with the general anomic qualities of the industrial epoch. Marginality thus becomes a basic way to confront and confound anonymity. It is a way to be heard, a way to be defiant of history; and ultimately a way to remake society.

The nineteenth century was not only the high point of capitalist development but in that period are the beginnings of what was to become a virtual storm of criticism attacking the idea of development itself. What the nineteenth century called progress the twentieth century calls despotism. Flaubert, in his early writings, said that men would always be unjust and every flag would be soiled with blood. Socialism would end in nothing but institutionalized dogmatism and the obliteration of the individual. As to why the individual should be safeguarded, his answer was significant. All important values were singular. The individual rises over and against the polity. Marginality thus becomes a statement of discontent, and eventually, of renewed faith in revolution. In short, the picture that emerges from European society of the nineteenth century is one in which Romanticism itself takes on a form of cultural and historical pessimism, in which the idea of development becomes challenged, in which marginality becomes something to be celebrated rather than something to live through.

The twentieth century is the high point of socialist development. But already the same tensions and strains that first appeared in industrial capitalism have emerged in industrial socialism. The same sorts of struggles between collectivism and individualism, sociality and egotism, internalized authority and externalized power, all appear in the context of socialist systems. Thus, if the nineteenth century was an age of pessimism, the twentieth century has rightfully been characterized by Camus and other existentialists as the century of cynicism. The velocity of change has produced instant heroes and instant villains, twenty-four hour cultural forms, rotating political leaderships. It has in the process made clear how much fear and trembling there is in the very act of survival. From technological warfare to mechanized transportation, all conspire to make life treacherous. In retrospect, the nineteenth century seems to be a model of stability and predictability. History still counted for something.

By midtwentieth century, history was reduced to decision making, and politics to strategic thinking. It is not that the present is less worthy or less noble than any past epochs, only radically different. The moral worth of man, his psychological conditionings, remain roughly the same. But the velocity of morals, and the turns of psychology all are accelerated by a technological-scientific era that is neutral to problems of men, but certainly not irrelevant to such problems. Instead of one class or one race being or feeling "marginal" as in the past eras, the entire social structure has produced a collective anomie and global alienation that has made each individual feel the sense of marginality—and hence, made each man a potential agent of revolutionary social change (Vekemans *et al.,* 1969, pp. 375–398). Thus the velocity of change in the objective world is matched by the sense of the need for change in the subjective worlds of each person. In this way, all things have become political once more—and the much hoped for unity of society and polity that Aristotle hoped for, and the equally vaunted unity of theory and practice that Marx dealt with, have never been nearer to the touch. Out of marginality must come unity. The emergence of marginality announces the rebirth in revolutionary sentiment—and it is for this reason that history must always pay careful attention to losers as well as winners—since the vissicitudes of change often lead to the last becoming first and the first coming in dead last.

REFERENCES

Bottomore, T. B. (1964) "The Administrative Elite," in I. L. Horowitz, ed., *The New Sociology.* New York: Oxford University Press.

Dubnow, S. (1958) "The Sociological View of Jewish History," in his *Nationalism and History.* New York: World.

Graña, C. (1964) *Bohemian versus Bourgeois: French Society and the French Man of Letters in the Nineteenth Century.* New York: Basic Books.

La Palombara, J. (1963) *Bureaucracy and Political Development.* Princeton, N.J.: Princeton University Press.

Lynd, S. C. (1970) "Guerrilla History," *Social Education,* vol. 34, no. 5 (May), p. 527.

Talmon, J. L. (1960) *Political Messianism: The Romantic Phase.* London: Secker & Warburg.

Vekemans, R. I. S. Fuenzalida, and J. Giusti (1969) *Marginalidad en America Latina: Un Ensayo de Diagnostico.* Santiago de Chile: Desal.

NAME INDEX

SUBJECT INDEX